VISUAL BASIC 5
INTERACTIVE
COURSE

JOHN HARRINGTON, MA̶R̶K̶ ̶̶̶K̶,
HEIDI BRUMBAUGH, C̶L̶I̶F̶F̶ ̶̶̶D̶

WAITE GROUP PRESS™

A Division of

Sams Publishing

Corte Madera, CA

PUBLISHER • Mitchell Waite
ASSOCIATE PUBLISHER • Charles Drucker

ACQUISITIONS EDITOR • Joanne Miller

EDITORIAL DIRECTOR • John Crudo
PROJECT EDITOR • Lisa H. Goldstein
DEVELOPMENTAL EDITOR • Scott Rhoades
TECHNICAL EDITORS • Frank Sommer, Matt Tagliaferri
COPY EDITORS • Deirdre Greene, Bruce Tracy, Abigail Johnston/Creative Solutions

PRODUCTION DIRECTOR • Julianne Ososke
PRODUCTION MANAGER • Cecile Kaufman
SENIOR DESIGNER • Sestina Quarequio
DESIGNER • Karen Johnston
PRODUCTION EDITORS • Kate Talbot, Sally St. Lawrence
PRODUCTION • Andy Stone, Shawn Ring, Bud Livengood, Mary Ellen Stephenson, Ginny Bess
COVER ILLUSTRATION • © Steven Hunt/Image Bank

© 1997 by The Waite Group, Inc.
Published by Waite Group Press™
200 Tamal Plaza, Corte Madera, CA 94925

Waite Group Press is a division of Sams Publishing.

Printed in the United States of America
99 98 97 • 10 9 8 7 6 5 4 3 2 1

Library of Congress Cataloging-in-Publication Data
Visual Basic 5 interactive course / John Harrington . . . [et al.].
    p.   cm.
    Includes index.
    ISBN 1-57169-077-8
    1. Microsoft Visual Basic. 2. BASIC (Computer program language)
I. Harrington, John, 1936-
QA76.73.B3V565   1997
005.26'8--dc21

97-1819
CIP

www.waite.com/ezone
eZone Guided Tour

The Interactive Course title in your hands provides you with an unprecedented training system. *Visual Basic 5 Interactive Course* is everything you're used to from Waite Group Press: thorough, hands-on coverage of this important, cutting edge programming language. There is far more, however, to the Interactive Course than the pages you are now holding. Using your Internet connection, you also get access to the eZone where you'll find dedicated services designed to assist you through the book and make sure you really understand the subject.

FREE TUTORS, TESTING, CERTIFICATION, AND RESOURCES

The eZone provides a host of services and resources designed to help you work through this book. If you get hung up with a particular lesson, all you have to do is ask an online mentor, a live expert in the subject you're studying. A mailing list lets you exchange ideas and hints with others taking the same course. A resource page links you to the hottest related web sites, and a monthly newsletter keeps you up to date with eZone enhancements and industry developments. Figure 1 shows the page.

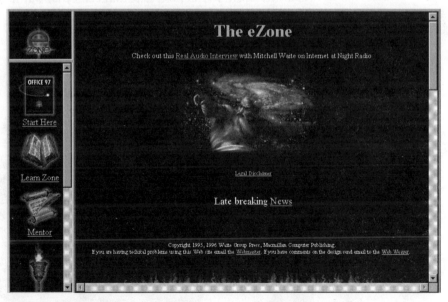

Figure 1
The eZone home page...a whole new way to learn

You'll also be able to work toward a certificate of completion. You can take lesson quizzes online, receive an immediate grade, track your progress through the course. The chapters are available online, too, so that you can refer to them when you need to. Once you've finished the course with a passing grade, you can print a personalized certificate of completion, suitable for framing.

Best of all, there's no additional cost for all of these services. They are included in the price of the book. Once you journey into the eZone, you'll never want to go back to traditional book learning.

EXPLORING THE EZONE

You'll find the eZone on the World Wide Web. Fire up your Web browser and enter the following site:

`http://www.waite.com/waite/ezone`

From there, click the eZone icon and you're on your way.

NOTE

If your browser does not support frames, or if you prefer frameless pages, click the No Frames link instead of the eZone icon. Your browser must support "cookies," so Microsoft Internet Explorer (version 3.01 or later) or Netscape Navigator (version 3 or later) is required.

Navigating the eZone

As you can see in Figure 2, the screen is divided into three frames. The eZone icon in the top left frame is always visible. This icon is a link back to the eZone home page. No matter where you are, you can always find your way home by clicking this icon.

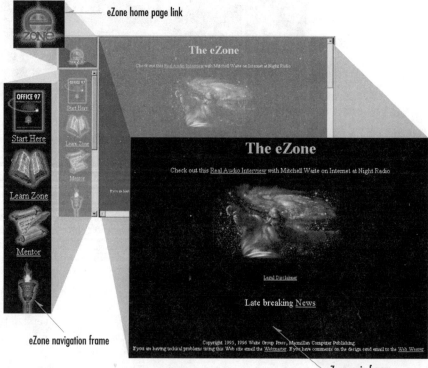

Figure 2
There are three frames in the eZone

Beneath the eZone icon is a navigation frame containing several icons. Each of these icons links to an area of the eZone. You'll learn about each of these areas as you read through this guide.

The largest frame on the page is the main frame. This is where you'll find the information. Scroll down this frame and you'll see text-based links to the eZone areas. Keep going and you'll find the latest eZone news and information, updated regularly. Be sure to check out this information each time you enter the eZone.

Start Here

Click the *Start Here* icon in the navigation frame. This takes you to the Getting Started page where you'll find different sets of instructions. Your options are:

```
I am a GUEST and visiting the EZONE.
I HAVE the EZONE BOOK and I am ready to start the course.
I want to BUY an EZONE COURSE and get my Book.
```

Clicking on these options provide instructions for how to sign on as a Guest, register for a course for which you have a book, or sign up for a course and order the corresponding book.

In the next couple of pages, you'll see how to explore the eZone as a Guest, register yourself, enroll in a course, and take advantage of the many service areas provided at no additional charge.

Signing on as a Guest

On your first visit to the eZone, consider signing on as a Guest, even if you have a book and are anxious to get started. Signing on as Guest lets you roam the eZone and familiarize yourself with its various areas and features before setting any options. You can view the first chapter of any available course and take the quizzes for that chapter (although Guests' scores aren't saved).

You can ask support questions, view the latest news, and even view the FAQs for a course. Until you register, you can't ask the mentors any questions, sign up for the eZone newsletter, or access the resource links page, but there's still plenty of stuff to check out as a Guest.

To explore the eZone as a Guest, click the *Learn Zone* icon in the navigation frame or on the word "Learn" at the bottom of the main frame. The first time you do this, the Registration Page appears. As a Guest, you can ignore this form.

Just click the *Guest* link, and the Course Matrix appears. From here, you can navigate the eZone in the same manner as registered course members. Remember, however, that access for Guests is limited.

THE INITIATE ZONE

Once you're comfortable navigating the eZone, we know you'll be anxious to start learning and taking advantage of this cutting edge training system.

The first thing you have to do is create an entry for yourself in the eZone records by registering. Click the Initiation icon in the navigation frame or on the Initiate link at the bottom of the main frame, and you move into the *Initiate Zone*, shown in Figure 3.

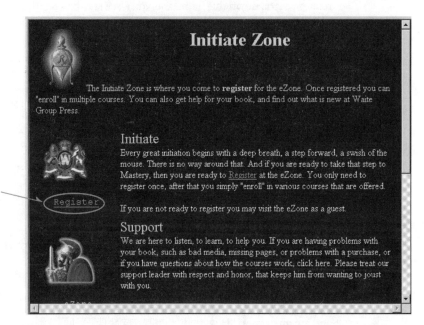

Click here to begin eZone registration

Figure 3
Go to the Initiate
Zone to start your
training

The Initiate Zone contains three options: *Initiate (Register), Support,* and *Announcements and What's New*. Use the *Support* option to report difficulties you are having with your Interactive Course material and services: problems with the book or CD, trouble getting eZone to work, whatever you need. This is not, however, where you'll ask questions related to the course content. Answering those questions is the mentor's job. The *Announcements and What's New* option lets you quickly find out about the latest additions and deletions at the eZone. It also contains information about upcoming courses.

Initiate (Register)

But what you want right now is the *Initiate (Register)* option. Click the *Register* link and a registration form appears.

> **NOTE**
>
> You don't need a book to register in the eZone; in fact, you can pre-register and order an Interactive Course title while you're online. When your copy arrives, you'll already have a recognized password and ID, so that you can enroll immediately in your course of choice.

You need to fill out the registration form completely. Click inside each text box, then type in the appropriate information; pressing the [TAB] key cycles you through these text fields. In addition to a little information about yourself, you'll need to enter:

`Requested User ID`—Type the name you'd like to use online.

`Password (5-8 Characters)`—Type the password you'd like to use online.

`Password (Verify)`—Retype your selected password, to be sure it's properly recorded.

Once you've supplied all the information, click the *Register* button to submit the form to the eZone's data banks. A confirming message lets you know that you've successfully registered. Registration is important. If you don't register, you can't take advantage of the full power of the eZone.

Entering the eZone as a Registered User

Once you've registered, you'll use your unique ID and password to enter the eZone. Next time you enter the eZone, you need only click the *Learn Zone* icon in the navigation frame or the *Learn* link in the main frame. A simple two-line form pops up, allowing you to type in the user ID and password you created when you registered.

THE LEARN ZONE

Now that you're registered, it's time to get down to business. Much of the course work is done in the *Learn Zone*, shown in Figure 4. To get here, click the *Learn* icon in the navigation frame.

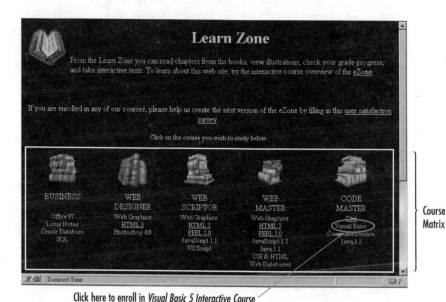

Figure 4
Use the Course Matrix in the Learn Zone to select courses

Click here to enroll in *Visual Basic 5 Interactive Course*

The Course Matrix

When you enter the Learn Zone, you'll see lists of courses and certification programs. This is called the Course Matrix, and it provides a way to select the various eZone cours-es. Under each discipline—such as Web Designer, Business, or Code Master—are a list of core courses. To select the *Visual Basic 5 Interactive Course* using this Course Matrix, click on the *Visual Basic 5* link in the column labeled "Code Master." In a moment, a three-columned table appears.

Verification

The first time you select a specific course, you must enroll. You'll need a copy of the book to do so. You will be asked to provide a specific word from the book. This verifies that you have the proper book for the selected course. The verification process uses the familiar page-line-word formula; in other words, you'll need to look and enter a word from a specified line of text on a specified page of your book. Click your mouse in the text box and type the specified word to verify that you have the course book.

Passing Percentage

You can also set a minimum passing percentage for your course. This determines what percentage of test questions you need to answer correctly in order to pass the course. The percentage is preset at 70%, but you can select 50%, 60%, 70%, 80%, 90%, or 100%.

To set a minimum passing percentage, click the text box for this option to see a list of choices, then click the option you prefer. Once you've typed in the correct word and set the desired passing percentage, click the *Verify* button to enroll in the course. The Chapters Grid appears.

The Chapters Grid

The table shown in Figure 5 displays the 18 chapters of this book, and it shows your completion status and average score for each of them.

Click here to go back to the Course Matrix

Click on a Chapter to view the Quizzes within

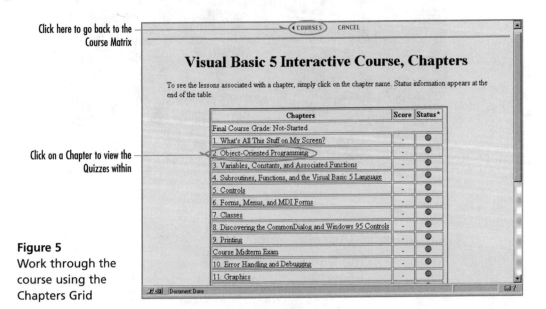

Figure 5
Work through the course using the Chapters Grid

The left-hand column lists the chapters of the book; clicking on a chapter lets you view the lessons within it. The middle column, Score, shows your current overall grade for the section (as a percentage). The Status column uses a colored indicator to let you know with a glance whether you've passed (green), failed (red), are still working through (yellow), or have not yet started (gray) a particular chapter.

Click a Chapter, and the Lessons Grid appears. (Remember, only the first lesson is enabled for Guests.)

The Lessons Grid

As you take the course, the Lessons Grid (Figure 6) tracks your performance within each section of the book. You can use it to read a chapter lesson or take the related lesson quiz.

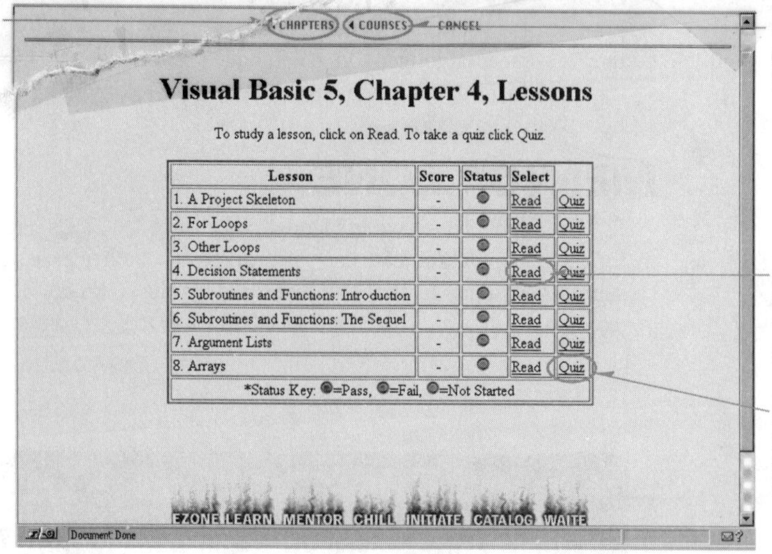

Click here to see the Chapters Grid

Click here to go back to the Course Matrix

Click here to view Lesson 4, "Decision Statements"

Click here to take the quiz for Lesson 8, "Arrays"

Figure 6
The Lessons Grid organizes each chapter

To read a lesson, click the *Read* link in the Select column. To take a quiz, click the *Quiz* link in the Select column. The LEDs in the status column show whether you've passed (green), failed (red), or not yet started (gray) each quiz. A percentage grade appears for each completed quiz in the Score column.

Most likely, you'll achieve the best results if you read through the lessons, then take the quiz. If you prefer, however, you can jump directly to the corresponding quiz, without reading through the lesson.

Testing

Each quiz is a multiple choice questionnaire. In some quizzes, there is only one answer to each question, but others allow more than one answer. Read the instructions for your course so you know how the quizzes work.

Taking Quizzes

To answer a quiz question, click the check box next to the answer you w.
choose. When you've answered all the questions, click the *Grade My Choices* b
Your quiz is corrected and your score shown. To record your score, click either the *L*
or *Chapters* link at the top of the main frame.

CAUTION

Do not use your browser's Back button after taking a quiz. If you use the Back butto
instead of the Lessons or Chapters link, your score will not be recorded.

Midterm and Final Exams

The Interactive Course includes midterm and final examinations. The midte
ers the *first half* of the book, while the final is comprehensive. These exams fo
same multiple-choice format as the quizzes. Because they cover more, h
they're somewhat longer. Once you have successfully passed all the quizzes,
the midterm and final exams, you'll be eligible to download a certificate of co
from Waite Group Press.

MENTOR ZONE

In the *Mentor Zone*, shown in Figure 7, you can review FAQs (Frequently Asked Questions)
for each chapter. You can also ask a question of a live expert, called a mentor, who is
standing by to assist you. The mentor is familiar with the book, an expert in the subject, and can provide you with a specific answer to your content-related question, usually

Click on this pull down menu
to see a list of chapters.
Click on the chapter to which
your question relates.

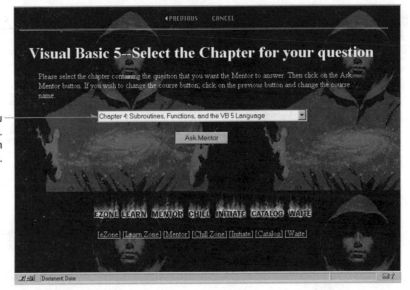

Figure 7
Get personalized
help in the
Mentor Zone

within one business day. You can get to this area by clicking on the Mentor icon in the navigation frame.

Just the FAQs

Before you ask a mentor a question, you're first shown a set of FAQs. Be sure to read through the list. Since you have a limited number of questions you may ask, you'll want to use your questions carefully. Chances are that an answer to your question has already been posted, in which case you can get an answer without having to ask it yourself. In any event, you may learn about an issue you hadn't even considered.

If the FAQ list does not contain the answer you need, you'll want to submit your own question to the mentor.

Ask Your Mentor

eZone students may ask 10 questions of their course mentor. This limit ensures that mentors will have the opportunity to answer all readers' questions. Questions must be directly related to chapter material. If you ask unrelated or inappropriate questions, you won't get an answer; however, the question will still be deducted from your allotment.

If the FAQ doesn't provide you with an answer to your question, click the button labeled *Ask Mentor*. The first time you contact the mentor, the rules and conditions for the mentor questions are provided. After reading these, click the *Accept* button to continue. In a moment, a form like the one shown in Figure 8 appears.

This form specifies the course, the chapter, and other information pertinent to your question. The mentor e-mails the answer to your question directly to you, but keep in mind that Mentor Zone questions must be *directly* related to the chapter subject matter.

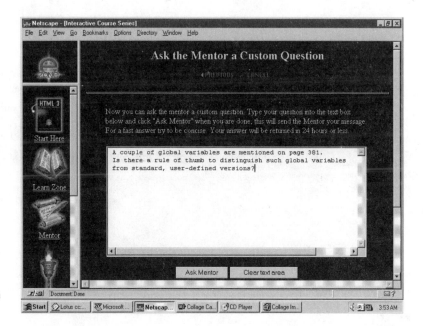

Figure 8
Use this form to send your question to your mentor

More Assistance

Keep in mind that there are other sources of assistance in the eZone, too. If you are experiencing technical problems with the book or CD, you'll want to contact the Webmaster; you'll find a link on the eZone's main page. If you want to discuss related issues, such as developments and applications, check out the newsgroups available in the Chill Zone. There are other ways to discuss issues with real people, as you'll discover, when you visit the eZone.

CHILL ZONE

Think of the Chill Zone as your student lounge, a place where students hang out and discuss their classes. But the Chill Zone does a student lounge one better—it's also a library chock full of information. It's a place where you can interact with others reading the same book and find expert resources to assist you as you develop and use your new skills. Perhaps the coolest thing about the Chill Zone is that its options are all included with the cost of your book.

To get into the Chill Zone, click the Chill Zone icon in the navigation frame. Once there, you can click three Chill Zone options:

Discussion List—You can subscribe (or unsubscribe) to a dedicated newsgroup centered on your book.

Newsletter—Select this option to subscribe (or unsubscribe) to the quarterly eZone newsletter.

Resources—These are links to Web sites, tools, and other useful materials related to the course subject.

To select a Chill Zone option, click the link and follow the on-screen instructions.

THE EZONE AWAITS

As you have seen from this tour, this Interactive Course book is a lot more than the pages before you. It's a full-blown, personalized training system—including textbook, testing, guidance, certification, and support—that you can pick up and work through at your own pace and at your own convenience.

Don't settle for just a book when you can get a whole education. Thanks to this comprehensive package, you're ready to log on and learn in the eZone.

Dedication

For Barbara, whose encouragement is my inspiration.

—John Harrington

To the love of my life, my wife Lisa, for her love and incredible support (including her editing ability) throughout this project.

—Mark Spenik

This book is dedicated to everyone who always thought programming was "too mysterious" or "too hard." Telling a computer what to do isn't the exclusive domain of people who possess some innate talent for it. It's simply something you learn. I hope this book makes learning Visual Basic 5 a smooth and enjoyable experience for you.

—Heidi Brumbaugh

About the Authors

Like so many in the computer business, **John Harrington** has enjoyed a checkered career. After selling life insurance, building houses, teaching electronics, and establishing a practice in hypnotherapy, he has settled into consulting and contracting as a Visual Basic programmer. John's first computer was a home-built Cosmac Elf, but it was Microsoft Extended Basic on the TRS80 Model 1 that really got him hooked. After forays into half a dozen other programming languages, he is back to BASIC. He is currently a partner in Tampa Programming Group, programming business applications in Visual Basic.

Mark Spenik is the manager of client/server technology at Keiter Stephens Computer Services, Inc., located in Richmond, Virginia. Mark, a graduate of George Mason University in Fairfax, Virginia, entered the computer industry in 1985. He has designed and coded large-scale client/server (C/S) applications and has consulted with numerous firms in C/S development, implementation, and migration. He has a broad programming background that includes assembly language, C, C++, and Visual Basic. Visual Basic is his language of choice, and he has been using it since its early days. Mark is a frequent speaker at Microsoft Developer Days and is a Microsoft Certified Solution Developer and charter member. He is also certified in Microsoft SQL Server administration, SQL Server database implementation, and Windows NT. Mark is the co-author of the *Microsoft SQL Server DBA Survival Guide* by Sams Publishing. You can reach him at `mspenik@kscsinc.com`.

Heidi Brumbaugh is an editor and writer living in the San Francisco Bay area. She has worked in the computer publishing industry for 10 years and programmed in Basic for 15 years. She has edited over two dozen books for The Waite Group. She is currently working on hypertext training systems for Microsoft Windows.

Cliff Diamond works as an information technology consultant specializing in investment banking. His work consists of the design and development of large, often worldwide, distributed client/server systems, principally for the securities industries. Visual Basic is very important to him as a strategic development environment for client systems. He's been using Visual Basic since Version 1, and it is his development language of choice. He lives in Edgeware, England (right outside London), with his wife and two daughters.

Table of Contents

Introduction	. . . .	.xxii
Chapter 1	What's All That Stuff on My Screen?	.1
Chapter 2	Object-Oriented Programming	.31
Chapter 3	Variables, Constants, and Associated Functions . .75	
Chapter 4	Subroutines, Functions, and the Visual Basic 5 Language	.153
Chapter 5	Controls	.219
Chapter 6	Forms, Menus, and MDI Forms	.273
Chapter 7	Classes	.327
Chapter 8	Discovering the CommonDialog and Windows 95 Controls	.375
Chapter 9	Printing	.453
Chapter 10	Error Handling and Debugging	.499
Chapter 11	Graphics	.537
Chapter 12	Files	.597
Chapter 13	Data Access	.661
Chapter 14	Advanced Features	.739
Chapter 15	Interfacing with Excel and Other Programs 787	
Chapter 16	Roll Your Own: Creating Your Own ActiveX Controls	.837
Chapter 17	Register Your Programs: Using the Windows Registry	.887
Chapter 18	Visual Basic 5 Communications	.919
Appendix A	Quiz Answers	.1001
Appendix B	Internet Explorer 3.0: A Field Guide	.1015
Index	. . . .	.1027

CONTENTS

Chapter 1   What's All That Stuff on My Screen?. 1
Lesson 1   Getting Started. 2
Lesson 2   Customizing the Development Environment. 7
Lesson 3   The Application Wizard. 12
Lesson 4   Add-Ins 18
Lesson 5   Help! 22

Chapter 2   Object-Oriented Programming 31
Lesson 1   Objects. 32
Lesson 2   Forms: Your First Program. 37
Lesson 3   Getting Things Done 42
Lesson 4   The File Picker Gets Better 48
Lesson 5   The Development Environment. 53
Lesson 6   Looking Closely at Forms 60
Lesson 7   The File Picker: Better Still 64
Lesson 8   It's a Wrap 71

Chapter 3   Variables, Constants, and Associated Functions . . . 75
Lesson 1   Variables: Getting Started. 76
Lesson 2   The Code Window Explored 83
Lesson 3   **If** and More Variable Types. 92
Lesson 4   Introduction to Strings 102
Lesson 5   String Manipulation. 115
Lesson 6   Times and Dates 127
Lesson 7   Other Date and Time Support Functions 136
Lesson 8   Variables Concluded 144

Chapter 4   Subroutines, Functions, and the
Visual Basic 5 Language. 153
Lesson 1   A Project Skeleton 154
Lesson 2   **For** Loops 158
Lesson 3   Other Loops. 165
Lesson 4   Decision Statements. 175
Lesson 5   Subroutines and Functions: Introduction 185
Lesson 6   Subroutines and Functions: The Sequel 191
Lesson 7   Argument Lists 204
Lesson 8   Arrays 209

Chapter 5 **Controls** 219
Lesson 1 The TextBox Control 220
Lesson 2 Labels and the **MsgBox** Function 227
Lesson 3 Command Buttons and Check Boxes 236
Lesson 4 Option Buttons and Frames. 243
Lesson 5 The ListBox Control. 251
Lesson 6 Advanced ListBox Techniques and the ComboBox Control 259
Lesson 7 Control Arrays 265

Chapter 6 **Forms, Menus, and MDI Forms** 273
Lesson 1 Forms 274
Lesson 2 An MDI Application 278
Lesson 3 Creating Forms at Runtime 283
Lesson 4 Further Form Techniques 288
Lesson 5 Adding Menus to Your Project. 294
Lesson 6 Filling In the Blanks: Programming the File Menus. 303
Lesson 7 Filling In the Blanks: Programming Edit Menus 310
Lesson 8 Filling In the Blanks: Finishing Up SuperPad 319

Chapter 7 **Classes** 327
Lesson 1 Classes and Objects. 328
Lesson 2 The **Form** Class 331
Lesson 3 Control Classes 336
Lesson 4 Introducing User-Defined Classes 343
Lesson 5 A Class Act: Modifying SuperPad 349
Lesson 6 Collections. 355
Lesson 7 User-Defined Properties. 364
Lesson 8 Why Use Classes? 369

Chapter 8 **Discovering the CommonDialog**
and Windows 95 Controls. 375
Lesson 1 Introducing the CommonDialog Control 376
Lesson 2 The RichTextBox Control and the Font and Color Dialog Boxes. 387
Lesson 3 The ToolBar and ImageList Controls 395
Lesson 4 The StatusBar Control 404
Lesson 5 The TabStrip Control. 410
Lesson 6 The TreeView Control 420
Lesson 7 The ListView Control. 437
Lesson 8 The ProgressBar and Slider Controls 448

Chapter 9   Printing 453
   Lesson 1   Introducing Printing 454
   Lesson 2   Using Fonts 460
   Lesson 3   The Printer and the CommonDialog 469
   Lesson 4   Printer Capabilities 475
   Lesson 5   Combining Text and Graphics. 479
   Lesson 6   Printing Reports from Visual Basic 485
   Lesson 7   Formatting Numeric Output. 488
   Lesson 8   Formatting Dates for Output. 494

Chapter 10   Error Handling and Debugging. 499
   Lesson 1   Errors in Visual Basic 5 Programs 499
   Lesson 2   Error Handlers. 505
   Lesson 3   Debugging: The Noble Art. 511
   Lesson 4   Debugger Bugs. 524
   Lesson 5   How to Write Code That Is Easy to Maintain 526
   Lesson 6   Advanced Debugging Techniques 531

Chapter 11   Graphics. 537
   Lesson 1   Understanding Coordinates. 538
   Lesson 2   Using Graphical Controls 544
   Lesson 3   Using Graphical Methods 549
   Lesson 4   Drawing Shapes. 556
   Lesson 5   Colors 564
   Lesson 6   Picture Control Versus Image Control 572
   Lesson 7   Simple Animation 577
   Lesson 8   Miscellaneous Graphics Issues. 583

Chapter 12   Files 597
   Lesson 1   Using the File System Controls 598
   Lesson 2   Making the File System Controls Work Together 602
   Lesson 3   Opening, Reading, and Closing a File 609
   Lesson 4   Sequential and Random Access Files. 618
   Lesson 5   Binary File Access 630
   Lesson 6   A Notepad Application 645
   Lesson 7   Using Files in Development Time Versus
                Stand-alone Applications. 656

Chapter 13   Data Access 661
   Lesson 1   What Is a Database? 662
   Lesson 2   Using the Data Control 667
   Lesson 3   Accessing Data with Code 675
   Lesson 4   Using the Bound Controls 685
   Lesson 5   Managing Your Data with SQL 706
   Lesson 6   Creating Reports 716
   Lesson 7   Designing a Database 723
   Lesson 8   Understanding ODBC 730

Chapter 14   Advanced Features 739
   Lesson 1   Using the Windows API 740
   Lesson 2   Timer Control 748
   Lesson 3   Understanding the Architecture 754
   Lesson 4   Idle Time 757
   Lesson 5   DDE 762
   Lesson 6   Creating an Executable 770
   Lesson 7   Using the Setup Wizard 775
   Lesson 8   Application Optimization 781

Chapter 15   Interfacing with Excel and Other Programs 787
   Lesson 1   What Is OLE? 788
   Lesson 2   Using the OLE Container Control 793
   Lesson 3   What Is OLE Automation? 800
   Lesson 4   Object Hierarchy and the Object Browser 803
   Lesson 5   Using OLE Automation with Microsoft Word and Microsoft Excel 809
   Lesson 6   Exposing Your Own Classes: Creating OLE Servers 817
   Lesson 7   Using Visual Basic Built-In Objects 828
   Lesson 8   Thinking in Objects 832

Chapter 16   Roll Your Own: Creating Your Own
             ActiveX Controls 837
   Lesson 1   What Is ActiveX? 838
   Lesson 2   Running the Control at Design Time 843
   Lesson 3   The Key Events of a User Control Object 848
   Lesson 4   Drawing the Control 852
   Lesson 5   The Ins and Outs of Events 857
   Lesson 6   Give Your Control a Property Page 863
   Lesson 7   The Control Interface Wizard 870
   Lesson 8   Compiling and Distributing Your Control 879

Chapter 17 Register Your Programs:
Using the Windows Registry 887
Lesson 1   Using the Registry with Built-In VB Commands 890
Lesson 2   Using the Registry API 895
Lesson 3   Adding Values to Subkeys 904
Lesson 4   Reading Registry Values 910
Lesson 5   Deleting Values and Subkeys 914

Chapter 18 Visual Basic 5 Communications 919
Lesson 1   The MSComm Control 920
Lesson 2   More from the Modem 931
Lesson 3   Communications with MSComm 938
Lesson 4   Connect to the World Wide Web 960
Lesson 5   Files, Files, Files: Using FTP 972
Lesson 6   Grand Finale 1000

Appendix A Quiz Answers 1001

Appendix B Internet Explorer 3.0: A Field Guide 1015

Index   1027

Acknowledgments

Building a book, it turns out, is a lot like building a house: It is not a one-man job. I would like to thank everybody who made this book happen. Thanks to Barbara, who tolerated all the agonies of this birthing. Thanks, also, to my partner, Les, who practically ran the business without me as I worked on this project.

And thanks, especially, to the Waite Group and the team they gave me to do this. Thanks to Joanne Miller, who took a big chance when she signed me to the project. Big thanks to Lisa Goldstein, who held my hand across the country and guided the whole process to fruition. Thanks to the production editors, Kate Talbot and Sally St. Lawrence, who guided me through the intricacies of formatting. And to those behind the scenes, those I did not meet by e-mail and telephone, but whose hand I noticed in the editing. I don't know your names, but I know your work, and it is good.

Finally, thanks to the hundreds of Visual Basic programmers who post questions and answers on the Usenet newsgroups. You do more good than you know.

—John Harrington

I want to thank my wife, Lisa, for her enduring love and support. Lisa was the behind-the-scenes editor who kept this project going during some tough edits and changes. I would also like to thank Lisa Goldstein of Waite Group Press for coming to the rescue and pulling this project together. To my big family—John, Denise, David, Kim, Adam, Chris, Gary, Debbie, Lisa, David and all my nieces and nephews—thanks for the support! To the Meyer family (Sam, Marge, and Jonathan) and the Rimes family (Denise and Pat) for all their encouragement. To my father, John, and my late mother, Anna Jane, thanks for the great childhood and for giving me the tools to succeed. To everyone at Keiter Stephens Computer Services, Inc., for the support and feedback. Special thanks to Troy Rackley and Anne Hutchinson for their help and tips. Last but not least, to everyone at Waite Group Press who helped make this project a reality!

—Mark Spenik

I have been editing computer books for Mitch Waite for over five years, but was nonetheless completely taken by surprise by how difficult it is to write one. Thanks go mostly to Lisa Goldstein and John Crudo for their tireless and unwavering support, and to the production department for meeting an insane schedule. Thanks to my husband, Jim Kent, for helping to come up with devious wrong answers for the multiple choice quizzes, and for taking care of the kids when I snuck up to my office to write. Thanks to Scott Rhoades, Frank Sommer, and Matt Tagliaferri for editing the manuscript. Thanks also to Jim Kent (the senior) and Karen Engbretson for their helpful feedback on Chapter 1.

—Heidi Brumbaugh

INTRODUCTION

This book is a hands-on course in Visual Basic 5, the language that makes programming for Windows as visual as Windows itself. This is a beginner's book. It assumes no previous knowledge of programming. If you already program in some other language, you can use this book to get up to speed on Visual Basic.

What's in the Book?

The book starts by guiding you around the Visual Basic workspace, familiarizing you with the windows and dialog boxes of the development environment. Then, Chapter 2 fearlessly demystifies object-oriented programming, or OOP, which is at the heart of Windows programming.

Once the definitions are out of the way, the book takes you step by step through program creation. You will write dozens of sample programs, and you will understand how each line of code works and, better yet, why it is important.

Chapters 3 and 4 introduce variables, tell you how programs make decisions, and put it all to work manipulating strings and other data. Chapters 5 and 6 describe the variety of controls and forms you can use to make your Visual Basic projects really take shape. By the time you finish Chapter 6, you will have a powerful replacement for Windows NotePad program.

Chapter 7 explains how to use classes in your programs. And Chapter 8 shows you how to add professional features to your programs using the Windows CommonDialog controls. In Chapter 9, you will learn all the ins and outs of Visual Basic's **Printer** object, which lets you send data and pictures to your printer in any format you want.

Chapter 10 dives into error handling and the noble art of debugging. You will learn how to troubleshoot your programs and how to prevent bugs instead of having to fix them. Chapter 11 introduces you to graphics programming. You will learn to use graphical controls and methods and do some simple animation.

In Chapter 12, you will learn to read and write disk files. You will learn to use the file system controls and to handle sequential access, random access, and binary access file types.

Much of business programming involves databases. In Chapter 13, you will learn simple techniques for creating and managing database files. The chapter introduces structured query language (SQL) and teaches you how to create classy reports with Crystal Reports.

This book does not stop with the basics. Chapter 15 teaches you how to use object linking and embedding. You can link your programs to Microsoft Office products like Microsoft Word and Microsoft Excel. The chapter also shows you how to link two of your own programs together as client and server.

In Chapter 16, you will learn how to make your own custom controls, which you can use in other programs you write. In Chapter 17, you will find two different ways to access the Windows Registry so you can save parameters from your programs.

The final chapter, Chapter 18, delineates two different techniques for computer communications and then teaches you how to connect to the Internet. You will learn how to add a Web browser and an FTP client to your programs.

The Waite Group Interactive Series

The main way this book differs from other Visual Basic books is that it's a Waite Group Interactive book. This isn't just publisher's hype. By connecting you to the Waite Group via the World Wide Web, this new approach plays a significant role in helping you learn Visual Basic. There are many aspects to the Interactive series. We won't dwell on them here, but the details are presented in the eZone Guided Tour at the beginning of this book. You should note, though, that this book was written, from the ground up, as part of the Interactive series.

First, each chapter is divided into short, easily digestible lessons. Each lesson is devoted to a specific topic and requires only an hour (approximately) to read and understand. This makes it easy to sit down with this book and learn something, even if your time is limited.

Each lesson is followed by a quiz to ensure that you've understood the material. You can answer the quizzes by yourself, or you can do them on the Web, which will grade them automatically.

The Waite Group Web site offers many other advantages. A principle one is mentoring, which is the ability to ask questions and get answers back, just as you would if you were taking a class at a university and could talk to the professor.

About the CD-ROM

The CD-ROM contains all the source code in the book as well as several useful utilities and controls. The directory structure of the CD-ROM is shown in Table CD-1. Following the table are descriptions of each of the items that include installation instructions.

Table CD-1 Directory structure of the CD-ROM included with this book

Location	Description
SOURCE	Source code from the book
Chap01	
Chap02	
Chap03	
Chap04	
Chap05	
Chap06	
Chap07	
Chap08	
Chap09	

continued on next page

continued from previous page

Location	Description
Chap10	
Chap11	
Chap12	
Chap13	
Chap14	
Chap15	
Chap16	
Chap17	
Chap18	
EXPLORER	Internet Explorer 3.01
IE301M95.EXE	Windows 95
IE301MNT.EXE	Windows NT 4
WIN31NT3.51	Internet Explorer 3.0
SETUP.EXE	Setup for Windows 3.1x and NT 3.51
UTILITIES	Third-party controls that can simplify and enhance your Visual Basic programs
ACROBAT	
ACTIVE3D	
ALARM	
BARCOD	
DFINFO	
FIRE	
FLABEL	
HITIME	
JOYSTK	
LED	
PERCNT	
RESIZE	
ROTEXT	
SBLIST	
VSDATA	
VSFLEX	
VSVIEW	

Source Code

All the examples in the book are placed under the **SOURCE** directory. Examples from each chapter are placed in their own subdirectory, specified by the chapter number.

To use the examples, you must copy them to your hard disk drive. When files are saved to a CD-ROM, they are automatically made read-only files. Copying them to your hard drive does not change their read-only attribute. To save you the trouble of manually changing the properties for all the files, a simple batch file is included on the CD.

Assuming that your CD-ROM is drive D: and you want the source code on your C: drive, the following steps copy the files from the CD to your hard drive. The batch file creates the **VB5Interactive** directory on your hard disk and copies all the source code into the new directory.

To use the batch file:

1. Click on the Start button in Windows 95.

2. Click on Run.

3. Enter D:\SOURCE D: C: in the text box.

4. Click on OK.

A DOS window opens as the batch file runs. When it is finished, you must close it manually. If your CD-ROM is other than D: or you want to copy the files to a different drive, change the appropriate drive letter.

Explorer

This directory contains the latest version (3.01) of Microsoft Internet Explorer (IE). IE, or some of its components, is required for the Internet programs in this book. This directory contains self-extracting EXEs for Windows 95 and Windows NT 4. Installation is a matter of double-clicking on the correct EXE file and answering a few questions. They are probably the most automatic, trouble-free installation programs you will ever see.

The **WIN31NT3.51** subdirectory contains Internet Explorer 3.0 for Windows 3.1x and Windows NT 3.51. If you want to install it, select RUN from the FILE menu. Type **D:\EXPLORER\WIN31NT3.51\SETUP** and click on OK. If your CD-ROM is other than D: or you want to copy the files to a different drive, change the appropriate drive letter.

Utilities

This directory contains third-party controls and utilities that can simplify your programming by making formerly difficult and tedious programming tasks easy. Most of them are demonstration versions of the products, which means that you can't distribute programs that use them until you register (and pay for) them. Your author is particularly fond of **RESIZE.OCX** and **SBLIST.OCX**.

OCX controls work only with Visual Basic 5. If you're working with an older, 16-bit version of Visual Basic, you need the VBX versions of the controls, which, if available, are included on the CD-ROM.

Descriptions and installation instructions for each of the controls and utilities are listed below.

ACROBAT Reader

Many sources of information provide documents in the Portable Document Format (PDF). Adobe Acrobat Reader gives you instant access to documents in their original form, regardless of what computer platform you're on. With the Acrobat Reader, you can view, navigate, print, and present any PDF file.

To install Acrobat Reader, run `AR32E30.EXE`.

ACTIVE3D

This is a collection of enhanced 3D controls. It includes

- *SSCheck control*: A flexible, multimedia-enabled replacement for the standard Windows CheckBox control.

- *SSCommand control*: An extended version of the standard Windows command button. It is functionally identical to a regular command button, but it provides a greater range of interface features, including sound, picture, and animation.

- *SSOption control*: A flexible, multimedia-enabled replacement for the standard Windows option button control.

- *SSPanel control*: A container control that groups other controls both visibly and functionally. It provides a unified, distinctive area suited to the creation of control groupings such as toolbars and control panels. The SSPanel can also function as a progress indicator, showing the percentage of a task's completion both graphically and textually.

- *SSRibbon control*: Similar to the SSCommand button except that when it is clicked, it toggles between two states (up and down). It also displays the same exclusive behavior as an option button, but its exclusivity is determined by a property of the control rather than its grouping inside a container.

- *Ssplitter*: A container control that organizes the controls it contains into resizable panes, which are separated by splitter bars that can be dragged with the mouse. It provides functionality similar to that of the frames found on Web pages that use the HTML 2.0 (or greater) specification.

To install ACTIVE3D, run `SETUP.EXE`.

ALARM

Alarm Custom Control (VBX/OCX). This control lets you set an alarm (or multiple alarms) to go off at a particular time(s). An event is fired at the time(s) specified. You can specify times such as 10:45 pm, every hour on the hour, every 10 minutes, and so forth.

To install, run **ALARM.EXE**.

BARCOD

Bar Code Custom Control (VBX/OCX) makes it very simple to display bar code. Just pick the orientation, set the size, and pick the bar code style. Then, set the text to whatever you want the bars to be.

To install, run **BARCOD.EXE**.

DFINFO

Disk and File Info Control (VBX/OCX) gives you disk and file information that VB doesn't provide (including the drive's serial number). It also allows you to change some aspects of a file (attributes, size, date, time, and so on).

To install, run **DFINFO.EXE**.

FIRE

FireEvent Custom Control allows you to fire events in applications. It could be used to add events to Visual Basic objects that you create.

This is a very useful control for the intermediate-to-advanced VB programmer. You must use the 32-bit version if you're working with Visual Basic 5.

To use the FireEvent custom control, you must copy the file to your Windows system directory. The 32-bit version file name of the FireEvent custom control is **FIREVE32.OCX**. The 16-bit version is called **FIREVE16.OCX**. If you are using Windows 95, drag the 32-bit version of the FireEvent OCX to your **WINDOWS\SYSTEM32** directory. If you are using Windows 3.x, drag the **FIREVE16.OCX** to your **WINDOWS\SYSTEM** directory, using the File Manager. Once you have copied the OCX to the proper Windows system directory, you will need to register the custom control. Using Visual Basic 5, from the main menu select Tools and the item Custom Controls; a dialog box appears. From the dialog box, click on the Browse button. Highlight the FireEvent custom control and click the OK button. The custom control will register itself and will appear in the list of custom controls. Check the check box by the FireEvent custom control in order to add the control to your Visual Basic toolbar.

FLABEL

Formatted Label Custom Control (VBX/OCX), FLabel is a label control that lets you format the text within it. You can have different fonts, different colors, multiple paragraphs, paragraph formatting, and so on. Using properties, you can print your text. All this and it's bound, too.

To install, run **FLABEL.EXE**.

HITIME

High Resolution Timer (VBX/OCX) is a high-resolution timer custom control for Visual Basic. It allows you to have timer events come in nearly every millisecond, as opposed to every 55 milliseconds with the normal Visual Basic Timer control.

To install, run **HITIME.EXE**.

JOYSTK

Joy Stick Custom Control (VBX/OCX) gives joystick information (movement, buttons) for your programs. It supports two joysticks, one 4-button joystick or one 3D joystick.

To install, run **JOYSTK.EXE**.

LED

LED Custom Control (VBX/OCX) behaves like an LED. 3D effects and colors are all user-definable.

To install, run **LED.EXE**.

PERCNT

Percentage Bar Custom Control (VBX/OCX) displays a percentage bar. It makes status reporting very simple. 3D effects, fonts, and colors are all user-definable.

To install, run **PERCNT.EXE**.

RESIZE

ReSize is an invisible Visual Basic custom control. When placed on a form, it causes all controls on the form to resize proportionally as the form is resized. You don't have to write any code or set any properties. ReSize does this automatically. Registered users can use the control in both design and stand-alone VB modes. The shareware version is fully functional, but it will only operate in the VB development environment.

To install, follow the instructions in the **README.TXT** file in the **RESIZE** directory.

Check the file date of the **MFC40.DLL** file in your **WINDOWS\SYSTEM** directory. If it is newer than 10/15/96, skip step 2 in the installation instructions.

ROTEXT

Rotated Label Custom Control (VBX/OCX) lets you put a label on your form at any angle of rotation.

To install, run **ROTEXT.EXE**.

SBLIST

SBList 32-bit OCX (sblist.ocx) is an extended list box that allows embedded bitmaps, multiple font attributes, variable color text and backgrounds, table formatting, and grid lines. It's simple to use, and there is a demo included.

To install, run **SETUP.EXE**.

VSDATA

A replacement for the JET Database Engine. Multimedia-aware.
To install, run `SETUP.EXE`.

VSFLEX

A powerful replacement for the databound grid. Multimedia-aware.
To install, run `SETUP.EXE`.

VSVIEW

Adds a word processor control to your programs. Adds enhanced printing control, too.
To install, run `SETUP.EXE`.

Some of the software included on the bundled CD, including Adobe Acrobat™, is shareware, provided for your evaluation. If you find a shareware product useful, you are requested to register it as discussed in its documentation and/or in the About screen of the application. Waite Group Press has not paid the registration fee for this shareware.

CHAPTER 1

WHAT'S ALL THAT STUFF ON MY SCREEN?

ven if you've been programming for a while, your first look at Visual Basic 5 (VB 5) is likely to startle you. There sure is a lot of *stuff* there! True, and a lot of it is new to Visual Basic. In this chapter, you will learn to maneuver around the Visual Basic 5 integrated development environment and to set it up for convenient programming. You won't be writing any programs, but learning these techniques can be a big time saver for you. Even if you are upgrading from VB 3 or VB 4, you will find something new here.

1

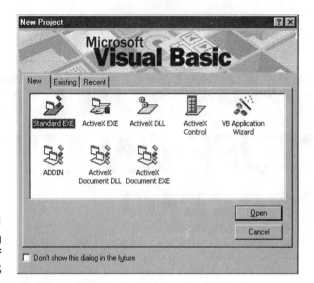

Figure 1-1
The opening
dialog box of
Visual Basic 5

GETTING STARTED

We all have to start *sometime*. If you haven't done so already, double-click on the VB 5 icon and let's take a ride.

The Opening Screen

The first thing you get when you double-click on the VB 5 icon is an opening dialog box that offers a confusing array of choices. The dialog box is shown in Figure 1-1.

Wow! Let's take a look at what all those icons mean.

Your Mileage May Vary

There are three different versions of Visual Basic 5. Some of the features available in the Professional and Enterprise Editions are not available in the Learning Edition. The screens shown throughout this book are from the Enterprise Edition. They may vary in some detail from the screens you see.

All these choices exist because Visual Basic 5 can compile your programs into several different types of files:

● Standard .EXE files, which are normal programs.

- ActiveX .EXE files, which are programs that allow other programs to access their data. These are known as *out of process servers* because they operate in their own process space—memory that Windows sets aside for programs to use.

- ActiveX .DLL files—*dynamic link libraries*, which are collections of functions and procedures that can be accessed by other programs. DLL files are known as *in-process servers*; they operate in the same memory space as the program that uses them.

- ActiveX Controls, which are components that you add to your program. You will learn about controls in Chapter 5, Controls.

- ActiveX Document .DLL and .EXE files that are programs that have been modified to work within Web browser programs such as Internet Explorer. They are suitable for distribution and viewing over the Internet.

- Add-in files, which can be "added in" to the Visual Basic programming environment. They are used to automate things that you do over and over again.

- The VB Application Wizard, which builds a part of your program for you. Obviously it doesn't know what you want the program to do, but it can create a large part of the program's user interface.

Most of the applications in this book use the standard EXE option.

There are three tabs on this opening screen. To open a project file from the disk, select the Existing tab. A dialog box like the one in Figure 1-2 opens.

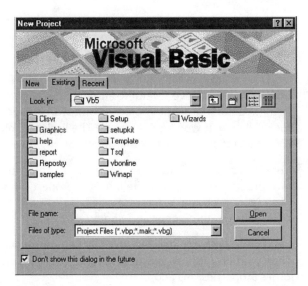

Figure 1-2
The Existing tab

As you can see, this is a lot like the standard Windows 95 Explorer window, and you negotiate it the same way. Later in the book, you will learn to include windows like this in your own programs.

The third tab is the Recent tab. As you might expect, it contains a list of the most recent projects you have been using. Figure 1-3 shows the Recent tab.

You will find this tab handy as you work through the lessons in this book.

The Development Environment

Go back to the New tab and select Standard EXE. Click on Open to begin a new project, and let's take a look at where you will work. The default development environment is shown in Figure 1-4.

There's a *lot* there! Let's take a closer look at the default items on the screen.

- Visual Basic 5 creates Windows programs. The user interface for Windows programs is a window. (Tough stuff!) Each window that your program uses is created on a *form* in the development environment. Think of a form as a blank window on which you will draw the part of program that the user sees.

- When you are writing the program that makes a form work (called the *code*), you use the Code window.

- The items on a form are called *controls.* All the controls that you can use in your project are in the toolbox. Microsoft supplies several controls that are not automatically included in the toolbox. You can also purchase or download other controls, called *third-party controls*. These extra controls add functionality to your VB programs. Later in this book, you will see how to add more controls to the toolbox.

- The toolbar provides quick access to things that are found in the menus. There are several specialized toolbars, too. The standard toolbar is the one you will use the most.

- The Project Explorer window lets you access the different parts of your project. You may have several forms and any number of classes and program modules in a single project. (Don't worry if some of this is mysterious right now. It won't be for long!) The Project Explorer gives you instant access to any part of the project at any time.

- Properties are attributes of your form or an object on your form. You have properties, too. You have a height property, a weight property, and a hair color property. You can set the properties of the form or a control on the form in the Properties window.

- The Form Layout window lets you set the position your form will take when your program begins to run. It is a visual way to set two of the form's properties, Top and Left.

Figure 1-3
The Recent tab

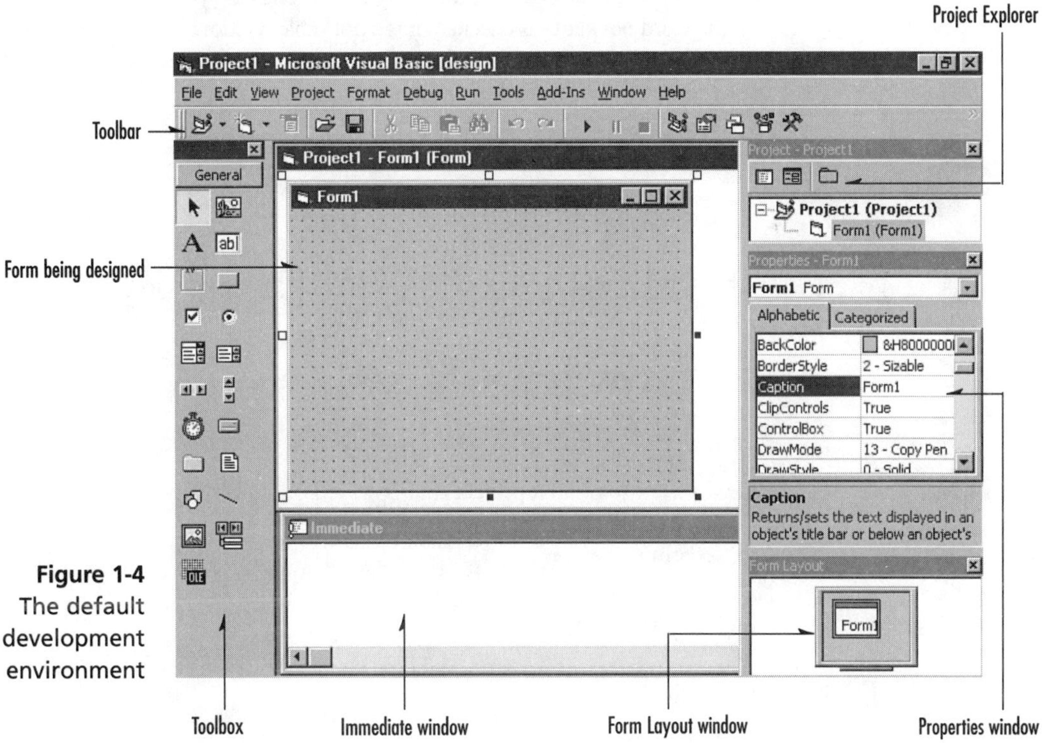

Figure 1-4
The default
development
environment

Project Explorer

Toolbar

Form being designed

Toolbox   Immediate window   Form Layout window   Properties window

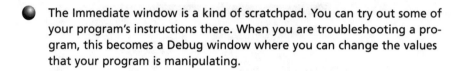

The Immediate window is a kind of scratchpad. You can try out some of your program's instructions there. When you are troubleshooting a program, this becomes a Debug window where you can change the values that your program is manipulating.

Dockable?

All the windows except the Form window have a property of their own: They are dockable. A dockable window is one that attaches itself to the nearest edge of the screen or to the nearest other dockable window. When you move a dockable window, it "snaps" to the location. A docked window is dominant. If you drag the toolbox to the top of the screen, for example, it docks there and all the other windows change size to accommodate it.

Windows that have their **Dockable** property enabled also have another property. They are "always on top." If they are open, they are visible and not hidden behind another window.

You can view the **Dockable** property by right-clicking your mouse inside the window. If the word **Dockable** is checked, it is a dockable window. You can, of course, change that property. If a window is not docked, it is a "floating" window.

Whether you choose to have a window docked or not is a matter of personal preference.

1. The New tab offers several choices for creating a new project. If you just want an ordinary program you should select:
   a. Standard EXE
   b. ActiveX EXE
   c. ActiveX DLL
   d. ActiveX Control

2. If you want to open a project that is stored on your disk, select the:
   a. Recent tab
   b. Existing tab
   c. ActiveX DLL icon
   d. Cancel button

3. The _____ window helps you access the different parts of a project.
   a. Properties
   b. Immediate
   c. Project Explorer
   d. Toolbox

4. Select the controls for your form from the _____ window.
   a. Properties
   b. Immediate
   c. Project Explorer
   d. Toolbox

5. Set the attributes of your form in the _____ window.
   a. Properties
   b. Immediate
   c. Project Explorer
   d. Toolbox

CUSTOMIZING THE DEVELOPMENT ENVIRONMENT

All these wonderful windows are handy, but you don't really need all of them all the time, and the screen is awfully cluttered. If you increase the size of your form, for example, the dockable windows on either side of the form will hide part of it, and you will have to use the scroll bars to view different parts. Worse yet, you will have problems visualizing the overall appearance of the form. It makes sense, then, to close at least some of the windows and perhaps to undock others.

Start by clicking on the Maximize button of the form. Find Window State in the Properties window. Set Window State to Maximized by clicking in the Window State label, then clicking on the drop-down arrow that appears and selecting Maximized from the drop-down list. Note that a portion of the Form window is clipped and scroll bars let you view the hidden parts. You may find it more convenient to see more of the form and to close most of the other windows.

The Project Explorer

The Project Explorer is an essential window. As your project grows, you will need it to get from one part of the project to another. But while you are designing the user interface (the form), the Project Explorer is in the way. Click on the Close button in the upper-right corner of the Project Explorer to close this window. You can get it back when you need it by selecting Project Explorer under the View menu, by pressing CTRL-R, or by selecting the Project Explorer icon on the toolbar. Close this window now.

The Form Layout Window

You use the Form Layout window only once for each form in the project, and sometimes not at all. The form in the current project opens maximized—it takes up the entire screen. There is no need to position it. Also, you often position your program's forms in the program code. As a rule of thumb, use the window when you first add a form to your project, then close it. You can reopen it from the View menu or by selecting its icon on the toolbar, but there is no keyboard shortcut. Close it now.

The Immediate Window

You won't need the Immediate window very often. When you do, it is accessible from the View menu or by pressing CTRL-G. Close it now.

The Properties Window

You need the Properties window to set the properties of the form and all of the controls you place on the form. If you also want to view parts of your form that the Properties window normally covers, you can drag it to another part of the screen. If you close the Properties window, you can reopen it from the View menu, by pressing F4, or by selecting it on the toolbar. You can also drag it into another part of the screen. Leaving it floating is often more convenient than docking it.

The Toolbox

While you are designing the user interface of a form, the form's layout, you need the toolbox available. Once you have placed all your controls, however, you may want to close it to give you a better view of the form for setting properties and positioning the controls more precisely. You can reopen the toolbox from the View menu, by pressing CTRL-X, or by selecting it on the toolbar. Leaving the toolbox floating is often more convenient than docking it.

On the Toolbar

Thought we weren't going to tell you? Figure 1-5 shows the right end of the standard toolbar, where you can find the icons for these necessary windows. There is no reason to worry about closing one of these windows because they are all so easy to recover.

A More Convenient Work Space?

Figure 1-6 shows a work space that we find convenient for form layout. The toolbox is showing, but it is floating instead of docked. It is easy to drag around the screen to get it out of the way. All the other windows are closed, but they are only a mouse click away. Your own preferences dictate the most convenient work space for you.

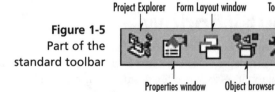

Figure 1-5
Part of the
standard toolbar

Project Explorer   Form Layout window   Toolbox

Properties window   Object browser

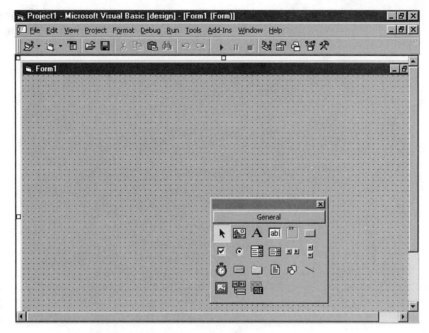

Figure 1-6
A more convenient
work space

This arrangement provides good access to the form, most of which can be accessed without using the scroll bars. It is a great aid for form design.

Don't forget that all these windows are *sizable*, too.

Customizing Your Toolbars

There are several options that are not on the standard toolbar that you may decide you would like to have available with the click of your mouse. For example, the Immediate window is not part of the default toolbar settings, but you may wish to add it. As you gain more experience in programming, you will probably find other features that you use frequently that are not on any of the available toolbars.

Fortunately, it is easy to customize a toolbar. Let's add a few of items to the standard toolbar so you can see how it is done.

1. Right-click in the standard toolbar and select Customize from the pop-up menu that appears. The Customize window shown in Figure 1-7 opens.

2. Select the Tools tab.

3. Click on View in the Categories list box

4. Grab the icon for the Immediate window and drag it to the standard toolbar, as shown in Figure 1-8. Drop it just to the right of the Toolbox icon. This is called "drag and drop."

5. Repeat with the View Object and View Code icons. They will come in handy later.

Figure 1-7
The Customize window

Dropping the icon on the toolbar

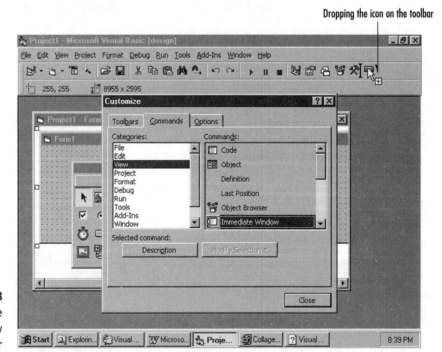

Figure 1-8
Dropping the Immediate window icon on the toolbar

Setting the Dockable Property

You can set the **Dockable** property of all the windows in a single step. Click on the Tools menu and select Options. When the dialog box appears, select the Docking tab. Figure 1-9 shows the Docking tab. The check boxes indicate which windows are dockable and which are not. As an experiment, click on the check box for the Properties window and then click on OK. When you have returned to the development environment, open the Properties window by clicking on its icon.

You may find this version of the Properties window more convenient to use. Note, however, what happens when you click on the form. The Properties window disappears! It is no longer always on top, so when it does not have the focus, it falls behind the window that does have focus.

It is all a matter of taste; set your development environment up the way you like it. You can always change it.

While you are in the Options window, make one more change. Select the Environment tab and click in the check box next to Prompt To Save Changes, then click on OK. When you run a Visual Basic program, VB 5 asks whether you want to save any changes you have made. In most cases, the correct answer is Yes.

1. What windows need to be open while you are laying out a form?
   a. Form, Form Layout, Properties, Toolbox
   b. Form, Form Layout, Properties, Toolbox, Project Explorer
   c. Form, Toolbox
   d. Form, Form Layout, Properties, Project Explorer

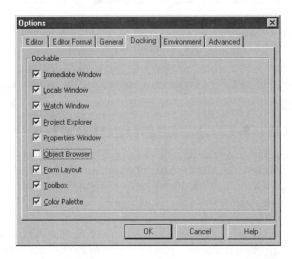

Figure 1-9
VB 5's Docking tab

2. Which of the standard windows is *not* accessible from the toolbar?
   a. The Toolbox window
   b. The Project Explorer window
   c. The Properties window
   d. The Immediate window

3. You can add new functions to a toolbar by using the _____ window.
   a. Immediate
   b. Customize
   c. Options
   d. Form Layout

4. You can select which windows are dockable using the _____ window.
   a. Immediate
   b. Customize
   c. Options
   d. Form Layout

5. Which of the standard windows do you need to select different parts of a project?
   a. The Toolbox window
   b. The Project Explorer window
   c. The Properties window
   d. The Immediate window

THE APPLICATION WIZARD

Microsoft has added wizards to almost everything it produces, and Visual Basic 5 is no exception. In this lesson, you will use the Application Wizard to see how VB 5 creates a ready-to-modify application framework that can make your programming efforts look professional with a minimum of work. This book is dedicated to teaching you how to write and understand the code, so we will not use the wizards a lot. After you have mastered the art of programming, you might find some of them very helpful.

Running the Application Wizard

Select New Project under the File menu. (The keyboard shortcut is CTRL-N if you prefer keys.) When the opening dialog box appears, select the Application Wizard. The Application Wizard—Introduction screen shown in Figure 1-10 appears. You probably won't want to see this screen again, so click on the Skip This Screen In the Future check box, then click on Next.

This brings up the Application Wizard—Interface Type screen shown in Figure 1-11, which offers three types of user interface. It's too early to get really fancy, so select

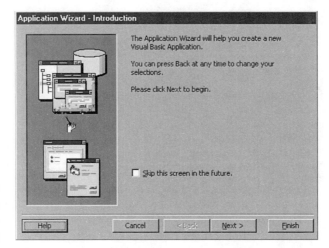

Figure 1-10
The Application
Wizard—
Introduction screen

Single Document Interface; then click on Next. (Honest, we will talk about the others later in the book!)

The next screen you see is the Application Wizard—Menus screen, shown in Figure 1-12. Many programs will have three standard menus, File, Edit and Help, but we are going to go whole hog here, so click in the check box next to View as well. The Wizard adds all four menus to your program. Click on Next to move on.

The next screen is the Application Wizard—Resources screen. Building resource files is an advanced topic that we will not cover in this book. Note that the No option is already selected. Just click on Next to move on.

You see the Application Wizard—Internet Connectivity screen. Yep, it can be that easy! Well, almost that easy. As nice as it would be to add an Internet browser to your

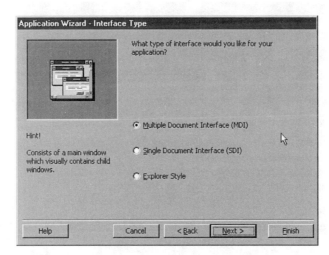

Figure 1-11
The Application
Wizard—Interface
Type screen

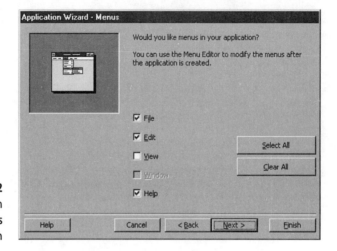

Figure 1-12
The Application
Wizard—Menus
screen

new application, it is far too early. Chapter 18, Visual Basic 5 Communications, shows you how to build a Web browser. Be sure that No is selected and click on Next.

Which brings you to the Application Wizard—Standard Forms screen, shown in Figure 1-13. *Now* you have some choices to make.

You can design forms that you will use again and again and save them in a standard forms template collection. Actually, Microsoft has provided you with 19 standard form templates in the **TEMPLATE\FORMS** subdirectory for Visual Basic 5, but you can add as many more as you wish. Click on the Form Templates button to get an idea of the choices. They don't all show up because most of your selections are made using the check boxes. Close the Standard Forms dialog box and let's make our choices.

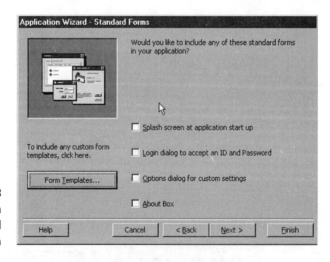

Figure 1-13
The Application
Wizard—Standard
Forms screen

Splash Screen

A splash screen is a screen that comes up immediately and gives the user something to look at while the real working screens are being loaded. You see them all the time; Visual Basic 5 starts out with a splash screen, as do most other large programs. Splash screens give the illusion that your program loads more quickly than it actually does.

Based on the questions that appear in the Visual Basic Internet newsgroups, splash screens are not easy to do. Not any more! VB 5 can create one for you. All you have to do is modify it a little to make it uniquely your own. Click on the Splash Screen check box to select it.

You can get a lot of help and a lot of ideas from the Usenet newsgroups. As of this writing, four are devoted to Visual Basic. They are

> comp.lang.basic.visual.thirdparty
> comp.lang.basic.visual.announce
> comp.lang.basic.visual.database
> comp.lang.basic.visual.misc

There are also special newsgroups available at Microsoft's Visual Basic Web site, `http://www.microsoft.com/vbasic`. And if you enjoy the World Wide Web, a recent search found more than 83,000 documents about Visual Basic.

Login Dialog

Some programs need security, which requires a login screen where the user must enter a name and a password before he or she is granted entry to the program. VB 5 can build the login screen for you, but you are not ready to use it yet, so skip this choice.

Options Dialog for Custom Settings

The best programs let you customize the way they look and, to some degree, the way they work. You have already customized Visual Basic 5, so you have a pretty good idea what that is all about. Customizing settings is pretty sophisticated for a first effort, so skip this choice.

About Box

If you pull down the Help menu in any good Windows program, you see an option called About .... The program's distributor uses the About box to display copyright notices and version information. *Really* sophisticated programs include a choice here to allow the user to get system information.

VB 5 can build the About box for you. Some modification is required to personalize it, but the hard part is done. Put a checkmark next to About Box; then click on Next.

The next screen is the Application Wizard Data Access Forms screen. You aren't writing a database application yet, so just remember that it is there and click on Next.

The Finished! Screen

The next screen you see is the Finished! screen. All that remains is to give your project a name and you are ready to try it out! Enter `GeeWhiz` (all one word) in the text box and click on Finish. Your hard drive whirs and whizzes for a while, your screen flashes and flickers and gives you tantalizing views of sophisticated-looking forms, and finally you are rewarded with the screen in Figure 1-14.

There's no end to the wonders of this program! Here is a set of instructions about what you can do next! You can read the instructions on this screen and choose to close the screen or to save the instructions to a text file and then close the screen. For now, just close it.

If your Project Explorer is not open, open it now.

The Wizard-Created Program

According to the Project Explorer, you have three forms and a module in your program. This might not make a lot of sense to you right now, but you will get it. For now, you just want to see what VB 5 has wrought. Press F5 to run the program.

Pretty neat! And you have yet to write a single line of code! There you are with a nifty (so we exaggerate a bit!) splash screen; when the main form comes up, just *look* at everything there. Four menus, a toolbar, and a status bar at the bottom of the screen.

Check out the menus. Under the File menu, select Open. You get a standard Windows file selection screen. Go ahead and select a file, perhaps a text file or a bitmap. It seems to load, but nothing happens. Try Print under the File menu. Aha! Now you begin to see what *your* job is.

Try a few of the icons on the toolbar. Except for File Open, none of them have any working code. Let your mouse pointer rest on one of the icons for a moment. Tooltips! Another new toy from Visual Basic 5.

Now let's look at some real sophistication. Select About under the Help menu. The About box has a place to put a picture—your logo, perhaps? There is space for the version number and a description of the application, or maybe a plug for your company. There is an ominous space labeled `Warning...`, which is where you will put your copyright notice.

Figure 1-14
Your application
has been created

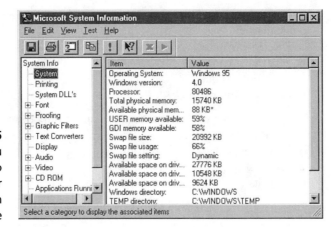

Figure 1-15
Everything you
always wanted to
know about your
system—and then
some

And there is a System Info button. Go ahead, click it! (If you are scared, take a look at Figure 1-15.)

The System Info window is a standard Microsoft component that can be accessed from Visual Basic 5. Not too long ago, people spent a couple hundred dollars for programs that could tell them some of what this utility provides in your About box!

What's Missing

You can see that the wizard did a lot of useful work for you, but a lot of work remains to be done. Except for a few standard functions, you must write the code to make all the menu items work. And the main form is blank except for the menus and the toolbar. That's a good thing. After all, if Visual Basic could write the whole program, there wouldn't be a need for programmers!

The purpose of this book is for you to learn how to fill in the blanks, the remainder of the program, and how to create programs that differ from the "standard" patterns that the wizard will develop. If you play with the Application Wizard, you will discover, for example, that the toolbar is always included, although your programs may not require one—or may require a toolbar with completely different options. To adapt the output of the wizards to your own tasks, you must understand the details of the programming language. Read on!

1. What type of program interface will the Application Wizard create?
   a. Multiple Document Interface
   b. Single Document Interface
   c. Explorer Style Interface
   d. All of the above

2. Several standard menus are available in the wizard. The ones found in most programs are:
   a. File, Edit, Window
   b. File, Edit, Help
   c. View, Edit, About
   d. File, Edit, Insert

3. Form designs that you use over and over again can be saved as:
   a. `Form1.FRM`
   b. Templates
   c. Patterns
   d. Formats

4. The _____ is used to display the version number and the copyright notice.
   a. Login screen
   b. Data access forms
   c. Options dialog
   d. About box

5. The program that the wizard creates is:
   a. A complete, ready to run program
   b. A pattern that you can copy for your own work
   c. An application framework that you must modify to have a functional program
   d. None of the above

REVIEW

John: Wow! I am impressed with that Application Wizard!

Lisa: Yes. I especially liked the System Info button. I was surprised how complete it was.

John: And we didn't even write a program to make it happen.

Lisa: It won't be long before we know how to do that, too.

John: I hope so. This looks like fun!

ADD-INS

Visual Basic 5 comes with several *add-ins*. Add-ins are extensions of the Visual Basic development environment—utilities and wizards that simplify some of the more common tasks. If you have the Professional or Enterprise Editions of Visual Basic 5, you can even create your own add-ins.

Adding Add-Ins

Add add-ins? Well, the default setup for VB 5 includes only one of the add-ins as a standard, the Visual Data Manager. You may find other add-ins that are not yet built lurking around in the `Samples` directory.

Select the Add-Ins menu. The default Add-Ins menu is shown in Figure 1-16.

There are only two items in the Add-Ins menu at the moment: the Visual Data Manager and the Add-In Manager. Select the Add-In Manager. Your screen looks something like Figure 1-17.

Some of the add-ins might not show up on your system. Different versions of Visual Basic support different features. As of this writing, full information on which features will be included with which version is not available.

Let's take a quick look at the add-ins shown in Figure 1-17.

Visual Data Manager

The Visual Data Manager lets you create databases without having to go to the expense of purchasing Microsoft Access. You will learn to work with databases in Chapter 13, Data Access.

API Viewer

Windows programs are built around a standard set of features known as the *application program interface*, or API. All programs call on the API for most of their functions. But some of the API functions are not accessed directly from Visual Basic. You can still

Figure 1-16
The Add-Ins menu

Figure 1-17
The Add-In
Manager screen

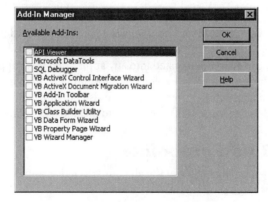

use them, as you will see in Chapter 14, Advanced Features, and again in Chapter 17, Register Your Programs: Using the Windows Registry.

Using the API is not difficult, but the API is picky. Everything must be just so, and much of what you have to add to your programs is quite detailed. The API viewer allows you to cut and paste the required declarations. It helps you avoid errors and is a great time saver.

The Microsoft Data Tools

The Data Tools add-in helps you build data-aware Internet applications. It requires Internet Explorer and Microsoft's SQL Server software. Its use goes beyond the scope of a beginning programmer's book.

SQL Debugger

SQL stands for *Structured Query Language*. You will learn some SQL in Chapter 13, Data Access, but the SQL Debugger add-in is meant to be used with Microsoft's SQL Server software. Its use goes beyond the scope of a beginning programmer's book.

The VB ActiveX Control Interface Wizard

Visual Basic 5 lets you build your own ActiveX controls, which you will do in Chapter 16, Roll Your Own: Creating Your Own ActiveX Controls. The ActiveX Control Interface Wizard helps you create the public interface for a Visual Basic-generated ActiveX control after you have created your user interface. The public interface includes properties, methods, and events. (Yes, you will understand all this terminology, and soon, too!)

The VB ActiveX Document Migration Wizard

The programs you create with Visual Basic 5 can become ActiveX documents. That means that they can be viewed and operated with browsers such as the Internet Explorer and they can be made available on the Internet or in company-wide intranets. The Document Migration Wizard does most of the work for you. You will migrate an application in Chapter 18, Visual Basic 5 Communications.

What is ActiveX, anyhow? ActiveX is a programming standard that integrates software components in a networked environment. ActiveX controls can be integrated into Web pages. They can also be integrated into any application that supports ActiveX controls, including Microsoft Internet Explorer, Microsoft Office 97, Visual Basic, and Netscape Navigator via plug-ins. Other companies are also building ActiveX capabilities into their products, allowing developers (that's you!) to include new controls in their applications.

The VB Add-In Toolbar

The VB Add-In toolbar lets you use all your selected add-ins with a single mouse click instead of having to use the Add-In menu.

The VB Application Wizard

We covered the Application Wizard in Lesson 3. You haven't forgotten already, have you?

The VB Class Builder Utility

Classes are the blueprints for *object-oriented programming*, and object-oriented programming is the foundation of all modern programming languages, including Visual Basic 5; you will be exposed to the concepts of object-oriented programming throughout this book. Although you don't *need* it, the Class Builder utility helps you build and organize your classes.

The VB Data Form Wizard

Database programming involves a lot of attention to detail. Databases can store tremendous amounts of data arranged in a bewildering array of tables and fields. The Data Form Wizard creates forms (screens) that display your data. Like all the other wizards, the Data Form Wizard leaves some of the finer details to you, but it can be a big time saver.

The VB Property Page Wizard

As you work with some of the controls in Visual Basic, you will discover that they have *property pages*, which are tabbed pages that help you customize the way a control or looks and behaves. When you create your own ActiveX controls, the Property Page Wizard helps you add this sophisticated feature to your own controls.

The Wizard Manager

Just in case there aren't enough wizards to satisfy your taste, the Wizard Manager helps you build your own wizards. If you find yourself building the same kind of application time after time, or adding the same functionality to all your applications, you can build a wizard that automates the process for you.

Summary

Add-ins, builders, wizards! Visual Basic 5 makes every effort to provide you with the tools that simplify and speed the process of creating your own applications. If you already program in Visual Basic 3 or 4 or in another language, you will be amazed to discover how quickly Visual Basic 5 can do things that you used to spend hours doing. If you are a new programmer, you will be able to turn out professional-looking (and -acting) applications even while you learn Visual Basic.

1. Add-ins can be included in the Visual Basic development environment by using the:
   a. Add-In toolbar
   b. Visual Data Manager
   c. Wizard Manager
   d. Add-In Manager

2. The _____ add-in helps you build forms for database programs.
   a. SQL Debugger
   b. Property Page Wizard
   c. Data Form Designer
   d. ActiveX Document Migration Wizard

3. You can create your own controls for Visual Basic with the help of:
   a. The ActiveX Control Interface Wizard
   b. The Visual Data Manager
   c. The ActiveX Document Migration Wizard
   d. The Wizard Manager

4. You can build your own wizards with:
   a. The ActiveX Control Interface Wizard
   b. The Visual Data Manager
   c. The ActiveX Document Migration Wizard
   d. The Wizard Manager

5. You can access your add-ins with a single mouse click with the:
   a. Add-In toolbar
   b. Visual Data Manager
   c. ActiveX Document Migration Wizard
   d. Wizard Manager

HELP!

This may be the single most important lesson in the entire book. There is no way that any book can hope to cover all the features of Visual Basic 5, or all the possibilities you may uncover for using them. Finding and solving new problems is one of the joys of programming.

Visual Basic 5 comes with a large collection of Help files. Knowing how to find what you need by using the Help files is one of your most valuable skills.

Using Help

If you have been using Windows for any length of time, you already know how to use Help. You might be surprised to know how many Visual Basic users ask questions that are answered in the Help files! Open the Help menu; a menu something like the one shown in Figure 1-18 appears.

Hmmm. There's more here than the usual Help and About listings. Let's take a look at them.

Microsoft Visual Basic Help Topics

This is where you will spend most of your time in Help. You will spend some time visiting this section later in this lesson.

Search Reference Index

As of this writing, this choice takes you to exactly the same place as Help Topics.

Search Master Index

Included on the Visual Basic 5 CD is a version of Microsoft's Books Online database. The Master Index referred to here is the index of the VB Books Online file.

Obtaining Technical Support

Microsoft offers technical support in several different venues. The information in this menu provides the latest information on how to get official Microsoft technical support.

Microsoft on the Web

This menu option provides the URL for Microsoft's Web pages. It also includes the Internet address of the Microsoft FTP sites for Visual Basic. If you have Internet access, the WWW pages are the best way to keep up with changes, problem solutions, and ideas.

About Microsoft Visual Basic

This option displays the standard About box, including, of course, that System Info button you found in GeeWhiz.

Figure 1-18
The Visual Basic 5
Help menu

A Closer Look

Let's take a closer look at the Microsoft Visual Basic Help Topics selection. Click on that now and a menu like the one shown in Figure 1-19 appears.

Familiar enough, of course; Microsoft did not suddenly reinvent the Help system just for Visual Basic. What it *has* done is use the Help system to its fullest. Double-click on Objects, then on the C: book, and finally on the CheckBox Control icon. A screen like Figure 1-20 appears.

You selected the check box because you are already familiar with it, although this is certainly a lot more detail than you had before, when you just clicked in it. Don't pay a lot of attention to what it says about the CheckBox control for now; you will work with that in Chapter 2, Object-Oriented Programming. Notice, instead, the choices offered at the top of the screen. As we discuss each one, click on it to see what it offers.

See Also

The See Also choice points you to other Help topics that have some bearing on the CheckBox control. Because some Help topics cover items that are closely related to other Help topics, you will find this invaluable in tracking down all the references you need to get a task done.

Example

If you are looking up a command or a function, the Help system will often give you an example of how to use it. You can even cut and paste the example into your own programs! There are no examples for most of the controls, and Example is grayed out in that case.

Figure 1-19
Visual Basic
Help topics

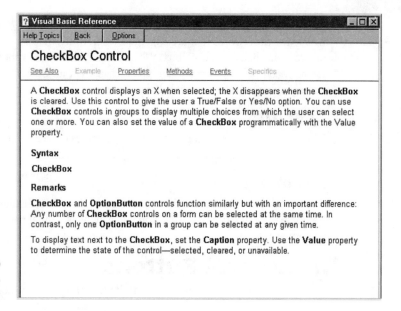

Figure 1-20
Help on the
CheckBox control

Properties

Properties are attributes or characteristics, like color and size. If you click on the Properties choice, you see a list of the control's properties, as shown in Figure 1-21.

Again, don't pay a lot of attention yet. What you need is to learn how to find things in the Help files. You will have plenty of time to dig out more details later.

Methods

Methods are things you can do to a control. You can, for example, move it or give it focus (make it the active control). Methods are often thought of as "verbs" like *MoveThis* or *DoThat*. Try clicking on the Methods choice to get an idea. The CheckBox has only a few methods. Other controls have many more.

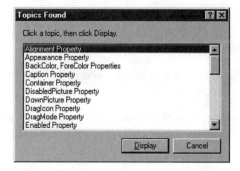

Figure 1-21
The properties
of a check box

Events

Events are procedures that are triggered when things happen to a control. For example, you can click on a check box. When you do, the `Click` event is fired and the control can respond to what you have done. Once again, there are only a few events for a CheckBox control, whereas other controls have dozens.

Specifics

When a topic requires a lot of detail, the Specifics choice is enabled. Because a check box is a pretty simple control, Specifics is grayed out.

Summary

The Summary choice is not shown for a check box. It is displayed for topics like the Database Object, where the topic you are viewing is a small part of a collection of related controls.

The Control Buttons

There are also three control buttons at the top of the screen. Let's take a look.

Help Topics

The Help Topics button takes you back to the Table of Contents screen.

Back

Windows Help keeps a history of the choices you have made during a Help session. If you have selected a series of Help topics, the Back button lets you move backward through the list of topics you have viewed. This is often handier than trying to find the topic again.

Options

The Options button offers several more choices. You can

- Annotate the topic: Write notes on the topic that you can then view the next time you bring the topic up. The same choice lets you read notes you have written.

- Copy the topic to the clipboard: Once the topic is copied, you can paste it into any Windows document.

- Print the topic: Use this sparingly unless you have reams of paper and are an excellent organizer.

- Change the font size: The three choices are small, normal, and large, which is helpful on those late nights after a 16-hour stint at the keyboard.

- Keep Help on top, or not, depending on your taste: It is always on top by default.

- Use System Colors for Windows Help: If you have a favorite color scheme, you can have Help use the same colors.

But Wait! There's More!

The main Help screen has three tabs, and you have looked at only one of them. The others can sometimes be your biggest help.

The Index Tab

The Help files have an index, which can usually help you find what you are looking for faster than the table of contents. Switch to the Index tab now and type `check` into the text box at the top. You see something like Figure 1-22.

Turns out that there is more to this topic than you originally saw! Not really, but the index seems to be a quicker way to find things.

The Find Tab

The Find tab is even more flexible. The first time you select Find, the computer wants to do a conversion of the word list. Tell it OK, then go get some coffee and a couple of donuts—it takes a while. Even after the Find database has been created, the Find tab takes a few seconds the first time you click on it so it can "load the word list." It is more than worth the wait.

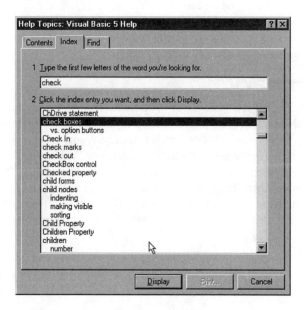

Figure 1-22
Index finding `check`

Figure 1-23
Find finding check

Click on Find now and type **check** in the text box at the top of the Find tab's dialog. The Find tab looks something like Figure 1-23.

Now *there* is a collection of information! You can even tailor the search if you are looking for something in a specific area. You can change the time when the search begins and how much of what you type in is a required part of the search key. All that is handled by the Options button.

By default, the Find tab begins searching when there is a pause in your typing, it searches for all references that begin with the characters you typed, and it searches through the entire collection of VB 5 Help files.

Summary

Practice using the Visual Basic Help files. Practically everything you need to know is included in there somewhere, and it is available whenever you need it. You might have to dig for your information, but if you persist, you can find it.

This lesson has concentrated on Visual Basic 5's Help files. The Contents tab offers well-organized, single-topic selections; the Index tab widens the scope of your search; and the Find tab gives you the broadest search capabilities. You will find that all these tabs are handy, but chances are you will find yourself using one more than the other two combined. Which one that is will be a matter of personal taste.

1. The VB 5 Help system provides information about the _____ for controls.
   a. Properties, methods, and events
   b. Color, position, and size
   c. Syntax
   d. None of the above

2. The first tab in the Help system is the _____ tab.
   a. Contents
   b. Index
   c. Find
   d. Options

3. The _____ button lets you visit Help topics you have viewed before.
   a. Contents
   b. Help
   c. Back
   d. Go

4. The _____ button lets you change the font size or add annotations to the Help files.
   a. Index
   b. Options
   c. Find
   d. Contents

5. The broadest search in the Help system is provided by the _____ tab.
   a. Contents
   b. Index
   c. Find
   d. Options

CHAPTER 2

OBJECT-ORIENTED PROGRAMMING

Visual Basic 5 is based on the concept of *objects*. An object is a distinct unit in a program that has certain characteristics and can do certain things. In *object-oriented programming*, you approach a programming problem by asking How can I break down this task into objects? What will each object look like? How will it behave? and then, How do the objects interact?

The advantage of object-oriented programming, or OOP, is that well designed objects are reusable in other applications. The most visible example of this technique is Microsoft Windows itself. The elements you commonly use to interact with your computer—windows, buttons, menus, and so on—are all objects. As a Visual Basic programmer, you add these types of objects to your programs. You control their characteristics—such as whether or not a window is sizable—and what happens when your program's user interacts with them—for example, by clicking on a button. However, many of the tasks that are common to all objects of the same type are handled automatically by Windows.

OBJECTS

The word *object* has a particular meaning in software development terminology. An object also means different things to different people. We are going to concentrate on the definition of objects and OOP from the perspective of Visual Basic 5.

The Evolution of Object-Oriented Programming

In the past, programmers were taught to take complex problems and break them down into smaller, less complex ones. This process, termed *decomposition*, may be familiar to you as the traditional top-down approach to software design. Decomposition continues until you are left with a finite set of *procedures*—small units of code—that fully define the solution to the problem.

The problem with procedural design is that the resulting software is inherently inflexible. Small changes to one localized section of the design can affect large amounts of code. Even well-structured software designed by highly experienced analysts is affected in this way. Eventually, the software becomes difficult, or even impossible, to maintain and debug. When it reaches this stage, the only option is to start all over again.

When the computer software industry was in its infancy, the idea that software had to be ultimately disposable was largely accepted. As software became more complex and, therefore, more expensive, the fact that the software itself needed to be more durable and accepting of change became clear. It also became clear that the design techniques themselves were flawed.

So that they could understand more about software design, software designers and methodologists turned to other industries to see if anything could be learned from their design and construction techniques. The construction industry itself is a good example. After all, it would be ridiculous if you had to dismantle your house every time you wanted to redecorate. Yet this was what had been happening to software for many years.

Eventually, it was recognized that although computing was a new industry, it didn't necessarily require new design strategies. Like a construction project, a software project could be seen as a system that programmers would build up from lots of small, self-contained objects.

Objects surround us. This is obvious. We intuitively know what a real-world object is because we can use our senses to determine that it exists. Some examples of real-world objects are trees, cars, people, computers, desks, and chairs. Let's have a look at the characteristics all objects have in common:

- Each individual object is a self-contained unit. The existence of one particular object is not dependent on the existence of another.

- Although individual objects are unique, each object can be identified as belonging to a particular classification through its properties.

- Objects can respond to certain predefined external stimuli only.

- Objects can interact with each other and with the outside world in a predefined and limited manner.

- Although each object behaves in a different way, many of the things objects know how to do can be given the same name. For example, for humans to walk, we have to coordinate moving two legs. For dogs to walk, they have to coordinate four legs. Both can walk, but neither is concerned at a strategic level with the actual processes involved.

And So...What?

How does this understanding of objects relate to computer software?

Imagine that a sports equipment manufacturer has hired you as an information technology consultant. The company has decided to launch a new range of soccer balls for both the professional and the home markets. To achieve its goal (argh), the company has to transform a basic design concept into a fully operational manufacturing process.

To begin with, the company has only a vague idea about the final products and their performance specifications. For example, it knows that the top-of-the-line professional ball will have to be made of a number of black and white hexagonal and square pieces of leather, stitched together to form a sphere. It knows that the ball will contain an inner tube that will have to be inflated to a certain air pressure, with the air inlet protected by a valve to prevent the air from escaping.

Compare this with the bottom-of-the-line ball for the home market. This will be made of two molded hemispherical pieces of plastic, which will then be bonded together. Unlike the professional ball, this version will be inflated during the manufacturing process and, instead of a valve, a solid piece of plastic will be molded into the air inlet hole to prevent the air from escaping.

The company needs to determine the type and grade of materials that will be used in the construction of the various versions of the ball. Criteria such as durability, bounce, and burst pressure will all affect the choice of materials and the manufacturing processes eventually chosen. Factors such as the grade of leather and thread used, as well as the stitching technique itself, will affect the durability of the professional ball. Similarly, the type of plastic and the plastic welding technique used to bond the two halves of the domestic ball together must produce a strong enough bond to meet the specification for that product.

Traditionally, the company has relied on prototyping to determine that both the materials and manufacturing processes will meet the required standards. However, prototyping is expensive and time-consuming, so instead the company has come to you to write a computer system to model the performance of balls made from different materials and manufacturing processes.

Thinking in Objects

Object-oriented programming requires you to think first of the *things* you are trying to model in your software. (In procedural-oriented design, by contrast, you would first think about how those things work.) This does not imply that analyzing how things work is unimportant, but it is not of central importance and does not influence the higher-level design.

The first problem most software analysts have is working out what an object is in their particular project. They often have difficulty identifying where the boundaries between objects lie. Some objects have boundaries that are fairly intuitive. For example, it is easy to tell that, in your prototyping system, you need to think of a ball as an object, because it directly relates to something that exists in the real world. Although the objects in each particular project vary each time, there is a broad rule that you can apply. Try to think of every *thing* in object-oriented terms. In other words, assume that everything you can represent by a noun in the system that you are trying to model is an object. Examples in this project would include a ball, an inner tube, and an air inlet.

Object-oriented analysis is all about understanding the properties and behavioral characteristics of the objects in your project. Once you have identified what the objects are, you need to consider the following:

- An object's properties, which help identify it as being an object of a particular type

- The common external events to which objects of a particular type need to respond

- The common abilities that objects of a particular type need to exhibit to make them useful

Objects Have Properties

To classify objects as belonging to a particular type, you need to identify the properties that distinguish them from other types of objects.

In the prototyping example, the professional ball might have the following properties:

- The length of one side of one hexagonal shape: Because the number and arrangement of hexagonal and square shapes is fixed, you only need to vary the size of each component piece to produce a ball of a different size. It is possible to write an algorithm to calculate the entire surface of the ball from this one measurement. (An *algorithm* is a way of going about solving a problem.)

- Internal and external air pressure expressed in pounds per square inch: You would need this property to model how well the ball might bounce.

- Strength of outer skin expressed on a percentage scale: You would need this property to help assess the durability of different grades of leather over time.

Obviously, a real prototyping system would need to implement more properties than these for an accurate representation of a soccer ball. This list does, however, convey the kinds of properties that objects have.

Objects Have Events

To exist in an environment, objects must be able to react with that environment and with other objects that share that environment. For example, in the prototyping system, consider how you might model how well a soccer ball bounces. Provided you have an algorithm for modeling how a ball moves when it comes into contact with some external surface, you simply have to recognize that, to make the ball bounce, it has to be able to respond to the event of hitting the other surface. Let's call this event Touch. Therefore, every time a ball comes into contact with another surface, a Touch event occurs, and your simulation of the ball reacts to the event.

Similarly, each time the ball moves to a different position, it will be necessary to redraw the ball on the screen. So the list of events that the ball would have to respond to would have to include a ReDraw event.

Objects Have Methods

Objects also have to perform functions of their own. It isn't usually enough that the object exists. After all, the whole point of creating an object is that the object does something useful. These additional functions are known as *methods* in OOP terms.

In the prototyping example, one of the methods that the soccer balls would have to implement would be the functionality that draws the ball on the screen. Earlier, we talked about the example of humans and canines, who both know how to walk. The processes are different, but the verb is the same. Similarly, you'll be able to draw a ball in your project simply by using the verb "draw," because each ball will contain the source code it needs to be able to draw itself on the screen.

It is legitimate to connect an object's methods to the events that it responds to so that the object can perform useful tasks in response to external events. Given the example of a ball object responding to a ReDraw event, the ball could simply call its Draw method every time it receives a ReDraw event to update the screen.

Objects Are Instances of Classes

Until now, we have talked about different classifications or types of objects. You have also seen how an object can be defined by its properties, events, and methods. Object-oriented terms use the word *class* to refer to the properties, events, and methods that uniquely define a type of object.

When we refer to a *class*, we are not referring to a tangible object, either in the real world or in the context of the computer program. Rather, a class is the information that we need to create an object of that class.

Each object in a program is said to be an *instance* of its class. The form and controls you use to build a program are actually instances of their respective classes.

You should now be able to see another benefit of object-oriented design. Each object is a separate unit, consisting of the code *and* the data, which together refer to that particular instance of the class. In the prototyping example, it would therefore be a simple matter to model more than one ball on the screen at the same time. You could simply create a new instance of one particular class of ball. To model two or more professional balls at the same time, you could just create the number of professional ball objects that you require. It would also be a simple matter to create instances of different types of balls and model them all on the screen at the same time.

Some objects naturally fit into a schema in which multiple instances of the objects might exist. The soccer ball is a good example. Others do not, however. For instance, take the screen around which the soccer balls are bouncing. Remember that everything in your object-oriented world should be considered an object. Accordingly, the environment in which your soccer ball objects bounce around must be an object itself. It would not make sense, however, to have more than one screen object.

Objects Have Life Cycles

Now that you have seen that objects are instances of their classes, you may recognize that objects have life cycles. That is to say that in order to be used, they have to be created. At some point, when they are not needed any more, they can be destroyed. You should also note that, before an object is created, it doesn't exist and therefore it doesn't take up any of the computer's resources (memory). Similarly, when an object is destroyed, the memory that was being used by that object is freed and is then available for reuse.

Conclusion

You should now understand what is meant by the terms object, instance, class, property, event, and method. Let's start putting these concepts to work.

1. A *property* is best defined as:
   a. Something that an object has
   b. Something that an object knows how to do
   c. The size of something, such as the side of a soccer ball
   d. A characteristic of an object

2. A *method* is best defined as:
   a. A function that calls an object
   b. A function that an object knows how to do
   c. Walking
   d. A type of event

3. Which of the following is *not* an object that might appear in a printing application?
   a. A printer driver
   b. A file
   c. A font
   d. The number of pages to print

4. After defining the characteristics of a *class*, how do you add an object of that class to your program?
   a. Generate an *instance* of that class.
   b. Generate a *method* of that class.
   c. Add a **Name** property to refer to it.
   d. You don't have to do anything further; defining the class automatically creates the object.

5. Destroying an object when you're done using it:
   a. Is heartless and unnecessary
   b. Frees up system resources for reuse
   c. Takes more processing time than it is worth
   d. Is no longer necessary in Windows 95

FORMS: YOUR FIRST PROGRAM

Sure, you've heard how easy it is to program in Visual Basic. How easy?

Off and Running

Double-click on the Visual Basic 5 program icon and select Standard Exe. Now click on Start under the Run menu. The program that's running represents Visual Basic's default project: a single blank window called Form1. Even though you haven't done anything, this window, shown in Figure 2-1, behaves as you would expect it to. You can move it around, minimize or maximize it, or resize it. This is because Windows already knows how this object is supposed to behave.

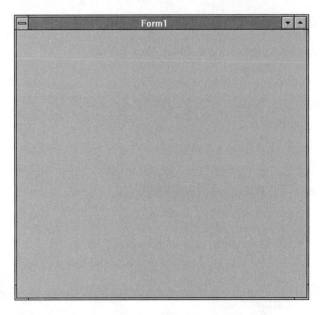

Figure 2-1
This really is a
program

Now close the program by clicking on the window's Close box and selecting the Close menu option. (The Close box and its menu are shown in Figure 2-2.) You return to the Visual Basic design screen.

In Visual Basic, this window object is called a *form*. The form contains most of the other objects that make up your program. In Figure 2-2, the form is a generic sizable window.

A form can be large, such as a program's main screen, or small, such as a dialog box. A form can even be hidden from view, performing tasks in the background. You specify all the characteristics of the forms in your program. When your program is running, Microsoft Windows handles much of the form's behavior automatically.

Figure 2-2
Click on the Close
option to quit

Looking Pretty

A program can have one or many forms. The form that comes up when the user first runs your program is called the *startup* form. By default, this is called Form1. Let's change this name to something more descriptive.

The description of the form that appears on the title bar is called a *caption*. A caption is one of the many characteristics or *properties* an object can have.

You can change most properties at *design time,* which is when you are laying out your application and writing code. You can also change most properties at *runtime* as well, which is when your program is running.

The Visual Basic title bar indicates whether you are currently in design or runtime mode.

Notice the Properties window, shown in Figure 2-3. The property names are in the left column; the corresponding values are in the right. The long list of properties for Form1 gives you an idea of the power Visual Basic provides over your form design. Luckily for you, the default settings describe a fairly typical window and are fine for now. Click on the Caption property and type in File Picker, as shown in the figure. Note that VB copies the caption to the title bar as you type it.

Visual Basic's visual editing system lets you "draw" your program to your specifications. What you see on the screen is pretty much what you'll get when the program runs. Test this by resizing the form and running the program again to see your changes reflected.

Stay in Control

Tired of looking at an empty window? Let's add some objects to the form.

Visual Basic has several types of objects. Forms are one type. *Controls* are another. A Visual Basic control is the most common component of VB programs. Typical controls are small, with a specific function, such as a Command button or check box. Other controls offer more elaborate functionality, such as the Data control and MCI (multimedia) control.

Figure 2-3
The Properties
window

Under the View menu, click on Toolbox. This brings up the selection window for the Visual Basic 5 controls, as shown in Figure 2-4. Note that the *tooltips* feature is implemented; when you hold the mouse cursor over an icon for a few seconds, you can see the name of the control that icon represents.

Click on the Command button icon indicated in the figure. The CommandButton control puts a standard gray Windows button on the screen. When the program is running, the user can click on the button to issue a command.

Now "draw" the button onto the form by holding down the mouse button and drawing a rectangle. When you let go of the mouse, the button appears in the size and location you specified. Notice how you can pick up the button with the mouse and move it around, or resize it as you would a window.

Let's change the text that the user sees on the Command button. Like a form, a Command button uses the Caption property to specify a label. Click on the Command button once to select it. Note the properties available to this control.

The Properties window lists the properties for the currently selected form or control. The name of this control is noted on the title bar of the Properties window. It's a good idea to get in the habit of checking to make sure the correct object is specified. Otherwise, you may change a property value for the wrong control; if the change is minor, it might take some time before you catch the mistake. To change the active object in the Properties window, select a new property from the drop-down list box right beneath the title bar.

Select the Caption property for the Command button and enter Done. The change is reflected immediately.

Figure 2-4
The toolbox lets you add controls to your project

Run the program again by clicking on Run under the Start menu. You can click on this button to your heart's content and it automatically receives the focus and "presses" in and out. What's that you say? But it doesn't do anything? Microsoft Windows can handle common tasks, but unfortunately it can't read our minds. If you want that button to do something, you have to tell it what to do! Quit the program by clicking on the Close box and then selecting Close.

1. Although there are many advantages to OOP, the *main* advantage is:
    a. You get to feel you're on the leading edge of software design.
    b. It's easier to learn.
    c. Breaking a task down into objects is less work than breaking it down into functions.
    d. Well-designed objects can be reused in different applications.

2. A Visual Basic form is most like:
    a. A window
    b. A list of items you can select from
    c. A file selector
    d. A button

3. The Caption property:
    a. Lets the user type in a new value for the title bar
    b. Is a value you set at run- or design time to label an object for the user
    c. Requires complicated programming gyrations to define
    d. Is always `Command1`

4. Which of the following tasks is likely *not* handled automatically by Microsoft Windows?
    a. Displaying a window on screen
    b. Minimizing or maximizing a window
    c. Performing a specific task, such as adding a list of numbers, in response to the user's request
    d. Making a button looked "pressed" when the user clicks on it

5. A Command button:
    a. Lets the user type in a command
    b. Is a type of form
    c. Is a control you can draw on the screen, label, and then let the user "press" to carry out a function
    d. Is a button labeled OK or Cancel

GETTING THINGS DONE

Objects *have* things, they *do* things, and they can *respond* to things. In Visual Basic lingo, the characteristics that describe an object are known as its *properties*. An action that an object performs is called a *method*. Finally, an object responds to system *events*. In this lesson, we'll talk about events.

The Main Event

An event is something that happens in the environment. This can be triggered by a user (clicking on a control), by another program (messages), or by something like a timer going off.

In Lesson 2, you saw the Properties window, which shows all the properties associated with each control. Now let's take a look at the events associated with each control. While still in design mode, double-click on the button labeled Done. You'll see the Code window shown in Figure 2-5. The *list box* to the left contains all the objects in the current project that have events associated with them. A list box is a standard Windows interface element that gives the user a list of items and lets the user select one of them.

By Any Other Name

Notice that the name of the current object is Command1, not Done. That's because the Caption property value—the label the user sees—is completely separate from the name that you use to identify the object *within* the program. Internally, the property that identifies a control is the **Name** property. The **Name** property is a unique name that lets you refer to the object's other property values, the events associated with the object, and the methods the object can perform. You've already seen this property used in the Properties window. Visual Basic assigns all objects a default name (**Form1**, **Command1**) when you create them. Later, you'll change these names to make them more descriptive.

Figure 2-5
The Code window

Take another look at Figure 2-5. The list box to the right contains all the events that can be triggered for the current object. The Code window comes up with a default event for the current object. In this case it's the `Click` event, which is what you want. The `Click` event is fired when the user clicks on the form or control.

Events are processed in *subroutines* or *procedures*—logical groupings of code. This subroutine is bracketed by the keywords `Private Sub` and `End Sub`. The name of this routine is `Command1_Click()`. Whatever source code you place inside this routine executes whenever the associated event is fired.

Event routine names are always in the form:

```
ControlName_Event([parameters])
```

(Don't worry about parameters for now.)

Know the Code

It's time to start adding source code.

Visual Basic 5 has a rich and powerful language in which you'll write the procedural aspects of your projects. Visual Basic has a nice feature called *automatic syntax checking*. When you press ENTER after typing in a line of code, Visual Basic alerts you if there's an error in that line.

A programming language is a command set that lets you instruct the computer to perform certain tasks. Types of commands typically include *assignments*, system commands, conditional instructions, and *looping* instructions. Additionally, you can call *subroutines* and *functions* to perform complex tasks and build subroutines and functions of your own. Because Visual Basic 5 is an object-oriented language, many (if not most) of the routines you'll be working with will have to do with defining the behavior of the objects that make up your program.

Make sure the cursor is between the `Private Sub` and `End Sub` lines and enter the following line of code:

```
End
```

The `End` statement ends the program and returns control to the operating system or shell (if the program is compiled) or the Visual Basic development environment (if not). The screen should now look like Figure 2-6. Go ahead and run the program; clicking on the Done button now ends the program as advertised.

In some programming languages, instructions are *case-sensitive*. That is, something called student is different from something called STUDENT. Other languages are *case-insensitive*; you could use the two expressions interchangeably. Visual Basic handles case in a slightly different way.

Figure 2-6
Real source code in
place

Instructions are case-insensitive; you can type **end**, **End**, or **END** and it all means the same thing. However, Visual Basic has a preferred case usage for keywords, and it automatically converts whatever you type to that usage. Thus if you type in

```
end
```

as soon as you press (ENTER), Visual Basic changes the command to

```
End
```

VB 5 similarly changes **form1** to **Form1**, **label1** to **Label1**, and so on.

Furthermore, VB forces all your variable names to have the same case usage everywhere they appear. Thus, if you declare a variable to be named **NumStudents**, and enter a line such as

```
numstudents=5
```

when you press (ENTER), VB will change it to

```
NumStudents=5
```

Moving Right Along

By now you should be getting a feel for the Visual Basic development process, sketched out in broad strokes in Figure 2-7. Visual editing lets you "draw" the interface for the program. Then you add the code, the functionality, to your program. Finally, you test your work.

In practice, this process is cyclical; once you've tested a component, you move on to add the next piece. This illustration also omits the design and architecture phase, which takes place before you even load up Visual Basic.

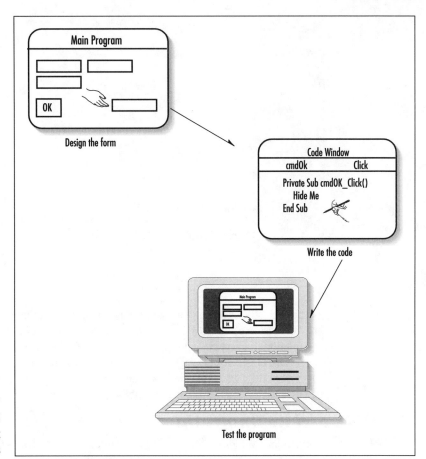

Figure 2-7
The VB 5
development
process

Visual Basic's File Controls

Let's add some more controls to the form to make this program more functional. Drag three new controls onto the form: a FileListBox control, a DirListBox control, and a DriveListBox control. The icons for these controls are indicated in Figure 2-8. These three controls pack a lot of functionality. In fact, you'll notice that as soon as you put them on the form, they fill in with information about the current directory and drive, even though you're still in design mode.

The FileListBox control is a list box that Visual Basic automatically fills with the contents of the current directory. The `FileName` property of the control contains the currently selected file name.

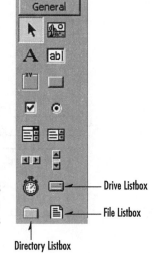

Figure 2-8
The file selection
controls

Drive Listbox

File Listbox

Directory Listbox

The DirListBox control is a list box that Visual Basic automatically fills with the current directory's subdirectories. The **Path** property of the control contains the currently selected directory name. This selection defaults to the current directory.

The DriveListBox control is a list box that Visual Basic automatically fills with the drives currently available on the system. The **Drive** property of the control contains the currently selected drive name. This selection defaults to the current drive.

Sizing Things Up

The standard Windows file selector is adequate, but we always find we have to spend a lot of time on the scroll bars. Let's make the FileListBox and DirListBox controls nice and long. To resize a control, click on it to select it, then grab (hold down the mouse button) the lower-right sizing square to the new position. Run the program again; the screen should look roughly like Figure 2-9.

Looking good! Notice that even though the file selection controls and the CommandButton control have vastly different functionality, from your perspective they work more or less the same. You drop them where you want them and let them do their thing. If you play with this program a little, you'll notice it doesn't really "work"; selecting a new drive or directory has no effect. Here, again, is where Windows leaves off and we pick up. You'll add this functionality via code in Lesson 4.

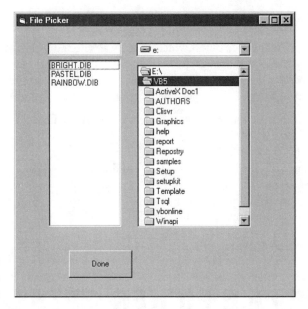

Figure 2-9
Program with file
selection controls

1. In Visual Basic terms, an *event* is:
   a. Something the user does, such as clicking on something or moving a form
   b. Something that Windows does, such as setting off a timer or letting you know when something's changed
   c. Something another program does, such as sending a message to your program
   d. Any of the above

2. The Code window:
   a. Is where you enter code for your program
   b. Can be accessed only at runtime
   c. Is where you output debugging statements
   d. Is accessible only via a secret decoder ring

3. The property used internally to identify an object is:
   a. The **Caption** property
   b. The **Name** property
   c. The **Variable** property
   d. The **Label** property

4. When the user clicks on an object:
   a. The mouse cursor changes to a button.
   b. You need to detect which object was selected by analyzing the x,y coordinates of the mouse.
   c. Windows figures out what you probably want that object to do and does it.
   d. A `click` event is generated for that object.

5. If you want to let your user select from a list of files, the best choice would be to:
   a. Add a DirListBox control
   b. Read the current directory from the operating system and generate the list of files that way
   c. Add a FileListBox control
   d. Add a DriveListBox control

THE FILE PICKER GETS BETTER

So far, you've built a little program that looks like it should do something but actually doesn't. Let's go back into the file picker and add some functionality. Recall that the program is made up of the components shown in Table 2-1.

Table 2-1 The file picker objects

Object	Property	Value
Form	Name	Form1
	Caption	File Picker
CommandButton	Name	Command1
	Caption	Done
FileListBox	Name	File1
DirListBox	Name	Dir1
DriveListBox	Name	Drive1

The File Control's Properties

The file selection controls all have built-in functionality. To access this functionality, you'll have to get to know the properties of the controls that relate to this functionality. These properties are summarized in Table 2-2.

Table 2-2 Important file selection properties

Property	Applies to	Description
Drive	DriveListBox	Sets or returns the currently selected drive. Not available at design time.
Path	DirListBox, FileListBox	For the DirListBox, sets or returns the currently selected path. For the FileListBox, sets or returns the path containing the currently displayed list of files. Not available at design time.
FileName	FileListBox	Sets or returns the name of the currently selected file. Not available at design time.

Because these are all runtime properties, you won't see them in the Properties window. You'll need to access them directly in code.

To access the value of an object's property, create an identifier consisting of the object's name, a period, and the property name. For example:

```
Form1.Caption = "The Amazing File Picker"
File1.Path   = Dir1.Path
```

Zeroing In on the Task

Figure 2-10 illustrates how the controls need to interrelate. When the user selects a new drive, the directory list box is updated. When the user selects a new directory, the file list box is updated. To implement this behavior, rely on the **Change** event, which occurs whenever the contents of the control change. Another feature you're going to add to your program is to change the current drive and directory whenever one of these changes occurs. This way the user will always go back to the last directory chosen.

Let's enter some code. Double-click on the drive list box to bring up the code window. You should already be in the **Change** event. Enter the code shown in Listing 2-1. You don't need to retype the first and last lines; they are included in the listing so you can be sure where the code is supposed to go.

Listing 2-1 A change to the drive list box propagates a change to the directory box

```
Private Sub Drive1_Change()
     Dir1.Path = Drive1.Drive
     ChDrive Drive1.Drive
End Sub
```

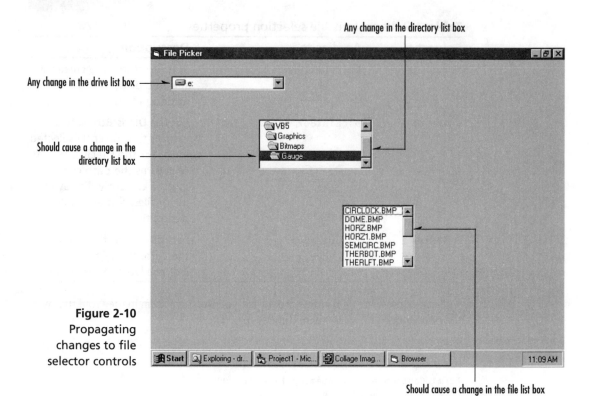

Figure 2-10
Propagating
changes to file
selector controls

We'll discuss the first statement below. The `ChDrive` statement changes the current drive. The current drive and directory are the first places programs (or file selectors) look for files.

Now let's add corresponding code in the directory list box `Change` event. From the Object: drop-down list on the top left of the Code window, select Dir1. This puts you in the `Change` routine. Now enter the code in Listing 2-2.

Listing 2-2 A change to the directory list box propagates a change to the file box

```
Private Sub Dir1_Change()
    File1.Path = Dir1.Path
    ChDir Dir1.Path
End Sub
```

The `ChDir` statement changes the current directory.

All set, no kidding! Run the program again. Double-click on a drive to select it, and see the changes in the other controls.

Assignments

Let's take a closer look at what you did. (If you're not new to programming, you can skip ahead to the quiz.) The statement

```
Dir1.Path = Drive1.Drive
```

makes an *assignment*. In computer programming, an assignment means you take a value and copy it somewhere else. In this case, you assign the value in the Drive1 control's `Drive` property to the Dir1 control's `Path` property.

The = Operator and Expressions

The equal sign has two functions in Visual Basic: It works as an assignment operator and it works as a comparison operator. (We'll cover comparison operations in Chapter 3, Variables, Constants, and Associated Functions.) When you invoke the equal sign as an assignment operator, it evaluates the *expression* on the right side of the equation and then puts the result into the contents of the left side of the equation. An expression can be

- A constant, such as File Picker

- The result of an operation, such as 4+5

- The return value of a function, such as Sqr(9)

- The contents of a variable (or property), such as `NumStudents` or `Form1.Caption`

- Any combination of the above

An expression yields a numeric or string result.

Assignments to and from property values are simple to carry out and are immensely powerful. It's as if you can reach in with your virtual fingers and tweak, twist, and fine-tune the object instances you've created, molding them in your hands to the perfect form to carry out the function you want.

1. The property you'd use for accessing the path currently being pointed to by the `DirListBox` is:
   a. `ChDir`
   b. `DirListPath`
   c. `Path`
   d. `Drive`

2. The `FileName` property:
   a. Is common to the DirListBox, FileListBox, and DriveListBox controls
   b. Is set automatically by Visual Basic to the current project name
   c. Needs to be typed in by the user
   d. Returns the name of the currently selected file in the File List box

3. Which of the following does *not* identify an object's property?
   a. `Form1.Caption`
   b. `Dir1.Path`
   c. `frmMain_Click`
   d. `cmdOk.Caption`

4. The `Change` event:
   a. Is fired whenever the contents of the control are changed
   b. Is of no use whatever
   c. Happens only when another program sends you a message
   d. Was inspired by a David Bowie song

5. Which of the following would be considered an expression?
   a. `A+B`
   b. `Sqr(25)`
   c. `PI`
   d. All of the above

Run four or five of the Windows programs on your desktop, such as the calculator, the notepad, your word processor, or spreadsheet. Note which elements all the programs have in common. Think about these elements as objects. How might you use similar types of objects in your own programs?

REVIEW

John: Visual Basic programming isn't as hard as I thought it would be. Even though we haven't learned very much of the programming language, I feel like I've got a good idea about how to get things done.

Lisa: I know. It would almost be better to say "Visual Basic development" or "Visual Basic design" rather than "Visual Basic programming." What I like is the way you just "draw" the way you want the form to look by dragging and dropping the controls.

John: And I like how much you *don't* have to do, like worrying about making the button look "pushed" or resizing the window. Those file controls are great! They do everything you need.

Lisa: Almost everything. I've already got my own ideas for a file selector; one thing I want is to bring up only certain files, depending on their file extensions. That's probably a complex programming task, though.

John: I wouldn't be so sure. If what we've seen is any indication, it may be a simple matter of setting a property value to, say, `*.DOC`.

THE DEVELOPMENT ENVIRONMENT

Visual Basic programs are called *projects*, which are made up of various components. So far, you've seen a project with a single form and the source code associated with that form. In fact, a project can contain many forms and code modules, which perform functions in the background, as well as class modules, which are new to VB 5. Although we expect the components of our project to come together flawlessly and become something greater than the sum of its parts, keeping track of all the pieces can be troublesome.

Visual Basic 5 doesn't require a project's files to be in a separate directory. However, it's a good practice to create a new directory for each project. This prevents confusion and possibly overwriting other projects. Switch over to the File Manager or Windows Explorer to create a new directory (folder in Windows 95) called FILEPICK.

So far, you've been taking the Visual Basic development environment for granted. Let's take a closer look at Visual Basic's main screen and the tools it makes available to you. If you've had any experience with Microsoft Windows, many of the elements of Figure 2-11 may already be familiar to you.

The Menu Bar

Visual Basic's menu bar is pretty typical. Click on the File menu (shown in Figure 2-12). Notice that there are different options for files and projects. Each module of a project is saved in a separate file; the project file pulls all the information together. Click on Save Project As... Because you haven't saved the form to a file yet, VB asks if you want to do this. Click on Yes, and then switch to the FILEPICK directory and enter FILEPICK.FRM and press ENTER. Next it's time to save the project; enter FILEPICK.VBP.

Visual Basic 5 and Visual Basic 4 projects have the extension `.VBP`; previous versions of Visual Basic used the extension `.MAK`.

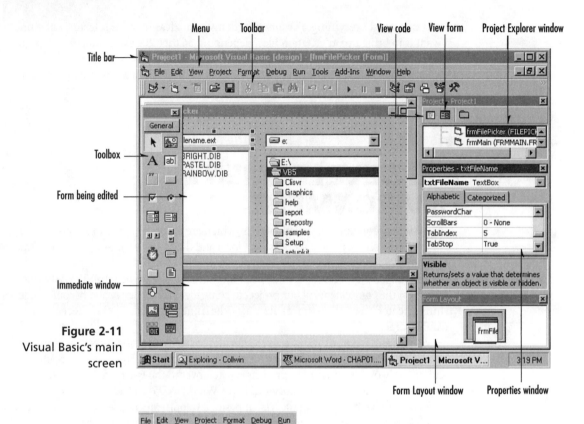

Figure 2-11
Visual Basic's main screen

Figure 2-12
The File menu reflects the fact that projects are made up of one or more files

So far, the only other menus you've used are View and Run. Like most larger software products, Visual Basic 5 has a range of options that won't be important to you until later. We'll be talking about more advanced options as the book unfolds.

Click on Code under the View menu. You'll see the Code window you've previously brought up by double-clicking on an object. There is actually one other way to get to this screen.

The Project Window

If the Project window is not showing, click on Project under the View menu. This brings up the Project window. Right now this isn't a very useful feature, because you have only one file in your project. Let's add another file to make things more interesting.

Click on Add Form under the Project menu. A blank form labeled Form2 comes up. Now look at the Project window (shown in Figure 2-13). You can select between the elements of the project and choose to view either the code or the form.

Notice that as you add to the project, you'll realize that the default names Visual Basic assigns aren't very helpful. Let's make the project a little more understandable.

The Properties Window, Part 2

Make sure Form2 is selected in the Project window. Then bring up the Properties window, either by clicking on it or by clicking on Properties under the View window.

You can also bring up the Properties window for the current form by pressing F4.

Let's change the caption of the new form. Click on the Caption property, then enter Browser. At this point, you should also give your forms better names. Click on the Name property and enter frmMain. To change the name of the other form, you first need to select that form. You can do this either by clicking on it or by selecting its name from the Project window and then clicking on View Form. Next, go back to the Properties window (which should now say Properties - Form1 on the title bar) and click on the Name property. Enter frmFilePicker as the new name.

You'll be using frmFilePicker as a dialog box, which you'll call from frmMain in response to certain user actions.

View code

Figure 2-13
The Project window
helps you manage
the elements of
your project

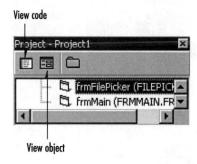

View object

The Menu Editor

Let's advance the professional look of the program by adding a menu to the main screen. Select the frmMain form by clicking on it (or using the Project window). Click on Menu Editor... under the Tools menu to bring up the dialog box shown in Figure 2-14. The first two fields are the familiar Caption and Name. Menus and menu items look and act like the other objects you've seen. Like the Command button you entered earlier, the Caption is the label, and the Name refers to the object internally. When you're ready to add code, the Click event will let you know when the user selected the item.

Enter File in the caption field, a standard first menu. Press TAB to advance to the next field and type mnuFile as the name. Although this dialog box has other options, this is all the information you need to enter for now.

The Visual Basic 5 development environment has extensive context-sensitive help. You can press F1 to bring up a description of any dialog box.

Click on the Next button. This adds another item to the menu. Type Open... for the caption and mnuFileOpen for the name. The horizontal arrow icons to the left of the Next button set the level of the menu item. Click the right arrow button now to make Open... subordinate to the File menu.

Press ENTER to start a new entry. (This is the same as clicking on Next.) Let's add a separator bar. In the Caption field, enter a single hyphen. The hyphen has a special meaning to the menu editor. It tells the editor to create a separator bar, like the one between Open Project... and Save File in the Visual Basic File menu.

Even though you won't be assigning code for this entry, each menu item needs a name. Call this item mnuSeparator. Finally, create a menu item with the caption Exit and name it mnuFileExit. Your screen should look like Figure 2-15.

Figure 2-14
The Menu Editor

Figure 2-15
Creating a file
menu

Exit the Menu Editor by clicking on OK. Look at the menu as it appears on the design-time form. Note that the separator bar automatically extends across the menu box. Click on a menu item to bring up the Code window for that item's **Click** event. You'll be filling in the code in Lesson 6.

Each Form in Its Place

Let's run the program now. Rather than selecting Start from the Run menu, you can use the VCR-style controls on the toolbar, shown in Figure 2-16. Other toolbar buttons you might find useful are the ones to switch to the menu editor, Properties window, and Project window. Remember, you can find out what a button does by holding the mouse over it for a few seconds and reading the drop-down tooltip.

Currently, only the Start button is enabled. Click on it now to run the program. This also enables the Break and End buttons. Hey! That's not what you want! When the program runs, the file picker comes up, not the main menu screen. Once again, Visual Basic fails miserably at reading your mind. Exit the program, this time by pressing the toolbar End button to exit.

Figure 2-16
The Visual Basic 5 toolbar

What's happening is that the first form in a project is assumed to be the *startup* form—the one first displayed. To change which form is the startup form, click on Properties... under the Project menu. The Properties dialog box has four sets of options: settings for General, Make, Compile, and Component. Select a set of options by clicking on the tab label. For now, click on General to bring up the screen shown in Figure 2-17. This dialog box is mostly used for setting options relating to projects that will be used as OLE Automation Servers. (This topic is covered in Chapter 14, Advanced Features.) The Startup Form drop-down list is the one you want. As you saw when you ran the program, this is currently set to frmFilePicker. Change this now to frmMain.

Note that there is a third item on the list—Sub Main. Occasionally, you may not want a form to gain control when your project starts. If this is the case, you can pass control to a special subroutine called **Main**. The **Main** subroutine must appear in a code module somewhere in your project, and there can be only one **Main** subroutine per project. You can use this feature to produce hidden Windows programs that do not have a visible interface but that perhaps add functionality to a client application via OLE automation.

At this point, you don't need to worry about the other options on this screen. The Project Name setting, for example, is confusingly not where you need to name your project. This is for OLE automation naming purposes. You already saved the name of the project file when you saved the project to disk.

Click on OK to close the dialog box. Now, when you run the program, the main screen comes up first. Because you still haven't added any functionality, exit the program by pressing the End button on the VCR-style controls on the toolbar. For now, disregard the middle Break button in Figure 2-16; you'll use that when you learn about debugging in Chapter 9, Printing.

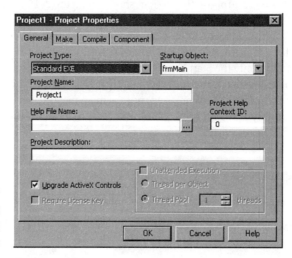

Figure 2-17
The Project
Properties dialog
box

1. A Visual Basic project:
    a. Can be made up of multiple forms and modules
    b. Refers to the source code that tells the computer what to do
    c. Must start with the first (default) form
    d. Can have a maximum of eight class modules

2. The Visual Basic Project window:
    a. Is where you enter code for your projects
    b. Isn't very helpful, because you have to use the default names of Form1 and Form2
    c. Lets you switch between your forms in design mode
    d. Lets you switch between your forms in runtime mode

3. The menu editor:
    a. Is a Visual Basic menu
    b. Lets you name your menu items, but then you use a resource editor to draw them on the screen
    c. Is where you enter code to respond to menu selections
    d. Is where you define the menu characteristics, information VB uses to draw and maintain your window

4. To bring up Visual Basic's context-sensitive help:
    a. Press F1.
    b. Press F2.
    c. Press F3.
    d. Press CTRL-H.

5. The VCR-style controls on the Visual Basic toolbar:
    a. Let you run, pause, and end your program by pressing icons
    b. Let you exit Visual Basic
    c. Are icons you can drag onto your form to add functionality
    d. Let you hook up your computer to your VCR

Start a new project and add the following menus to it:

File	Edit
New	Undo
Save	Cut
Save As...	Copy
Close	Paste
Exit	

Give the menu items names that tell you something about the functionality.

LOOKING CLOSELY AT FORMS

When you run the File Browser program, the main window comes up on the screen. So far, you've pretty much taken this for granted, but that's what's happening only from a user's perspective. What's happening from your (more sophisticated, of course) programming perspective?

The Mother Load

Running a program causes the startup form to *load*. Windows generates an instance of the window and sets up all the internal housekeeping it needs to keep track of it. Put another way, running a program generates a **Load** event for the startup form. In addition to letting Windows perform its necessary functions, Visual Basic also executes any code the programmer has placed in the form's **Load** event.

The Load Event

The **Load** event occurs when a form loads. A form loads

- When the application runs, if the form is a startup form
- Via code by calling the Load statement for a form
- When any reference is made to an unloaded form's properties or controls

Let's add some source code to the main form's **Load** event and watch this happen. Double-click on frmMain, or select frmMain from the Project window and click on View Code. Notice that the **Load** event is the default event for this object. Enter the following code:

```
Private Sub Form_Load()
        MsgBox "Hello world"
End Sub
```

Figure 2-18
Inside the Load
routine

The **MsgBox** function displays a box on the screen with a message to the user. Chapter 4, Subroutines, Functions, and the Visual Basic 5 Language, covers this function in detail. Run the program and you'll see the message box in Figure 2-18.

A Method to the Madness

Now let's invoke a **Load** event from inside the program. The type of command you're going to use to do this is called a *method*. A method is a command that is applied to an object.

A method is invoked with the syntax:

```
[objectname.]methodname [parameters]
```

For example,

```
pictButterfly.Move 100,100,200,200
```

The details of this syntax, of course, depend on the particular method you're invoking.

In the Lesson 1 discussion of classes, we said you could think about humans and canines as being examples of classes. In that analogy, a task such as walking is a method: It is a function members of both types of objects can carry out. Thus, if you have an instance of a human named Julia and an instance of a canine named Fido, you could invoke their respective walk methods by saying

```
Julia.Walk
Fido.Walk
```

These commands would actually call different routines, because walking is a different procedure, depending on whether you have two legs or four. However, once the classes and the methods for those classes are defined, you can access the methods without any further consideration as to how the task is accomplished. You tell the object, in effect, just go do it.

Visual Basic objects such as forms and controls have a wide range of built-in methods, as you might imagine. Visible objects contain methods to move, drag, and refresh the display of themselves. Objects to hold and manipulate data, such as list boxes, contain methods to manipulate the data they contain. Specialized controls often have methods that contain powerful functionality; the **Database** object contains a method to execute an SQL query on any ODBC database, for example.

Calling All Forms

Let's invoke a fairly straightforward method, the **Show** method. Its syntax is

```
[form.]Show [style]
```

Show displays a form and gives that form the *focus*. A form or a control with the focus is the object that will receive input.

Remember from the event description of **Load** that a **Load** event is invoked automatically whenever you reference a form or a form's controls or properties. Therefore, just by calling the **Show** method, you automatically load the form if it isn't loaded already.

Remove the **MsgBox** function from the **Form_Load** routine. While in design mode, click on Open... under frmMain's File menu. This brings you to the Code window. Enter the code in Listing 2-3.

Listing 2-3 Displaying the file picker form

```
Private Sub mnuFileOpen_Click()
      frmFilePicker.Show
End Sub
```

While you're at it, let's implement the Exit option. In the Code window's Object dropdown list box, select mnuFileExit and enter the code in Listing 2-4.

Listing 2-4 Code to end the program

```
Private Sub mnuFileExit_Click()
      End
End Sub
```

Run the program once again. This time when you click on Open..., the file picker comes up.

In Windows, you can tell which window has the focus because its title bar is highlighted. In a dialog box, you can tell which control has the focus because its caption is surrounded by a dotted rectangle.

The program is starting to behave, at least a little bit. But again things aren't quite right.

Going in Style

Switch over to your program's main window by clicking on it. Now switch back to the file picker dialog box. Any problem? OK, that was a trick question. You shouldn't be able to switch back and forth—at least, not from the standpoint of typical Windows interface design. Exit the program by clicking on the Exit option, which now works. Under the Visual Basic 5 File menu, click on Save File As.... When the file selector comes up, without clicking on OK or Cancel, try to get back to Visual Basic's main screen. Clicking on an area outside the dialog box causes VB to beep in protest. This is because the Save

File As... dialog box is *modal*; nothing else can happen in the program until the dialog box closes. Click on Cancel now and look at the VB environment from this new perspective. Note that while you're in design mode, you can freely move between the forms in your project. Additionally, you can move between the Project window, the Properties window, and so on without restriction. These windows are said to be *modeless* style.

Modal Versus Modeless: Although the difference between these types of forms is simple enough to grasp (either you temporarily give up control of the program flow or you don't), sometimes it's hard to remember which style is which. Here's an easy way to remember the difference between the terms: A modal dialog box takes over ALL of the running program.

After the user selects Open..., you don't want her or him to do anything else before picking a file name. This is because, eventually, the line after the `Show` command will go off and open the file. The program won't behave predictably if the user can do something else in between.

Change the frmFilePicker dialog box to a modal style by modifying the `Show` method in the `mnuFileOpen_Click` subroutine. The value for the style parameter can be modal (`1`) or modeless (`0`). Modeless style is the default. Bring up the `mnuFileOpen_Click` routine in the Code window and change the command as shown in Listing 2-5.

Listing 2-5 Showing the form in modal style

```
Private Sub mnuFileOpen_Click()
        frmFilePicker.Show vbModal
End Sub
```

Now when you run the program and click Open..., you can't go back to the main form. To exit, click on the Done button.

1. Which event is generated when Windows creates an instance of a window?
   a. `Show`
   b. `Load`
   c. `UnHide`
   d. No event is generated; Windows handles everything.

2. In the example of a human and a dog both walking, what point is being made about class methods?
   a. Walking is always the same function, no matter how many legs you have.
   b. `Julia.Walk` and `Fido.Walk` both call the same routine, because the name is the same.
   c. Even though Julia and Fido use different functions to walk, you can invoke the method without particular concern as to how the task is accomplished.
   d. The best approach to programming is to break down a task such as walking into small, manageable subtasks, such as extending a leg.

3. In the File menu's **Open Click** event, you didn't need to explicitly load the file picker form because:
   a. It was implicitly loaded when it was referenced by the **Show** method.
   b. All forms are loaded when the program runs.
   c. It was the startup form.
   d. The code is wrong; you were supposed to load it explicitly.

4. A modal window:
   a. Is the same as a form
   b. Is any window that operates in some kind of mode
   c. Lets you switch freely between windows
   d. Takes over ALL of the application

5. If you call the **Show** method without any parameters:
   a. The form is displayed in modal style.
   b. The form is displayed in modeless style.
   c. The form is displayed in the same style as the calling form.
   d. You get an error message (a parameter is required).

THE FILE PICKER: BETTER STILL

Thus far, you've been throwing controls around without really thinking much about what you wanted to do with them. Let's formalize what we want this application to do.

It Slices, It Dices...

Let's make the program a browser so the user can pick a file from the file picker and view the file's contents on the main screen. Because you don't know anything about file operations yet, you'll view only files that Visual Basic can handle for you. It turns out the picture box control has a built-in method to load pictures, so let's make the program a picture browser for now.

When the user runs the program, the form is blank. When he or she clicks on Open..., the file picker comes up. You want the file picker to act a little more like a standard file selector, so make a few changes to it. For example, you want functional OK and Cancel buttons instead of the Done button you have now, and you need a place to put the file name. You also want to limit the file list to picture files, because that's all you know how to view. Finally, if the user clicks on OK, you need a place to view the picture.

Everything's OK

Select the File Picker form. Click once on the Done button to select it. Now go to the Properties window. Click on Caption and type OK, then click on Name and type cmdOk. Now go to the toolbox and select another Command button, draw it on the form, and change the Caption property to Cancel and the Name property to cmdCancel.

From here out, we'll use tables to show you concisely which controls to create and what the property values should be. Only the properties you need to change will be listed, for example:

Control	Property	Value
CommandButton	CaptionOK	
	Name	cmdOk

Now add a text box to the form. Figure 2-19 shows the icon for the TextBox control. The text box is a remarkably powerful control that displays—or lets the user enter—alphanumeric characters. We'll explore the text box in more detail in Chapter 5, Controls, when we use it as the centerpiece of a notepad application.

Edit the text box's properties as shown in Table 2-3. Size and arrange the controls so that the design is pleasing and the layout seems accessible. The finished form looks something like Figure 2-20.

Table 2-3 Property values for file picker's TextBox control

Control	Property	Value
TextBox	Text	filename.ext
	Name	txtFileName

Getting It Working

Because you'll view only picture files, let's limit the file list box to list only those files. This makes it easier for the user to find the picture files and prevents the user from selecting a file you can't display. Fortunately, the FileListBox control has a built-in property to limit which files are displayed: the **Pattern** property.

The Pattern *Property*

The **Pattern** property limits the files displayed in the list box. The value of the property follows the standard Windows/MS-DOS convention of using *wildcards* to mean "any" value. An asterisk matches any number of characters, for example, ***.*** or ***.EXE**. A question mark matches any single character, for example, **CHAP??.*** matches CHAP01.DOC and CHAP24.DOC but not CHAPTERS.TXT.

Figure 2-19
The TextBox control

Text box on form

TextBox on toolbox

Figure 2-20
The smoothed-over
File Picker

The default value of the **Pattern** property is ***.*** (all files). You can specify more than one pattern by separating the values by semicolons, for example, ***.EXE;*.BAT**.

To limit the file list box to all the image types the picture box knows how to read, enter ***.bmp;*.wmf;*.emf;*.rle;*.ico;*.dib;*.cur;*jpg;*.gif** for the pattern value. Because you won't change this value at runtime, this is all you need to do with this property.

The Text *Property*

You saw in Lesson 4 how to propagate changes across the drive, directory, and file controls. Let's see how to get the selection from the file list box into the text box. You'll use two properties: **FileName** and **Text**. The **Text** property sets or returns the text in the editable area of the control.

You probably see where this is going.

Double-click on the FileListBox control to bring up the Code window. Again, the default event for this control is what you want, the **Click** event. Enter the following code:

```
Private Sub File1_Click()
    txtFileName.Text = File1.FileName
End Sub
```

That should handle the user's selections. There's one other detail to handle, however. Back when you defined the text box, you initialized the Text field to filename.txt. This made it so it was easy to see what the runtime result would look like when you positioned the controls on the form. You could clear this value in the Properties window, but it's just as easy to do it at runtime in code. This approach allows you to retain the design-time self-documentation.

Double-click on the File Picker form to get to the **Load** event and enter the following code:

```
Private Sub Form_Load()
    txtFileName.Text = ""
End Sub
```

The two quotation marks in a row set the value to nothing.

A string is a type of value that can contain any combination of alphanumeric characters. The contents of the text box's Text field is a string, as is the **Caption** property and a few other properties you've seen. We'll be covering strings extensively in Chapter 3, Variables, Constants, and Associated Functions. For now, the important thing to keep in mind is that when you set these values in code, you must enclose the string in quotation marks. Two quotation marks in a row are called an empty string and clear the property's value.

Now you know where the value you want will be. How do you get at it?

The Hide *Method*

After selecting a file name, the user clicks on OK or Cancel to dismiss the dialog box. At that point, you need to shut down the File Picker form so that program control goes back to the main form. The command to do that is the **Hide** method. The syntax is

```
[object.]Hide
```

This method hides a form from view but doesn't unload it from memory. It hides the form that has the focus if *object* is omitted.

Bring up the **cmdOk_Click** event procedure and enter the following code into it.

```
Private Sub cmdOk_Click()
      Hide
End Sub
```

Because this form was shown in the modal style, everything else in the program essentially came to a halt. Hiding the form returns you to where you were before file picker displayed—in other words, right after the **Show** command in the **mnuFileOpen_Click** event. Let's go back to the main form and see what you need to do to display a picture.

A Thousand Words

The PictureBox control displays a graphic .GIF image file, .JPG image file, bitmap (.BMP) file, icon (.ICO) file, Windows metafile (.WMF), run-length encoded (.RLE) file, or Windows enhanced metafile (.EMF). Select a picture box from the toolbox (shown in Figure 2-21) and place it on the main form. Because you don't know how big the picture is going to be, don't worry about how big to draw the box.

Figure 2-21
The PictureBox icon

The AutoSize *Property*

In the Properties window for this control, select the **AutoSize** property, which is currently set to **False**. The **AutoSize** property determines whether or not a control is automatically resized to fit the image it contains.

Notice that when you select this property, a drop-down arrow appears to the right of **False**. Click on the arrow and select **True** to change the value.

Whenever a property has a limited set of values it can contain, you can select from those values at design time, using a drop-down list in the Properties window.

The Picture *Property*

The **Picture** property determines the graphic to be displayed in the control. At design time, you set the **Picture** property in the Properties window. Click on the **Picture** property and notice that an ellipsis icon (...) appears to the right of the property name. This means you need to use a dialog box to fill in the value of the property. Click on the ellipsis now. A file selector box comes up. This is where you load the image at design time. Click on Cancel for now; you want to start with a blank picture.

To set the value of the **Picture** property at runtime, you need to learn one more command, the last new language element of the chapter: the **LoadPicture** function.

The LoadPicture *Function*

The **LoadPicture** function loads an image from a file into an object. The syntax is

```
LoadPicture([filename])
```

For example,

```
Picture1.Picture = LoadPicture("happy.bmp")
```

Remote Control

Now the question is simply, How do we get the file name from the file picker? From *inside* the file picker, the file name value is

```
txtFileName.Text
```

It turns out that accessing a control from *outside* the form is a simple matter of putting the form name, separated by a period, in front of the control.

*Note*Accessing Controls Outside the Current Form

Syntax: *formname.controlname.propertyname*

Examples: `Form1.CommandButton1.Caption`

`frmMain.mnuOption.Checked`

Go back to the **mnuFileOpen_Click** routine and add the highlighted line after the existing code, as shown in Listing 2-6.

Listing 2-6 Loading the picture

```
Sub Open_Click
      frmFilePicker.Show 1
      Picture1.Picture = LoadPicture(frmFilePicker.txtFileName.Text)
End sub
```

Run the program and try it out. Click on Open..., select a file, and click on OK. Majestic! Load another file. Live it up! However, if you experiment with all the buttons, you'll soon see you have a slight problem: The Cancel button doesn't work yet. Sigh. A programmer's work is never done. Exit the program and go into the frmMain Code window. Select the cmdCancel Click event. There are (you'll see later) a few fancy techniques you can use for forms to communicate with each other about what the user did. However, in this case, you're kind of going to cheat.

It turns out that assigning a blank string to the **LoadPicture** function clears the contents of the picture box. This effect will be fine if the user presses Cancel. All you need to do, then, is clear the contents of the text box and hide the form as you did when the user pressed OK. This code is shown in Listing 2-7.

Listing 2-7 The Cancel button

```
Private Sub cmdCancel_Click()
   txtFileName.Text = ""
   Hide
End Sub
```

Conclusion

The file picker might not have the broadest functionality, but it's not bad for your first project. You know only a handful of controls and language statements, yet you have all the tools to build something that performs a useful function in the real world.

Save your work now. In Lesson 8, we'll review what you've learned and apply it to another project.

1. The TextBox control:
   a. Is a modal dialog box to request input from the user
   b. Has a Caption property so you can use it as a label
   c. Is read-only at runtime
   d. Is a control you add to a form to let the user type in alphanumeric characters

2. Which of the following is *not* an example of a valid `Pattern` property?
   a. `*.*`
   b. `INV*.DOC`
   c. `FIG??.BMP`
   d. `D:\MYDIR`

3. A null string is:
   a. Two quotation marks in a row (`""`) designating an empty string
   b. The same as the space bar
   c. `0`
   d. Illegal in many string operations

4. To assign a value to the `Picture` property of a picture box:
   a. Assign the file name, as in `Picture1.Picture = "SMILEY.BMP"`
   b. Set the `AutoSize` property to `True`
   c. Use the `Show` method on the `Picture` control
   d. Call the `LoadPicture` function, as in `Picture1.Picture = LoadPicture("SMILEY.BMP")`

5. Which of the following expressions refers to the contents of the text box txtFile in frmSource (assume you're outside of frmSource)?
   a. `frmSource_txtFile.Text`
   b. `frmSource.txtFile.Text`
   c. `frmSource.txtFile.Caption`
   d. `frmSource.txtFile_Caption`

EXERCISE

Modify the file picker so that the user can enter a pattern in the text field and then press a Change Pattern button to adjust the contents of the list box.

IT'S A WRAP

Visual Basic 5 and Windows handle so many details for you, you can focus on the fun part of programming: designing and building a project that performs exactly how *you* tell it to. You still have a lot to learn about programming—variables, program flow and structure, object design, logic, and debugging—but as we move from this introduction through the book to more advanced topics, you'll see that a large part of learning Visual Basic 5 will be absorbing more of the same type of things you learned here. You'll need to learn the rest of the common controls, more property values, events, and methods. If you already understand the concepts in this chapter, the work ahead won't be particularly difficult: We'll combine the same types of tools in different ways. If you feel some of the concepts are still a little fuzzy, that's OK too. As you do more of this type of work, these concepts will come into clearer and clearer focus.

Summary

Let's take a look at the VB language elements you've learned thus far and review vocabulary. Tables 2-4, 2-5, 2-6, 2-7, and 2-8 summarize the language elements covered in this chapter.

Table 2-4 The objects introduced in this chapter

Object	Description
CommandButton	A control that draws a button on the screen for the user to click.
DirListBox	A list box the user can select from that is automatically filled with the directories in the current drive.
DriveListBox	A list box the user can select from that is automatically filled with the drives available to the system.
FileListBox	A list box the user can select from that is automatically filled with the files in the current directory.
Form	The main window that contains the other objects in your program.
Menu	A control that puts up a menu on the screen from which the user can make selections.
PictureBox	Displays a graphic bitmap, icon, or metafile.
TextBox	Displays or lets the user enter text.

Table 2-5 The properties introduced in this chapter

Property	Description
AutoSize	Determines whether or not a control is automatically resized to fit the image it contains
Caption	Provides a label to describe the form or control to the user
Drive	Sets or returns the currently selected drive on the DriveListBox
FileName	Sets or returns the file name of the currently selected file in the FileListBox
Name	A descriptor that identifies the object internally
Path	Sets or returns the currently selected path for the DirListBox; for the FileListBox, sets or returns the path containing the currently displayed list of files
Pattern	Limits the files displayed in the FileListBox
Picture	Determines the graphic to be displayed in the control
Text	Sets or returns the text in the editable area of the control

Table 2-6 The events introduced in this chapter

Event	Description
Change	Occurs when the contents of the control change
Click	Occurs when the user clicks on an object
Load	Occurs when a form is loaded

Table 2-7 The statements and functions introduced in this chapter

Statements and Functions	Description
ChDir	Changes the current directory on the system
ChDrive	Changes the current drive on the system
End	Ends the program and returns control to the operating system or shell
LoadPicture()	Loads an image from a file into an object
MsgBox()	Puts up a message on the screen

Table 2-8 The methods introduced in this chapter

Methods	Description
Show	Displays a form and gives that form the focus
Hide	Hides a form from view but doesn't unload it from memory

Table 2-9 lists the terms related to OOP you've seen in this chapter.

Table 2-9 OOP terms introduced in this chapter

Terms	Definition
Class	The properties, events, and methods that uniquely define a type of object.
Decomposition	The traditional, top-down approach to software design in which you break down complex problems into smaller, less complex ones.
Event	Something that happens in the environment.
Instance	An object in a program is an *instance* of its class.
Method	A function that an object knows how to do.
Object	A distinct unit in a program that has certain characteristics and can do certain things.
Object-oriented programming	An approach to programming in which you first break a programming task into the objects that make it up.
Programming language	A command set that lets you instruct the computer to perform certain tasks.
Property	A characteristic of an object.
Subroutines/procedures	Logical groupings of code.

1. Which property was common to *all* the controls you learned about in this chapter?
   a. Caption
   b. Name
   c. Pattern
   d. Text

2. Which of the following commands unloads a form from memory?
   a. `End`
   b. `Hide`
   c. `Change`
   d. `ChDir`

3. Which is the best definition of a programming language?
   a. An approach in which you first break down a task into smaller tasks to perform
   b. A tool that lets you draw forms and controls on the screen
   c. A command set that lets you instruct the computer to perform certain tasks
   d. An object

4. Which of the following tasks do you already possess all the tools to perform in Visual Basic?
   a. Track the mouse's movements to draw on the screen
   b. Create a new program that displays a different picture at regular intervals
   c. Modify the file picker to read text files as well as pictures
   d. Modify the browser to clear the text box field before the file picker comes up

5. In VB 5 terminology, what's the difference between an event and a method?
   a. There's no difference; these are both terms meaning "command."
   b. An event is a `command` statement; a method is a way you go about solving a problem.
   c. An event is something that happens in the environment; a method is a function that an object knows how to do.
   d. Only an event can return a value.

VARIABLES, CONSTANTS, AND ASSOCIATED FUNCTIONS

n Chapter 2, Object-Oriented Programming, you learned about many of the fundamentals of the Visual Basic 5 (VB 5) development environment and the components of a VB 5 program. This chapter concentrates on the different types of variables and constants. You'll see how to use them and how to declare them. This chapter also covers many support functions provided by Visual Basic that perform specific actions on different variable types. Additionally, we'll explore the VB environment a little more and start to learn about program flow.

VARIABLES: GETTING STARTED

Variables are containers that store data in our programs. A variable is like a place holder for a value. In programming, variable names are usually descriptive of the contents they hold. For example, a program to analyze student test scores might contain variables called `NumStudents`, `TotalScores`, and `AverageScore`.

To learn how to use variables, you'll create a new project called CD Maker. This program analyzes data about a list of songs and computes whether the songs will fit on an audio CD.

CD Maker

Create a new directory called **CDMAKER**. Create a new project by clicking on New Project under the File menu. Select the program's main form (all right, the only form) by clicking on it; then bring up the Properties window, and set the property values shown in Table 3-1.

Table 3-1 The CD Maker's main form's property values

Object	Property	Value
Form	Name	frmCDMaker
	Caption	CD Maker

Visual Basic 5 comes with an icon library from which you can import images to spice up your programs. Let's add a CD image to the program. Select the PictureBox control from the toolbox and draw it in the upper-left region of the form. Don't worry about the size. Set the property values described in Table 3-2. Note that the path to your Visual Basic Graphics directory may be different.

Table 3-2 The PictureBox's property values

Object	Property	Value
PictureBox	AutoSize	True
	Picture	VB\ICONS\COMPUTER\CDROM01.ICO

If a property value has a limited set of values to choose from—such as the `AutoSize` property, which can be either `True` or `False`—you can quickly switch between them in the Properties window by double-clicking on the property name.

The Label Control

Next we'll add another common control to your repertoire: the Label control.

The Label control lets you display textual information to your user via the Label's `Caption` property. The Label control is typically not used for input. You can set the label's caption at design or runtime.

Draw a label next to the CD icon. Again, you don't need to worry about the size because the Label control also has an `AutoSize` property. Assign the property values shown in Table 3-3.

Table 3-3 The Label control's property values

Object	Property	Value
Label	AutoSize	True
	Caption	This program figures out how many songs will fit on a CD.
	Font	Arial, bold, 10 points

The Font *Property*

Notice that we used a new property, the `Font` property. In design mode, setting this property is easy. Click on Font in the Properties window and then click on the ellipses (…) button that appears to bring up the Font selection dialog box shown in Figure 3-1. Setting the property in code is a little more complicated. We'll get to that in Chapter 9, Printing.

Add one more label and also an Exit Command button to the form, as described in Table 3-4.

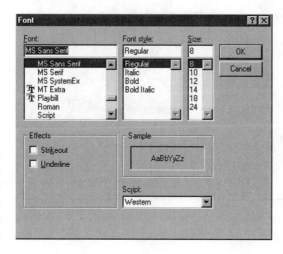

Figure 3-1
The Font dialog box lets you easily set font characteristics at design time

Table 3-4 More property values for CD Maker

Object	Property	Value
Label	Name	lblTimeAvailable
	AutoSize	True
	Caption	There are x minutes available.
CommandButton	Name	cmdExit
Caption	Exit	

The screen should look like Figure 3-2.

Declaring Variables

Let's add some source code to the program. First we'll program the Exit button. Enter the code in Listing 3-1 in the **cmdExit** button's **Click** event routine. This should be familiar to you by now.

Listing 3-1 The Exit routine

```
Private Sub cmdExit_Click()
    End
End Sub
```

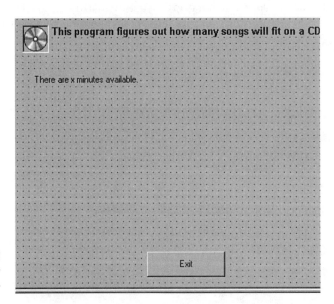

Figure 3-2
The CD Maker
thus far

Now you need to *declare* the variables you'll use. Declaring a variable tells Visual Basic about that variable: what its name is and what type of value it contains. Visual Basic uses different declaration statements to cope with different situations. The most commonly used declaration statement is the `Dim` statement. The `Dim` statement has the following syntax:

```
Dim varname [([subscripts])] As [New] type [, varname ...]
```

for example,

```
Dim MyVar As Integer
```

Variable declarations for a form are handled outside the event routines. In the Code window, click on the drop-down list next to Object:. Select the very first item, General. This will take you to the Proc: item (Declarations), which is what you want. Enter the following declaration:

```
Dim TotalCDTime As Integer
```

This tells VB, in effect, that you're going to be using a variable in this program called `TotalCDTime` that will contain integer values. Integers are whole numbers in the range of -32768 to +32767.

Initializing Variables and &

Now let's use this variable to store some data. Go to the `Form_Load` routine and add the code in Listing 3-2.

Listing 3-2 Initializing values

```
Private Sub Form_Load()

' Initialize
TotalCDTime = 60
lblTimeAvailable.Caption = "There are " & TotalCDTime & " minutes available."
End Sub
```

The `&` operator lets you build string expressions by combining integer and string expressions.

Before we move on, notice there's a new element to this code. The line

```
' Initialize
```

is a *comment*, a notation that explains what the code is doing but isn't itself source code to be executed. You can precede comments with either an apostrophe or the keyword `Rem` (short for Remark). Commenting source code is part of good programming. Even if you use meaningful variable names, it's sometimes hard, when you go back later, to remember what each section of code does. It is even harder to read someone else's code that hasn't been well commented.

In this case, we're *initializing* variables—that is, setting them to an initial value. The startup form's `Form_Load` event is typically a good place to initialize values, because it's the first code that gets executed when the program runs.

Run the program, and you'll see that the variable was correctly assigned and used in the expression, as shown in Figure 3-3. Exit the program.

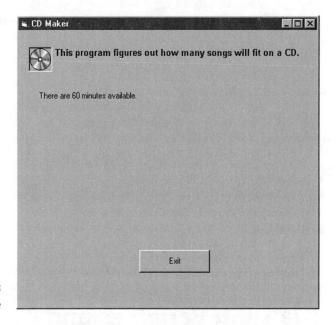

Figure 3-3
The first variable

Manipulating Variables

Assigning values to variables is pretty straightforward. This is, of course, the same operation you performed in Chapter 2, with property values. Let's add a few more variables to the program and see how to manipulate them.

Add the controls shown in Table 3-5 to the form. The form should now look like Figure 3-4.

Table 3-5 More and more property values for CD Maker

Object	Property	Value
Label	Name	lblLengthSong1
	AutoSize	True
	Caption	Your first song is x minutes long.
Label	Name	lblLengthSong2
	AutoSize	True
	Caption	Your second song is x minutes long.
Label	Name	lblTotalLength
	AutoSize	True
	Caption	Together the songs are x minutes long.
CommandButton	Name	cmdCompute
	Caption	Compute

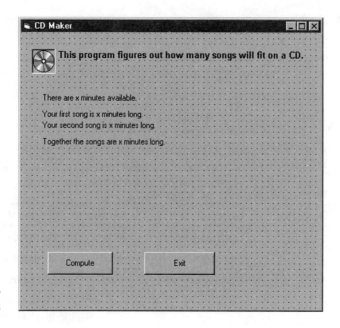

Figure 3-4
CD Maker expands

Add the code shown in Listing 3-3 to the (General) Declarations section. Changes are in bold.

Listing 3-3 Variables to hold song lengths

```
Dim TotalCDTime As Integer
Dim Song1Length As Integer
Dim Song2Length As Integer
Dim TotalLength As Integer
```

Add the code in Listing 3-4 to the **Form_Load** routine.

Listing 3-4 Giving the user more information

```
Private Sub Form_Load()

' Initialize
TotalCDTime = 60
Song1Length = 3
Song2Length = 5

' Update Captions
lblTimeAvailable.Caption = "There are " & TotalCDTime & " minutes available."
lblSong1.Caption = "Your first song is " & Song1Length & " minutes long."
lblSong2.Caption = "Your second song is " & Song2Length & " minutes long."

End Sub
```

Finally, add the code in Listing 3-5 to the **cmdCompute** button's **Click** event routine.

Listing 3-5 Adding the lengths

```
Private Sub cmdCompute_Click()
TotalLength = Song1Length + Song2Length
lblLength.Caption = "Together the songs are " & TotalLength & " minutes long."
End Sub
```

Arithmetic Operators

The arithmetic operators built into the Visual Basic language are summarized in Table 3-6.

Table 3-6 Arithmetic operators

Operator	Name	Example	Description
^	Exponentiation	x^y	Raises x to the power of y
–	Negation	–y	Negates y
*	Multiplication	x*y	Multiplies x and y
/	Division	x/y	Divides x by y and returns a floating point result
\	Integer division	x\y	Divides x by y and returns an integer result
Mod	Modulo	x Mod y	Divides x by y and returns the remainder
+	Addition	x + y	Adds x and y
–	Subtraction	x – y	Subtracts y from x

Precedence

In programming terms, *precedence* refers to the order in which arithmetic operations are carried out. For example, the expression **4+5*2** evaluates to **40**, because the multiplication operator has a higher precedence than the addition operator. Table 3-6 lists the arithmetic operators in order of precedence, with exponentiation being the highest. (Multiplication and division actually have the same precedence, as do addition and subtraction.)

You can override operator precedence by enclosing expressions in parentheses. Operations inside parentheses are always evaluated first (although, if there are multiple operators inside the parentheses, normal rules of precedence apply). Thus the equation **(4+5)*2** evaluates to **18**, because the addition is performed first.

In Lesson 2 you'll expand the program further, using more arithmetic operators and learning some new language features.

1. A variable is:
   a. A kind of property
   b. A container to store data
   c. Any arithmetic operation
   d. A number

2. Which of the following controls is typically *not* used for input?
   a. Label
   b. TextBox
   c. CommandButton
   d. DriveListBox

3. When you click on a property name in the Properties window and an ellipses (...) button appears next to the property value, it means:
   a. You must enter a string value.
   b. The property is read-only at design time.
   c. You can click on the button to bring up a dialog box from which you can select the value.
   d. You can't set the value in code.

4. Which of the following lines declares an integer value to store a high score?
   a. `Dim HighScore as Integer`
   b. `Declare HighScore as Integer`
   c. `Initialize HighScore as Integer`
   d. `Dim HighScore as Integer = 0`

5. What is the result of the equation $(2 + 3 * 10) \setminus (4 + 2)$?
   a. 5.333
   b. 5
   c. 8.333
   d. 8

THE CODE WINDOW EXPLORED

In this lesson, you'll expand your program to include some further math operations and use the first math function. You'll also explore the Visual Basic environment some more, especially the Code window.

Still More Labels

Add two more labels to the CD Maker screen, as described in Table 3-7.

Table 3-7 Two more CD Maker labels

Object	Property	Value
Label	Name	lblAverage
	AutoSize	True
	Caption	The average song length is x.
Label	Name	lblRoom
	AutoSize	True
	Caption	You have room for x more songs.

Because lblRoom, lblAverage, and lblResult don't really apply until after the user has clicked on the Compute button, let's hide these values until then.

The Visible Property

The Visible property specifies whether or not the user sees the object. Set the Visible property to False for lblRoom, lblAverage, and lblResult.

You can set property values for more than one control at once. Click on the controls to select while holding down the (CTRL) key. Notice that the Properties window now contains the properties common to all the selected controls. Set the values you want. Remember you can toggle a value by double-clicking on it.

Computer Computes

Now let's program some more computations. Go into the Code window and select the (General) Declarations section. You'll need a few more variables. Enter the declarations shown in Listing 3-6.

Listing 3-6 Variables to hold computation results

```
Dim TotalCDTime As Integer
Dim Song1Length As Integer
Dim Song2Length As Integer
Dim TotalLength As Integer
Dim AverageLength As Integer
Dim RoomLeft As Integer
```

You'll add some source code to the cmdCompute_Click event routine, but first let's learn a little more about the Code window and its features.

Splitting the Screen

In a case like this, it would be helpful to see both the Declarations section and the routine where you're going to use those variables. That way you can make sure you're using the same variable name as the one you declared. Fortunately, there's a way to see two routines at once in the Code window. To split the screen, move the mouse to the space directly above the vertical scroll bar, shown in Figure 3-5, until the mouse cursor turns into two vertical arrows separated by a bar. (This icon is also used in Word for Windows and other programs with split-screen functionality.) Now hold down the mouse button, and you'll see a line appear across the width of the window. Move that line, holding down the mouse button, to about halfway down the screen. When you release the mouse button, you'll see the window is separated into two panes, which can be scrolled independently of one another.

Now select **cmdComputer** under the Object: list box of the Code window. The **Click** event routine displays in whichever window currently contains the cursor, as shown in Figure 3-6.

Figure 3-5
Click on the area above the scroll bar to split the screen

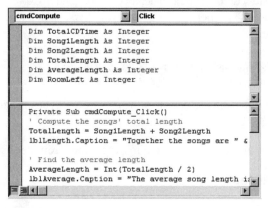

Figure 3-6
The split screen

Enter the computations in Listing 3-7 in the `cmdCompute_Click` event routine.

Listing 3-7 Computing average length and room left

```
Private Sub cmdCompute_Click()
' Compute the songs  total length
TotalLength = Song1Length + Song2Length
lblLength.Caption = "Together the songs are " & TotalLength & " minutes long."

' Find the average length
AverageLength = TotalLength / 2
lblAverage.Caption = "The average song length is " & AverageLength & "."

' See how much room is left over.
' Use parentheses to force precedence.
RoomLeft = (TotalCDTime - TotalLength) / AverageLength
lblRoom.Caption = "You have room for " & RoomLeft & " more songs."

End Sub
```

The Int *Function*

Both `AverageLength` and `RoomLeft` are integer values, so if the division results in a fractional value, it will automatically be converted to an integer. If you attempt to put a *real* number (numbers with fractional parts are called *real numbers*) into an integer variable, VB automatically truncates it into an integer. You can make this more explicit by using the `Int` function, which removes the fractional portion of a value.

Functions are routines that return a value. Visual Basic has numerous built-in functions of different types. You can also create your own functions. Functions often take *arguments*, values that you pass to the function. *Argument* is another word for *parameter*, which was mentioned in Chapter 2. For example, the `Int` function takes as an argument the value to convert to an integer. The syntax of the `Int` function is therefore

```
Int(expr)
```

Because functions return a value, they can be used in expressions, just as you've been using variables, property values, and numbers. Some valid uses of this function might be

```
Answer = Int(Question)
LblAnswer.Caption = "The answer is " & Int(3.4) & "."
Result = msgbox ("The integer value is " & int(OtherValue) & ".")
```

Similarly, you can include an entire expression as an argument to a function, as in

```
Answer = Int(Question/3)
```

Modify the lines shown in bold in the compute routine shown in Listing 3-8.

Listing 3-8 Forcing integer values

```
Private Sub cmdCompute_Click()
' Compute the songs' total length
```

```
TotalLength = Song1Length + Song2Length
lblLength.Caption = "Together the songs are " & TotalLength & " minutes long."

' Find the average length
AverageLength = Int(TotalLength / 2)
lblAverage.Caption = "The average song length is " & AverageLength & "."

' See how much room is left over.
RoomLeft = Int((TotalCDTime - TotalLength) / AverageLength)
lblRoom.Caption = "You have room for " & RoomLeft & " more songs."

End Sub
```

The True *and* False *Keywords*

Next you need to display the labels. In the Properties window, you changed the **Visible** property from **True** to **False**. It turns out that **True** and **False** are *keywords* in Visual Basic. That means they have predefined values and you can use them naturally in an expression. Add the final bits of code to your routine, as shown in Listing 3-9.

Listing 3-9 Making the controls visible

```
Private Sub cmdCompute_Click()
' Compute the songs' total length
TotalLength = Song1Length + Song2Length
lblLength.Caption = "Together the songs are " & TotalLength & " minutes long."

' Find the average length
AverageLength = Int(TotalLength / 2)
lblAverage.Caption = "The average song length is " & AverageLength & "."

' See how much room is left over.
RoomLeft = Int((TotalCDTime - TotalLength) / AverageLength)
RoomLeft = (TotalCDTime - TotalLength) / AverageLength
lblRoom.Caption = "You have room for " & RoomLeft & " more songs."

' Make the labels visible
lblLength.Visible = True
lblAverage.Visible = True
lblRoom.Visible = True

End Sub
```

Notice the color scheme VB uses as you type in code. Comments are green, keywords are blue, and the rest of the code is black.

Your color scheme may be different. You can select the colors that you want to use. Open the Tools menu and select Options. The color scheme is set on the Editor Format tab.

Run the program and click on the Compute button. The result should look like Figure 3-7.

Figure 3-7
CD Maker and the
computed values

Context-Sensitive Help in the Code Window

Before we move on, go back to the design-mode Code window. Visual Basic 5 implements extensive context-sensitive help as you're programming. In the `cmdCompute_Click` event routine, move the cursor so that it's on the property name `Caption`. Press F1. If the help system finds more than one instance of the word, you'll see the dialog box shown in Figure 3-8. At this point you'll generally pick VB (or VBA for Visual Basic for Applications). Click on Help to continue to the help system.

Next go back to the Code window (either by exiting Help or by pressing ALT-TAB to switch between Windows applications). Put the cursor on the word `Int` and press F1. You'll see the Int, Fix Functions help screen. Click on See Also, then select Math Functions. You'll see the hypertext list shown in Figure 3-9. It's never too soon to get in the habit of using VB 5's online help engine as a primary reference. It's faster to look up keywords in here than it is to look them up in the manual, and it's easier to move around in Help. Putting the cursor on a keyword and pressing F1 is particularly helpful when you know the command you want but don't remember the exact syntax or order of arguments.

Another convenient feature of VB 5 is the Auto Quick Info feature, which displays the correct syntax for a keyword as you type it. If Auto Quick Info is not turned on, open the Tools menu and select options. Auto Quick Info is on the Editor tab. You can also access Quick Info by placing your mouse pointer on a keyword and pressing CTRL-I.

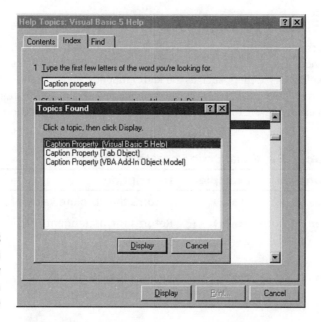

Figure 3-8
Sometimes you need to specify which Help screen is applicable

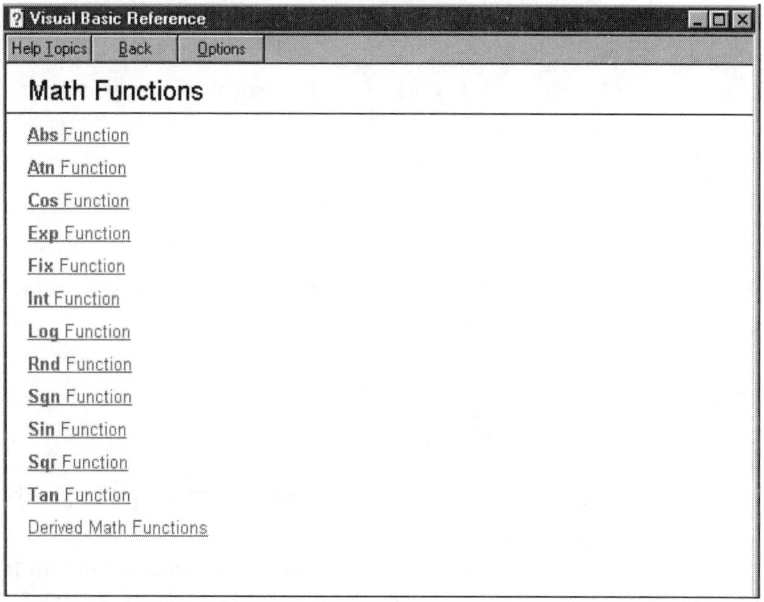

Figure 3-9
The math functions

Math Functions

Let's take a closer look at the list of math functions shown in Figure 3-9. Some of these functions—particularly the trigonometric functions `Sin()`, `Cos()`, and so on—are self-explanatory. Others, such as the `Rnd()` function, require more explanation and will be covered in detail later. Table 3-8 summarizes these math functions. Don't worry about memorizing all the functions at once. This is just to give you an idea of what's available.

Table 3-8 Visual Basic 5's math functions

Function	Example	Description	Note
Abs	Abs(x)	Returns the absolute value of x.	
Atn	Atn(x)	Returns the arctangent of x.	Returns an angle in radians.
Cos	Cos(x)	Returns the cosine of x.	x expresses an angle in radians.
Exp	Exp(x)	Returns e (the base of natural logarithms) raised to the power of x.	
Fix	Fix(x)	Returns the integer portion of x.	See the online help screen for the difference between Int and Fix.
Int	Int(x)	Returns the integer portion of x.	See the online help screen for the difference between Int and Fix.
Log	Log(x)	Returns the natural logarithm of x.	
Rnd	Rnd(x)	Returns a random number less than 1 but greater than or equal to 0.	

Function	Example	Description	Note
Sgn	Sgn(x)	Returns: 1 if x is greater than 0. 0 if x equals 0. −1 if x is less than 0.	
Sin	Sin(x)	Returns the sine of x.	x expresses an angle in radians.
Sqr	Sqr(x)	Returns the square root of x.	
Tan	Tan(x)	Returns the tangent of x.	x expresses an angle in radians.
Derived Math Functions			See the online help system for formulas to derive functions that aren't predefined, such as cotangent.

1. Which of the following statements shows a label that was previously invisible to the user?
   a. `lblTotalSongs.Visible = True`
   b. `Show lblTotalSongs`
   c. `Show lblTotalSongs.Visible`
   d. `lblTotalSongs.Show = True`

2. Which of the following statements puts an integer value in `Result`?
   a. `Result = TotalLength\2`
   b. `Result = Int(TotalLength/2)`
   c. `Dim Result As Integer Result = TotalLength/2`
   d. All of the above

3. In order to make an assignment to `True` or `False` valid, you first need to:
   a. Declare `True` and `False` as Booleans.
   b. Do nothing; they are predefined keywords.
   c. Assign −1 to `True` and 0 to `False`.
   d. Assign 1 to `True` and 0 to `False`.

4. To look up a Visual Basic keyword from the Code window, put the cursor on the keyword, and press:
    a. F1
    b. F2
    c. F3
    d. F4

5. Most VB math functions are pretty self-explanatory. The **Sin** function, for example:
    a. Returns the sine of an angle
    b. Returns the cosine of an angle
    c. Returns the sine of an exponent
    d. Converts the angle to degrees

IF **AND MORE VARIABLE TYPES**

In this lesson you'll learn some new variable types. But first, we'll start with a discussion of *program flow*. So far, all the source code you've written has been linear within the routine it's contained in. That is, first one statement is executed, then the next, and so on until the end of the routine. Although this is fine for very short tasks, soon you'll need to know program flow statements to make your programs do what you want. Most program flow statements fall into one of the following categories:

● *Conditional*, or *decision* statements, in which code is executed based on whether or not a condition is met

● *Looping* statements, in which code is executed repeatedly either a certain number of times or until a condition is met

● *Branching* statements, in which program execution switches to a different part of the program, usually based on some condition

This lesson deals with a very common decision statement, the **If** statement.

The **If** Statement (Introduction)

It's time to make a decision.

The **If...Then...Else** statement lets you say, in effect, "If this is true, then do this; otherwise, do that." This statement can be used in two different ways:

● As a single-line statement

● As a multiple-line statement

The syntax for the single-line **If** statement is

```
If expression Then statement(s) [Else statement(s)]
```

The multiline **If** statement syntax is

```
If expression Then
    [statement(s)]
[Else]
    [statement(s)]
End If
```

The statements following the **If** statement are executed if the expression evaluates to **True**. Conversely, the **Else** block of statements is executed if the expression evaluates to **False**. The expression used in **If...Then** is a *Boolean expression*. Boolean expressions have two possible values: **True** or **False**. Numerically, **False** is equal to minus 1, and **True** is defined as *not false*.

Note The use of the **Else** block in both versions of the **If** statement is optional.

Here is an example of the single-line syntax:

```
If lblScore.Visible = True Then lblScore.Caption = Score Else Score = 0
```

The multiline structure of this statement is preferred, as it is generally much easier to read:

```
If lblScore.Visible = True Then
    lblScore.Caption = Score
Else
    Score = 0
End If
```

Comparison Operators

Note that, in the above example, the equal sign is being used both as an assignment statement (**Score = 0**) and as a *comparison operator* (**lblScore.Visible = True**). A comparison operator compares two values and returns the result of the comparison (either **True** or **False**). Table 3-9 lists the arithmetic comparison operators in Visual Basic, in order of precedence.

Table 3-9 Comparison operators

Operator	Name
=	Equality
<>	Inequality
<	Less than
>	Greater than
<=	Less than or equal to
>=	Greater than or equal to

CD Maker Gets Smarter

Let's use these new language elements to give CD Maker a little logic. On the main form, add the label described in Table 3-10.

Table 3-10 Yet another CD Maker label

Object	Property	Value
Label	Name	lblResult
	AutoSize	True
	Caption	Your songs will/will not fit.
	Visible	False

Go to the **cmdCompute** click event and modify the code as shown in Listing 3-10.

Listing 3-10 Implementing a conditional statement

```
Private Sub cmdCompute_Click()
' Compute the songs' total length
TotalLength = Song1Length + Song2Length
lblLength.Caption = "Together the songs are " & TotalLength & " minutes long."

' Find the average length
AverageLength = Int(TotalLength / 2)
lblAverage.Caption = "The average song length is " & AverageLength & "."

' Can they fit on the CD?
If TotalLength <= TotalCDTime Then
   lblResult.Caption = "Your songs will fit."

   ' See how much room is left over.
   RoomLeft = Int((TotalCDTime - TotalLength) / AverageLength)
   lblRoom.Caption = "You have room for " & RoomLeft & " more songs."
   lblRoom.Visible = True
Else
   lblResult.Caption = "Your songs will not fit."
End If

' Make the labels visible
lblResult.Visible = True
lblLength.Visible = True
lblAverage.Visible = True

End Sub
```

The conditional statement in this code segment reads, **"If the total length is less than or equal to the total time on the CD, then..."** Notice that the **lblRoom** property assignments are now inside the conditional statement block, because if there isn't enough room on the CD for the two songs, there won't be room for any more. Run the program again and click the Compute button. You'll see the screen in Figure 3-10. Try changing the values of `Song1Length` and `Song2Length` to 45 and 20 and running the program again.

That about does it for the CD Maker. Go ahead and save the form as `CDMAKER.FRM` and the project as `CDMAKER.VBP` inside the `CDMAKER` directory. After a few digressions, we'll start a new sample project.

Constants

So far, we have considered only variables in the programs. Visual Basic allows you to declare *constants* as well. Constants are rather like variables, except that their value never changes. Consider the following example:

```
If Action = 3 Then
    ' execute code for action number 3
End If
```

The problem with the above example is that `action number 3` isn't very meaningful. It would be much better if we could write the code as:

```
If Action = CANCELORDER Then
    ' execute code to cancel the order
End If
```

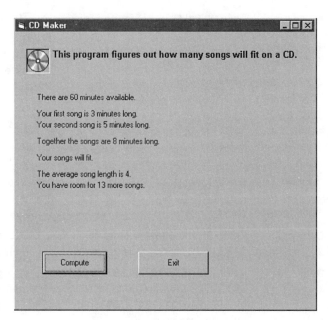

Figure 3-10
The CD Maker
knows what will fit

In this example, **CANCELORDER** is a constant that we have predefined to take the number **3**. Constants are declared anywhere in your project, but you will most likely declare your constants in the General Declarations sections of your modules. Constants are declared using the **Const** keyword, which has the following syntax:

```
[Public | Private] Const constname [As type] = expression
```

For example:

```
Const CANCELORDER As Integer = 3
```

The keywords **Public** and **Private** refer to scope, which we'll talk about in Chapter 4, Subroutines, Functions, and the Visual Basic 5 Language.

Variable Types

So far, the variables you've declared have all been integers (although we talked in Chapter 2, Object-Oriented Programming, about string values for some properties). VB 5 has a range of additional types as well. Table 3-11 lists all of VB's built-in types.

Table 3-11 The VB 5 variable types

Type	Range	Note
Byte	0-255	Occupies only 1 byte of memory.
Boolean	True or False	This is actually stored internally as an integer.
Integer	-32767 to 32768	Each integer occupies 2 bytes of memory.
Long	-2,147,483,648 to 2,147,483,647	Longs hold integers, but use 4 bytes of memory.
Single	See below.	Single-precision floating-point variable; occupies 4 bytes of memory.
Double	See below.	Double-precision floating-point variable; occupies 8 bytes of memory.
Currency	-922,337,203,685,477.5808 to 922,337,203,685,477.5807	Occupies 8 bytes of memory.
Dec	+/-79,228,162,514,264,337,593,543,950,335 as a whole number +/-7.9228162514264337593543950335 with decimal places	Occupies 12 bytes of memory.
String	See Lessons 4 and 5.	

Type	Range	Note
Date	See Lessons 6 and 7.	
Variant	See Lesson 8.	
Object	See Chapter 14, Advanced Features.	

Byte

A byte is the smallest numeric data type. It can hold unsigned numbers (positive only) between 0 and 255. Bytes are quite useful when you want to conserve memory space and you know that the numbers you need to process will never be greater than 255. Consider the example in Listing 3-11, which assumes that the form has the Command buttons `cmdApples`, `cmdBananas`, `cmdOranges`, and `cmdGroceryOrder`.

Listing 3-11 Replacing numbers with meaningful constants helps readability

```
Const APPLES As Byte = 1
Const BANANAS As Byte = 2
Const ORANGES As Byte = 3
Dim Fruit As Byte

Private Sub cmdApples_Click()
Fruit = APPLES
End Sub

Private Sub cmdBananas_Click()
Fruit = BANANAS
End Sub

Private Sub cmdOranges_Click()
Fruit = ORANGES
End Sub

Private Sub cmdGroceryOrder_Click()
If Fruit = ORANGES Then
    MsgBox "Sorry, oranges are out of season."
End If
End Sub
```

By replacing the numeric values with symbolic constants, you made the code easier to read. Because you know you'll have less than 255 kinds of fruit, you're conserving memory as well by using the Byte data type.

Boolean

Boolean types are special in that they can be set to only one of two values: `True` or `False`. Internally, the Boolean type is actually an Integer data type. The value `True` is represented by the value `-1` and `False` is represented by `0`. When you print the value of a `Boolean` variable, Visual Basic converts these internal representation to the string `"True"` or `"False"`.

Booleans are generally used in two ways:

- To hold the result of an expression evaluation
- As flags to indicate whether or not a particular condition has been satisfied

Booleans to Hold the Result of an Expression Evaluation

To use a Boolean to hold the result of an expression, simply assign the expression to the Boolean as in Listing 3-12.

Listing 3-12 Code fragment to assign a value to a Boolean

```
Dim Higher As Boolean
Dim Num1 As Integer, Num2 As Integer

' Perform assignments or get data here.

Higher = Num1 > Num2
If Higher Then
    ' Do whatever
EndIf
```

You might want to do this if you'll be using the result of the expression in more than one place or if the value of `Num1` or `Num2` might change, but you still want to remember the results of the original comparison.

Booleans to Keep Track of Whether a Condition Has Been Satisfied

Start a new Visual Basic project with the Command buttons listed in Table 3-12. It doesn't matter where on the form you put the buttons.

Table 3-12 Controls for Boolean flag example

Control	Property	Value
CommandButton	Caption	Click once, at least!
	Name	cmdClick
CommandButton	Caption	Exit
	Name	cmdExit

This program uses a Boolean flag, `Clicked`, to keep track of whether the user has clicked the first button. You'll use the value in the `Exit` routine to prevent the user from quitting before clicking. The code to do this is shown in Listing 3-13.

Listing 3-13 Boolean flag example

```
Dim Clicked As Boolean

Private Sub cmdClick_Click()
' Set flag to True
Clicked = True
End Sub

Private Sub cmdExit_Click()
If Not Clicked Then
    MsgBox "Sorry, you have to click at least once!"
Else
    End
End If
End Sub

Private Sub Form_Load()
' Initialize flag to False
Clicked = False
End Sub
```

Integer

You have already seen integers in action in the CD Maker program. Integers are whole numbers in the range of -32767 to 32768. Each integer occupies 2 bytes of memory.

Long

Longs are another type of integer, except they occupy 4 bytes of memory rather than 2. Correspondingly, they can hold much larger numbers.

A long can hold numbers in the range of -2,147,483,648 to 2,147,483,647.

Single

Single-precision floating-point variables occupy 4 bytes of memory. Singles and doubles are used for storing numbers that have a decimal point. You should be aware, however, that the accuracy of the representation of floating-point numbers is as dependent on how many digits there are before the decimal point as on how many there are after.

For example:

```
Dim MySingle As Single
MySingle = 123456.123456
lblOutput.Caption = MySingle
```

The original value assigned to MySingle doesn't survive the assignment. This is because, although single-precision floating-point variables can store very large or very small numbers, by using their exponent component, they can hold only a small number of actual numbers (seven at the most).

The full range of valid numbers for singles is

- -3.402823E38 to -1.401298E-45 for negative numbers

- 1.401298E-45 to 3.402823E38 for positive numbers

- 0

The numbers above are expressed in *scientific notation*. Scientific notation is a system used to express very large and very small numbers using the powers of ten. Briefly, 1E3 evaluates to 1000 and 1E-3 evaluates to 0.001. The number following the *E* tells you how far to move the decimal point and the sign of the number tells you which way to move it.

Double

Double-precision floating-point variables use 8 bytes of memory for each variable and, accordingly, can store a greater range and precision of numbers. The full range of valid numbers for doubles is

- -1.79769313486232E308 to -4.94065645841247E-324 for negative numbers

- 4.94065645841247E-324 to 1.79769313486232E308 for positive numbers

- 0

Be careful when using single- and double-precision floating-point variables in the same program unless it doesn't matter if you lose some decimal places during your calculations. For example, if you need to do monetary calculations, use the Currency data type rather than Single or Double.

Currency

The **Currency** data type is provided for the express purpose of holding money values. It can hold amounts in the range -922,337,203,685,477.5808 to 922,337,203,685,477.5807.

Currency data types can hold numbers down to four decimal places, because some currencies around the world need such accuracy.

Currency variables use 8 bytes of memory space.

Decimal

If you are calculating *really* big numbers, like this month's electric bill, you can use the new **Decimal** data type. This little gem uses 12 bytes of memory and holds numbers in the range (hold on to your hat!) +/-79,228,162,514,264,337,593,543,950,335 for zero-scaled numbers, that is, numbers with no decimal places. If you need decimal places, you can have up to 28 of them, and the range becomes +/-7.9228162514264337593543950335. The smallest possible non-zero number is 0.0000000000000000000000000001.

As of this writing, you can't *declare* a Decimal data type, but you can *create* one from a variant. To see how to do this, open a new form and put a text box on it. Enter the following code in the form's **Load** event:

```
Private Sub Form_Load()

Dim MyCurr As Currency, MyDec As Variant
MyCurr = CCur(234.456784)    ' MyCurr is a Currency.
MyDec = CDec(MyCurr * 8.2 * 0.000000000000001)    ' Convert result to a Decimal
Text1.Text = MyDec

End Sub
```

Now run the program by pressing F5.

Note the use of the *variant* data type in the code. A variant is a catch-all data type that can be used to hold any kind of data. Most programmers avoid them when possible because they use more memory than the other data types, but sometimes, as in this code, they are required.

1. **If** is an example of:
   a. A looping statement
   b. A branching statement
   c. A conditional statement
   d. A function

2. What is the difference between:

   ```
   If...Then...Else...
   ```

   and
   ```
   If...Then
   ...
   Else
   ...
   End If
   ```

   a. The first usage can execute only one statement per condition.
   b. The first usage cannot really implement an **Else** clause.
   c. They are functionally equivalent, but the second usage is easier to read.
   d. Both a and b are true.

3. In which of the following statements is = being used as a comparison operator?
   a. `HighScore = 50`
   b. `HighScore = lblScore.Caption`
   c. `lblScore.Caption = HighScore`
   d. `If HighScore = 50 Then ...`

4. How would you declare a constant to hold a value representing a grocery item?
   a. `Dim Const FRESHDILL As Integer = 23`
   b. `Dim FRESHDILL = 23`
   c. `Const FRESHDILL As Integer = 23`
   d. `Dim FRESHDILL As Integer FRESHDILL = 23`

5. Which of the following lists of variable types is in the order of least memory to store to most memory to store?
   a. Byte, Single, Integer
   b. Integer, Long, Double
   c. Integer, Currency, Single
   d. Single, Double, Boolean

INTRODUCTION TO STRINGS

Strings are variables and constants that hold alphanumeric values. These are values that you want to display but will not usually use for mathematical calculations. You've already been using strings since Lesson 2 in Chapter 2, Object-Oriented Programming. In Visual Basic, a sequence of alphanumeric characters treated as a single value is considered a string. The **Caption** property, **Text** property, **FileName** property, and so on all contain string values. Literal strings are assigned by enclosing the value in quotation marks, as you've already seen. For example:

```
lblMessage.Caption = "Sorry, oranges are out of season."
```

Working with a string's contents is more complicated than working with numbers because the characters that make up the string give you not just one value, but have a separate value for each character in the string. Fortunately, VB has a wealth of string manipulation functions. How you use them depends on how closely you need to analyze a string's contents. Before we proceed, let's take a look at a new, fast way to look at variables' values.

The Immediate Window

The Immediate window is a window to which you can output information that you might need for purposes of program development and debugging. You might use the Immediate window to check a variable's value quickly or to evaluate an expression without interrupting the flow of your program.

The Immediate window is actually Visual Basic's built-in **Debug** object. The **Debug** object is an example of a class that has only one instance. The **Debug** object is automatically created by Visual Basic for you, so there is no need for you to provide any additional programming support to create it. The **Debug** object provides you with a single method only—the **Print** method.

The Print *Method*

The **Print** method outputs a value. What **Print** does depends on the object being acted on. To try out the Immediate window, start a new project, double-click on the form to bring up the Code window, and enter the code in Listing 3-14 in the **Form_Load** event.

Listing 3-14 Testing the Immediate window

```
Private Sub Form_Load()
    Dim FullName As String
    FullName = "c:\vb\vb.exe"
    Debug.Print FullName
End Sub
```

Run your program. The Immediate window may be hidden behind the main form. To bring it to view, click on Immediate Window under the View menu. You'll see your output as in Figure 3-11.

You can leave the **Debug** statements in your program when you compile it, because they are ignored by the compiler. We will often use the Immediate window in this way to help demonstrate the values that variables take in our examples.

In the future, when we use short code snippets with **Debug.Print** as examples, we won't specify the **Form_Load** event every time. This will be assumed, because that's the natural place to put code you want to run immediately. You may want to resize or move the main form and the Immediate window in design mode so that the Immediate window is visible when the program runs.

To learn to use strings, you will create a new project called Address Book. This program accepts data entry and separates it into the appropriate strings for address book entries. (The program will not save your entries. Chapter 12, Files, and Chapter 13, Data Access, deal with techniques for saving data like this to disk for later use.)

Figure 3-11
The Immediate
window

Address Book

Create a new directory called **ADDRESS BOOK**. Create a new project by clicking on New Project under the File menu. Select the program's main form and press F4 to bring up the Property window. Set the form's property values as shown in Table 3-13.

Table 3-13 The Address Book form's property values

Object	Property	Value
Form	Name	frmAddressBook
	Caption	Address Book

The Icon *Property*

You will add an icon to this project to change its look. When you compile a project that has one or more icons set, the first icon the compiler finds will become the icon for the project's EXE file. Click on the **Icon** property of the form; then click on the ellipses that appear in the right edge of the property list. A File Open list box will appear. The collection of icons is in the **GRAPHICS\ICONS** directory. Select the **WRITING** directory; then select **NOTE14.ICO**.

If you select an icon or a bitmap picture that you later decide to delete, you cannot remove it by selecting None again—VB will not offer you that choice. You can remove it by highlighting the word Icon or Bitmap—drag the mouse pointer across the selection in the Properties window—and pressing DEL.

Add three labels, a text box, and a Command button to **frmAddressBook**. Assign the property values shown in Table 3-14.

Table 3-14 New properties for the Address Book project

Object	Property	Value
Label	Name	lblInstructions
	Caption	Enter Last Name, First Name
	AutoSize	True
TextBox	Name	txtName
	Text	txtName
Label	Name	lblFirstName
	AutoSize	False
	Caption	False

Object	Property	Value
Label	Name	lblLastName
	AutoSize	False
	Caption	False
CommandButton	Name	cmdSave
	Caption	&Save

For **lblFirstName** and **lblLastName**, select the **BackColor** property and change the color to white (**&H00FFFFFF&**).

Arrange the controls on the form as shown in Figure 3-12. The two white blocks in the center are **lblFirstName** on the left and **lblLastName** on the right. Note that **txtName**, **lblFirstname**, and **cmdSave** are aligned on the left.

You can align controls easily in VB 5. Select all the controls you wish to align by holding down (SHIFT) as you click on each control. Now select Align from the Format menu. You will get a cornucopia of alignment and sizing options. Try it!

Before we add code to this project, let's look at some basic facts about strings.

Strings

Strings hold character data. Visual Basic 5 can store strings up to 2 billion characters in length! There are two types of strings:

- Variable-length
- Fixed-length

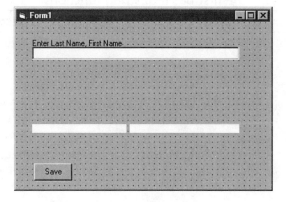

Figure 3-12
The Address Book
project

Variable-Length Strings

Variable-length strings are declared simply by using the `String` type name when you declare the variable. For instance:

```
Dim MyVarString As String
```

Variable-length strings have an overhead of 10 bytes per string. They occupy 10 additional bytes over and above the length of the string itself.

Fixed-Length Strings

Fixed-length strings are declared by specifying the length of the string in the declaration of the string variable. For instance:

```
Dim MyFixedString As String * 30
```

declares a 30-character string. It will always be 30 characters, even if you assign less data to it. For example:

```
MyFixedString = "ABCDE"
```

automatically right-pads the string with 25 spaces.

String Functions

Sometimes you don't care what's in a string. A string is just a thing that you pass from one part of your program to another without regard for its contents. Other times, however, you need to know what's inside. You might need to verify its contents, modify it in some way, or extract a specific piece of information from it. There are enough core string functions that two lessons are required in order to cover them all. The string functions you'll learn in this lesson are summarized in Table 3-15.

Table 3-15 The first batch of string functions

Function	Example	Description
Len	Len(String)	Returns the integer length of String
InStr	InStr ([StartPosition,] String, ⇐ SubString [, Compare])	Searches String for occurrences of SubString
Left	Left(String,Length)	Returns the leftmost Length characters of String
Right	Right(String, Length)	Returns the rightmost Length characters of String

Function	Example	Description
Mid	Mid(String, Start, Length)	Returns Length characters from String, starting at position Start

Many of these functions are helpful in *parsing*, extracting smaller pieces from the string. Throughout this session, you'll explore the task of breaking a string into components and checking the values of specific parts of a string.

Code for Address Book

Now let's add the code for the Address Book project. Because you will be doing the same thing to several different strings before you are done, add some functions to the project.

All the work to begin with will be done in the **cmdSave_Click** event. Enter the code in Listing 3-15 or copy it from the CD that comes with this book.

Listing 3-15 The cmdSave_Click event

```
Private Sub cmdSave_Click()
'    message for sMsgbox
Dim sSMsg As String
'    The name, separated into first and last names
Dim sFirstName As String, sLastName As String
'    where is the comma in the name
Dim iCommaPosition As Integer
'    The length of the name as entered
Dim iLength As Integer
'    Where the space is
Dim iSpacePosition As Integer
'    The city, state and ZIP code
Dim sCity As String, sState As String, sZip As String

'    First make sure the name was entered
If Len(txtName.Text) = 0 Then
    '    Create the warning message
    sMsg = "No Name Entered"
    '    make it visible
    MsgBox sMsg
    '    set focus back to txtName
    txtName.SetFocus
    Exit Sub
End If
'    now check for the comma
If InStr(txtName.Text, ",") = 0 Then
    '    Create the warning message
    sMsg = "Must have a comma between" & vbCrLf
    sMsg = sMsg & "Last Name and First Name"
    '    make it visible
    MsgBox sMsg
```

continued on next page

continued from previous page

```
'    set focus back to txtName
    txtName.SetFocus
    Exit Sub
End If
'   if we got here the name was probably entered correctly
'   get the length
iLength = Len(txtName)
'   find the comma
iCommaPosition = InStr(txtName.Text, ",")
'   Pull the First name from the textbox
'   The -1 is so we don't get the comma, too
sLastName = Left(txtName, iCommaPosition - 1)
'   Pull the last name from the textbox
'   Start by testing for a space after the comma
If Mid(txtName, iCommaPosition + 1, 1) = " " Then
    iCommaPosition = iCommaPosition + 1
       'move the start position one place to the right
End If
sFirstName = Right(txtName.Text, iLength - iCommaPosition)
'   display the separated names
lblFirstName.Caption = sFirstName
lblLastName.Caption = sLastNameEnd Sub
End Sub
```

A Look at the Code

Let's take a look at the code and see what is happening.

```
'   message for sMsgbox
Dim sSMsg As String
'   The name, separated into first and last names
Dim sFirstName As String, sLastName As String
'   where is the comma in the name
Dim iCommaPosition As Integer
'   The length of the name as entered
Dim iNameLength As Integer
```

This section of code declares the variables you will be using in the **Click** event. It is using a *naming convention* that helps you remember what kind of variable you are using. For example, the **s** in **sMsg** reminds you that it is a string variable and the **i** in **iNameLength** reminds you that it is an integer variable. Naming conventions like this can help avoid mistakes, especially on large projects.

Because computer users are human, input errors are quite possible. The code in **cmdSave_Click** begins with a couple of tests to be sure the data was input in the correct format. (Sorry, we can't do anything about spelling!)

```
If Len(txtName.Text) = 0 Then
    '   Create the warning message
    sMsg = "No Name Entered"
    '   make it visible
    MsgBox sMsg
```

```
'    set focus back to txtName
txtName.SetFocus
 'the entry is incorrect, do not process it
Exit Sub
End If
```

The first routine checks to make sure that something was actually entered in **txtName**. It uses the **Len()** function to verify that something is in the box.

The Len *Function*

The **Len** function counts the characters in a string and returns the length as an integer. The syntax is

```
Length = Len(String)
```

Knowing how long a string is can help you in cases where you need to verify that the string will fit in a certain field. You also might use this function when you need to perform some operation for every character in the string, when you need to compare the relative sizes of two strings, or in other situations.

In this case, if **Len** returns a **0**, it tells you there are no characters in the string. If that is the case, the program uses a built-in Visual Basic function, the Message Box, to let the user know that there is no text in the text box. The code lines

```
sMsg = "No Name Entered"
MsgBox sMsg
```

build a message to be displayed and then display the message in a *modal* form. A modal form is one that must be closed before the program can continue. Much more can be done with the **MsgBox** object, but we will stick to this simple method for now.

When the user clicks OK in the message box, the line

```
txtName.SetFocus
```

sets the focus back to the text box so a name can be entered.

Remember that spaces are characters, too, and will be counted.

Back to the Code

The next block of code makes sure that the user has followed instructions by separating the last name and first name with a comma.

```
If InStr(txtName.Text, ",")= 0 Then
    '    Create the warning message
    sMsg = "Must have a comma between" & vbCrLf
    sMsg = sMsg & "Last Name and First Name"
    '    make it visible
    MsgBox sMsg
    '    set focus back to txtName
    txtName.SetFocus
     'the entry is incorrect, do not process it
    Exit Sub
End If
```

This code uses the **InStr** function to be sure that a comma has been entered. If there is no comma, a **MsgBox** informs the user and focus is returned to the text box. Note that when the message is built, this time we use *string concatenation*. Concatenation is a 75-cent word for "pasting together." The first line,

```
sMsg = "Must have a comma between" & vbCRLF
```

ends with **& vbCRLF**. The **&** tells VB to add two strings together. The **vbCRLF** is a built-in Visual Basic constant that represents a carriage return and a linefeed. The next line,

```
sMsg = sMsg & "Last Name and First Name"
```

adds another string to the first. Because of the **vbCRLF** at the end of the first line, the message will be shown on two lines in the **MsgBox**.

The InStr *Function*

The **InStr** function returns the first position of a string inside another string. If the substring (the string you're looking for) isn't found, **InStr** returns a **0**. The syntax of **InStr** is

```
InStr([StartPosition,] String, SubString [, Compare])
```

where

- **StartPosition** is a numeric expression that sets the start position for the search of **SubString** in **String**. (The first character is position 1.) If **StartPosition** is omitted, **InStr** begins searching at the first position.

- **String** is the string being searched.

- **SubString** is the string you are looking for in **String**.

- **Compare** determines how to go about the comparison of the two strings. If you omit **Compare** or specify a value of 0, **InStr** performs a straight comparison, which is usually the type you want to use. If you are working mostly with text and want to use a case-insensitive **Compare**, specify 1 for the **Compare** parameter.

Here's a simple example of **InStr**:

```
Debug.Print InStr("Hello in there","in")
```

This line displays **7**. On the other hand,

```
Debug.Print InStr(8,"Hello in there","in")
```

returns a value of **0**, because the substring **"in"** doesn't appear at or after the eighth character.

InStr is helpful simply to see *whether* a string is in a substring, as in this example to validate input.

```
If  InStr(txtName.Text,",") = 0 Then
```

```
    lblMessage.Caption = "Please separate names with a comma."
Else
    ' (Go off and process the data.)
End If
```

However, `InStr` really shows its power when you need it to track the position of characters. We'll be looking at this use more below, in conjunction with the other string functions.

The Rest of the Code

Both of the tests will detect a problem with the data entered (or not entered) in `txtName`. You don't want to process that bad data, so both tests have the line

```
Exit Sub
```

just before the `End If`. `Exit Sub`, of course, exits from the `sub cmdSave_Click` without executing any more of the commands.

The next block of code assumes correct entry of the data; the name has been entered last name first, with a comma separating the last name from the first name. Data processing applications should really be written so that the two names are entered separately, but this program uses the next block of code to do the separation.

```
'   get the length
nLength = Len(txtName)
```

gets the length of the string.

```
iCommaPosition = InStr(txtName.Text, ",")
'   Pull the Last name from the textbox
'   The -1 is so we don't get the comma, too
sLastName = Left(txtName, iCommaPosition - 1)
```

uses the left function to extract the left end of the string in `txtName` into its own variable, `sLastName`. We will look at the `Left`, `Right`, and `Mid` functions after these blocks of code.

```
'   Pull the First name from the textbox
'   Start by testing for a space after the comma
If Mid(txtName, iCommaPosition + 1,1) = " " Then
    iCommaPosition = iCommaPosition + 1
End If
```

You don't want a space as the first character of the first name, so check to see if the user entered one by using the `Mid` function. If you find one (you should) then increment `iCommaPosition` by 1.

```
sFirstName = Right(txtName.Text, iLength - iCommaPosition)
```

Next, use the `Right` function to extract the first name from `txtName`. Then, using techniques you already know, display the separated names in their own labels.

```
'   display the separated names
lblFirstName.Caption = sFirstName
lblLastName.Caption = sLastName
End Sub
```

The Left *Function*

The Left function returns characters from the left-hand side of String. For example, the Left function has the following syntax:

```
Left(String, Length)
```

where

● String is the string from which you are returning characters.

● Length is the number of characters to return. If Length = 0, then a zero-length string is returned. If Length is greater than the length of the string, then the entire string is returned. You can try out the sample code by placing it in Form_Load and viewing the results in the Immediate window.

```
Dim Alphabet As String, EasyPart As String
Alphabet = "ABCDEFGHIJKLMNOPQRSTUVWXYZ"
EasyPart = Left(Alphabet,3)
Debug.Print "It's easy as " & EasyPart
```

This creates and prints out a new string consisting of Alphabet's first three characters, ABC. Here's another example.

```
Dim FullPathName As String, Drive As String
FullPathName = "c:\vb\vb.exe"
Drive = Left(FullPathName,1)
Debug.Print "Searching drive " & Drive & "..."
```

The Right *Function*

The Right function returns characters from the right-hand side of the string. It has the following syntax:

```
Right(String, Length)
```

where

● String is the string from which you are returning characters.

● Length is the number of characters to return. If Length = 0, then a zero-length string is returned. If Length is greater than the length of the string, then the entire string is returned.

The Mid *Function*

The Mid function returns characters from any part of a string.

The Mid function has the following syntax:

```
Mid(String, Start [,Length])
```

where

● String is the string from which you are returning characters.

● Start is the character position in string at which the part to be taken begins. If Start is greater than the number of characters in the string, Mid returns a zero-length string.

● Length is the number of characters to return. If this is omitted or if there are fewer than Length characters in the text (including the character at the start), all characters from the start position to the end of the string are returned.

For example,

```
Dim MyString As String, NewString As String
MyString = "ABCDEFGHIJKLMNOPQRSTUVWXYZ"
NewString = Mid(MyString, 11, 10)
Debug.Print NewString
```

outputs

```
KLMNOPQRST
```

Note that the third parameter refers to the length of string that you want to return, not the end character in the original string. If Length is omitted, all characters from Start to the end of the string are returned.

Running the Code

Now run the code for Address Book.

● Start by clicking on the Save button without putting any text in the text box. Note the appearance of the message box.

● Enter a name in the text box, but omit the required comma. Note what happens when you click on the Save button; the two-line message adds a touch of professionalism to the box.

● Add the comma between the first and last names in the text box. Again note what happens when you click on the Save button: The first and last names now appear in their specified display labels.

● Save the project. You will be working with it more in Lesson 5.

1. The statement:

   ```
   Debug.Print "The answer is 10."
   ```

   a. Outputs a single string to the Immediate window
   b. Won't do anything until you create an instance of the **Debug** object
   c. Will have to be removed manually before you can ship the compiled version
   of your product
   d. Won't work, because the argument is a string literal

2. String functions such as **Mid**, **InStr**, and **Len** are useful:
   a. When you need to perform close analysis of a string's contents
   b. When you are passing a string as a single value from one part of your
   program to another
   c. When you need to assign a string variable to an object property
   d. All of the above

3. The statement

   ```
   Debug.Print InStr(4, "c:\windows\system.ini","\")
   ```

   prints out:
   a. **3**
   b. **4**
   c. **11**
   d. **10**

4. The statement

   ```
   Dim MyString As String
   MyString = "ABC;123;QRS"
   Debug.Print Mid(MyString,InStr(MyString,";"),3)
   ```

   outputs:
   a. **123**
   b. **QRS**
   c. **;12**
   d. Nothing; the line has a syntax error.

5. If you have the following variables:

   ```
   Dim FullName As String
   FullName = "WINWORD.EXE"
   ```

   which of the following statements will *reliably* print out the extension? (Assume
   FullName can be any valid file name with an extension.)

```
a. Debug.Print Right(FullName,3)
b. Debug.Print Right(FullName,InStr(FullName,"."))
c. Debug.Print Right(FullName,InStr(FullName,".")+1)
d. Debug.Print Right(FullName,Len(FullName)-InStr(FullName,"."))
```

Write a program to print out the drive or device name of a file, given the full path name. Assume the device name is preceded by a colon and may be more than one character long. Let the user know if there isn't a device name present.

LESSON 5

STRING MANIPULATION

This session covers such string-handling techniques as converting a string to upper- or lowercase and trimming the excess spaces from a string. These functions are summarized in Table 3-16. After that, we'll round out our string machinations with sections on string concatenation and string comparison.

Table 3-16 The second batch of string functions

Function	Example	Description
UCase	UCase(String)	Converts string to all uppercase
LCase	LCase(String)	Converts a string to all lowercase
LTrim	LTrim(String)	Strips leading spaces from a string
RTrim	RTrim(String)	Strips trailing spaces from a string
Trim	Trim(String)	Strips leading and trailing spaces from a string
Asc	Asc(StringChar)	Returns the numeric equivalent of a character
Chr	Chr(Number)	Returns the character corresponding to a code value
Space	Space(Number)	Returns a string consisting of a number of spaces

continued on next page

continued from previous page

Function	Example	Description
String	String(Number, Character)	Returns a string consisting of a single character repeated a number of times
LSet	LSet String1 = String2	Left-justifies one string within another
RSet	RSet String1 = String2	Right-justifies one string within another
StrComp	StrComp(string1, string2[, compare])	Returns a value indicating the result of a string comparison

Improving Address Book

Open the Address Book project and add two new text boxes and six new labels to the form.

Look ahead at Figure 3-13. You will see that the new text boxes are exactly the same size as the original text boxes. You can make copies of VB controls just the same way you make copies of text in a word processor. Click in **txtName** and press CTRL-C to copy the control to the clipboard. Then press CTRL-V to paste it down on the form. VB will ask you if you are making a control array—answer No and it will insert a copy of the control in the upper-left corner of the form. While the control is selected, you can move it by holding down CTRL and using the arrow keys to move the control or by dragging it with the mouse. If you need to resize a control, select it and use SHIFT and the arrow keys to adjust the size, or use the mouse to resize the control.

Set the properties of the new controls according to Table 3-17.

Table 3-17 Properties for the new controls

Object	Property	Value
TextBox	Name	txtAddress
TextBox	Name	txtCityStateZip
Label	Name	lbl1
	AutoSize	True
	Caption	Name
Label	Name	lbl2
	AutoSize	True
	Caption	Address

Object	Property	Value
Label	Name	lbl3
	AutoSize	True
	Caption	City, State Zip
Label	Name	lblAddress
	Caption	lblAddress
	BackColor	&H00FFFFFF&
Label	Name	lblCity
	Caption	lblCity
	BackColor	&H00FFFFFF&
Label	Name	lblState
	Caption	lblState
	BackColor	&H00FFFFFF&
Label	Name	lblZip
	Caption	lblZip
BackColor	&H00FFFFFF&	

Use Figure 3-13 as a guide to placing these new control objects.

Changing the Tab Order

Move from control to control in a running VB program by pressing the TAB key. The *order*, or sequence of the controls as you tab through a form is initially set to be the same as the order in which you created the controls. On this form, with all its new controls, the tab order is no longer correct. If you enter data in **txtName** and press TAB, you may want to go to **txtAddress**, but you will go to **cmdSave**.

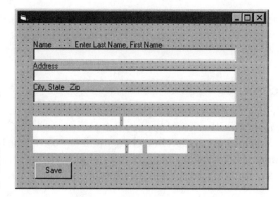

Figure 3-13
The improved
Address Book form

The following steps make it easy to change the tab order:

- Select the control you want to be last in the tab order and change its `Tab Index` property to 0.

- Select the next to last control and change its `Tab Index` property to 0.

- Continue to work your way backward through the controls, setting each control's `Tab Index` property to 0.

As you change each control's **Tab Index** property to **0**, all the controls "below it" are automatically changed to the next higher index. The effect ripples through all the previously set controls and your tab indexes are automatically reset to the order you wanted.

Enabling (ENTER)

You want to make some improvements to what you already have before you add code for the new controls. For example, some people find it more natural to finish entering data into a text box by pressing the (ENTER) key rather than by pressing (TAB), which is the standard "computer" way to move from field to field. You could do that by placing the following code in the **KeyPress** event of every text box:

```
If KeyAscii = 13 then
    KeyAscii = 0
    SendKeys "{Tab}"
End If
```

That wouldn't be too hard now—you have only three text boxes. But some programs have a lot more text boxes. Instead, you can use a formwide technique:

- Set the `KeyPreview` property of `frmAddressBook` to `True`.

- Put the code shown above in the `Form_KeyPress` event.

It is standard Windows practice to use (ENTER) to operate a "default key," usually either OK or Close. This alternative use of (ENTER) is included because some clients just don't *want* to be "standard."

KeyAscii

The **KeyPress** event occurs (surprise!) every time a key is pressed in a control. **KeyAscii** is the ASCII value of the key that was pressed. ASCII stands for American Standard Code for Information Interchange and represents the binary number for the letters, numbers, and control characters you can generate from the keyboard. Each character has its own code number. For example, the ASCII code for the letter A is **65** and the ASCII code for the letter a is **97**. There is a table of ASCII values under *Character Set* in online help.

ASCII **13** is the value of the carriage return, or ENTER. By default, if you press ENTER in a text box, the computer will beep. But if you detect the 13 and change it to a 0, the beep will disappear.

SendKeys

The **SendKeys** event sends one or more keystrokes to the active window as if typed at the keyboard.

The syntax for **SendKeys** is

```
SendKeys string[, wait]
```

where

 String is the keystroke or keystrokes you want to send.

 Wait is a Boolean value specifying the wait mode. If it is **False** (default), control is returned to the procedure immediately after the keys are sent. If it is **True**, keystrokes must be processed before control is returned to the procedure. If **Wait** is missing, it is **False** by default.

The only way out of the text box without using the mouse is the TAB key, so you will fool the computer by sending TAB out of the **KeyPress** event using the **SendKeys** statement. The string **"{Tab}"** represents TAB for **SendKeys**. The listing of special keystrokes is in online help.

More Improvements to Address Book

Users might enter their data in all uppercase or all lowercase letters, whereas we want to store (later) and display them in more normal fashion, with only the first letter capitalized. Find

```
sLastName = Left(txtName, iCommaPosition - 1)
```

in the code and add the following lines after it:

```
'    convert to all lower case
sLastName = LCase(sLastName)
'    Change first letter to upper case
Mid(sLastName, 1, 1) = UCase(Mid(sLastName, 1, 1))
```

Then find

```
sFirstName = Right(txtName.Text, nLength - iCommaPosition)
```

in the code and place the following lines after it:

```
'    convert to all lower case
sLastName = LCase(sFirstName)
'    Change first letter to upper case
Mid(sFirstName, 1, 1) = UCase(Mid(sFirstName, 1, 1))
```

These few lines of code use two new VB functions and a new VB statement.

The LCase *Function*

The **LCase** function returns a string with all letters converted to lowercase.

The syntax for **LCase** is

```
LCase(string)
```

The **string** argument is any valid string expression. If **string** contains **Null**, **Null** is returned.

The UCase *Function*

The **UCase** function returns a string with all letters converted to uppercase.

The syntax for **UCase** is

```
UCase(string)
```

The **string** argument is any valid string expression. If **string** contains **Null**, **Null** is returned.

For **UCase** and **LCase**, only the alphabetic characters are acted on; these functions will not affect numbers or punctuation or other printable symbols.

The Mid *Statement*

The **Mid** statement replaces a specified number of characters in a string variable with characters from another string. At first glance, it looks exactly like the **Mid** function, which returns the value of a specified part of a string, but its behavior is completely different.

The syntax for the **Mid** statement is

```
Mid(stringvar, start[, length]) = string
```

where

- **stringvar** is the name of the string variable to modify.

- **start** is the character position in **stringvar** where the replacement of text begins.

- **length** is the number of characters to replace. If this is omitted, all of **string** is used.

- **string** is the string expression that replaces part of **stringvar**.

In this code, the strings that are extracted from **txtName.Text** are first converted into lowercase letters; then the **Mid** statement is used to replace the first character of each string with an uppercase letter.

The New Code for Address Book

Now you are ready to add the code for handling the two new text boxes on frmAddressBook. You will add some declarations at the beginning of the cmdSave_Click event, immediately following the last Dim statement:

```
Dim sCity As String, sState As String, sZip As String
Dim iSpacePosition As Integer
```

The following code will be placed at the end of the cmdSave_Click event. Between the last line,

```
lblLastName.Caption = sLastName
```

and

```
End Sub
```

insert the code shown in Listing 3-16.

Listing 3-16 The new code for Address Book

```
'    new code for Lesson 5
'    Separate city, State and Zip
'    First check for length, if there is nothing here
'    skip these steps
If Len(txtCityStateZip) = 0 Then Exit Sub
'    Check for comma between city and state
iCommaPosition = InStr(txtCityStateZip, ",")
If iCommaPosition = 0 Then
    '    Create the warning message
    sMsg = "Must have a comma between" & vbCrLf
    sMsg = sMsg & "City and State"
    '    make it visible
    MsgBox sMsg
    '    set focus back to txtName
    txtCityStateZip.SetFocus
    Exit Sub
End If
'    Get length
nLength = Len(txtCityStateZip)
'    Extract City
'    again -1 to skip the comma
sCity = Trim(Left(txtCityStateZip, iCommaPosition - 1))
'    Make only first character upper case
sCity = LCase(sCity)
Mid(sCity, 1, 1) = Chr(Asc(Mid(sCity, 1, 1)) - 32)
'    Check for a space after the comma
If Mid(txtCityStateZip, iCommaPosition + 1, 1) = " " Then
    iCommaPosition = iCommaPosition + 1
End If
'    Find the space after the state
iSpacePosition = InStr(iCommaPosition + 1, txtCityStateZip, Chr(32))
```

continued on next page

continued from previous page

```
'    Extract State
If iSpacePosition > iCommaPosition Then
    sState = Trim(Mid(txtCityStateZip, iCommaPosition, iSpacePosition -⇐
iCommaPosition))
End If
'    Make only first character upper case
sState = LCase(sState)
If Len(sState) <> 0 Then _
    Mid(sState, 1, 1) = Chr(Asc(Mid(sState, 1, 1)) - 32)
'    Extract Zip
If nLength > iSpacePosition + 1 Then
    sZip = Trim(Right(txtCityStateZip, nLength - iSpacePosition + 1))
End If
'    display the results
lblCity = sCity
lblState = sState
lblZip = sZip
```

What's New in Address Book?

Much of what you added to Address Book in this session is only more of the same stuff you've seen before. There are a couple of new functions, though.

The `Trim` *Functions*

The `Trim` functions return a copy of a string without leading spaces (`LTrim`), trailing spaces (`RTrim`), or both leading and trailing spaces (`Trim`).

The syntax of the `Trim` functions is

```
LTrim(string)
RTrim(string)
Trim(string)
```

The `string` argument is any valid `string` expression. If `string` contains `Null`, `Null` is returned. In this program, you used `Trim` to remove all leading and training spaces. In some cases, you may want to remove spaces from only one end. Then you would use either `LTrim` or `RTrim`.

The `Asc` *Function*

The `Asc` function returns the character code corresponding to the first letter in a string.

The syntax of the `Asc` function is

```
Asc(string)
```

The `string` argument is any valid string expression. If the string contains no characters, a runtime error occurs.

The Chr **Function**

The **Chr** function returns the character associated with the specified character code. The syntax of the **Chr** function is

```
Chr(charcode)
```

The **charcode** argument is a number that identifies a character. The numbers are the ASCII character set, which includes numbers from 0 to 255. You should remember that ASCII codes above 127 represent what is called the Extended ASCII character set. These codes are valid only in IBM-type computers.

Explanation of the New Code

Some of the things you did in the new code are different ways of doing things you did in earlier code. The line

```
If Len(sState) <> 0 Then _
    Mid(sState, 1, 1) = Chr(Asc(Mid(sState, 1, 1)) - 32)
```

is really a difficult way of converting the first character to uppercase.

```
Asc(Mid(sState, 1, 1)
```

returns the ASCII code for the first character in the string. In the ASCII character set, the numbers for lowercase letters are higher than the numbers for the uppercase letters by exactly 32. So subtracting 32 from a lowercase letter converts it to an uppercase letter. The **Chr** function then converts the number back to a letter so you can put it back into the string. (Yes, this is the hard way, but now you know about the **Asc** and **Chr** functions and something about the ASCII character set.)

Running the New Code

Now run the code for Address Book. Enter names, cities, and states in all uppercase or all lowercase or mixed-case letters. Leave **txtCityStateZip** empty to see what happens. Enter text in **txtCityStateZip** without the comma to see what happens. Try leaving out the space between **AnyCity,State**.

More String Functions

You have learned a lot about string manipulation in the last two lessons, but there are still a number of string functions that we have not covered! We will provide examples of them, displaying their results in the Immediate window.

The Space **Function**

The **Space** function returns a string consisting of the specified number of spaces. The syntax of the **Space** function is

```
Space(number)
```

The **number** argument is the number of spaces you want in the string.

Use the **Space** function to fill a fixed-length string with spaces. Strange as it may seem, when you create a fixed-length string, it is still an *empty* string. The following code demonstrates that fact by using **InStr** to look for the first space before and after you use the **Space** function.

```
Dim sString As String * 20
Debug.Print Len(sString),
Debug.Print InStr(sString, " ")
sString = Space(10)
Debug.Print Len(sString),
Debug.Print InStr(sString, " ")
```

The string *length* is always 20 characters, but until you run **sString = Space(10)**, all the characters are composed of the *empty string*.

The empty string is represented by **""** (quotation marks with nothing between them). The empty string is a handy way of clearing text boxes and string variables. The code **sFirstName = ""** would fill **sFirstName** with the empty string. In other words, you would clear any other string from the variable. You also use the empty string to see if code has assigned a value to a string:

```
If sFirstName = "" Then debug.print "sFirstName is Empty"
```

The String *Function*

The **String** function returns a repeating character string of the length specified.
The syntax of the **String** function is

```
String(number, character)
```

where

 number is the length of the returned string. If number contains **Null**, **Null** is returned.

 character is the character code specifying the character or string expression whose first character is used to build the return string. If **character** contains **Null**, **Null** is returned.

If you specify a number for a character greater than 255, **String** converts the number to a valid character code using the formula **character Mod 256**.
This code demonstrates the effect of **String**:

```
Dim sString As String * 20
sString = String(20, 169)
Debug.Print sString
```

If you have changed the default font for your form, the results will vary, but you will get 20 of them, whatever they are.

The LSet *Statement*

The **LSet** statement left-aligns a string within a string variable.
The syntax is

```
LSet stringvar = string
```

where

- **●** stringvar is the name of the string variable.

- **●** string is the string expression to be left-aligned within stringvar.

The **LSet** statement replaces any leftover characters in **stringvar** with spaces.
If **string** is longer than **stringvar**, **LSet** places only the leftmost characters, up to the length of the **stringvar**, in **stringvar**. Try the following code:

```
Dim sString As String * 20
sString = String(20, 169)
Debug.Print sString
LSet sString = "Hello"
Debug.Print sString
```

The RSet *Statement*

The **RSet** statement right aligns a string within a string variable.
The syntax is

```
RSet stringvar = string
```

where

- **●** stringvar is the name of the string variable.

- **●** string is the string expression to be left-aligned within stringvar.

Leftover characters in **stringvar** are replaced with spaces, back to its beginning.
Try the following code:

```
Dim sString As String * 20
sString = String(20, 169)
Debug.Print sString & " Dolly"
RSet sString = "Hello"
Debug.Print sString & " Dolly"
```

LSet, **RSet**, and **String** are especially useful when you are working with data files stored on disk, where the different fields are of a specific length.

String Comparison

Now that you know how to manipulate strings, you need to know how to tell if two strings are equal. Not only that, you need to be able to test for equality in two different ways, case-sensitive and case-insensitive. In case-sensitive comparisons, capital letters have a different "value" than lowercase letters. Remember that the ASCII value of a lowercase letter is greater than the capital letter by 32; `Asc("A")` = `65` and `ASC( "a")` = `97`. In case-sensitive comparisons, `"A"` < `"a"` and in case-insensitive comparisons, `"A"` = `"a"`. If you are doing a case-sensitive comparison, `"A"` = `"a"` returns `False`.

The `StrComp` *Function*

The `StrComp` function returns a value indicating the result of a string comparison. The syntax is

```
StrComp(string1, string2[, compare])
```

where

- `string1` is any valid string expression.

- `string2` is any valid string expression.

- `compare` specifies the type of string comparison.

The `compare` argument can be omitted, in which case Visual Basic does a case-sensitive comparison. This is the same result you would get if you specified `0`. Specify `1` to perform a textual comparison, which is case-insensitive, as shown in Table 3-18.

Table 3-18 The return values for `StrComp`

Return Value	Comparison
-1	string1 < string2
0	string1 = string2
1	string1 > string2
Null	string1 or string2 is Null

The following code snippet demonstrates the different possibilities for the `StrComp` function:

```
Dim sString1 As String, sString2 As String
sString1 = "Abcdefgh"
sString2 = "AbcdefgH"
Debug.Print "Result     Comparison"
Debug.Print StrComp(sString1, sString2, 0); "   --- s1>s2,Compare = 0"
Debug.Print StrComp(sString2, sString1, 0); "   --- s2<s1,Compare = 0"
Debug.Print StrComp(sString1, sString1, 0); "   --- s1=s1,Compare = 0"
Debug.Print StrComp(sString1, sString2, 1); "   --- s1>s2,Compare = 1"
Debug.Print StrComp(sString2, sString1, 1); "   --- s2<s1,Compare = 1"
Debug.Print StrComp(sString1, sString1, 1); "   --- s1=s1,Compare = 1"
```

In this code, **sString2** is *less* than **sString2** by virtue of the uppercase *H* in the string. The two strings evaluate as equal when the **control** parameter = **1**, but the comparison is case-sensitive when the **control** parameter = **0**.

1. The **Mid** statement is used for:
   a. Testing for the presence of one string within another
   b. Changing one or more characters within a string
   c. Counting the number of characters in a string
   d. Testing a string for a null string

2. The **Chr** function returns:
   a. The characters in a string, sorted into ascending order
   b. The number of characters in a string
   c. The ASCII value of a character
   d. The character represented by an ASCII value

3. **StrComp ("One", "one", 0)** returns:
   a. **1**
   b. **-1**
   c. **0**
   d. Nothing; there is a syntax error in the statement.

4. What function would you use to remove all spaces from both ends of a string?
   a. **LSet**
   b. **LTrim**
   c. **RTrim**
   d. **Trim**

5. The code reads
   ```
   dim sString As String * 20
    sString = String(15, "*")
   ```

   This code will:
   a. Compare **sString** with **String15**
   b. Fill **sString** with 15 *****s and pad the left end of the string with spaces
   b. Fill **sString** with 15 *****s and pad the right end of the string with spaces
   d. Fill **sString** with 15 *****s and leave the remainder of the string empty

TIMES AND DATES

Visual Basic has a powerful **Date** data type and some useful functions to go with it. Both this lesson and Lesson 7 discuss this data type, which you will find extremely useful in your programs.

First, the basics.

The **Date** data type is capable of storing dates and times in the range January 1, 100, to December 31, 9999, inclusive. Each date that you declare occupies 8 bytes of memory.

The **Date** data type is actually stored internally as a double-precision floating-point number. The integer portion (the whole part) to the left of the decimal point is used to represent the date. The decimal portion (to the right of the decimal point) is used to represent the time. Times can be stored to single-second accuracy in the range 00:00:00 (midnight) to 23:59:59.

The Timesheet Program

To show you how the time and date functions work, we'll create a new sample program. Create a new directory called **TIMESHET**. Click on New Project under the File menu. Add the objects and property values described in Table 3-19 to the form.

Table 3-19 Objects and properties for the Timesheet program

Object	Property	Value
Form	Name	frmTimeSheet
	Caption	Timesheet
Label	Caption	Date:
	AutoSize	True
Label	Caption	Time In:
	AutoSize	True
Label	Caption	Time Out:
	AutoSize	True
Label	Caption	Total
	AutoSize	True
Label	Name	lblTotal
	Caption	x hours and x minutes
	AutoSize	True
	Visible	False
TextBox	Name	txtDate
	Text	[blank]
TextBox	Name	txtTimeIn
	Text	[blank]

Object	Property	Value
TextBox	Name	txtTimeOut
	Text	[blank]
CommandButton	Name	cmdCompute
	Caption	Compute
CommandButton	Name	cmdExit
	Caption	Exit
CommandButton	Name	cmdNowIn
	Caption	Now
CommandButton	Name	cmdNowOut
	Caption	Now

Lay out the controls so the form looks like Figure 3-14. Program the Exit button as shown in Listing 3-17 to make it a little easier to run and test the program.

Listing 3-17 The Exit button

```
Private Sub cmdExit_Click()
    End
End Sub
```

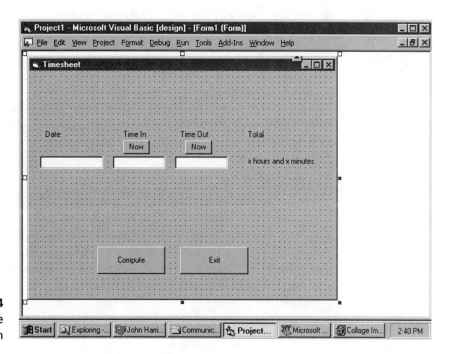

Figure 3-14
Layout for the
Timesheet program

Representing Dates and Times as Literals

You often need to represent dates and times as literal values in your programs. Visual Basic allows tremendous flexibility over how you do this. All the following are valid date formats and result in the same date (February 1, 1995) being placed in the `MyDate` variable.

```
Dim MyDate As Date

MyDate = "2/1/95"
MyDate = "2/1/1995"
MyDate = "2 1 95"
MyDate = "2 1 1995"
MyDate = "1 Feb 95"
MyDate = "Feb 1 1995"
MyDate = "February 1 1995"
MyDate = "1 February 1995"
MyDate = "1995 Feb 1"
MyDate = "1995 2 1"
MyDate = "95 1 Feb"
```

Visual Basic is even sensitive to the locale settings in the control panel. For example, if you set the country setting to the United Kingdom and rerun the above example, the first four dates are interpreted as the 2nd of January, rather than the 1st of February. If you are writing programs for international use, you need to take care that your program can adapt to such occurrences.

Visual Basic's date handling goes a little way toward solving this problem. Consider the following date literal:

```
15/1/95
```

Depending on which country you are in, this date could be interpreted as either a valid date (January 15, 1995) or an invalid date. However, if you try this with the country setting set to the United States, an error does not occur. Visual Basic recognizes that even though this date has not been entered in the correct format for the current locale, it would be a valid date if the month and day were swapped.

Date Literals

The above examples assign string values to dates. This works fine and, indeed, you would need to work with string values if you were assigning the date from a value entered by the user as a string. However, what's happening internally is that Visual Basic needs to create a temporary string variable before making the assignment. In the above examples, it would be more efficient to tell the VB compiler to treat the date literal as a **Date** type from the outset. You do this by surrounding the date with **#** (the pound sign) rather than with quotation marks.

```
MyDate = #1 Feb 1995#
```

Enter this line of code, and you can see Visual Basic converting the type up front. VB changes the representation of the date literal as soon as you type it into the Code window. It appears as

```
MyDate = #2/1/95#
```

Note that the displayed representation of the date when used with literals in your program remains fixed. It does not vary with the locale setting.

Date Functions

Visual Basic provides a wealth of date functions that can be used to manipulate dates. The first set of date functions we'll look at is summarized in Table 3-20. You'll learn about the remaining date functions in Lesson 7.

Table 3-20 VB 5 Time and Date functions

Syntax	Type of Language Element	Description
Now	Function	Returns the current date and time from your computer's built-in clock
Date	Function/Statement	Reads or sets the date from your computer's clock
Time	Function/Statement	Reads or sets the time from your computer's clock
IsDate(strexp)	Function	Returns a Boolean indicating whether or not the string is a valid date
DateValue(date)	Function	Optional, Returns a Date data type from a string representation of a date
TimeValue(time)	Function	Optional, returns a Date data type from a string representation of a time
Day(date)	Function	Returns an integer representing the day portion of the date parameter
Month(date)	Function	Returns an integer representing the month portion of the date parameter
Year(date)	Function	Returns an integer representing the year portion of the date parameter

continued on next page

continued from previous page

Syntax	Type of Language Element	Description
`Hour(time)`	Function	Returns an integer representing the hour portion of the time
`Minute(time)`	Function	Returns an integer representing the minute portion of the time
`Second(time)`	Function	Returns an integer representing the second portion of the time

The Now *Function and Statement*

The **Now** function returns the current date and time from your computer's built-in clock in a single **Date** variable.

For example:

```
Dim Today As Date
Today = Now
Form1.Caption = "Running: " & Today
```

The Date *Function and Statement*

The **Date** function reads or sets the date portion of the current system date. You can change the date on your system's clock simply by assigning **Date** a new value. Let's use this value in the Timesheet program to set the default date in the text box. In the **Form_Load** routine, enter the code in Listing 3-18.

Listing 3-18 Assign the current date to the text box

```
Private Sub Form_Load()
    txtDate.Text = Date
End Sub
```

The Time *Function and Statement*

Visual Basic provides you with a built-in **Time** variable that you can use to read or set the time from your computer's clock. Let's add functionality to the two Now buttons so the user doesn't have to type in the current time. Add the code in Listing 3-19.

Listing 3-19 Give the user access to the system clock

```
Private Sub cmdNowIn_Click()
    txtTimeIn.Text = Time
End Sub

Private Sub cmdNowOut_Click()
    txtTimeOut.Text = Time
End Sub
```

The IsDate *Function*

The **IsDate** function returns a Boolean value to indicate whether the string passed contains a valid date. Let's allow the user to edit the date field directly, but verify that he or she entered a valid date. To do this, you need to know about a new event, the **LostFocus** event.

The GotFocus *and* LostFocus *Events*

Recall that the object with the focus is the object that is currently receiving input. An event is fired both when the object gets the focus (**GotFocus**) and when it loses the focus (**LostFocus**). The **LostFocus** event of a text box is a good place to verify input, because it gives the user a chance to enter (and, if necessary, edit) the value. Add the code in Listing 3-20 to the Timesheet program.

Listing 3-20 Validate the date the user entered

```
Private Sub txtDate_LostFocus()
If Not IsDate(txtDate) Then
    txtDate = "<Invalid date>"
End If
End Sub
```

The Not *Operator*

Notice that we slipped in a new operator, **Not**. As you'd expect, this operator negates the current expression. Using it in context has the benefit of being very easy to read. We'll talk more about **Not** and other logic operators in Chapter 4, Subroutines, Functions, and the Visual Basic 5 Language.

The DateValue *Function*

The **DateValue** function returns a **Date** data type from a string representation of a date that is passed to it.

For example:

```
Dim MyDate As Date
Dim MyString As String
MyString = "1 May 1995"
MyDate = DateValue(MyString)
```

You may have noticed that the **DateValue** function is optional. As you saw in the section Representing Dates and Times as Literals, you could have written the above code as simply:

```
Dim MyDate As Date
Dim MyString As String
MyString = "1 May 1995"
MyDate = MyString
```

In this case, Visual Basic converts the string data type to a **Date** data type implicitly. Although this works, performing the operation explicitly is more pedantic and possibly more reliable. We will look at other types of conversion in Lesson 8 and you will see that Visual Basic does quite a lot of data type conversion behind the scenes.

The TimeValue *Function*

Similarly to the DateValue function, TimeValue takes a string representation of the time and converts it to a Date data type. For example:

```
Dim MyDate As Date
Dim MyString As String
MyString = "15:30:00"
MyDate = TimeValue(MyString)
```

You can also use implicit conversions rather than calling TimeValue. However, in the interest of clarity, let's use TimeValue to get at the times in your program. Add the code in Listing 3-21 to the cmdCompute click event.

Listing 3-21 Computing the time difference

```
Private Sub cmdCompute_Click()
Dim Timediff As Date
Dim TimeIn As Date, TimeOut As Date
TimeIn = TimeValue(txtTimeIn)
TimeOut = TimeValue(txtTimeOut)
Timediff = TimeOut - TimeIn

' Output the results
lblTotal.Caption = Timediff
lblTotal.Visible = True

End Sub
```

Run the program and try it out. See what happens if you enter an invalid date in the Date box. (Because you didn't check the time formats, trying to compute using bad values will cause the program to crash.) Play with the Now buttons. Notice that you can use either a 12- or a 24-hour clock. If you use a 12-hour clock, you'll need to specify PM values, as shown in Figure 3-15. Although the program correctly computes the time difference, it displays the value in a time format, which is not what you want. You need to learn a few more functions before adding the last bit of code.

Day, Month, *and* Year *Functions*

The Day, Month, and Year functions are used to extract integer representations of the day, month, and year, respectively, from a Date data type.

Try the example in Listing 3-22.

Listing 3-22 Displaying the date in the form caption

```
Private Sub Form_Load()
Dim MyDate As Date
Dim MyDay As Integer, MyMonth As Integer, MyYear As Integer
MyDate = Now
MyDay = Day(MyDate)
MyMonth = Month(MyDate)
MyYear = Year(MyDate)
Form1.Caption = "Today: " & MyMonth & "/" & MyDay & "/" & MyYear
End Sub
```

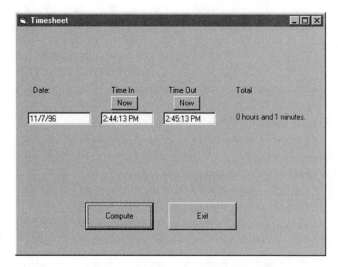

Figure 3-15
Entering values in
the Timesheet
program

Obviously, the actual values printed depend on the current setting of your computer's clock; however, using these three functions, you can extract integers that you can then use for date calculation or for some other purpose, such as storing information in a database.

Hour, Minute, **and** Second **Functions**

Visual Basic provides functions for displaying the components of the time as well. Add the final code to the `cmdCompute` routine, as shown in Listing 3-23.

Listing 3-23 Output the difference in a more readable format

```
Private Sub cmdCompute_Click()
Dim TimeDiff As Date
Dim HoursDiff As Integer, MinutesDiff As Integer
Dim TimeIn As Date, TimeOut As Date
TimeIn = TimeValue(txtTimeIn)
TimeOut = TimeValue(txtTimeOut)
TimeDiff = TimeOut - TimeIn
HoursDiff = Hour(TimeDiff)
MinutesDiff = Minute(TimeDiff)

lblTotal = HoursDiff & " hours and " & MinutesDiff & " minutes."
lblTotal.Visible = True
End Sub
```

As you can see, Visual Basic gives you access to every component of the Date data type. We'll cover the remaining date functions in Lesson 7.

Save the Timesheet program as `TIMESHET.FRM/TIMESHET.VPB`. You've been dated!

1. The *most explicit* way to represent a date literal in code is:
   a. **"2/1/95"**
   b. **"Feb 1 1995"**
   c. **#2/1/95#**
   d. It depends on the date settings of the Control Panel.

2. The difference between **Date** (used as a function) and **Now** is that:
   a. **Now** returns the date and time; **Date** returns just the date.
   b. **Now** returns the time; **Date** returns the date.
   c. **Date** returns the date and time; **Now** returns just the date.
   d. Nothing. The functions are equivalent.

3. Because a user may type many characters or make corrections in a text box, a good time to get input from the text box is in the _____ event.
   a. **GotFocus**
   b. **LostFocus**
   c. **Change**
   d. **Click**

4. Which of the following statements assigns a time to the **Date** variable declared

   `Dim MyTime As Date`

   a. **MyTime = Time**
   b. **MyTime = "03:45 PM"**
   c. **MyTime = TimeValue("03:45 PM")**
   d. All of the above

5. To get the month of a specific date as an integer value, you would:
   a. Use the **DateValue** function.
   b. Use the **Date** command.
   c. Use the **Day** function.
   d. Use the **Month** function.

OTHER DATE AND TIME SUPPORT FUNCTIONS

Some other useful functions relate to dates and times. Let's complete our look at the Date data type by considering these functions, summarized in Table 3-21.

Table 3-21 Remaining Date/Time functions

Syntax	Type of Language Element	Description
DateSerial	Function	Returns a Date data type from a year, month, and day
TimeSerial	Function	Returns a time from the hours, minutes, and seconds
Weekday	Function	Returns the day of the week
Timer	Function	Returns the number of seconds past midnight

The DateSerial Function

The **DateSerial** function returns a Date data type from the individual **year**, **month**, and **day** parameters that you pass to it. The syntax is

```
DateVar = DateSerial(Year, Month, Day)
```

For example:

```
Dim MyDate As Date
MyDate = DateSerial(1995, 5, 1)
Debug.Print MyDate
```

This code prints out

```
5/1/95
```

You can also use **DateSerial** to do some date calculations. Let's say you want to work out what the date will be in 50 days from May 1, 1995. Using the following:

```
MyDate = DateSerial(1995, 5, 1 + 50)
```

Visual Basic correctly determines that the new date is June 20, 1995.

The **DateSerial** function isn't doing anything particularly clever when you phrase this parameter as **1 + 50**. Visual Basic does the calculation **1 + 50** first, and then passes the number **51** to the function. The **DateSerial** function is capable of taking the date that you've asked for (May 51, 1995, effectively) and turning that into a correct date representation. It's quite a useful feature.

The TimeSerial Function

The **TimeSerial** function returns a time from individual hours, minutes, and seconds. The syntax is

```
TimeVar = TimeSerial(Hour, Minute, Second)
```

For example:

```
Dim MyDate As Date
MyDate = TimeSerial(13, 0, 5)
Debug.Print MyDate
```

This example returns a time of 1:00:05 PM.

You can also use `TimeSerial` to perform some math operations on times. For example:

```
Dim MyDate As Date
MyDate = TimeSerial(13, 0, 75)
Debug.Print MyDate
```

returns a time of 1:01:15 PM.

Consider the following example:

```
Dim MyDate As Date
MyDate = TimeSerial(23, 59, 75)
Debug.Print MyDate
```

This outputs

```
12/31/1899 12:00:15 AM
```

Why did this happen? Remember that **Date** data types are no more than double-precision floating-point numbers internally. You simply overflowed the decimal portion of the **Date** variable and accidentally placed an integer value in the floating-point number.

Let's prove this by rerunning that example; however, instead of directly printing the value of the date in the Immediate window, first assign it to a standard **Double** data type and then print that. The new example is shown in Listing 3-24.

Listing 3-24 Viewing a date as a Double

```
Dim MyDate As Date
Dim MyDouble As Double
MyDate = TimeSerial(23, 59, 75)
MyDouble = MyDate
Debug.Print MyDouble
```

You see that the value printed is **1.00017361111111**. It just so happens that the date represented by the integer number **1** is December 31, 1899.

Try rerunning some of the above examples, but this time assign the **Date** values to **Doubles** and print them out. This will give you a good understanding of how dates are represented internally in **Date** variables.

Weekday **Function**

In Lesson 6, you saw functions to return the month, year, and day of a date. Occasionally, however, you need to determine what the day of the week is. Luckily,

VB 5 has a built-in function to give you this information: the **Weekday** function. The syntax is

```
DayVar = Weekday(date [, firstdayofweek])
```

Weekday returns an integer value representing the day of the week. For example:

```
Debug.Print Weekday(Now)
```

displays a number from 1 to 7, representing Sunday through Saturday. The number corresponds to whatever day today is.

Visual Basic 5 provides built-in constants for the values **1** to **7** to use in your programs so that you don't have to refer to a particular day as just a number. The constants are as summarized in Table 3-22.

Table 3-22 Visual Basic's weekday constants

Constant	Value
vbSunday	1
vbMonday	2
vbTuesday	3
vbWednesday	4
vbThursday	5
vbFriday	6
vbSaturday	7

This, of course, assumes that you expect the week to begin on a Sunday. You might want the week in your program to start on a different day, say, a Monday. You can tell the **Weekday** function that it should return **1** for a Monday by adding one parameter to the function—the day of the week constant that you want to be the first day of the week. Therefore:

```
Debug.Print Weekday(Now, vbMonday)
```

will return **1** if today is a Monday and **7** if today is a Sunday.

The `Timer` **Function**

The **Timer** function is useful for implementing simple timed operations. It returns a value representing the number of seconds that have elapsed since midnight. Because there are 86400 seconds in a day (24 hours * 60 minutes * 60 seconds) and an integer cannot hold values greater than 32,767, **Timer** cannot return an integer. Let's see what type of variable it returns:

```
Dim MyVar As Variant
MyVar = Timer
Debug.Print TypeName(MyVar)
```

You might be surprised to find that `Timer` returns a single-precision variable. This is because of the way the timer is implemented inside Visual Basic. Again, the reason is largely historical, but `Timer` is capable of timing to subsecond intervals. However, the subsecond values are not really accurate because they are not tied to any hardware time base.

To see how you might use `Timer` in a typical timed operation, let's implement a loop that executes repeatedly until a predetermined number of seconds (10 in this case) has passed:

```
Dim EndTime As Single
EndTime = Timer + 10
Do While Timer < EndTime
    ' these statements will be executed repeatedly until
    ' the value returned by Timer is greater than or equal to EndTime
Loop
```

Although you will see how to use loops in detail in Chapter 4, Subroutines, Functions, and the Visual Basic 5 Language, it should be clear how `Timer` might be used to implement a simple timer.

Date and Time Calculation Functions

You saw earlier how `DateSerial` and `TimeSerial` could be used to perform date calculations. Visual Basic 5 also provides some specific functions to do this job more explicitly. These functions are

● `DateAdd`

● `DateDiff`

● `DatePart`

The `DateAdd` *Function*

The `DateAdd` function has the following syntax:

```
DateAdd(Interval, Number, Date)
```

The first parameter, `Interval`, is a string that represents the type of interval that is being added to or subtracted from the date in the third parameter. The `Interval` string must be one of the values summarized in Table 3-23.

Table 3-23 Values for the `DateAdd` interval parameter

Interval	Description
yyyy	Year
q	Quarter
m	Month
y	Day of year

Interval	Description
d	Day
w	Weekday
ww	Week
h	Hour
m	Minute
s	Second

The second parameter, **Number**, is a Long integer that represents the number of units of type **Interval** to add to the date in the third parameter. If **Number** is negative, the function subtracts the number of intervals, rather than adding. The **DateAdd** function, despite its name, can therefore be used for both adding to and subtracting from dates.

The third parameter, **Date**, must be a date variable that contains a valid date. The function acts on the date contained in the variable and returns the resulting date.

Let's see **DateAdd** in action. The example in Listing 3-25 returns the date one week from October 1, 1996.

Listing 3-25 The DateAdd function

```
Dim DateVar As Date
Dim NextWeek As Date
DateVar = #10/1/96#
NextWeek = DateAdd("ww", 1, DateVar)
Debug.Print DateVar
Debug.Print NextWeek
```

This code outputs

```
10/1/96
10/8/96
```

The **DateAdd** function always tries to return a valid date. For example, try the following code:

```
Dim MyDate As Date, NextMonthEnd As Date
MyDate = #31 Jan 1996#
NextMonthEnd = DateAdd("m", 1, MyDate)
Debug.Print NextMonthEnd
```

The **DateAdd** function hasn't just added one month to the date and produced an invalid date of February 31, 1996. Instead, it has done exactly what you asked of it, and found the last day of the next month (February 29, 1996). Try the example again, but this time use a start date of February 29, 1996.

```
Dim MyDate As Date, NextMonthEnd As Date
MyDate = #29 Feb 1996#
NextMonthEnd = DateAdd("m", 1, MyDate)
Debug.Print NextMonthEnd
```

This time, because March 29, 1996, is a valid date, that is the date returned.

The DateDiff *Function*

The DateDiff function returns the difference between two dates in the interval that you select.

The full syntax for DateDiff is

```
DateDiff(Interval, Date1, Date2[, FirstDayOfWeek[, FirstWeekOfYear]])
```

The Interval parameter is a string that denotes the interval in which the difference should be expressed. The same settings are used as those listed in Table 3-24 for DateAdd.

Date1 and Date2 are the two dates to be used. Date1 is subtracted from Date2, and the result is returned in the unit specified in Interval.

For example:

```
Debug.Print DateDiff("m", #2/29/96#, #3/29/96#)
```

returns 1 (one month).

For that matter, so does

```
Debug.Print DateDiff("m", #2/29/96#, #3/31/96#)
```

However, the following example returns two months:

```
Debug.Print DateDiff("m", #2/29/96#, #4/1/96#)
```

This is because, although two months have not elapsed, the difference in the two dates spans two calendar months. You have to be careful when using DateDiff that you ask for the answer you expect.

The DateDiff function has two optional parameters: FirstDayOfWeek and FirstWeekOfYear. Most of the time, you can probably ignore these, because they customize how the function works. The FirstDayOfWeek parameter is the same parameter as you saw in the Weekday function. It uses the day constants (vbSunday to vbSaturday) to specify which day should be treated as the first day of the week.

The FirstWeekOfYear parameter works slightly differently. It controls calculations where the function has to calculate the first week of the year.

This parameter takes the constants summarized in Table 3-24.

Table 3-24 Constants for DateDiff's FirstWeekOfYear parameter

Constant	Meaning
vbFirstJan1	Week in which January 1 appears
vbFirstFourDays	First week in January with at least four days
vbFirstFullWeek	First full week in January

The DatePart *Function*

The DatePart function uses the same interval string settings to return the part of the date specified.

Its full syntax is

```
DatePart(Interval, Date [, FirstDayOfWeek [,FirstWeekOfYear]])
```

In its simple form, `DatePart` returns the same information as the `Day`, `Month`, `Year`, `Hour`, `Minute`, `Second`, and `Weekday` functions.

For example:

```
Debug.Print DatePart("m", Now)    ' these two statements
Debug.Print Month(Now)            ' are equivalent
```

However, `DatePart` can also be used with the `FirstDayOfWeek` and `FirstWeekOfYear` parameters to customize your view of when the week and the year begin.

1. What date does the following line print out?

   ```
   Debug.Print DateSerial(1985,3,32)
   ```

   a. 3/32/85
   b. 3/31/85
   c. 4/1/85
   d. None. VB prints an error message.

2. Assuming April 1, 1985, is a Monday, what will

   ```
   Debug.Print Weekday("April 1 85",3)
   ```

   print out?
   a. 7
   b. 3
   c. 5
   d. 6

3. What sort of data type does the `Timer` function return?
   a. Long
   b. Integer
   c. Single
   d. Date

4. What does the following statement print out?

   ```
   Debug.Print DateAdd("m",1,#8/31/90#)
   ```

   a. 9/31/90
   b. 9/30/90
   c. 9/28/90
   d. 10/1/90

5. What is the difference between the **"w"** and **"ww"** interval settings in the
DateAdd function?
   a. There is no difference.
   b. **"w"** is Weekday; **"ww"** is Weekend.
   c. **"w"** is Week; **"ww"** is Weekday.
   d. **"w"** is Weekday; **"ww"** is Week.

VARIABLES CONCLUDED

By now, you should have a good idea of what variables are and how to use them. We'll
conclude this chapter by talking in a little more detail about variable declaration and
variable types.

Variable Declaration

Variables can be declared in two different ways: explicitly (via the **Dim** statement) or
implicitly.

Explicit Declaration

To use explicit declaration, you simply declare the variable using one of Visual Basic's
declaration statements. This is what you've been doing all along in this chapter with
the **Dim** statement. Typical declarations are

```
Dim TestScore As Integer
Dim FullFileName As String
```

Visual Basic's declaration statements are not executed in the same way as other language statements. Instead, they are really instructions to Visual Basic 5's compiler to
create the variable when the program is compiled rather than when it is run.

There is one caveat when regarding the **As** keyword. Although you can declare more
than one variable on a line, **As** refers only to the variable immediately preceding it. For
example,

```
Dim Var1, Var2 As Integer
```

looks like it declares two integer variables. However, because **Var1** has no corresponding
As statement, it's actually declared as a variant.

Let's take a look at how variables are treated by VB before you assign a value to them.
Add the following code after the declarations above:

```
Debug.Print TestScore
TestScore = 5
Debug.Print TestScore
```

Now run the project by pressing [F5]. Visual Basic outputs

0
5

Before you actually assign anything to **MyVar**, it has the value **0**. Visual Basic automatically initializes all variables when they are declared. All numeric variables are therefore initialized to **0**. This can be quite useful: You do not need to assign **0** expressly to a variable, as you do with some other languages.

You can force the use of explicit declarations by adding **Option Explicit** as the first line in the Declarations section of your code. That requires that you explicitly declare every variable before you use it in your programs, which helps you detect mistyped variable names in your code. Visual Basic will add **Option Explicit** to your code automatically if you select Options under the Tools menu and place a check beside Require Variable Declaration on the Editor tab. **Option Explicit** is discussed in more detail later in this chapter.

Implicit Declaration

Let's repeat the above test. This time, though, let's use implicit declaration. Remove the **Dim** statements from the **Form_Load** subroutine and run the project again.

You don't actually need to remove these statements. Instead, you can just comment out both lines.

```
'Dim TestScore As Integer
'Dim FullFileName As String
Debug.Print TestScore
TestScore = 5
Debug.Print TestScore
```

When Visual Basic encounters the assignment statement, it declares the variable and performs the assignment. This is implicit declaration and works only because the **Option Explicit** statement is not present in the module. When you run the example above, only **5** is printed out.

Consider the following example using implicit declaration:

```
MyVar = 5
MyVar = 5.1
```

The above code would cause a runtime error if you had explicitly declared **MyVar** to be an integer. What type of variable is Visual Basic declaring?

Visual Basic is actually declaring **MyVar** to be a variant type variable. A variant is a special data type that is capable of becoming any of the other built-in types. This is why **MyVar** can be an integer one moment and something else the next.

Let's prove that this is happening by using the **TypeName** function.

The TypeName *Function*

The **TypeName** function returns a string containing the name of the type of the variable passed to it.

For example, enter the code in Listing 3-26.

Listing 3-26 The `TypeName` function

```
Debug.Print TypeName(MyVar)
MyVar = 5
Debug.Print TypeName(MyVar)
MyVar = 5.1
Debug.Print TypeName(MyVar)
MyVar = "Five point 1"
Debug.Print TypeName(MyVar)
```

This program fragment outputs

```
Empty
Integer
Double
String
```

When the first statement is executed, `MyVar` hasn't been declared yet, so Visual Basic implicitly declares it as a variant. However, because you haven't assigned any data to it, the variant is unitialized and has the type name of `Empty`.

The second time you call `TypeName`, you have already assigned an integer number to `MyVar`. When that assignment took place, Visual Basic changed the variant from the uninitialized type `Empty` to an `Integer`.

The third time, `MyVar` has changed to a `Double`; the fourth time, it has become a `String`.

At first sight, implicit declaration appears to have some distinct advantages over explicit declaration. However, there are some distinct disadvantages to using implicit declaration.

1. Variants occupy more memory than most other variable types. If you rely on implicit declaration, your programs consume more memory than they would using explicit declaration.

2. Implicit declaration is a little too forgiving of typing errors. If you incorrectly entered `MyVar` as `MuVar`, for example, Visual Basic would simply declare another variable. In a real program, the error might be difficult to find.

3. Because variants can change type, there is a small overhead in their use. Each time some data is assigned to them, Visual Basic has to determine whether or not the type needs to change. This happens very quickly, of course, but if you use variants in long loops, for example, the code will take slightly longer to execute than if you used specific data types and explicit declaration.

Good programming practice dictates, and we firmly recommend, that you use explicit declaration in your programs. You can use variants in your programs on those rare occasions when they are necessary, as long as you explicitly declare the variables as such.

```
Dim MyVar As Variant
```

Option Explicit

The `Option Explicit` statement is placed in the General Declarations section of a module. It tells Visual Basic that all variable declarations in that module must be by explicit declaration only. In other words, you must declare every variable you use. In Chapter 9, Printing, you will learn that this helps avoid a common programming error. The Environment Options dialog box controls whether Visual Basic automatically puts this statement in the General Declarations sections of your modules. Display the Environment Options dialog box now by opening the Tools menu and selecting the Options... menu option from the Tools menu. The Editor tab, shown in Figure 3-16, displays automatically, because it is the first tab in the dialog box.

The setting you want is a check box labeled Require Variable Declaration. If it is not already set, click on it now. If the check box is off, any modules that you add to your project will not have the `Option Explicit` statement added to them automatically. This does not mean that you cannot add `Option Explicit` to a module manually; it is just that Visual Basic will not do it for you. If the `Option Explicit` statement is present, Visual Basic insists that you explicitly declare your variables and generates an error at compile time if you try to use a variable without declaring it first. Note that checking this option will not add `Option Explicit` to modules that already exist in your projects; it will only cause it to be added to future modules that you create.

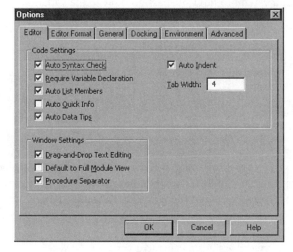

Figure 3-16
Environment
Options dialog box

Variants

You have already seen variants in action. Variants are capable of becoming any of the other built-in data types. However there is a small overhead in their use because Visual Basic has to do some behind-the-scenes work to determine whether or not it needs to change the data type represented by the variant.

Sixteen bytes of memory are used when variants are combined with numeric data. If you use variants to hold string data, each variant has an overhead of 22 bytes of memory on top of the space required to store the string.

Variants can, in addition to storing the built-in data types, take three further values:

- Empty
- Null
- Error

Empty

You have already seen that uninitialized variants are declared as Empty.

Null

Null is different from Empty and the two should not be confused with each other. Null is an explicit value that you can assign to variants only. It indicates that you intend the variant to contain no data. If you use variants in your programs, you will find it useful to be able to distinguish between variants that contain no data because they have not been initialized yet (Empty) and variants that intentionally contain no data (Null).

To set a variant to Null, just assign Null to the variant:

```
MyVariant = Null
```

Error

Variants can also hold special error values when used in conjunction with functions. We will look at this aspect of variant behavior later when we consider functions and error handling (Chapter 10).

Variable Assignment

In the examples in this chapter, we have assigned values to variables by using the assignment operator =. This is actually a shorthand way of assigning data to variables. There is a special keyword that you can use, called Let.

Let

The Let keyword assigns a value to a variable.

```
[Let] Var = Expression
```

The use of the **Let** statement is entirely optional and largely ignored by programmers. Its inclusion in the language is historical, because the earliest BASIC languages required its use.

Type Declaration Characters

Visual Basic offers a shorthand way of forcing a number to be a particular data type. Consider the following:

```
Dim MyInteger As Integer
Dim MyDouble As Double
MyInteger = 5
MyDouble = 5
```

You saw earlier when you took a quick look at variants that Visual Basic treats whole numbers within the range of an integer as integers. Therefore, the first assignment statement is self-explanatory. You are simply assigning an integer number to an integer variable.

The second assignment, however, requires a little more work on the part of Visual Basic. In the second case, **5** still starts out life as an integer. However, Visual Basic does a little bit of conversion work behind the scenes to turn the integer **5** into a double-precision floating-point variable.

To prevent Visual Basic from doing this work at runtime, you can use type declaration characters with both numbers and variables to force Visual Basic to treat them as specific data types. For example, we could have written

```
MyInteger = 5%
MyDouble = 5#
```

The **%** symbol is the type declaration character for an integer and **#** is the character for a double-precision floating-point number.

You can also use type declaration characters when you declare your variables. For example:

```
Dim MyInteger%
Dim MyDouble#
```

The use of the type declaration character obviates the need for the **As** keyword part of the declaration.

The full range of type declaration characters is summarized in Table 3-25.

Table 3-25 Type declaration characters

Data Type	Character	Data Type	Character
Byte	None	Date	None
Boolean	None	Currency	@
Integer	%	String	$
Long	&	Object	None
Single	!	Variant	None
Double	#		

Most of the time, you do not need to use type declaration characters, although you may prefer to if you feel it makes your choice of type declaration more obvious.

One occasion where it makes sense to use type declaration characters is when you use implicit declaration. For example, if you implicitly declare the following:

```
MyVar1 = 5
MyVar2% = 5
```

this code declares **MyVar1** as a variant and **MyVar2** as an integer.

Just My Type

Before wrapping up this chapter, let's take a look at a few functions that help you work across string and numeric types. These functions are particularly helpful because many of your input mechanisms (text boxes) and output mechanisms (captions) assume a string variable, but your program data may be numeric.

The Val *Function*

The **Val** function takes a string that contains the string representation of a number and converts it into a true numeric data type.

The **Val** function has the following syntax:

```
Val(String)
```

Because **Val** is designed to cope with any numeric type, it always returns a double-precision floating-point number. For example:

```
Dim MyString As String
MyString = "123"
Debug.Print TypeName(Val(MyString))
```

outputs

```
Double
```

If you change the code to **MyString = "Fred"**, **Val(MyString)** returns 0.

The Str *Function*

The **Str** function is the opposite of the **Val** function. It takes a numeric value and converts it to a string. The **Str** function has the following syntax:

```
Str(Number)
```

Listing 3-27 is an example.

Listing 3-27 The Str function on a positive value

```
Dim MyString As String
Dim MyInteger As Integer
MyInteger = 123
MyString = Str(MyInteger)
Debug.Print MyString
```

Note that **MyString** is set to a string that has a leading space. This is because **Str** works according to some very basic formatting rules that state that if the number being converted is negative, then the string representation of that number will begin with a minus sign, as in Listing 3-28.

Listing 3-28 The **Str** function on a negative value

```
Dim MyString As String
Dim MyInteger As Integer
MyInteger = -123
MyString = Str(MyInteger)
Debug.Print MyString
```

When that number is positive, **Str** places a space at the beginning of the string so that both negative and positive numbers line up if displayed. Again, this behavior has more historical than practical significance nowadays. This behavior was required by versions of the BASIC language before we had graphical user interfaces. Today, if we want our numbers to line up when displayed (or printed), we have access to other functions and techniques that give us more control over how numbers display than is possible with the simple **Str** function.

One of those techniques is the use of the **Format** function, which we discuss in more detail in Chapter 8, Discovering the CommonDialog and Windows 95 Controls.

1. To declare a variable implicitly:
   a. Use the **Dim** statement.
   b. Use the variable in a statement.
   c. Declare the variable a variant.
   d. Set the **Option Explicit** field of the Environment dialog box.

2. To find out a variable's type, call the _____ function.
   a. **Type**
   b. **TypeName**
   c. **TypeAs**
   d. **MyType**

3. Which of the following is never a valid type for a variant?
   a. **Empty**
   b. **String**
   c. **Null**
   d. All are correct.

4. Why might an implicitly declared variable have a type declaration character, as in:

```
Alphabet$ = "ABCDEFGHIJKLMNOPQRSTUVWXYZ"
```

   a. No reason.
   b. It forces the variable to be a string, avoiding the overhead of a variant.
   c. To prevent confusion with another variable of the same name.
   d. Variants can't take alphabetic characters as values.

5. The **Str** function:
   a. Converts a numeric value into a string
   b. Returns a string of a corresponding character code
   c. Returns a string **num** spaces long
   d. Adds a leading space to negative numbers

EXERCISE

Add a column to the Timesheet program that displays (from the date) the day of the week corresponding to an entry. Add another output label, called **lblCumulative**, that updates a cumulative time variable every time the user presses Compute, so that the user can use the program to add up more than one time period. Add a text box where the user enters an hourly rate, and compute from that the total paycheck due for the cumulative time. (Hint: Use the Currency data type as appropriate.)

SUBROUTINES, FUNCTIONS, AND THE VISUAL BASIC 5 LANGUAGE

This chapter builds on what you've already learned about variables and their related functions to complete the tutorial of the VB 5 programming language. Specifically, this chapter covers in detail:

- For...Next and other Loop statements
- Decision statements
- Subroutine and function syntax
- Procedure and variable scope
- Arrays

You've already seen many of the main elements of a VB 5 program. You know how to add controls to a form; how to customize the look of your program by setting object properties at design or runtime; and how to tie source code to events, such as quitting the program when the user presses a button. Additionally, you've learned the rudiments of computer programming. You can assign values to variables, call functions to manipulate your data, make decisions based on what your variables contain, and output results to the user.

Of course, there's still a lot to learn. But much of the work ahead of you has to do with expanding your familiarity with these basic building blocks and, with practice, gaining confidence in creatively recombining these processes. We hope that as you proceed through the exercises in this book, you take time to experiment, to test your own theories about what's happening by modifying the code to see the new result or by outputting variable values to the Debug window. You won't hurt anything by experimenting. But, as always with computers, you may want to save your work first!

A PROJECT SKELETON

In this chapter, you'll learn about program flow. We'll try out new language elements by progressively expanding a new project: the Number Adder. Create a new directory called ADDER.

The World's Most Annoying Adding Machine

Build the "skeleton" of the project first, just as you've done in previous chapters. Fill in the source code as you go along. Start a new project with the objects and properties summarized in Table 4-1. Lay out the controls as shown in Figure 4-1.

Table 4-1 Initial objects and properties for the Number Adder

Object	Property	Value
Form	Name	frmAdder
	Caption	The Number Adder
Picture	Picture	vb\icons\misc\misc18.ico
	AutoSize	True
Label	Caption	It's the world's most super amazing adding program!
	Font	Name: Monotype Corsiva (or other script font)
		Size: 24
Label	Name	lblOutput
	AutoSize	True
	Caption	[The Answer!]

Object	Property	Value
	Font	Name: Monotype Corsiva (or other script font)
		Size: 18
CommandButton	Name	cmdAdd
	Caption	Add!!!
	Font	Name: MS Sans Serif
		Size: 12
CommandButton	Name	cmdExit
	Caption	Exit
	Font	Name: MS Sans Serif
		Size: 12

Add source code to quit the program, as shown in Listing 4-1.

Listing 4-1 The familiar `Exit` routine

```
Private Sub cmdExit_Click()
    End
End Sub
```

Overblown Fanfare: The First OLE Object

The theme of this project is much ado about nothing. This program takes way too much pride in accomplishing a simple task. We'll convey the program's personality by adding a sound effect that plays when the program adds a number. Because playing a

Figure 4-1
The Number Adder
(initial design)

sound effect is a task the Sound Recorder that comes with Microsoft Windows already knows how to do, you'll add the sound as an OLE object. Don't panic! This will be easy, really.

Click on the OLE container control icon indicated in Figure 4-2.

Draw the control anywhere on the form. When you let go of the mouse cursor, the Insert Object dialog box shown in Figure 4-3 comes up. Click on Create From File, and then enter (or select via the Browse button) the file name **c:\windows\tada.wav**. Click on OK.

The sound object is represented by a microphone, as shown in Figure 4-4. OLE container control objects have a special pop-up menu that can access them. To bring up this window, click the right mouse button on the microphone icon. If you have a sound card, you can click on Play now to hear the sound.

Figure 4-2
The OLE container control

Figure 4-3
The Insert Object dialog box

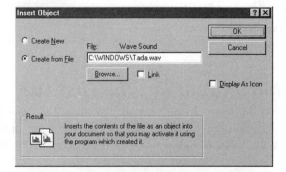

Figure 4-4
The microphone icon represents the sound

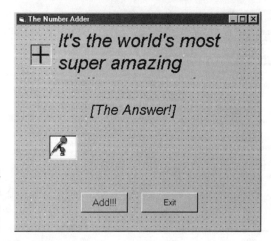

In Chapter 14, Advanced Features, you'll learn amazing things about OLE automation and programmable objects. For now, however, all you need to know is that objects have methods (that shouldn't surprise you!), just as the controls you've been using all along have methods. Although the methods available depend, of course, on the object and its features, many objects have a default method. You can access this method using the **DoVerb** method:

```
objectname.DoVerb
```

(This is actually just a small part of what **DoVerb** can do; you'll learn more about it in Chapter 14, Advanced Features.) Give your OLE object a meaningful name—**oleTada**—and go into the **cmdAdd_Click** routine. Enter the code to add numbers, as shown in Listing 4-2.

Listing 4-2 Ta da!

```
Private Sub cmdAdd_Click()
Dim Sum As Integer
'  If there is no sound card, skip to following line
On Error Resume Next
Sum = 2 + 2

lblOutput.Caption = Sum & " !!!"
oleTada.DoVerb

End Sub
```

The line **On Error Resume Next** is a simple error handler to take care of those of us who do not have sound cards in our computers. You will learn about error handlers in Chapter 9, Printing.

Because you probably don't want the microphone icon on your program's main screen, you can either set the OLE container control's **Visible** property to **False** or just move it out of sight by enlarging the **frmAdder** window, dragging the icon off out of the way, and then putting the form back to its previous size. Go ahead and save the form as **ADDER.FRM** and the project as **ADDER.VBX**. This skeletal project will provide a good place to experiment with the language flow commands coming up in this chapter.

1. Adding an OLE object that has a narrow function, such as a sound effect, to a program is:
   a. Not going to be covered until Chapter 14
   b. Incredibly difficult
   c. Incredibly, impossibly difficult, something you shouldn't even aspire to
   d. Actually not all that hard

2. Which of the following are valid techniques for watching what's happening in a program?
   a. Printing out variables with `Debug.Print`
   b. Showing values or state information with `MsgBox`
   c. Changing things around a little and watching what happens
   d. All of the above

3. Which statement best describes computer programming?
   a. Analyzing data (from user input or other sources), manipulating the data, making decisions based on the data's contents or from a program's state, and continuing this process until a desired result is achieved
   b. Using the `Debug.Print` statement for output
   c. Assigning values to variables
   d. Evaluating `True/False` expressions

4. The OLE object method `DoVerb`:
   a. Requires a verb name as a parameter
   b. By itself, executes a default action for an object
   c. By itself, always opens the object for user editing
   d. Is restricted to use by Microsoft-anointed gurus

5. Adding sound, graphics, and special fonts to your program:
   a. Is pretentious
   b. Wastes memory and system resources
   c. Makes your program more professional and accessible, often conveying something about the character of your task
   d. Is time-consuming and complicated, but generally worth it

For **LOOPS**

Visual Basic 5 provides a number of different types of loops that you can use to implement repetitive operations. We will start our look at loops by considering the most commonly used loop—the `For...Next` loop.

For...Next

The `For...Next` loop executes a series of statements a specific number of times. The basic syntax is

```
For countervariable = start To end
      ' Do something
Next countervariable
```

Here's how it works.

When VB executes the `For` line, the variable `countervariable` takes on the value of `start`. Thus, if the line is

```
For I = 1 to 10
```

then `I` starts life holding the value `1`.

After the first line is executed, all the commands up until the `Next` statement are executed. The code inside the `For...Next` loop can be any combination of regular `Basic` commands.

When VB gets to the line `Next countervariable`, it increments `countervariable` by 1. In the example above, `I` would now have a value of `2`.

VB then loops—goes back to the `For...` line. This time `I` is compared to the `end` value, `10`. If `I` is less than or equal to `10`, the statements through `Next` are executed again. Otherwise, program execution resumes at the line following the `Next` statement.

Let's watch a simple loop in action. In the `Form_Load` event of the Adder program, enter the following code:

```
Dim I As Integer
For I = 1 to 10
      Debug.Print "Hi, I =  & I
Next I
Debug.Print "Out of loop, I = " & I
```

Run the program to see the word `Hi` and the value of I printed 10 times. When the value of I reaches 11, program flow will exit from the loop, just as you might expect. Then the program will tell you the value that `I` has reached when it exits from the loop.

The `Counter` variable, in this case `I`, is a variable like any other variable. You can use it in an expression, print it out—even change its value (*not* a good idea). Printing out the value of the loop counter is also a frequent debugging tool. It lets you see exactly what your loop is up to.

Now remove this code from the program.

Adding Up

Let's do something useful. Well, marginally useful. Replace the `cmdAdd_Click` routine contents with the code in Listing 4-3. This adds up the numbers from 1 to 10.

Listing 4-3 Adding the numbers from 1 to 10

```
Private Sub cmdAdd_Click()
' Declare variables
Dim I, Sum As Integer

' Add the numbers from 1 to 10.
For I = 1 To 10
    Sum = Sum + I
Next I

Sub Output(Result As Variant)
```

continued on next page

continued from previous page

```
' Output the results with fanfare
' if there is no sound card, skip to next line
On Error Resume Next
lblOutput.Caption = Result & " !!!"
oleTada.DoVerb

End Sub
```

Let's look at the `For...Next` loop a little more closely. Its full syntax is

```
For countervariable = start To end [ Step step ]
    [ statements ]
    [ Exit For ]
    [ statements ]
Next [ counter ]
```

The counter must be a numeric variable—any numeric variable type will do. Generally, you use an integer for the counter, but this is by no means a requirement of the statement.

The start and end values are *numeric expressions* that evaluate to numbers of the type that can be stored in the `Counter` variable. By numeric expression, we mean any valid Visual Basic statement that returns a number.

Consider the example in Listing 4-4.

Listing 4-4 Using variable loop parameters

```
Dim StartVar As Integer
Dim EndVar As Integer
Dim Counter As Integer
StartVar = 1
EndVar = 1000
For Counter = StartVar To EndVar
    ' your statements
Next Counter
```

In this example, the start and end values have been replaced by variables. Using variables makes the code more flexible than entering the numbers directly, also called *hardcoding* numbers. Now if you wanted to use `StartVar` and `EndVar` somewhere else, you could be sure the values were the same. If you need to change the values, you need to do so only once.

Numeric expressions can also be the result of functions that return numeric values. Listing 4-5 is an example of using a function's return value in a `For` expression.

Listing 4-5 Using a function's return value in a loop parameter

```
Dim MyString As String
Dim Counter As Integer
MyString = "Visual Basic 5"
For Counter = 1 To Len(MyString)
    ' your statements
Next Counter
```

The Step *Keyword*

In its simplest form, the For...Next loop increments the Counter variable by 1 each time it goes through the loop. You can change the increment amount by using the Step keyword.

For example:

```
Dim QuarterMonth As Integer
For QuarterMonth = 1 To 12 Step 3
    ' your statements
Next QuarterMonth
```

In this example, the loop will execute four times, with the Counter variable QuarterMonth taking the values 1, 4, 7, and 10, respectively, on each pass through the loop. On the fifth pass through the loop, QuarterMonth will take the value 13, which is greater than the end expression 12. Accordingly, on the fifth pass through the loop, the loop will terminate.

You can also use the Step keyword to reverse order through the loop. For example:

```
Dim I As Integer
For I = 10 To 1 Step -1
    Debug.Print I
Next I
```

prints out

```
10
 9
 8
 7
 6
 5
 4
 3
 2
 1
```

What do you think will happen if you leave out the Step -1 part of the statement in the above example? Try it. Your code should appear as follows:

```
Dim I As Integer
For I = 10 To 1
    Debug.Print I
Next I
```

The loop terminates without executing the Debug.Print statement. This is because the For statement takes into account whether a Step keyword has a positive or negative increment when making its decision whether or not to pass through the loop. The Step keyword therefore has two functions:

- ● To control the amount by which the Counter variable is incremented or decremented

- ● To control the decision process over whether or not to pass into the loop

Remember that the `Step` amount does not have to be a whole integer; it just has to be an expression that evaluates to the same type of variable as `Counter`, `Start`, and `End`.

The Exit For Command

There are occasions where you need to break out of a `For...Next` loop. Consider the example in Listing 4-6.

Listing 4-6 The Exit For command

```
Dim FileName As String
Dim Counter As Integer
FileName = "VB.EXE"
For Counter = 1 To Len(FileName)
    ' Search for period
    If Mid(FileName, Counter, 1) = "." Then
        Exit For
    End If
Next Counter
Debug.Print Counter
```

In this example, you are searching a file name for a period. Once you find the period, you use the `Exit For` statement to forcibly terminate the `For` loop. The `Debug.Print` statement shows that `Counter` is set to **3** after the end of the loop—the position of the character `.` in the string `FileName`.

Nested Loops

You can put a `For...Next` loop inside of another `For...Next` loop. Consider the example in Listing 4-7.

Listing 4-7 Nested For Next...loops

```
Dim Counter1 As Integer
Dim Counter2 As Integer
For Counter1 = 1 To 10
    For Counter2 = 1 To 10
        ' your statements
    Next Counter2
Next Counter1
```

This example demonstrates nested `For...Next` statements. The statements inside the inner loop will execute 10 * 10 times.

It turns out that VB doesn't require you to use variables after the `Next` statement. The following code is functionally the same:

```
For Counter1 = 1 To 10
    For Counter2 = 1 To 10
        ' your statements
    Next
Next
```

Visual Basic treats each **Next** statement as the end of the last specified **For** loop. Therefore, the first **Next** statement terminates the **Counter2** loop, and the last **Next** statement terminates the **Counter1** loop. However, it is good practice to specify the **Counter** variable in the **Next** statement because it makes your code more readable.

When you use nested **For...Next** statements, you can terminate all your loops with one **Next** statement by specifying each **Counter** variable in the **Next** statement, separated by commas. You must specify the **Counter** variables with the one specified in the innermost **For** statement first. For example:

```
For Counter1 = 1 To 10
    For Counter2 = 1 To 10
        ' your statements
Next Counter2, Counter1
```

Onward

Save the Adder program for now. You'll continue building that project a little later in the chapter. You can either start a new project now to use for entering short examples in the **Form_Load** routine or enter the code examples directly in Adder's **Form_Load** event and simply delete them when you've seen how they work. Next, we'll examine VB 5's other looping constructs.

1. Which of the following code fragments outputs

```
10   10.1   10.2   10.3   10.4   10.5
```

a.
```
Dim I As Integer
For I = 10 to 10.5
    Debug.Print I;
Next I
```
b.
```
Dim I As Double
For I = 10 To 10.5
    Debug.Print I;
Next I
```
c.
```
Dim I As Double
For I = 10 to 10.5 Step .1
    Debug.Print I;
Next I
```
d.
```
Dim I as Double
For I = 10.1 To 10.5 Step .1
    Debug.Print I;
Next I
```

2. Which of the following code segments outputs the number 5?

   a.
```
Dim I As Integer
For I = 5 To 1
Next I
Debug.Print I
```

   b.
```
Dim I As Integer
For I = 1 To 5
Next I
Debug.Print I
```

   c.
```
Dim I As Integer
For I = 1 To 10
    If I = 5 Then Exit For
Next I
Debug.Print I
```

   d. All of the above

3. Which of the following types is *not* a valid loop counter?

   a. `Variant`
   b. `String`
   c. `Integer`
   d. `Double`

4. Which of the following is an invalid statement?

   a. `For I = 1 To EndVar`
   b. `For Counter = 0 To Len(SomeString)`
   c. `For J = StartVar To StartVar + 10 Step Increment`
   d. `For 2 = StartVar To EndVar Step 2`

5. What is the output of the following code:
```
Dim I As Integer
For I = 1 To 6
      If I = 3 Then
              I = 5
      End If
      If I = 4 Then
              Exit For
      End If
      Debug.Print I;
Next I
Debug.Print "Done! I is " & I
```

   a. 1 2 5 6 Done! I is 7
   b. 1 2 3 5 6 Done! I is 7
   c. 1 2 3 Done! I is 4
   d. 1 2 3 4 Done! I is 4

OTHER LOOPS

Although `For...Next` loops are useful when you know in advance how many times you want to execute the loop, there are occasions when you do not have this information in advance. Visual Basic provides other types of loops that you can use in these circumstances:

● `Do` loop

● `While...Wend` loop

The `Do` Loop

Visual Basic provides a very flexible general-purpose loop known as a `Do` loop. It has the following syntax:

```
Do [{ While | Until } expression ]
    [ statements ]
    [ Exit Do ]
Loop
```

or

```
Do
    [ statements ]
    [ Exit Do ]
Loop [{ While | Until } expression ]
```

This type of loop is very flexible, because the expression that controls whether the loop continues or terminates can be phrased in two different ways, using the keywords `While` or `Until`. Furthermore, the expression can be placed at either the beginning or the end of the loop.

You can even leave out the expression. See what happens when you enter the following code in the `Form_Load` event:

```
Do
    Debug.Print "Hi!"
Loop
```

Run the program and behold: Computers really are stupid enough to do exactly what you tell them. This is an example of an *infinite,* or endless, loop. Because nothing inside the program will get it to stop, you need to cause a break from the interpreter. To do this, hold down the (CTRL) key and press the (BREAK) button on your keyboard. You can now end the program by clicking on the square VCR-style stop button on the toolbar or by selecting End from the Run menu.

Let's move on to a less reckless example.

Do While

Using the `While` keyword and an expression tells VB to execute the loop while the expression is `True`. Let's program the adding program's poor relation. Replace the infinite loop tester code with the following:

```
Sum = 0
Do While Sum < 100
        Sum = Sum + 1
Loop
Debug.Print Sum
```

When this loop is finished, it prints out **100**. This routine can add, but only up to 100. Each time through, the loop evaluates `Sum < 100`. When the expression is no longer `True`, that is, when `Sum` is equal to (or greater than) 100, program execution occurs at the line after the `Loop` statement.

Do Until

The `While` loop executes until a condition is `False`; the `Until` keyword instructs the loop to execute until a condition is `True`. Replace the tester code with the example in Listing 4-8.

Listing 4-8 The `Do Until` loop

```
FileName = "vb.exe"
Pos = 0
Char = ""
Do Until Char = "."
    Pos = Pos + 1
    Char = Mid(FileName, Pos, 1)
Loop
Debug.Print Char & " found at position " & Pos
```

This program assigns each character in the file name in turn to `Char`. The loop terminates when `Char` is a period. This code outputs

```
. found at position 3
```

What happens if the exit condition is met even before the loop is executed? Try the example in Listing 4-9.

Listing 4-9 Checking the `Do Until` exit condition

```
I = 10
Do Until I >= 10
    Debug.Print "In the loop."
    Debug.Print "Incrementing I..."
    I = I + 1
Loop
Debug.Print "Out of loop; I is " & I
```

Guess what the output will be before trying it out. Here's what happens:

```
Out of loop; I is 10
```

With both `Do While` and `Do Until`, the loop isn't necessarily executed once. The program always evaluates the exit condition before entering the loop.

Loop While

To make sure that the loop executes at least once, place the exit condition at the `Loop` statement, rather than at the `Do` statement, as in Listing 4-10.

Listing 4-10 Loop While

```
I = 10
Do
    Debug.Print "In the loop."
    Debug.Print "Incrementing I..."
    I = I + 1
Loop While I < 10
Debug.Print "Out of loop; I is " & I
```

This version outputs

```
In the loop.
Incrementing I...
Out of loop; I is 11
```

 When checking a variable for an exit condition, you might not get the result you anticipate if you just check for equality or inequality. It is safest to use comparison operators such as less than, greater than, less than or equal to, and greater than or equal to. In the example above, if the exit condition had been

```
Loop While I <> 10
```

the program would have gone into an infinite loop, because `I` is incremented past its initial value of **10** before the value is checked.

Loop Until

You can similarly put the `Until` condition at the end of a loop. In the example above, where you were searching a string for a character, you knew you wanted to go through the loop at least once. By putting the `Until` statement at the end, you don't need to worry about the initial value of `Char`. Listing 4-11 demonstrates this principle.

Listing 4-11 Loop Until

```
FileName = "vb.exe"
Pos = 0
Do
    Pos = Pos + 1
    Char = Mid(FileName, Pos, 1)
Loop Until Char = "."
Debug.Print Char & " found at position " & Pos
```

The variations of the `Do...Loop` statement are summarized in Table 4-2.

Table 4-2 The `Do...Loop` statement

Loop	Description
`Do While` *condition* `Loop`	Enters loop if *condition* is `True`.
`Do Until` *condition* `Loop`	Enters loop if *condition* is `False`.
`Do Loop While` *condition*	Always executes loop once. Loops if *condition* is `True`.
`Do Loop Until` *condition*	Always executes loop once. Loops if *condition* is `False`.

The `While...Wend` Loop

Visual Basic 5 also provides another general-purpose loop statement called the `While ...Wend` loop. (The `Wend` keyword is short for "while end.") The `While...Wend` loop is equivalent to the `Do While` loop and is really provided only for compatibility with software written for earlier versions of Visual Basic that may not have the `Do Loop` statement. Because the `Do` loop is more expressive, we recommend that you use `Do While` rather than `While...Wend`.

The `While...Wend` loop has the following syntax:

```
While [ expression ]
    [ statements ]
Wend
```

Boolean Expression Evaluation

Both the `While` and `Until` loops work by evaluating Boolean expressions, just as you did in Chapter 3, Variables, Constants, and Associated Functions, when you learned the `If` statement. Now it's time to talk a little more about what's really going on behind the scenes.

You have seen how `Do` and `While` loops use Boolean expressions to decide whether to continue or terminate the loop. For example:

```
Dim I As Integer
Do Until I = 3
    I = I + 1
Loop
```

The above loop executes three times. Why? Each time the Boolean expression in the `Do Until` statement is evaluated, Visual Basic actually determines whether the Boolean expression is `True` or `False`. Each time the loop goes around, Visual Basic asks the question, "Is I equal to 3?"

The first time around the loop, `I` is equal to `0` because it has not yet been initialized to anything. Therefore the Boolean expression `I = 3` evaluates to `False`. Just before we go round the loop for the second time, the Boolean expression `I = 3` is evaluated again. This time, **I** equals **1**, so the Boolean expression evaluates to **False** again. This continues until after we have been around the loop three times. Just before we go round for a fourth time, the Boolean expression is evaluated again. This time **I** does equal **3**, so the Boolean expression evaluates to **True**, and this loop terminates.

You can see how expressions evaluate by looking at the result directly. To do this, we'll begin using the Debug window in a new way.

Break Mode

So far you've dealt with Visual Basic in only two modes: runtime and design time. There is actually a third mode, called *break* or sometimes *immediate* mode. During this time, the program is still running but it's temporarily stopped. You can examine or change variable values at this point or access a range of debugging features we'll talk about more in Chapter 9, Printing. For now, what interests us is that break mode provides full access to the Debug window.

Run whatever program is currently up. Click on Debug window under the View menu. Try to type something in the Debug window. Because the program is running, you can use Debug only for output, from inside your code.

There are several ways to enter break mode. The one we'll use here is to click on the Break button on the toolbar, shown in Figure 4-5. Click on the Break button now.

The Visual Basic title bar notes the change in the mode. Both the Play and Stop buttons on the toolbar are active, except now the "forward" button actually means "continue." Put the cursor in the Debug window and notice that you can now type. In fact, in immediate mode you can use this window to type in a VB 5 command and it executes immediately. Try typing

```
Print 2+3
```

You don't need to specify **Debug.Print**, because the method acts on the active object by default.

A question mark (**?**) is shorthand notation for the **Print** method. Thus

```
Print FullName
```

and

```
? FullName
```

both do the same thing.

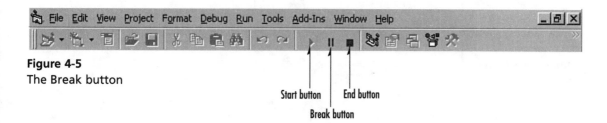

Figure 4-5
The Break button

Start button

Break button

End button

In immediate mode, you can access the current program variables. Try typing

```
FullName = "c:\winword\winword.exe"
Print FullName
```

You can even exit the program by typing **End**, as shown in Figure 4-6.

Immediate Boolean Expression Evaluation

While in break mode, try executing the following statement in the Debug window:

```
Print 0 = 3
```

VB prints the word **False** in the Debug window, because 0 is definitely not equal to 3. Now try

```
Print 3 = 3
```

Yes, as expected, VB prints the word **True**.

Realizing that Boolean expressions evaluate to a simple **True** or **False** value is important, because Boolean expressions are used frequently in Visual Basic. Sometimes they can become very complex indeed. Part of a programmer's skill in debugging software is the ability to determine what the result of a Boolean expression should be.

Now consider the following example:

```
Dim I As Integer
I = 5
Do While I
    I = I - 1
            Debug.Print I
Loop
```

Figure 4-6
You can execute basic commands in immediate mode

In this example, the Boolean expression being evaluated is actually a straightforward integer variable. How does Visual Basic evaluate such Boolean expressions? It turns out that Visual Basic treats any nonzero value as `True` and any value of 0 as `False`. Therefore, this program prints out

```
4
3
2
1
0
```

Combining Boolean Expressions: Logical Operators

You can combine Boolean expressions using Visual Basic's *logical operators*, such as `And`, `Or`, and `Not`. (You already saw this in Chapter 3, Variables, Constants, and Associated Functions, when you used `Not` to evaluate an `If` expression.) For example, see the code in Listing 4-12.

Listing 4-12 Combining Boolean expressions

```
FileName = "vb.exe"
Pos = 0
Char = ""
Do
    Pos = Pos + 1
    Char = Mid(FileName, Pos, 1)
Loop Until Char = "." Or Pos > Len(FileName)
If Char = "." Then
    Debug.Print Char & " found at position " & Pos
Else
    Debug.Print "Couldn't find period."
End If
```

The program now exits the loop either when the period is found, or when `Pos` is greater than the length of the string. This neatly handles the case of a `FileName` value without a period.

The logical operators are summarized in Table 4-3. Tables 4-4, 4-5, 4-6, 4-7, 4-8, and 4-9 show the results of the operators' behavior.

Table 4-3 The logical operators

Operator	Syntax	Behavior
And	Expr1 And Expr2	Returns `True` if (and only if) both expressions are `True`.
Eqv	Expr1 Eqv Expr2	Equivalence: Returns `True` if both expressions are the same.

continued on next page

continued from previous page

Operator	Syntax	Behavior
Imp	Expr1 Imp Expr2	Implication: Returns True *unless* Expr1 is True and Expr2 is False.
Not	Not Expr	Returns True if Expr is False and False if Expr is True.
Or	Expr1 Or Expr2	Returns True if Expr1 or Expr2 (or both) are True.
Xor	Expr1 Xor Expr2	Exclusive or: Returns True if either (but not both) of the expressions are True.

Table 4-4 The And operator

Expr1	Operator	Expr2	Result
True	And	True	True
True	And	False	False
False	And	True	False
False	And	False	False

Table 4-5 The Equ (Equivalence) operator

Expr1	Operator	Expr2	Result
True	Eqv	True	True
True	Eqv	False	False
False	Eqv	True	False
False	Eqv	False	True

Table 4-6 The Imp (Implication) operator

Expr1	Operator	Expr2	Result
True	Imp	True	True
True	Imp	False	False
False	Imp	True	True
False	Imp	False	True

Table 4-7 The Not operator

Operator	Expr2	Result
Not	True	False
Not	False	True

Table 4-8 The Or operator

Expr1	Operator	Expr2	Result
True	Or	True	True
True	Or	False	True
False	Or	True	True
False	Or	False	False

Table 4-9 The Xor (Exclusive Or) operator

Expr1	Operator	Expr2	Result
True	Xor	True	False
True	Xor	False	True
False	Xor	True	True
False	Xor	False	False

Bitwise Operations

You can also apply these operators to numeric values. In that case, the operators perform a *bitwise* operation on the numbers. That means each bit in a binary (base 2) representation of the number is evaluated. Bitwise operations are sometimes used in advanced programming techniques, particularly graphics techniques. Let's look at the example of

```
6 And 4
```

In a bitwise And operation, the result is **1** if and only if both bits in the same position are **1**. The binary representation of 6 is **110**; the binary representation of 4 is **100**. Line these numbers up, to see that

```
110             And
100
-----Evaluates to
100
```

1 And 1 evaluate to **1**; 1 And 0 evaluate to **0**; and 0 And 0 evaluate to **0**. The result, converted back to decimal, is 4. You can test this out in the Debug window with

```
Print 4 And 6
```

If you want to experiment with bitwise operations, a quick way to convert numbers to and from binary is to use the Windows calculator in scientific view.

1. What is the output of the following program segment?

```
I = 25
Do While I < 30
    I = I + 1
Loop
Debug.Print I
```

a. 25

b. 30

c. 29

d. 31

2. Assume **I** and **Pos** are implicitly declared variants. Which code segment outputs

```
Position found at 6.
```

a.
```
For I = 1 To Len("Split|Me")
            Pos = Mid("Split|Me", I, 1)
Next I
Debug.Print "Position found at " & Pos
```

b.
```
Do
            I = I + 1
              Pos = Mid("Split|Me", I, 1)
Loop Until I >= Len("Split|Me")
Debug.Print "Position found at " & Pos
```

c.
```
Do While I <= Len("Split|Me")
            If Mid("Split|Me", I, 1) = "|" Then
                    Pos = I
        End If
Loop
Debug.Print "Position found at " & Pos
```

d.
```
Do While I <= Len("Split|Me")
            I = I + 1
            If Mid("Split|Me", I, 1) = "|" Then
                    Pos = I
            End If
Loop
Debug.Print "Position found at " & Pos
```

3. What is the output of this code?

```
Debug.Print (5 ^ 2) + 12 = 37
```

  a. `True`
  b. `False`
  c. `37`
  d. `0`

4. Which loop is *not* executed at least once? Assume `I` is initialized to `10`.

  a.
```
For I = 1 To 10
        Debug.Print "Loopy"
Next I
```

  b.
```
Do
        Debug.Print "Loopy"
        I = I + 1
Loop Until I = 10
```

  c.
```
Do Until I = 10
        Debug.Print "Loopy"
        I = I + 1
Loop
```

  d.
```
Do While I = 10
        Debug.Print "Loopy"
        I = I + 1
Loop
```

5. Which Boolean expression evaluates to `False`?

  a. `Debug.Print True Xor 10 = 2 * 5`
  b. `Debug.Print 10 = 2 * 5 And 20 = 2 * 10`
  c. `Debug.Print Not 10 = 5 + 2`
  d. `Debug.Print 10 = 2 * 5 Or True`

DECISION STATEMENTS

In Chapter 3, Variables, Constants, and Associated Functions, you used the `If` statement to make a decision. In this lesson, we'll look at the `If` statement in more detail. We'll also look at the VB application language's other decision statement: `Select Case`.

If...Then...Else

As you saw in Chapter 3, Variables, Constants, and Associated Functions, the two forms of the `If` statement are

```
If expression Then statement(s) [Else statement(s)]
```

and

```
If expression Then
    [statement(s)]
[ElseIf]
    [statement(s)]
[Else]
    [statement(s)]
End If
```

The statements following the `If` statement are executed if the Boolean expression evaluates to `True`. Conversely, the `Else` block of statements is executed if the expression evaluates to `False`.

The : Statement Separator

You can execute multiple statements in a single-line `If` statement by separating the individual statements with statement separators (`:`) as follows:

```
' "Move" the traffic light pictures.
Car = (Car.Visible = True)
If Car Then Green.Visible = True: Car.Visible = False: Message.Caption = "Go!"
```

In fact, you can use the statement separator on any VB line:

```
Dim Counter As Integer : Counter = 0
```

performs the same task as

```
Dim Counter As Integer
Counter = 0
```

However, most programmers prefer only a single statement per line. This makes the code easier to read, analyze, and debug. If you use longer (more meaningful) variable names, placing more than one command on a line could make the code extend past the visible part of the window. In fact, you may want to break your statements into more than one line. To do this, place a space and the underscore character (`_`) before the carriage return.

The `If` statement below could be all on one line without the `_` character, but it is easier to read this way.

```
If InStr(filename, ".") = 0 And _
   InStr(filename, "\") = 0 And _
   InStr(filename, ":") = 0 Then
        MsgBox "Nothing to parse!"
End If
```

The Picture Pusher

For this section, create a new test project named PUSH. Create a directory for the project. Add the objects and properties summarized in Table 4-10. Arrange the controls as shown in Figure 4-7.

Table 4-10 The Picture Pusher project

Object	Property	Value
Picture	Name	Car
	AutoSize	True
	Picture	c:\vb\icons\traffic\trffc16.ico
Picture	Name	Green
	AutoSize	True
	Picture	c:\vb\icons\traffic\trffc10A.ico
Picture	Name	Yellow
	AutoSize	True
	Picture	c:\vb\icons\traffic\trffc10B.ico
Picture	Name	Red
	AutoSize	True
	Picture	c:\vb\icons\traffic\trffc10C.ico
Picture	Name	Right
	AutoSize	True
	Picture	c:\vb\icons\arrows\arw04rt.ico
Label	Name	Output
	AutoSize	True
	Caption	Parked

Else *and* ElseIf

Let's generate some code that performs multiple actions based on a variety of circumstances. If the car is present, turn on the green light. If the green light is on, turn on the yellow light, and so on. Add the code in Listing 4-13 to the right arrow button Click routine.

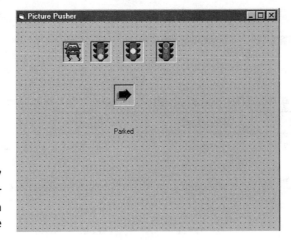

Figure 4-7
The Picture Pusher
project at design
time

Listing 4-13 "Move" the pictures

```
Private Sub Right_Click()
' "Move" the traffic light pictures.
    If Car.Visible Then
        Green.Visible = True
        Car.Visible = False
        Message.Caption = "Go!"
    Else
        If Green.Visible = True Then
            Yellow.Visible = True
            Green.Visible = False
            Message.Caption = "Slow!"
        Else
            If Yellow.Visible = True Then
                Red.Visible = True
                Yellow.Visible = False
                Message.Caption = "Stop!"
            Else
                ' Red must be visible
                Car.Visible = True
                Red.Visible = False
                Message.Caption = "Parked"
            End If
        End If
    End If
End Sub
```

Making sure the opening/closing blocks line up helps readability, but this code is still hard to read. You can improve it using the **ElseIf** statement. Add the improved code in Listing 4-14 to the right arrow picture's **Click** event.

Listing 4-14 More readable routine with ElseIf

```
Private Sub Right_Click()
' "Move" the traffic light pictures.
    If Car.Visible Then
        Green.Visible = True
        Car.Visible = False
        Message.Caption = "Go!"
    ElseIf Green.Visible = True Then
        yellow.Visible = True
        Green.Visible = False
        Message.Caption = "Slow!"
    ElseIf yellow.Visible = True Then
        red.Visible = True
        yellow.Visible = False
        Message.Caption = "Stop!"
    Else
        ' Red must be visible
        Car.Visible = True
        red.Visible = False
        Message.Caption = "Parked"
    End If
End Sub
```

This method is somewhat easier to read and is equivalent to the nested If statements used before. The If statement now requires only one End If. Go ahead and save the project.

Select Case

The Select Case statement differs from the If (and nested If) statement by providing a structured way to execute alternative blocks of code depending on the *value* of a numeric expression, rather than on a True/False *evaluation* of the expression. The syntax of Select Case is as follows:

```
Select Case expression
    Case expression
        [statements]
    [Case Else]
        [statements]
End Select
```

Chapter 3, Variables, Constants, and Associated Functions, showed the listing for a sample Grocery program. This program used a set of constants and the Byte variable Fruit, as shown in Listing 4-15. If you created this program, load it now; otherwise, load it from the book's CD.

Listing 4-15 Constants for Grocery program

```
Const APPLES As Byte = 1
Const BANANAS As Byte = 2
Const ORANGES As Byte = 3
Dim Fruit As Byte
```

Replace the Grocery button code with the code in Listing 4-16.

Listing 4-16 Expanded Grocery program

```
Private Sub cmdGroceryOrder_Click()
Select Case Fruit
    Case APPLES
        lblMessage.Caption = "An apple a day..."
    Case BANANAS
        lblMessage.Caption = "Monkeyin' around!"
    Case ORANGES
        lblMessage.Caption = "Sorry, oranges are out of season."
    Case Else
        lblMessage.Caption = "Please click a fruit button."
End If
End Sub
```

Select Case *Ranges and Types*

The **Select Case** statement can be used with all variable types. An example is shown in Listing 4-17.

Listing 4-17 Select Case with strings

```
Dim I As String
I = "A String"
Select Case I
    Case "A"
        'This block will not be executed
    Case "B"
        'This block will not be executed
    Case "A String"
        'This block will be executed
    Case Else
        'This block will not be executed
End Select
```

You cannot use the **Like** comparison operator in a **Case** statement.

You can also specify ranges in the **Case** expressions. Listing 4-18 is an example.

Listing 4-18 Case ranges

```
Dim I As Integer
'set I to something
Select Case I
    Case 1 To 5
        'all values of I in the range 1 through 5
    Case Else
        'all other values of I
End Select
```

If you want to execute the same block of code for different values of the test expression, you can do so by specifying the different case expressions in one **Case** statement, separated by commas, as shown in Listing 4-19.

Listing 4-19 Evaluating more than one condition

```
Select Case I
    Case 1,5,9
        'this block of statements will be executed
        'when I is equal to 1 or 5 or 9
    Case 10 To 15
        'this block of statements will be executed
        'when I is equal to any number in the range 10 through 15
    Case Else
        'this block of statements will be executed
        'when I is equal to any value other than 1 or 5 or 9 or 10 to 15
End Select
```

You can nest **Select** statements, but you must ensure that each **Select** has a corresponding **End Select**. Listing 4-20 is an example.

Listing 4-20 Nested Select Case statements

```
Select Case I
    Case 1 To 3
        Select Case I
            Case 1
                'This block of statements will be executed
                'when I equals 1
            Case 2
                'This block of statements will be executed
                'when I equals 2
            Case 3
                'This block of statements will be executed
                'when I equals 3
        End Select
    Case Else
End Select
```

The Is *Keyword*

You can also use the **>**, **<**, **>=**, and **<=** operators to set up ranges in a **Case** statement. If you do so, you must use the **Is** keyword to refer to the **Select Case** value.

```
Select Case I
    Case Is > 15
        'This block of statements will be executed
        'when I is greater than 15
    Case Is < 10
        'This block of statements will be executed
        'when I is less than 10
End Select
```

In all the above examples, if the value being tested does not fall within the range of one of the **Case** statements, program flow falls through the **Select** statement without executing any code, unless a **Case Else** statement is present.

To combine more than one range of values in a single **Case** statement, you can use the logical operators **And** and **Or**. Note that the example in Listing 4-21 uses **Is** for the first reference to the **Select Case** variable, but not for references after **And** or **Or**.

Listing 4-21 Combining ranges

```
Select Case NumVar
    Case Is > 15 Or NumVar <= 10
        'This block of statements will be executed
        'if NumVar is greater than 15 or less than or equal to 10.
    Case Is >= 11 And NumVar <= 13
        ' executes when NumVar is 11, 12, or 13
    Case Else
        'This block of statements will be executed
        'for any other value of NumVar
End Select
```

The **Select Case** statement is remarkably flexible. Any time your **If...Then... Else** constructions start to get unwieldy, analyze whether you could be using a **Select Case** statement instead.

Now that you've got more programming skills under your belt, let's move on to subroutines and functions.

1. Recall that a semicolon after a **Print** statement prevents the output from advancing to the next line. Using a comma enters tabs, so you can space your output by columns. With that in mind, which segment prints:

```
stopped          True             True
```

   a.
```
Go = True
If Go Then Stopped = True: Go = False: Msg = "stopped"
Debug.Print Msg, Stopped, Go
```

   b.
```
Go = True
If Go Then
        Stopped = True
        Go = False
        Msg = "stopped"
End If
Debug.Print Msg, Stopped, Go
```

c.
```
Go = True
If Not Go Then
            Stopped = False
            Go = False
            Msg = "Not going"
End If
Debug.Print Msg, Stopped, Go
```

d.
```
Go = True
If Not Go Then
            Stopped = False
            Go = True
            Msg = "Not going"
Else
            Stopped = True
            Msg = "stopped"
End If
Debug.Print Msg, Stopped, Go
```

2. Which symbol lets you put more than one statement on a line? Which symbol (respectively) lets you extend a statement across more than one line?

   a. _ and :
   b. : and _
   c. : and '
   d. ' and :

3. In the following program, which condition needs to be True for Umbrella to evaluate to True?

```
If Cold Then
    Wear = "Coat"
    If Rainy Then
        Umbrella = True
    Else
        Umbrella = False
    End If
ElseIf Sunny Then
        Wear = "T-Shirt"
        Umbrella = False
ElseIf Patchy Then
        Wear = "Sweater"
        Umbrella = False
Else
        Wear = "Unknown"
End If
```

   a. Rainy
   b. Cold and Patchy
   c. Cold and Rainy
   d. Cold

4. In the following program, what does the numerical value of **Sky** have to be for the output to be, **Let's go to the beach!**?

```
Const CLOUDY = 1
Const OVERCAST = 2
Const FOGGY = 3
Const RAINY = 4
Const CLEAR = 5
Const BEAUTIFUL = 6

' (Sky is assigned in here.)

Select Case Sky
    Case CLOUDY Or OVERCAST
        Debug.Print "Brrrrr."
    Case FOGGY
        Debug.Print "Drive carefully."
    Case RAINY
        Debug.Print "Please run umbrella program."
    Case CLEAR, BEAUTIFUL
        Debug.Print "Let's go to the beach!"
    Case Else
        Debug.Print "Unknown forecast."
End Select
```

a. Less than 6
b. Greater than or equal to 6
c. 1, 2, or 4
d. 5 or 6

5. Which **Case** statement evaluates to **True** if **TheValue** is greater than **10**, given a **Select** statement:

```
Select Case TheValue
```

a. `Case Is > 10`
b. `Case TheValue > 10`
c. `Case TheValue Is > 10`
d. `Case Is > TheValue`

REVIEW

John: I'm understanding most of the concepts, but I feel like I need to sit down and get more hands-on experience.

Lisa: I know. I just need more practice experimenting with all the little details.

John: Like the difference between all those **Do...Loop** constructs...

Lisa: And combining all the logical operators...

John: And knowing which loop to use when...

Lisa: Reading this chapter has made me think about how important and helpful it is to use meaningful variable names. Like

```
Do While Position <= Len(TargetString)
```

is a lot more understandable than

```
Do While I <= Num
```

John: Agreed.

Lisa: But I still think we're learning a lot of the ins and outs of the Visual Basic language.

John: Right, and there's a lot more to come!

SUBROUTINES AND FUNCTIONS: INTRODUCTION

You shouldn't need much of an introduction to subroutines and functions: You've already used them! Look at the following examples of routines from previous lessons. A routine is a generic term that refers to either a subroutine or a function.

```
Private Sub mnuFileExit_Click()
    End
End Sub

Private Sub Form_Load()
    txtFileName.Text = ""
End Sub

AverageLength = Int(TotalLength / 2)
Length = Len(String)
EasyPart = Left(Alphabet,3)
```

In the first two examples, the event routines are actually subroutines you're defining.

When you *define* a subroutine or function, you are specifying the name of the subroutine or function, the parameters it takes (if any), and the code that executes when the routine is called.

The last three examples all *call* a routine (actually, in these cases, a function).

When you *call* a subroutine or function, you tell Visual Basic to execute the code associated with that routine. When you call a subroutine or function, you specify the *arguments* you want to pass to the routine, that is, the value or values you want the routine to work on.

In this lesson, you'll learn how to define and call your own subroutines and functions.

A Dip in a Sub

The basic syntax for defining a subroutine is

```
Sub name [( argumentlist)]
    [ statements ]
    [ Exit Sub ]
    [ statements ]
End Sub
```

Lesson 6 will expand on this syntax, but this is all you need to know to define a subroutine. Similarly, here is the basic syntax to define a function:

```
Function name [( argumentlist)] [As type]
    [ statements ]
    [ name = expression ]
    [ Exit Function ]
    [ statements ]
    [ name = expression ]
End Function
```

The only difference between a subroutine and a function is that a function returns a value.

Programmers use subroutines and functions to break code into smaller tasks. This makes code easier to read and debug. Also, routines can be called from different sections of the program, reducing duplication.

Load the Adder program from Lessons 1 and 2. Let's separate some of the code into a subroutine. We'll devote the **cmdAdd_Click** routine to actual addition and create a new subroutine to output the sum.

To begin a new subroutine, simply place the cursor at the beginning of a line either just before another **Sub** statement or just after an **End Sub** statement and enter

```
Sub Output(Result As Variant)
```

Visual Basic automatically creates the new routine in the General section of the form and makes this the prominent routine in the Code window. Note that the closing line

```
End Sub
```

is also added automatically. The **Output** routine takes one parameter—**Result**—which is the number to output. Fill in the subroutine as shown in Listing 4-22.

Listing 4-22 The Output subroutine

```
Sub Output(Result As Variant)

' Output the results with fanfare
' if there is no sound card, skip to next line
On Error Resume Next
lblOutput.Caption = Result & " !!!"
oleTada.DoVerb

End Sub
```

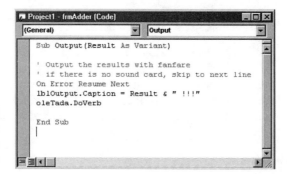

Figure 4-8
The Output
subroutine in the
Code window

Your screen should look like Figure 4-8.

Now, if you decide to reformat the output in any way, the changes you make get compartmentalized in the **Output** routine. The rest of the code doesn't need to know about the details. If you expand the program and include routines to, say, perform subtractions (sacrilege!), you can call this routine to output a different value.

Next you need to remove the output code from the **cmdAdd_Click** routine and call this subroutine instead. Here is the syntax to call a subroutine:

```
[Call] subname [argumentlist]
```

The **Call** keyword is optional. If you use the **Call** keyword, the argument list must be included in parentheses, as in

```
Call Output(Sum)
```

If you don't include the **Call** keyword, you must not use parentheses, as in

```
Output Sum
```

Modify the **Add button** routine as shown in Listing 4-23.

Listing 4-23 Calling the Output routine

```
Private Sub cmdAdd_Click()
' Declare variables
Dim I, Sum As Integer
' Add the numbers from 1 to 10.
For I = 1 To 10
    Sum = Sum + I
Next I

Output Sum

End Sub
```

One thing to notice is that **cmdAdd_Click** calls the routine with the argument name **Sum**, whereas the function definition is **Output(Result)**. The reason this works is that **Result** takes on any value that is passed to the function; the variable names are completely separate. We could just as easily have said

```
Output ANumber
Output 35
Output Len(SomeString)
```

Note Why use **Call**? Because the **Call** statement is optional, you might wonder why you should bother to use it. The fact is, there *is* no good reason. Some programming languages require **Call**, and programmers who were trained in those languages tend to use **Call** from force of habit.

An Added Routine

Functions, as we said above, differ from subroutines in that they return a value. One way to describe functions is to think about a black box that processes input, as shown in Figure 4-9. The code calling the function doesn't need to know how the function calculates the result; it just takes the output it needs and goes on its merry way.

Let's write a short function for the adding program: a function to add two numbers. Yes, yes, Visual Basic already knows how to add two numbers, but our silly program thinks addition is important enough to merit its own function. Add the **Sum** routine shown in Listing 4-24. As before, you just need to type the first line of the function anywhere in the Code window, and VB creates the function definition block.

Listing 4-24 The **Sum** function

```
Function Sum(Num1 As Variant, Num2 As Variant) As Variant
    Sum = Num1 + Num2
End Function
```

Listing 4-24 sets the function's return value by assigning the value to the name of the function. The function definition includes a type identifier at the end. You're using variants here because you don't know what kinds of numbers you'll add. Because variants are the default data type, you don't actually need the **As Variant** statement, but including it makes it clear that you explicitly decided to use variants.

You call a function any time you use that function's return value in an expression:

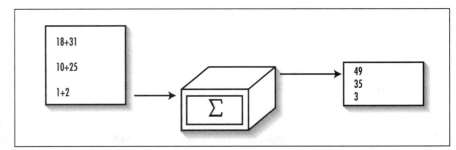

Figure 4-9
The black box

```
Answer = Sum(1,2)
Output Sum(Start, End)
lblOutput.Caption = "2 + 2 make " & Sum(2,2)
```

are all valid ways of calling the function. You can also call a function *without* using the return value, as in

```
MsgBox "Hello!"
```

In this case, **MsgBox** would have returned the button the user clicked, but because you're using the default message box, which contains only one button, disregard the return value.

Note that user-defined functions look exactly like VB's functions when you call them:

```
Answer = Sum(x,y)
Answer = Sin(x)
```

Function Type Casting

Functions don't have to return numbers; they can return any data type. Let's create a function that returns a Boolean, expressing whether or not the user has already clicked the Add button. Enter the function definition in Listing 4-25.

Listing 4-25 The `AlreadyAdded` function

```
Function AlreadyAdded() As Boolean
    'See if output label has changed.
    If lblOutput.Caption = "[The Answer!]" Then
        AlreadyAdded = False
    Else
        AlreadyAdded = True
    End If
End Function
```

Now integrate these functions into the main **cmdAdd_Click** routine, as shown in Listing 4-26.

Listing 4-26 Calling our routines

```
Private Sub cmdAdd_Click()
' Declare variables
Dim I, Number As Integer
' Add the numbers from 1 to 10.

' Don't bother to do anything if answer is already displayed.
If Not AlreadyAdded Then
    For I = 1 To 10
        Number = Sum(Number, I)
    Next I

    Output Number
End If

End Sub
```

Because the Number Adder is so short, you didn't really gain much by separating things out as procedures. The program still works pretty much the same as before. (But it won't "Ta da" more than once per run now.) But then, you already knew these routines were for demonstration purposes. By keeping them simple, it makes it easy to see the basic syntax and usage.

Next, we'll talk about procedures in more detail and variable scope in particular.

1. An argument to a procedure is:
   a. A value that is passed when the procedure is called
   b. Available only to functions
   c. Necessarily numeric
   d. Passed with a variable that has the same name in the called procedure as the calling procedure

2. The difference between a function and a subroutine is:
   a. There is no difference.
   b. Only a function can have arguments.
   c. A function can return a value.
   d. You always call a function with the `Call` statement.

3. A function definition that doesn't include a type definition character:
   a. Generates a syntax error
   b. Generates a runtime error
   c. Defaults to a variant type, just like variables without type declaration
   d. Must return a number

4. Which function returns the difference between the first and second numbers?
   a.
```
Function Diff(Num1, Num2) As String
    Diff = Num1 - Num2
End Function
```

   b.
```
Function Diff(Num1,Num2)
    Num1 = Num1 - Num2
End Function
```

   c.
```
Function Diff(Num1, Num2)
    Diff = Num1 - Num2
End Function
```

   d.
```
Function Diff(Num1,Num2)
    Exit Function
    Diff = Num1 - Num2
End Function
```

5. In the Adder program examples, which would be a valid way to call the `Sum` function?

   a. `Call Sum(2,2)`

   b. `Answer = Sum(2,2)`

   c. `Sum 2,2`

   d. All of the above

EXERCISE

Write a function that uses a loop to convert the characters in a string to asterisks. Return the result. Spaces don't get converted. If the function reaches a | character, it should chop off the | and everything past that point. Thus,

`hello there`

becomes

`***** *****`

and

`hello out| there`

becomes

`***** ***`

Include code to test the function with several strings and print the result.

LESSON 6

SUBROUTINES AND FUNCTIONS: THE SEQUEL

The Visual Basic programming environment is modular, in some cases to a fault. Take the Code window, for example. Load the Adder program and, in design mode, double-click on the Add button. The Code window that comes up compartmentalizes the `cmdAdd` routine, as shown in Figure 4-10, to the point where you might think the routine was alone in the universe. This layout is useful when you are focusing on a specific event or function, but there are times when you want to get the big picture.

Under the Tools menu, click on the Options... item. Select the Editor tab, and then click to turn on the check box labeled Full Module View. If the Procedure Separator box is not checked, click on that, too. The Options dialog box looks like Figure 4-11. Click on OK and go back to the Code window.

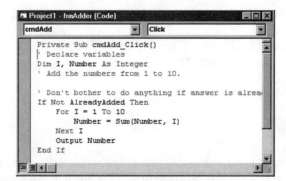

Figure 4-10
The Code window showing a single routine

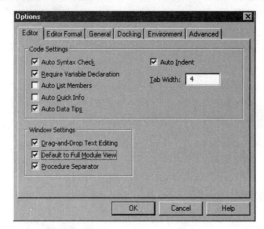

Figure 4-11
Set full module view in the Options dialog

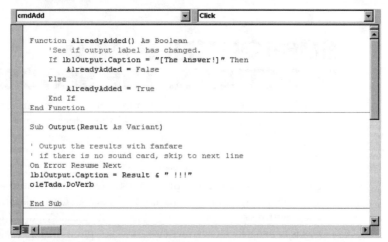

Figure 4-12
The Code window in full module view

Whoa! The code for the form module is really just a collection of subroutines, as shown in Figure 4-12. But then, you were probably starting to suspect that.

The Big Picture

So, the code for the form module is really just a collection of subroutines. What does that mean to us? To explore this question, let's work through another example.

This will be a multiple-form project called Sender. Each form will have a text box and a button. All the forms will be accessible at all times. The Main form's button will exit the program. The buttons on the other forms will send the contents of that form's text box to the Main form's text box. The user can change the contents of a text box and then send the results to the Main form's text box. Granted, this isn't a very useful program, but it will provide a chance to practice communication between forms.

Create a directory called **SENDER** for the project files. Click on New Project under the VB 5 File menu. Make the window rather small and put it near the center of the screen. Add the objects and properties described in Table 4-11 to the form. The result will look something like Figure 4-13.

Table 4-11 Objects and properties for the main form

Object	Property	Value
Form	Name	frmMain
	Caption	Main
TextBox	Name	txtBox
	Text	
CommandButton	Name	cmdExit
	Caption	Exit

Now add another form to the project by clicking on Add Form under the Project menu. This form looks very similar to the Main form. It is about the same size and has the same controls. The objects' names and captions are slightly different, however, as seen in Table 4-12.

Figure 4-13
Sender's Main form
(design mode)

Table 4-12 Objects and properties for the sender forms

Object	Property	Value
Form	Name	frmSender1
	Caption	Sender
TextBox	Name	txtBox
	Text	
CommandButton	Name	cmdSend
	Caption	Send

Next, create two more forms that are exactly the same, except the form names are
frmSender2 and **frmSender3**. It doesn't matter that the control names are the same
in different forms, because you can use the form names to identify them.

To copy one or more controls, click on each of the controls *while holding down* SHIFT.
The selected controls will turn light gray. Select Copy from the Edit menu, select a new
form by clicking on it, and then select Paste from the Edit menu.

Select Form Layout window under the View menu. Drag it from its corner of the
screen and resize it so you can get a good idea of how the forms will appear at runtime.
Arrange the forms as shown in Figure 4-14.

Code It

This program won't require much code. In the Code window for the Main form, enter
the code in Listing 4-27. The Exit button is self-explanatory. The code in the **Load** routine shows the other three forms, so that all four forms are available at runtime.

You want the user to be able to switch freely between all the forms, so call the **Show**
method in the default "modeless" state.

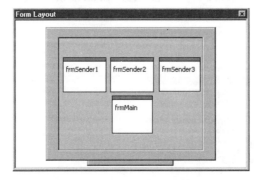

Figure 4-14
The sender forms

Listing 4-27 The Main form routines

```
Private Sub cmdExit_Click()
    End
End Sub
Private Sub Form_Load()
    Show frmSender1
    Show frmSender2
    Show frmSender3
End Sub
```

Now double-click on one of the Send buttons. You want to put the contents of the text box into the main text box, so let's use the technique of specifying the text box that is outside the current form with the destination form name followed by a period. Add the code in Listing 4-28 to the **Click** event routine.

Listing 4-28 Sending text across forms

```
Private Sub cmdSend_Click()
    frmMain.txtBox.Text = txtBox.Text
End Sub
```

Copy this command into the **cmdSend_Click** routines in the other two Sender forms as well. To copy a single line of text, move the mouse to the left of the line until the cursor turns into a right-pointing arrow, and then click once to select the line. Click on Copy under the Edit menu to copy it and Paste to paste it to the destination.

Run the program. Type into any of the text boxes, and then click on the Send buttons to see how it works. The runtime program is shown in Figure 4-15.

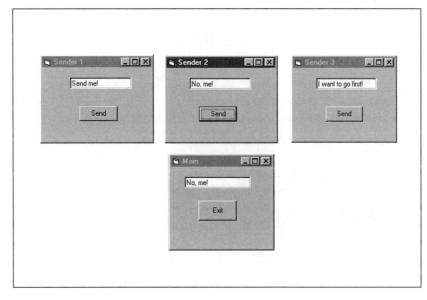

Figure 4-15
Sending, sending

Now let's keep track of when "messages" are sent. In the Sender 1 form, double-click on the Send button. Add the first attempt at keeping track of message sending by entering the code shown in Listing 4-29. (Additions are in boldface.)

Listing 4-29 Sender 1 form's first attempt at keeping a log

```
Private Sub cmdSend_Click()
    Dim MailTime As Date
    Dim MessageSent As Boolean
    frmMain.txtBox.Text = txtBox.Text
    MailTime = Time
    MessageSent = True
End Sub
```

Now add a new button to that form, as described in Table 4-13.

Table 4-13 The View Mail Log button

Object	Property	Value
CommandButton	Name	cmdViewMailLog
	Caption	View Mail Log

The design-time form should look like Figure 4-16. Add the code shown in Listing 4-30.

Listing 4-30 Sender 1 form tries to read the log

```
Private Sub cmdViewMailLog_Click()
If MessageSent Then
    MsgBox "Message sent at " & MailTime & ", boss."
Else
    MsgBox "Message hasn't been sent!"
End If

End Sub
```

Run the program, enter a message in the Sender 1 text box and send it to the Main form, and then click on the View Mail Log button. You get the message shown in Figure 4-17. What happened?

Figure 4-16
Sender 1's new
button

Figure 4-17
You didn't think it
would be that easy,
did you?

Scoping Out Scope

All variables, procedures, and objects have what is called *scope*. Scope defines the visibility of the item to other parts of the program.

All variables declared with the **Dim** statement have *private* scope within the routine in which they are declared. This means they are available only to that procedure. This is true for variables whether they have been explicitly or implicitly declared. Keep in mind that because variables are private, you can have variables with the same name in different procedures that won't influence each other whatsoever. Save the Sender program, start a new project, and enter the program in Listing 4-31.

Listing 4-31 Private variables are separate, even if they have the same name

```
Option Explicit
Sub Proc1()
    Dim Message As String
    Message = "Hello from Proc1"
    Debug.Print Message
End Sub
Private Sub Form_Load()
    Dim Message As String
    Message = "Hello from Form_Load"
    Debug.Print Message
    Call Proc1
    Debug.Print Message
End Sub
```

This program outputs

```
Hello from Form_Load
Hello from Proc1
Hello from Form_Load
```

Even though **Proc1** assigns a value to its **Message** variable, the separate **Message** variable in **Form_Load** isn't affected.

In the Sender example, the **cmdViewMailLog_Click()** couldn't "see" the variables that had been defined in **cmdAdd_Click**. When VB came to the line

```
If MessageSent Then
```

it implicitly declared **MessageSent**, and then evaluated its contents to **False**. (If your program has an **Option Explicit** statement in the Sender General Declarations section, you won't even get this far. Try it!)

Module Scope

What happens if you declare a variable in the General Declarations section of a module? Well, it too has private scope, but within the module as a whole. Type in Listing 4-32 to see an example.

Listing 4-32 Module scope

```
Option Explicit
Dim Message As String
Sub Proc1()
    Debug.Print Message
End Sub
Private Sub Form_Load()
    Message = "Hello from Form_Load"
    Debug.Print Message
    Call Proc1
    Debug.Print Message
End Sub
```

This version prints out

```
Hello from Form_Load
Hello from Form_Load
Hello from Form_Load
```

OK, so what happens if you declare a variable in the General Declarations section of a module that has the same name as a variable in one or more procedures? For example, look at Listing 4-33.

Listing 4-33 Competing variables?

```
Option Explicit
Dim Message As String
Sub Proc1()
    Dim Message As String
    Message = "Hello from Proc1"
    Debug.Print Message
End Sub
Private Sub Form_Load()
    Dim Message As String
    Message = "Hello from Form_Load"
    Debug.Print Message
    Call Proc1
    Debug.Print Message
End Sub
```

This listing outputs

```
Hello from Form_Load
Hello from Proc1
Hello from Form_Load
```

This is the same output as Listing 4-31. When the program runs, the **Message** string in the General Declarations section is immediately created and has module scope. Any subroutine or function in the form can see and use it. But in **Form_Load**, you declare another **Message**. Any reference to **Message** in **Form_Load** automatically refers to the variable declared in that subroutine.

Note that although the **Message** in the **Form_Load** subroutine takes precedence, both **Message** variables are still in scope. Visual Basic 5 allows you to identify the module-level **Message** within **Form_Load** by placing the name of the module (**Form1**), followed by a dot, before its name. For example,

```
Debug.Print Form1.Message
```

Now reload the Sender program. Move the **Dim** statements from the **cmdAdd** routine to the General Declarations section of Sender. Listing 4-34 shows the new code. Now these variables have module scope, so the program works as advertised.

Listing 4-34 Sender 1 with module scope variables

```
Dim MailTime As Date
Dim MessageSent As Boolean
Private Sub cmdSend_Click()
    frmMain.txtBox.Text = txtBox.Text
    MailTime = Time
    MessageSent = True
End Sub
```

The World at Large

Let's try to poke around in Sender 1's private stuff. Add a Command button form named **cmdSnoop** and labeled **Snoop** in the **frmMain**. Add the line in Listing 4-35 to the **Click** event routine.

Listing 4-35 The Snoop button

```
Private Sub cmdSnoop_Click()
If frmSender1.MessageSent Then
    MsgBox "Sender 1 sent a message at " & frmSender1.MailTime
End If
End Sub
```

Run this program. When you try to snoop, you get a message that says **Method or data member not found**.

Private and Public Declarations

So far, we've used only the **Dim** statement to declare variables. Normally, you don't need to specify whether a variable is declared as public or private, because most of the time you want your variables to have private scope. Furthermore, variables declared within a subroutine or function are automatically private and cannot be declared public.

Visual Basic has two additional declaration statements that affect the scope of variables declared in the General Declarations section of a module, however. These are **Public** and **Private**.

Both **Public** and **Private** statements have the same syntax as the **Dim** statement. In fact, the **Private** statement is equivalent to the **Dim** statement. You might use it instead to underline the fact that you intend a particular variable to have private scope in the General Declarations section of a module.

In the Sender program, change the declarations in Sender 1 from

```
Dim MailTime As Date
Dim MessageSent As Boolean
```

to

```
Public MailTime As Date
Public MessageSent As Boolean
```

Run the program, send a message, and then try the Snoop button again. You're a regular Private Eye!

Procedure Scope

It is now time to consider subroutines and functions in more detail. Let's start by looking at the full syntax for subroutines and functions.

Subroutines have the following syntax:

```
[Private | Public] [Static] Sub name [( argumentlist)]
    [ statements ]
    [ Exit Sub ]
    [ statements ]
End Sub
```

Whereas the syntax for functions is

```
[Private | Public] [Static] Function name [( argumentlist)] [As type]
    [ statements ]
    [ name = expression ]
    [ Exit Function ]
    [ statements ]
    [ name = expression ]
End Function
```

Private Versus Public

The **Private** or **Public** keyword determines the scope of the subroutine or function. If you omit this part of the declaration, the subroutine or function will be public by default. Public subroutines and functions can be called from any module in your project, whereas private ones can be called only from within the module in which they are declared.

Standard Modules

So far, all the source code you've entered has been in form modules. There are two other types of modules in Visual Basic 5: class modules (which we'll discuss in Chapter 6, Forms, Menus, and MDI Forms) and standard modules. (In previous versions of Visual Basic, these were called code modules.) Standard modules contain only declarations and source code. Standard modules are a good place to put routines that may be common to several other forms or modules in a project.

Let's add a standard module to Sender. Under the Project menu, click on Add Module. VB opens up a Code window for the module. Notice that there is only one item under the Object drop-down menu in the Code window: General. Add the routine in Listing 4-36. Next bring up the Properties window for the module by pressing F4. There is only one property to change: the **Name** property. Change it now to **Code**.

Listing 4-36 A public Sub in a standard module

```
Public Sub Notify()
    MsgBox "Message has been sent to main form."
End Sub
```

Now you can call the routine from any of the other modules with the command

```
Code.Notify
```

To finish up, add this line to the Send button routines. For example, the Send button routine for the Sender 2 form looks like Listing 4-37.

Listing 4-37 Calling a standard module routine

```
Private Sub cmdSend_Click()
    frmMain.txtBox.Text = txtBox.Text
    Code.Notify
End Sub
```

Now when you save the project, VB prompts you to save the standard module, which uses the extension **.BAS**. Save it as **CODE.BAS**. As you build up module libraries of useful routines, you can add them to future programs simply by selecting the Add File... option of the File menu.

You can call public routines from outside a module without specifying the module name. For example, you could say **Notify** instead of **Code.Notify**. If you have a routine of the same name in the calling module, however, remember that Visual Basic always looks inside the current module first when trying to resolve references. This applies to subroutines, functions, variables, and constants. Visual Basic will not complain that there is a naming conflict because, as far as it is concerned, there isn't. It simply will look no further in trying to resolve a reference once it has been found.

Persistence of Variables

The life of a variable is termed its *persistence*. Normally, unless you expressly state otherwise, a variable has what is called *automatic persistence*. This means that the variable is automatically created when the procedure in which it exists is called.

To demonstrate this, consider Listing 4-38.

Listing 4-38 Automatic persistence

```
Private Sub Form_Load()
    AddSub
    AddSub
End Sub

Private Sub AddSub()
Dim Sum As Integer
    Sum = Sum + 1
    Debug.Print Sum
End Sub
```

The example outputs

```
1
1
```

In this example, when **AddSub** is called for the first time, **Sum** is declared with automatic persistence. This means that when **AddSub** ends, **Sum** is destroyed. (Do not confuse scope and persistence. They are two separate effects.)

You can alter the way you declare a variable if you wish it to have static persistence. Instead of using the **Dim** statement to declare it, use the **Static** statement. The **Static** statement has the same syntax as **Dim**, except that the variables declared with it survive between calls to the procedures in which they are contained. Change the **AddSub** routine in the above example, as shown in Listing 4-39.

Listing 4-39 Static persistence

```
Private Sub AddSub()
Static Sum As Integer
    Sum = Sum + 1
    Debug.Print Sum
End Sub
```

The **Sum** statement now keeps its value between calls, so the program now outputs

```
1
2
```

Compare the persistence of a variable declared in a subroutine or function with one declared in the General Declarations section of a module. Remember that variables declared in the General Declarations section are no different from variables declared anywhere else, except that they have module scope. The persistence of such variables doesn't change. They are created when the module is created, and they are destroyed when the module is destroyed.

The `Static` *Keyword*

You saw how the `Static` keyword controls the persistence of variables within the subroutine or function. The `Static` keyword in a subroutine or function declaration controls how *all* the variables in that procedure are declared. If you declare a procedure with the `Static` keyword, any variables declared within the body of the procedure will be static by default. You cannot override the persistence of variables in a procedure that has been declared `Static`.

Listing 4-40 shows the **AddSub** routine from the previous example rewritten to apply static variable persistence to all variables in the routine.

Listing 4-40 Static in subroutine definition

```
Private Static Sub AddSub()
    Dim Sum As Integer
    Sum = Sum + 1
    Debug.Print Sum
End Sub
```

1. What does the following code print out?

```
Const Dingo = "Dingo"
Const Salamander = "Salamander"
Private Sub Form_Load()
    Const MuskRat = "Loaded_MuskRat"
    Const Salamander = "Loaded_Salamander"
    Debug.Print Salamander, Dingo, MuskRat
End Sub
```

    a. `Loaded_Salamander`   `Dingo`   `Loaded_MuskRat`
    b. `Salamander`   `Dingo`   `Loaded_MuskRat`
    c. `Salamander`   `Dingo`   `MuskRat`
    d. `Loaded_Salamander`   `Loaded_Dingo`   `Loaded_Muskrat`

2. What does the following program print out?

```
Private Sub Form_Load()
    Dim Platypus, Dingo
    Dim Jack
    Platypus = "Platypus"
    Dingo = "Dingo"
    Jack = Hopping(Dingo)
    Debug.Print Jack, Platypus, Dingo
End Sub

Function Hopping(Animal)
    Platypus = "Jump, jump, platypus!"
    Hopping = "Hopping " & Animal
    If Animal = "Dingo" Then Dingo = "Hopping Dingo"
End Function
```

```
a. Hopping Dingo    Platypus                Dingo
b. Hopping Dingo    Jump, jump, platypus!   Dingo
c. Hopping Dingo    Jump, jump, platypus!   Hopping Dingo
d. Hopping Dingo    Platypus                Hopping Dingo
```

3. If a form named `frmDataSource` wants to make a variable called `InterestingStuff` available to a form named `frmWantsStuff`, which of the following declarations would produce this result?

   a.
   ```
   Private Sub Form_Load()
        Dim InterestingStuff
   End Sub
   ```

   b.
   ```
   Private Sub Form_Load()
        Public InterestingStuff
   End Sub
   ```

   c.
   ```
   Dim InterestingStuff
   Private Sub Form_Load()
   End Sub
   ```

   d.
   ```
   Public InterestingStuff
   Private Sub Form_Load()
   End Sub
   ```

4. If `frmWantsStuff` wants to display this value, which statement would it use?
   a. `MsgBox InterestingStuff`
   b. `MsgBox Public.InterestingStuff`
   c. `MsgBox frmDataSource.InterestingStuff`
   d. `MsgBox frmWantsStuff.InterestingStuff`

5. The `Static` keyword:
   a. Makes a variable available to outside functions
   b. Makes a variable maintain its value between procedure calls
   c. Forces a variable to reinitialize each time the procedure is called
   d. Refers to that stuff that makes your clothes stick to your socks

ARGUMENT LISTS

Both functions and subroutines can take arguments, values that they need to manipulate. The argument list has its own syntax that requires separate consideration.

The syntax for each argument in an argument list is

```
[Optional][ByVal | ByRef][ParamArray] varname As VarType [, ...]
```

PASSING MULTIPLE ARGUMENTS

You can declare as many parameters as you wish in the argument list of a subroutine or function, provided you separate each parameter with a comma. The basic syntax is to specify a name for the variable and the type of variable.

For example:

```
Private Sub PrintNumbers(Var1 As Integer, Var2 As Integer)
Debug.Print Var1
Debug.Print Var2
End Sub
```

You then call **PrintNumbers** from **Form_Load**, specifying the arguments after the subroutine name as follows:

```
Private Sub Form_Load()
PrintNumbers 1, 2
End Sub
```

Execute the above example, and the values **1** and **2** are successfully passed to **Var1** and **Var2**.

Var1 and **Var2** require no further declaration syntax. It is enough to declare them in the parameter list of the subroutine or function. Don't forget that when you pass arguments to functions, or to subroutines with the **Call** statement, you must enclose the arguments within parentheses.

ByVal *and* ByRef

When you pass parameters to a subroutine or function, you can do so in two ways: either by value (**ByVal**) or by reference (**ByRef**). Let's look at the distinction between the two methods.

ByVal means that the *value* of the variable used in the parameter list of the call will be passed to the called procedure. The contents of the variable will be unchanged by anything you do to the destination variable in the called procedure.

This is demonstrated by the example in Listing 4-41.

Listing 4-41 Passing parameters by value

```
Private Sub Form_Load()
    Dim ANumber As Integer
    ANumber = 1
    Inc ANumber
    Debug.Print "Value after function is: " & ANumber
End Sub

Private Sub Inc(ByVal IncSubsNumber As Integer)
    Debug.Print "Inc was passed: " & IncSubsNumber
    IncSubsNumber = IncSubsNumber + 1
    Debug.Print "New value is: " & IncSubsNumber
End Sub
```

This program outputs

```
Inc was passed: 1
New value is: 2
Value after function is: 1
```

ANumber in Form_Load is unaffected by the addition in Inc. This is because only the value of ANumber has been passed to IncSubsNumber. IncSubsNumber is a completely separate variable.

Now try this example again, but change ByVal in Inc to ByRef as follows:

```
Private Sub Inc(ByRef IncSubsNumber As Integer)
```

This time the output is

```
Inc was passed: 1
New value is: 2
Value after function is: 2
```

A *reference* to ANumber is passed to IncSubsNumber, not the value. Therefore, as far as the computer is concerned, both ANumber and IncSubsNumber are referencing the same integer in memory.

You can remove the keyword ByRef and the routine will still increment ANumber. This is because unless you specify otherwise, all variables are passed by reference.

Optional Arguments

There are times when it is inappropriate to pass all the variables in a parameter list to a subroutine or function. This is typically the case when parameters later in the list are dependent on specific values of variables earlier in the list. To declare a parameter as optional, include the Optional keyword in the parameter declaration.

For example, in the subroutine in Listing 4-42, Var1Length applies only if Var1 is a string.

Listing 4-42 Optional arguments

```
Private Sub MySub (Var1 As Variant, Optional Var1Length As Variant)
If TypeName(Var1) = "String" Then
    Debug.Print Var1Length
Else
    Debug.Print "Not a string"
End If
End Sub
```

There are some restrictions in the use of optional parameters. For instance, when you declare a parameter as optional, all subsequent parameters in the list must also be optional. Also, variables that are declared Optional can only be variants.

Named Arguments

Normally, when you pass parameters to subroutines and functions, you do so in the order specified in the parameter list of the called procedure. You do not have to do this, however, because Visual Basic allows you to name which parameter applies to which variable. For example, the following subroutine requires three parameters:

```
Private Sub MySub (IntVar As Integer, StringVar As String, NumVar As Double)
Debug.Print IntVar
Debug.Print StringVar
Debug.Print NumVar
End Sub
```

You could call this subroutine in the following way:

```
Private Sub Form_Load()
MySub 5, "Hi", 3.14
End Sub
```

Alternatively, you can name the parameters in the call and vary the order in which the parameters appear when you make the call:

```
Private Sub Form_Load()
MySub NumVar := 3.14, IntVar := 5, StringVar := "Hi"
End Sub
```

The `:=` syntax ensures that the correct parameter is referenced by the compiler. Most of VB 5's built-in procedures support named parameters. To find out the parameter names, look up the online help topic entry.

Type Declaration Characters

In Chapter 3, Variables, Constants, and Associated Functions, you saw type declaration characters used in variable declaration. However, you can also use them when declaring functions and subroutines. For instance, the following two functions are equivalent:

```
Public Function MoneyFunction (Var1 As Integer, Var2 As String) As Currency
End Function

Public Function MoneyFunction@(Var1%, Var2$)
End Function
```

Note how the second declaration of `MyFunction` doesn't require the `As Currency` syntax at the end of the declaration. It is simply enough to append the type declaration character `@` to the function name to indicate that it returns a currency data type.

You're almost finished with your tour of the Visual Basic 5 applications language. There's one last topic to master before you graduate, however: arrays.

Hint: As a rule, avoid the use of type declaration characters. (There are places where they are necessary, as you will see in Chapter 12, Files.) It is far easier to declare variable types explicitly and to name your variables with a naming convention that tells you what type they are than to try to remember whether to use # or % with a variable name.

1. Which subroutine cannot change the value of the argument passed to it?
   a. `Sub Changes(ByRef var)`
   b. `Sub Changes(ByVal var)`
   c. `Sub Changes(var)`
   d. `Sub Changes(Optional var)`

2. What is the output of the following program?

```
Dim A
Public C
Private Sub Form_Load()
    Dim B
    A = 1
    For C = 1 To 3
     B = PartyTime(C)
    Next C
    Debug.Print A, B, C, D
End Sub

Function PartyTime(D)
    Static A
    A = A + 1
    PartyTime = D
   D = D + 2
End Function
```

   a. 2   1   4
   b. 4   3   4
   c. 4   3   3
   d. 1   1   4

3. Which of the following is the only valid function call for:

```
Sub SendMe(AString$, ANumber%, ADate@, Optional MaybeMe)
```

   a. `Call SendMe(Him$, It%, ThisString$)`
   b. `SendMe Her$,ADate := LastDay@, It%`
   c. `SendMe ADate:=LastDay@, AString:=It%, ANumber:=Num%`
   d. `SendMe Its$, Num%, MaybeMe:=Her$, ADate:=LastDay@`

4. What is the output of the following program?

```
Private Sub Form_Load()
    Var1 = 0
    Process Var1
    Debug.Print Var1
End Sub

Sub Process(ByVal Var)
    Var = Var + 10
```

```
        Wring Var
    End Sub

    Sub Wring(ByVal Var1)
        Var1 = Var1 * Var1
        ShakeOut Var1
    End Sub

    Sub ShakeOut(Var1)
        Var1 = Var1 + 159
    End Sub
```

   a. 10
   b. 100
   c. 259
   d. 0

5. Which of the following is a valid use of the `Optional` keyword?
   a. `Sub Sub1(v1$, v2 As Integer, Optional v3 As Integer, v4 as Date)`
   b. `Sub Sub1(v1$, v2 As Integer, Optional v3 As Integer)`
   c. `Sub Sub1(v1$, v2 As Integer, Optional v3)`
   d. `Sub Sub1(v1$, v2 As Integer, Optional v3$)`

ARRAYS

An array is essentially a grouping of identical variable types, arranged together in one or more dimensions. One way to think about an array is as a list of related values. You can look at any one element in the list by accessing its *index*, its position in the list. This is best explained by looking at a working example. Let's assume you need to store a set of four currency variables, representing the sales figures for four departments of a company for one month of the year. To do this, you could simply declare four separate variables, as follows:

```
Dim SalesDept1Jan As Currency, SalesDept2Jan As Currency
Dim SalesDept3Jan As Currency, SalesDept4Jan As Currency
```

Although this would work, it is not the most efficient way of programming a solution to this particular problem. For instance, if you wanted to add all the figures together, you would have to do so explicitly, as follows:

```
TotalSalesAllDeptsJan = SalesDept1Jan + SalesDept2Jan + SalesDept3Jan + SalesDept4Jan
```

If the number of departments were much larger, say 100, it would be impractical to refer to each variable individually in any calculation. There is also the inherent inflexibility of such a solution. If the number of departments were to change, it would be a lot of work to make the corresponding changes to your program.

The Dim **Statement Revisited**

Declaring an array in your program is called *dimensioning* an array, and was, once upon a time, the exclusive use of the **Dim** statement. Arrays cannot be implicitly declared. Recall that the **Dim** statement syntax is

```
Dim varname [([subscripts])] As [New] type [, varname ...]
```

In the basic array declaration, the subscript's parameter is the array's upper bound. In the example above, you could achieve the same functionality using an array of four elements, where each element represents one department, as follows:

```
Dim SalesJan(4) As Currency
```

This declaration creates the currency variables with the same variable name. Each variable in the array can be accessed by specifying its index, in parentheses, after the name of the array. Start a new project and enter Listing 4-43 to see how this works.

Listing 4-43 Array

```
Private Sub Form_Load()
Dim SalesJan(4) As Currency
Dim TotalSales As Currency
Dim Counter As Integer

SalesJan(1) = 150000
SalesJan(2) = 220000
SalesJan(3) = 125000
SalesJan(4) = 183000

For Counter = 1 To 4
    TotalSales = TotalSales + SalesJan(Counter)
Next Counter
Debug.Print TotalSales
Stop
End Sub
```

Run the program. The output is

```
678000
```

Index Numbering

When you declared the array, you specified the upper bound of the highest-numbered element in parentheses. The first (base) element in the array, however, has an index of 0. This is because index numbering in Visual Basic begins at 0, unless you specify otherwise. Listing 4-43 has a **Stop** statement, so when you run the program you go into break mode. Go to the Debug window and type

```
Print SalesJan(0)
```

This statement outputs

0

because you haven't assigned a value to element **0**.

Changing the Base Index

You can change the index number that represents the first element in the array in two ways.

● Using the **Option Base** statement

● Within the **Dim** statement itself

Option Base

The **Option Base** statement sets the number of the first element in an array (the base element) to either 0 or 1. If you do not include an **Option Base** statement in your program, the default option base is 0, as you have already seen.

You must place the **Option Base** statement in the General Declarations section of a module. It cannot appear inside a subroutine or function. When it appears in a module, it affects all the arrays in that module.

Dim *Statement*

You can specify the base index at the time you declare your array by using the **To** keyword in the declaration of the array subscript as follows:

```
Dim SalesJan(1 To 4) As Currency
```

This way, you can use index ranges that apply to the particular situation you are coding for. Note that when you use this method, you can use any numbers you choose as lower and upper boundaries.

```
Dim HighArray(100 To 200) As Integer
Dim LowArray(-200 To -100) As Integer
```

If you try to access an array element outside the lower or upper bound, you get the **Subscript out of Range** runtime error.

Multiple Dimensions

All arrays must have some dimension. The simplest array, the type you have seen, has one dimension. More complex arrays may have two, three, or more. For example, let's expand the array by keeping track of the whole year's sales at each of the four departments:

```
Option Base 1
Dim Sales(12, 4) As Currency
```

Here, the first dimension in the array represents the month of the year, and the second dimension represents the department. For example, `Sales(1,1)` refers to the January figures in the first department. So, to display the sales figures for December for the third department, you would write

```
Debug.Print Sales(12, 3)
```

To access each element in the array, you would write a nested loop, such as:

```
Dim Month As Integer, Dept As Integer
For Month = 1 To 12
    For Dept = 1 To 4
        ' Do something with Sales(Month, Dept)
    Next Dept
Next Month
```

Dynamic Array Sizing

Some of the time, you will find that you know the number of elements that you will need for an array when you write your program. For instance, an array such as ours has 12 elements in the first dimension, corresponding to the 12 months of the year. Because this figure is static, you can safely hardcode the number of elements in the first dimension.

However, you can also allow for situations in which the number of elements is not fixed. In these situations, use the `Dim` statement in conjunction with the `ReDim` statement. When you declare your array using `Dim`, leave the number of elements and dimensions blank, so that your array declaration is as follows:

```
Dim Sales() As Currency
```

You have told Visual Basic that `Sales` is to be an array, but you do not yet know the array's dimensions. Before you can use the array, you have to provide this information using the `ReDim` statement. For example:

```
ReDim Sales(12, 4)
```

These two statements are equivalent to the single `Dim` statement used earlier, except that the `ReDim` statement can be called as many times as you wish and the array bounds can be passed as variables. (Array boundaries declared with `Dim` must be numbers or constants.)

You could therefore write

```
Dim Sales() As Currency
Dim Months As Integer, Depts As Integer
Months = 12
Depts = 4
ReDim Sales(Months, Depts)
```

When you use dynamic array sizing, you must use one of the two standard base index numbering schemes (0 or 1). You cannot use the `To` keyword in the `Dim` statement to declare your own base index.

Each time you `ReDim` the array, the contents of the array are destroyed. In fact, the array is completely destroyed, and the memory it was using is released. Then a new array is created according to the new specification.

There are times when you want to retain the contents of the array and just change the size of one of its dimensions. Visual Basic allows you to do this using the `Preserve` keyword in the `ReDim` statement. This is particularly useful when you wish to "grow" an array at runtime. For example, assume you want to read some information from a file, but you do not know how many items of information are in the file. You could read through the file once, counting how many items there are, and then use a single `ReDim` statement to allocate an array large enough. However, what if the information were coming from a communications line? In that situation, you wouldn't have the opportunity of preparsing the data to determine the number of items. The solution is to use the `Preserve` keyword in conjunction with `ReDim`, as shown in Listing 4-44.

Listing 4-44 The `Preserve` keyword

```
Dim MyArray() As String
Dim NumElements As Integer
Dim MoreData As Boolean

'Read data from communications line and set MoreData to True if data was read
Do While MoreData
    NumElements = NumElements + 1
    ReDim Preserve MyArray(NumElements)
    'code to assign data to MyArray
    'Read data from communications line
    'and set MoreData to True if data was read
Loop
```

For Each...Next **Loop**

The `For Each...Next` loop is a special type of loop designed to be used with arrays and collections. We will consider collections in Chapter 6, Forms, Menus, and MDI Forms, when we look at classes and objects. The `For Each...Next` loop has the following syntax:

```
For Each element In array
    [statements]
    [Exit For]
    [statements]
Next [element]
```

The `For Each...Next` loop works by cycling through each element in an array without you having to specify the element's index. Each time through the loop, the variable element is assigned the contents of the next item in the array. To continue the previous example, which involved growing an array using `ReDim Preserve`, you could then use a `For Each...Next` loop to print out each element of the array as follows:

```
Dim Element As Variant
For Each Element In MyArray
    Debug.Print Element
Next Element
```

The loop starts at the first element in the array (**MyArray(0)**) and loops for each element in that array. Notice that the **Element** variable has to be **Variant**, no matter what type of array **MyArray** is.

The Erase Statement

The way the **Erase** statement works depends on the type of array you are using it with. If you use it with a statically sized array, it sets each element in the array to its preinitialized value. For example:

```
Dim StringArray(10) As String
Dim IntArray(10) As Integer
Erase StringArray      'Each element set to ""
Erase IntArray         'Each element set to 0
```

If you use it with an array of variants, each variant is set to **Empty**. However, if you use it with a dynamically sized array, the memory used by the array is freed:

```
Dim MyArray() As Currency
ReDim MyArray(6,7,8)
Erase MyArray    'memory used by MyArray is freed,
                         'as if the ReDim statement had not been executed
```

You can specify more than one array to erase by separating the names of the arrays with commas. For example:

```
Dim MyStringArray(10) As String
Dim MyCurrencyArray(10) As Currency
Dim MyIntegerArray(10) As Integer
Erase MyStringArray, MyCurrencyArray, MyIntegerArray
```

LBound and UBound

These two functions return the lower and upper bound indexes in the array. For example:

```
Dim MyArray(10) As String
Debug.Print LBound(MyArray)
Debug.Print UBound(MyArray)
```

If an array has more than one dimension, you can specify the dimension as an optional second parameter to these functions:

```
Dim MyArray(10, 11, 6 To 12)
Debug.Print LBound(MyArray, 3)
```

This code prints **6**—the lower bound index of the third dimension.

ParamArray

In Lesson 7, you learned about passing arguments to procedures. There is one additional keyword you can use in procedure declarations: `ParamArray`. The `ParamArray` keyword allows you to pass an arbitrary number of different types of arguments in an argument list.

To use a `ParamArray`, just specify the last parameter in a parameter list as a `ParamArray Variant` array, as shown in Listing 4-45.

Listing 4-45 The `ParamArray` keyword

```
Private Sub Form_Load()
Dim A As Integer, B As String
Dim C As Single, D As Currency, E As Double
A = 5
B = "Some Text"
C = 3.14
D = 100.45
E = 1 / 5.6
MySub 1, 2, A, B, C, D, E
End Sub

Private Sub MySub(Num1%, Num2%, ParamArray Param3() As Variant)
Dim Var As Variant
Debug.Print "Lower bound: " & LBound(Param3)
Debug.Print "Upper bound: " & UBound(Param3)
For Each Var In Param3
    Debug.Print Var
Next Var
End Sub
```

This code outputs

```
Lower bound: 0
Upper bound: 4
 5
Some Text
 3.14
 100.45
 0.178571428571429
```

Wow! You know a lot. In Chapter 5, Controls, you'll start to have some real fun using these wonderful commands to explore the VB controls in more detail.

1. An array is:
   a. Kind of like a list
   b. A grouping of identical variable types
   c. A way of thinking about (and treating) similar variables together
   d. All of the above

2. How many elements are in the following array?

```
Option Base 0
Dim Sales(4) As Currency
```

a. 4

b. 5

c. 0

d. Impossible to tell without more information

3. What is the output of the following program?

```
Option Base 1
Private Sub Form_Load()
    Dim UnderWater(-10 To 10)
    Dim Normal(10)
    Dim AbNormal(0 To 10)
    Debug.Print LBound(UnderWater), LBound(Normal), LBound(AbNormal)
End Sub
```

a. 0   1   0

b. 10   0   0

c. −10   1   0

d. −10   0   1

4. What is the total number of elements in the following array?

```
Option Base 1
Dim TwoLevel(2,3) As Integer
```

a. 2

b. 3

c. 5

d. 6

5. What is the output from the following program?

```
Option Base 1
Private Sub Form_Load()
    Dim Letters() As String
    Dim Word As String
    Dim I As Integer
    Dim Element As Variant
    Word = "good"
    For I = 1 To Len(Word)
                ReDim Preserve Letters(I)
      Letters(I) = Left(Word, I)
    Next I
    For Each Element In Letters()
      Debug.Print Element
    Next
End Sub
```

a.
g
go
goo
good
b.
good
good
good
good
c.
good
d.
good

EXERCISE

Rewrite the **Sum** routine for the **Adder** program so that it takes an arbitrary number of arguments, adds them all, and returns the result. Include code to test the program with several sets of input and output the results.

CHAPTER 5

CONTROLS

earning to program in Visual Basic isn't just about learning the language. As you've already seen, Visual Basic comes complete with a wide variety of controls that you can use in your programs. Because these controls offer so much built-in functionality, learning to use the controls adeptly is half the game.

In this chapter, we'll look in more detail at the controls you've already used, and we'll introduce many of VB's other controls. To demonstrate the controls, we'll build a data entry application. This will help you understand not only *how* to use the individual controls but *when* to use them.

The controls you'll explore in this chapter are

- TextBox
- Label
- CommandButton
- CheckBox
- OptionButton
- Frame
- ListBox
- ComboBox

Additionally, we'll talk about tab order, accelerator keys, how to use the values in one control to affect the behavior of other controls, and some new, useful properties. Finally, we'll cover the advanced topic of control arrays.

THE TEXTBOX CONTROL

Different controls perform different roles in your programs. As you've seen, however, they all conform to the same fundamental programming interface. Once you've learned how to use one control, you should find it quite straightforward to apply what you've learned to a different one.

Let's begin our look at controls with the TextBox control. As you saw in Chapter 1, What's All That Stuff on My Screen?, TextBox is a control that allows the user to type in text from the keyboard and store it in your program. Some people call it an edit control, because it allows you to edit text.

The Data Entry Program

Here's the scenario: You've been given the task of writing a data entry program as part of a suite of programs that store and retrieve information about the members of a video library and the videotapes they have borrowed. You need to design a data entry form that can be used for a number of different purposes:

- To allow registration of a new member
- To allow an existing member's personal details to be retrieved
- To register when a member withdraws or returns a tape

Start a new project and place a text box on the default form. (Peek ahead at Figure 5-2 to get an idea about placement.)

TextBox Properties

Select the text box and press F4 to bring up the Properties window. Let's take a closer look at how property values work.

Select the **Appearance** property and click to view its possible values. Notice (Figure 5-1) that the actual text is **0 - Flat** and **1 - 3D**, as opposed to simply **Flat** and **3D**. Remember that properties are simply variables that exist inside the control. Therefore, each property must be a specific type of variable.

It turns out that the **Appearance** property is an integer. The list box that lets you set the value of the **Appearance** property provides you with a textual description of the two possible values. When you change the property from **3D** to **Flat**, you are actually changing it from **1** to **0**. It is often important to know what type of variable a particular property is, particularly if you wish to read or set the property value in your program code. For example, to change the TextBox style to **Flat**, you would code

```
Text1.Appearance = 0
```

When you change the appearance from **3D** to **Flat**, the text box is immediately redrawn, but without the 3D appearance it had earlier. (Change it back to **3D** now, because you want to keep the 3D appearance throughout this data entry program.)

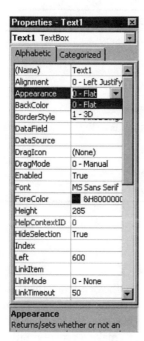

Figure 5-1
Changing the
Appearance
property from
3D to flat

An easy way to find out what a particular property does and what the values mean is to select the property using the mouse and then press the F1 key. Visual Basic displays a Help window telling you how to use that property.

Now change the name of this text box to **txtMemID**. The three-letter prefixes we've been using, **txt**, **lbl**, and **cmd**, are a convention that many programmers use to help identify their controls by their type. We'll introduce other prefixes for the other standard controls as we go along, although there's nothing to stop you from choosing your own conventions.

The Text *Property*

You've already used the **Text** property for input in other example programs. The **Text** property is a string that contains the text that the user has typed in.

The default value of this property is **Text1**. If you don't delete this text from the **Text** property prior to running your program, the text box will display **Text1** when the program runs. There will probably be times when you want to use this feature of preloading the **Text** property with some text to serve as a default value. However, you don't want to do this now, so remove the text before you continue.

Now add three more text boxes to **Form1**. The text boxes you've added to the form so far are summarized in Table 5-1.

Table 5-1 The TextBox controls

Object	Property	Value
TextBox	Name	txtMemID
	Text	None
TextBox	Name	txtFirstName
	Text	None
TextBox	Name	txtSurname
	Text	None
TextBox	Name	txtAddress
	Text	None

Try to position the controls so that they appear in roughly the same positions as those shown in Figure 5-2.

The MultiLine *Property*

The difference between the address text box and the other text boxes is that you want the address text box to store more than one line of text. If you run the program as it stands and attempt to enter an address into txtAddress, you'll find that making the address text box large enough isn't sufficient to make it accept multiple lines of text.

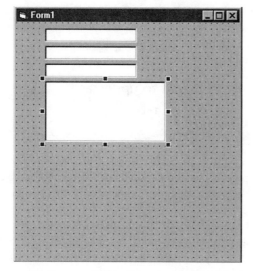

Figure 5-2
View of Form1
after name and
address text boxes
have been added

To add the functionality you want, you need to change the **MultiLine** property of the text box txtAddress to **True**. Rerun the program and enter an address (street, city, state, and Zip code). You'll find that you can now enter more than one line of text by pressing (ENTER) at the end of a line.

The ScrollBars *Property*

The only remaining problem with the address text box is that you cannot enter an address that is wider than the actual width of the text box. The text box automatically wraps the text for you, rather like a word processor. It would be better if the text box displayed a scroll bar to allow the user to scroll the contents of the text box. The **ScrollBars** property lets you switch on this functionality.

This property can be set to **None**, **Horizontal**, **Vertical**, or **Both**. If you like, experiment with the different settings to see how they affect the text box's behavior. When you're done, set the value to **3 - Both**.

Now that you've added all the text boxes that you need, let's look at how you can interact with them in your program.

The KeyPress *Event*

Let's say that to adhere to the product specification, the text box containing the member ID should automatically capitalize all the text typed into it. Double-click on the TextBox control to bring up the Code window. This puts you in the **Change** event, the default event for the text box. This particular event is one that is called *after* the text in a text box has changed. You need to convert each character typed into uppercase *before* the character has been added, so you want the **KeyPress** event.

Select the Code window's Proc ComboBox to create an event subroutine for the **KeyPress** event. Visual Basic adds the full declaration for the subroutine for you. This is nice, especially for routines such as this one with parameters.

Add the code in Listing 5-1 to the **KeyPress** subroutine.

Listing 5-1   Convert the key pressed to uppercase

```
Private Sub txtMemID_KeyPress(KeyAscii As Integer)
  KeyAscii = Asc(UCase(Chr(KeyAscii)))
End Sub
```

The **KeyAscii** parameter is an integer that represents the character that's been pressed. When the user presses a key on the keyboard, Visual Basic converts that key to a number in the ASCII character set. For example, the lowercase letter a is converted by Visual Basic to the ASCII number 97.

You passed the number to the **Chr** function, which, as you saw in Chapter 2, Object-Oriented Programming, converts ASCII numbers to strings. You then take the character that's been returned to you by the **Chr** function and passed that to the **UCase** function, which converts lowercase characters to uppercase characters. Finally, you converted the result back to an ASCII value with the **Asc** function. Note that in cases like this, when you use "nested" function calls, the innermost expression, in this case, **Chr(KeyAscii)**, is *always* evaluated first. Note also that because the **KeyAscii** parameter is passed by reference, changing its value in the function changes the character the user sees on the screen.

Run your program now and see the effect this one line of code has had on your text box.

If you don't want the text box to accept the key that the user has entered, you can "throw it away" by setting the value of **KeyAscii** to **0**.

Validating User Input

Many data entry programs need to perform some sort of validation on the text that has been entered into a text box. Typically, you want this validation to take place after the user has completed the entry in the text box.

You'll use the **LostFocus** event here, as you did to validate the date the user entered in the Timesheet program in Chapter 3, Variables, Constants, and Associated Functions. You'll also learn a new method—**SetFocus**—that you'll use to force the user to stay in the text box until he or she enters valid data.

The SetFocus *Event*

Let's add some new functionality to **txtMemID**. You want to make sure that only alphabetical (A to Z) or numeric characters (0 to 9) have been entered. If the user enters invalid characters, the **SetFocus** method forces the cursor to move back onto the text box so the user can correct the input. Recall that the syntax for calling an object's method is

```
ControlName.MethodName
```

Use the Code window to add the declaration for the **LostFocus** event subroutine for the txtMemID control, and then add the code in Listing 5-2 to the subroutine.

Listing 5-2 Validating user input

```
Private Sub txtMemID_LostFocus()
Dim I As Integer
Dim Character As String

For I = 1 To Len(txtMemID.Text)
    Character = Mid(txtMemID.Text, I, 1)
    If (Character < "A" Or Character > "Z") And _
        (Character < "0" Or Character > "9") Then
        Beep
        txtMemID.SetFocus
        Exit For
    End If
Next I
End Sub
```

The **If** statement in the listing is saying that an invalid character has been entered if the character is outside the range A to Z and the range 0 to 9. The check relies on the ordering of characters in the ASCII character set. The character A has the lowest ASCII value of the uppercase characters, and the character Z has the highest. Similarly, the digit 0 has the lowest value in the character range 0 to 9.

Once you've detected that there's a character outside either of these ranges in the **Text** property of the control, beep the speaker once and return the focus to the text box. Now run your program and type

ABCD****1234

into the membership number text box. You can type the four asterisks, but when you try to move the focus to one of the other text boxes, you will find that you are unable to do so.

The program is a little user-unfriendly now, though. The user can type in that text box all day long and never figure out why he or she can't seem to leave it. You need a touch more code. Change the original code in the **LostFocus** event by adding the new code, shown in bold print below.

```
Private Sub txtMemID_LostFocus()
Dim I As Integer
Dim Character As String
For I = 1 To Len(txtMemID.Text)
    Character = Mid(txtMemID.Text, I, 1)
    If (Character < "A" Or Character > "Z") And _
        (Character < "0" Or Character > "9") Then
            MsgBox "Enter only letters and numbers, please", 48, "Note:"
        txtMemID.SetFocus
        Exit For
    End If
Next I
End Sub
```

Notice that the "beep" has been removed; your user does not want everybody in the office to know he or she has made a mistake. Now a message box tells the user how to fix the problem. When the user clicks on OK, he or she will be back in `txtMemID`, ready to fix the problem. We will look more closely at the `MsgBox` function in Lesson 2.

1. If you don't change the default value of the `Text` property for a text box, what displays in it when the program runs?
   a. Nothing.
   b. No answer; you must set this value.
   c. The caption.
   d. The same default value that VB gives the `Name` property, such as `Text1`

2. How do you set up a text box to allow more than one line of input?
   a. Instruct the user to press ENTER or SHIFT-ENTER at the end of a line.
   b. Set the `MultiLine` property to `True`.
   c. Set the `ScrollBars` property to `1-Horizontal`.
   d. Set the `ScrollBars` property to `2-Vertical` or `3-Both`.

3. What are the type and contents of the variable passed to the `KeyPress` event routine?
   a. `String`; the key pressed
   b. `String`; the text entered so far
   c. `Integer`; `1` for A, `2` for B, and so on
   d. `Integer`; the ASCII value of the key pressed

4. Validate input in the `KeyPress` routine if it's important to:
   a. "Catch" the input before it appears on-screen
   b. Validate an entire string of input
   c. Validate input after the control loses focus
   d. Use `SetFocus` to force the user to stay on the control

5. What is the name of the event that is triggered when the focus moves away from a control?
   a. `Change`
   b. `LostFocus`
   c. `Click`
   d. `GotFocus`

LABELS AND THE MsgBox FUNCTION

You've already used Label controls both for captions and for message output. In this lesson, you'll learn more about how to use these ubiquitous objects. Additionally, we'll take a closer look at one of Visual Basic's more versatile functions, **MsgBox**.

Label Controls

You should try to make your forms as intuitive as possible to use. Where you position your labels will have an important effect on the overall form design. Typically, labels are to the left of the controls they describe.

Add the four labels described in Table 5-2 to the form. Table 5-2 also includes a Command button; add this now so you have a place to output results.

Table 5-2 The video membership labels

Object	Property	Value
Label	Caption	Membership Number
Label	Caption	First Name
Label	Caption	Surname
Label	Caption	Address
CommandButton	Caption	Ok
	Name	cmdOk

The Alignment *Property*

The Label control has an **Alignment** property. You can use this to left-, right-, or center-align the label's caption on the form. Try right-aligning the labels. It's more pleasant to look at a form that has right-aligned labels because the gap between the end of the caption and the beginning of the text box to which the caption relates is kept to a minimum. Try to make your form appear as in Figure 5-3.

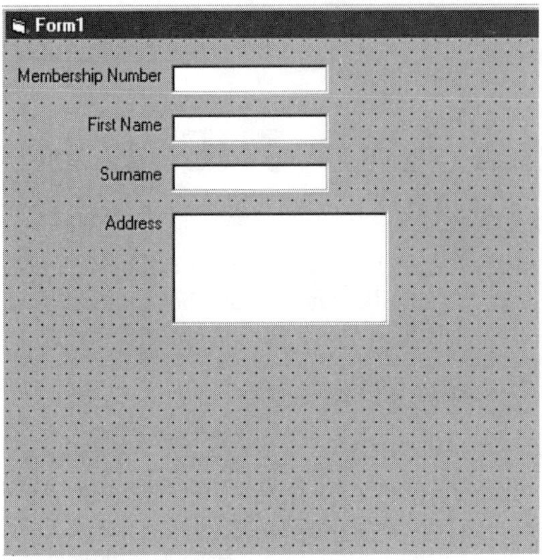

Figure 5-3
Form1 with right-aligned labels

Tab Order and the `TabIndex` *Property*

When your program is running, you can move from control to control on the form by pressing TAB or SHIFT-TAB. Each time you press TAB, the cursor jumps to a different control. In fact, the cursor is following a set order when it jumps from one control to another. This order is called the *tab order*, and it is controlled by the value of the `TabIndex` property. Any control that is capable of receiving the focus has a `TabIndex` property.

Accelerator Keys

When forms have many controls on them, it can be helpful to your program's users to give them shortcuts for moving about a form. Many people still prefer to use the keyboard when entering data. This is where *accelerator keys* come in.

Visual Basic's development environment uses accelerator keys all the time. Take a look at any of the dialog boxes (say, the Options dialog box in the Tools menu), and you'll see that each label has a caption in which an underline appears below one of the letters. That letter is the accelerator key for that control in that dialog box.

Accelerators work by letting the user press a combination of ALT and the character under which the underline appears. In the Environment Options dialog box, therefore, you can press ALT-A to set or clear the Align Controls to Grid check box.

You can provide the same functionality in your own programs by adding an accelerator to an object's caption or, if the object doesn't have a caption, to the caption of the label preceding the object.

To add an accelerator key to a caption, simply place an ampersand (&) just before the letter in the caption that you want to be the accelerator. Label1's caption should therefore read &Membership Number, Label2's &First Name, Label3's &Surname, and Label4's &Address.

If you want to use an & character in a label without its being interpreted as an accelerator, there are two techniques you can use. One is to use two ampersands in a row. The Label control will interpret an **&&** sequence as a single ampersand character.

Another way to achieve the same effect is to set the Label control's **UseMnemonic** property to **False**. This has the effect of turning off the interpretation of & characters as accelerators.

After you add the ampersand character to a caption, you'll see the caption has an underline underneath the accelerator character (see Figure 5-4).

If you run the program now, your accelerators may not work as expected. Go back to design mode and take a look at the **TabIndex** values for your labels and text boxes. If you've added the controls to the form in the order that we've prescribed, you'll find that they are set as in Table 5-3.

Table 5-3 Default TabIndex values

Control	TabIndex **Value**
txtMemID	0
txtFirstname	1
txtSurname	2
txtAddress	3
Label1	4
Label2	5
Label3	6
Label4	7
cmdOk	8

Visual Basic 5 sets the **TabIndex** value to the next available number when you add controls to a form. In addition to controlling the order in which the focus jumps from one control to another, the **TabIndex** value is important because it also controls how the accelerators on a Label control work. The focus will jump to the next control in the tab order when you press the accelerator key for a particular label because the label itself is unable to receive the focus. It is therefore important that you set the **TabIndex** values for all your controls in a logical order; otherwise, the accelerators on your labels will not work as expected.

Set the **TabIndex** values for the eight controls as in Table 5-4.

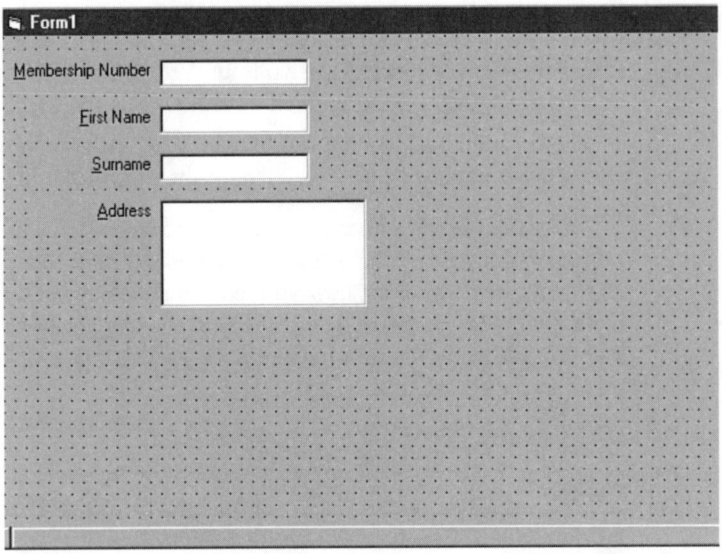

Figure 5-4
Form1 after
accelerators have
been added

Table 5-4 TabIndex values for accelerator keys

Control	TabIndex **Value**
Label1	0
txtMemID	1
Label2	2
txtFirstname	3
Label3	4
txtSurname	5
Label4	6
txtAddress	7
cmdOk	8

Sometimes you may have a control that you do not want to receive focus in the tab order. The `TabStop` property provides the answer. Set `TabStop` to `False` and the control will no longer be part of the tab sequence.

Make sure you start changing the `TabIndex` values of the control that you want to take the lowest value. Change Label1 first. If you don't do this and try to change the values in a random order, Visual Basic may have to alter the `TabIndex` values to fit what you've asked it to do, which is probably not what you *wanted* it to do.

The MsgBox *Function*

Now that the Video Store program has enough of an interface to begin testing it, it's time to program a routine to do something with the input. You'll use the **MsgBox** function inside **cmdOk**'s **click** routine to display the data the user enters.

You've used the **MsgBox** function a few times already to output brief messages with a single OK button to the user. This usage, such as

```
MsgBox "Hello out there!"
```

is simple and will serve you well for as long as you program in Visual Basic. However, this example barely scratches the surface of **MsgBox**. Its complete syntax is

```
MsgBox(prompt[, buttons][, title][, helpfile, context])
```

As you've seen, the **prompt** parameter gives the message (or prompt) to show to the user. If you need to build a long output string, as you'll do in a little while, you may want to put this value in a variable.

We'll talk about the **buttons** parameter below. The **title** parameter is simply the text that appears across the title bar of the message box. This defaults to your application's name. The **helpfile** and **context** arguments implement context-sensitive help for the message box. See the VB online help for more details.

The **MsgBox** function can have one, two, or three buttons. The function returns which button the user pressed. Before we talk about these values, however, we need to take a quick detour and talk about VB 5's predefined constants.

Predefined Constants

Recall that a constant is a way of representing a number symbolically. In the grocery program example in Chapter 3, Variable, Constants, and Associated Functions, for example, you assigned numbers to constant fruit names. You could therefore refer to an apple as APPLE, rather than having to remember that an apple is number 1. Using constants in code prevents bugs because you are less likely to assign incorrect values. Also, constants make the code easier to write and read.

Visual Basic 5 has a number of predefined constants you can use with its functions, properties, and commands. These constants all have the prefix **vb**. Like constants you define in your own programs, predefined constants make code more readable. Constants also save you from having to remember (or spend time looking up) values for parameters. Using predefined constants, you can show a form as modal, for example, with the statement:

```
Form2.Show vbModal
```

rather than

```
Form2.Show 1
```

To browse through VB 5's predefined constants, search the help system for Visual Basic constants, or just constants.

MsgBox *Constants*

The **button** parameter of **MsgBox** can take the values summarized in Table 5-5. You can combine values by adding them together.

Table 5-5 Constants for the **MsgBox button** parameter

Constant	Description
vbOKOnly	OK button only (default).
vbOKCancel	OK and Cancel buttons.
vbAbortRetryIgnore	Abort, Retry, and Ignore buttons.
vbYesNoCancel	Yes, No, and Cancel buttons.
vbYesNo	Yes and No buttons.
vbRetryCancel	Retry and Cancel buttons.
vbCritical	Critical message.
vbQuestion	Warning query.
vbExclamation	Warning message.
vbInformation	Information message.
vbDefaultButton1	First button is default (default).
vbDefaultButton2	Second button is default.
vbDefaultButton3	Third button is default.
vbApplicationModal	Application modal message box (default).
vbSystemModal	System modal message box.

Visual Basic also has **MsgBox** constants you can use to analyze the value the function returns. They are summarized in Table 5-6.

Table 5-6 Constants for the **MsgBox** return value

Constant	Button User Clicked
vbOK	OK
vbCancel	Cancel
vbAbort	Abort
vbRetry	Retry
vbIgnore	Ignore
vbYes	Yes
vbNo	No

Finally, you can use the **Chr** constants defined in Table 5-7 to format your output. In fact, you can use these constants in other strings as well, for example, any time you need to extend output across multiple lines.

Table 5-7 Nonprinting character constants

Constant	Description	Chr **Equivalent**
vbCrLf	Carriage return/linefeed	Chr(13)+Chr(10)
vbCr	Carriage return	Chr(13)
vbLf	Linefeed	Chr(10)
vbTab	Tab	Chr$(9)

Below are a few example calls to **MsgBox** and the resulting message boxes.

```
Answer = MsgBox("Do you want to continue?", _
          vbYesNo + vbQuestion, "Continue")
```

This produces the message box in Figure 5-5.

```
Continue = MsgBox("Error:" & vbTab & "File not found.", _
      vbAbortRetryIgnore + vbCritical)
```

This produces the message box in Figure 5-6.

```
If MsgBox("Do you want to perform another search?", _
          vbYesNo + vbDefaultButton2, "Search") = vbYes Then
      ' Perform Search
End If
```

This produces the message box in Figure 5-7.

Figure 5-5
MsgBox with vbYesNo + vbQuestion

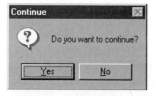

Figure 5-6
MsgBox with VbAbortIgnoreRetry + vbCritical

Figure 5-7
MsgBox with vbYesNo + vbDefaultButton2

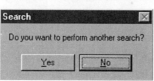

Add the source code for the Ok button as shown in Listing 5-3.

Listing 5-3 The Ok button

```
Private Sub cmdOK_Click()
' Ouput name and address
Dim Msg As String
Dim Answer As Integer

Msg = txtMemID.Text & vbCr
Msg = Msg & txtFirstname.Text & " " & txtSurname.Text & vbCr
Msg = Msg & txtAddress.Text & vbCr

Msg = Msg & vbCr & "Are these values correct?"

' Check info
Answer = MsgBox(Msg, vbYesNo, "Video Store")
If Answer = vbYes Then
    ' Do something; possibly store data to file
    ' and clear values for next entry
    ' For now, just quit.
    End
End If
' (If user clicked no, we'll just return to form
' where they can make corrections.)

End Sub
```

The program's output is shown in Figure 5-8.

During software development, it's often helpful to give controls values that you use only for testing purposes. For example, after you're done testing the member ID validation routine, you could preset text box values to a membership number and your name and address. That way you don't have to retype them every time you run the program. It's a simple enough matter to clear the values before distributing the application once everything's working.

Although you already know how to use buttons, the next lesson talks about these important controls in more detail. You'll learn, for example, how to make the Video Store Ok button look and act like a standard Ok button.

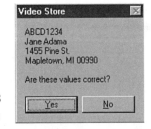

Figure 5-8
Output from MsgBox

1. The tab order is best defined as:
    a. A constant you define to insert a tab indent in a string
    b. The order in which controls are accessed when the user presses TAB
    c. An index
    d. The order of the Command buttons only

2. Which of the following caption definitions will result in a label that reads exactly:

    `Reilly & Sons`

    a. `Reilly & Sons`
    b. `Reilly "&" Sons`
    c. `Reilly && Sons`
    d. `Reilly _& Sons`

3. Which of the following message boxes *cannot* be generated by the `MsgBox` function?
    a. The message "Are you sure you want to continue?" with the buttons Yes, No, and Cancel
    b. The message "Continue?" with the buttons Ok and Cancel and a big question mark icon
    c. The message "I'm going to continue." with the button Ok and a big exclamation point
    d. The message "Do you want to continue?" with the buttons Continue and Stop

4. The return value for `MsgBox`:
    a. Is inaccessible, because you must call `MsgBox` in the form of a statement
    b. Is always **1** for the left button, **2** for the center button, and **3** for the right button
    c. Is easily accessible via predefined constants such as `vbOK`, `vbAbort`, and `vbYes`
    d. Cannot be used in a `Select Case` statement

5. To advance to the next line within a `MsgBox` prompt string:
    a. Insert a carriage return character (`vbCr`).
    b. Insert a tab character (`vbTab`).
    c. Press ENTER in the Code window.
    d. Press ENTER and an underscore (_) in the Code window.

COMMAND BUTTONS AND CHECK BOXES

Look around you at the appliances in your home. There are buttons everywhere: push buttons, light switches, round buttons, square buttons, buttons that stay in when you push them, and buttons that don't. Even the keys on a computer keyboard are buttons.

Buttons are an important part of the design of your program's user interface, just like they are an important part of the panel of a stereo.

Visual Basic 5 provides you with three standard button controls for you to use in your forms:

● CommandButton

● CheckBox

● OptionButton

This lesson discusses the Command button in more detail than you've seen before and introduces the CheckBox. Lesson 4 covers the Option button.

Command Button

You've already seen how easy it is to program a Command button and how it acts from the user's point of view. Let's take a look at some of its other properties and events.

Users are used to seeing two buttons on this type of form: the Ok button to tell the program to accept information and the Cancel button to tell the program to ignore what the user has entered. You already have an Ok button, so add the Cancel button shown in Table 5-8.

Table 5-8 The Cancel button

Object	Property	Value
CommandButton	Name	cmdCancel
	Caption	Cancel

There's a bit more to these controls than just setting the captions, however.

The Default Property

You gave accelerators to the text boxes, and you could do that for the Command button as well by including an ampersand in the caption name. However, your user will probably expect your Ok button to follow convention and respond to ENTER. To do this,

Visual Basic 5 provides the `Default` property. The `Default` property is a Boolean value that, when set to `True`, sets that particular Command button to be the default one for the form. The default Command button is the one that is pressed when a user presses ENTER on the keyboard, even if the focus is set to a different control. Only one Command button on a form can have the `Default` property set to `True`.

Set the `Default` property of the `cmdOK` button to `True`. When you do this, you will find that the Ok button is redrawn slightly differently—it now has a thicker border (Figure 5-9).

Effect on a Multiline Text Box of Default Button: You may have noticed a small inconsistency here. Earlier, you set the `MultiLine` property of the txtAddress text box to `True` so that the user could use ENTER to end each line. Now, however, you're using ENTER for the default button. You'll find that now, if you press ENTER while the focus is set to the txtAddress text box, the Ok button is pressed.

You now have to press SHIFT-ENTER to terminate each line.

In fact, it's good practice to instruct users of your software to get into the habit of pressing SHIFT-ENTER on a MultiLine text box. This is because the text box will always accept SHIFT-ENTER as the line break regardless of whether or not the form also has a default Command button.

The Cancel Button

There is also a convention for the Cancel button's accelerator: ESC (the escape key). To support this, the Command button also has a `Cancel` property, which you can set to `True`. Do this now for your Cancel button so that it will respond correctly to ESC. Like

Figure 5-9
The default
Command button
has a slightly
thicker border

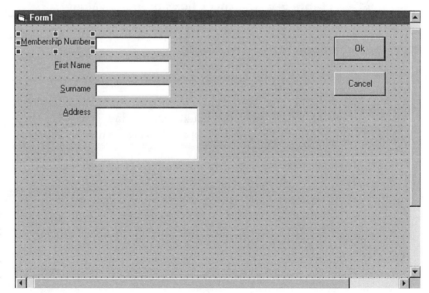

the `Default` property, only one button on the form can have the `Cancel` property set to `True` at any one time.

Add the code shown in Listing 5-4 to end the program in the `Cancel` routine.

Listing 5-4 The `Cancel` event routine

```
Private Sub cmdCancel_Click()
End
End Sub
```

Run the program. Notice that ⌷ENTER⌷ presses the Ok button regardless of which control in the form has the focus. ⌷ESC⌷ now ends the program.

Next you'll learn how to use a different type of button: the check box.

The CheckBox Control

Although it looks quite different from the Command button, the check box is really just another type of button. It is typically used where you want to provide your users with a way to indicate a Boolean choice: something that may be either `True` or `False`.

Let's add a check box to the form in the example to indicate whether or not the member has provided proof of identity. Of course, the video club requires a member to provide proof of identity before he or she can rent films. This shouldn't prevent a member's details from being entered into the system, however. Market research shows that 25 percent of all video club members decide to join on impulse and don't have the required proof of ID with them. We have to allow someone to join the club now but show an ID later.

Add a CheckBox control to the form. Figure 5-10 shows you what the check box looks like on the toolbox. Set the property values as shown in Table 5-9.

Table 5-9 The check box's property values

Property	Value
Name	chkID
Caption	Proof of &ID

Note that this time you're using an accelerator character directly in the caption of the button. The form should appear as in Figure 5-11.

The check box's caption displays next to the check box. It's a bit like having a built-in Label control.

Figure 5-10
The CheckBox
control

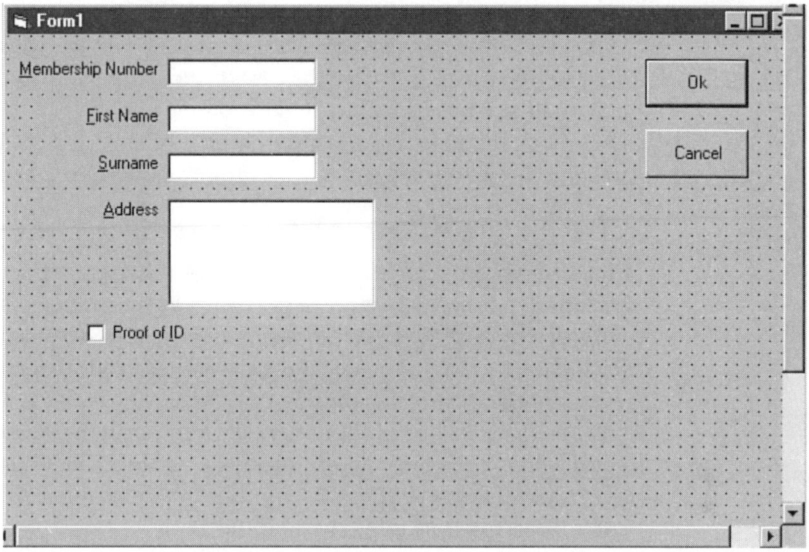

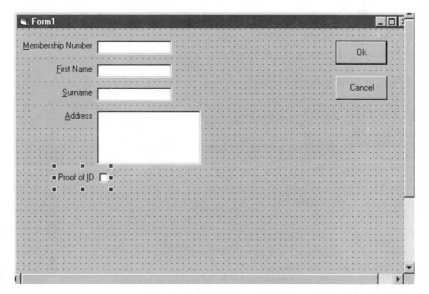

Figure 5-11
Form1 with check
box added

The Check Box Alignment *Property*

You can vary which side of the caption the check box appears on by changing the value
of its **Alignment** property. Change it now so that it appears to the right of the caption
by setting its **Alignment** property to **1 – Right Justify**. Adjust the size of the check
box so that it appears as in Figure 5-12.

Figure 5-12
View of Form1
with right-aligned
check box

The check box will now work automatically when you run the project. Let's see it in action. Run the project now and experiment with the check box at runtime. You'll find that you can set and clear the checkmark in the check box by clicking on the check box itself, or on its caption with the mouse by pressing its accelerator key ((ALT)-(I)) or by pressing the space bar when the check box has the focus. Like the Command button, the check box will generate a `Click` event when it is clicked.

The Value *Property*

The `Value` property reflects the current state of a button. For example, when the Command button is in its normal, unpressed state, its `Value` property is set to `False`. However, when you click on it, its `Value` property changes to `True`. Because a value of `True` means the button is pressed, you could use this value in code to invoke a Command button's `Click` routine programmatically.

Although you normally don't need to worry about the `Value` property for Command buttons, this property is important for the check box. The `Value` property sets or returns the current state of the check box. You can set this value at design time if you want the control's default state to be checked. To check the box in code, you would write

```
chkID.Value = True
```

and to turn it off, you would write

```
chkID.Value = False
```

Add the highlighted code in Listing 5-5 to the `cmdOK` button's `Click` event subroutine to print the current `Value` setting for the check box when the Ok button is pressed.

Listing 5-5   Evaluate the check box value

```
Private Sub cmdOK_Click()
' Ouput name and address
Dim Msg As String
Dim Answer As Integer

Msg = txtMemID.Text & vbCr
Msg = Msg & txtFirstname.Text & " " & txtSurname.Text & vbCr
Msg = Msg & txtAddress.Text & vbCr

If chkID.Value Then
    Msg = Msg & "Member has shown ID." & vbCr
Else
    Msg = Msg & "Note: Member has not yet shown ID." & vbCr
End If

Msg = Msg & vbCr & "Are these values correct?"

' Check info
Answer = MsgBox(Msg, vbYesNo, "Video Store")
If Answer = vbYes Then
    ' Do something; possibly store data to file
    ' and clear values for next entry
```

```
End If
' (If user clicked no, we'll just return to form
' where they can make corrections.)

End Sub
```

The Enabled *Property*

Let's add another button to the form. This will be where you'll add the functionality to rent a videotape. However, don't give the user access to the videotape until the Proof of ID button is checked. To disable controls and make them appear gray, set the `Enabled` property. Add the button with the properties described in Table 5-10.

Table 5-10 Properties for the Rent button

Object	Property	Value
CommandButton	Name	cmdRent
	Caption	Rent a &Tape
	Enabled	False

When the program runs, the Rent button is disabled, as shown in Figure 5-13. Note that you also can't access the button via the accelerator key while the `Enabled` property is `False`.

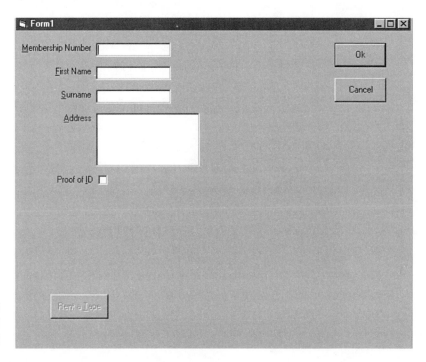

Figure 5-13
The button's initial
state is disabled

To enable the button at the appropriate time, enter the source code for the `chkID_Click` routine shown in Listing 5-6.

Listing 5-6   Enable a button if a value is checked

```
Private Sub chkID_Click()
If chkID.Value Then
    cmdRent.Enabled = True
Else
    cmdRent.Enabled = False
End If
End Sub
```

Alternately, you can shorten this code by replacing the entire `If...End If` block with the statement

```
cmdRent.Enabled = chkID.Value
```

Note how easy it is to express relationships between the values of the controls on a form. Of course, if this were a complete application, you'd probably need more validation. For example, you might want to make sure the name, address, and membership number were completed before enabling the Rent button. But the procedure to do this would be essentially the same as in Listing 5-6.

1. To make a button the default button for a form:
   a. Set the `Ok` property to `True`.
   b. Set the `Default` property to `True`.
   c. Program an accelerator using &-ENTER.
   d. Enter a caption of `Ok`; Visual Basic is smart enough to know what you mean.

2. To advance to a new line of a multiline text box on a form that has a default Ok button:
   a. Press ENTER (VB temporarily disables the default button functionality).
   b. Press SHIFT-ENTER.
   c. Press the down arrow key.
   d. Use the horizontal scroll bar.

3. Setting the `Value` property of a Command button to `True`:
   a. Has no effect
   b. Makes the button look "pressed"
   c. Calls the `Click` event routine for that button
   d. Does nothing; the Command button doesn't have a `Value` property!

4. For which situation is a CheckBox control *not* a good choice?
   a. When there is a button to turn on or off other options on a form
   b. When there is a button the user can press to indicate whether or not a condition is true
   c. When there is a box to display whether a condition is true and that the user can't click
   d. When there is a box on a form for the user to answer a yes/no question

5. How do you make a control appear "gray" and inaccessible?
   a. Set the **Enabled** property to **False**.
   b. Set the **Visible** property to **False**.
   c. Set the **Disabled** property to **True**.
   d. Apply the **Hide** method.

 *LESSON 4*

OPTION BUTTONS AND FRAMES

In this lesson, we're going to look at two new controls. One of these, the Option button, is a button similar to the Command button. The second, the frame, is the first control you've met that is not really used on its own. Intrigued? Read on.

The OptionButton Control

Option buttons are sometimes called radio buttons. The idea is that only one button can be pressed at one time, just like the preset buttons on a radio. Option buttons therefore work in groups, which is the one fundamental difference between them and the other types of buttons.

Figure 5-14 shows how the Option button appears on the toolbox.

Option buttons are useful when you have a small number of options of which only one can apply at a time. Let's add some option buttons to Form1 to show the member's marital status. Add option buttons to Form1 now with the property settings described in Table 5-11. Lay out the controls as shown on Figure 5-15. To make the label's accelerator work correctly, be sure to add the Label control first.

Figure 5-14
Adding an Option
button to the form

Table 5-11 The Marital Status radio buttons

Object	Name	Caption
Label	lblMaritalStatus	Marital Stat&us
OptionButton	optSingle	Sin&gle
OptionButton	optMarried	Ma&rried
OptionButton	optDivorced	&Divorced
OptionButton	optSeparated	Se&parated

Option buttons respond to the same stimuli as the CommandButton and CheckBox controls. They also generate a `Click` event and have a `Value` property. The difference is that only one at a time in a group can have its `Value` property set to `True`. By contrast, any number in a group of check boxes may have a value of `True` at any one time.

Add the highlighted code in Listing 5-7 to the Ok button routine. Run your program now and see how the Option buttons operate at runtime.

Listing 5-7 `Select Case` is a natural way to access the Option button values

```
Private Sub cmdOK_Click()
' Ouput name and address
Dim Msg As String
Dim Answer As Integer

Msg = txtMemID.Text & vbCr
Msg = Msg & txtFirstname.Text & " " & txtSurname.Text & vbCr
Msg = Msg & txtAddress.Text & vbCr
```

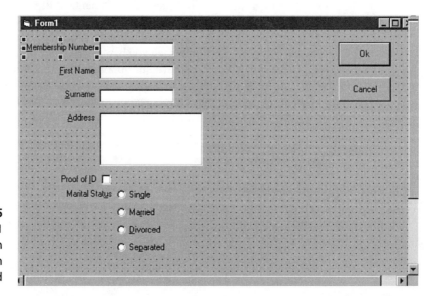

Figure 5-15
View of Form1
after Option
buttons have been
added

```
Msg = Msg & "Marital Status:" & vbCr
' Output marital status.
Select Case True
    Case optSingle.Value
        Msg = Msg & vbTab & "Single" & vbCr
    Case optMarried.Value
        Msg = Msg & vbTab & "Married" & vbCr
    Case optDivorced.Value
        Msg = Msg & vbTab & "Divorced" & vbCr
    Case optSeparated.Value
        Msg = Msg & vbTab & "Separated" & vbCr
    Case Else
        Msg = Msg & vbTab & "Unknown" & vbCr
End Select

Msg = Msg & vbCr & "Are these values correct?"

' Check info
Answer = MsgBox(Msg, vbYesNo, "Video Store")
If Answer = vbYes Then
    ' Do something; possibly store data to file
    ' and clear values for next entry
End If
' (If user clicked no, we'll just return to form
' where they can make corrections.)

End Sub
```

The Frame Control

The Frame control (shown in Figure 5-16) is different from the other controls that you have seen because it doesn't really do anything by itself. Instead, you use it to group other controls together, both visually and functionally. A Frame control works by letting you add other controls on top of it.

Add a Frame control to your form.

The Frame control is a rectangle with a caption along the top side. As you size the control, the size and shape of the frame change. Figure 5-17 shows you how the frame appears when you first add it to the form.

The frame has a `Caption` property just like a label does. Like the Label control, the Frame control can have an accelerator in its caption that, when keyed at runtime, will set the focus to the control with the next `TabIndex` value. Set the Frame control's `Caption` property as shown in Table 5-12.

Figure 5-16
Adding a frame to the form

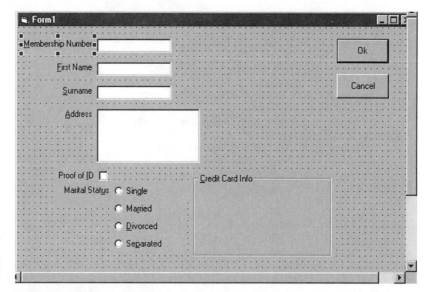

Figure 5-17
Form1 with Frame
control added

Table 5-12 The Frame control's caption

Object	Property	Value
Frame	Caption	&Credit Card

You're going to use the Frame control to store some further detail about each member. This time you're going to record the type and number of the credit card the member has selected to use in case he or she fails to pay for a rental or overdue tape. The video rental store accepts Visa, MasterCard, and its own store card.

Add controls to a frame simply by drawing them on top of the frame. You can tell an object belongs with a frame because if you drag the frame around the control, all its objects move with it. Also, you can move controls around on a frame, but you cannot move them outside the frame.

If a control is already on a form, you can't simply drag it onto a frame to make the object belong to the frame. Here is a way to move it onto a frame: Select the control by clicking on it. Cut it out by clicking on Cut under the Edit menu. Now select the frame you want to own the control. When the frame is selected, click on Paste under the Edit menu.

Add three additional OptionButton controls to the frame, one for each type of card. This raises another important issue. You already have a set of OptionButton controls on the main part of the form. If you add more Option buttons to the form, how can you tell Visual Basic to treat the two groups separately? As well as acting as a visual frame to group controls together, the Frame control groups OptionButton controls together functionally.

Add the controls shown in Table 5-13 to the frame.

Table 5-13 The Credit Card Option buttons

Object	Property	Value
OptionButton	Name	optVisa
	Caption	&Visa
OptionButton	Name	optMastercard
	Caption	&Mastercard
OptionButton	Name	optStore
	Caption	&Store card
Label	Caption	&Number:
	Autosize	True
TextBox		txtCardNum
	Text	<none>

You'll also need to add an additional TextBox control to store the credit card number. Call it txtCardNum. Your form should now look like Figure 5-18.

Now check the TabIndex values of your controls. If necessary, modify them so that they appear in the same order as Table 5-14.

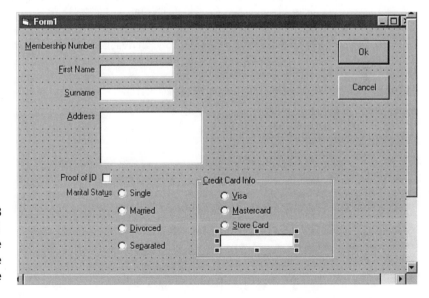

Figure 5-18
View of Form1 after controls have been added to the frame

Table 5-14 The form's tab order

Control	TabIndex	Control	TabIndex
Label1	0	optSingle	10
txtMemID	1	optMarried	11
Label2	2	optDivorced	12
txtFirstname	3	optSeparated	13
Label3	4	Frame1	14
txtSurname	5	optVisa	15
Label4	6	optMastercard	16
txtAddress	7	optStore	17
chkID	8	txtCardNum	18
lblMaritalStatus	9	cmdRent	19

If more than one control on a form has the same accelerator, pressing the accelerator once advances you to the first control in the tab order that has that accelerator, pressing it again advances you to the next control with that key, and so on.

Now add the highlighted lines in Listing 5-8 to the Ok button's **Click** event subroutine. This code accesses the Credit Card radio buttons. You should note that even though these new controls are contained within the Frame control, there is no special syntax to use to access them. You can treat controls positioned within a frame for programming purposes as if they were placed directly on the form.

Listing 5-8 Accessing the credit card info

```
Private Sub cmdOK_Click()
' Ouput name and address
Dim Msg As String
Dim Answer As Integer

Msg = txtMemID.Text & vbCr
Msg = Msg & txtFirstname.Text & " " & txtSurname.Text & vbCr
Msg = Msg & txtAddress.Text & vbCr

Msg = Msg & "Marital Status:" & vbCr
' Output marital status.
Select Case True
    Case optSingle.Value
        Msg = Msg & vbTab & "Single" & vbCr
    Case optMarried.Value
        Msg = Msg & vbTab & "Married" & vbCr
    Case optDivorced.Value
        Msg = Msg & vbTab & "Divorced" & vbCr
    Case optSeparated.Value
```

```
            Msg = Msg & vbTab & "Separated" & vbCr
        Case Else
            Msg = Msg & vbTab & "Unknown" & vbCr
    End Select

Msg = Msg & "Credit Card:" & vbCr
Select Case True
    Case optVisa.Value
        Msg = Msg & vbTab & "Visa" & vbCr
    Case optMastercard.Value
        Msg = Msg & vbTab & "Master Card" & vbCr
    Case optStore.Value
        Msg = Msg & vbTab & "Store Card" & vbCr
    Case Else
        Msg = Msg & vbTab & "None" & vbCr
End Select

Msg = Msg & vbTab & txtCardNum.Text & vbCr
Msg = Msg & vbCr & "Are these values correct?"

' Check info
Answer = MsgBox(Msg, vbYesNo, "Video Store")
If Answer = vbYes Then
    ' Do something; possibly store data to file
    ' and clear values for next entry
End If
' (If user clicked no, we'll just return to form
' where they can make corrections.)

End Sub
```

You are now ready to run the project. Note how the Option buttons work and how they are evaluated when you click on Ok.

1. The Option button differs from the Command button and check box in that:
    a. It has a `Value` property that tells whether the button option is on or off.
    b. It doesn't have a `Click` event.
    c. You can't use an accelerator to access it.
    d. Only one option in a group may be selected at any time.

2. If you have three Option buttons in a group—`optRockyRoad`, `optMintChocolate`, and `optFudgeSwirl`—and Rocky Road is selected, what's the easiest way to turn off `optRockyRoad` and turn on `optFudgeSwirl` in code?
    a. `optFudgeSwirl.Value = True`
    b. `optRockyRoad.Value = False : optFudgeSwirl.Value = True`
    c. `optRockyRoad.Value = False`
    d. `optFudgeSwirl.Pressed = True`

3. An accelerator key implemented on a frame's caption:
   a. Sets the focus to the Frame control when pressed
   b. Sets the focus to the first editable control inside the frame when pressed
   c. Sets the focus to the next editable control in the tab order when pressed
   d. Isn't implemented, because it wouldn't make sense to put the focus on a frame

4. To distinguish two or more sets of Option buttons on a form functionally:
   a. Put at least one other control between the tab orders of the sets of buttons.
   b. Put one or both of the groups on its own frame.
   c. Give options in the same group the same prefix name.
   d. Give options in the same group the same accelerator name.

5. To access the properties of a control that is on a frame:
   a. You don't need to do anything special.
   b. Precede the control name with the frame name and a period.
   c. Precede the control name with the frame name and an underscore.
   d. Put the code you want to execute in the frame's **Change** event.

EXERCISE

Create a program to order a pizza by filling out a form. Users can select toppings by clicking on check boxes next to the toppings' names. They can also click on a button to select a small, medium, or large pizza (but they can only select one item from that category). Display prices for each size of pizza. When the user has completed the form, figure out how much the pizza costs if toppings are 50 cents each. Display the total amount due to the user in some sort of message box or on the form. Be creative!

REVIEW

Lisa: Buttons, buttons everywhere.

John: I know. There certainly seems to be one for every situation.

Lisa: I can think of ways to use these buttons for data entry, report forms, dialog boxes...

John: And it's great to know how easy it is to make controls look and act like buttons in professional programs. Accelerator keys are a snap, and I was wondering how to make an Ok button.

Lisa: You can use some of these buttons, like the check box, to get state information rather than keeping track of it separately in a global state variable. It's going to make code more straightforward.

John: It seems the more we know, the easier it is to learn new controls, because they have so many elements in common with each other.

Lisa: I'm starting to get ahead of the book a little bit, exploring the Properties window for each new control and trying to guess what the properties mean.

John: I knew I picked the right study partner! Speaking of getting ahead of the book, next we'll learn how to do something really useful: Let the user select a string from a list of items.

Lisa: Lists? That sounds like the arrays we learned about at the end of Chapter 4, Subroutines, Functions, and the Visual Basic 5 Language.

THE LISTBOX CONTROL

The data entry program is beginning to take shape, but it's not yet complete. What you need is a way to display a list of any video titles that a member has borrowed. Because the number of titles that a member could borrow at any one time is variable, you need a flexible way to display as many titles as needed. The control that will let you do this is the list box.

Figure 5-19 shows you how the list box appears on the toolbox. You add it to the form in the same way as you added the previous controls. A list box lets your user select an item from a list of choices. In the Windows file selector, for example, you use list boxes to select the file name and directory. A ListBox control is a little more complicated than the other controls you've seen, because you need to manage the items it contains, but its usage is nonetheless not very difficult.

Add a label and a list box to the form as described in Table 5-15. Remember to add the label first so the accelerator key works correctly.

Table 5-15 Adding a list box and label to the form

Object	Property	Value
Label	Caption	Tit&les Rented
ListBox	Name	lstTitlesOut

Make the list box roughly the same size and position as that shown in Figure 5-20.

Adding Items to the List

Now you'll program the Rent a Tape button to let the user type in a videotape name and then add the name to the list. Visual Basic has a nice built-in function to accept text from the user. Of course, if this were a complete program, you'd probably get a list of all the videos in the store from a database and let the user select from that instead of having to type in the title.

Figure 5-19
Selecting the
ListBox control
from the toolbox

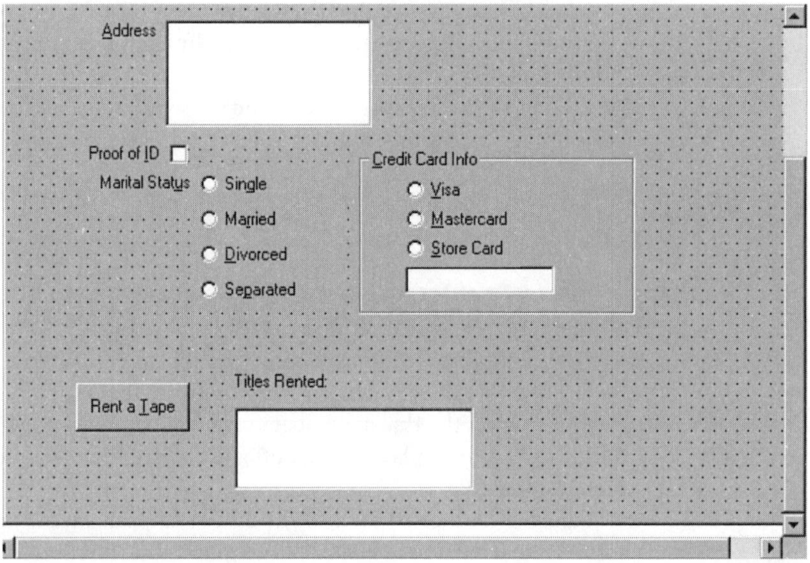

Figure 5-20
View of Form1
after the list box
has been added

The InputBox *Function*

The **InputBox** function accepts one or more lines of text from the user. It has its limitations. It isn't nearly as versatile as the text box, for example. However, there may be times when you need an input box's ease of use. The syntax for this function is

```
InputBox(prompt[, title][, default][, xpos][, ypos][, helpfile, context])
```

For this example (and probably for most cases), you need only the **prompt** argument. The input box is a dialog box that displays the prompt, a text box for data entry, and an OK and Cancel button. The **title** parameter is the text displayed in the title bar (if this is omitted, VB uses the application name). You can set the x and y position of the input box; if these parameters are omitted, the box is centered on screen. (See the online help page of this function for more details.)

The AddItem *Method*

Add the video title to the list box using the **AddItem** method, which appends the string to the list. The **AddItem** method has the following syntax:

```
object.AddItem item [, index]
```

Enter the **cmdRent** function in Listing 5-9. This is the most basic way to use the **AddItem** method, where you simply specify the string expression (a variable will do) to add to the list box. In this case, the string is always added to the end of the list box. If you were adding text to the list box from a real database, you would probably want to place the call to the list box's **AddItem** method in a loop, calling it once for each line of data extracted from the database.

Listing 5-9 Adding a video title to the list box

```
Private Sub cmdRent_Click()
Dim TapeName As String

TapeName = InputBox("What tape would you like to rent?")
If TapeName <> "" Then
    lstTitlesOut.AddItem TapeName
End If
End Sub
```

Run the program and see how the Proof of ID check box enables the Rent button, and how that button in turn lets you add titles to the list, as shown in Figure 5-21. The ease with which Visual Basic controls interrelate makes building this type of functionality a snap.

One thing to note about the **InputBox** function is that it returns a zero-length string if the user cancels, regardless of the text box's contents. Because the **cmdRent_Click** routine checks for this, if the user cancels (or doesn't enter a string) then nothing happens.

Add two or three video titles using the Rent a Tape button. Once there are some items to choose from, notice how you can use the mouse to select items or use arrows to scroll down the list when the list box has the focus. Notice also that when there are more items than will fit on the box, VB automatically adds scroll bars, as shown in Figure 5-22. Next we'll look at how to read user input from the list box.

Selecting List Box Items

When you select an item in a list box, the list box generates a **Click** event that you can trap using the list box's **Click** event subroutine. Similarly, when the user double-clicks on an item in a list box, VB generates a **DblClick** event. Often, nothing happens right away when the user clicks on an item, but if he or she then clicks on Ok (or some other button), the choice is read and processed. As a shortcut, the user can often simply double-click on an item to select it and perform the default processing.

Text, List, ListIndex, *and* ListCount *Properties*

There are two ways you can find out which item was selected. If you need the full text of the item, simply read the list box's **Text** property, which returns the text of the currently selected item. For example,

```
UserChoice$ = lstSomeListOfStuff.Text
```

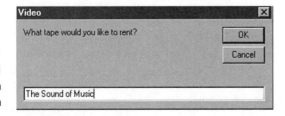

Figure 5-21
The input box in action

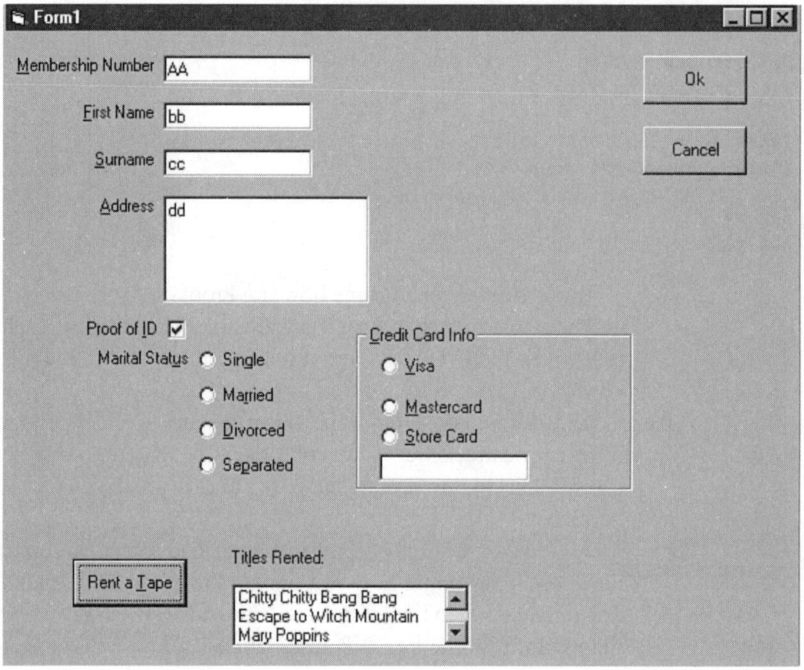

Figure 5-22
VB adds scroll bars
automatically when
the list gets long

The other way to access the selected item is to treat the contents of a list box as an array—which, it turns out, is what it really is. The array is accessed via the **List** property; the **ListCount** property contains the number of elements in the list. Because **List** is a 0-based array, a loop to print out the contents of a list box would look like this:

```
For Index = 0 to lstSomeListOfStuff.ListCount - 1
    Debug.Print lstSomeListOfStuff.List(Index)
Next Index
```

You may need to know the index number of the line the user selected. You can do this by referring to the list box's **ListIndex** property. This property is a simple integer that represents the index number of the selected item. If an item has not been selected, the **ListIndex** property will be set to **-1**.

Add the lines of code in Listing 5-10 to the **DblClick** event subroutine to see how these properties work.

Listing 5-10 Determining the selected item

```
Private Sub lstTitlesOut_DblClick()
    Dim Msg As String
    Msg = "You selected " & lstTitlesOut.Text & ";" & vbCr
    Msg = Msg & "Index number " & lstTitlesOut.ListIndex
    Msg = Msg & " out of " & lstTitlesOut.ListCount & "."
    MsgBox Msg
    MsgBox "And a fine choice it was, too."
End Sub
```

Note that you can set the list items at design time via the Properties window. However, the other properties can be read only at runtime. These are read-only properties that have no meaning until your program is running.

You can add items to a specific position in a list by using the `index` parameter of the `AddItem` method. For example,

`lstTitlesOut.AddItem TapeName, 0`

inserts the tape name at the beginning of the list.

Multiselect List Boxes

So far, we've considered only single-selection list boxes. These are list boxes that allow you to select only one entry at a time. For much of the time, you'll probably find that single-selection list boxes are enough for most of your programming tasks. However, some tasks require your users to select more than one entry from the list box at a time.

In our example, for instance, the rented-out list box could be used to identify the tapes that a member has returned. What would happen if a member returns more than one tape? If you used a single-selection list box, as you currently are doing, that would mean that the user would have to select one tape and then press a Command button to indicate that the tape had been returned. You haven't added such a button yet, but assume for the moment that one exists. The user would then have to repeat this process for each returned tape.

The `MultiSelect` *Property*

It would be better to let the user select more than one tape and press the button once. The list box can behave in this way thanks to the `MultiSelect` property. By default, the `MultiSelect` property is set to `0 - None`, but you can also set it to `1 - Simple` or `2 - Extended`.

Simple Versus Extended Multiselect List Box

A simple multiselect list box lets your user select more than one entry in the list box by clicking on each item with the mouse or by pressing the space bar. The user can select only individual entries, not groups of entries. This is the main difference between the simple and the extended MultiSelect types.

If you set the `MultiSelect` property to `2`, your list box becomes an extended multiselect list box. The user can select a group of items together by dragging them with the mouse or by pressing (SHIFT) and clicking on the item that you want to be the last item selected. The user can also use the mouse with (CTRL) depressed to select and deselect individual items.

Try experimenting with the `MultiSelect` property now until you are satisfied that you appreciate the differences between the simple and the extended multiselect list box styles. Before you continue, set the `MultiSelect` property for your list box to `2 - Extended`.

The Selected *Property*

The list box's **Text** property provides you with the text of the currently selected list box item. But what if your list box is a multiselect list box and it has more than one selected item? The **Selected** property helps you solve this problem.

The **Selected** property is an array of Boolean values that allows you to determine whether a particular item in the list box is currently selected. The **List** property allows you to access the text of any item in the list box regardless of whether or not it is currently selected. Both of these properties are arrays, indexed from 0. You can therefore use these two properties together with the **ListCount** property to scan through the items in the list box and determine which items are selected and which are not.

Listing 5-11 shows how to do this.

Listing 5-11 Finding selected items

```
Dim I As Integer
For I = 0 To lstTitlesOut.ListCount - 1
    If lstTitlesOut.Selected(I) = True Then
        Debug.Print lstTitlesOut.List(I)
    End If
Next I
```

Remember that the **ListCount** property returns the actual number of items in the list box, whereas the **Selected** and **List** properties reference the entries from an index of 0.

Removing Items from a List Box

Let's add a button to the form for returned tapes. Add the button described in Table 5-16 below the Rent a Tape button.

Table 5-16 The Return button

Object	Property	Value
CommandButton	Caption	&Return a Tape
	Name	cmdReturn

The RemoveItem *Method*

Individual items can be removed from a list box by calling the list box's **RemoveItem** method. The syntax is

object.RemoveItem *index*

The method requires a parameter, the index number of the item to be deleted. Any item can be deleted, not only selected ones. However, the way you typically use list boxes is to first let the user select the items and then let the user issue a command to perform the deletion.

If you were using a single-selection list box, the code needed to delete the selected entry would be

```
If lstTitlesOut.ListIndex <> -1 Then
    lstTitlesOut.RemoveItem lstTitlesOut.ListIndex
End If
```

You're using the `ListIndex` property as a parameter to the list box's `RemoveItem` method.

Things get a little more complicated with multiselect list boxes. If you think about it, when you have a list box that has multiple items selected, each time you remove one item, the indexes of the other items change. In fact, they decrease by one as each item is removed. You have to use a little more care when coding multiselect list box deletion routines, otherwise your program will not work as expected.

Add the routine in Listing 5-12 to the `Return Button` event routine.

Listing 5-12 Removing selected items from a list

```
Private Sub cmdReturn_Click()
Dim I As Integer
I = 0
Do
    If lstTitlesOut.Selected(I) Then
        lstTitlesOut.RemoveItem I
    Else
        I = I + 1
    End If
Loop Until I > lstTitlesOut.ListCount - 1
End Sub
```

If you delete an item, you don't increment the index counter. For example, if you delete item number 2, the item that was previously index number 3 is now 2. By not incrementing the counter, you make sure to check that item's `Selected` property as well.

The `Clear` *Method*

Should you need to remove all the items from a list box in one step, you can use the list box's `Clear` method. This will completely clear the list box:

```
lstTitlesOut.Clear
```

1. Which line adds the item "Apple" to the list box?
   a. `lstFruit.AddItem "Apple"`
   b. `lstFruit_AddItem "Apple"`
   c. `InputBox("Apple").AddItem = lst.Fruit`
   d. `AddItem "Apple" To lstFruit`

2. What value does the **ListIndex** property take when no items are selected in the list box?

   a. **0**

   b. **1**

   c. **−1**

   d. The number of elements in the list + 1

3. Which loop correctly prints out all the items in a list box? (Assume **Counter** is an integer with an initial value of **0**.)

   a.

   ```
   While Counter < lstFruit.ListCount
       Debug.Print lstFruit.Text(Counter)
   Wend
   ```

   b.

   ```
   For Counter = 1 to lstFruit.ListCount
       Debug.Print lstFruit.Text(Counter)
   Next Counter
   ```

   c.

   ```
   For Counter = 0 to lstFruit.ListCount - 1
       Debug.Print lstFruit.List(Counter)
   Next Counter
   ```

   d.

   ```
   For Counter = 1 to lstFruit.ListCount
       Debug.Print lstFruit.List(Counter)
   Next Counter
   ```

4. The difference between a simple multiselect list box and an extended multiselect list box is that:

   a. A simple list box lets you select only one list element.

   b. A simple list box doesn't let you deselect items.

   c. An extended list box lets you double-click to select the entire list.

   d. An extended list box lets you select a group of items using standard Windows interface conventions.

5. Which loop correctly prints out the selected item(s) in a list box? (Assume **Counter** is an integer with an initial value of **0**.)

   a.

   ```
   For Counter = 0 to lstFruit.ListCount - 1
       If lstFruit.Selected(Counter) Then
           Debug.Print lstFruit.List(Counter)
       End If
   Next Counter
   ```

b.

```
For Counter = 0 to lstFruit.ListCount - 1
    If lstFruit.List(Counter) = lstFruit.Text Then
        Debug.Print lstFruit.List(Counter)
    End If
Next Counter
```

c.

```
For Counter = 1 to lstFruit.ListCount
    If lstFruit.Selected(Counter) = True Then
        Debug.Print lstFruit.List(Counter)
    End If
Next Counter
```

d.

```
For Counter = 0 to lstFruit.ListCount - 1
    If lstFruit.Index(Counter) Then
        Debug.Print lstFruit.List(Counter)
    End If
Next Counter
```

ADVANCED LIST BOX TECHNIQUES AND THE COMBOBOX CONTROL

Before we move on to consider the combo box, there are a couple of advanced list box techniques that we did not consider in Lesson 5. These are

- Using the Columns property

- Storing numbers in a list box

- Sorting list boxes

- Searching the list box at runtime

The Columns Property

The list box style that you used in Lesson 5 scrolls through a single list of items vertically. When the list box fills up, it displays a vertical scroll bar that can be used to bring the hidden items into view.

You can divide the list box into columns and scroll horizontally instead by setting the `Columns` property to the number of columns you want. (By default, this property is set to `0`.) Each column is given the same width so, if you set `Columns` to `2`, each column occupies half the overall width of the list box. Note that the number of columns in this property represents the number of columns *displayed* at one time, not the number of columns altogether.

Try setting the `lstTitlesOut` list box's `Columns` property to `2` and then rerun the project. When the first column fills up, items will display in the second column. When the second column fills up, a horizontal scroll bar will be displayed, allowing you to bring the hidden columns into view.

Storing Numbers in a List Box

As well as storing text in a list box item, the list box also can store a number alongside the text. The number is never displayed, but it can be stored and retrieved by your program. This list of numbers can be used for anything. It might be an index into a database, an index into another list box, or even a list of ages to correspond to a list of names.

The property you need for this feature is called `ItemData`. The `ItemData` property is an array of `Long` integers, one for each item in the list box. When you add a new item into the list box, the `ItemData` value starts out at zero. You could write something such as

```
lstTitlesOut.ItemData(lstTitlesOut.ListCount - 1) = MyNumber
```

which would set the `ItemData` value for the last entry in the list box to a `Long` integer called `MyNumber`.

Sorted List Boxes

Normally, when you enter items into a list box, they are added in the order in which you enter them (unless you use the optional `index` parameter in the `AddItem` method). However, if you set the list box's `Sorted` property to `True`, the list box automatically performs an alphabetical sort on the items, ensuring that they remain in alphabetical order.

Set `Sorted` to `True` and run the program. Notice that when you add new titles they display in alphabetical order.

By changing the order in which the items are displayed in the list box, any attempt to add a number using `ItemData` no longer works. What you need is a way to tell what index number the last item was added to. Another property gives you this information. It is called `NewIndex` and it returns the index number of the last item added to the list box. This is very useful when using sorted list boxes. Listing 5-13 provides an example of this technique.

Listing 5-13 The `NewIndex` property

```
Dim I As Integer
Dim S As String
```

```
For I = 0 To 99
    S = "Entry " & I
    lb.AddItem S
    lb.ItemData(lb.NewIndex) = I
Next I
```

Searching the List Box at Runtime

One useful feature the list box provides is a built-in search facility. Once the focus is set to the list box, your user can key in the beginning of the selection he or she is interested in. Enter some movie titles, such as *One Flew Over the Cuckoo's Nest*, *The Wizard of Oz*, and *Terminator*. Move the focus to the list box. Try entering the letters **TH** at runtime. When you press the letter T, the selection bar moves to the first title beginning with T (*Terminator*). When you then press the letter H, the two characters together are used to move the selection bar to the only title beginning with those two letters (*The Wizard of Oz*). This feature gives the user an alternative to scrolling through all the items in the list box. It is a particularly useful feature when the list box contains a large number of items.

The ComboBox Control

A combo box is a combination of two other controls—TextBox and ListBox. One of the disadvantages of single selection list boxes is that they occupy a lot of real estate on your form. Once you have made your selection, you rarely need to see the remaining entries that lie unselected in the list box, but they are still there and still taking up space. As you will discover when you start writing your own real-life programs, space on forms is at a premium. It would be nice if list boxes could just be folded up and set aside until they were needed again.

The combo box provides a tidy solution to this problem in that it contains a single-selection list box that remains hidden until it is needed. Instead, all that stays visible at all times is the text box portion of the control and a small *drop-down* button (a down arrow bitmap button), which the user can press to display the list box at runtime.

What's more, you can use a combo box where you previously used a group of Option buttons. Although the code required to support the control would be different, a combo box can be viewed as functionally similar to a group of Option buttons.

You could have used combo boxes, for example, in place of the Marital Status or Credit Card groups of Option buttons. If you find yourself in a situation like this and are unsure which control to use, here are some pointers to help you make your choice:

- If you have a small, set number of options, you should use the Option button.

- If you have a larger set of options, or the text for the options is not fixed, then use the combo box.

Figure 5-23 shows how the ComboBox control appears on the toolbox.

Figure 5-23
Adding a combo
box to the form

Add the label and combo box described in Table 5-17 to Form1. You'll use the combo box to store a list of special promotions that the store is offering at any particular time. A combo box is appropriate in this case because the names and number of promotions can vary and there could be so many that it would be impractical to use Option buttons.

Table 5-17 The Promotions combo box

Object	Property	Value
Label	Caption	Promotions:
ComboBox	Name	cboPromotions

Figure 5-24 shows the combo box at design time. To get everything to fit, enlarge the form and put the Rent, Return a Tape, and Titles Rented list boxes a little closer together.

You can select multiple controls and move them together by drawing a "rubberband" box around them by holding down the mouse button and drawing a rectangle. Selected controls are highlighted.

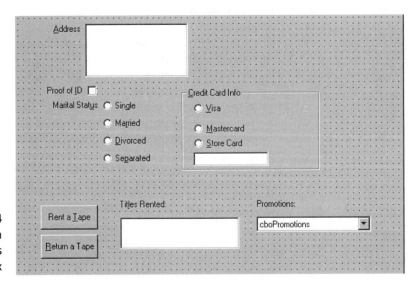

Figure 5-24
Video Store form
with Promotions
combo box

The Style **Property**

Although the combo box has now been added to Form1, you need to do a little more work before you can go ahead and start programming it. First, you need to look at its Style property. This property controls how the combo box behaves at runtime. There are three different styles for you to choose from:

- Drop-down combo

- Simple combo

- Drop-down list

To see how these controls work, you first need to add some entries to the list box part of the combo box so that you've got something to select from at runtime.

Add the code in Listing 5-14 to Form1's **Form_Load** subroutine. The combo box has an **AddItem** method that you can use in the same way as a normal list box's **AddItem** method. If you look at the Properties window for the combo box, you'll also see that it shares many of the same properties as the ListBox control.

Listing 5-14 Filling the combo box

```
Private Sub Form_Load()
' Initialize ComboBox
cboPromotions.AddItem "None"
cboPromotions.AddItem "Rent three get one free!"
cboPromotions.AddItem "Gold star tape"
cboPromotions.AddItem "Extra day rental free"
cboPromotions.AddItem "New member first tape free"
End Sub
```

Now let's look at each style in turn.

Drop-Down Combo

This style is characterized by the text box part of the combo box. The text box in this style of combo box is editable, which means that your users have a choice of either selecting an entry from the list box part of the combo box or typing in their own entry into the text box part.

The combo box has a **Text** property that you should use with this style to obtain the text selected or entered in the text box. You have to use the **Text** property to determine the entered text because you cannot be certain that the text has come from the list box part of the control.

This ComboBox control also provides a search facility. In this case, the user can key in the first part of the desired entry and then press (ENTER). If the keyed entry matches the beginning of an item in the list box portion, then that item is selected.

For instance, if you press the drop-down button, type **G**, and then press (ENTER), the Gold star tape promotion would be selected for you. You need to key in only the text that uniquely identifies the item in the list box portion. To select the New member first tape free promotion, key in **Ne**, to distinguish the promotion from the entry **None**. You could key in **ne** or **NE** because the search is not case-sensitive.

Simple Combo

The main difference between the simple combo and the other styles is that the list box portion is always displayed. Therefore, you have to be careful to set the height of the combo box at design time, because the height you set determines the height of the list box portion at runtime. If you don't set the height of the combo box, you won't see the list box at all and the combo box will look just like an ordinary text box.

This combo box style also allows the user to key in the text; you can use its **Text** property to see the text the user entered. This combo box has no search facility.

Drop-Down List

This style of combo box is the one you want to use in your program. The main difference between this and the other two styles is that the text box portion of the combo box is now protected so that the user cannot type anything into it. The **Text** property is now read-only at runtime. This means you can read the **Text** property to see the text in the text box, but you cannot assign a value to it (at least without generating a runtime error).

Set this value and run the program. The combo box in action is shown in Figure 5-25.

Before you continue to the next lesson, save the sample program as **VIDEO.FRM/VIDEO.VBP**.

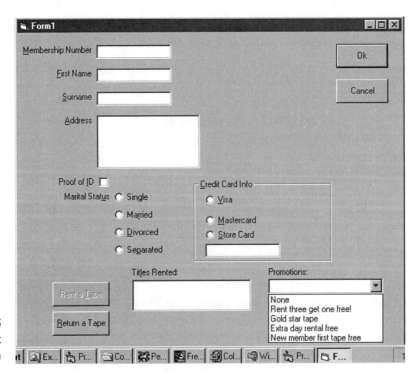

Figure 5-25
The combo box
in action

1. A `Columns` property value of **2** on a list box means:
   a. Your list is broken into two columns and can be scrolled horizontally or vertically.
   b. Your list is broken into multiple columns the user can scroll horizontally, two of which are visible at once.
   c. The items are split into two list boxes.
   d. Any nonzero value for this property splits the list into two columns.

2. Which property returns the index value of the last item added to a list box?
   a. `NewIndex`
   b. `ListIndex`
   c. `ListCount`
   d. `ListCount - 1`

3. A combo box is a combination of which two controls?
   a. ListBox and Label
   b. ListBox and CommandButton
   c. TextBox and OptionButton
   d. TextBox and ListBox

4. Which type of list box would you use if you wanted a bare-bones list box that a user could use to type an item or select it and that stays the size it was given at design time?
   a. ListBox
   b. Drop-down combo-style combo box
   c. Simple combo-style combo box
   d. Drop-down list-style combo box

5. Which type of list box would you use to save the most screen real estate, while at the same time not letting the user type in a value?
   a. List box
   b. Drop-down-style combo box
   c. Simple-style combo box
   d. Drop-down list-style combo box

CONTROL ARRAYS

So far, you have set about the task of designing forms in a pretty consistent way. You have always added the controls that you need to a form using the toolbox and then simply loaded the form (either implicitly or explicitly) at runtime and relied on Visual Basic 5 to create the control objects for you.

This is fine when you know in advance how many instances of a particular control you will need. The problem is that there are many occasions when you do not have this information when you develop your project.

Control Arrays

Let's say you want to store information on more than one credit card for each member, including the account number and expiration date. You don't know in advance how many and what types of card a member is going to want to use. One way to tackle this problem would be to design a form that allows for a theoretical maximum number of cards and to duplicate the controls required for each card that many times. Although such an approach would work, it isn't very elegant and there's bound to be one credit card junkie out there with more cards than you allowed for.

Instead, you're going to use a technique to generate any number of sets of identical controls at runtime. Load the saved **VIDEO.VBP** project. To make room for this lesson's example, remove the Marital Status option buttons, the Promotions combo box, and the Credit Card Info frame and its contents. You also need to remove (or comment out) the code that refers to these controls in the Ok button routine. Now add a set of controls that describe a single credit card. These controls are summarized in Table 5-18. Resize and move controls around on the form so that the layout is similar to Figure 5-26. Save this version of the program as **VIDEO2.VBP**.

Table 5-18 The Credit Card Info controls

Object	Property	Value
Label	Caption	Credit Card Type
ComboBox	Name	cboCardName
	List	Visa
		MasterCard
		Store Card
	Style	2 - Dropdown List
Label	Caption	Account Number
TextBox	Name	txtCardNumber
	Text	None
Label	Caption	Expiration Date
TextBox	Name	txtExpDate
	Text	None

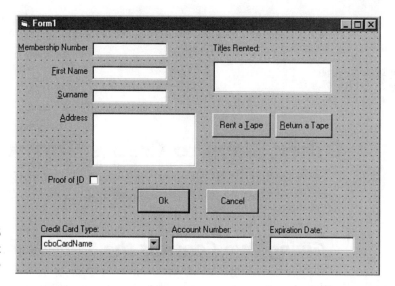

Figure 5-26
Credit Card form at
design time

Notice that the new controls have plenty of blank space beneath them. The idea is that you are going to create as many control objects as you need at runtime from these three controls.

Visual Basic 5 always creates the first set of three controls for you. If for any reason you do not want to display the first set of controls when the form displays, you must set its **Visible** property to **False** at design time.

In this example, assume that the member has at least one credit card to register. Therefore, you always need to display at least one set of these three controls.

The Index *Property*

The next thing to do, and this is the key to the solution to this problem, is to set the **Index** property of each of these three editable controls to zero (**0**) while you're still in design mode. Do this so each of these three controls becomes a *control array*. A control array is a mechanism for creating instances of controls at runtime.

What Is a Control Array?

A control array isn't conceptually much different from any other type of array, such as an array of integers, which you learned about in Chapter 3, Variables, Constants, and Associated Functions. Like an array of integers, a control array is a grouping together of identical variables, except that in the case of a control array, the variables are control object variables that contain references to control objects, rather than just integers. Also, like an array of integers, each individual control object is accessed by specifying its index number in parentheses after the name of the control itself.

If you have an array of, say, 10 text boxes all called Text1, you could print the contents of their **Text** properties to the Debug window by using the following simple **For...Next** loop.

```
Dim I As Integer
For I = 0 To 9
    Debug.Print Text1(I).Text
Next I
```

Other Ways to Create Control Arrays

We've just shown you one way to create a control array—by setting the control's **Index** property to **0**. There are two other ways to create a control array: by giving two controls the same name and by copying a control using the Copy and Paste commands from VB's Edit menu.

Giving Two Controls the Same Name

This method involves creating two or more controls of the same type at design time on the same form. We'll use a TextBox control as an example.

Draw a new text box somewhere on the form. Change its **Name** property to **txtTest**. Now draw another text box on the form and change *its* **Name** property to **txtTest** as well. Visual Basic 5 asks you if you want to create a control array, as shown in Figure 5-27.

VB asks you this only the first time that you set two controls to have the same name. If you press the Yes button, Visual Basic 5 sets the name of both controls to **txtTest** and sets the index of the two controls to different values. It gives one **txtTest** control an index of **0** and the other an index of **1**.

Copying a Control

Copying a control involves placing a control on a form and then using the Copy and Paste options from Visual Basic 5's Edit menu to place an additional control with the same name on the form. Again, Visual Basic 5 asks you to confirm that this is what you intend to do and, if you press the No button, it creates the new control with a unique name. Although the method to create the control array is different, Visual Basic 5 behaves in the same way with regard to the creation of the control array itself.

Figure 5-27
Creating a control
array at design
time

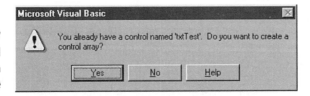

Creating New Instances of Controls at Runtime

When the program runs, VB creates only as many of each control in an array as you created at design time. To create more elements in the control array than you specified at design time, you have to tell VB to do it in code.

Now that you know what a control array is and how to create one, the next problem to solve is how to create further instances of each control at runtime.

The Load *Statement*

In the credit card example, create five additional instances of these three controls. Use the **Load** statement, which creates controls at runtime. Delete the txtTest controls (if you added them in the previous example) and add the highlighted code in Listing 5-15 to the form's **Load event** subroutine.

Listing 5-15 Loading controls at runtime

```
Private Sub Form_Load()
Dim I As Integer

' Load additional control arrays.
For I = 1 To 5
    Load cboCardName(I)
    Load txtCardNumber(I)
    Load txtExpDate(I)
    cboCardName(I).Visible = True
    txtCardNumber(I).Visible = True
    txtExpDate(I).Visible = True
Next I

End Sub
```

In this example, **I** is the **Index** value for the new control object. **Index** 0 references the existing control object in each of your three arrays; to create subsequent controls in the array, you must start with **I** set to a value of **1**.

Control object arrays are always indexed from 0, regardless of any **Option Base** that you may have set for the form.

When each new control is created, its properties are, with a few exceptions, set to the same values as the control on which it was based. The **Visible** property, however, is automatically set to **False**, so you need to change this value.

If you run the program, you still won't see the new controls, however. That's because they all occupy the same position on the form: The **Top**, **Left**, **Height**, and **Width** properties—which describe the object's position on the form—are the same as the control on which the other controls are based. As a result, you have to move each object so that you can see it at runtime. The method used here is simply to calculate a new position for the control based on its position in the control array. The changes are highlighted in Listing 5-16. Don't worry too much about the details here; we'll cover coordinates in more detail in Chapter 8, Discovering the CommonDialog and Windows 95 Controls.

Listing 5-16 The controls so you can see them

```
Private Sub Form_Load()
Dim I As Integer

' Load additional control arrays.
For I = 1 To 5
    Load cboCardName(I)
    Load txtCardNumber(I)
    Load txtExpDate(I)
    cboCardName(I).Visible = True
    txtCardNumber(I).Visible = True
    txtExpDate(I).Visible = True

    cboCardName(I).Top = cboCardName(0).Top _
                    + (I * cboCardName(0).Height)
    txtCardNumber(I).Top = txtCardNumber(0).Top _
                    + (I * txtCardNumber(0).Height)
    txtExpDate(I).Top = txtExpDate(0).Top _
                    + (I * txtExpDate(0).Height)
Next I

End Sub
```

This code will move the new controls to a position relative to the original control's height and the new control's position in the array. Figure 5-28 shows you the form at runtime.

Referencing Indexed Controls in Your Code

We said earlier that the way to use an indexed control variable at runtime is to specify the **Index** property value of the control object that you want to access in parentheses after the variable name. Well, Visual Basic 5 is pretty clever in that it recognizes when an event has occurred in a control object that is part of a control array and it provides you with the **Index** value in the event subroutine as a parameter to the subroutine.

Take a look at the **GotFocus** event subroutine for the **txtCardNumber** control:

```
Private Sub txtCardNumber_Click(Index As Integer)

End Sub
```

Figure 5-28
Form with
additional controls
created at runtime

The subroutine has a parameter, **Index As Integer**, which it wouldn't otherwise have. The **Index** parameter contains the **Index** property value of the control that triggered the event. Try experimenting for yourself by entering the following line in this event routine:

```
txtCardNumber(Index).Text = "I'm index number " & Index
```

Now you can click on a Card Number text box to see its index number. This is how you can create a single set of code that is run for all the control objects in a control array. It's a pretty powerful feature!

1. Which of the following statements is *not* a reason to use a control array?
   a. A control array is useful when you don't know ahead of time how many controls you'll need during runtime.
   b. A control array is useful when you are dealing with a group of nearly identical controls.
   c. A control array lets you efficiently add functionality for each instance of the control.
   d. A control array lets you group related controls, such as a label and the object it describes.

2. Assume you created a control at design time named Text1. What do you need to do to be able to create elements of a Text1 control array at runtime?

    a. Set the **Array** property to **True**.

    b. Set the **Index** property to **0**.

    c. Create a second Text1 at design time and set its **Visible** property to **False**.

    d. Nothing; you can create control arrays from any control.

3. In the same situation as Question 2, which statement creates an element in the Text1 control array at runtime?

    a. `Create Text1(1)`

    b. `Load Text1(1)`

    c. `Load.Text1(1)`

    d. `Text1(1) = True`

4. Finally, what additional processing do you need to do for Text1(1)?

    a. Initialize its contents to **Null**.

    b. Set the focus to the control.

    c. Assign it different coordinates from Text1(0) and make it visible.

    d. Copy all the data from Text1(0) into Text1(1).

5. How does Visual Basic 5 let you know which specific instance of a control in a control array triggered an event?

    a. The **Index** property passed to the control's routine refers to the index number of the control that generated the event.

    b. VB doesn't need to let you know; which control generated the event is irrelevant.

    c. VB sets up a separate event routine for each control.

    d. The value of **Index** is **True** for the control that generated the routine.

EXERCISE

Create a program to let the user select a picture from a list of file names (by double-clicking) and view the picture on the form. Hardcode some file names into the list in the **Form_Load** routine, but let the user add items to the list by entering the file names in a text box and clicking on an Add button. Also, give users a way to delete pictures they don't like (just from the list, not from disk!).

CHAPTER 6

FORMS, MENUS, AND MDI FORMS

Although you've been using forms since Chapter 1, What's All That Stuff on My Screen?, you've been using them in a very simple way. Forms, like controls, have properties, events, and methods. You can customize the way the form looks and acts depending on your application's needs. Furthermore, there is more than one type of form for you to use.

In this chapter, we're going to address some of the design aspects that you need to consider when using different types of forms. As we progress, we'll build a new application based on the MDI (Multiple Document Interface) style of form, which we'll use as a platform for demonstrating the ideas that we introduce.

Learning about forms, handling form variables and properties across instances of the same forms, and studying related concepts such as form collections will give you the skills and confidence to build programs that look and act like professional Windows applications.

FORMS

So far in your projects, you have been using a form called **Form1** as part of the default project. This form is actually a type of window called a *single document interface* (SDI) window.

Don't get confused between the terms "window" and "form." For our purposes, they are one and the same thing. You already know from experience that Windows applications work by displaying windows on your computer's screen. Well, a "form" is just the name given to a window in a Visual Basic project.

The word "document" in single document interface is important because many Windows programs work with documents of one type or another.

What Is a Document?

We all know what a document is in the real world—think of legal documents, insurance documents, and don't forget tax documents (how could you!). However, whereas a real-world document is an official piece of paper, we are using the word in a different sense, to describe a collection of data that can be worked on as a unit by a particular application program. In fact, Visual Basic itself is an example of a program that works with documents of a particular type—in this case, your project.

How does all this affect the design of your applications? When we designed the Video Store application in Chapter 5, Controls, we didn't have documents in mind. Instead, we designed the form around the individual data items (name, address, and so on) that the application had to process. Applications that are designed this way are *data-centric* applications. If you change the structure of the data, you usually have to make sweeping changes to the structure of the application.

Although there isn't anything wrong with designing data-centric applications, Windows programs are particularly suited to working in a different way—in a *document-centric* way. In this chapter, we are going to look at using forms in the context of a document-centric application. But more on that in a moment.

Single Document and Multiple Document Interface

Document-centric applications can let the user work on either one document at a time (single document) or more than one document at a time (multiple document).

Windows WordPad, for example, can work on only one document at a time. If you try to create a new document or open an existing one, WordPad has to store the currently loaded document to disk or abandon it first. If you want to have two different documents loaded at the same time, you have to run two copies (we call them *instances*) of WordPad and load each document into its own copy of WordPad.

So, WordPad is a single document interface (SDI) application. However, you don't have to design your projects to work on just one document at a time; with careful preparation, you can build applications capable of working on more than one document with very little extra work. Such applications are known as multiple document interface (MDI) applications.

You can use Visual Basic to create both styles of applications. In the next lesson, you will begin to develop an MDI application to demonstrate how this is done. For the moment, however, let's stick to finding out more about document-centric user interfaces and how such a user interface might influence application design.

A Typical SDI Application

Let's take a brief look at another document-centric application: Windows Notepad. (This application is in the Accessories folder if you're using Windows 95 or the Accessories program group of Windows 3.*x*.)

When you run NotePad, it displays a window as shown in Figure 6-1.

NotePad is basically a text editor—a kind of baby word processor. You use it to create or edit documents that contain only printable characters, such as letters and numbers, rather than any special formatting. You can't make words **bold**, *change their font,* or *italicize them* as you can with a proper "grown up" word processor. NotePad is a useful little application, though, and for our purposes, it's a great example of a document-centric SDI application.

Document-centric Windows applications follow certain fundamental conventions in the way their user interfaces are designed. Although those conventions are not cast in stone, it's a big help to your users if your programs work in a way that is similar to applications that they're already using.

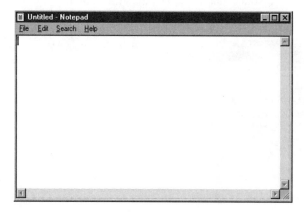

Figure 6-1
Notepad running
under Windows

NotePad's User Interface

Let's look at NotePad's user interface a little more closely.

First, when you started NotePad, what did it do? It created a fresh document of the type that it works on, a text document, ready for you to start editing. Visual Basic 5 also creates a fresh "document," the default project, ready for you to start editing. Although the detail of the documents is different, the overall behavior of both applications is the same.

Let's now look in more detail at the window NotePad displays.

The Title Bar

At the top of NotePad's window is a title bar. NotePad uses it to display both the title of the document that it is working on and its own name. This is another convention that document-centric applications follow. In NotePad's case, it has called the new text document Untitled. Visual Basic 5 works slightly differently. It gives the default project the name Project1.

The Menu

Below the title bar is the menu bar. The menu is the way in which your program's users can tell your program what to do. It's important that your programs follow a menu design similar to other document-centric applications.

Notice that both NotePad and Visual Basic have File, Edit, and Help menus and that both programs use the same accelerator keys for those menus: ALT-F, ALT-E, and ALT-H. These three menus are the minimum menus that any SDI document-centric application should have.

The File Menu

The File menu, shown in Figure 6-2, is where you put the commands that relate to your document as a whole. This is where your users can create new documents, load existing ones, and save them to disk. If you look at both NotePad and Visual Basic 5's File menus, you will see these commands under the names New, Open ..., Save, and Save As .... Notice that the accelerators used are the same.

Figure 6-2
The File menu

Figure 6-3
The Edit menu

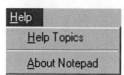

Figure 6-4
The Help menu

The Edit Menu

The Edit menu, shown in Figure 6-3, is where you put the editing commands. Both NotePad and Visual Basic share certain Edit menu commands. They both have Cut, Copy, Paste, and Delete options. These are the standard menu commands that use the Windows clipboard. You will see how to program access to the clipboard later in this chapter.

The Help Menu

The Help menu, shown in Figure 6-4, is where you would place the commands concerned with context-sensitive help for your application. You would also place a menu command to display an About box, a window that gives some basic information about your application—such as its version number or about the people who wrote it. Again, this is something we'll do in this chapter.

1. What does SDI stand for?
   a. Single document interface
   b. Simple document interface
   c. Silly document interface
   d. Single document information

2. What is a document, from a program's point of view?
   a. A structured database
   b. A collection of text, possibly with formatting information
   c. Any collection of related data that can be worked on as a unit
   d. A form you fill out, such as a tax form

3. Which of the following menus is generic—something you would include in most applications?
   a. Draw
   b. Format
   c. Edit
   d. Table

4. Although there is room for creativity in developing an application, which caption in the title bar would be most familiar to your user?
   a. Click on F1 for help.
   b. Super Spreadsheet - work1.xls.
   c. The result of the last calculation is: 139.50.
   d. The Date is: 01/01/98. The Time is: 13:50.

5. Where is a good place to put program information such as copyright and version number?
   a. The first page of the Help system
   b. In an About box under the File menu
   c. In an About box under the Help menu
   d. Printed across the status bar

AN MDI APPLICATION

Now that you appreciate more of what's involved in the user interface of a document-centric application, you're going to use that information to develop a sort of super NotePad, one that works with multiple documents. We'll call it SuperPad!

Building SuperPad's User Interface

The major departure from what we've done before is that SuperPad is going to be an MDI application. As part of learning how to build up the user interface of such an application, you'll also learn more about defining and programming menus, and you'll learn how to use the clipboard.

The only functions that we don't cover in this chapter are printing—the use of the common dialog control to provide Open..., Save As..., and Print dialogs—and toolbars. Printing is covered in Chapter 9, and the CommonDialog controls are covered in Chapter 8.

Adding an MDI Form to your Project

Run Visual Basic or start a new project. Go to the Project menu and add an MDI form to your project by selecting the Add MDI Form menu entry.

An MDI form is basically a frame inside which other windows are displayed. The advantage of having an MDI application is that the user can work on more than one document within the same application.

Although your project can have multiple SDI forms, it can have only one MDI form at a time. If you look at the Insert menu, you'll find that the MDI Form entry is now disabled (grayed out).

So, **MDIForm1** will become the startup form, providing the frame to display the individual document windows inside. You will use **Form1** as the form for the individual documents.

Naming the Forms

The next thing you have to do is change **MDIForm1**'s name to something more appropriate. Call it **frmMain** because it's the main form in your project. You should also change the name of **Form1** for the same reasons. Call it **frmDocument**.

The Title Bars

The text in a form's title bar is determined by the text in its **Caption** property. Set the **Caption** property of **frmMain** to **SuperPad**. Similarly, set the **Caption** property of **frmDocument** to **Untitled**, which is the default name that you want to give to new documents. That way, when the user creates a new document at runtime, the document will automatically have the caption **Untitled**, and you can use the text in the form's **Caption** property as the name of the document.

You now need to think about the type of document that you want to be able to edit. Remember that our definition of a document is any collection of information that can be treated as a unit. In this particular case, you want the user to be able to edit a text document, so your document will consist of the individual characters that make up its text. Use the standard **TextBox** control to display and edit the text.

SuperPad's Text Box

Select the **TextBox** control in the toolbox and try to drag it onto **frmMain**. It won't go! An MDI form is a frame for other forms. You can't drag any old control onto it. There are certain controls that you can place on an MDI form, but they are special-purpose controls used to implement toolbars and status bars. You will see how to use those controls in Chapter 7, Classes. (Additionally, you'll see in Lesson 5 how to add menus, which are actually a kind of control, to an MDI form.)

The text box is going to have to sit on **Form1**, the SDI form. Add the text box described in Table 6-1 to **Form1**. It doesn't matter where you place the text box on the form or what size you make it. You will tackle the problem of changing the size of the text box shortly.

Table 6-1 The SDI form's text box

Object	Property	Value
TextBox	Name	txtDocument
	Text	None
	MultiLine	True
	ScrollBars	2 - Vertical

The MDIChild Property

All SDI forms are capable of being displayed within the frame of an MDI form, but to enable that behavior, you have to set a property in the form first. The property is called the MDIChild property and it is normally set to False. Set it to True now for frmDocument.

A Little Bit of Code

You need just a little code to peek at what all of this will look like—two lines, to be exact. Open the frmMain Code window and add the following code:

```
Option Explicit
Dim frmPad As New frmDocument

Private Sub MDIForm_Load()
    frmPad.Show
End Sub
```

We will expand on this later; for now all you want to do is take a look at the MDI form with one child window open. Run the program now. You can see (as in Figure 6-5) that the window relationships are visually and functionally apparent. If you move the SuperPad window, the document moves with it. Similarly, you can move the document around, but not outside, its parent form. You can resize the child window, maximize it, and minimize it. If you close it, however, you will lose it because you have not yet inserted code to create new child forms.

The Icon Property

When you run any Windows application, you do so by clicking on its icon (from the Start button in Windows 95 or from an appropriate program group in other versions of Windows).When the user minimizes an application's main window, the program is represented by the same icon on the computer's desktop. Unless you specify otherwise, Visual Basic 5 uses default icons for both frmMain and frmDocument. These are basic icons signifying that frmMain is an MDI form and frmDocument is an SDI form. Figure 6-6 shows you what the standard icons look like.

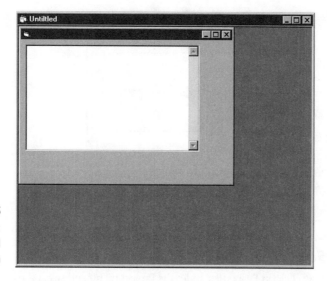

Figure 6-5
The `frmDocument` inside the MDI form

Visual Basic 5 comes complete with a library of icons. You are going to use two icons from the `icons\writing` directory to represent what your program does. To assign an icon to a form, simply select the `Icon` property for that form and then select the file name, just as you did to preload a picture into a PictureBox control. Set `note03.ico` for `frmMain` and `note07.ico` for `frmDocument`. These are shown in Figure 6-7.

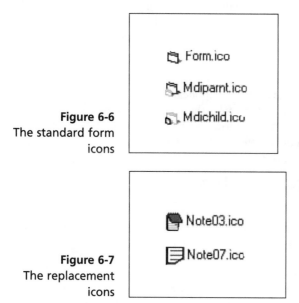

Form.ico

Mdiparnt.ico

Figure 6-6
The standard form icons

Mdichild.ico

Note03.ico

Note07.ico

Figure 6-7
The replacement icons

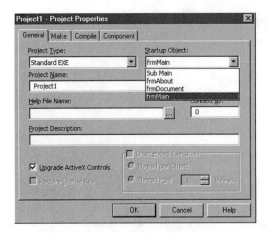

Figure 6-8
Setting the Startup
form to frmMain

Set the Startup Form

Now click on Properties under the Project menu and select the General tab. Set the start-up form to be **frmMain**, as shown in Figure 6-8.

Well, that's basic visual editing completed. We can now move on to the other aspects of this project.

1. Which object *cannot* serve as a container for other objects?
   a. **MDIForm**
   b. **Frame**
   c. **PictureBox**
   d. **CommandButton**

2. What is the main advantage of an MDI application?
   a. The user can open and work on more than one document at once.
   b. The MDI form can be a startup form.
   c. The MDI form has more controls and functionality.
   d. The MDI form lets you edit text.

3. Which object can you put on an MDI form?
   a. **TextBox**
   b. **Form**
   c. **CommandButton**
   d. All of the above

4. How would you make the regular form **frmBaby** a child of MDI form
   frmMommy?
   a. Set **frmBaby's** **MDIChild** property to **frmMommy**.
   b. Draw **frmBaby** on **frmMommy**.
   c. Set **frmMommy's** **MDIChild** property to **frmBaby**.
   d. Set **frmBaby's** **MDIChild** property to **True**.

5. The icon file assigned to a form's **Icon** property:
   a. Displays when the user minimizes the form
   b. Is ideally a graphic representation of the form's function and/or contents
   c. Is the icon the user presses to launch the program
   d. All of the above

CREATING FORMS AT RUNTIME

One of the main things your program has do is to create new documents, each of which
will display in a separate **frmDocument** window. There are three occasions when you
will want to do this:

● When your application starts so that your user has a default document to
work with

● When your user uses the menu to create a new document

● When your user uses the menu to open an existing document

An AddForm **Function**

Place code to display a form in a function called **AddForm** in the **frmMain** module. Bring
up the Code window for **frmMain** by selecting the **frmMain** form in the Project window. Then press the Project window's View Code button. Select Add Procedure... from
the Tools menu and fill out the Add Procedure dialog box to insert an **AddForm** function with **Private** scope, as shown in Figure 6-9.

Now press the OK button on the Insert Procedure dialog box and Visual Basic 5 creates the function declaration for you. It appears as in Figure 6-10.

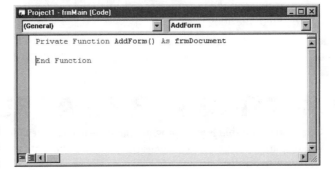

Figure 6-9
Complete the Add
Procedure dialog
box as shown

Figure 6-10
Code window with
`AddForm` function

Because this function is going to add a form to the application, you need to modify its return value to return a variable of type **Form**:

```
Private Function AddForm() As Form

End Function
```

In case you don't quite understand how a form can be represented by a variable, think about what happens when you specify that a form should be the startup form. A variable is automatically created for you with the same name as the form, allowing you to access that form's properties and methods. You've been doing this with **Form1** for some time now, although you probably didn't think of **Form1** as a variable. When you create a form at runtime, you need to obtain a similar variable to access the new form. Listing 6-1 shows the code to do this.

Listing 6-1 Adding a new form at runtime

```
Private Function AddForm() As Form
    Dim frmNewDoc As Form
    Set frmNewDoc = New frmDocument
    frmNewDoc.Show vbModeless
    Set AddForm = frmNewDoc
End Function
```

We'll look at this function line by line so that you see exactly what it's doing.

Form Variables

First, you declare a new variable of type **Form**. You're not actually creating a form at this point, just the variable where you will store the reference to the actual form.

```
Dim frmNewDoc As Form
```

The New Keyword

At this stage, **frmNewDoc** could be used to refer to any form in the application, even **frmMain**. Before you can use it, you have to assign a form to it. This is done in the second line:

```
Set frmNewDoc = New frmDocument
```

This line is doing all the hard work. It's actually doing two jobs. The code to the right of the equal sign is the part that's creating the new form. It's using **frmDocument** as a mold to create an identical copy of that form, complete with controls. It then assigns a reference to the form to the variable **frmNewDoc** so that you can access that form's properties and methods.

Showing the Form

Now that you have assigned the new form to a form variable, you can call its methods. Prior to this statement, although the form existed, it had not been displayed. To display it, you have to call its **Show** method. Call this method with the built-in constant **vbModeless**, because you want the user to be able to switch between the forms in the application.

```
frmNewDoc.Show vbModeless
```

The Set Statement

Finally, you assign the form variable **frmNewDoc** to the name of the function **AddForm** with the line:

```
Set AddForm = frmNewDoc
```

This is so you can return a form variable to the procedure that calls this function, so that it too can obtain a copy of the form variable.

Notice that you're using the **Set** statement when you assign form references, rather than just using a standard assignment operator (=) on its own. You cannot simply write

```
AddForm = frmNewDoc
```

because **frmNewDoc** is a form variable, rather than a built-in data type. However, the analogy between the two types of assignments is sound.

Calling the AddForm Function

All that's left to do now is call this function to create a new document, a new instance of the document form. For now, add it at the point at which the application begins, in the **Load** event handler for the **frmMain** form. Add this code, as shown in Listing 6-2.

Listing 6-2 The `MDIForm_Load` routine

```
Private Sub MDIForm_Load()
    AddForm
End Sub
```

For the moment, you aren't doing anything with the form variable that **AddForm** returns. Although you could store it somewhere, at present you're just throwing it away. This doesn't mean that the form won't exist anymore. In fact, the form continues to exist until the user closes it. This just means that you have lost your copy of the variable that references the form. You will see that this is not necessarily as important as it may appear at first, because there are techniques that you can use to obtain the form variable when you need it. We'll show you those techniques in the next lesson.

This is a good time to save the file. Save **frmDocument** as **SuperDoc.Frm** and **frmMain** as **SuperMDI.Frm**. Save the project as **SuperPad.VBP**. Run the program. SuperPad looks the same as it did back in Figure 6-5, except this time the Editing window is opened in code instead of because it is the startup form.

Although the text box doesn't look quite right yet, you'll find that the windows behave just as you would expect them to. You can drag their borders to change their size and minimize and maximize them. When you maximize the document window, the title bar of the **frmMain** form reflects this by adding the name of the document to its title, just like NotePad and Visual Basic! This is shown in Figure 6-11.

You can even close the document window, although you can't create a new one yet.

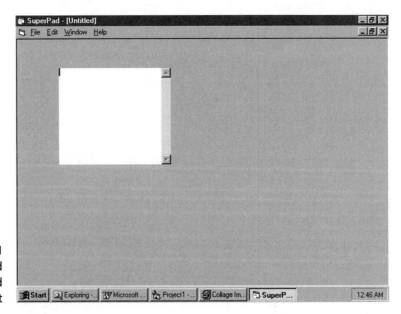

Figure 6-11
View of SuperPad
with maximized
document

Optimizing AddForm

Before you add further functionality to SuperPad, let's return to **AddForm** for a moment. The version of **AddForm** that you've written is not exactly optimized. To tell the truth, it's written in a way that helps clarify the steps involved in creating a new form at runtime. Now that you understand these steps, you can reduce that function from four lines of code to just two. Replace **AddForm** with the code in Listing 6-3. You'll find the program runs just as before.

Listing 6-3 Optimized **AddForm**

```
Private Function AddForm() As frmDocument
    Set AddForm = New frmDocument
    AddForm.Show vbModeless
End Function
```

Note that you changed the declaration of the function slightly. It no longer returns a variable of type **Form**. Now it's returning a variable of type **frmDocument**.

Hang on a moment, **frmDocument** is something *you've* added to the project. How can you suddenly use a form that you've added to the project as if it were a built-in data type, like an integer? Well, this is exactly what you can do. It's a pretty powerful feature. Furthermore, it means that you don't have to declare a new **Form** variable explicitly within the body of the function. Remember that by declaring that a function has a return value, you declare a new variable and you can use that variable in the function by using the name of the function to refer to the variable.

So, by declaring **AddForm** to return a **frmDocument** variable, you have declared a variable that you can use during the function. Of course, you still have to create the form, assign the newly created form to the **AddForm** return variable, and show the form. This time, however, you can use the return variable to access the form's **Show** method.

1. Concerning the design of your application, when would you not need to generate a new document?
   a. When the user clicks on File New
   b. When the application starts—if it makes sense to the application
   c. When the user clicks File Close
   d. When the user opens an existing file

2. You can use a form as a variable, much like other variable types. Which of the following statements is not a valid example of this technique?
   a. `Set Form = frmMain`
   b. `Dim frmMain As Form`
   c. `Private Function CreateForm() As Form`
   d. `frmNewForm = CreateForm()`

3. Each choice below is a line of code in a routine to load a new form. Assume `frmTemplate` was created at design time. Which line has a bug?
   a. `Dim frmTextDocument As Form`
   b. `frmTextDocument = New frmTemplate`
   c. `frmTextDocument.Caption = "New doc"`
   d. `frmTextDocument.Show vbModeless`

4. The sample program's `Form_Load` routine call to `AddForm` doesn't assign `AddForm`'s return value to a form variable because:
   a. There are other techniques to identify forms you'll be learning shortly.
   b. `AddForm` is a subroutine and doesn't return a value.
   c. You can't use a form-type variable in that way.
   d. We forgot.

5. From your experience with SuperPad, which doesn't have much code yet, which statement below would you say is *not* an automatic characteristic of child forms?
   a. The user can't move a form out of a parent window.
   b. Maximizing a child causes its caption to be concatenated to the parent's caption.
   c. Maximizing a parent automatically resizes a child and its controls.
   d. Only one child can have the focus at any time.

FURTHER FORM TECHNIQUES

We said we'd fix that text box and show you some techniques for obtaining the form variable, so let's do both of these right now. We'll also show you another tip for getting the most out of your forms.

Prepping the Text Box for Editing

At the moment, the text box is just sitting there, looking rather sorry for itself. It's not behaving correctly. Every time the user resizes the document window, for example, the text box stays the same size.

When the new instance of `frmDocument` is created, it is displayed at first with a certain size and at a particular position. In fact, the size of the new document form is related to the size of its MDI parent form. You can prove this by changing the size of `frmMain` before you run your project. The `frmDocument window`, which is an MDI child window, is sized proportionally to the size of `frmMain`.

Also, once `frmDocument` has been created, there is nothing to stop your users from changing its size and position. In short, you can never tell how big to make the text box on the document form at design time. You have to wait until that form is running.

The Resize *Event*

The solution to this problem is to find out whenever the size of an instance of the `frmDocument` form changes and to change the size of that one form's text box at that time. Fortunately, there is an event that lets you do this: the `Resize` event.

Use the Code window to display the event subroutines for the `frmDocument` form. You will find the `Resize` event in the list of event procedures for the form in the `Proc` combo box.

Create a declaration for the event by clicking on the `Resize` event in the `Proc` combo box. The declaration will appear as follows:

```
Private Sub Form_Resize()

End Sub
```

When you create a new form at runtime, Visual Basic 5 creates a completely fresh copy of the form you originally designed. Using the object-oriented terms you learned in Chapter 2, Object-Oriented Programming, the runtime form is an *instance* of that form's class. Each instance of that form has its own copy of the form properties and any form variables that you've declared. So changing the properties of one instance of the form does not affect any other instance. However, although the data associated with each instance of the form is different each time, the program code that runs is shared between *all* instances of the form. This means that you have to go to only one place, the Code window for `frmDocument`, to program all the document forms in your running application.

Let's use the `Resize` event subroutine to change the size of the `txtDocument` text box. You want to make it the same size as the inside of `frmDocument`. The code to do that is shown in Listing 6-4.

Listing 6-4 The Resize event routine

```
Private Sub Form_Resize()
    Me.txtDocument.Top = 0
    Me.txtDocument.Left = 0
    Me.txtDocument.Width = Me.ScaleWidth
    Me.txtDocument.Height = Me.ScaleHeight
End Sub
```

Run the project again just to satisfy yourself that this code works. Resize and move the document window. SuperPad now sizes its text box correctly, as shown in Figure 6-12.

Now let's take a look at the code you added.

The Me *Keyword*

Each line of code makes some use of the keyword **Me**, as in

```
Me.txtDocument.Top = 0
```

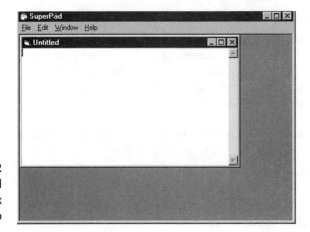

Figure 6-12
View of SuperPad
with the text box
fixed up

The **Me** keyword is a reserved keyword in Visual Basic 5 that refers to a particular running instance of a form. It is equivalent to the form variable for that form. You can use **Me** to refer to the form that is *in context*. For example, **Me** in a line of code in **frmMain** refers to the **frmMain** form, whereas **Me** in a line of code in the **frmDocument** form refers to one instance of the **frmDocument** form. When you have only one instance of a form in an application, such as **frmMain** in this application, it's easy to tell which window **Me** refers to. However, imagine you have five or six **frmDocument** windows. How can you tell which form **Me** will relate to in those circumstances?

In a multiple document scenario, **Me** always relates to the document that triggered the event. So you can safely use **Me** in the **Form_Resize** subroutine to access the properties of any instance of **frmDocument**. If the first instance of **frmDocument** was the one resized, that form's text box would be changed, and so on. You don't have to use any other technique to obtain the form's form variable.

The Top, Left, Width, *and* Height *Properties*

So far, you haven't had to worry very much about the coordinates of controls. It's so convenient to use the mouse to draw the controls where you want them that you haven't had to think about what's going on behind the scenes. The properties that set the coordinates (and size) of an object are **Top**, **Left**, **Width**, and **Height**. All objects have these properties; when you position them with the mouse, VB figures out the coordinates and assigns the values for you.

You can see this in action very easily. In design mode, bring up the form view of **frmDocument** and position the Properties window so that you can see both windows at the same time. Now move the text box around on the form. Notice when you let go of the text box in a new position that the values of **Top** and **Left** change. Similarly, resize the text box and see **Width** and **Height** change.

You can set these values manually in the Properties window at any time. You may want to do this, for example, if you're lining up controls on a form, as you did in Chapter 5, Controls, for the Video Store program. It might be easier to set all the **Left** properties to the same number, rather than trying to line up the controls by sight. The Format menu lets you do this even more easily; a few mouse clicks and everything is aligned.

Similarly, you can set the values in code, just as you would any other property value, which is what you're doing in the **Resize** event.

Changing Object Coordinates in Code

The **Top** and **Left** property values are always relative to an object's container control. For example, use the Properties window to set **frmDocument**'s **Top** property to 0. The form moves to the top of the screen. Now run the program. The form is now at the top of the MDI form, because at runtime that window is the container for the **frmDocument**.

Similarly, the lines

```
Me.txtDocument.Top = 0
Me.txtDocument.Left = 0
```

in the **Resize** event above set the text box's position *within* the document form. The position of the form on the screen doesn't affect this.

Now let's move on to the lines

```
Me.txtDocument.Width = Me.ScaleWidth
Me.txtDocument.Height = Me.ScaleHeight
```

Here you're setting the width and height of the text box. However, the expressions **Me.ScaleWidth** and **Me.ScaleHeight** require a little explanation.

The **ScaleWidth** property of a form, at runtime, returns the internal width of the form. This is the width from the inside edge of the left border to the inside edge of the right border. Similarly, the **ScaleHeight** property returns the internal height of the form. These measurements are different from the standard **Width** and **Height** properties of a form, which measure the form to its *external* edges. This is important. If you tried to set the width and height of the **TextBox** control to the external width and height of the form, the text box would be too big for the form! This is a common mistake made by many programmers new to Visual Basic.

That's all there is to it. You'll now find that no matter how you size the document form at runtime, the text box resizes itself correctly. It's fixed!

The Move Method

Before we move on to looking at some other techniques, let's do a little optimization on the code that you've just written. It turns out you can replace the four lines of code that you've just written with a single line of code! It reads as follows:

```
Me.txtDocument.Move 0, 0, Me.ScaleWidth, Me.ScaleHeight
```

Here you are calling the text box's **Move** method. The four parameters are the values that will be placed into the **Top**, **Left**, **Width**, and **Height** properties of the control. You can also use this method to move an object without resizing it; the **Width** and **Height** parameters are optional.

Now you have a document form that automatically resizes its text box every time it is resized. The `Resize` event is triggered when the form is first displayed, so you don't need to provide the same functionality in any other event subroutine for the form.

Screen Resolution

One trap you should be careful not to fall into is using fixed-sized forms. Bear in mind that, although you might be working with a top-of-the-range computer monitor capable of displaying very high resolutions, your users may be running on something more down to earth. You've already seen that Visual Basic 5 faithfully reproduces the size and position of your MDI forms to the same size as you left them at design time. The same is true for ordinary (non-MDI child) SDI forms, too. Unless you're careful, you could easily end up trying to display a form that is too large for the physical screen on which it is being displayed.

One "technique" is to assume that your users have simple VGA resolution screens and to size all your forms accordingly. This is the "lowest common denominator" approach. A far more satisfactory solution would be to change the position and size of the main window when that window is created but before it is actually displayed. The form's **Load** event subroutine is ideal for implementing this.

The Screen *Object*

Visual Basic 5 supplies a built-in object, called the `Screen` object, that you can use to determine the size of the physical screen on which your application is displayed at run-time. The `Screen` object has two properties that you can use to help calculate how large to make your forms. Say you want to size **frmMain** so that it is 75% of the width and height of the screen and it is centered in the middle of the screen, regardless of how large the physical screen is.

The code to do this is presented in Listing 6-5.

Listing 6-5 Center SuperPad on any size screen

```
Private Sub MDIForm_Load()
Me.Height = Screen.Height * 0.75
Me.Width = Screen.Width * 0.75
Me.Move (Screen.Height - Me.Height) / 2, (Screen.Width - Me.Width) / 2

AddForm
End Sub
```

Here you are setting the height and width of the form to 75 percent of the actual height and width of the screen. Once you've done this, you can center the form on the screen by moving it as shown. All you're doing is taking the height and width of the screen, subtracting the new height and width of the form, and dividing the remaining space by 2 to center the form on the screen. SuperPad will have proportionally the same size no matter what screen resolution you run it on.

1. Because `Form_Resize` is called whenever a form is drawn or redrawn on screen, which case would *not* generate this event?
   a. The form is displayed with `Show`.
   b. The user moves the form with the mouse.
   c. The user changes the form's size.
   d. The user clicks on a picture box inside the form.

2. What is shared across each instance of a form?
   a. The form's variables
   b. The form's properties
   c. The form's controls
   d. The form's source code

3. How does an event in a form know which instance of the form generated the event?
   a. The form's number is passed via the `Index` property.
   b. The form's `Selected` property is `True`.
   c. The form is passed as a `Form`-type parameter to the event.
   d. The keyword `Me` refers to the form.

4. If a form is a child of an MDI form, a value of `0` for the `Top` property means:
   a. The top of the child is aligned with the parent's inner top border.
   b. The top of the child is aligned with the top of the parent's outer border (the child's title bar covers the parent's).
   c. The top of the child is the top of the screen object.
   d. The default `Top` position for new controls added to the form is `0`.

5. What is the difference between a form's `Width` and `ScaleWidth` property?
   a. It's a trick question; only controls have a `Width` property.
   b. The `Width` property measures the form's external edge; `ScaleWidth` measures the form's internal width.
   c. The `ScaleWidth` property is always scaled to the screen's width.
   d. There's no difference.

Exercise

Set up an MDI parent form and a child document. Set up the project so that when the program is run, no child document is displayed. Create a File menu with two options: New and Quit. Enable the options so that when the user clicks on New, a new form is generated.

REVIEW

Lisa: There's a lot of elegance to Visual Basic. Positioning controls on Frame controls is kind of like positioning controls on a form, is kind of like putting child windows on an MDI form...

John: And in each case you'd use the same language: The parent object is the *container* object.

Lisa: Right. Because the relationships are applied consistently, it's easier to learn new material.

John: Agreed. As soon as I started thinking about a form as a type of variable, it got easier to understand how the functions manipulating the forms worked.

Lisa: In Chapter 5, Controls, we learned about control arrays, which was made easier because we already knew about arrays. That makes it easier to think about a collection of MDI child forms as kind of being an array of forms, right down to the usage of `Forms(I)`.

John: Another way to think about this topic is to go back to Chapter 1, What's All That Stuff on My Screen?, where we read about instances and classes. Each `frmDocument` that the `AddForm` function created is an *instance* of a form class.

Lisa: Keep talking like that and you'll get a job in Silicon Valley before we even finish this book! What's up next, smart stuff?

John: Menus, menus, and more menus.

Lisa: I thought we already knew how to do menus. Just give it a name in the menu editor and treat it as a control you can click on.

John: So you don't think we have any more to learn?

Lisa: Well, maybe a few details!

ADDING MENUS TO YOUR PROJECT

Now it's time to look at adding menus to the project. From the earlier look at NotePad's menus, you've got a pretty good idea what menus you want to add to SuperPad. You used the menu editor in Chapter 2, Object-Oriented Programming, to add a rudimentary menu to the file picker. Let's take a closer look at menus, now that you're older and wiser.

What Is a Menu?

A menu in Visual Basic 5 terms is a type of control. As such, it has a lot in common with the controls that you've already used. Menus, like other controls, have properties and events. However, they don't have any methods. Also, each menu item is a separate menu control. You can set some of the properties of a menu when you add the menu item using the menu editor. Alternatively, after you have completed adding a menu item to a form, you can use the Properties window to change the properties of an individual menu item. We'll show you how to do this later in this lesson.

Before you display the menu editor, you have to display the form to which you want to add the menu. Display `frmMain` and then select Menu Editor from the Tools menu.

Learning to Use the Menu Editor

The Menu Editor is shown in Figure 6-13.

Adding Top-Level Menu Items

At the top of the window is a text box labeled `Caption`. This is where you enter the text that will appear on the menu bar. Initially, you want to add three top-level menus to the menu bar: the File, Edit, and Help menus. Let's deal with the File menu first.

Add the text `&File` to the `Caption` text box. You can add an accelerator to a menu as easily as you can to a Label control by prefixing the accelerator character with an ampersand.

The next thing to do is to give this menu item a name. Like a control, each individual item in the menu, from top-level items down, has to have a name. Use a naming convention similar to the one used for controls and forms and call this menu item `mnuFile`. Set the `Name` text box to `mnuFile`.

The menu editor should now appear as in Figure 6-14.

The next task is to add the Edit and Help menus to the menu bar. At the bottom of the menu editor is a list box that currently contains one item, the File menu that you just added. This list box represents the menu hierarchy and can display every menu item, regardless of its level in the menu hierarchy.

To add a new top-level menu after the File menu (this will be the Edit menu), just click on the Next button. Figure 6-15 shows you the empty entry highlighted.

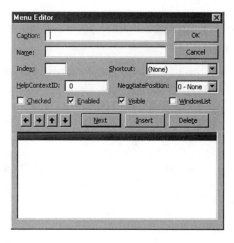

Figure 6-13
Menu Editor dialog window

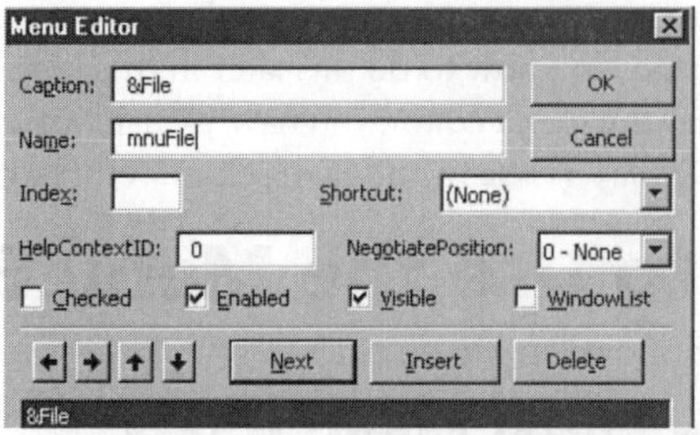

Figure 6-14
Completed Menu
Editor dialog
window

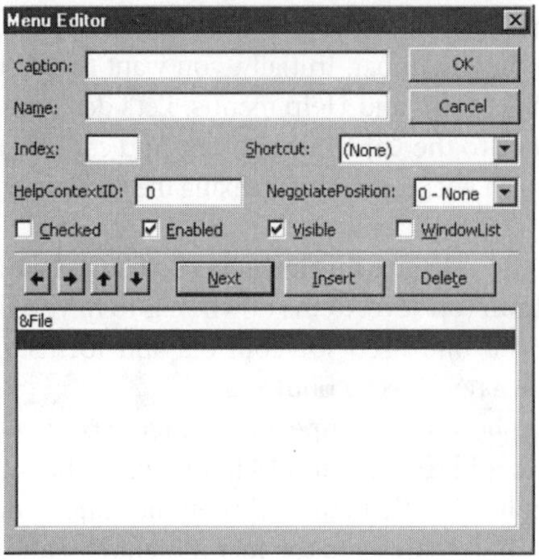

Figure 6-15
Adding a menu
item to the end of
the menu

Enter the name `mnuEdit` and the caption `&Edit` for the Edit menu. Then add a menu for `&Help/mnuHelp`. Now when you press the OK button, the menu bar contains all three menus, as shown in Figure 6-16.

Adding Subordinate Menu Items to the Top-Level Menus

Now that you've added the top-level menus, you need to add the individual menu items that your users can select to send commands to SuperPad.

Return to the menu editor. Select the Edit menu item on the list box and then press the Insert button. You now have a blank item you can use to add an item under the File menu, as shown in Figure 6-17. Note that Insert always inserts the new menu item *above* the selected menu item.

Set the caption to `&New` and the name to `mnuFileNew`. Structuring the name in this way serves as a reminder to you that this "new" menu should be a submenu item of the File menu. Recall that the arrow keys above the list box in the menu editor control the position of each menu item in the menu. You can move a menu item up or down the list by pressing the up or down arrows. Similarly, you can make an individual menu item a subordinate to the item that appears directly above it in the list box by pressing the right arrow key. This is shown for the New menu item in Figure 6-18.

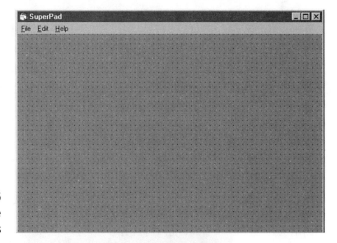

Figure 6-16
The design mode
frmMain with menus

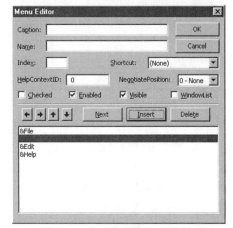

Figure 6-17
Inserting a menu
item

Figure 6-18
Making mnuFileNew
a submenu of
mnuFile

Add the rest of the menus now. The captions and names for the menus are detailed in Tables 6-2, 6-3, and 6-4.

Table 6-2 mnuFile menu items

Caption	Name
&New	mnuFileNew
&Open...	mnuFileOpen
&Close	mnuFileClose
&Save	mnuFileSave
Save &As...	mnuFileSaveAs
Print Set&up...	mnuFilePrintSetup
&Print...	mnuFilePrint
E&xit	mnuFileExit

Table 6-3 mnuEdit menu items

Caption	Name
Cu&t	mnuEditCut
&Copy	mnuEditCopy
&Paste	mnuEditPaste
De&lete	mnuEditDelete
Select &All	mnuEditSelectAll
Time/&Date	mnuEditTimeDate
&Word Wrap	mnuEditWordWrap

Table 6-4 mnuHelp menu items

Caption	Name
&About SuperPad	mnuHelpAbout

As you can see, you have quite a bit of additional functionality to add to SuperPad yet, some of which we won't tackle until later in the book.

Shortcut Keys

If you look at NotePad's menus, you will see additional "shortcut" keys that you can use to access specific menu items quickly. For instance, to add the time and date to the document, you can simply press the F5 key. You want to reproduce these types of shortcuts in SuperPad. The menu editor assists you in this task.

Return to the menu editor. Below the Cancel button, you will see a Shortcut combo box that you can use to add shortcuts to your menu items. Figure 6-19 demonstrates adding a CTRL-N shortcut to the mnuFileNew menu item.

Add the shortcuts listed in Table 6-5.

Table 6-5 SuperPad's shortcut key assignments

Menu Item	Shortcut
mnuFileNew	CTRL-N
mnuFileOpen	CTRL-O
mnuFileSaveAs	CTRL-A
mnuFilePrint	CTRL-P
mnuEditCut	CTRL-X
mnuEditCopy	CTRL-C
mnuEditPaste	CTRL-V
mnuEditDelete	DEL
mnuEditTimeDate	F5

Now when you select frmMain's menus, you'll see the shortcut keys displayed.

Adding Separator Bars

You'll notice that NotePad spaces out its menu items by introducing separator bars. You can do this too by using the menu editor. Add separators between mnuFileClose and mnuFileSave, between mnuFileSaveAs and mnuFilePrintSetup, and between mnuFilePrint and mnuFileExit.

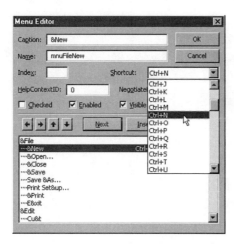

Figure 6-19
Adding a shortcut
to a menu item

In the menu editor, insert a blank menu item between the two menu items that you want to separate. This menu item will become the separator bar. Then give the new menu item a – caption. That's a single hyphen character. The menu editor will generate a separator bar for that menu item. You still have to give the menu item a name, so call the first one in the File menu `mnuFileSep1`, the second `mnuFileSep2`, and so on.

You can now do the same for the Edit menu. Add a separator between `mnuEditDelete` and `mnuEditSelectAll` and between `mnuEditTimeDate` and `mnuEditWordWrap`. Figures 6-20, 6-21, and 6-22 show how your three submenus should now look.

The Word Wrap Menu Item

Notice that we've included the Word Wrap menu in the SuperPad implementation. If you try out this menu item in the real NotePad, you'll find that a check box appears in the menu when Word Wrap is on.

Remember that each menu item is actually a control on the form. There is a property called `Checked` that you can set to `True` or `False` at runtime when the user selects that particular menu item.

Figure 6-20
View of File menu

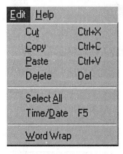

Figure 6-21
View of Edit menu

Figure 6-22
View of Help menu

You can preset the **Checked** property to **True** using the menu editor. You can also set it using the Properties window after the menu has been added to the form. There is a check box on the Menu Editor window with the caption **Checked**. If you set it for a menu item, that menu item will immediately appear with a checkmark next to it.

Context-Sensitive Menus

Finally in this lesson, we'll talk about how to make your menu items context-sensitive. If you look at NotePad's menus, you will see that some of them are disabled (grayed out). This means that you cannot select them, because selecting them would be inconsistent with NotePad's current state. For instance, the Edit menu's Cut, Copy, and Paste commands remain grayed out until you select some text in the document.

Let's add the same feature to SuperPad. However, this time use the Properties window to set the property for the menu item because the menu item already exists.

Display the Properties window for the form. At the top of the window is a combo box. When you click the mouse on it, it drops down to reveal all the controls on the form, including all the menu items that you've just added. Find the menu items in Table 6-6 and set their **Enabled** properties to **False**.

Table 6-6 Disable these menu items

Menu Item
mnuFileClose
mnuFileSave
mnuFileSaveAs
mnuFilePrint
mnuEditCut
mnuEditCopy
mnuEditPaste
mnuEditDelete
mnuEditSelectAll
mnuEditTimeDate
mnuEditWordWrap

Now when you run your program, these items will be disabled by default when the program starts. You can enable and disable individual menu items at runtime by setting the **Enabled** property accordingly. You will write a subroutine to set up these context-sensitive menus in the next lesson.

1. In the VB 5 menu editor, to make a menu item subordinate to a menu that will appear across the top of the screen, position the cursor after the menu, press the Insert button, type in the name and caption, and then:
   a. Press the right arrow button above the list box.
   b. Press the up arrow button above the list box.
   c. Change the `Negotiate Position` value to `3 - Right`.
   d. That's all; positioning the item beneath the menu is enough.

2. To give the user keyboard access to the menu, you can program an accelerator via the `Caption` property or:
   a. Type in the key equivalent to the caption, such as `Open... Ctrl O`.
   b. Use the `Set` command in `Form_Load` to set the shortcut.
   c. Choose the keyboard equivalent from the menu editor's shortcut drop-down list.
   d. Select Customize from the Tools menu.

3. How can you place a checkmark next to a menu item to indicate that a choice can be on or off?
   a. Set the value in the Properties window.
   b. Click on the Checked button in the menu editor.
   c. Take care of it in code, as in

   ```
   mnuEditWordWrap.Checked = True
   ```

   d. All of the above.

4. Which statement about separator bars is *false*?
   a. You can use them to break menu items into logical (but not functional) groups.
   b. They tend to "break up" a menu visually, making items easier to scan and find.
   c. They need a `Name` property, even though they aren't functional.
   d. You need to make them up of many hyphens, so they'll extend across like a bar.

5. A context-sensitive menu is:
   a. A menu with its items grayed out
   b. A menu with checkmarked items
   c. A menu with specific items grayed out, allowing only selections that make sense in the program's current state
   d. A menu that applies to an MDI form

FILLING IN THE BLANKS: PROGRAMMING THE FILE MENUS

It's time to start programming!

Even though you haven't added code to the menu events, the user can still send commands to the program using Windows conventions. Just as changing the window's size generates a **Resize** event, double-clicking on the window's Close box generates an **Unload** event. You've actually already used this feature. It provides a way to exit a program that doesn't have that functionality programmed in. This is because closing the last window in a program ends the program.

Confirming a Close Command

Let's add a feature to SuperPad. If the user tries to close a document before saving any changes, bring up a message box reminding the user that he or she will lose the changes.

First, you need a way to tell when the text in a document has changed since it was last saved. You can do this by adding a **Boolean** variable to the General Declarations section of **frmDocument**. Adding a variable in this way is rather like adding an additional property to the form. Go to the Code window for **frmDocument** and add the following declaration to the General Declarations section:

```
Dim Changed As Boolean
```

Because the default value for a **Boolean** variable is **False**, you don't have to assign anything to this variable. When a new document is created, its **Changed** variable will be created and initialized to **False** by default.

You know that the document has changed when the user types something in the text box. There is a **TextBox** event that you can use just for this purpose: the **Change** event.

The Change Event

Add the code in Listing 6-6 to the **Change** event subroutine for **txtDocument**.

Listing 6-6 Setting the form-level change flag

```
Private Sub txtDocument_Change()
   Changed = True
End Sub
```

Look at the way that you've accessed the **Changed** form variable. Each instance of the form will have its own copy of **Changed**, and, accordingly, only that copy will be affected when the code runs. You could also have written

```
Me.Changed = True
```

Note that this is the same syntax that you would have used if `Changed` were a property of the form. Now you can see why we said earlier that form variables are like adding your own properties to a form.

You now have a way to tell if a document needs to be saved or not. You can use this variable to handle the situation of the user closing the form without saving it first.

The Unload *Event*

Let's have a look at the `Unload` event subroutine for `frmDocument`.

Visual Basic declares the `Unload` event as follows:

```
Private Sub Form_Unload(Cancel As Integer)

End Sub
```

The event is generated when a form is closed, regardless of the method used to close it. The same event is generated if you close a form by using the `Unload` statement or if your user manually closes it with the mouse. You'll notice that the subroutine includes a `Cancel` parameter. If you set that parameter to `True` in the body of the subroutine, the form will stay open and the operation to close it will be canceled. Add the code in Listing 6-7 to the `Unload` event subroutine for `frmDocument`.

Listing 6-7 The `Unload` event routine

```
Private Sub Form_Unload(Cancel As Integer)
If Changed Then
    Select Case MsgBox("The text in the " & Me.Caption & _
                       " file has changed." & vbCr & vbCr & _
                       "Do you want to save the changes?", _
                       vbExclamation + vbYesNoCancel, frmMain.Caption)
        Case vbYes
            'Perform save
        Case vbNo
            'Allow form to close
        Case vbCancel
            'Cancel close form
            Cancel = True
    End Select
End If
End Sub
```

As you can see, you're checking the value of the form's `Changed` variable when the form is unloaded. If changes were made to the text in the text box, a modal message box prompts the user to decide whether to save the changes, ignore them, or cancel the close operation. Look carefully at the `If` statement that includes the call to the `MsgBox` function. It incorporates a number of techniques, including

- Returning the key pressed directly to the `Select Case` statement

- Forcing the message text to be displayed on more than one line by embedding a carriage return character—vbCr—in the message text

- Selecting the button combinations to display using a built-in constant

- Selecting the Exclamation Mark icon to be displayed by adding two constants together

- Specifying that the text in `frmMain`'s title bar should be used in the title bar of the message box

The message box that is produced by this function is reproduced in Figure 6-23. SuperPad is beginning to behave like a professional Windows application now!

You're not going to add the code to save the text now, so you've left that option in the `Select Case` statement empty. If the user presses the No button in the message box, you need do nothing else. You can just allow the form to close, losing the text in the text box. Finally, if the user decides to cancel the close operation, you can handle that case by setting the `Cancel` variable to `True`.

The File New Menu Item

Now let your users create new document windows by selecting the File New menu item. Because you've already written the `AddForm` function that does this, introducing this functionality should be quite straightforward. First, display the Code window for the `frmMain` form. This is where the programming will take place because the menu item is part of `frmMain`.

Locate the `mnuFileNew` menu in the `Object` combo box. When you select the menu entry in the combo box, the `Click` event subroutine declaration is added to the Code window. Add the call to the `AddForm` function, as shown in Listing 6-8.

Listing 6-8 The `File New` routine

```
Private Sub mnuFileNew_Click()
    AddForm
End Sub
```

When you run the program now, you'll be able to create as many new documents as you can fit into your PC's memory. Go on—try it!

Figure 6-23
The confirmation
message box

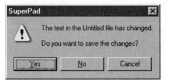

Context-Sensitive Menus: Using the Forms Collection

In Lesson 5, you disabled the Close, Save, Save As..., and Print menu items by default. You also disabled the Edit menus. You did this for a very good reason—if you close all the documents in SuperPad, those menus go "out of context." In other words, those menus are applicable only when there is at least one active document. To prevent users from selecting menus that are out of context, well-behaved Windows programs make sure that such menus are disabled.

Let's write a subroutine that you can use to enable or disable the context-sensitive menus accordingly. Go into the **frmMain** Code window and enter the subroutine in Listing 6-9. You can either type in the **sub** definition, as described in Chapter 3, Variables, Constants, and Associated Functions, or click on Procedure... under the Insert menu and fill it out, as shown in Figure 6-24.

Listing 6-9 Setting up context-sensitive menus

```
Public Sub SetupCSMenus()
Dim Found As Boolean
Dim I As Integer
For I = 0 To Forms.Count - 1
    If Forms(I).Name = "frmDocument" Then
        Found = True
        Exit For
    End If
Next I
mnuFileClose.Enabled = Found
mnuFileSave.Enabled = Found
mnuFileSaveAs.Enabled = Found
mnuFilePrint.Enabled = Found
End Sub
```

You're declaring this subroutine as **Public** because you will need to call it from the **frmDocument** form.

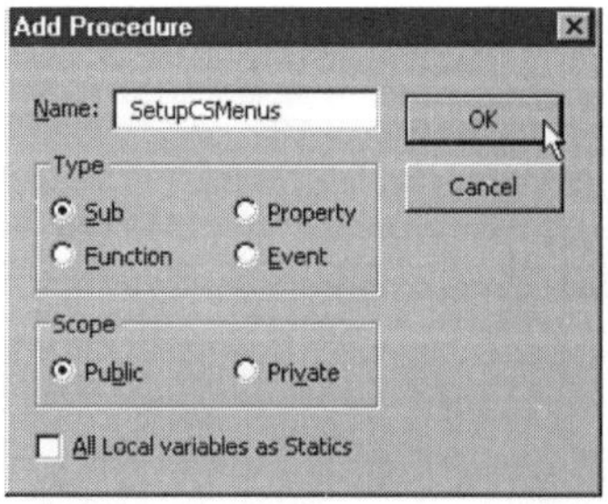

Figure 6-24
The context-sensitive menu procedure definition

The Forms Collection

One line that's interesting in this subroutine is the `For` statement:

```
For I = 0 To Forms.Count - 1
```

When you create forms in Visual Basic 5, they are automatically added to something called the *forms collection*. A collection is a way of grouping together similar objects in Visual Basic 5 so they can be retrieved or manipulated easily. Because Visual Basic 5 adds new forms to the forms collection for you, you might as well make use of this functionality.

The `Count` Method

Collections have a `Count` property that you can use to find out how many items are in the collection. The `Forms.Count` property is an integer, the total number of forms in your running application. Be careful—the count includes `frmMain`!

You can access an individual item in the collection by specifying its index in parentheses, as in the statement:

```
If Forms(I).Name = "frmDocument" Then
```

Because the indexes in the collection start at 0, it is necessary to fix the value of `I` by subtracting 1 from the number of forms returned from the `Count` method. If there are two forms in the collection, the variable `I` will take the value `0` on the first pass through the loop and `1` on the second pass.

Together, these two lines allow you to cycle through each form in the collection and find out if one of them is a `frmDocument` type of form by checking the value of the form's `Name` property. The rest of the subroutine is straightforward. You're setting a `Boolean` variable to note if you found such a form and enabling or disabling the menu items accordingly.

Calling `SetupCSMenus`

All that's left to do is to find a suitable point to call this subroutine from. You need to call it from two places: once when you create a new form and again when a form is closed. When a form is created, its `Load` event is triggered; when it is closed, its `Unload` event is triggered. Listing 6-10 is the code to add to `frmDocument`'s `Load` event subroutine.

Listing 6-10 Setting up the menus when a form is loaded

```
Private Sub Form_Load()
    frmMain.SetupCSMenus
End Sub
```

Notice how you preceded the call to `SetupCSMenus` with the name of the form in which the subroutine is contained. Because you've declared the subroutine to be `Public`, you can call it from `frmDocument`, but if you don't prefix it with the name of the form, Visual Basic 5 will assume it is a part of `frmDocument` and, accordingly, will not be able to find it.

Before you can add the same line to **frmDocument**'s **Unload** event, there is a small hurdle to overcome.

You see, the **Unload** event subroutine is called just *prior* to the form being destroyed. **SetupCSMenus** will find the form that is being unloaded in the forms collection because it hasn't been destroyed yet. To get around this, you need a way to let **SetupCSMenus** know which form is being unloaded so it can ignore that form when it is found in the forms collection.

Tracking Unloading Forms

The answer to this little problem is to add an additional **Boolean** form variable to **frmDocument**. Add it now and modify the **Unload** event subroutine for **frmDocument** as shown in Listing 6-11. (Changes are in bold.)

Listing 6-11 Calling SetupCSMenus from Form_Unload

```
Public Closing As Boolean

Private Sub Form_Unload(Cancel As Integer)
If Changed Then
    Select Case MsgBox("The text in the " & Me.Caption & _
                    " file has changed." & vbCr & vbCr & _
                    "Do you want to save the changes?", _
                    vbExclamation Or vbYesNoCancel, frmMain.Caption)
        Case vbYes
            'Perform save
        Case vbNo
            'Allow form to close
        Case vbCancel
            'Cancel close form
            Cancel = True
    End Select
End If
Closing = Not Cancel
frmMain.SetupCSMenus
End Sub
```

You're declaring **Closing** as **Public** so that **SetupCSMenus** can see it in the form. In **Form_Unload**, you're setting the **Closing** form variable to **True** after the user has confirmed that he or she wants to close the form. Then, of course, you modify **SetupCSMenus** as in Listing 6-12 to check this variable so it ignores that form as being an open document. Again, the changed lines are highlighted in bold.

Listing 6-12 The Closing variable

```
Public Sub SetupCSMenus()
Dim Found As Boolean
Dim I As Integer
For I = 0 To Forms.Count - 1
    If Forms(I).Name = "frmDocument" Then
        If Forms(I).Closing = False Then
            Found = True
            Exit For
```

```
        End If
    End If
Next I
mnuFileClose.Enabled = Found
mnuFileSave.Enabled = Found
mnuFileSaveAs.Enabled = Found
mnuFilePrint.Enabled = Found
End Sub
```

The File Close Menu

Now that SuperPad handles forms being closed correctly and the File menus are truly context-sensitive, you can add the code to close a form from the File Close menu. Use the Code window to add the `Click` event subroutine for the `mnuFileClose` menu. Then complete the subroutine as in Listing 6-13.

Listing 6-13 The `File Close` routine

```
Private Sub mnuFileClose_Click()
    Unload frmMain.ActiveForm
End Sub
```

This line of code is important. It demonstrates another way you can obtain access to a form variable.

The ActiveForm *Property*

The `ActiveForm` property is one of the MDI form's properties. It is the MDI child form that is currently active. Of course, it is the active MDI child form that you want to close.

You don't have to worry about an MDI child form not being available because the Close menu is context-sensitive. If no `frmDocument` forms are open, the Close menu will be disabled.

Well, we covered quite a lot of ground in this lesson, and now it's crunch time. Run SuperPad again and watch how your menus are affected when you have no documents open compared to when you have one or more open. Now is a good time to practice testing your program thoroughly. Try running the program through its paces with one window open, with no windows open, with many windows open, with some changes made to the text box, with no changes made to the text box, and so on.

Don't worry about the Edit menus for the moment—we'll come to them next.

1. How can you prevent a form from being closed after the user has tried to close it with the mouse?
   a. Press the Cancel button.
   b. Set the `Cancel` argument to the `Unload` procedure to `True`.
   c. Set the form `Closing` flag to `True`.
   d. Disable the user's ability to click on the Close button in the first place.

2. What's the easiest way to find out how many forms are open in your application?
   a. Keep track of them as they're opened.
   b. Ask the user via an Input box.
   c. Access the forms collection `Count` method.
   d. Access the parent form's `MDIChildCount` property.

3. How can you obtain a reference to the active MDI child form in an MDI application from the MDI form?
   a. Via the `ActiveForm` property, which returns a reference to the form
   b. Via the `ActiveForm` property, which returns an index into the forms collection
   c. Via the `Me` keyword, which refers directly to the active form
   d. Via the `Index` parameter of the form routine

4. If a form has multiple instances, how can you access a form variable of a particular instance, say, `Forms(I)`, from outside that form, say, from a parent form?
   a. By putting the variable name after the form name, separated by a period, as in

   `Forms(I).DocumentChanged`

   b. By putting the variable name before the form name, separated by a period, as in

   `DocumentChanged.Forms(I)`

   c. By including the keyword `Me`, as in

   `Me.Forms(I).DocumentChanged`

   d. By putting the variable name after the form name, separated by an underscore, as in

   `Forms(I)_DocumentChanged`

5. Although we've only scratched the surface of this topic, what do you think might be another use of forms collections?
   a. Looping through the forms in a project and passing all or some of the forms as `Forms(Counter)` to a procedure that accepts form variables
   b. Checking to see if there are any open documents before quitting an application
   c. Getting a list of open forms to add to a Window menu
   d. All of the above

LESSON 7

FILLING IN THE BLANKS: PROGRAMMING EDIT MENUS

Like the File menus, you need to make the Edit menus fully context-sensitive. However, doing this is more complex than you might think at first.

Enabling/Disabling Menu Options

The first point to recognize is that the Edit menu items need to be enabled and disabled at different times. Table 6-7 shows you the conditions under which each menu must be enabled or disabled.

Table 6-7 When to enable/disable Edit menu items

Menu	Enable When	Disable When
mnuEditCut	At least one form document is present and text in that document is selected	No forms are present or the active document has no text selected
mnuEditCopy	Same as mnuEditCut	Same as mnuEditCut
mnuEditPaste	At least one form document is present and text is present in the Windows clipboard	No forms are present or there is no text present in the Windows clipboard
mnuEditDelete	Same as mnuEditCut	Same as mnuEditCut
mnuEditSelectAll	At least one form document is present	No forms are present
mnuEditTimeDate	Same as mnuEditSelectAll	Same as mnuEditSelectAll
mnuEditWordWrap	Same as mnuEditSelectAll	Same as mnuEditSelectAll

Notice that all the menus require at least one form to be present before they are enabled. Some of the menus have additional requirements, but that basic requirement must be satisfied first. This can be done by adding the highlighted code in Listing 6-14 to the end of the **SetupCSMenus** subroutine.

Listing 6-14 Adding Edit menu to Setup routine

```
Public Sub SetupCSMenus()
Dim Found As Boolean
Dim I As Integer
For I = 0 To Forms.Count - 1
    If Forms(I).Name = "frmDocument" Then
        If Forms(I).Closing = False Then
            Found = True
            Exit For
        End If
    End If
Next I
mnuFileClose.Enabled = Found
mnuFileSave.Enabled = Found
```

continued on next page

continued from previous page

```
mnuFileSaveAs.Enabled = Found
mnuFilePrint.Enabled = Found

' enable / disable Select All, TimeDate, and WordWrap
' edit menus according to whether or not there is
' an active document
mnuEditSelectAll.Enabled = Found
mnuEditTimeDate.Enabled = Found
mnuEditWordWrap.Enabled = Found
If Found = False Then
    ' disable Copy, Cut, Delete and Paste menus
    ' when no forms are found
    mnuEditCopy.Enabled = False
    mnuEditCut.Enabled = False
    mnuEditDelete.Enabled = False
    mnuEditPaste.Enabled = False
    ' remove any check mark from the Word Wrap menu
    mnuEditWordWrap.Checked = False
End If
End Sub
```

Notice that you're also forcing the `Checked` property of the Word Wrap menu to `False`, so that any checkmark that may be set against that menu item is cleared when the menu goes out of context.

The Select All, Time/Date, and Word Wrap menu items can be enabled and disabled on the basis of whether or not a document is present. On the other hand, the Copy, Cut, Delete, and Paste menus must be disabled if no documents are present, although they have special requirements that must be satisfied before you can enable them.

The SelLength *Property*

The additional requirement for Copy, Cut, and Delete is that they can be enabled only when text has been selected in the active `frmDocument`'s text box. You can determine whether text is currently selected in the text box by checking its `SelLength` property. The `SelLength` property is available only at runtime, so you won't find it in the list of properties in the text box's Property window. If `SelLength` is `0`, there is no text selected. If it's greater than `0`, then that many characters of text have been selected. Now modify the `If` statement that you've just added to `SetupCSMenus` so that it reads as shown in Listing 6-15.

Listing 6-15 Special cases for the Edit menu

```
If Found = False Then
    ' disable Copy, Cut, Delete and Paste menus
    ' when no forms are found
    mnuEditCopy.Enabled = False
    mnuEditCut.Enabled = False
    mnuEditDelete.Enabled = False
    mnuEditPaste.Enabled = False
    ' remove any check mark from the Word Wrap menu
```

```
        mnuEditWordWrap.Checked = False
Else
    If frmMain.ActiveForm.txtDocument.SelLength > 0 Then
        ' Enable Copy, Cut and Delete menus if there is
        ' an active form and text is selected in it.
        mnuEditCopy.Enabled = True
        mnuEditCut.Enabled = True
        mnuEditDelete.Enabled = True
    Else
        ' Disable Copy, Cut and Delete menus if there is
        ' an active form and there is no text selected in it.
        mnuEditCopy.Enabled = False
        mnuEditCut.Enabled = False
        mnuEditDelete.Enabled = False
    End If
End If
```

If a form is present and text is selected in that form's text box, the Copy, Cut, and Delete menus are now enabled. Note that you still need to disable these menus expressly when there is no text selected to allow for when the focus has moved from a document form that has text selected to one that does not.

At the moment, you're calling only **SetupCSMenus** when a **frmDocument** form is loaded or unloaded. You now need to accommodate for the following events: when a user selects some text and when a user switches from one document form to another.

The KeyUp *and* MouseUp *Events*

You have a small problem. No specific event is called when a user selects some text in a text box. How can you get around this? If you think about it, there are two ways that a user can select some text: either by clicking and dragging the mouse over the text or by using the keyboard equivalent of pressing the cursor keys with the (SHIFT) key depressed.

Two events signal the end of these operations: the **MouseUp** and **KeyUp** text box events. Add a call to **SetupCSMenus** to both of these subroutines in the **txtDocument** control, as shown in Listing 6-16.

Listing 6-16 Calling Setup routine when user selects text

```
Private Sub txtDocument_KeyUp(KeyCode As Integer, Shift As Integer)
    frmMain.SetupCSMenus
End Sub

Private Sub txtDocument_MouseUp(Button As Integer, Shift As Integer, X As Single, Y⇐
As Single)
    frmMain.SetupCSMenus
End Sub
```

The Activate *Event*

To make sure that the menus behave correctly when the user moves from one document to another, you need to add another call to **SetupCSMenus**, this time from **frmDocument**'s **Activate** event. This code is shown in Listing 6-17.

Listing 6-17 The Form Activate event routine

```
Private Sub Form_Activate()
    frmMain.SetupCSMenus
End Sub
```

A form's **Activate** event is called when the form becomes the active form. This happens when a form is created and the user clicks on it, making it the active form when more than one MDI child document form is present. (There is a corresponding **Deactivate** event, which is called when a form loses the focus, but you don't need to use it.)

Before you can run SuperPad with these changes, you have to do one more thing. In **SetupCSMenus**, you are now making a reference to the text box on **frmDocument** in the line that reads

```
If frmMain.ActiveForm.txtDocument.SelLength > 0 Then
```

If you run the program now, you will get a runtime error when this statement is reached. The reason is that when a document form is created during the **AddForm** function, the form's **Load** event subroutine is called. However, although the **Load** event subroutine is called after the form itself has been created, the controls on that form aren't created until the **Load** event is completed.

The error occurs because you're making a reference to a control that doesn't yet exist. You can use two techniques to overcome this.

1. Add a call to the form's **Show** method in its **Load** event subroutine prior to calling **SetupCSMenus**. This will force Visual Basic 5 to create the controls and display the form. Because the form is already loaded, the **Load** event isn't triggered a second time, which is just as well, because otherwise you would enter an endless loop!

2. The other technique is to move the call to **SetupCSMenus** from the **Load** event subroutine to the form's **Activate** event subroutine. The **Activate** event is called first after the form and its controls have been created and the form becomes active.

Luckily, you already have a call to **SetupCSMenus** in the **Activate** event subroutine for **frmDocument**, so the easiest way to get around the error is to remove the call to **SetupCSMenus** from **frmDocument**'s **Load** event subroutine.

That's it! The Cut, Copy, and Delete menus will now be context-sensitive.

Try running SuperPad again and experiment with selecting text and moving from one document to another.

The Paste Menu Item and the Clipboard *Object*

You have already disabled the Paste menu if there are no document forms loaded. However, the Paste menu can be enabled only when there is text in the clipboard. The clipboard is a storage area available for use by all the programs running on your Windows desktop. Visual Basic 5 has a built-in **Clipboard** object that represents the Windows clipboard. The **Clipboard** object has a number of methods that you can use. One of them, **GetFormat**, can tell you if there is any text on the clipboard that can be pasted into your document.

Modify the **If** statement at the end of the **SetupCSMenus** subroutine, which should now read

```
If Found = False Then
    ' disable Copy, Cut, Delete and Paste menus
    ' when no forms are found
    mnuEditCopy.Enabled = False
    mnuEditCut.Enabled = False
    mnuEditDelete.Enabled = False
    mnuEditPaste.Enabled = False
    ' remove any check mark from the Word Wrap menu
    mnuEditWordWrap.Checked = False
Else
    If frmMain.ActiveForm.txtDocument.SelLength > 0 Then
        ' Enable Copy, Cut and Delete menus if there is
        ' an active form and text is selected in it.
        mnuEditCopy.Enabled = True
        mnuEditCut.Enabled = True
        mnuEditDelete.Enabled = True
    Else
        ' Disable Copy, Cut and Delete menus if there is
        ' an active form and there is no text selected in it.
        mnuEditCopy.Enabled = False
        mnuEditCut.Enabled = False
        mnuEditDelete.Enabled = False
    End If
    If Clipboard.GetFormat(vbCFText) Then
        mnuEditPaste.Enabled = True
    Else
        mnuEditPaste.Enabled = False
    End If
End If
```

You have used another of Visual Basic 5's built-in constants (**vbCFText**, which stands for clipboard format text) to find out if there is any text on the clipboard. The **GetFormat** method returns a Boolean value representing whether any data of the requested format was found. If there is any text on the clipboard, you can enable the Paste menu; otherwise, disable it.

Copying Text into the Clipboard

Both the Copy and Cut edit menus need to copy the selected text from the text box to the clipboard. The Cut and Delete menus also have to remove the selected text physically.

The SetText Method

Let's write a subroutine to copy the text from the text box to the clipboard. Place the subroutine in **frmMain**. It should read as shown in Listing 6-18.

Listing 6-18 Copying text to the clipboard

```
Private Sub CopyTextToClipboard()
    Clipboard.SetText frmMain.ActiveForm.txtDocument.SelText
End Sub
```

Here you're using another **Clipboard** method, **SetText**, to copy the selected text to the clipboard. You're also obtaining that text by using the **SelText** text box property. The **SelText** property is available only at runtime. It contains the selected text—very useful. All you need to do now is add a call to **CopyTextToClipboard** to both the **mnuEditCopy** and **mnuEditCut Click** event subroutines, as shown in Listing 6-19.

Listing 6-19 The Cut Menu item

```
Private Sub mnuEditCopy_Click()
    CopyTextToClipboard
    SetupCSMenus
End Sub

Private Sub mnuEditCut_Click()
    CopyTextToClipboard
    SetupCSMenus
End Sub
```

Deleting the Selected Text from the Text Box

Additionally, both the Cut and Delete Edit menus need to delete the selected text from the text box. Unfortunately, there isn't a single method that will do the job for you, but you can do it quite easily by using a combination of the text box's **SelStart**, **SelLength**, and **Text** properties. Create a new subroutine in **frmMain** as follows:

```
Private Sub DeleteSelectedText()
    Dim Text As String
    Dim SelStart As Long
    Dim SelLength As Long
    ' Put the text in a local string variable
    Text = frmMain.ActiveForm.txtDocument.Text
```

```
    ' Get the begining and ending positions of the selected text.
    SelStart = frmMain.ActiveForm.txtDocument.SelStart
    SelLength = frmMain.ActiveForm.txtDocument.SelLength
    ' Replace text box with a string containing what's before
    ' and what's after the selection.
    frmMain.ActiveForm.txtDocument.Text = Left(Text, SelStart) & _
            Right(Text, Len(Text) - (SelStart + SelLength))
    ' Reset the cursor
    frmMain.ActiveForm.txtDocument.SelStart = SelStart
End Sub
```

At first sight, this subroutine may seem a little daunting, so let's break it down line by line.

The SelStart and SelLength Properties

The first three lines are straightforward. You're making local copies of the **Text**, **SelStart**, and **SelLength** text box properties to use later in the subroutine. You already know about **Text** and **SelLength**. The **SelStart** property gives you the offset into the text of the text box at which the selection starts. If **SelLength** is greater than **0**, it means that some text is selected. The **SelStart** property tells you at which character position in the text the selected text begins.

The fourth line in the subroutine removes the selected text. It chops the text into two portions using the **Left** and **Right** string functions. The two portions are the strings to the left and right of the selected text. It then uses the string concatenation operator (&) to join them back together, minus the selected portion, and places the result in the text box.

The final line positions the text box's text cursor to where the selection started; otherwise, it would be positioned back at the beginning of the text box, which would look strange. You can try cutting text out of the text box without the last line to see what we mean. The last line also demonstrates another use for **SelStart**. If **SelLength** is set to **0**, **SelStart** sets or returns the position of the text cursor. This is pretty complex stuff and shows just how much you can do with a "simple" text box.

Finally, you need to add calls to **DeleteSelectedText** from the Cut and Delete menus' **Click** event subroutines, which now read like Listing 6-20.

Listing 6-20 Calling the Delete routine

```
Private Sub mnuEditCut_Click()
    CopyTextToClipboard
    DeleteSelectedText
    SetupCSMenus
End Sub

Private Sub mnuEditDelete_Click()
    DeleteSelectedText
    SetupCSMenus
End Sub
```

OK, you now have working Cut, Copy, and Delete menus. All that's left to do is finish off the Paste and other Edit menus and add an About box, and SuperPad will be complete. We've got one more trick up our sleeve that we'll show you in the next lesson. For now, run SuperPad again and experiment with cutting and copying text to the clipboard. You can use the clipboard viewer program that comes with Windows to see the text on the clipboard if you wish. You can also use the [SHIFT]-[INSERT] key combination to paste text, because that is a built-in Windows function.

1. The **Clipboard** object is an object like many others you've seen in VB 5. Which of the following is a method or property of the **Clipboard** object?
   a. **Text**
   b. **SetText**
   c. **SelStart**
   d. **SelLength**

2. Which of the following is the most efficient and reliable approach to implementing context-sensitive menus?
   a. Disable appropriate menu items at design time.
   b. Track needed program state in form variables, place enabling/disabling code in a single routine, and call the routine when the state might change.
   c. Disable or enable options directly whenever the user state changes.
   d. Group routines to enable/disable items by function, such as clipboard routines, to reduce redundant execution.

3. Which of the following is not a use of the **SelLength** property?
   a. To determine the cursor position when no text is selected
   b. To determine whether the user has selected text
   c. To determine the length of the selection
   d. To determine, with **SelStart**, the ending position of the selection

4. Which event triggers when a loaded form gets the focus?
   a. **GotFocus**
   b. **Activate**
   c. **Show**
   d. **Load**

5. **If** statements inside other **If** statements, called nested **If** statements:
   a. Are always difficult to read and should be avoided
   b. Are limited to one nested **If** statement per block
   c. Are helpful in evaluating conditions and subsets of those conditions
   d. Shouldn't be indented; they waste system resources

FILLING IN THE BLANKS: FINISHING UP SUPERPAD

All that's left to do is to wrap up the Edit menus and add an About box, but don't forget the extra trick we mentioned. We'll save that for the end. The Edit menu items that you have left to program are Paste, Select All, Time/Date, and Word Wrap. Let's get right to it and consider the Paste menu.

Pasting Text from the Clipboard

The `Clipboard` object provides a method, called `GetText`, that you can use to obtain the text on the clipboard so that you can paste it into the text box. You have already seen how to determine if there is any text on the clipboard and how to set the context of the Edit menus accordingly. However, the fact that text was on the clipboard at the time you enabled the Paste menu doesn't mean that it will still be there at the time you actually paste it in. For example, in the meantime the user may have switched to a graphics application and used Cut and Paste to move some graphics data around. Unfortunately, the `Clipboard` object has no events, so it cannot tell your program when its contents have changed.

To overcome this problem, you should double-check when you paste in the text that there is still text there to paste.

There is one other consideration as well. Although the clipboard provides you with the basic method to obtain the text, you still have some work to do to support the paste itself.

With all that taken into consideration, the finished Paste menu's `Click` event subroutine for `frmMain` should look like Listing 6-21.

Listing 6-21 The `Paste` command

```
Private Sub mnuEditPaste_Click()
Dim Text As String
Dim ClipboardText As String
Dim SelStart As Long
If Clipboard.GetFormat(vbCFText) Then
    ' Replace selected text (if any)
    If frmMain.ActiveForm.txtDocument.SelLength > 0 Then
        DeleteSelectedText
    End If
    ' Move stuff we need to variables
    Text = frmMain.ActiveForm.txtDocument.Text
    SelStart = frmMain.ActiveForm.txtDocument.SelStart
    ClipboardText = Clipboard.GetText
    ' Concatenate new text string and replace text box
```

continued on next page

continued from previous page

```
        ' contents with it.
        frmMain.ActiveForm.txtDocument.Text = Left(Text, SelStart) & _
            ClipboardText & Right(Text, Len(Text) - SelStart)
        ' Restore cursor position.
        frmMain.ActiveForm.txtDocument.SelStart = SelStart
    Else
        SetupCSMenus
    End If
End Sub
```

When you paste text into a document, you have to check first if any text is already highlighted. If so, the text you are pasting in should replace the highlighted text. That's what the nested **If** statement is doing.

The next two lines obtain local copies of the **Text** and **SelStart** text box properties.

You are then using the clipboard's **GetText** method to obtain the text that is currently on the clipboard. It's being assigned to another local variable, **ClipboardText**.

The next line is the one that is doing the job of adding the text. Note that you're adding the clipboard text at the current position of the text cursor, which is what you expect when pasting text from the clipboard.

Finally, the last line repositions the text cursor to the point at which you pasted in the text, as you did in the Cut menu.

The Remaining Edit Menu Items

You're through with the **Clipboard** functions now. Let's finish up the Edit menu items.

Select All

The Select All menu simply selects all the text in the text box. This is pretty straightforward to program using the text box's **SelStart** and **SelLength** properties. The **Select All** routine is shown in Listing 6-22.

Listing 6-22 Select all the text

```
Private Sub mnuEditSelectAll_Click()
    frmMain.ActiveForm.txtDocument.SelStart = 0
    frmMain.ActiveForm.txtDocument.SelLength = _
    Len(frmMain.ActiveForm.txtDocument.Text)
    SetupCSMenus
End Sub
```

By setting the text box's **SelStart** property to **0** and its **SelLength** property to the length of the text in its **Text** property, you select all the text in the text box. Finally, don't forget to call **SetupCSMenus** because text is now selected in the document and the context-sensitive Edit menus may need to be updated. It's as easy as that!

Time/Date

When you use the Time/Date menu option in NotePad, it adds the current time and date, in Windows short format, to the document. The routine shown in Listing 6-23 will do the same thing.

Listing 6-23 Adding the date and time

```
Private Sub mnuEditTimeDate_Click()
    Dim Text As String
    Dim SelStart As Long
    ' Replace selection (if any)
        DeleteSelectedText
    If frmMain.ActiveForm.txtDocument.SelLength > 0 Then
    End If
    ' Use our regular trick to get the text,
    ' add what we want to it, and replace the
    ' text box contents with the result.
    Text = frmMain.ActiveForm.txtDocument.Text
    SelStart = frmMain.ActiveForm.txtDocument.SelStart
    frmMain.ActiveForm.txtDocument.Text = Left(Text, SelStart) & _
    Now & Right(Text, Len(Text) - SelStart)
    frmMain.ActiveForm.txtDocument.SelStart = SelStart
    ' Menus may need to be updated.
    SetupCSMenus
End Sub
```

Again, while you're adding text to the document, you need to check if there is any selected text to be deleted first. Then you get on with the job of adding the time and date text to the correct position in the text box.

Word Wrap

We pointed out earlier that it isn't possible to provide a word wrap facility using the standard TextBox control. The application that you're trying to emulate, NotePad, implements word wrap by removing the horizontal scroll bar. When word wrap is turned on, the text is forced to wrap at the end of each physical line of text according to the size of the document window. Unfortunately for you, the standard text box does not let you set the scrollbar's property at runtime. You can find out what the property is currently set to, but if you try to change its value, a runtime error is generated.

There are advanced techniques that you can use to overcome this problem, but they involve using the Windows API and are outside the scope of this book.

Therefore, for the moment, implement the Word Wrap menu as far as providing the code to implement the checkmark in the menu itself.

The Word Wrap menu's **Click** event subroutine should therefore read

```
Private Sub mnuEditWordWrap_Click()
    mnuEditWordWrap.Checked = Not mnuEditWordWrap.Checked
End Sub
```

This is a straightforward way to toggle the checkmark. If there is no checkmark, the menu's `Checked` property will be `False`. Therefore, `Not False` is `True` and vice versa.

Adding an About Box

All great Windows programs have great About boxes. This is when you get the chance to put your artistic abilities to the test and try to code the most exciting About box possible. Check out the About boxes of your favorite applications. You'll find a whole range of styles used, from straightforward text to animated graphics.

The About box that you're going to add to SuperPad will contain the basic information that you need to add to any About box. You need a place to display the copyright and version information of the program, together with a copy of the icon used for `frmMain`.

The About box starts out life as a straightforward SDI form. So, first add a new form to the project, name it `frmAbout,` and set its `Caption` property to `About SuperPad`.

The BorderStyle **Property**

Next, set the form's `BorderStyle` property to `3 - Fixed Dialog`. In the forms you've used so far, you haven't expressly set this property. You've always used the default setting of `2 - Sizable`. However, this About box is going to be a dialog-style form. As such, it must not have sizable borders. Its size has to be fixed. To do this, set its `BorderStyle` property to `3 - Fixed Dialog`. You'll see from the Properties window that you can use a number of different styles. You will come across some of the other styles later in this book.

Set the `MinButton` and `MaxButton` properties to `False`. In this way, you prevent the form from being minimized or maximized, which is just what you need for the About box.

There is also a property called `ControlBox` that you can set to hide the control box on the form's title bar. It's not doing any harm there, so leave it alone, but you can experiment with removing it if you wish.

The Image Control

Previously, you added pictures to forms using a PictureBox Control. Visual Basic's Image control can also contain a picture. The difference between the two controls is that the PictureBox control has more functionality. You can tell this by glancing at the list of properties for the controls. Also, the PictureBox control can double up as a container for other controls, just like the frame. You can therefore use it as a captionless Frame control even without using it to display a picture. The PictureBox control is also one of the few controls that you can drag directly onto an MDI form. For these reasons, it is arguably the more flexible of the two controls.

However, the trade-off here is that the Image control uses fewer system resources and repaints faster than the PictureBox control. If you don't need the PictureBox control's extra bells and whistles, the Image control will do the job.

Add an Image control to the form. You will use an Image control to display a copy of SuperPad's icon in the About box. Figure 6-25 shows how the Image control appears on the toolbox.

You can add a copy of the **note02.ico** icon to the Image control by setting its **Picture** property to the icon file, as you did earlier for the icon properties in **frmMain** and **frmDocument**. You might also want to set the **Icon** property of the form to the same file. Although you can't minimize the About box, Windows 95 displays the icon in the title bar. If you don't add your own icon, you'll see the standard SDI form icon instead.

Finally, you can add Label controls as appropriate and set their **Caption** properties to whatever you want to say in your About box. The only control that's mandatory here is an OK button to close the form. That source code is shown in Listing 6-24.

Listing 6-24 Dismissing the About box

```
Private Sub Command1_Click()
    Unload Me
End Sub
```

Note how the **Me** keyword has uses for any old form, not just child forms.

Back at **frmMain**, program the About box menu option as in Listing 6-25. You could have done that without peeking!

Listing 6-25 Calling the About box

```
Private Sub mnuHelpAbout_Click()
    frmAbout.Show vbModal
End Sub
```

Figure 6-26 shows what the About box form looks like when SuperPad is running.

Figure 6-25
Adding an Image
control to the
About box

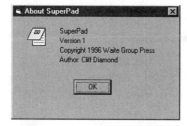

Figure 6-26
SuperPad's About
box

Something Up Our Sleeve!

Great, SuperPad's nearly done. But we did mention that we were holding back a final trick till the end. The trick is an extra menu, called the Window menu. All the best MDI applications have one, so SuperPad mustn't be left out. A Window menu serves two purposes. One is to hold a "window list." This is a list of the open MDI child windows. The other is to provide the `Cascade` and `Tile` commands that your users can use to help organize the documents open in the MDI frame.

The first thing you have to do is add the Window menu itself. Do this using the menu editor, placing it between the Edit and Help menus. When you add the Window menu, make sure you click on the WindowList check box. This is a great time-saving Visual Basic feature, because Visual Basic completely manages the window list for you. Figure 6-27 shows you the completed entry in the menu editor.

When you run SuperPad, you'll see a list of the open windows in the Window menu. What's more, you can move around the open documents by selecting their entries in the Window menu, even if the document window is minimized. Figure 6-28 shows you what this looks like with six open documents.

Finally, there are the menu commands to add to arrange the windows. There are a total of four different commands that you can add: Cascade, Tile Horizontally, Tile Vertically, and Arrange Icons. Add these menus to the Window menu using the menu editor. Use the names `mnuWindowCascade` and the like. Don't worry about where the window list will go; Visual Basic always adds it to the end of the menu.

Listing 6-26 shows the code to place in each menu.

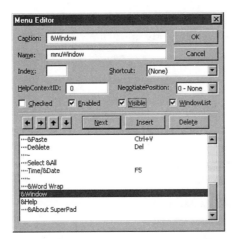

Figure 6-27
Adding a Window
List menu

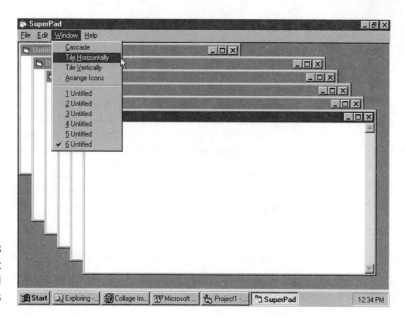

Figure 6-28
The window list
with six untitled
documents

Listing 6-26 Code to rearrange windows

```
Private Sub mnuWindowArrangeIcons_Click()
    frmMain.Arrange vbArrangeIcons
End Sub

Private Sub mnuWindowCascade_Click()
    frmMain.Arrange vbCascade
End Sub

Private Sub mnuWindowTileHorizontally_Click()
    frmMain.Arrange vbTileHorizontal
End Sub

Private Sub mnuWindowTileVertically_Click()
    frmMain.Arrange vbTileVertical
End Sub
```

Yes! Just one line of code per menu—we said we had a trick up our sleeve! As you can see, the MDI form has a method called **Arrange** that does the job for you. Now you can organize your documents with a click of a mouse.

QUIZ

1. In the context of the `Clipboard` object, what is `GetText`?
   a. A method that returns the text in the clipboard
   b. A property containing the value of the clipboard
   c. An event that triggers when the clipboard text changes
   d. A method that returns `True` if there is text on the clipboard

2. If you programatically insert text in a text box, such as by pasting from the clipboard, what should happen if there is highlighted text?
   a. The inserted text goes before the selected text.
   b. The inserted text goes after the selected text.
   c. The inserted text replaces the selected text.
   d. The program should ask the user whether to replace the text.

3. Which property controls whether the user can resize a window by dragging the corner with the mouse?
   a. `MaxButton`
   b. `MinButton`
   c. `Resize`
   d. `BorderStyle`

4. Windows About boxes come in all styles, but which element(s) is common to all of them?
   a. An image of the program's icon
   b. Program name and copyright info
   c. A nifty animated sequence
   d. A Help button

5. Which function is *not* easily implemented under the Window menu via a VB 5 built-in feature?
   a. Viewing and being able to select from a window list
   b. Generating a copy of the current window
   c. Arranging icons in a "cascade"
   d. Arranging icons in a vertical "tile"

EXERCISE

Rewrite the Sender program (from Chapter 4, Subroutines, Functions, and the Visual Basic 5 Language) so that the Sender forms are all child forms of `frmMDISender`. Make `frmMain` a regular form. Implement the program with the same functionality as before.

CHAPTER 7

CLASSES

For you to make the most of Visual Basic 5's object-oriented features, it is important that you have a complete understanding of *classes*. In this chapter, you'll see precisely what the relationship is between a class and an object. You'll learn about the classes already built into Visual Basic 5 and how to create your own classes.

You'll learn how an apparently complex problem can be simplified by applying object-oriented design techniques to it and how useful classes can be reused. You'll also discover how you have been using many of the object-oriented features of Visual Basic 5 since Chapter 1, What's All That Stuff on My Screen?.

CLASSES AND OBJECTS

A *class* is a category of things. An *object* is a thing, and each object belongs to a class. Car is a class. Your brother's '87 Honda Civic is an object of class car.

A class is a description of a set of characteristics. An object contains specific characteristics that can change over the period of time the object is in existence. We can describe the chair class as having (at minimum) a place to sit and legs to hold it up. We can further describe the chair class as having optional characteristics such as a back, armrest, rockers, cushion, and so on. In your house, you may have the objects stool (three legs and a seat), desk chair (with ergonomic back rest), and dining room chair (with designer cushion and arm rest).

A class is abstract; it doesn't really exist. An object exists. An architecture professor engages her students in many discussions on the house class, but these discussions are all theoretical. Not until after he graduates will the student design and see to completion his first house object.

Class Design Techniques

Imagine you're designing a computer keyboard. You start by designing a key for the letter A; it has everything. It is beautiful with round edges. It has a spring thingy and a click thingy and makes just the right clicking sound before it bounces back up. The boss loves it, but what about the rest of the keys?

In this example, it would be better to start out with a generic design—in other words, a class design. The design would have all the information you need to produce an object. With a key class design, it takes only the slightest effort to generate the key for the letter B. If the client comes back and says, oh, we don't want a click sound after all, you simply make the changes to the class design and all the key objects created from the class automatically act the way you want.

You've already seen this approach in action in the SuperPad example in Chapter 6, Forms, Menus, and MDI Forms. In design mode, you made a document form you can think of as a prototype. When the program runs, the program can generate one document window after another, at the whim of the user. These objects are all based on the single design prototype. If you change any of the characteristics of the design—as indeed you'll do in Chapter 8, Discovering the CommonDialog and Windows 95 Controls—these changes will be reflected in each new document object the next time the program runs.

Instances

An object is an *instance* of a class. The terms object and instance have similar meanings. In fact, they can often be used interchangeably. However, in programming, if you refer to an instance, you are really keeping the class in the front of your mind. You can talk about an object, on the other hand, as a fairly independent entity.

SuperPad, for example, is based on a form class designed for text entry. When the program runs, SuperPad generates one or more instances of the form class. The user can edit text in each instance independently. (In other words, the user can edit text in each window object independently.) The user can move and resize these objects, a feature found in most other Windows programs.

Classes, Classes Everywhere

Classes are intrinsic to Visual Basic 5. As an example, consider one of the most commonly used classes in Visual Basic 5—the form.

When you move the mouse over a form object at runtime, the form object reacts by generating MouseMove events. However, when you move the mouse over a form class at design time, no event is generated. The two forms that you see at design time and runtime may appear similar, but they are quite different conceptually.

Think of what happens when you add controls to a form class at design time. The controls are visually displayed on the form class but, like the form class itself, they don't work yet. This is because they, too, are classes.

When you run a project, what happens? Not only is an instance of the form class created, but an instance of each control class is created too.

You can begin to see that Visual Basic 5 is intuitively object-oriented. In fact, it's difficult to think of using Visual Basic 5 without using one type of object or another.

Other Class Types

Visual Basic 5 has a number of different types of classes. Forms and controls are two of the types. The other class types that you can use fall into the following four categories.

- Single-instance classes
- User-defined classes
- Database classes
- Miscellaneous classes

Predefined Single-Instance Classes

Visual Basic 5 creates a few special objects based on single-instance classes when you run your project. They are special in that they represent single items in the environment in which your project runs. Because VB generates these objects automatically, they are always available to your running program.

Objects created based on single-instance classes are already familiar to you. You've used three of these objects: the Screen, Clipboard, and Debug objects.

See Table 7-1 for a list of Visual Basic 5's predefined single-instance objects.

Table 7-1 Visual Basic 5's predefined single-instance objects

Object	Description
App	Represents your running application
Clipboard	Represents the clipboard
Err	Represents an error
Debug	Represents the Debug window
Printer	Represents the printer attached to your PC
Screen	Represents the physical screen on your PC

User-Defined Classes

User-defined classes are very important, and much of this chapter is devoted to showing you how to use them. They are the real key to making your own applications object-oriented. With user-defined classes, you can invent your own classes with properties and methods that you define.

Database Classes

Use of the database classes is a large topic on its own. Chapter 12, Files, is dedicated to showing you how to use databases and the classes that go with them.

Miscellaneous Classes

There are three miscellaneous classes that you might find of use in your projects. These are shown in Table 7-2.

Table 7-2 Miscellaneous classes

Class Type	Description
Collection	A grouping of objects
Font	Represents a font
Picture	Represents a graphical image

1. Which of the following statements about classes is false?
   a. A class is abstract.
   b. A class includes a set of general characteristics.
   c. A class is a kind of thing.
   d. A class is abstract only until the first object is created from it.

2. Which of the following statements about objects is false?
   a. An object is an instance of a class.
   b. An object's characteristics can never change.
   c. In many cases, you can have any number of objects based on a single class.
   d. Object is to class what "that Saturn out front" is to "car."

3. What happens when you move the mouse over a form at design time?
   a. A `MouseMove event` is generated.
   b. The control under the mouse is activated.
   c. Nothing
   d. The Code window opens.

4. When you run a program:
   a. An instance of the form class is created.
   b. An instance of each control class in the project is created.
   c. The form and other objects begin responding to events.
   d. All of the above

5. How do you create an instance of a single-instance class, such as the `Printer`?
   a. We won't learn that until later this chapter.
   b. With the `New` statement
   c. With the `Declare` statement
   d. We don't need to; the single-instance class objects are automatically generated by VB 5 at runtime.

THE Form **CLASS**

Now we're going to look at how objects are actually implemented and managed in Visual Basic 5. We'll start out in this lesson demonstrating certain features that are common to all classes. We're using forms as an example because you are already familiar with them. In the next lesson, we'll turn our attention to the control classes; later in this chapter, we'll introduce user-defined classes, which are central to designing fully object-oriented applications.

Let's start out by showing you what really happens when Visual Basic creates an object from a class.

Let's start with a nice new default project and review what you already know.

The Form1 Class

When you run the default project, Visual Basic 5 starts by creating an instance of the Form1 class. Once the form object has been created, you are able to access the running form object by using its name in your code, as in:

```
Form1.Show vbModeless
```

Note that in this syntax, Form1 is actually a type of variable known as an *object variable*.

An object variable isn't terribly complex conceptually. It's really just a variable, and in that respect it's no different from an Integer or a String variable. However, the object variable doesn't store data in the same way that an Integer or String variable stores data. Instead, it stores something called an *object reference*. The reference is a bit like a signpost; it tells Visual Basic 5 where the actual object is. Of course, Visual Basic 5 does all this behind the scenes so that by the time the form object's Load event subroutine is called, the object variable is ready for you to use.

Creating Your Own Form1 *Object*

We can show you how this works by writing a program to do what VB does automatically.

Click on Module under the Insert menu to begin a new code module. Give it the name modMain by bringing up the module's Properties window. Next, create a public subroutine called Main. Now make Sub Main the startup form. Do this by clicking on Options (you don't need to show the ellipsis on menu options) under the Tools menu, then click on the Project tab. Under Startup Form, select Sub Main.

Once this has been done, add the code in Listing 7-1 to the Main subroutine.

Listing 7-1 Loading a form via code

```
Public Sub Main()
' Create the object variable
Dim Form1Variable As Form1
Debug.Print "Created a " & TypeName(Form1Variable) _
        & " variable"
' Create an instance of Form1 and assign a reference to
' it to Form1Variable.
Set Form1Variable = New Form1
Debug.Print "Now it's a " & TypeName(Form1Variable) _
        & " variable"
' Now use the variable name to call one of the
' object's methods.
Form1Variable.Show vbModeless
End Sub
```

This piece of code does the same job Visual Basic 5 does when you specify that **Form1** should be the startup form. However, we changed the name of the variable that Visual Basic 5 creates to emphasize that it is a variable that has been created.

The statement

```
Dim Form1Variable As Form1
```

creates the variable. The line is saying "Create a variable that can contain a reference to a **Form1** object."

The **Print** command uses the **TypeName** function to find out what sort of object **Form1Variable** is connected to. Remember that at this stage, all you have done is create the variable itself. You haven't assigned a reference to a running form object to it yet. Therefore, TypeName returns the text Nothing.

The next line:

```
Set Form1Variable = New Form1
```

creates the new form object and completes the job of assigning its reference to **Form1Variable**. (Recall from Chapter 6, Forms, Menus, and MDI Forms, that you need to use the Set statement when dealing with objects.) You then prove that this has worked by asking for the TypeName of the object referenced by **Form1Variable** again. This time, TypeName returns **Form1**.

To prove that the object is really there and that the connection to it works correctly, you then call its **Show** method to display it on the screen.

So, objects are accessed through object variables, and different types of object variables are used to access different types of objects. The really clever part is that you can create your own specific form classes merely by changing the **Name** property of each form module added to your project. You'll see later that the same is true for the user-defined classes.

Referencing an Object More Than Once

If an object variable simply contains a reference to an object, does this mean that two object variables can reference the same object?

The answer is Yes! Let's show you how this works.

Modify Main so that it reads as shown in Listing 7-2.

Listing 7-2 Two variables reference the same form

```
Public Sub Main()
' Create the object variables
Dim Form1Variable As Form1
Dim AnotherForm1Variable As Form1

' Create an instance of Form1 and assign a reference to
' it to Form1Variable.
Set Form1Variable = New Form1
```

continued on next page

continued from previous page

```
' Assign the form to the second variable
Set AnotherForm1Variable = Form1Variable
If AnotherForm1Variable Is Form1Variable Then
        MsgBox "The two variables point to the same object."
End If
Form1Variable.Show vbModeless
AnotherForm1Variable.Left = 0
AnotherForm1Variable.Width = Screen.Width
End Sub
```

Here you're creating two object variables, both capable of storing references to instances of the **Form1** class. You then go on to create a new form and assign a reference to it to **Form1Variable**, just like you did in the previous example. The next line takes the reference stored in **Form1Variable** and assigns it to **AnotherForm1Variable**. Now both **Form1Variable** and **AnotherForm1Variable** contain the same object reference.

The Is *Statement*

Just as you can't assign object references with the normal equal sign as you can with other variable types, you can't compare two object references with the equal sign. Instead, use the **Is** operator, as in the expression

```
AnotherForm1Variable Is Form1Variable
```

This expression returns **True** if the two variables point to the same object; otherwise, it returns **False**.

Note that you can use either the **Form1Variable**

```
Form1Variable.Show vbModeless
```

or **AnotherForm1Variable**

```
AnotherForm1Variable.Left = 0
AnotherForm1Variable.Width = Screen.Width
```

to access the objects methods and properties.

Form Object Types

In the above example, you created a form based on the **Form1** class. To do that, you declared an object variable of the type **Form1**, created the form itself (with **New**), and then assigned the reference to the form to the variable. Now assume you want to write a subroutine to center the form on the screen.

Listing 7-3 shows you one possible solution.

Listing 7-3 Passing a form as a procedure argument

```
Public Sub CenterForm(AnyForm1Form As Form1)
AnyForm1Form.Move (Screen.Width - AnyForm1Form.Width) / 2, _
                (Screen.Height - AnyForm1Form.Height) / 2
End Sub
```

As you can see, to complete this task, the subroutine needs access to the form's **Move** method and its **Width** and **Height** properties. The way to do this is to pass the reference to the form that you want to center to another object variable that is a parameter of the subroutine. The code that you would use to call this subroutine from the form's **Load** event subroutine would be

```
CenterForm Me
```

The **Me** keyword provides the reference that you need to the form object called the subroutine.

Although that solution would work, it is limited in one important way. It can be used only to center forms that are instances of the **Form1** class. If you have another form class in your project, say **Form2**, you wouldn't be able to use the same subroutine, because Visual Basic 5 would complain that you are attempting to pass a **Form1** object reference to a **Form2** object variable. It's a bit like trying to store a String in an Integer: The two class types are completely different as far as Visual Basic 5 is concerned, even though they are both forms.

The solution is to use a more generic class type. Visual Basic 5 has a built-in class type called Form. An object variable of type Form can be used to hold a reference to any form object, be it a **Form1** object or whatever. Let's modify **CenterForm** so that it will work for any type of form. The final version is shown in Listing 7-4.

Listing 7-4 Centering any form on the screen

```
Public Sub CenterForm(AnyForm As Form)
AnyForm.Move (Screen.Width - AnyForm.Width) / 2, _
             (Screen.Height - AnyForm.Height) / 2
End Sub
```

Now you can call **CenterForm** from a **Form1** form, a **Form2** form, or any type of form, including an **MDI** form.

1. In the line

    ```
    Form1.Top = 0
    ```

    Form1 is actually a(n):
    a. Class
    b. Class type
    c. Object variable
    d. Instance

2. How does an object variable differ from some other type of variable, such as a String?
   a. The names of object variables must begin with `Form`.
   b. You must use the `Set` statement to assign a value to an object variable.
   c. Object variables cannot be passed to subroutines.
   d. Object variables must be written in C++.

3. The `Is` operator is used to:
   a. Perform "fuzzy" matching in string comparisons
   b. See if two variables reference the same object
   c. See if an object is of a specific class
   d. Tell if a form is loaded

4. The `New` statement:
   a. Creates a new file
   b. Creates an object
   c. Redimensions an array
   d. Prepares an object for reuse

5. In the following code fragment:

```
Public Sub MoveForm(A As Form, X as Integer, Y as Integer)
```

the first parameter, `A`:
   a. Can be any class of form you create
   b. Must be an instance of class `Form`
   c. Is a syntax error
   d. Can refer to any object

CONTROL CLASSES

Now that you appreciate what's going on behind the scenes when form objects are created, you can move on to considering the object-oriented nature of controls—or, to give them a more accurate title, *control classes*.

Although controls are classes, they differ from forms and the other classes in Visual Basic 5 in two important ways.

● They cannot exist on their own. They have to be contained within a form. In fact, a form class is known as a *container* for the control classes that appear on it. Therefore, when you delete a form class from your project, all the control classes that are contained within it are deleted, too.

🔵 Whereas forms and other classes are implemented within Visual Basic 5 itself, controls can be implemented outside, as separate programs that conform to the ActiveX Control Extension (OCX) standard.

Through the OCX standard, third-party suppliers can produce their own specialist controls. (We'll call these controls OCX controls from now on.) This is an important way in which Visual Basic 5's functionality can be extended. If you want to add some special functionality to your project, it is likely that someone has already written an OCX that does what you need. If they haven't, you can write your own. OCXs couldn't be written in VB4 and had to be implemented in C++. One of the important improvements in Visual Basic 5 is the ability to create your own OCXs in Visual Basic. We will cover that in detail in Chapter 16, Roll Your Own: Creating Your Own ActiveX Controls.

What Are OCX Controls?

The great thing about OCX controls is that they are as easy to use in Visual Basic as the standard controls. This is because they have properties and methods and fire off events in just the same way. The only difference is that the standard controls are permanently built in to Visual Basic 5 and cannot be removed from the toolbox, whereas OCXs are packaged as separate files. Because of this, you have to go through a small procedure to tell Visual Basic 5 that you want to use a particular OCX in your project. This procedure is known as *referencing* the OCX.

Referencing OCXs

The tool that you use to reference an OCX is the Custom Controls dialog box. Display it by selecting Custom Controls from the Tools menu. This dialog box is reproduced in Figure 7-1.

The first thing you'll want to do is find out which OCXs are available for use on your computer. To do this, make sure that the Selected Items Only check box in the lower-right corner of the dialog is not checked. This way, all the OCXs installed on your PC are displayed, rather than just the ones currently in use. Visual Basic can do this because each OCX file has already been *registered* with Windows. This happened when the OCX was installed. To the left of each entry in the list box is a small check box. Use it to signal to Visual Basic 5 that this is an OCX that you want to use in this project. Just click on the check box with the mouse so that a checkmark appears next to the description of the OCX. The full path name of the currently highlighted OCX file is displayed at the bottom of the dialog box so that you can check which OCX file is going to be used.

Each OCX file can contain more than one control class. For example, the Common Windows 95 Control OCX (COMCTL32.OCX) contains a total of eight controls. (We'll show you these controls in Chapter 8, Discovering the CommonDialog and Windows 95 Controls.)

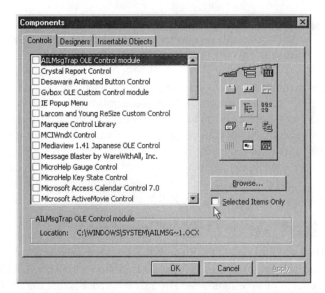

Figure 7-1
Custom Controls
dialog box

After you press the OK button, Visual Basic 5 loads the control classes from the OCX file and updates the toolbox with the new controls. Once the controls have been added to the toolbox, you can add them to your forms in the usual way.

When you save your project to disk, the reference to the OCX is saved with it so that when you next load your project, the OCX is loaded too. Similarly, when you compile your project, the references to the OCXs are stored in the compiled program, so that the correct OCX files can be found at runtime.

What About VBX Controls?

VBX controls are 16-bit controls and cannot be used in the 32-bit environment of Visual Basic 5.

Object Variables for Controls

You need to be aware of one important restriction when using controls. Whereas form object variables can be declared in your code by the name you have given to the form, control classes can be referenced only by their class name.

A quick example should prove the point. Start with the default project and add a text box to it. The text box has its **Name** property set to **Text1** by default. If this were a form, you could create an object variable of type **Text1** and then assign a reference to it. Controls, however, behave slightly differently. Try running the following one-line example:

```
Private Sub Form_Load()
   Debug.Print TypeName(Text1)
End Sub
```

When you run the above code, `Text1`'s type name is displayed as TextBox, rather than as Text1. You can still create a separate object variable and assign the text box's reference to it, however, the same way that you did with a form:

```
Private Sub Form_Load()
    Dim TextBoxVariable As TextBox
    Set TextBoxVariable = Text1
    Text1.Text = "Some text"
    Debug.Print TextBoxVariable.Text
End Sub
```

As you can see, the reference to the TextBox object in the variable `Text1` is being assigned to the variable called `TextBoxVariable`, which you have created. You are assigning it in exactly the same way that you assigned form object variables, using the `Set` statement.

After the assignment, both `Text1` and `TextBoxVariable` are left referencing the same physical TextBox control object.

Passing Control References

Control references can be passed in the parameters of a subroutine or function in a similar way to a form reference. Here's how you do it.

Using the previous example, add a subroutine to `Form1` as follows:

```
Private Sub ControlRefTest (TextBoxVariable As TextBox)
    TextBoxVariable.Text = "Got here!"
End Sub
```

Call the subroutine from the form's `Load` event subroutine:

```
Private Sub Form_Load
    ControlRefTest Text1
End Sub
```

What's clever about this is that you can pass control references to subroutines and functions that are in code modules outside the context of the form. You can, therefore, develop common procedures that work, for example, on all of your text boxes. This can be extremely useful. Imagine that you want to perform some special validation on the text that has been entered into a text box. The example in Listing 7-5 performs some rudimentary checking on the text in a text box to make sure that it is in a valid time format. (The code expects the time to be represented in the format `hh:mm:ss`.) If the text fails the validation check, a separate subroutine, called `SetTextBoxError`, is called to select all the text in the text box so that the entire entry can be easily rekeyed. The PC's speaker beeps and the focus is set back to the text box that failed the validation check.

Listing 7-5 Using a common routine for data checking

```
Public Sub ValidateTime(MyTextBox As TextBox)
Dim Hour As Variant, Min As Variant, Sec As Variant
Dim I As Integer
```

continued on next page

continued from previous page

```
If Len(MyTextBox.Text) = 8 Then
    For I = 1 To 8
        If I = 3 Or I = 6 Then
            If Mid(MyTextBox.Text, I, 1) <> ":" Then
                SetTextBoxError MyTextBox
                Exit Sub
            End If
        Else
            If Not IsNumeric(Mid(MyTextBox.Text, I, 1)) Then
                SetTextBoxError MyTextBox
                Exit Sub
            End If
        End If
    Next I
    Hour = Left(MyTextBox.Text, 2)
    Min = Mid(MyTextBox.Text, 4, 2)
    Sec = Right(MyTextBox.Text, 2)
    If Hour < 0 Or Hour > 23 Or Min < 0 Or Min > 59 _
            Or Sec < 0 Or Sec > 59 Then
        SetTextBoxError MyTextBox
        Exit Sub
    End If
Else
    SetTextBoxError MyTextBox
    Exit Sub
End If
End Sub

Private Sub SetTextBoxError(MyTextBox As TextBox)
MyTextBox.SelStart = 0
MyTextBox.SelLength = Len(MyTextBox)
Beep
MyTextBox.SetFocus
End Sub

Private Sub Text1_LostFocus()
ValidateTime Text1
End Sub
```

The **ValidateTime** routine should be called from the text box's **LostFocus** event subroutine. The call is also shown. Both **ValidateTime** and **SetTextBoxError** can be added to a standard code module. You then only have to call **ValidateTime** from the **LostFocus** event subroutine of an individual text box to add this functionality to it. This will work for all text boxes, no matter which form they are contained on.

The Control Data Type

Visual Basic 5 also has a generic type called Control that you can use in place of the individual class name of a control. This is useful if you want to perform a more general operation on a control in a subroutine or function and you want to pass a reference to more than one type of control to that procedure. The Control type is analogous to the Form type, which can be used to hold references to all types of forms.

We'll demonstrate this with a subroutine that disables a control by setting its `Enabled` property to `False`. This subroutine can be used with any control that has an `Enabled` property, which is almost all of them:

```
Public Sub DisableControl(AnyControl As Control)
    AnyControl.Enabled = False
End Sub
```

TypeName **and** If TypeOf

At times, it can be useful to determine what type of control a control variable is currently referencing. This is particularly true in common procedures where a reference has been passed to a Control type variable.

You can do this in the same way that you would find out the class name of a form object, by passing the reference to the `TypeName` function. For example,

```
Debug.Print TypeName(AnyControl)
```

Alternately, you can use the `TypeOf` keyword in an `If...Then` statement. The syntax for this expression is

```
If TypeOf objectname Is objecttype Then
```

For example, to disable only `TextBox` controls, you would use

```
Public Sub DisableControl(AnyControl As Control)
    If TypeOf AnyControl Is TextBox Then
        AnyControl.Enabled = False
    End If
End Sub
```

Finally, to disable anything but `TextBox` controls, use the `Not` operator:

```
If Not (TypeOf AnyControl Is TextBox) Then
    AnyControl.Enabled = False
End If
```

Working with Objects: The With Statement

Sometimes you will want to perform multiple operations on the same object. For example, you might want to set multiple coordinates of a control, as in

```
ThatForm.txtTheBox.Left = 0
ThatForm.txtTheBox.Top = 0
ThatForm.txtTheBox.Width = 200
ThatForm.txtTheBox.Height = 200
```

Visual Basic provides a shorthand way to do this, without having to retype the entire object reference. This is the **With** statement, which has the syntax

```
With object
     [statements]
End With
```

To phrase the above example more concisely, you would write

```
With ThatForm.txtTheBox
    Left = 0
    Top = 0
    Width = 200
    Height = 200
End With
```

You actually get a double benefit from using **With**. First, you reduce your typing load (and the possibility of fat-finger mistakes) because you type the reference **ThatForm.txtTheBox** only once. Second, your program will run faster because Visual Basic has to dereference it only once. (Dereferencing is a fancy word for "figure out where it is.") In a short demonstration program like this, the second benefit is insignificant, but in a full-blown application, it can make a significant difference.

1. Which of the following statements about OCXs is true?
   a. It is likely that someone has already written an OCX that does what you need.
   b. OCXs can be written in Visual Basic 5 Professional and Enterprise editions.
   c. OCX stands for OLE Control Extension.
   d. All of the above

2. How do you add a new control to your toolbox?
   a. You can't add new controls to the toolbox
   b. By dropping COMCTL32.OCX into the Systems folder
   c. By referencing the OCX via the Custom Controls dialog box
   d. By activating the toolbox window and pressing [INSERT]

3. If you have a TextBox control called **Text1**, what would you expect to be returned from:

   ```
   TypeName(Text1)
   ```

   a. **Text1**
   b. **Control**
   c. Nothing is printed unless you previously assigned it a value.
   d. **TextBox**

4. How would you declare a subroutine to set a Command button's caption to Click Me? The subroutine takes only a Command button as an argument.

a. `Public Sub SetCaption(TheButton As Control)`

b. `Public Sub SetCaption(TheButton As CommandButton)`

c. `Public Sub SetCaption(TheButton As Command1)`

d. `Public Sub SetCaption(Caption As Property)`

5. To determine if the control `SomeControl` is a Command button, which statement would you use?

a. `If SomeControl Is CommandButton Then`

b. `If TypeOf SomeControl Is CommandButton Then`

c. `If TypeOf SomeControl = CommandButton Then`

d. `If TypeName(SomeControl) Is CommandButton Then`

Write a program with four or five different controls of various types, including a label called lblClicked. Write a routine that takes a control as an argument and displays in lblClicked the name and type of the control, such as:

```
"You clicked Command1, a CommandButton."
```

Implement the functionality so that the label always displays the last control pressed.

INTRODUCING USER-DEFINED CLASSES

User-defined classes are really the key to making the most of Visual Basic 5's object-oriented features. Without them, your project cannot be considered fully object-oriented.

Although you've been using classes for some time now, the classes that you have been using to date have been limited in two important respects.

● They have been written by someone else. You have been reusing them rather than creating your own. The reusability of classes is an important feature of object-oriented programming and, of course, you have been able to customize the behavior of these classes by setting their properties, calling their methods, and programming their events. So far, however, you have been unable to develop your own classes from scratch.

● They have been mainly concerned with the user interface of your project. The single-instance classes are used for accessing operating system services such as the clipboard, but if you consider the two main types of class that you have used so far (forms and controls), it should be clear that they address only the user interface of your projects.

Why You Might Implement Your Own Classes

Before we go any further, it is important that you understand why there should be a need for you to implement your own classes. The problem is that your project's user interface may account for only a fraction of the code that you have to write.

We can show you what we mean by looking back at some of the projects that you've developed so far. Take the video store project, for example. In that project, it was clear that all you were implementing was the user interface of a much larger application. Accordingly, the types of objects you were concerned with were display objects (controls) required to display information on a form.

What you didn't consider were all the other types of objects that could exist in such an application. Real-world objects such as members, videotapes, credit cards, and accounts would all need to be represented somehow if you were going to complete that application and make it fully object-oriented.

SuperPad, too, has the same problem because it should ideally introduce a new type of object to the world—a SuperPad document. It's important that you recognize that the data that SuperPad processes doesn't consist only of the characters stored in the `Text` property of the TextBox control. Instead, you need to think of a SuperPad document as an autonomous object independent of the text box. It just so happens that a text box was a convenient control to use for manipulating the text of the document for editing purposes. The document itself could and should be completely independent.

SuperPad's Document *Object*

Armed with this knowledge, let's see how we sneakily got around this problem. In Chapter 6, Forms, Menus, and MDI Forms, you managed to get away without having to create a separate user-defined SuperPad document object by relying on the fact that the TextBox control satisfied some of your requirements for the document, whereas the form you used for the document window, `frmDocument`, provided the remaining functionality. Specifically, the form provided a mechanism to name the document and determine whether its contents had changed since it was last saved, and the text box contained within the form provided the ability to store and edit the text of the document.

This is, in fact, how many Visual Basic 5 programmers go about their programming: reusing forms, controls, and other classes to provide a "best fit" approach to program design. After all, if objects that you need to create in your projects fit well into an existing class such as a form or a control, then there's no real reason to go to the additional effort of implementing the object as a separate class. However, there are cases in which there are benefits to going to this extra effort. If you later want to replace the TextBox control with a different control, for example, you may experience incompatibility problems between the two controls. In Chapter 8, Discovering the CommonDialog and Windows 95 Controls, you're going to do just that when you replace the text box in SuperPad with one of the Windows 95 controls, the RichTextBox control. This will allow you to change the font and color attributes of the text in your SuperPad document and make it truly a "super" document.

We're now going to look at the changes that you need to make to SuperPad to implement the document as a separate user-defined class. Open the SuperPad project as you left it at the end of Chapter 6, Forms, Menus, and MDI Forms.

The Class Module

The key to creating your own classes at runtime is the class module. SuperPad doesn't have one, so let's start out by adding a class module to it. This class module will become the SuperPad document class.

The CD included with this book contains two versions of SuperPad in the directory for Chapter 7. The version in the OldSPad subdirectory has not been modified. The version in the SuperPad directory includes the changes described in this chapter. Understanding how to create and implement classes is crucial to your success in object-oriented programming. Open the version in OldSPad so you can follow this step-by-step example.

Add a class module to the project by selecting Add Class Module from Visual Basic 5's Project menu. This brings up the Add Class Module dialog box for class modules, as shown in Figure 7-2.

Your Add Class Module dialog box may differ, depending on the version of Visual Basic 5 you have. The Class Builder and ADDIN Builder are supplied only with the Professional and Enterprise Editions of Visual Basic 5.

The Existing tab is included with all editions of Visual Basic 5. As its name implies, it allows you to add class modules that you have already written to your project. Reusability is one of the main features of object-oriented programming; once you have a class that works correctly, you do not need to "reinvent the wheel" each time you need the functionality of that class.

Select Class Module in the Add Class Module dialog box. VB 5 adds the class to your project, and it appears in the Project Explorer as Class1 (Class1). This is shown in Figure 7-3.

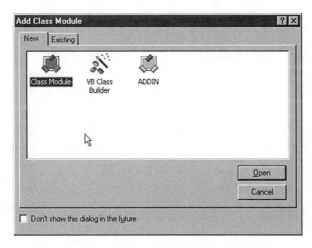

Figure 7-2
The Add Class
Module dialog box

Figure 7-3
The class has been
added to your
project

Notice, also, that the Add Class dialog has brought you straight to the Code window for your class. This is shown in Figure 7-4.

Going straight to the Code window for your class is important because the class module has no visual interface of its own. However, apart from this, class modules are, in all other respects, identical to forms. Because you are so used to forms now, this should come as good news. In fact, everything that you will learn about class modules in this lesson can be equally applied to form modules.

Figure 7-4
Code window
displayed for the
class module

Before we continue with programming SuperPad's new document class, there are a couple of points to note:

1. A class module is a class—it doesn't become an object until an instance of it is created at runtime. Think of it as a blueprint for an object. It's up to you to decide what a class module represents in your project. It might represent a customer, an item of stock, a bank account, a currency, or anything you like. It's entirely up to you.

2. You cannot begin a project by specifying that a class module should be the startup form. If, for any reason, you need to start your project by creating an instance of a class module, you can achieve the same result by using the Sub Main startup method and creating an instance of your class module manually.

What Does a Class Module Contain?

A class module can contain three things:

● Subroutines and functions that you add to its General Declarations section: These become the methods of the class.

● Properties that you add to the class module: These are the variables that the class will manipulate. Some of the properties are declared as Public, accessible from any part of the supporting program, and some are Private, accessible only from within the class.

● Events that you add to the class module: Events are different from methods. Events are procedures that are called from within the class and have an effect on objects outside the class object. They are *outgoing* interfaces. Methods are procedures that are called from outside the class module and have an effect on the class object. They are *incoming* interfaces.

You should be quite familiar with adding subroutines, functions, variables, and constants by now. However, what you haven't seen is the concept of a user-defined property. By the word "property," we don't just mean Public variables. Instead, we're talking about something much closer to the properties that you see in the Properties window. These properties are not added to the Properties window. You can make them work in the same way as "real" properties, but they remain something that you add to the class module via the Code window.

1. How does a user-defined class differ from the classes you have been using to date?
   a. The user-defined class is primarily concerned with the user interface of your project.
   b. The other classes were written by someone else.
   c. You cannot customize the other classes (such as by programming their events).
   d. All of the above

2. Which of the following would likely *not* be a reason to implement your own class?
   a. Classes help you design the aspects of your program that *aren't* concerned with the user interface.
   b. The built-in controls don't necessarily provide all the functionality you need.
   c. You might want a class that is independent of the controls that implement it.
   d. You might want to modify the "look and feel" of your user interface controls.

3. How do you add a new class module to your project?
   a. Click on Add File under the File menu.
   b. Click on Class Module under the Insert menu.
   c. Click on Module under the Insert menu.
   d. Click on Class under the Insert menu.

4. In what way does a class module differ from a form?
   a. A class module doesn't have a General Declarations section.
   b. Variables declared in a class module are necessarily private.
   c. The class module has no visual interface.
   d. The class module has methods instead of subroutines and functions.

5. How do you add properties to the class module?
   a. A property is really the same as a public variable.
   b. Via the Properties window
   c. Via the Code window
   d. You cannot add "real" properties to user-defined classes.

REVIEW

Lisa: We've really been working with classes and objects all along.

John: Well, we kind of knew that from Chapter 2, Object-Oriented Programming, but it's nice to look at the terms again now that we've been using them for a while.

Lisa: I never particularly thought about how we were using control and form names, such as `Form1.Show` and `txtABox.Text = "Something"`, but now that we know they're really object variables, it makes a lot of sense.

John: Right. It makes it easy to understand. For example, passing an object as an argument to a function—it's just like any other argument.

Lisa: I like the `With...End With` statement. Sometimes it gets cumbersome typing those object names.

John: Especially if the object is in a separate module.

Lisa: One thing I'm not sure about is properties. I don't really see the difference between a property and a variable.

John: Well, think about it. Although a property does hold a value, sometimes it does something else as well. Changing the coordinate properties of an object, like `Left` and `Width`, resize the object automatically. I think that's what they mean by "real" property behavior.

A CLASS ACT: MODIFYING SUPERPAD

Now let's make the changes needed to make SuperPad more object-oriented.

Building the Class

Of course, this would all have been a lot easier if you had begun the SuperPad project as an object-oriented design. You didn't, and you will have to make several changes before you can implement clsDocument and have it work. Let's take them a step at a time.

The Class Module's Properties

The first thing to do is to give the new class module a suitable name. Call it clsDocument instead of Class1. To change the name, use the Properties window and look at the properties for the class module. The class module has only one property, `Name`. Any other properties that the class has are user defined. Before you go any further, save the class. Open the File menu and select Save objDocument.cls.

Now add some properties to clsDocument. In the General Declarations section of clsDocument, add the following declarations:

```
Option Explicit
Public Changed As Boolean
Public Closing As Boolean
Public DocName As String
Public DocumentForm As frmDocument
```

What you have really done here is to create four public *properties* for the new clsDocument object. Two of them, `Changed` and `Closing`, existed before as form-level variables. The other two are new. For now, that is all you need to do with the new class, but there is some work to be done in the original code of SuperPad.

Changes to frmDocument

Switch to the Code window of frmDocument and make the changes listed below:

1. Remove the following two lines from the Declarations section.

```
Dim Changes as Boolean
Public Closing as Boolean
```

2. Add the following line to the Declarations section.

```
Public objDocument as New clsDocument
```

3. Add the following code to `Sub Form_Load()`.

```
Private Sub Form_Load()
    Set objDocument.DocumentForm = Me
    objDocument.DocName = Me.Caption
End Sub
```

4. Change all references to `Changed` and `Closing` so that VB can access them from the class. The easiest way to make global changes like this is to click on Replace under the Edit menu from inside the frmDocument module. Visual Basic 5's Find and Replace dialog boxes let you make procedurewide, modulewide, or projectwide searches. (Additionally, you can opt to limit searches to selected text regions.)

5. Make sure the default scope of Current Module is checked, then enter Changed as the string to find and objDocument.Changed as the string to replace, as shown in Figure 7-5. Follow the same procedure to change Closing to objDocument.Closing. In this case, you'll need to change the occurrence of Closing in the frmMain module as well, so instead of the line in the SetupCSMenus routine that reads

```
If Forms(I).Closing = False Then
```

you will have

```
If Forms(I).objDocument.Closing = False Then
```

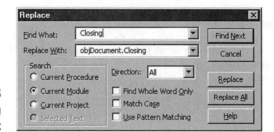

Figure 7-5
The Replace dialog box

Make the searches manually rather than clicking on Replace All, because you don't want to change occurrences of "changed" or "closing" in cases where the word is not used as a variable reference.

6. Switch to Sub Form_Unload() of frmDocument. There is a change to make here and an addition. The change is to the message displayed in the MsgBox function. It changes the reference from Me.Caption to objDocument.DocName. The addition is at the end of the procedure. All new text is in bold.

```
Private Sub Form_Unload(Cancel As Integer)
If objDocument.Changed Then
    Select Case MsgBox("The text in the " & objDocument.DocName & _
                       " file has changed." & vbCr & vbCr & _
                       "Do you want to save the changes?", _
                       vbExclamation + vbYesNoCancel, _
frmMain.Caption)
        Case vbYes
            'Perform save
        Case vbNo
            'Allow form to close
        Case vbCancel
            'Cancel close form
            Cancel = True
    End Select
End If
objDocument.Closing = Not Cancel
frmMain.SetupCSMenus
If Cancel = False Then
    Set objDocument = Nothing
End If
End Sub
```

7. Add the following changes to the Change event of txtDocument.

```
Private Sub txtDocument_Change()
    objDocument.Changed = True
    If Right(Me.Caption, 2) <> " *" Then
        Me.Caption = objDocument.DocName & " *"
    End If
End Sub
```

If you made the one change to frmMain when you ran the **Replace** function, your work is done. If not, make that change now (see Step 4).

A Look at the Code

The class you have created is the simplest of all possible classes. The properties were all declared as Public variables, and you created neither methods nor events. The DocName property is included so that you can remove the program's dependence on the caption of frmDocument. The name of the document needs to be a part of the class. The other new variable is an object variable that completes the encapsulation process by allowing you to access the document's form as a part of the class.

According to the principles of object-oriented programming, all the data for an object should be accessed only through references to that object. The class that defines the object is said to *encapsulate* the data. That means that the class can *protect* the data from changes that are not appropriate. In this case, little "protection" is necessary, but in some cases the data must not be allowed to assume certain values. For example, a variable that counts the number of transactions on a bank account may not have a negative value. You will see how properties are protected in Lesson 7.

Creating an Object

Once the blueprint is drawn, SuperPad needs to be able to create a new instance of **clsDocument** when it is opened and each time the **AddForm** function is called. The declaration

```
Public objDocument As New clsDocument
```

does the job. It *declares* the object as a variable, and the **New** in the line also creates an *instance* of the object. This is a convenient technique, and one that you will use in the future. As an alternative, you could have used

```
Public myDocument As clsDocument

Sub Form_Load()
    Set myDocument = New clsDocument
End Sub
```

to do the same thing. Either way you do it, it is called *instantiating* the object.

The **Form_Load** procedure creates a reference to the new object and sets the value of **DocName**.

```
Private Sub Form_Load()
    Set objDocument.DocumentForm = Me
    objDocument.DocName = Me.Caption
End Sub
```

The change you made to `Sub txtDocument Change()` adds a Windows convention to SuperPad. It is conventional to *tag* document titles with an asterisk if the document has been changed. The following code performs that function for you:

```
If Right(Me.Caption, 2) <> " *" Then
    Me.Caption = objDocument.DocName & " *"
End If
```

The Events in clsDocument

Even though you did not add any events to clsDocument, Visual Basic inserted two events by default. They are shown in Figure 7-6. The `Initialize` event is fired when an object is created (instantiated) from the class, and the `Terminate` event is fired when the class is destroyed. Often there will be no code in these events, but you may need them to create or destroy class-related objects.

Destroying the Object

Sounds drastic, doesn't it? Perhaps, but it is also important. Objects take up memory space, and that memory space is not relinquished by Visual Basic simply by unloading the object. When SuperPad is done using an instance of `objDocument`, the form `Unload` event contains the code

```
If Cancel = False Then
    Set objDocument = Nothing
End If
```

The `Nothing` keyword *does* remove the object from memory. If you do not do this, you will soon have all your available RAM filled up with unreferenced objects, a phenomenon called *memory leak* by old-hand programmers.

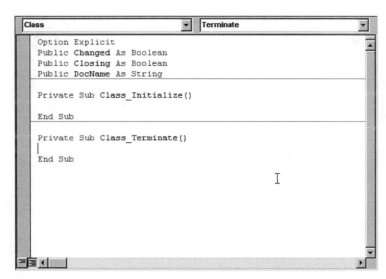

Figure 7-6
The default events
for a class

Visual Basic keeps an internal count of how many object variables are currently referencing a given object. When that count falls to zero, VB destroys the object that was referenced. This is a particularly useful feature. If Visual Basic did not keep this count for you, you would have to do it yourself to be sure you didn't pull the rug from under the feet of some code somewhere.

When you are programming with objects, do not use the End VCR button or the keyword **End** to exit from your programs. Both close your program abruptly, without using the form unload or query unload procedures. Similarly, don't exit from the development environment with a program running. In either case, you will generate memory leaks. Memory leaks are objects that are left in memory with no way to close them except rebooting the computer.

Running the Program

Now you are ready to run the new SuperPad. Try all the features that have been implemented to this point. About the only *visible* difference is the addition of .* to the end of Untitled in the caption of the form. Internally, though, it is a very different program.

1. What events are triggered when an instance of a class is created and when an instance of a class is destroyed?
   a. `Load` and `Unload`
   b. `Initialize` and `Terminate`
   c. `Add` and `Remove`
   d. `Add` and `Destroy`

2. Which of the following is one of a class module's predefined properties?
   a. `OLE`
   b. `Instancing`
   c. `Public`
   d. `Name`

3. How do you create an instance of a user-defined class using two lines of code?
   a.

```
Public objSomeObject As clsSomeClass
New objSomeObject = clsSomeClass
```

   b.

```
Public objSomeObject As clsSomeClass
Set objSomeObject = New clsSomeClass
```

c.

```
Public objSomeObject As clsSomeClass
Set objSomeObject = clsSomeClass
```

d.

```
Declare objSomeObject As clsSomeClass
Set objSomeObject = New clsSomeClass
```

4. How can you achieve the same results by using just one line of code?
   a. You can't; you must create the object separately.
   b. `Set objSomeObject = New clsSomeClass`
   c. `Public objSomeObject = Set New clsSomeClass`
   d. `Public objSomeObject As New clsSomeClass`

5. How do you destroy a user-defined object?
   a. Call the `Unload` event routine of the form that references the object.
   b. Set the object reference to a `Null` string (`""`).
   c. Set the object reference to `Nothing`.
   d. Set all the references to the object to `Nothing`.

COLLECTIONS

Now that SuperPad is more object-oriented than it was before, you can begin to use the additional features of Visual Basic 5 that are designed to make programming with classes even easier.

One of these features is the *collection*. In fact, you met collections in the guise of the forms collection in Chapter 6, Forms, Menus, and MDI Forms. Remember that every form that's created in your project is automatically added to the forms collection, which provides a convenient mechanism for gaining access to all the forms in your project. You relied on it in frmMain's SetupCSMenus subroutine. Now we're going to look at collections in detail, including how you can create your own.

To get started, think of a real-world collection, such as a stamp collection. A stamp collection consists of lots of individual stamps, each of which is an object. The stamp collection as a whole can also be thought of as an object, but one that contains lots of other stamp objects.

A stamp collection might physically consist of a binder in which the stamps are stored. The binder forms an intrinsic part of the collection. It keeps the stamps clean and prevents them from getting lost. It also enables you to organize the stamps so that you can locate individual objects in the collection quickly.

A collection in Visual Basic 5 terms is similar to the real-world stamp collection. A collection is a Visual Basic 5 object in its own right and is analogous to the binder in which the stamp objects are kept. Being an object, the collection also has methods that you can call to organize the objects it contains.

This is pretty neat. You can effectively ask the binder to find the right object for you.

Creating Collections

OK, how do we create a collection? Some collections are created and maintained for you automatically. The forms collection is one you've already seen. Others that you have yet to see include the printers collection and numerous collections used to access databases.

You're going to enhance SuperPad by adding all the clsDocument objects to a new collection. Say you want to provide a documentwide search facility. By storing all the clsDocument objects in one collection, you can search through them all with ease.

Because a collection is an object, creating one is just a matter of creating a new instance of the built-in Collection class. Add the statement in Listing 7-6 to the General Declarations section of frmMain.

Listing 7-6 Declaring the collection

```
Option Explicit
Public DocColl As New Collection
```

The variable is Public so that you can access it from outside frmMain.

Now when SuperPad is started and frmMain is created, the DocColl collection will be automatically created.

Destroying Collections

Now that you've created the collection, the question arises as to how to destroy it. You could rely on Visual Basic 5 to tidy up everything for you when the program terminates and do nothing explicitly. However, it's good programming practice to be tidy and destroy it yourself. Listing 7-7 presents the code to destroy the collection in frmMain's **Terminate** event.

Listing 7-7 Destroying the collection

```
Private Sub MDIForm_Terminate()
    Set DocColl = Nothing
End Sub
```

This is the same syntax used to destroy a user-defined object. The same rules about object destruction apply, so the **DocColl** collection object is destroyed only because its reference count has fallen to zero.

What Happens When You Destroy a Collection?

Destroying a collection can have far-reaching effects. Here's why. Visual Basic 5 maintains a count of how many references there are to each and every object. When that count falls to zero for an object, the object is destroyed. This is why you can use the same **Set ObjectVariable = Nothing** syntax both to dereference an object from a variable and to destroy the object itself.

This is important, because collections don't actually store objects. (OK, we know we said they did, but we were just trying to get you to understand the idea of a collection.) In fact, collections store only object references. The object isn't physically moved into the collection. Instead, a copy of its reference is created and that is stored in the collection. In this sense, you can think of a library card catalog as a collection of books, even though the books themselves are stored elsewhere.

Storing references in a collection is efficient and it has the advantage of hooking into Visual Basic 5's object deletion behavior. When you destroy a collection, you also destroy the object references contained within it. If the reference counts for the objects that were referenced by the collection fall to zero, those objects will also be destroyed.

As a result, it is possible to destroy all the objects in the collection just by destroying the collection. If you don't want those objects to be destroyed, you must make another reference to the objects before you destroy the collection.

Adding Object References to the Collection

The objects that you're going to add to this new collection are the clsDocument objects created in frmDocument's **Load** event.

Keys

Before you can add more clsDocument objects, you need some way of telling one from the other. Right now, you don't know which clsDocument object reference is which in the collection. You really have no means of distinguishing them. You need a fast way to locate the correct reference, either to access it or to remove it from the collection.

The answer to this problem is to use a *key* when adding the reference to the collection in the first place. A key is a string you define that is a unique identifier that you associate with that particular object.

You could, for example, add a static Integer variable to frmMain's General Declarations section and increment it each time you create a new clsDocument object. You could then convert that integer number to a string and use it as a key to the object reference. You could store the key in a form variable so that you would know which key to use to obtain the correct object reference from the collection. Below are the changes needed to implement this strategy.

Adding and Incrementing a Key

In frmMain, add a new Integer variable called `CollKeyIndex`, as shown in the code in Listing 7-8. The `CollKeyIndex` variable is automatically initialized to zero when SuperPad starts.

Listing 7-8 frmMain's general declarations

```
Option Explicit
Public DocColl As New Collection
Public CollKeyIndex As Integer
```

Now add a new Integer variable to frmDocument's General Declarations section, as shown in Listing 7-9. This new variable stores the key number used when adding the objDocument reference to the collection.

Listing 7-9 frmDocument's general declarations

```
Option Explicit
Public objDocument As New clsDocument
Dim CollKey As Integer
```

The Add Method

The easiest syntax to use to add the objects to the collection is

```
frmMain.DocColl.Add objDocument
```

Here, you're passing the object reference in objDocument to the collection's **Add** method. From now on, each object will be referenced by both the objDocument variable and a copy of the reference in the collection. Each object will have two active references. The effect of this is that you must set the objDocument variable to **Nothing** and remove the reference from the collection before Visual Basic 5 actually destroys the object.

The complete syntax for the **Add** method is

```
object.Add item [,key] [,before|,,after]
```

You have the option to specify before or after arguments to give the position in the collection. These values can either be integer values (indicating the position) or strings (indicating the key). You want to use only the key parameter, however. Modify frmDocument's **Load** event subroutine so that it appears as shown in Listing 7-10. The modified lines are highlighted.

Listing 7-10 Assigning keys to the collection members

```
Private Sub Form_Load()
frmMain.DocColl.Add objDocument, CStr(frmMain.CollKeyIndex)
CollKey = frmMain.CollKeyIndex
frmMain.CollKeyIndex = frmMain.CollKeyIndex + 1
Set objDocument.DocumentForm = Me
objDocument.DocName = Me.Caption
End Sub
```

The second parameter to the collection's **Add** method is the string equivalent of the current value of `CollKeyIndex` in frmMain. You're taking a copy of that value and storing it locally in frmDocument in the new Integer variable, `CollKey`, so that you can use it later when you need to find the object. You then increment `CollKeyIndex` in frmMain so that the next time you create an object, it will be stored with a different key.

Of course, this mechanism limits you to creating approximately 32,000 objects in one SuperPad session. This should be large enough, but you could always change `CollKeyIndex` and `CollKey` to be Long integers, in which case the limit could be extended to 4 billion objects in one session. It's just a theoretical limit, really, but you need to be aware of it. Of course, you could use a different mechanism to create the key that relies, for example, on large random numbers. That way, you could remove this limit altogether.

The Remove *Method*

You have to be careful to remove the object reference from the collection; otherwise, the `clsDocument` objects will not be destroyed. You need to add only one line to frmDocument's `Unload` event. The line is highlighted in Listing 7-11.

Listing 7-11 The Remove method

```
Private Sub Form_Unload(Cancel As Integer)
If objDocument.Changed Then
    Select Case MsgBox("The text in the " & objDocument.DocName & _
                    " file has changed." & vbCr & vbCr & _
                    "Do you want to save the changes?", _
                    vbExclamation + vbYesNoCancel, frmMain.Caption)
        Case vbYes
            'Perform save
        Case vbNo
            'Allow form to close
        Case vbCancel
            'Cancel close form
            Cancel = True
    End Select
End If
If Cancel = False Then
    objDocument.Closing = True
End If
frmMain.SetupCSMenus
If Cancel = False Then
    frmMain.DocColl.Remove CStr(CollKey)
    Set objDocument = Nothing
End If
End Sub
```

Just before the object is destroyed, you remove the reference to it from the collection.

Using the Collection to Provide a Search Facility

Now that the collection is available, here are the changes you need to make to implement a documentwide search facility.

Add a new menu item to the end of SuperPad's Edit menu, with the properties shown in Table 7-3.

Table 7-3 The Find item on the Edit menu

Property	Value
Name	mnuEditFind
Caption	&Find
Shortcut Key	CTRL - F
Enabled	False

Add a new form to SuperPad with the objects and properties shown in Figure 7-7 and summarized in Table 7-4.

Table 7-4 Objects and properties for frmFind

Object	Property	Value
Form	Name	frmFind
	Caption	Find
	BorderStyle	3 - Fixed Dialog
	ControlBox	False
	MaxButton	False
	MinButton	False
Label	Name	lblFind
	Caption	&Text to find
	AutoSize	True
	TabIndex	0
TextBox	Name	txtFind
	MultiLine	True
	TabIndex	1

Object	Property	Value
CommandButton	Name	cmdFind
	Caption	Find
	Default	True
	TabIndex	2
CommandButton	Name	cmdCancel
	Caption	Cancel
	Cancel	True
	TabIndex	3

Add the code in Listing 7-12 to mnuEditFind's Click event subroutine in frmMain.

Listing 7-12 mnuEditFind's Click event in frmMain

```
Private Sub mnuEditFind_Click()
    frmFind.Show vbModal
End Sub
```

In frmMain's SetupCSMenus subroutine, add the highlighted code shown in Listing 7-13 in the section of the routine that enables the Select All, Time/Date, and Word Wrap menu items.

Listing 7-13 Enable/disable the Find menu item in SetupCSMenus

```
' enable / disable Select All, TimeDate, WordWrap, and Find
' edit menus according to whether or not there is
' an active document
mnuEditSelectAll.Enabled = Found
mnuEditTimeDate.Enabled = Found
mnuEditWordWrap.Enabled = Found
mnuEditFind.Enabled = Found
```

Complete the cmdCancel button programming in frmFind as shown in Listing 7-14.

Listing 7-14 The Find form's Cancel button

```
Private Sub cmdCancel_Click()
    Unload Me
End Sub
```

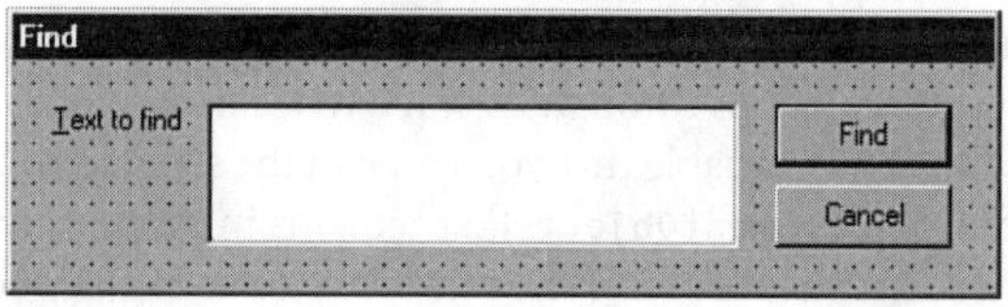

Figure 7-7
View of frmFind
form

The ZOrder **Method**

Finally, program the search routine itself in cmdFind's **Click** event subroutine as shown in Listing 7-15. This routine works by bringing the form that contains the found string to the front. It does this by calling the **ZOrder** method on the form, which sets the position of an object within its graphical level.

Listing 7-15 The Find routine

```
Private Sub cmdFind_Click()
Dim DocumentObject As clsDocument
Dim FindResults As Integer
For Each DocumentObject In frmMain.DocColl
    FindResults = InStr(DocumentObject.DocumentForm.txtDocument.Text, _
                        txtFind.Text)
    If FindResults > 0 Then
        DocumentObject.DocumentForm.ZOrder
        DocumentObject.DocumentForm.txtDocument.SelStart = FindResults - 1
        DocumentObject.DocumentForm.txtDocument.SelLength = Len(txtFind.Text)
        Exit For
    End If
Next DocumentObject
Unload Me
End Sub
```

How It Works

This search routine requires a little explanation.

The first line of interest is the collection version of the **For Each...Next** statement. Chapter 4, Subroutines, Functions, and the Visual Basic 5 Language, shows how to use the **For Each...Next** loop with arrays. For collections, the **For Each...Next** statement has the syntax

```
For Each element In group
    [statements]
    [Exit For]
    [statements]


Next [element]
```

The **For...Each...Next** statement is a lot like the **For...Next** loop you first saw in Chapter 4, Subroutines, Functions, and the Visual Basic 5 Language. The difference is that it works only with collections, and you don't need to know how many objects are in the collection.

This statement cycles through each reference in the collection and assigns the reference to the object variable that you name in the statement. You have declared a new object variable, **DocumentObject**, that remains in scope only for the duration of this subroutine. That variable receives a reference to each clsDocument object in the collection on each pass through the **For Each...Next** loop.

The search itself is accomplished using the `InStr` function and by accessing the text in the txtDocument text boxes directly. If the string is found, the document form containing the string is brought to the front of the `ZOrder` and the found text is selected so that it is visible in the document.

Other Ways to Access the Collection

Using the `For Each...Next` loop is just one way to access the collection. Remember that you have given each reference in the collection a key. Let's program an example of how to access the object through the key. Don't add this example to SuperPad, however.

The Item *Method*

To obtain an object reference for a key, you must use the collection's `Item` method. When you pass a string value to the `Item` method, it treats `Item` as the key and returns the object corresponding to that key.

```
DocColl.Item CollKey
```

To print the current value of the clsDocument object's `Changed` variable for a particular form, using its key to access the reference in the collection rather than its own copy of that reference in its `objDocument` variable, you would write

```
Debug.Print frmMain.DocColl.Item(CStr(CollKey)).Changed
```

The Count *Property*

You can also treat the objects in a collection as elements of an array, with `Item` corresponding to an array index. To find out the number of properties in a collection, use the `Count` property.

```
NumObjects = DocColl.Count
```

To iterate through the list, you would use

```
For I = 1 To NumObjects
    Debug.Print frmMain.DocColl.Item(I).Changed
Next I
```

1. Which statement about collections is false?
   a. A collection has methods you can call to organize the objects it contains.
   b. A collection is an object.
   c. Visual Basic 5 has some predefined collections that are automatically created for you at runtime.
   d. A collection is a kind of form.

2. How do you create a collection?
   a. Just as you would any other object, for example,

   ```
   Public objTheCollection As New Collection
   ```

   b. Using the Collection object's **Add** method
   c. Using the **CreateCollection** statement
   d. You never need to create collections; VB handles this automatically.

3. What should you be particularly careful about when destroying collections?
   a. Using the **Nothing** keyword to destroy a collection causes a runtime error.
   b. You need to destroy the contents of the collection individually before you can destroy it.
   c. If there aren't other references to the objects in the collection, destroying the collection destroys those objects as well.
   d. Destroying the collection can unload the form that contains it.

4. What is the advantage of having a key associated with a reference in a collection?
   a. There is no way to access members of a collection numerically via an array subscript.
   b. The key automatically corresponds to the class's **Caption** property.
   c. Assigning keys gives you an opportunity to keep a count of the collection members.
   d. A key can uniquely identify a reference with a descriptive string.

5. What collection method do you use to obtain a reference from a collection?
   a. **Count**
   b. **Item**
   c. **Key**
   d. **Add**

USER-DEFINED PROPERTIES

We said earlier in this chapter that it is possible to add your own properties to classes. Let's see why you might want to do this.

The Benefits of Properties

To see how a user-definable property might work, let's have a closer look at some of the properties built into the form class and see how they differ from ordinary class variables. Take the **Top**, **Left**, **Width**, and **Height** properties, for example. When the values of those properties are changed, the size or position of the form changes accordingly. The form's **Caption** property also does something spectacular. When you assign some text to it, that text magically appears in the title bar of the form.

You might think that this is pretty intuitive, but that's the whole point. There is no magic connection between the **Caption** property of a Visual Basic 5 form and the title bar of a window. Instead, the property is able to recognize and respond to changes in its value. This ability sets properties apart from mere class variables. It's as if they have a built-in event that gets triggered when the property is set to something.

This is important because the code that you write in an object-oriented program can be simplified somewhat if the properties of a class can react when they are accessed by code in other parts of the program.

One example of this in SuperPad is the class variable **Changed**. This variable records when a change occurs to the text of a document. That information is then used to determine whether the document needs to be saved when an attempt is made to close the form. Also, when the text has changed, an asterisk is added to the caption of the form so that the user can tell at a glance which documents need to be saved.

The code to add the asterisk is implemented in the **Changed** event of the form's txtDocument text box. There, you set the value of the clsDocument object's **Changed** variable to **True**. If the caption doesn't already end in an asterisk, you add it accordingly.

This isn't very object-oriented. It would be better if the **Changed** variable could react to a change in its current value and set or clear the asterisk in the caption itself. Later on, when you add the code to save the document, you will need to reset **Changed** to **False**, after the document has been successfully saved. You will need to add some more code to remove the asterisk at that time. So unless you introduce a user-defined property, you'll end up with code that adds and removes the asterisk from the form's caption in two different places in the project. This is inherently undesirable, because any time you have code in two places you have to maintain (debug or make changes to) the same code twice. This is extra work and it increases the chances of a bug slipping through.

Adding a Class Property

To make **Changed** a proper property, one that can react to changes in its value, go to the clsDocument module and replace **Public Changed As Boolean** in the Declarations section with **Private DocChanged As Boolean**. The declarations now look like this:

```
Option Explicit
Private DocChanged As Boolean
Public Closing As Boolean
Public DocName As String
Public DocumentForm As frmDocument
```

Now select the Add Procedure menu item from Visual Basic 5's Tools menu. Complete the Insert Procedure dialog box as shown in Figure 7-8. Be sure to check the Property option.

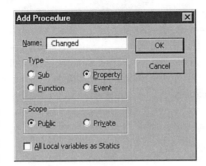

Figure 7-8
Adding a property
to the clsDocument
class

When you press the OK button, Visual Basic 5 adds the new property to the General Declarations section of the class.

The Property Get *and* Property Let *Events*

The property consists of two events: a **Property Get** event and a **Property Let** event. They appear in the Code window as shown in Figure 7-9.

As you can see, the new **Changed** property has been set as a variant. The parameter in the **Property Let** event, **vNewValue**, will be a variant by default unless you change it to something else. At this stage, you have to complete the programming of these events. The way the property works is that when you set the property to a specific value in your code, the **Property Let** event is triggered with the new value passed in the parameter. Similarly, when you obtain the current value of the property in your code, the **Property Get** procedure is called. The **Property Get** event works like a function, so you can return a value by modifying its declaration accordingly.

Let's see how these two procedures look once the correct code has been added to make them work. The revised contents of the class module are shown in Listing 7-16.

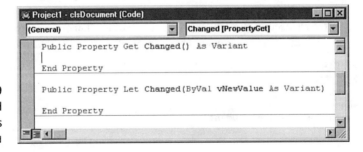

Figure 7-9
Property Get and
Property Let events
for Changed

Listing 7-16 The class module

```
Private DocChanged As Boolean
Public Closing As Boolean
Public DocName As String
Public DocumentForm As frmDocument

Public Property Get Changed() As Boolean
Changed = DocChanged
End Property

Public Property Let Changed(NewValue As Boolean)
DocChanged = NewValue
End Property
```

The first thing you've had to change is the name of the variable that was previously called **Changed**. This is because there would be a naming clash with the new **Changed** property. Instead, you have changed its name to **DocChanged**. You are still using it to hold the value associated with the new property, it's just that you no longer give the rest of SuperPad unlimited access to that variable. From now on, all access to the **DocChanged** variable will pass through the **Changed** property. You've even declared **DocChanged** as **Private** so that only the code in the clsDocument module can access it directly.

Finally, you can now move the asterisk code from the **Changed** event of txtDocument to the **Property Let** event for the new **Changed** property. You don't need to change any of the code in the rest of SuperPad that accesses this property because the syntax to access it is the same as when it was a variable. The new **Property Let** and **Changed** events are listed in Listing 7-17.

Listing 7-17 Updated Property Let and txtDocument_Change routines

```
Public Property Let Changed(NewValue As Boolean)
DocChanged = NewValue
If DocChanged = True Then
    If Right(DocumentForm.Caption, 2) <> " *" Then
        DocumentForm.Caption = DocName & " *"
    End If
Else
    If Right(DocumentForm.Caption, 2) = " *" Then
        DocumentForm.Caption = DocName
    End If
End If
End Property

'     The following is in frmDocument

Private Sub txtDocument_Change()
'     Delete the If...Then
    objDocument.Changed = True
End Sub
```

Try running SuperPad again. If you have made the changes exactly as we have speci-fied, you'll find that it runs correctly and that the new **Property Get** and **Property Let** events are triggered automatically.

Property Set

There is one further event that properties can respond to. This is the **Property Set** event. This book classifies this event as an advanced feature of Visual Basic 5, so we do not cover it in detail. The **Property Set** event is used when the variable behind a prop-erty is not just a simple variable, such as a Boolean, Integer, Long, or String, but an object variable. In other words, it is possible for a property to be a reference to another object.

In such a case, it would be necessary to use the Set statement to pass a reference to the object variable property. The **Property Set** event is triggered when a user-defined property is used in a **Set** statement. For example:

```
Set MyObject.MyProperty = MyObjectVariable
```

or

```
Set MyObject.MyProperty = New MyClass
```

Form Properties

There's one final point to be made about these properties. We've introduced only user-definable properties in a class context because they tend to get used primarily with class modules. However, there's nothing to stop you from adding them to form modules too.

1. What is the difference between an ordinary class variable and a property?
    a. There is no difference.
    b. Other elements of the class can respond to changes in the property value.
    c. Class variables are private.
    d. Class variables can be accessed from other modules, but via a syntax differ-ent from that used to access property values.

2. Which dialog box can you use to add properties to your form and user-defined classes?
    a. The Insert Property dialog box
    b. The Insert Class dialog box
    c. The Insert Procedure dialog box
    d. It's a trick question; you can't add properties to your form.

3. What event routine is triggered when another portion of the program attempts to set a value for a variant type property called `MyProperty`?
   a. `Public Property Let MyProperty(NewValue As Variant)`
   b. `Public Property Let MyProperty()`
   c. `Public Property Set MyProperty(NewValue As Variant)`
   d. `Public Property Set MyProperty()`

4. The `Property Let`, `Property Get`, and `Property Set` routines give you an opportunity to perpetuate changes to an object based on a change of the property value. But how do you keep track of the property value itself?
   a. You don't need to.
   b. By creating a `Private` variable with the same name as the property that will contain the value
   c. By creating a `Private` variable with a different name that will contain the value
   d. By creating a `Public` variable with a different name that will contain the value

5. How do you implement an object type of property?
   a. You can't implement object properties.
   b. Use the `=` assignment operator to set the value; use the `Property Set` event routine to respond to the change in value.
   c. Use the `Set` command to set the value; use the `Property Get` event routine to respond to the change in value.
   d. Use the `Set` command to set the value; use the `Property Set` event routine to respond to the change in value.

EXERCISE

Create a new project with a single Command button labeled Turn me on. Create a class for the project called clsSwitch. Add a single property to clsSwitch and a Boolean called `State`. Implement the following functionality:

When the user clicks the button, the `State` value switches from `True` to `False` or `False` to `True`. If the value is `True`, the caption on the button should read Turn me off. If the value is `False`, the caption should read Turn me on.

WHY USE CLASSES?

All this seems like a lot of work, and the program seems to do just about the same thing it did before you made all these changes. You might be wondering why bother. In this lesson, you will be reminded of the advantages of user-defined classes.

Easy Maintenance

In Lesson 7, we mentioned that if you did not use property procedures to insert and remove the asterisk from frmDocument's caption, the code would have to be repeated in two different parts of the program. Properties in some programs may be changed in many more than two sections of code. That means that if the program's requirements change, the code in many different parts of the program will have to be changed.

A classic example is the renowned "year 2000 problem" that is a topic of panic in newspapers and magazines. Most of the programs that suffer from the problem were written well before the advent of object-oriented programming. Programmers today are combing through hundreds of thousands of lines of code searching for any variable reference that might represent a date and making changes to each one. When they finish, they pray that they have not missed any. Had the date been handled as a date class, only a single code module would have to be changed!

Reusable Code

As you might imagine, programmers use the same routines in program after program. For years, the best programmers have maintained text files of their favorite procedures and functions and used cut-and-paste techniques to insert them into their programs. Then they had to rename variables and otherwise make the old routine fit the new program.

A big time saver? Sure, but you can save a class as a separate file and simply insert it into your program. Even if the events and properties in the class have the same name as procedures and variables in the new program, simply by referencing the class object you can invoke the correct event or change the correct property. This is known as a $5.00 word in object-oriented programming: *polymorphism*.

Sharing Code in Large Projects

Large projects are a particular nightmare to project managers. These projects may have dozens of programmers, all working on different parts of the same project. For example, Sally is handling the cash deposits portion of the code while Juan is dealing with cash balances and Jim is handling the code for withdrawals.

In the top-down model of programming, Sally, Juan, and Jim would need to know all the details of each others' code. Obviously, a deposit would affect the balance. Each person must be careful not to use a variable name that has been used by one of the others, and each must be aware of the rules that have been set for any variable in the project. A change in code written by any of the programmers has a direct impact on all of them.

Object-oriented programmers don't have these worries. Juan, handling the cash balance, needs to tell Sally and Jim only the names of the methods in his class module and the data types for the properties, the *interface* for the class. He does not need to know a thing about Sally's and Jim's code, and they don't need to know how his works. If Juan discovers the need to change how a property is handled, he can change the `Property Get` and `Property Let` procedures in his class module and the change will have no effect at all on the code that Sally and Jim are writing.

Data Hiding

Private properties are *hidden* from the rest of the program. The only way to change them is through the `Property Let` procedure and the only way to read them is through the `Property Get` procedure. The `Property Let` procedure can be written to include the business rules so that improper values are not allowed.

You can even implement read-only properties, properties that are changed only inside the class module but that can be read by the rest of the code. Juan could maintain a count of the number of deposits and the number of withdrawals in a month, for example, that Sally and Jim could read but could not explicitly change. To accomplish that, Juan would delete the `Property Let` procedure for both properties. In VB, the `BorderStyle` property, for example, is read-only at runtime.

The concept of data hiding is called *encapsulation* in object-oriented programming circles. Generally, all properties should be encapsulated except when there are no constraints on them. If a property can legally (and safely) hold any value that may be sent by the rest of the program, it is OK to use a public property. If there must be limitations, or if the value should not be changed or should not be changed after it has been set, use a `Private` property with `Property Let` and `Property Get` procedures. If you are not sure, lean toward `Private` properties.

Improved Program Design

Some programmers do it right the first time, but most of us start coding first and thinking later. Our programs, like Topsy, "just grow." Over the development period we make dozens of changes, most of them affecting more than one procedure. We add new procedures to "patch" what we did wrong in other procedures and soon wind up with a mishmash of code that will render us speechless when we look at it a few months down the line.

One of the side effects of object-oriented programming is that you must design the objects before you can even think of writing the code. It seems like an extra, time-consuming step, but it is really a big time saver because you will have fewer corrections to make during the testing stages. True, you could insert the think-before-you-program step into your normal program design stages, but it is so much easier just to sit down and start coding.

In other words, object-oriented programming results in better, more robust programs, not just because programming with objects is a better method (it is) but because it forces you to think before you code. In cooking, the sauce is everything; in programming, planning is everything. Let's look at the design process to get an idea of what that means.

Designing an Object-Oriented Program

For the sake of this simulation, let's say that you have finished this course and started the Handy Dandy Software Company. Pat Fixit, an appliance repairperson, has come to you for help.

"I need to keep track of the service calls I perform for my customers," Pat says. "I tried doing it on paper, but I just seem to keep getting it all tangled up."

As you question Pat further, Pat tells you of the need to keep a record of each appliance serviced for each customer, including the type of appliance, its model and serial number, and the nature of each repair. You know this will take a database, a topic we will cover in Chapter 12, Files, and you also have some ideas about the screens you will need for handling each type of entry.

Actually, you already have most of the information you need to do an object-oriented design. Look at the list of requirements that Pat gave you. Each of the nouns in that list is a potential object. We have appliance and customer as the primary nouns, and they suggest the main objects that you will need.

The nature of the object also tells you something about the properties for the object. The customer object, for example, will probably need

- Name (break it down into `Last_Name` and `First_Name`)
- Address
- City
- State
- Zip code
- Phone number

The appliance object needs

- `Type_of_Appliance`
- Make
- Model
- Serial number
- Repair
- `Repair_Date`

The properties, in turn, suggest the **Property Let** and **Property Get** procedures. The `Type_of_Appliance` property, for example, would probably be an integer, with **1** representing a washing machine, **2** a dishwasher, and so on. The **Property Let** procedure would limit the properties' values to those that are valid. The `Repair_Date` **Property Let** procedure would check to be sure its parameter is a valid date.

As you progress in your coding, or in your discussion of the project with Pat, you may find other items (properties) to add to these, but adding them is simplicity itself because they are encapsulated in a single place.

Summary

Object-oriented programming is different, but not difficult. This chapter details some of the reasons why you should prefer it over the top-down programming model. More scholarly texts go beyond this short list, but these are the most practical excuses for making the change. If you are a real coding maniac you can add one more—it's *fun*.

1. If a business rule changes for an object in your program, you must change
   a. The code in the class module
   b. All the code in the program
   c. None of the code
   d. The code in the class module and some of the program code

2. If you want to insert a class module you wrote for a different program into your current project, you must change
   a. All the property names in your class
   b. All the method names in your class
   c. All the event names in your class
   d. None of the above

3. If you need to share a class module with other programmers, they need to know
   a. All the inner workings of your class
   b. The names of the class methods and the data types of the class properties
   c. The names of the class methods and the names of the properties
   d. All of the above

4. When data in your class is hidden,
   a. It cannot be accessed from the program.
   b. It can be changed at random by the main program.
   c. It can be changed only through the **Property Let** procedure.
   d. It can be changed only through the **Property Get** procedure.

5. A side effect of object-oriented program is improved code because
   a. It just always works out that way.
   b. Object-oriented programmers are smarter.
   c. Object-oriented programs have better error handlers.
   d. Object-oriented programmers have to think before they can write any code.

CHAPTER 8

DISCOVERING THE COMMONDIALOG AND WINDOWS 95 CONTROLS

The end of Chapter 7, Classes, left SuperPad rather unfinished. SuperPad still lacks many of the professional features that you would expect to find in a modern Windows application—features such as a toolbar, a status bar, and tooltips. Also, SuperPad is still missing the Open and Save As dialog boxes. Luckily, with the Professional and Enterprise editions of Visual Basic 5, Microsoft provides 10 controls designed to solve just these sorts of problems. They are

- The CommonDialog control
- The RichTextBox control
- The ToolBar control
- The ImageList control
- The StatusBar control
- The TabStrip control
- The TreeView control

375

- The ListView control
- The ProgressBar control
- The Slider control

All controls are implemented as ActiveX control extensions (OCXs). This chapter begins by configuring a project to use them. The first lesson explains how to use the CommonDialog control. The remaining lessons use the other controls, using SuperPad as a demo platform.

INTRODUCING THE COMMONDIALOG CONTROL

Load the SuperPad project from Chapter 7, Classes. In Chapter 7, you learned how to reference OCXs to be able to use them in your own projects. Bring up the Components dialog box now by clicking on Components on the Project menu, or by pressing CTRL-T. Add the controls listed in Table 8-1 to the toolbox.

Table 8-1 OCX controls to reference

OCX Description	File Name
Microsoft CommonDialog Control 5.0	COMDLG32.OCX
Microsoft RichTextBox Control 5.0	RICHTX32.OCX
Microsoft Windows Common Controls 5.0	COMCTL32.OCX

Figure 8-1 shows the toolbox after the controls for this chapter are loaded. The toolbox must be widened so that all the controls can be seen.

There is also a Microsoft Common Controls 2 5.0 available that adds two more controls, an Animation control, and a Spin Button control. They are not used in this chapter.

The Microsoft RichTextBox control and the Microsoft Windows Common Controls form the group of controls that are known as the Windows 95 controls.

Introducing the CommonDialog Control

Some years ago, Microsoft recognized that many different Windows applications needed to perform common tasks, such as loading and saving files, printing, and choosing fonts and colors. To assist programmers in these tasks and to promote standardization,

Figure 8-1
Toolbox with
CommonDialog
and Windows 95
controls

Microsoft developed a group of ready-to-use dialog boxes and made them part of the Windows operating system. The Common Dialog boxes are still an intrinsic part of the various versions of Windows, and the CommonDialog control provides you with an easy way to use them. The toolbox icon for the CommonDialog control is shown in Figure 8-2.

One common misconception is that the Common Dialog boxes themselves are a part of the CommonDialog control. They are not. The CommonDialog control simply acts as a go-between between your project and the dialog boxes, which are buried inside the operating system itself, in the Windows Application Program Interface.

One interesting side effect of the dialog boxes being part of the operating system is that their look and feel differ among the different versions of Windows, most notably between the 16-bit versions of Windows, Windows 3.x, and Windows 95. However, by using the CommonDialog control, your programming interface into the dialog boxes remains consistent.

Figures 8-3, 8-4, 8-5, and 8-6 provide you with a sneak preview of how a few of the dialog boxes look under Windows 95.

Figure 8-2
The CommonDialog
control

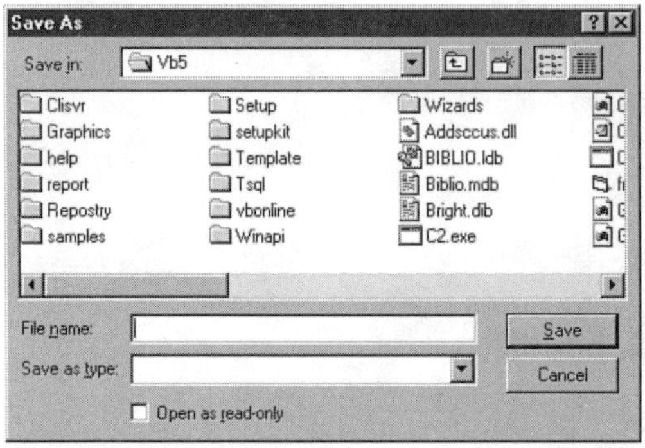

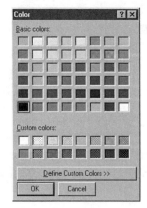

Figure 8-3
The Save As
dialog box

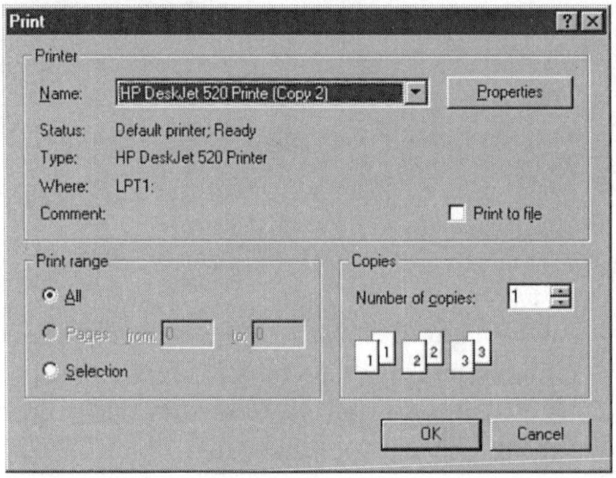

Figure 8-4
The Print setup
dialog box

Figure 8-5
The Color dialog
box

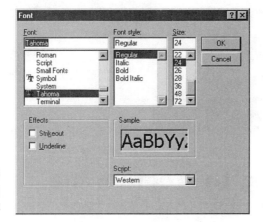

Figure 8-6
The Font dialog
box

What's great about these dialog boxes is that all the underlying functionality is pre-programmed. You get a professional look to your programs and you don't have to write a single line of code! What's more, you can even customize the dialog boxes to a certain extent.

A Control Without a User Interface

One of the features of the controls that you've used so far is that the control itself provides the graphical interface with which the users of your program interact. For example, the TextBox control is responsible for displaying a text box on the form at runtime. The CommonDialog control is different. At runtime, it is completely invisible. This is because it has no visual interface of its own. It is, in fact, one of a number of controls that do not directly interact with the user but instead provide an additional programming service. Examples of other controls that behave this way are the Timer and the MSComm (communications) controls.

A Control That Can Be Dragged onto an MDI Form

Open the SuperPad project and make **frmMain** the active form. You learned in Chapter 6, Forms, Menus, and MDI Forms, that you can't add just any control to an MDI form. The CommonDialog control is an exception. Select the CommonDialog control and drag it onto the form, shown in Figure 8-7. Yes, unlike other controls, the CommonDialog control is quite happy to be added to an MDI form.

As you can see, the control appears as a small icon. It can't be resized, although you can move it around the form. It doesn't matter where you place it; it is only providing a programming interface through its properties and methods.

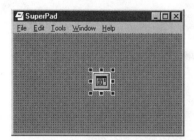

Figure 8-7
frmMain in design
mode with the
CommonDialog
control added

Learning to Program the CommonDialog Control

Now that the CommonDialog control has been added to **frmMain**, using it is a straightforward matter of learning how to use its properties and methods. The control has no events.

The first thing to note is that the same control can be used to access any of the Common Dialog boxes provided by Windows. This will become evident if you look at its properties, as shown in Figure 8-8.

Notice how some of the properties apply to one type of dialog box, whereas others are common to all types. For instance, **PrinterDefault**, **FromPage**, and **Copies** obviously apply to printing, whereas those that begin with the word **Font**, such as **FontBold** and **FontUnderline**, apply to the Font dialog box. Others, such as **CancelError** and **Flags**, are common to all the dialog boxes.

Click on Custom in the Properties window to open the Property Pages of the CommonDialog control, shown in Figure 8-9. The separate tabs on the Property Pages provide further emphasis on the versatility of the control.

Figure 8-8
CommonDialog
control Properties
window

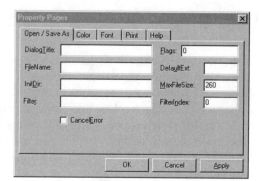

Figure 8-9
The Property Pages
for the
CommonDialog
control

The Flags **Property**

The **Flags** property is arguably the most important property. It allows you to customize how a dialog box appears before you display it. For example, the File dialog boxes (Open and Save As dialog boxes) in Figure 8-3 contain a check box labeled Open as read only. You may not want to make this feature available in your project unless you want to give your users the ability to read a document without changing it. You can turn off the display of that particular check box by setting a flag in the **Flags** property.

In fact, you can set a large number of customizable options. The examples in this book show you how to use many of the flags, but you should consult the online Help for a full list of the options and what they can do.

The File Dialog Boxes

The two dialog boxes associated with files are the Open and Save As dialog boxes. The code you need to add to the Open menu's **Click** event to display the Open dialog box is in Listing 8-1.

Listing 8-1 Bringing up the File Open dialog

```
Private Sub mnuFileOpen_Click()
    CommonDialog1.Filter = "Text files (*.txt)|*.txt|All files|*.*"
    CommonDialog1.ShowOpenc
End Sub
```

The call to the **ShowOpen** method displays the Open dialog box. The dialog box is displayed modally, so the call doesn't return until the user presses either the Open or the Cancel button.

The Filter *Property*

The **Filter** property applies only to the File dialog boxes. Its purpose is to select entries for the Files of type combo box. It allows users to select the file extensions that will be listed in the combo box. This is a feature of most Windows applications. Visual Basic's common dialog box, for example, defaults to **Project Files** (*.vbp, *.mak, *.vbg).

The syntax for the `Filter` string is

```
object.Filter [= description1 |filter1 |description2 |filter2...]
```

The `Filter` string requires some explanation. Each file type (or group of file types) is represented by a two-part string: a description and the actual file specification. The description appears in the combo box, whereas the CommonDialog control uses the file spec to select the files. The two parts of the filter string are separated by the pipeline symbol, the vertical bar that represents **Or** in syntax diagrams. (On most keyboards, the pipeline symbol is a broken vertical bar that shares a key with the backslash.)

You can add as many `Filter` strings as you want, separating the `Filter` strings with the same pipeline symbol. Each `Filter` string appears as a separate entry in the combo box. The code to use in SuperPad is

```
CommonDialog1.Filter = "Text files (*.txt)|*.txt|All files (*.*)|*.*"
```

The first `Filter` string is `Text files (*.txt)|*.txt`, which selects and displays all files with the `.txt` extension.

Figure 8-10 shows the user selecting `"Text files (*.txt)"` from the available types.

Determining Whether the User Canceled

The user has the choice of selecting a file to open and pressing the Open button (or double-clicking on the file of his or her choice), or pressing the Cancel button to cancel the whole operation. Then it's up to your program to respond correctly.

There are two ways to determine which button has been pressed. The first technique works only with file dialogs, whereas the second can be used with any of the Common Dialog boxes.

The Non-Error-Trapping Method

This method applies only to the File dialog boxes, because it checks the `FileName` property to determine whether or not a file name was selected. Before you call the `ShowOpen` method, assign an empty string to the `FileName` property. Then, when the method returns, check to see if the `FileName` property is still empty. The `FileName` property remains empty unless the user selected a file and pressed the Open button (or double-clicked on a file). The code to implement this strategy is shown in Listing 8-2.

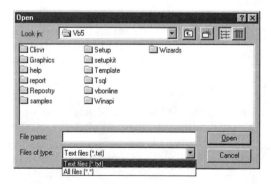

Figure 8-10
The Text files filter

Listing 8-2 Checking for Cancel without error handling

```
Private Sub mnuFileOpen_Click()
CommonDialog1.Filter = "Text files (*.txt)|*.txt|All files (*.*)|*.*"
    CommonDialog1.Filename = ""
    CommonDialog1.ShowOpen
    If CommonDialog1.Filename <> "" Then
    'A file was selected. Add the code to load it here
    End If
End Sub
```

Note that if a file is selected, the `FileName` property contains the full path to the file, not just the file name, so you have all the information you need to locate the selected file. If you want just the name, use the `FileTitle` property.

The `Error-Trapping` *Method*

The non-error-trapping technique of checking the `FileName` property works fine for the File dialog boxes. However, it doesn't work for the others. Instead, you need a sure-fire way of determining which button was pressed. That's what the error-trapping technique does.

Error trapping is a mechanism in Visual Basic 5 that allows your own code to be run when an error occurs at runtime. Without error trapping, a compiled EXE version of your project will terminate rather ungraciously when an error occurs. Visual Basic 5 allows you to set up something called an *error handler*. This is an entry point in your project that runs when an error occurs. Error handlers are covered in detail in Chapter 10, Error Handling and Debugging. You can use it with the CommonDialog control to determine when the Cancel button has been pressed.

To use error trapping, set the control's `CancelError` property to `True` and install a suitable error handler. Listing 8-3 shows how the `Click` event looks using the `Error-Trapping` method.

Listing 8-3 Checking for Cancel with error trapping

```
Private Sub mnuFileOpen_Click()
Dim Cancel As Boolean
On Error Goto ErrorHandler
Cancel = False
CommonDialog1.Filter = "Text files (*.txt)|*.txt|All files (*.*)|*.*"
CommonDialog1.CancelError = True
CommonDialog1.ShowOpen
If Not Cancel Then
    'The Open button was pressed. Add the code to load the file here
End If
Exit Sub

ErrorHandler:
If Err.Number = cdlCancel Then
    Cancel = True
    Resume Next
```

continued on next page

continued from previous page

```
End If
End
End Sub
```

The line that begins `On Error GoTo` is the line that installs the error handler. It says that if an error occurs in this subroutine at runtime, program execution should jump to the label `ErrorHandler`. By setting the `CancelError` property to `True`, the CommonDialog control forces an error to occur when the user presses the Cancel button. Each runtime error has a unique number in Visual Basic, so it's easy to check whether the error that occurred was the user pressing the Cancel button on a Common Dialog box. The error code is represented by the constant `cdlCancel`. The constant is made globally available to your project by the CommonDialog control itself. That's why you can use it in your project without specifically declaring it.

If a user presses the Cancel button in a Common Dialog box, the dialog box closes and an error is raised upon exiting from the dialog. Because of the error, the program jumps to the error handler instead of executing the instruction immediately following the call to `CommonDialog1`.

Each error in Visual Basic has a unique number. The error handler checks the error number to be sure that the error was caused by the dialog box's Cancel button. If it was, the variable `Cancel` is set to `True` and the `Resume Next` statement is executed. If it was not, the program simply exits from the `mnuFileOpen` procedure.

The `Resume Next` statement tells the computer to resume operation at the statement following the one that raised the error. In this procedure, the line that raised the error is the call to `CommonDialog1`, and the next line is `If Not Cancel Then`.

It's a lot easier to watch this than it is to read about. Place the cursor on the line

```
On Error Goto ErrorHandler
```

and press F9. (Don't worry about what is happening, it's covered in detail in Chapter 10, Error Handling and Debugging.) Then press F5 to run the program. When the program starts running, select Open from the File menu. The program stops running and highlights a line of code that is the next line to be executed. Press F8 and watch the highlight move to the next line. When you press F8 with `CommonDialog1.ShowOpen` highlighted, the Common Dialog File Open dialog box opens. Click on the Cancel button. When the program returns to the code window, the next statement highlight is on the first line of the error-handler code. Continue pressing F8 to watch the flow of the program. Repeat the same steps, this time selecting a file to load, and watch the flow of the program to load a file. (Because the file load procedure is not yet added, no file is actually loaded.)

What you just did is called *single-stepping* through a section of code. It's a perfect way to see exactly what is happening in a program. Now, back to work.

The Flags *Property*

The Open dialog box still has the Open as read-only check box. To get rid of it, you must set a flag in the `Flags` property just before you call `ShowOpen`:

```
CommonDialog1.Flags = cdlOFNHideReadOnly
```

You can set many flags that do neat things. For instance, the flag `cdlOFNFileMustExist` prevents users from attempting to open a file that doesn't exist. How could they do that? By typing in the name of a file that is not in the list. What's great about these flags is that they simplify your code tremendously. If it weren't for the `cdlOFNFileMustExist` flag, for example, you would have to write your own routine to check that the file actually exists.

To use more than one flag at a time, use the logical `Or` operator to combine them:

```
CommonDialog1.Flags = cdlOFNHideReadOnly Or cdlOFNFileMustExist
```

The constants are defined by the CommonDialog control. You don't have to declare them yourself.

Next add the code for the Save As dialog box, as shown in Listing 8-4.

Listing 8-4 `FileSaveAs` routine

```
Private Sub mnuFileSaveAs_Click()
Dim Cancel As Boolean
On Error Goto ErrorHandler
Cancel = False
CommonDialog1.DefaultExt = ".txt"
CommonDialog1.Filter = "Text files (*.txt)|*.txt|All files (*.*)|*.*"
CommonDialog1.CancelError = True
CommonDialog1.Flags = cdlOFNHideReadOnly Or _
                      cdlOFNOverwritePrompt
CommonDialog1.ShowSave
If Not Cancel Then
    'A filename was selected. Add the code to save the file here
End If
Exit Sub

ErrorHandler:
If Err.Number = cdlCancel Then
    Cancel = True
    Resume Next
End If
End Sub
```

The main difference between the Save As dialog box and the Open dialog box is in the use of the `DefaultExt` property. If you set `DefaultExt` to a file extension (we've used `.txt`) then if the user enters a file name without an extension, the CommonDialog control automatically adds the default extension. This way you can be certain that the file name returned in the `FileName` property will contain a full file name, complete with a valid extension.

We've also used a new flag, `cdlOFNOverwritePrompt`. This causes the dialog box to warn the user that the file already exists, preventing an accidental overwrite.

Note that when the CommonDialog control gets a file name from the user, it doesn't actually perform the Open or Save operation for you. You have to code that yourself. File I/O (that's input and output) is covered in Chapter 12, Files, but the File Open and Save As menu items are completed in the next lesson, which looks at one of the

Windows 95 controls, the RichTextBox control. The `FileOpen` and `SaveAs` methods are standard methods of the RichTextBox control.

1. Configuring your project to use an OCX is known as:
   a. Registering the OCX
   b. Referencing the OCX
   c. Referring the OCX
   d. Running the OCX

2. Which of the following controls is *not* specifically a Windows 95 control?
   a. The RichTextBox control
   b. The CommonDialog control
   c. The Slider control
   d. The ListView control

3. How can you add the CommonDialog control to an MDI form?
   a. You cannot. You can only add it to an SDI form.
   b. You can only do it by adding a control first that can act as a container for other controls, such as the PictureBox control.
   c. Just drag it onto the form.
   d. You have to use OLE automation.

4. Which property controls whether the CommonDialog control causes an error to occur when the user presses a dialog box's Cancel button?
   a. `CancelError`
   b. `TriggerError`
   c. `ForceError`
   d. `ErrorEvent`

5. Which of the following strings should you set the control's `Filter` property to if you want to apply a filter to files of type DOC, TXT, or All Files?
   a. `"Document files(*.doc)\*.doc\Text files (*.txt)\*.txt\All files\*.*"`
   b. `"Document files (*.doc)|Text files (*.txt)|All files (*.*)"`
   c. `"Document files (*.doc)|(*.doc)|Text files (*.txt)|(*.txt)|All files|(*.*)"`
   d. `"Document files (*.doc)|*.doc|Text files (*.txt)|*.txt|All files|*.*"`

THE RICHTEXTBOX CONTROL AND THE FONT AND COLOR DIALOG BOXES

Now that you've seen how the File Common Dialog boxes work, it's time to learn how to use the Font and Color dialog boxes. However, there is a small problem. At present, SuperPad can work only with simple text, because it uses the TextBox control. That simplifies the storage, display, and editing of the text in a document, but it is also a limiting factor. To use the Font and Color dialog boxes, you are going to have to change the way SuperPad works so that you can apply font and color changes to text.

What you really want is a replacement for the TextBox control—another control that works just like it but that also allows you to change the fonts and colors of its text. Fortunately, the RichTextBox control was designed to do just that. It is a direct, drop-in replacement for the TextBox control that fully supports all the TextBox control's properties, events, and methods. It also has some additional features that let you control the displayed fonts and colors.

What Is Rich Text?

The RichTextBox control gets its name from a Microsoft standard called rich text format (RTF). This is a standard for storing text with additional attributes, such as font and color. Quite a few word processors and other document editors can work with RTF, including WordPad and Microsoft Word.

RTF itself is very complex and would ordinarily require a considerable amount of programming effort to support fully. Luckily, with the RichTextBox control, all the hard work has been done for you. What's more, the RichTextBox control also provides methods to load and save RTF files and, because it's backward compatible with the TextBox control, you can still work with ordinary text if you want to.

Replacing the TextBox Control

To use the RichTextBox control, you must make a change to SuperPad that, at first sight, seems pretty drastic. You have to delete the TextBox control from `frmDocument` and replace it with a RichTextBox control. However, because the RichTextBox control has all the same properties, events, and methods as the ordinary TextBox control, it turns out that this replacement isn't as drastic as you might at first imagine. Furthermore, if you give the new RichTextBox control the same name as the control it's replacing, you actually need make no programming changes at all and the program will work exactly as it did before!

Try the changes now.

● Double-click on frmDocument in the Project Explorer window to bring the form to the front.

● Click on the text box to select it; then press the DELETE key.

● Select the RichTextBox control from the toolbox and draw it onto the form in place of the original text box.

Figure 8-11 shows the RichTextBox control icon.
Change the properties of the new control to those shown in Table 8-2.

Table 8-2 RichTextBox control properties

Property	Value
Appearance	0 – Flat
BorderStyle	0 – No border
Name	txtDocument

By default, the **Appearance** and **BorderStyle** properties are set so that the RichTextBox has a 3-D appearance. This isn't desirable for SuperPad because you want the control to extend to the inner edge of the document window.

Now try running SuperPad. It works exactly as before. In fact, you won't be able to tell that you're no longer using the TextBox control.

Setting Fonts and Color

The next thing to do is to provide some additional menus in SuperPad so that the user has access to the Font and Color Common Dialog boxes. This means that he or she will be able to use the Font and Color Common Dialog boxes to change the text in the rich text box.

Add two new menu items to SuperPad's Edit menu. These are specified in Table 8-3.

Table 8-3 Menu items to be added to SuperPad's Edit menu

Menu Name	Caption
mnuEditFont	F&ont...
mnuEditColor	Colo&r...

Figure 8-11
The RichTextBox
control icon

Ensure that both menu items are always enabled, because you will want to be able to change the current font settings as well as those of the selected text. The properties of the RichTextBox control that affect the selected text also affect the current font and colors if no text is selected.

The code for the Font menu's `Click` event is in Listing 8-5. Note the use of the `With...End With` structure to apply multiple property values to a single object.

Listing 8-5 Letting the user change the font

```
Private Sub mnuEditFont_Click()
CommonDialog1.Flags = cdlCFBoth Or cdlCFEffects
CommonDialog1.ShowFont
With frmMain.ActiveForm.txtDocument
    .SelFontName = CommonDialog1.FontName
    .SelFontSize = CommonDialog1.FontSize
    .SelBold = CommonDialog1.FontBold
    .SelItalic = CommonDialog1.FontItalic
    .SelStrikeThru = CommonDialog1.FontStrikeThru
    .SelUnderline = CommonDialog1.FontUnderline
    .SelColor = CommonDialog1.Color
End With
End Sub
```

As you can see, the code uses the CommonDialog control's `ShowFont` method to display the Font dialog box. It sets two flags. The first, `cdlCFBoth`, tells the Font dialog box to display both printer and screen fonts in its list of fonts. In fact, you can display a wide range of different font types in this dialog box, limiting the display to either printer or screen fonts, and even just to TrueType fonts that work on both screen and printer. If you don't specify the font type to display, no fonts will appear in the dialog box.

The second flag, `cdlCFEffects`, indicates that you want to see the attributes for the fonts, which include the **strikethrough**, **underline**, and **color** attributes. Note that you can use this one control to set the color of the fonts as well, although you cannot define custom colors with it. You need the Color dialog box to do that.

Figure 8-12 shows you how the Font dialog box appears with the **effects** flag set. Table 8-4 lists some additional flags for you to try. For more information on these flags, refer to the online Help.

Table 8-4 Try these additional flags with the Font Common Dialog box

Flag Constant	Description
cdlCFANSIOnly	Displays only fonts that contain a complete ANSI character set
cdlCFFixedPitchOnly	Displays only fixed-pitch fonts
cdlCFPrinterFonts	Displays only printer fonts
cdlCFScalableOnly	Displays only fonts that are scaleable
cdlCFScreenFonts	Displays only screen fonts
cdlCFTTOnly	Displays only TrueType fonts

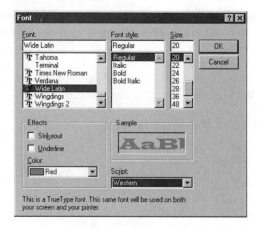

Figure 8-12
The Font dialog
with the
cdlCFEffects
flag set

Note that the constants shown in Table 8-3 do not provide any error handling to allow for the user pressing the Cancel button. This is purely for the sake of clarity. You should always install an error handler to check for the **cdlCancel** error code in your own code.

Applying the selected font styles is straightforward enough. You simply copy the font properties from the CommonDialog control. Note that the RichTextBox properties begin with **Sel**. This is because they apply only to the selected text, rather like the **SelStart** and **SelLength** properties that you saw in Chapter 6, Forms, Menus, and MDI Forms. Similarly, the changes apply to the current font settings if no text is selected.

Now add the code for the Color menu's **Click** event (see Listing 8-6). This will allow the user to set the **Color** property of the font.

Listing 8-6 Activating the Color dialog

```
Private Sub mnuEditColor_Click()

CommonDialog1.Flags = cdlCCFullOpen

CommonDialog1.ShowColor

frmMain.ActiveForm.txtDocument.SelColor = CommonDialog1.Color

End Sub
```

Again, it is the **Flags** setting that characterizes the way the dialog box works. The only flag the code uses is **cdlCCFullOpen**, which provides the full Color dialog box to allow the user to define his or her own custom colors or to select the standard colors from the prepared palette.

Figure 8-13 shows you how the full Color dialog box looks.

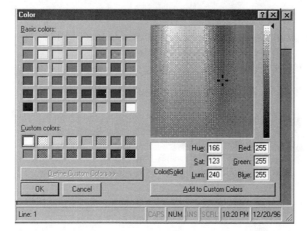

Figure 8-13
The full Color
dialog box

Loading and Saving Rich Text Files

All that's left now is to complete the programming of the Open and Save As dialog boxes by calling the RichTextBox's methods to load and save rich text files. The methods provided by the RichTextBox control for this purpose are called **LoadFile** and **SaveFile**. Both methods support loading either rich text or ordinary text files, as you will see from the completed **Click** event subroutines for the Open and Save As menus. The **Open** routine is in Listing 8-7.

Listing 8-7 Opening a rich text or text file

```
RichTextPrivate Sub mnuFileOpen_Click()
Dim Cancel As Boolean
    On Error GoTo ErrorHandler
    Cancel = False
    CommonDialog1.Filter = _
      "Text files (*.txt)|*.txt|All files (*.*)|*.*" & _
      "RichText files (*.rtf)|*.rtf|" & _
CommonDialog1.CancelError = True
    CommonDialog1.Flags = cdlOFNHideReadOnly Or _
      cdlOFNFileMustExist
    CommonDialog1.ShowOpen
    If Not Cancel Then
    ' Load a File
        If UCase(Right(CommonDialog1.filename, 3)) = _
          "RTF" Then
          ' It is an RTF file
            frmMain.ActiveForm.txtDocument.LoadFile _
              CommonDialog1.filename, rtfRTF
        Else
          ' It is a text file
            frmMain.ActiveForm.txtDocument.LoadFile _
              CommonDialog1.filename, rtfText
```

continued on next page

continued from previous page

```
            End If
            ' Set the document name
            frmMain.ActiveForm.objDocument.DocName = _
              CommonDialog1.filename
            ' Set FileChanged parameter
            frmMain.ActiveForm.objDocument.Changed = False
        End If
        ' All done here
        Exit Sub
    '
ErrorHandler:
        If Err.Number = cdlCancel Then
            Cancel = True
            Resume Next
        End If
End Sub
```

What's Happening Here?

The new code adds a filter string for RTF files to the Common Dialog File Open list. When a file is selected, the file name is passed to the load file routine. The load file routine uses the **LoadFile** method of the RichTextBox. The syntax of the **LoadFile** method is

```
object.LoadFile pathname, filetype
```

where

- **object** is the name of the RichTextBox object.

- **pathname** is the full path and file name of the file to load.

- **filetype** is either **rtfRTF**, which means the file must be a valid rich text file, or **rtfText**, which means the file can be any text file.

The code in Listing 8-7 contains an **If...Then...Else** to handle either case. The **SaveAs** routine is shown in Listing 8-8.

Listing 8-8 The SaveAs routine

```
Private Sub mnuFileSaveAs_Click()
Dim Cancel As Boolean
On Error GoTo ErrorHandler
Cancel = False
CommonDialog1.DefaultExt = ".rtf"
CommonDialog1.Filter = "RichText files (*.rtf)|*.rtf|" & _
                        "Text files (*.txt)|*.txt|All files (*.*)|*.*"
CommonDialog1.CancelError = True
CommonDialog1.Flags = cdlOFNHideReadOnly Or _
                      cdlOFNOverwritePrompt
CommonDialog1.ShowSave
If Not Cancel Then
```

```
    With frmMain.ActiveForm
        If UCase(Right(CommonDialog1.filename, 3)) = "RTF" Then
            .txtDocument.SaveFile CommonDialog1.Filename, rtfRTF
        Else
            .txtDocument.SaveFile CommonDialog1.Filename, rtfText
        End If
        .objDocument.DocName = CommonDialog1.Filename
        .objDocument.Changed = False
    End With
End If
Exit Sub

ErrorHandler:
If Err.Number = cdlCancel Then
    Cancel = True
    Resume Next
End If
End Sub
```

The changes to the Save As menu's Click event are similar to those you made to open a file. Again, an RTF entry is added to the Filter property and the code distinguishes between rich text and ordinary text files by means of the file extension.

To complete this lesson, you must also provide the code to go into the Save menu's Click event. See Listing 8-9. The Save menu should determine whether the current document has been saved to disk. If the document has not, the menu item should perform the same task as the Save As menu item. It does that by calling the Save As menu's Click event directly. If the document has already been saved, then the Click event just resaves the document using the current file name.

Listing 8-9 The Save routine

```
Private Sub mnuFileSave_Click()
With frmMain.ActiveForm
    If .objDocument.DocName = "Untitled" Then
        mnuFileSaveAs_Click
    Else
        If UCase(Right(.objDocument.DocName, 3)) = "RTF" Then
            .txtDocument.SaveFile .objDocument.DocName, rtfRTF
        Else
            .txtDocument.SaveFile .objDocument.DocName, rtfText
        End If
        .objDocument.Changed = False
    End If
End With
End Sub
```

As you can see, the code determines if the document has been saved by checking whether its name is still the default Untitled. If it is, the Save As menu's Click event is called directly; otherwise, the RichTextBox control's SaveFile method is called. The If...Then...Else to determine the file type parameter is the same as that in the SaveAs method.

Figure 8-14 shows how SuperPad now looks with a rich text document loaded.

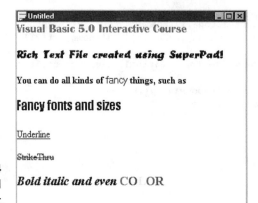

Figure 8-14
SuperPad
displaying rich text

1. The name of the RichTextBox property that controls whether text appears with a line through the middle of it is:
   a. StrikeThrough
   b. FontStrikeThru
   c. SelStrikeThrough
   d. SelStrikeThru

2. Which CommonDialog flag controls whether the effects attributes of the Font dialog box are displayed?
   a. cdlCFEffects
   b. cdlEffects
   c. cdlFontEffects
   d. cdlShowEffects

3. Which of the following lines of code will save a file in RTF (assuming the RichTextBox control's name is RichTextBox1)?
   a. RichTextBox1.SaveFile FileName, RTF
   b. RichTextBox1.SaveFile FileName, rtfRTF
   c. RichTextBox1.SaveFile rtfRTF, FileName
   d. RichTextBox1.SaveFile RTF, FileName

4. How do you tell the RichTextBox control to change its default font settings?
   a. You cannot. You can only change the font settings of selected text.
   b. Use the properties that begin DefaultFont rather than SelFont.
   c. Change to the properties that begin with SelFont to automatically apply default text when no text is selected.
   d. Set the Edit Font menu to Enabled.

5. Which of the following is *not* a valid flag setting for the Font dialog box?
   a. `cdlCFFixedPitchFonts`
   b. `cdlCFScreenFonts`
   c. `cdlCFPrinterFonts`
   d. `cdlCFTTOnly`

THE TOOLBAR AND IMAGELIST CONTROLS

Now to add a toolbar to SuperPad. A toolbar usually appears at the top of a program's main window and consists of a bar containing small buttons and, possibly, other controls. The idea of the toolbar is to give the user direct access to the most commonly used features of the program. Most of the time, toolbar buttons are used as direct replacements for equivalent functions on the program's menu. Toolbars are popular because the user can point and click at a toolbar button a lot more quickly and much more conveniently than navigating through a menu structure.

Toolbars also have another important function. They make your applications look a little friendlier. However, their little buttons just cry out to be pressed, so you should make sure that you disable them, as you do their menu equivalents, when the buttons go out of context.

Adding a Toolbar to Your Project

Adding a toolbar to your project involves using two Windows 95 controls. The first of these is called the ToolBar control. You use it to create the toolbar and the basic toolbar buttons. The second control is the ImageList control. The image list's job is to store the images displayed on the toolbar button tops. In fact, you can use an image list to store any images you like, not just the ones destined for a toolbar's buttons. Your only limitation is the amount of available memory. Remember that images are memory hogs!

Once the images are loaded into the image list, the toolbar buttons can be linked to the images. From that point on, the ToolBar control does the rest, automatically repainting its buttons in the down position when they get pressed and graying them out when they become disabled, so you need only one bitmap per button.

Figure 8-15 shows how the ToolBar and ImageList controls appear on the toolbox.

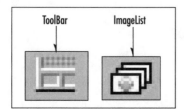

Figure 8-15
The ToolBar and ImageList controls

Add these two controls to `frmMain`. Like the CommonDialog control, the ImageList control will quite happily sit on the MDI form because it has no visual interface of its own and will be invisible at runtime. The ToolBar control automatically aligns itself to the top of the form, although you can change its alignment by setting its `Align` property. Leave it at the top of the form, where convention dictates a toolbar should be.

Figure 8-16 shows `frmMain` in design mode with both controls added.

The Image List's `MaskColor` *Property*

The `MaskColor` property affects the way the images contained in the image list are displayed. The purpose of this mask is to facilitate situations where an image is going to be displayed on top of an existing graphic. This is exactly what you are about to do in displaying an image on top of a button. The mask is a black-and-white image created from the original image in the image list. The `MaskColor` value determines which color in the image is going to be used as the "background" (and therefore which color will be transparent when the image is finally displayed). All other colors will be opaque. As a rule of thumb, the most predictable results occur when you use the button face color for the mask. The button top that the image is to be displayed on is gray, and you should use the same gray color as the mask color for this image list. Follow Figure 8-17 to set the `MaskColor` correctly.

At this stage, the toolbar doesn't look too exciting. For a start, it has no buttons. Your job—to add some.

Adding Buttons to the Toolbar

If you check out the toolbar's properties, you'll find one at the top of the Properties Windows called (Custom). Notice that the property name is in parentheses. This is because it isn't a property itself, but a link to a Properties Pages dialog box inside the OCX. Many of the Windows 95 controls have this (Custom) entry in their Properties windows. The reason it's there is that many of the properties of the control are too complex to be programmed directly from the Properties window. Some properties are interrelated and require a more structured editing tool than the ordinary Properties window. The Property Pages dialog box provides this additional structure.

Figure 8-16
SuperPad in design
mode with the
ImageList and
ToolBar controls
added

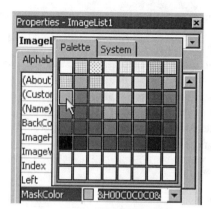

Figure 8-17
Applying a
MaskColor property
to the image list

When you select the (Custom) entry, a small button with ellipses on it appears. Press that button to display the Property Pages dialog box for the control. Use the dialog box to create three new toolbar buttons. These three buttons will be used:

- To create a new document
- To open an existing document
- To save the current document to disk

The dialog box that is displayed contains three tabs: General, Buttons, and Pictures. The first thing to do is to add the buttons themselves. Select the Buttons tab and press Insert Button three times. This is shown in Figure 8-18.

Each time you press the Insert Button button, a new button is added to the toolbar. What's actually happening here is quite interesting. The buttons you are creating at design time will be added to a Buttons collection at runtime. That's why this dialog box has a Key field. Just like any other collection, you can associate a key with the button object itself so that you can locate that button in the collection at runtime.

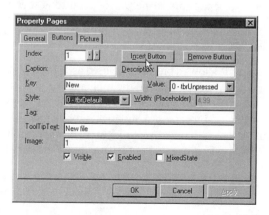

Figure 8-18
The ToolBar control
Property dialog

Note that you cannot rely on a button occupying the same index position in the collection when your program is run. This is because the toolbar is potentially customizable by the user, a feature that is covered at the end of this lesson.

Use the Spin button to set the Index to 1 and type New in the Key field. You can optionally add a caption that will appear beneath the button, but for this exercise leave the Caption field blank. (It is not conventional to have captions on toolbars.) Set the Key for Index 2 to Open, and set the Key for Index 3 to Save.

You can also set styles for the buttons. The standard toolbar button is tbrDefault, but you can select from other styles:

- tbrCheck
- tbrButton Group
- tbrSeparator
- tbrPlace Holder

Check Style

The Check style changes the way the button operates at runtime. Instead of emulating a standard Command button, this style makes the button work like a check box. The button stays in its down position when it is first pressed. It then has to be pressed once again to be released.

Button Group

When you set two or more buttons to be a button group, they behave just like Option buttons. In other words, when you push one and another in the group is already pressed, it pops back up. You can create more than one group of buttons on the toolbar by adding separator buttons to act as spacers between the groups.

Separator

A Separator button is not displayed as a button at all, but as a small gap between buttons. You can use separators to help group buttons together, both visually and functionally.

Placeholder Style

The Placeholder style allows a button to be used as a container for another control. This is how you can add other controls to the toolbar.

By using button groups, separators, and place holders, you can add all the features of a professional word processor to SuperPad's toolbar, such as a group of buttons to make text bold, italic, underlined, or strikethrough, and combo boxes to allow the user to select the font and font size without having to use the Font CommonDialog boxes.

Adding Images to the Buttons

Now that you have three buttons to play with, here's how to add bitmaps to the button tops. You can find the bitmaps to use in the `GRAPHICS\BITMAPS\TLBR_W95` subdirectory of Visual Basic's "home" directory.

The bitmaps to use are shown in Figure 8-19.

These three bitmaps must be loaded into the ImageList control. To do this, select the (Custom) properties of the ImageList control to display the ImageList Property Pages dialog box, and select the Images tab. On that tab is the Insert Picture button, which you can use to load the images into separate index positions in the image list. Figure 8-20 shows you this dialog box with the three bitmaps loaded. Bitmaps in the ImageList control can be referred to by index, or you can add a key, if you wish. For larger collections of images, keys are easier to remember; use the same key name for the bitmap as for the button.

You now have bitmaps that correspond to each of the three buttons. Each button is a **Button** object in the toolbar's Buttons collection and, correspondingly, each image is a **ListImage** object in the image list's List Images collection. Now all you have to do is link the images to the buttons.

At design time, the index numbers of the **ListImage** objects and the **Button** objects are fixed. In other words, the **Button** object with an index of **1** will always be the new button at design time. Similarly, the **ListImage** object with an index of **1** will always be the bitmap that is associated with that button.

To link the two together, return to the Custom Properties dialog box of the ToolBar control and display its General tab. The ImageList combo box allows you to link the toolbar to an image list. This is shown in Figure 8-21. When you open the combo box, it displays all the ImageList controls on the form.

Figure 8-19
Bitmaps for the
buttons

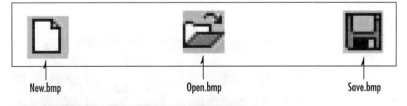

New.bmp   Open.bmp   Save.bmp

Figure 8-20
Loading images
into the ImageList
control

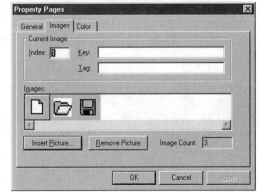

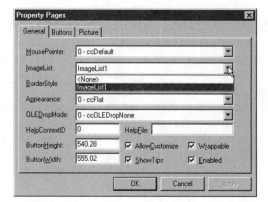

Figure 8-21
Linking the image
list with the
ToolBar dialog
box's General tab

Once the toolbar knows which image list to use, it has access to the List Images collection in that control. All that's left to do then is to specify which `ListImage` object in the collection to use for each button.

To do this, select the Buttons tab. A text box labeled Image is at the bottom of the displayed dialog box. In the text box, enter the index number of the `ListImage` object that you want on that button. (If you used keys for the images, you can add a key instead of an index number.) So, for button index one, enter a **1** in the Image text box. For button index two, enter a **2**, and so on.

A word of warning. Once you have connected the image list to the toolbar, you cannot add new images to the image list unless you remove all references to it from the toolbar. That can be a lot of work if you have a large toolbar. As always, the best strategy is to plan ahead.

That's all there is to it. Now when you run SuperPad, it will have a toolbar as shown in Figure 8-22, although the toolbar isn't fully functional yet.

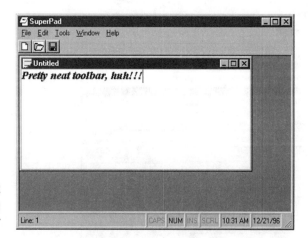

Figure 8-22
SuperPad running
with the toolbar

Disabling the Save Button

On the Buttons tab is an Enabled check box that you can use to enable or disable a button at startup. You should disable the Save button at startup for the same reasons that you disabled the Save menu item. Like the menu, you'll have to add a line to the **SetupCSMenus** subroutine to enable or disable the button at runtime. This is shown in Listing 8-10.

Listing 8-10 Making the toolbar context-sensitive

```
mnuFileClose.Enabled = Found
mnuFileSave.Enabled = Found
mnuFileSaveAs.Enabled = Found
mnuFilePrint.Enabled = Found
Toolbar1.Buttons("Save").Enabled = Found
```

As you can see from the single new line, it's easy to access the Save button at runtime using the key you set up at design time.

What Happens When the Button Is Pressed?

When a toolbar button is pressed, it generates a **ButtonClick** event. Listing 8-11 shows how to program the three buttons.

Listing 8-11 Programming the toolbar

```
Private Sub Toolbar1_ButtonClick(ByVal Button As Button)
Select Case Button.Key
    Case "New"
        mnuFileNew_Click
    Case "Open"
        mnuFileOpen_Click
    Case "Save"
        mnuFileSave_Click
End Select
End Sub
```

The **ButtonClick** event's **Button** parameter is a reference to the **Button** object that was pressed. All you have to do is check the **Key** property of that particular object to tell which of the three buttons generated the event. If you're finding the use of the word "Button" confusing, it's probably because the ToolBar control gives the **Button** object variable the same name as the **Button** class. That's why the declaration reads **Button As Button**. There's nothing to stop you from changing the name of the variable, so you could write the subroutine as shown in Listing 8-12 instead.

Listing 8-12 Same routine, different variable name

```
Private Sub Toolbar1_ButtonClick(ByVal TheButton As Button)
Select Case TheButton.Key
    Case "New"
        mnuFileNew_Click
    Case "Open"
        mnuFileOpen_Click
    Case "Save"
        mnuFileSave_Click
End Select
End Sub
```

Additional Toolbar Features

The toolbar has some nice additional features that you might want to use. These include tooltips and the ability to let the user reorganize the toolbar at runtime.

Tooltips

You know what tooltips are—those little pop-ups that appear when you point at something. Tooltips contain a small piece of text that describes what the object that you're pointing to does. This is a particularly helpful feature for your users because some toolbar button graphics can be rather obscure. Your users will want to know what that button with the little flying polygons on it does without having to press it.

The toolbar has support for tooltips built in, so adding tooltips is a trivial exercise. Just return to the Buttons tab on the toolbar's Custom Properties dialog box. In there, you'll find a field labeled **ToolTip Text**. Just add the text that you want to appear in the tooltip to this field and set the toolbar's **ShowTips** property to **True**, and the tooltip will be displayed at runtime. The text to add to your three buttons is **New file**, **Open file**, and **Save file**.

Figure 8-23 shows you SuperPad running with Tooltips.

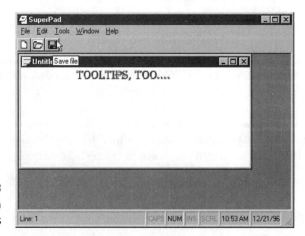

Figure 8-23
SuperPad with
Tooltips

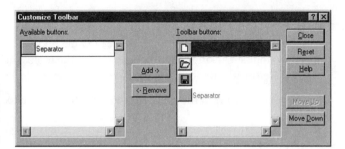

Figure 8-24
The toolbar's
Customize Toolbar
dialog box

Reorganizing the Toolbar's Buttons at Runtime

Did you know that your users can reorganize the toolbar at runtime? Try double-clicking on the background of the toolbar (any place other than a button) when SuperPad is running. The Customize Toolbar dialog box in Figure 8-24 appears. Your users can use this dialog box to move the buttons around. If you don't want your users to have this facility, you should set the toolbar's `AllowCustomize` property to `False`.

The text that appears next to each bitmap is a description of the button. However, this text is not picked up from the tooltip `Text` field on the Buttons tab. Instead, it comes from the `Description` field on the same tab. You'll have to add some text to that field or your dialog box will display just the buttons without the descriptive text.

1. What is the maximum number of images that can be stored in an ImageList control?
   a. 8
   b. 16
   c. 32
   d. It is limited only by available memory.

2. How does the ToolBar control store the individual button objects at runtime?
   a. I've no idea.
   b. In its Button collection
   c. In its Buttons collection
   d. In an array of button objects

3. Which of the following is not a valid toolbar button style?
   a. Placeholder
   b. Option button
   c. Separator
   d. Button group

4. How do you display the Customize ToolBar dialog box?
   a. By selecting the (Custom) entry on the toolbar's Properties window
   b. By calling the toolbar's `AllowCustomize` method
   c. By double-clicking on the background of the toolbar at runtime
   d. By setting the toolbar's `AllowCustomize` property to `True`

5. What is the name of the event that is generated when a toolbar button is pressed?
   a. `ButtonClick`
   b. `Click`
   c. `Button`
   d. `ButtonPressed`

THE STATUSBAR CONTROL

One feature that's missing from SuperPad is a status bar. This is a horizontal bar that sits at the bottom of the main window of an application. Its purpose is to display useful information about what's going on in the application. In SuperPad, this could include the current position of the cursor in the document and any other relevant information. Figure 8-25 shows you how the StatusBar control appears on the toolbox.

First, add the StatusBar control to **frmMain** in the usual way. Like the toolbar, the status bar knows where it is supposed to go, so it aligns itself to the bottom of the form. It has an **Align** property, just like the toolbar, so you can vary the alignment if you like. Figure 8-26 shows you how **frmMain** now looks with the status bar added.

Figure 8-25
The StatusBar
control

Figure 8-26
frmMain in design
mode with a
StatusBar control
added

Take a close look at the bar itself. It consists of three distinct regions. To the left is an indented panel that, at the moment, is empty. At the far right is a Windows 95-style sizing handle that can be used at runtime to resize the main window with the mouse. The remaining part of the bar is unused at present, and so it is empty. Try running SuperPad now. You can use the new resizing handle, although nothing appears yet in the indented panel.

What Do I Use the Status Bar For?

The first thing to work out is what information you want to display in the status bar. Typically, this will dictate how many panels you will need. The **Style** property controls whether the bar has just one panel or is capable of showing multiple panels. You are going to need multiple panels for this example.

Adding Panels

The StatusBar control stores each Panel object in a Panels collection, just like the ToolBar stores each Button object in a Buttons collection. You should realize now that Microsoft has designed the Windows 95 controls to be used in very similar ways.

You can define the number of panels and the properties of each Panel object by selecting (Custom) from the control's Properties window. Figure 8-27 shows the StatusBar's Panels Property dialog box.

Panels can be added to and removed from the status bar using this dialog box.

Panel Properties

Add six more panels with properties set according to Table 8-5.

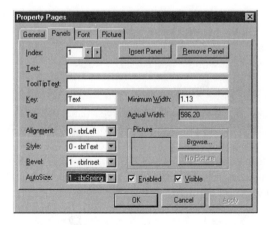

Figure 8-27
Panels Property
dialog box

Table 8-5 Panels to add to the status bar

Index	Key	Alignment	Style	Bevel	AutoSize
1	Text	0 - Left	0 - Text	1 - Inset	1 - Spring
2	Caps	1 - Center	1 - CAPS	1 - Inset	2 - Content
3	NumLock	1 - Center	2 - NUM LOCK	1 - Inset	2 - Content
4	Ins	1 - Center	3 - INS	1 - Inset	2 - Content
5	Scroll	1 - Center	4 - SCROLL	1 - Inset	2 - Content
6	Time	1 - Center	5 - Time	1 - Inset	2 - Content
7	Date	1 - Center	6 - Date	1 - Inset	2 - Content

The Key *Property*

The `Key` property defines the key that will be used to identify a Panel object in the Panels collection at runtime.

The Alignment *Property*

The `Alignment` property determines how the text in the panel will be positioned. You can choose `Justified`, `Left`, `Center`, or `Right`.

The Style *Property*

The `Style` property is an important property. It determines what is to be stored in a panel. The first panel is used to store some text. However, the other panels display the states of the (CAPS), (NUMLOCK), (INS), and (SCROLL) keys. The last two panels display the current time and date.

The Bevel *Property*

The `Bevel` property determines whether the panel is displayed inset into the status bar, raised from it, or flat with no bevel at all.

The AutoSize *Property*

The `AutoSize` property determines how large a panel is. The first panel is set to `Spring`, which means that it shrinks and grows according to the size of the status bar at runtime. The rest are sized according to their content. There is no need to set their sizes manually. Alternatively, you could set `AutoSize` to `None`, in which case you would have to set the minimum size of the `Panel` object at design time and then manually control its size at runtime by setting its `Width` property in your code.

Adding Text to a Text Panel

All that's left for you to do now is to add some text to the first panel to tell the user which line of the document contains the cursor. The RichTextBox assists in this task, because it has a couple of nice features that the ordinary TextBox lacks. One of these is the `GetLineFromChar` method and the other is the `SelChange` event.

The GetLineFromChar *Method*

Listing 8-13 shows the code for a new `Public` subroutine to add to `frmMain`. The `GetLineFromChar` method returns the line number of a character. To return the line number of the cursor, the program sends the selection `Start` as an argument.

Listing 8-13 Routine to display a line number

```
Public Sub DisplayLineNumber()
Dim LineNum As Integer

With frmMain.ActiveForm.txtDocument
    If .SelStart > 0 Then
        LineNum = .GetLineFromChar(.SelStart)
    End If
    frmMain.StatusBar1.Panels("Text").Text = "Line: " & CStr(LineNum + 1)
End With
End Sub
```

This subroutine needs to be called whenever a document form becomes the active form or whenever the position of the insertion point changes. One place to call it from is the `Activate` event in the `frmDocument` form, as shown in Listing 8-14.

Listing 8-14 Calling DisplayLineNumber

```
Private Sub Form_Activate()
frmMain.SetupCSMenus
frmMain.DisplayLineNumber
End Sub
```

As you can see, all you need to do is to call the subroutine.

The SelChange *Event*

The RichTextBox's `SelChange` event is triggered whenever the value of the `SelPos` property is changed. This occurs, of course, whenever the insertion point is moved; the `SelChange` event is a convenient event to use for this purpose. This is shown in Listing 8-15.

Listing 8-15 Calling DisplayLineNumber when the cursor moves

```
Private Sub txtDocument_SelChange()
frmMain.DisplayLineNumber
End Sub
```

Don't forget to clear out the text from the panel when a form is destroyed. You can implement this by making a small change to the `If Cancel = False Then...End If` statement block at the end of `frmDocument`'s `Unload` event, as shown in Listing 8-16.

Listing 8-16 Update to the Unload event

```
If Cancel = False Then
    frmMain.DocColl.Remove CStr(CollKey)
    Set objDocument = Nothing
    frmMain.StatusBar1.Panels("Text").Text = ""
End If
```

Just a few simple changes and you now have a working status bar that tells you which line of your document you are working on.

1. What is the name of the **StatusBar** property that controls what is to be displayed in a Panel object at runtime?
   a. Content
   b. Type
   c. Style
   d. Text

2. In the RichTextBox control, what event can you use to determine when the insertion point (text cursor) has been moved?
   a. Change
   b. KeyDown
   c. Move
   d. SelChange

3. Which of the following cannot be displayed in a panel?
   a. The state of the SHIFT key
   b. The state of the NUMLOCK key
   c. The status of the CAPSLOCK key
   d. The state of the INSERT key

4. What Panel property controls whether or not a panel is inset?
   a. Outline
   b. BorderStyle
   c. Bevel
   d. Border

5. Which of the following is correct syntax (assuming all names are valid)?
   a. Form1.StatusBar1.Panels("Panel1").Text = "Some text"
   b. Form1.StatusBar1.Panel1.Text = "Some text"
   c. Form1.StatusBar1.Panels.Panel1.Text = "Some text"
   d. Panels(Panel1).Text = "Some text"

Rewrite the File Picker/Browser from Chapter 2, Object-Oriented Programming. Use the Common Dialog file selector instead of the one you wrote. Implement new functionality: The user can "browse" text or RTF files in addition to pictures.

REVIEW

Lisa: I can't believe how easy it is to add all this great functionality to programs. It's like Microsoft has done all the grunge work so we can focus on being creative.

John: I know. We can combine these features in any combination. A word processor is an obvious example for the rich text box, but you could use the rich text box to add fonts, color, and effects to any other application.

Lisa: I like the ToolBar control. It's not hard to set up and it adds that extra professional look to the program.

John: The user can customize it, and we don't have to do any work!

Lisa: Think about it. These are just the controls that come with VB 5's professional edition. There are dozens of third-party companies out there churning out more OCXs for us to play with as we speak.

John: You know, this stuff used to take *a lot* of work. Every programmer who wanted to implement a fancy feature such as rich text support had to write the code himself.

Lisa: Ahem.

John: ... or herself. As a result, most applications didn't go as far as they might today.

Lisa: So what's up next?

John: More controls to make our programs look professional, including Windows 95-style controls such as TabStrips and TreeLists.

Lisa: Tab strips?

John: You know, those things inside dialog boxes that look like tabs in a card catalog, letting you switch between sets of options.

Lisa: Oh, sure. VB 5 uses those a lot. And tree lists—I know what they are. Hierarchical lists, like the Windows 95 Explorer uses.

John: We'll also see other ways to use the ImageList control.

Lisa: And let me guess, it will be very easy.

John: Not too bad, anyway.

THE TABSTRIP CONTROL

You already know what the TabStrip control looks like. It's the same control that you've seen in some of Visual Basic's own dialog boxes. The Project Options dialog box and the Windows 95 controls' Properties dialog boxes all make use of this versatile control to separate option screens into separate but related "tabs," much like a card index tab.

To see the features of the TabStrip control (and the remaining Windows 95 controls), add a new form to SuperPad. Call the form **frmOptions** and set its properties according to Table 8-6. The purpose of the new form is to provide an Options dialog box, rather like the one in Visual Basic itself. Actually, this lesson uses this form as a vehicle for demonstrating the remaining Windows 95 controls, but you could extend all manner of user-configurable settings to this dialog box if you wish.

Table 8-6　frmOptions properties

Property	Value
BorderStyle	3 - Fixed Dialog
Caption	Options
ClipControls	False
ControlBox	False
MaxButton	False
MinButton	False
Name	frmOptions

Two new menu items to add to **frmMain** that give you a way to display the dialog box are defined in Table 8-7.

Table 8-7　Menus to add to frmMain

Name	Caption	Menu Type
mnuTools	&Tools	Top level between mnuEdit and mnuWindow
mnuToolsOptions	&Options...	Submenu to mnuTools

Add the code in Listing 8-17 to the **mnuToolsOptions Click** event subroutine to display the new dialog box.

Listing 8-17 Bringing up the frmOptions dialog

```
Private Sub mnuToolsOptions_Click()
frmOptions.Show vbModal
End Sub
```

You're now ready to add a TabStrip control to **frmOptions**. Figure 8-28 shows you how the TabStrip control appears on the toolbox.

Drag a TabStrip control onto the form and add two Command buttons as shown in Figure 8-29. Set the **Name** of these three controls to **tabOptions**, **cmdOK**, and **cmdCancel**. Set the **Default** and **Cancel** properties of the two buttons accordingly.

Finally, add the code in Listing 8-18 to the Command buttons' **Click** events, so that the form gets unloaded when either button is pressed.

Listing 8-18 Unload the form

```
Private Sub cmdOK_Click()
Unload Me
End Sub

Private Sub cmdCancel_Click()
Unload Me
End Sub
```

How Does the TabStrip Control Work?

The TabStrip control has a lot in common with the other Windows 95 controls you have seen. It consists of a Tabs collection that contains individual Tab objects. Each Tab object relates to one tab on the TabStrip control. As with the ToolBar and the StatusBar, you can define how many Tab objects should be created and how their properties should be set at design time.

When you first add the tab strip to a form, the Tabs collection already contains one default Tab object. You can add more Tab objects to the Tabs collection by using the control's Properties dialog box. Display this dialog box the same way the other Windows 95 controls are displayed, by selecting the (Custom) entry in the control's Properties

Figure 8-28
The TabStrip
control

Figure 8-29
frmOptions form
with TabStrip
control and
Command buttons
added

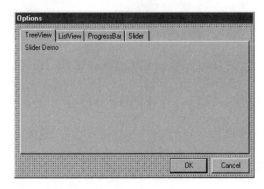

window. As you can see from Figure 8-30, the dialog box allows you to define everything that you would associate with each Tab object in the collection, including its Key, Caption, and ToolTip Text.

There's even an image index that you can enter if you want to add an image to the tab. This works in exactly the same way as adding pictures to toolbar buttons. You have to add an ImageList control to the form first. The General tab allows you to tie in the correct ImageList control from those that may already be on the form. The General tab is reproduced in Figure 8-31.

The project needs four tabs, one for each of the remaining Windows 95 controls. Use the Tabs tab in the Properties dialog box to add three more tabs. Set the properties for each tab to the values shown in Table 8-8.

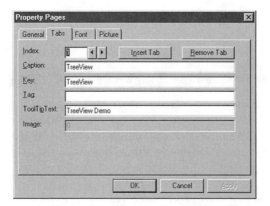

Figure 8-30
The Tabs tab

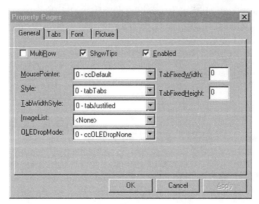

Figure 8-31
The General tab

Table 8-8 Tab object properties

Index	Caption	Key	ToolTip Text
1	TreeView	TreeView	TreeView Demo
2	ListView	ListView	ListView Demo
3	ProgressBar	ProgressBar	ProgressBar Demo
4	Slider	Slider	Slider Demo

Once you press the Properties dialog box's OK button, the changes you made are reflected in the on-screen tab strip.

Tabs or Buttons

The **Style** property allows you to choose between the standard Tab style or a Button style. Figure 8-32 shows you the tab strip using the Button style.

The Tab style is rather more intuitive than the Button style and is the accepted convention, but you can use buttons if you prefer. For this example, switch back to the Tab style.

Defining the Control Groups

The next stage is to define the groups of controls that appear when the tabs are selected. This is where things get a little complicated. The tab strip was not designed to be a container for other controls. Therefore, you cannot create the control groups by themselves, using the TabStrip control alone. You're probably wondering why you can't simply click on a tab and display the group that goes with that tab. Unfortunately, the TabStrip control really knows nothing about the control groups it is meant to display.

Creating the groups of controls themselves is easy. You can use any control that is capable of being a container for other controls. If you remember from Chapter 6, Forms, Menus, and MDI Forms, the PictureBox control supports this feature.

There are four Tab controls, so you need to add four PictureBox controls to **frmOptions**.

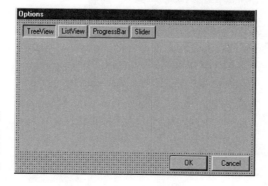

Figure 8-32
tabOptions using
Button style instead
of Tab style

Now for the tricky part. You must make the four picture boxes a control array by giving them the same name and setting their index values to 0, 1, 2, and 3, respectively. The array of picture boxes simplifies selecting the correct picture box at runtime.

● Draw a picture box on top of the TabStrip control. Size it so it fills the tab strip without covering the tabs.

● Click on the picture box to select it, then press CTRL-C to copy it onto the clipboard.

● Click on the form (not on the picture box!).

● Press CTRL-V to paste the copy of the picture box onto the form.

● Visual Basic asks if you want to start a control array. Answer Yes and click on OK.

● Drag the new picture box so it is a little below and a little to the right of the first picture box.

● Click on the form.

● Press CTRL-V to paste another copy of the picture box onto the form.

● Drag the new picture box so it is a little below and a little to the right of the second picture box.

● Click on the form.

● Press CTRL-V to paste another copy of the picture box onto the form.

● Drag the new picture box so it is a little below and a little to the right of the third picture box.

● Add a label to each picture box. Use Figure 8-33 as a guide.

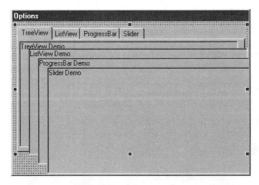

Figure 8-33
frmOptions with
PictureBox controls
added

Be careful when you add the picture boxes to the form. It's easy to make one picture box a child of another accidentally. You must click on the form before adding each picture box to ensure that the new picture box is contained by the form and not by the previous picture box. Figure 8-33 shows the design-time form with picture boxes added.

Note that the picture boxes occupy slightly different positions on the form. That is a design-time strategy that makes it easier to add other controls to the correct picture box. Once the design is completed, the four picture boxes must be moved so that they are superimposed on each other in the correct position on the tab strip.

Picture Box ZOrder

Recall from Chapter 7, Classes, that the ZOrder method sets the position of an object within its graphical level. Each picture box occupies a different position in the ZOrder of controls on the form. In other words, the four picture boxes appear to be stacked on top of each other. This is important because it is the key to using the tab strip.

The tab strip must have the lowest ZOrder so that all other controls appear to sit on top of it. To see why, click on the tab strip to select it and press (CTRL)-(J) to move it to the top of the ZOrder. That makes it hard to work, doesn't it? Press (CTRL)-(K) to move the tab strip back to the rear, where it belongs.

Click on the first picture box to select it. Look at the Properties window to be sure you have selected Picture1(0). Press (CTRL)-(J) to move it to the top of the ZOrder. Figure 8-34 shows the design-time frmOptions with Picture1(0) at the top of the ZOrder.

Linking the TabStrip Tabs to the Correct Picture Boxes

When the form is loaded, the picture box at the top of the ZOrder is the one that is visible and associated with the first tab. All that's left to do now is to make sure that when a different tab is pressed at runtime, the correct picture box is brought to the top of the ZOrder.

This is accomplished through the TabStrip's Click event. Add the code in Listing 8-19 to that event.

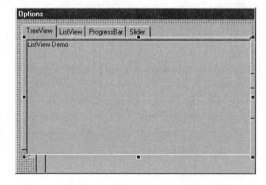

Figure 8-34
frmOptions with rearranged picture box ZOrder

Listing 8-19 Selecting the correct tab option

```
Private Sub TreeViewDemo()
End Sub

Private Sub ListViewDemo()
End Sub

Private Sub ProgressBarDemo()
End Sub

Private Sub SliderDemo()
End Sub

Private Sub tabOptions_Click()
Picture1(tabOptions.SelectedItem.Index - 1).ZOrder
Select Case tabOptions.SelectedItem.Index
    Case 1 'Run the TreeView demo
        TreeViewDemo
    Case 2 'Run the ListView demo
        ListViewDemo
    Case 3 'Run the ProgressBar demo
        ProgressBarDemo
    Case 4 'Run the Slider demo
        SliderDemo
End Select
End Sub
```

When you click on a tab, the **SelectedItem** property of the TabStrip indicates which tab you selected. The **SelectedItem** property is an integer that ranges from **1** to the number of tabs on the TabStrip—in this case, **4**. Recall that the indexes of **Picture1** range from **0** to **3**. All you need to do is associate a tab with a picture box by subtracting one from the **SelectedItem** property. Thus, the line:

```
Picture1(tabOptions.SelectedItem.Index - 1).ZOrder
```

sets the **ZOrder** of the correct picture box and brings it to the front.

The **Select Case** statement is a piece of advanced planning. Note that the code also creates the four demonstration procedures at this stage, although they are empty for now. Empty procedures like this are called *stubs* or *program stubs*. They are a convenience, allowing you to design your program without having to write all of it at once.

Run the program and select Options from the Tools menu to display the form at runtime. You can select the tabs and see the correct picture box displayed. Later, when you complete the four demonstration subroutines, each of the tabs will demonstrate a different ActiveX control.

Once you've seen the way this works, return to design mode and move the four picture boxes into the same position, so that they are positioned within the borders of the tab strip itself. Then set their **BorderStyle** properties to **None** and run SuperPad again. The result is shown in Figure 8-35.

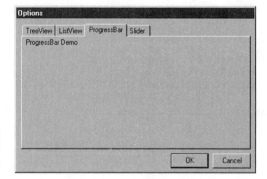

Figure 8-35
The completed
tab strip

You can, of course, add whatever controls you like to the picture boxes.

Working with Multiple Picture Boxes

Working with multiple picture boxes at design time can be a bit confusing. Probably the least confusing method is to resize and position the controls as shown in Figure 8-36.

This keeps all four picture boxes visible and easy to find. To add controls to one of the picture boxes, click on it and press (CTRL)-(J) to bring it to the top of the ZOrder. Then drag it to the top of the tab strip and size it to fill the tab strip while you add controls. When you are done with that picture box, make it smaller and drag it back to its original position.

This does require additional code, but it makes working with the picture boxes so much easier that it is worth more code. The changes in the code are shown in Listing 8-20.

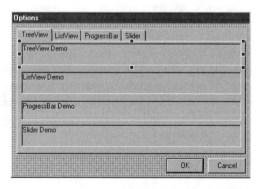

Figure 8-36
One approach to
working with
multiple picture
boxes

Listing 8-20   Using the `Move` method to position the picture boxes

```
Private Sub tabOptions_Click()
' Move the picture
Picture1(tabOptions.SelectedItem.Index - 1).Move _
   tabOptions.ClientLeft, tabOptions.ClientTop, _
   tabOptions.ClientWidth, tabOptions.ClientHeight
' Bring it to the top
Picture1(tabOptions.SelectedItem.Index - 1).ZOrder
' Give it time to draw
DoEvents
Select Case tabOptions.SelectedItem.Index
    Case 1 'Run the TreeView demo
        TreeViewDemo
    Case 2 'Run the ListView demo
        ListViewDemo
    Case 3 'Run the ProgressBar demo
        ProgressBarDemo
    Case 4 'Run the Slider demo
        SliderDemo
End Select
End Sub
```

The new code uses the `Move` method to reposition and size the correct picture box, then uses the `ZOrder` method to bring it to the top. The `ClientLeft`, `ClientTop`, `ClientWidth`, and `ClientHeight` properties define the inner dimensions of the tab strip and assure that the picture box fills the entire tab strip without covering the tabs and without overlapping the edges. The `DoEvents` command is needed because of the time it takes to draw the picture box in its new size and position.

Another approach to using multiple picture boxes is to size and position all of them to their final position and use CTRL-J and CTRL-K to change the design-time `ZOrder`. Try both techniques and use the one you prefer.

The `BeforeClick` Event

The TabStrip also has a useful event called `BeforeClick`. This event gets called when the user clicks on a tab but before the focus has moved away from the previous one.

The `BeforeClick` event is particularly useful for running "cleanup" code between tabs. The code in the next two lessons takes advantage of `BeforeClick`. You can also use this event to prevent the focus from moving from one tab to another. The `BeforeClick` event is issued with a `Cancel` parameter. You can set this parameter to `False` to cancel the `Click` event.

How to Display a Tab Programmatically

Another useful feature of the TabStrip control is that it allows you to select a tab from within your code. Each Tab object has a `Selected` property. Your code can read the `Selected` property or it can write it. Therefore, the following code will work for the TabStrip example. Try executing it from the Debug window when any tab is displayed other than the ProgressBar tab.

```
? tabOptions.Tabs("ProgressBar").Selected
```

This returns **False**. Alternatively:

```
tabOptions.Tabs("ProgressBar").Selected = True
```

makes the ProgressBar tab the selected one.

There is a perfectly good reason why you might want to use this feature in **frmOptions**. At present, the tab strip in **frmOptions** is dependent on the top-level picture box being the one for the TreeView demo. If the picture boxes on your form are arranged as in Figure 8-36, all four of them are visible in their reduced size when the form opens. Only after you click on a tab does the form arrive at its desired appearance. If you are using full-sized picture boxes, the one that shows will depend on the design-time **ZOrder**—if you have the Slide demo on top when you start the program, that is the picture box that is on top at runtime. Add the code in Listing 8-21 to make the **Form Load** event "click" a tab for you.

Listing 8-21 Setting the Tab control's initial value

```
Private Sub Form_Load()
Me.Move (Screen.Height - Me.Height) / 2, (Screen.Width - Me.Width) / 2
DoEvents
tabOptions.Tabs("TreeView").Selected = True
End Sub
```

By setting the TreeView's **Selected** property to **True**, the TabStrip's **Click** event is triggered and the TreeView's picture box is brought to the top of the **ZOrder**. However, if you don't display the form first, the picture box generates an error.

DoEvents

The **DoEvents** command tells Windows to finish processing any other events in its queue. In this example, **DoEvents** gives the form time to display. If you leave out **DoEvents**, you run the risk of trying to display the picture box before the form has had time to display itself.

1. Which of the following expressions returns the index number of the tab that is currently selected?
   a. `TabStrip1.SelectedItem`
   b. `TabStrip1.SelectedItem.Index`
   c. `TabStrip1.Tabs(SelectedItem)`
   d. `TabStrip1.Tabs(SelectedItem.Index)`

2. Which properties return the internal dimensions of the tab strip?
   a. `ClientHeight`, `ClientLeft`, `ClientTop`, and `ClientWidth`
   b. `Height`, `Left`, `Top`, and `Width`
   c. `ScaleHeight`, `ScaleLeft`, `ScaleTop`, and `ScaleWidth`
   d. `InternalHeight`, `InternalLeft`, `InternalTop`, and `InternalWidth`

3. If all the picture boxes on a tab strip are on top of each other and therefore have the same coordinates at design time, how do you display a given one as being on "top" at runtime?
   a. By calling the TabStrip's `SetTop` method
   b. By setting the picture box's `Top` property to `True`
   c. By making sure the `Index` property of the selected tab is the same as that of the current picture box
   d. By calling the `ZOrder` method to display the picture box associated with the selected Tab object

4. Which of the following programmatically sets the ProgressBar tab to be the currently selected tab?
   a. `tabOptions.Tabs("ProgressBar").Selected = True`
   b. `tabOptions.Tab("ProgressBar").Selected = True`
   c. `Set tabOptions.SelectedItem = tabOptions.Tabs("ProgressBar")`
   d. `tabOptions.SelectedItem = tabOptions.Tabs("ProgressBar")`

5. How would you prevent a new tab from being selected?
   a. Set the `Enabled` property of all the other Tab objects to `False`.
   b. Trap the `BeforeClick` event and set its `Cancel` parameter to `True`.
   c. Trap the `BeforeClick` event, note the current tab, and then, from the `Click` event, set that tab's `Selected` property to `True`.
   d. There is no way to prevent a tab from being selected.

THE TREEVIEW CONTROL

The Windows 95 user interface implements lists in a variety of styles. Frequently, the lists are hierarchical. The Windows Explorer is a typical example: It is a list of files and folders. This lesson explains how to program lists with the same look and feel. You can use them in file browsers and in many other applications.

Introducing the TreeView and ListView Controls

The TreeView and ListView controls are closely related. They are meant to be used together. A good example of the use of these two controls is in the Windows 95 Explorer, shown in Figure 8-37.

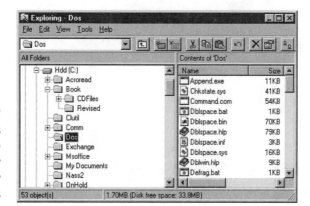

Figure 8-37
The Windows
Explorer makes use
of the TreeView
and ListView
controls

The TreeView control makes up the left pane of the Explorer. The ListView control is on the right.

The TreeView control is used to display a high-level chart of information. When a user selects an item from the TreeView control, the item is expanded and displayed in more detail in the ListView control. Although most people are familiar with the control combination for viewing directory and file hierarchies, you can use this combination for any hierarchical data. For example, you can use the TreeView control to display a company's list of accounts and the ListView control to display details about a selected account.

Adding a TreeView Control

Bring **Picture1(0)** to the front and size it to fill the tab strip's interior. Click on the TreeView icon in the toolbox and draw it in the picture box. The TreeView icon is shown in Figure 8-38.

Once you've added the control, size it so that it fills the area underneath the label. It should look like Figure 8-39.

The Sample Node entries that you see do not actually exist. They are merely there to give you an idea how the TreeView will look at runtime. This is a nice feature. It saves you the effort of running your code every time you want to change the properties that affect the TreeView control's appearance.

Figure 8-38
The TreeView icon

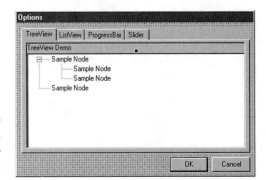

Figure 8-39
Initial appearance
of the TreeView
control

How Does the TreeView Control Work?

A good way to start thinking about the TreeView control is as a tree-structured list box. Like with a list box, you can add and remove individual lines of text. Each line can respond to the user clicking on it with the mouse. However, this is about as far as the similarity extends.

Instead of adding lines of text to the TreeView, you add Node objects to its Nodes collection. A Node object is an item in a TreeView control that can contain images and text. Furthermore, you can establish relationships between Node objects when the objects are added to the collection. A number of different relationships can be established, including parent-child, which is the key relationship in constructing a tree structure of nodes within the TreeView.

In some respects, the concept of adding Node objects to a Nodes collection is similar to the way the TabStrip, ToolBar, StatusBar, and ImageList controls work. Each of those controls contains a collection of objects of a specific type. However, the difference with the TreeView control is that it assumes that you will want to add Node objects to the Nodes collection at runtime only. Compare that to the other Windows 95 controls. They provide a special tab in their Properties dialog box that allows you to specify the objects to be added to their internal collections at design time. This is how you added Button objects to the toolbar, Panel objects to the status bar, and Tab objects to the tab strip.

Take a quick look at the TreeView control's Property dialog box. You get to it in the same way as with the other controls, through the (Custom) entry in the Properties window. The dialog box is reproduced in Figure 8-40. As you can see, it has no Nodes tab, which is a giveaway that you're going to have to do this work programmatically.

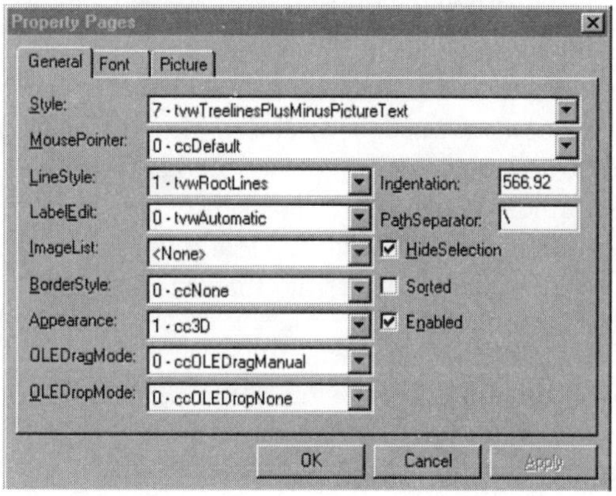

Figure 8-40
The TreeView
control's Property
dialog box

Adding a Node to the Nodes Collection

The following example shows you how to add a node to the TreeView control.

The first thing you must know is the text you want the node to display. The text may come from a database, a text file, or a directory listing. In this example, the text is hard-coded into the program. As your knowledge of Visual Basic increases through the use of this book, you can begin to imagine other sources.

Add the code in Listing 8-22 to the **TreeViewDemo** subroutine.

Listing 8-22 Adding nodes to a tree

```
Private Sub TreeViewDemo()
Dim MyNode As Node
Dim I As Integer
Dim Text As String

'Clear out any objects from the TreeView
TreeView1.Nodes.Clear

For I = 1 To 100
    Text = "Node " & CStr(I)
    Set MyNode = TreeView1.Nodes.Add(, , , Text)
Next I
End Sub
```

Note that the first thing the code in this example does is clear any preexisting Node objects from the Nodes collection with **TreeView.Nodes.Clear**. This is because this demo subroutine will be run every time you click on the TreeView's tab on the tab strip. If you don't clear out preexisting nodes, the code will attempt to add the new ones with the same key. As you remember from Chapter 7, Classes, keys must be unique.

This example adds 100 Node objects to the Nodes collection. The text for each node is made up of the word **Node** and a number from 1 to 100. The line that does all the work is the call to the Nodes collection's **Add** method. Here, the **Add** method returns a reference to the newly created Node object. The code is not doing anything with that reference, but it's coded this way to show you that the method is capable of returning the reference should you need it.

You can also code the **Add** method so that it doesn't return anything. Just treat the method as if it were a subroutine rather than a function, as follows:

```
TreeView1.Nodes.Add , , , Text
```

Figure 8-41 shows you how the TreeView looks when this example is run.

What Are All Those Commas?

Remember that the Nodes collection is a *collection*. Pretty obvious, isn't it? The syntax of the **Add** method for a TreeView Nodes collection is

```
object.Add(relative, relationship, key, text, image, selectedimage)
```

where

- **object** is the TreeView Nodes collection.

- **relative** is an optional parameter that is the node number or key of an existing Node object.

- **relationship** is an optional parameter that specifies the placement of the new object.

- **key** is an optional unique string that can be used to identify the Node object.

- **text** is the string that appears in the node.

- **image** is an optional parameter that is the index of an image in an image list.

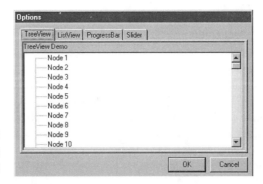

Figure 8-41
TreeView with
100 nodes

- `selectedimage` is an optional parameter that is the index of an image list image to be shown when the node is selected.

- The `relationship` parameter controls where the new node will be placed. The options are

  `tvwLast:`The node is placed after all other nodes and at the same level as the node named in `relative`.

  `tvwNext:` The node is placed immediately after the node named in `relative`.

  `tvwPrevious:` The node is placed immediately before the node named in `relative`.

  `tvwChild:` The node becomes a child node of the node named in `relative`. This is the default value.

  If no Node object is named in `relative`, the new node is placed in the last position of the top-node hierarchy and `relationship` has no effect.

So what about the commas? You assign each node a text string, and you probably *should* assign a key. But, if you just want the new node to be added to the end of the list, you can omit `relative` and `relationship`. If you used a line like:

```
TreeView1.Nodes.Add Key, Text
```

the compiler would assume that your key was really `relative`, because it is first in the list, and your test would be seen as (an incorrect) `relationship`.

When you leave out a parameter that precedes a parameter that you include, the empty space in the list must be marked by commas. So,

```
TreeView1.Nodes.Add , , , Text
```

has three empty spaces preceding the **Text** parameter. Note that the code leaves off the last two parameters, too. No commas are needed (or allowed) following the last parameter you include.

Displaying Images in the TreeView Control

The TreeView control is capable of displaying a small bitmap next to the text in a node. It can do this because it can optionally reference images that are stored in an ImageList control.

Obviously, to add images you must also add an ImageList control. Add it to **frmOptions** so it can also be used by other controls on the form. Leave it with its default name of **ImageList1**.

Modify the code in Listing 8-21 so that it reads as shown in Listing 8-23.

Listing 8-23 Adding nodes with images

```
Private Sub TreeViewDemo()
Dim MyImage As ListImage
Dim MyNode As Node
Dim I As Integer
Dim Text As String

'Clear out any objects from the TreeView and ImageList
TreeView1.Nodes.Clear
ImageList1.ListImages.Clear

'Add the closed file image to the ImageList
Set MyImage = ImageList1.ListImages.Add(, "closed", _
        LoadPicture("graphics\bitmaps\outline\closed.bmp"))

'Link the TreeView to the ImageList
Set TreeView1.ImageList = ImageList1

For I = 1 To 100
    Text = "Node " & CStr(I)
    Set MyNode = TreeView1.Nodes.Add(, , , Text, "closed")
Next I
End Sub
```

Before you run this code, make sure to set the ImageList's **MaskColor** property to **white**, as shown in Figure 8-42. If you don't do this, the images may not display correctly for the reasons described in Lesson 4.

As you can see, after you have cleared the nodes and List Images collections, you have to load the appropriate image into the image list. You can do this manually, using the ImageList control itself at design time, but here you're doing the same thing programmatically. The reason is to demonstrate using a single image list for multiple purposes.

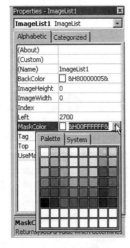

Figure 8-42
Setting the image list's MaskColor to the background color of the TreeView

Bear in mind that the single image list on this form is going to be used to demonstrate both the TreeView and the ListView controls. Therefore, each time you click on the TreeView or ListView tabs, you need to clear out any images that were left in the image list from the previous demonstration.

The image that you are adding to the image list is an image of a closed folder. The path is relative to Visual Basic 5's home directory.

The second parameter to the ImageList's List Images collection's **Add** method is the key for the ListImage object. The key is simply **closed**. Later, when you need to retrieve this image to use it in the TreeView's node, you can use the same key to locate the correct ListImage object.

Note that there's nothing to prevent you from adding more than one image to the image list. Although each node that you add to the TreeView can have only one image associated with it, different Node objects can reference different ListImage objects from the same ImageList control.

At this stage, you need to link the ImageList control to the TreeView. Again, this can be done at design time through the TreeView's General tab in its Properties page. However, this code is doing the job programmatically.

The only difference in your use of the Node collection's **Add** method this time is that you're now telling the TreeView control to create the node with the image that has the key **closed**. When you run the example, the node text is displayed next to the image of a closed folder, as shown in Figure 8-43.

Node Relationships

You learned earlier that it is possible to establish relationships between Node objects. There are, in fact, four different relationships that you can establish.

- Before
- After
- Last
- Child

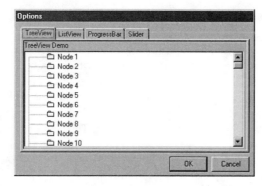

Figure 8-43
The TreeView control displaying images in each node

The relationship that you'll probably want to use most is child, so try that one first. Type in the example in Listing 8-24.

Listing 8-24 Child nodes

```
Private Sub TreeViewDemo()
Dim MyImage As ListImage
Dim MyNode As Node
Dim I As Integer
Dim J As Integer
Dim ParentKey As String
Dim ChildKey As String
Dim Text As String

'Clear out any objects from the TreeView and ImageList
TreeView1.Nodes.Clear
ImageList1.ListImages.Clear

'Add the closed file image to the ImageList
Set MyImage = ImageList1.ListImages.Add(, "closed", _
        LoadPicture("graphics\bitmaps\outline\closed.bmp"))
'Add the leaf image to the ImageList
Set MyImage = ImageList1.ListImages.Add(, "leaf", _
            LoadPicture("graphics\bitmaps\outline\leaf.bmp"))

'Link the TreeView to the ImageList
Set TreeView1.ImageList = ImageList1

For I = 1 To 10
    ParentKey = "Node" & CStr(I)
    Text = "Parent node " & CStr(I)
    Set MyNode = TreeView1.Nodes.Add(, , ParentKey, Text, "closed")
    For J = 1 To 3
        ChildKey = "Node" & CStr(I) & "\" & CStr(J)
        Text = "Child node " & CStr(I) & "\" & CStr(J)
        Set MyNode = TreeView1.Nodes.Add(ParentKey, _
tvwChild, ChildKey, Text, "leaf")
    Next J
Next I
End Sub
```

The TreeView control that results from the above example is shown in Figure 8-44. Double-click on a node to expand it to show its children.

This exercise starts by adding two bitmaps to the image list. The second bitmap (which is given a key of **leaf**) represents a leaf node, which is a node that has no children.

The program adds 10 top-level (parent) nodes, each of which has three children.

Look at the differences between the two TreeView **Add** methods. The outer one, which adds the parent node, is virtually the same as the call made earlier, except that this time it is added to the Nodes collection with a key. The key is specified in the third parameter. This is important, because you need to know the parent's key when you later add the nodes that are children.

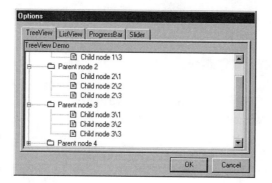

Figure 8-44
TreeView control
with child nodes

The inner **Add** method adds the child nodes. Here, for the first time, the code specifies values in the first and second parameters of the **Add** method. The first parameter identifies the parent node. This is known as the *relative node*. The second parameter is a constant that specifies what the relationship is going to be. In this case, the relationship is a child relationship. The constant **tvwChild** is predefined by the TreeView control, so you don't have to declare it yourself.

Other Relationships

There are four relationships in total. Table 8-9 describes the remaining three.

Table 8-9 Other node relationships

Constant	Relationship
tvwLast	The new node is positioned at the end of the level in which the relative node is positioned.
tvwNext	The new node is positioned immediately after the relative node.
tvwPrevious	The new node is positioned immediately before the relative node.

Deleting Nodes

To delete a single node from the TreeView control, just specify the node to be deleted in the Node collection's **Remove** method. You can specify either the index or the key of the node to be deleted. For example:

```
TreeView1.Nodes.Remove 1
```

will remove the Node object that has an index of **1**, or

```
TreeView1.Nodes.Remove "Fred"
```

will remove the Node object that has a key of **Fred**.

If you remove a node that is the parent of child nodes, the child nodes will be removed also.

Sorting Nodes

If a node contains child nodes, the children can automatically be sorted alphabetically by setting the parent Node object's **Sorted** property to **True**. Try the example in Listing 8-25, which demonstrates this.

Listing 8-25 Sorting demo

```
Private Sub TreeViewDemo()
Dim MyImage As ListImage
Dim MyNode As Node

'Clear out any objects from the TreeView and ImageList
TreeView1.Nodes.Clear
ImageList1.ListImages.Clear

'Add the closed file image to the ImageList
Set MyImage = ImageList1.ListImages.Add(, "closed", _
Loadpicture("graphics\bitmaps\outline\closed.bmp"))
'Add the lead image to the ImageList
Set MyImage = ImageList1.ListImages.Add(, "leaf", _
Loadpicture("graphics\bitmaps\outline\leaf.bmp"))

'Link the TreeView to the ImageList
Set TreeView1.ImageList = ImageList1

Set MyNode = TreeView1.Nodes.Add(, , "Parent key", "Parent", "closed")
MyNode.Sorted = True
Set MyNode = TreeView1.Nodes.Add("Parent key", _
tvwChild, "Child J", "J", "leaf")
Set MyNode = TreeView1.Nodes.Add("Parent key", _
tvwChild, "Child I", "I", "leaf")
Set MyNode = TreeView1.Nodes.Add("Parent key", _
tvwChild, "Child H", "H", "leaf")
Set MyNode = TreeView1.Nodes.Add("Parent key", _
tvwChild, "Child G", "G", "leaf")
Set MyNode = TreeView1.Nodes.Add("Parent key", _
tvwChild, "Child F", "F", "leaf")
Set MyNode = TreeView1.Nodes.Add("Parent key", _
tvwChild, "Child E", "E", "leaf")
Set MyNode = TreeView1.Nodes.Add("Parent key", _
tvwChild, "Child D", "D", "leaf")
Set MyNode = TreeView1.Nodes.Add("Parent key", _
tvwChild, "Child C", "C", "leaf")
Set MyNode = TreeView1.Nodes.Add("Parent key", _
tvwChild, "Child B", "B", "leaf")
Set MyNode = TreeView1.Nodes.Add("Parent key", _
tvwChild, "Child A", "A", "leaf")
End Sub
```

The order in which you add the 10 child nodes doesn't matter; the TreeView always displays them in alphabetical order, as shown in Figure 8-45.

The ExpandedImage **Property**

In the above examples, the parent node always displays the closed folder bitmap, even when you double-click on it to expand it. Wouldn't it be better if, when you expanded the node, the bitmap changed to show that the node was now expanded? You can achieve this effect by using the node's **ExpandedImage** property. Modify the parent-child example from Listing 8-23 so that it reads as shown in Listing 8-26 (add the lines in bold).

Listing 8-26 The ExpandedImage property

```
Private Sub TreeViewDemo()
Dim MyImage As ListImage
Dim MyNode As Node
Dim I As Integer
Dim J As Integer
Dim ParentKey As String
Dim ChildKey As String
Dim Text As String

'Clear out any objects from the TreeView and ListView
TreeView1.Nodes.Clear
ImageList1.ListImages.Clear

'Add the closed file image to the ImageList
Set MyImage = ImageList1.ListImages.Add(, "closed", _
        LoadPicture("graphics\bitmaps\outline\closed.bmp"))

'Add the open file image to the ImageList
Set MyImage = ImageList1.ListImages.Add(,"open", _
        LoadPicture("graphics\bitmaps\outline\open.bmp"))

'Add the lead image to the ImageList
Set MyImage = ImageList1.ListImages.Add(, "leaf", _
        LoadPicture("graphics\bitmaps\outline\leaf.bmp"))

'Link the TreeView to the ImageList
Set TreeView1.ImageList = ImageList1

For I = 1 To 10
    ParentKey = "Node" & CStr(I)
    Text = "Parent node " & CStr(I)
    Set MyNode = TreeView1.Nodes.Add(, , ParentKey, Text, "closed")
    MyNode.ExpandedImage = "open"
    For J = 1 To 3
        ChildKey = "Node" & CStr(I) & "\" & CStr(J)
        Text = "Child node " & CStr(I) & "\" & CStr(J)
        Set MyNode = TreeView1.Nodes.Add(ParentKey, _
```

continued on next page

continued from previous page

```
        tvwChild, ChildKey, Text, "leaf")
            Next J
        Next I
    End Sub
```

Now when you run this example and double-click on a closed folder, the node expands and changes its bitmap to the open folder. Double-click on the node to close it and the bitmap reverts to the closed folder. This is shown in Figure 8-46.

Specifying a Selected Image

You can also display an image when a node is selected. There is a sixth parameter to the **Add** method that you haven't used. You can specify another image key in this parameter and that image displays when the node is selected, regardless of whether it is expanded or not.

Style **and** LineStyle **Properties**

These two properties control how the information in the Nodes collection is presented when the TreeView is displayed. Try running the previous example again, but this time try different combinations of these two properties. You'll find that you can get the TreeView to display a small Plus/Minus box, which indicates whether a node is

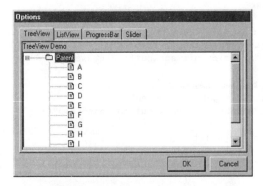

Figure 8-45
Using the node's
Sorted property

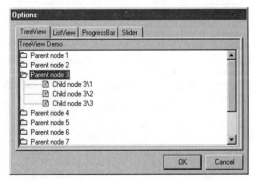

Figure 8-46
TreeView using the
ExpandedImage

expanded, by setting **LineStyle** to **1 - RootLines**. You can also control which visual components of the node are displayed by setting the control's **Style** property to different values. Figure 8-47 shows the previous example running with root lines instead of tree lines. It is accomplished by adding the line

```
TreeView1.LineStyle = tvwRootLines
```

You can add that line almost anywhere in the **ListViewDemo** code.

Tables 8-10 and 8-11 define the constants to use for each value.

Table 8-10 LineStyle Property Constants

Constant	Value	Description
tvwTreeLines	0	Displays lines between sibling nodes and their parents
tvwRootLines	1	Displays lines between root nodes and a small Plus/Minus box to indicate if a node is currently expanded

The **Style** property determines the graphical appearance of the TreeView control. Table 8-11 lists the constants you can use.

Table 8-11 Style property constants

Constant	Value	Description
tvwTextOnly	0	Displays text only
tvwPictureText	1	Displays picture and text
tvwPlusMinusText	2	Displays the Plus/Minus box and text only
tvwPlusPictureText	3	Displays the Plus/Minus box and picture and text
tvwTreeLinesText	4	Displays tree lines and text only
tvwTreeLinesPictureText	5	Displays tree lines, picture, and text
tvwTreeLinesPlusMinusText	6	Displays tree lines, the Plus/Minus box, and text
tvwTreeLinesPlusMinusPictureText	7	Displays all the components

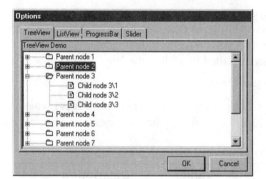

Figure 8-47
TreeView displaying
root lines instead
of tree lines

Editing the Text in a Node

The `LabelEdit` property controls whether or not the text in the TreeView's nodes is editable. This property can be set to two values, `lvwAutomatic` and `lvwManual`. If the property is set to `lvwAutomatic` (which is the default setting), clicking on the text of a selected node displays a text box, allowing the user to edit the node's text. At this point, the TreeView's `BeforeLabelEdit` event is triggered, allowing you to perform any preparation work for the impending change. When the edit is completed, the control's `AfterLabelEdit` event is called. You can use this event to pick up the changed text and act on the change if required.

Alternatively, if the `LabelEdit` property is set to `lvwManual`, you have to call the control's `StartLabelEdit` method before any editing can begin. The Windows 95 Explorer uses this feature to allow you to rename folders and files easily.

Detecting When a Node Is Clicked

Two events can be triggered when the user clicks on a Node object. These are `Click` and `NodeClick`.

The `NodeClick` event supplies a reference to the node that was selected. Also, the `NodeClick` event is called whenever a node is selected, by whatever means (mouse or keyboard).

The `Click` event, however, is triggered specifically by a mouse click on any part of the node's entry in the TreeView. This means that a `Click` event is fired when you click on a Plus box to expand a node, whereas the `NodeClick` is not. Try the example in Listing 8-27.

Listing 8-27 Testing the node's `Click` events

```
Private Sub TreeView1_NodeClick(ByVal MyNode As Node)
Debug.Print "NodeClick event: "; MyNode.Key, MyNode.Text
End Sub

Private Sub TreeView1_Click()
Debug.Print "Click event"
End Sub
```

The NodeClick and Click events are often triggered by the same physical event, in which case the NodeClick event is always triggered first.

Programmatically Selecting a Node

The Node object has a Selected property that you can both read and set. If you set a node's Selected property to True, it will become the selected node.

Locating the Parent of a Child Node

To obtain a reference to a child's parent node, use the child node's Parent property. Be aware, however, that a top-level node will have no parent, and attempting to read its Parent property will generate a runtime error.

Expanding and Collapsing a Node

You can both expand and contract individual nodes in the collection by setting their Expanded property accordingly. The example in Listing 8-28 will expand every node in the collection. Add the code to the end of the TreeViewDemo subroutine.

Listing 8-28 Expanding the nodes

```
For Each MyNode In TreeView1.Nodes
    MyNode.Expanded = True
Next MyNode
```

Similarly, to contract them all, use

```
For Each MyNode in TreeView1.Nodes
    MyNode.Expanded = False
Next MyNode
```

Other TreeView Features

The TreeView control has a number of additional features. For instance, to find out if a node has any children, you can check its Children property. This will return the number of children that the node currently has. You could combine this property with the Expanded property to ensure you expand only Node objects that have children, as shown in Listing 8-29.

Listing 8-29 Expanding selected nodes

```
For Each MyNode in TreeView1.Nodes
    If MyNode.Children > 0 Then
        MyNode.Expanded = True
    End If
Next MyNode
```

Another useful property is `FullPath`. This returns the fully qualified path of a node. The full path will consist of the text in each node from the root down to the target node. Each text component is separated by the character that is set in the TreeView's `PathSeparator` property (which is a \ character by default).

Next up is a look at the closely related ListView control.

1. How many different images can you associate with a node in a TreeView list?
   a. 1
   b. 2
   c. 8
   d. The number is limited only by available memory.

2. What value would you set the `LineStyle` property to if you wanted to display the Plus/Minus box to the left of a parent node?
   a. `tvwPlusMinus`
   b. `tvwTreeLinesPlusMinusPictureText`
   c. `tvwTreeLines`
   d. `tvwRootLines`

3. What constant value would you use to add a node to the end of a list of nodes?
   a. `tvwLast`
   b. `tvwNext`
   c. `tvwPrevious`
   d. `tvwChild`

4. Which node feature would you use to contract an expanded node in your code?
   a. `Expand` method
   b. `Expanded` property
   c. `Contract` method
   d. `Contract` property

5. How would you prevent the text in a node from being edited?
   a. Set the TreeView's `LabelEdit` property to `lvwAutomatic`.
   b. Set the TreeView's `LabelEdit` property to `lvwManual` and ensure that you never call its `StartLabelEdit` method.
   c. Ignore the `BeforeLabelEdit` and `AfterLabelEdit` events.
   d. You cannot prevent the text from being edited.

THE LISTVIEW CONTROL

Now that you've mastered the TreeView control, you'll be happy to know that the ListView control works in a remarkably similar way. However, there is one major difference. The ListView control contains two collections instead of just one. They are

- ListItems
- ColumnHeaders

The ListItems Collection

ListItems is the main collection in this control. It stores the individual ListItem objects displayed in the List view. You can view the items in one of four different ways:

- Large icons
- Small icons
- List
- Report

Figures 8-48, 8-49, 8-50, and 8-51 show each of the four different views using the List view in the Windows 95 Explorer.

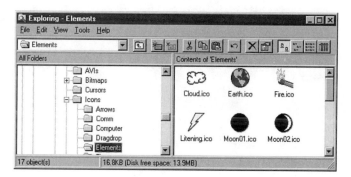

Figure 8-48
Large icon view

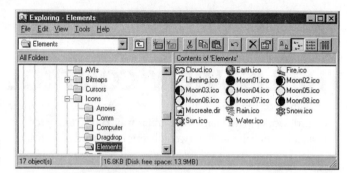

Figure 8-49
Small icon view

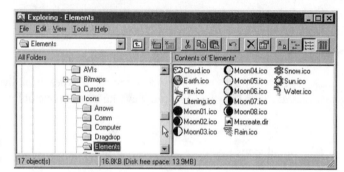

Figure 8-50
List view

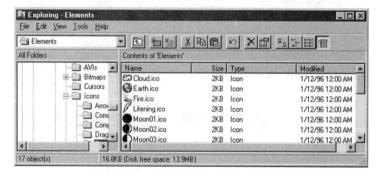

Figure 8-51
Report view

The ColumnHeaders Collection

Look at the report view in Figure 8-51. Note that it's fundamentally different from the others. Not only does it display more information about each ListItem object, but that information is presented in a series of columns. What's more, each column has a header. This header is provided by the ColumnHeaders collection.

The header isn't just for presentation purposes. It is functional, too. If you click on any of the headers, the items will be sorted by that column.

Adding ListItems Objects to the List View

In this example, you are going to add a ListView control to SuperPad's **frmOptions** form and then simply add some ListItem objects to it.

Start by resizing **Picture1(0)**, which you used in the previous lesson, so it is out of the way. Then resize the List view picture box, **Picture1(1)**, to fill the tab strip and press CTRL-J to bring it to the top of the **ZOrder**.

Add a ListView control to **Picture1(1)** and size it to fill the picture box. Figure 8-52 shows the icon for the ListView control.

Figure 8-53 shows you how **frmOptions** should appear with the ListView added. Now add the code in Listing 8-30 to the **ListViewDemo** subroutine.

Figure 8-52
The ListView
control icon

Figure 8-53
frmOptions with
ListView added

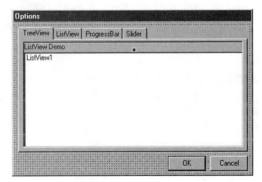

Listing 8-30 The ListView demo

```
Private Sub ListViewDemo()
Dim I As Integer
Dim MyItem As ListItem
Dim MyImage As ListImage
Dim ImageKey As String
Dim Key As String
Dim Text As String

ListView1.ListItems.Clear
ImageList1.ListImages.Clear

For I = 1 To 18
    ImageKey = "note" & CStr(I)
    Set MyImage = ImageList1.ListImages.Add(, ImageKey,⇐
LoadPicture("graphics\icons\writing\note" & Format(I, "00") & ".ico"))
Next I

Set ListView1.Icons = ImageList1

ListView1.View = lvwIcon ' Set to large icons view

For I = 1 To 18
    ImageKey = "note" & CStr(I)
    Key = "ListItem" & CStr(I)
    Text = "List item " & CStr(I)
    Set MyItem = ListView1.ListItems.Add(, Key, Text, ImageKey)
Next I
End Sub
```

This example loads the 18 note icons (**note01.ico** to **note18.ico**) from the icon library into the image list. It then sets the List view's **Icons** property to reference the ImageList control on the form so that the List view can obtain the icons from the image list by key. Figure 8-54 shows how the List view appears with this example running.

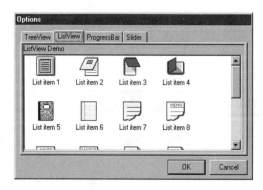

Figure 8-54
Example of
ListView running in
large icon view

As you can see from the code, the ListItems collection's **Add** method performs the task of creating the **ListItem** objects and adding them to the collection. Like the other **Add** methods you have used, you can obtain a reference to the newly created list item, as the code is doing here, or you can discard the reference by treating the **Add** method as a subroutine.

Disassociating the Image List from a Control

At this point, we need to demonstrate a technique for reusing an ImageList control. In these examples, we've tried to simplify matters by using and reusing a single image list (**ImageList1**). However, unless you are very careful, you can run into a problem. To see this problem for yourself, try switching between the ListView and TreeView demonstrations by clicking on their respective tabs. This generates a runtime error, as shown in Figure 8-55.

This error is caused when the TreeView demonstration attempts to clear the ListImages collection in the ImageList control after the ListView demonstration has been run. This happens because the ListView was set to reference the ImageList in the line that reads

```
Set ListView1.Icons = ImageList1
```

In other words, the ImageList has been told that the ListView still needs the images it contains and is raising the error when the TreeView demonstration attempts to clear the ListImages collection.

You need a way to disassociate the ListView from the shared ImageList when the demonstration is over.

It is here that the TabStrip's **BeforeClick** event comes into its own. Stop SuperPad by pressing the error dialog box's End button and then add the code in Listing 8-31 to the TabStrip's **BeforeClick** event.

Figure 8-55
Runtime error
caused by reusing
the ImageList

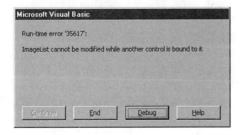

Listing 8-31 Disassociating the shared ImageList

```
Private Sub tabOptions_BeforeClick(Cancel As Integer)
Select Case tabOptions.SelectedItem.Index
    Case 1 'TreeView cleanup code
        Set TreeView1.ImageList = Nothing
    Case 2 'ListView cleanup code
        Set ListView1.Icons = Nothing
    Case 3 'ProgressBar cleanup code
    Case 4 'Slider cleanup code
End Select
End Sub
```

As you can see, this code uses the **BeforeClick** event to remove the association between the ImageList and the TreeView or ListView when the tab focus moves from one of these demonstrations. Now that the ImageList is not associated with any control, you are free to reuse it however you want and no error is generated.

Note that we've allowed a place for some additional cleanup code for both the ProgressBar and the Slider demonstrations in the next lesson.

Small Icon View

If you look at Figures 8-48 and 8-49, you can be forgiven for thinking that the ListView somehow automatically converts large icons to small ones. Unfortunately, it does not. The feature as demonstrated by the Windows 95 Explorer is part of the Explorer and is not part of the ListView control itself.

This means that you have to create the images that you want to use for small icons. The ListView distinguishes between large and small icons by means of its **SmallIcon** property. This performs the same function as the **Icon** property, except that the ImageList referenced by **SmallIcon** is used when displaying the ListView in small icon, list, or report view. The **Icon** property is used only for displaying large icons.

There is nothing to prevent you from using the same ImageList control for both **Icon** and **SmallIcon**, provided you use different images within that control for the large and small icons. Any type of image can be used. You aren't restricted to purely icon files.

Listing 8-32 modifies the previous example to add an additional image to **ImageList1**. This contains a small bitmap to display instead of the note icons when the ListView is switched to small icon view.

Listing 8-32 Small icon view

```
Private Sub ListViewDemo()
Dim I As Integer
Dim MyItem As ListItem
Dim MyImage As ListImage
Dim ImageKey As String
Dim Key As String
Dim Text As String

ListView1.ListItems.Clear
```

```
ImageList1.ListImages.Clear

For I = 1 To 18
    ImageKey = "note" & CStr(I)
    Set MyImage = ImageList1.ListImages.Add(, ImageKey, _
      LoadPicture("graphics\icons\writing\note" & _
      Format(I, "00") & ".ico"))
Next I
Set MyImage = ImageList1.ListImages.Add(, "small", _
    LoadPicture("graphics\bitmaps\bitmaps\assorted\w.bmp"))

Set ListView1.Icons = ImageList1 'large icon ImageList
Set ListView1.SmallIcons = ImageList1 'small icon ImageList

ListView1.View = lvwSmallIcon ' Set to small icons view

For I = 1 To 18
    ImageKey = "note" & CStr(I)
    Key = "ListItem" & CStr(I)
    Text = "List item " & CStr(I)
    Set MyItem = ListView1.ListItems.Add(, Key, _
      Text, ImageKey, "small")
Next IEnd Sub
```

The small icon's key is provided in the fifth parameter to the ListItems collection's **Add** method. The program did not provide anything for this parameter last time.

You must also make a change to the **BeforeClick** event. Add the line in bold.

```
Case 2 'ListView cleanup code
        Set ListView1.Icons = Nothing
        Set ListView1.SmallIcons = Nothing
```

Now the ListView has enough information to work out which image should be displayed in both large and small icon views. To change between views, set the ListView's **View** property to the appropriate constant.

Figure 8-56 shows the List view displaying small icons.

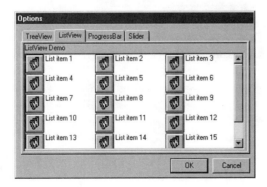

Figure 8-56
Small icon view

List View

No additional coding is required to display the ListView control in List view (apart from setting the `View` property to `lvwList`). Figure 8-57 shows the previous example running in List view. As you can see, the only difference between small icon view and list view is that the icons are arranged horizontally in small icon view and vertically in List view. The List view still displays the small icons.

Report View

Before you can display the List view in Report mode, you have to add some `ColumnHeader` objects to the ColumnHeaders collection. The objects in this collection can be defined at design time, however.

To begin with, display the Column Headers tab in the ListView's Custom Properties dialog box by selecting the (Custom) entry from the Properties window. This appears as shown in Figure 8-58.

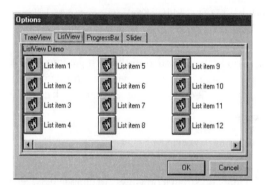

Figure 8-57
List view

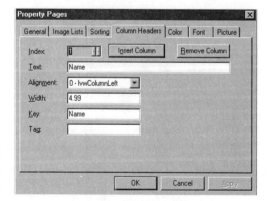

Figure 8-58
The Column
Headers tab

Insert three columns as shown in Table 8-12.

Table 8-12 Column header definitions

Index	Text	Alignment	Width	Key
1	Name	0 – Left	1440	Name
2	Size	1 – Right	722	Size
3	Type	2 – Center	1440	Type

Now modify the previous example so that the code reads as shown in Listing 8-33. The lines that are added or amended are shown in bold.

Listing 8-33 Report view demo

```
Private Sub ListViewDemo()
Dim I As Integer
Dim MyItem As ListItem
Dim MyImage As ListImage
Dim ImageKey As String
Dim Key As String
Dim Text As String

' In case this tab is clicked twice
Set ListView1.Icons = Nothing
Set ListView1.SmallIcons = Nothing
'
' Clear the ListView and the ImageList
ListView1.ListItems.Clear
ImageList1.ListImages.Clear

For I = 1 To 18
    ImageKey = "note" & CStr(I)
    Set MyImage = ImageList1.ListImages.Add(, ImageKey, _
      LoadPicture("graphics\icons\writing\note" & _
      Format(I, "00") & ".ico"))
Next I
ImageKey = "small"
Set MyImage = ImageList1.ListImages.Add(, ImageKey, _
  LoadPicture("graphics\bitmaps\assorted\w.bmp"))

Set ListView1.Icons = ImageList1
Set ListView1.SmallIcons = ImageList1

ListView1.View = lvwReport ' Set to report view

For I = 1 To 18
    ImageKey = "note" & CStr(I)
    Key = "ListItem" & CStr(I)
    Text = "List item " & CStr(I)
    Set MyItem = ListView1.ListItems.Add(, Key, Text, _
```

continued on next page

continued from previous page

```
        ImageKey, "small")
    MyItem.SubItems(1) = CStr(CInt(Rnd(1) * 10000))
    MyItem.SubItems(2) = Key
Next I


End Sub
```

As you can see from the example, each ListItem object contains an array of SubItem strings. The first element in this string array (element **0**) refers to the text contained in the ListItem object. This is why we named the first ColumnHeader object **Text**. Element **0** is already populated with the text of the object, so there is no need for you to set it. Elements **1** and **2**, however, relate to the second and third ColumnHeader objects that you defined at design time. All we're doing is setting the size to a random number and the type to the key name for the ListItem object. Figure 8-59 shows how the ListView control appears in Report view.

Sorting the Report View

To sort the report view, you must respond to the user clicking on a header of the report. The ListView generates a **ColumnClick** event when this occurs. Listing 8-34 shows you how to program the ListView to sort the three columns correctly.

Listing 8-34 Sorting the report

```
Private Sub ListView1_ColumnClick(ByVal MyColumnHeader As ColumnHeader)
ListView1.SortKey = MyColumnHeader.Index - 1
ListView1.Sorted = True
End Sub
```

The minimum amount of information you need to supply is the **SortKey** by which the list will be sorted. This is always the **ColumnHeader Index** less one, because the **Index** values run from **1** to **3** (in our example), whereas the **SortKey** is always indexed from **0**.

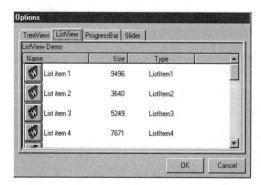

Figure 8-59
The ListView
control in Report
view

You can additionally specify whether the list should be sorted in ascending or descending order by setting the **SortOrder** property. For example, to specify that the list should be sorted in descending order, you would set **SortOrder** to the constant **lvwDescending** (**lvwAscending** is the other constant). Again, these constants are provided by the ListView control itself.

1. What is the name of the collection that contains information on the headers in the ListView?
   a. Columns
   b. ColumnHeaders
   c. ColumnHeadings
   d. ColumnHeads

2. Which constant value would you use to display the ListView control in Report view?
   a. **lvwReport**
   b. **lvwReportView**
   c. **lvwReportMode**
   d. **lvwViewReport**

3. Which event is generated when the user clicks on a header when in Report view?
   a. **Click**
   b. **ClickHeader**
   c. **ClickColumn**
   d. **ColumnClick**

4. How do you get the ListView control to sort its list?
   a. Call its **Sort** method.
   b. Set its **Sorted** property to **True**. The ListView control will automatically resort itself when **SortKey** is changed.
   c. Set its **Sorted** property to **True** and then call its **Sort** method.
   d. Set its **SortKey** and then call its **Sort** method.

5. Which parameter to the ListView control's **Add** method does the small icon key go in?
   a. Parameter **2**
   b. Parameter **3**
   c. Parameter **4**
   d. Parameter **5**

LESSON 8

THE PROGRESSBAR AND SLIDER CONTROLS

Finally, it's time to consider how to program the ProgressBar and Slider controls.

The ProgressBar Control

The ProgressBar control provides a graphical display that gives your users a rough estimation of the progress of a lengthy operation within your software. You might be saving a file to disk, for example, or printing a document. The icon for this control is shown in Figure 8-60.

To show how the ProgressBar control works, enlarge **Picture1(3)** and bring it to the top of the runtime **ZOrder**. Add a ProgressBar control to the picture box. Size the control so that it appears as in Figure 8-61.

Whatever the operation that you're programming is, the first thing you need to do is decide the minimum and maximum numbers that the progress bar will represent. For example, if you want the progress bar to represent the percentage of how complete the operation is, the minimum is 0 and the maximum is 100. Alternatively, assume that you are printing a document with 10,000 characters in it. You might then select a scale from 0 to 10,000, updating the progress bar after each character is printed. (Not a very practical example, but you get the idea.) Indeed, you can establish any minimum and maximum values for the progress bar to use by setting its **Min** and **Max** properties accordingly. You can even use negative numbers. The only restriction is that the **Max** property

Figure 8-60
The ProgressBar
control icon

Figure 8-61
ProgressBar control
added to
frmOptions

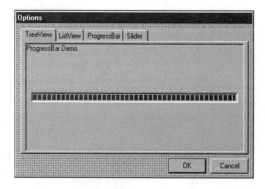

must be greater than the **Min** property, which is pretty self-explanatory. **Min** and **Max** are set to **0** and **100**, respectively, by default.

Listing 8-35 shows you the how to use the ProgressBar.

Listing 8-35 `ProgressBar` demo

```
Private Sub ProgressBarDemo()
Dim Min As Single
Dim Max As Single
Dim I As Integer
Dim SaveTime As String
Min = 0
Max = 10
ProgressBar1.Min = Min
ProgressBar1.Max = Max
SaveTime = Time
For I = Min To Max
    Do While Time = SaveTime
    Loop
    SaveTime = Time
    ProgressBar1.Value = I
Next I
End Sub
```

This demonstration code simply increments the ProgressBar's **Value** property by 1 each second. (Remember the **Time** function returns the current time in a **String** variable.) That's all there is to it!

The Slider Control

The Slider control is a useful control that gives you the sort of functionality you would expect from a volume control or something similar. You can use it to control changes in any value. It also establishes minimum and maximum values for the value being set.

To learn how to use it, enlarge **Picture1(3)** and bring it to the top of the design-time **ZOrder**. Add a Slider control to the picture box. The Slider icon is shown in Figure 8-62.

Add a TextBox called **txtSliderValue** and clear its **Text** property. Arrange the two controls so that they appear as in Figure 8-63.

Note the setting of the Slider control's **Min** and **Max** properties. Set them to **0** and **10**, the same values you used for the corresponding properties in the ProgressBar.

Figure 8-62
The Slider control icon

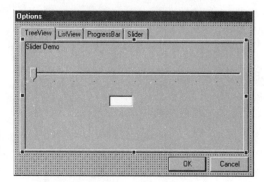

Figure 8-63
The Slider control
on frmOptions

The `SmallChange` and `LargeChange` properties control how far the slider will move in the event of a small or large movement. A small movement is achieved by dragging the slider handle to the next tick (the small dots underneath the slider itself). A large movement is achieved by clicking on the slider bar rather than dragging the slider handle. Leave these values set to **1** and **5**, respectively, which are suitable for your purposes.

The slider provides two events that you can use to monitor its value. These are

 Scroll

 Change

The Scroll *Event*

The `Scroll` event is triggered whenever the `Value` property of the Slider changes, whether you are in the process of dragging the slider handle or using the cursor keys to control the slider.

The Change *Event*

The difference between the `Change` event and the `Scroll` event is that `Change` is generated once the change to `Value` is completed. Therefore, if you drag the slider's handle with the mouse, the `Change` event will not occur until you release the mouse.

Populate the `txtSliderValue` TextBox as shown in Listing 8-36. This should give you a clear idea of how the control works.

Listing 8-36 Slider demo

```
Private Sub SliderDemo()
txtSliderValue.Text = Slider1.Value
End Sub

Private Sub Slider1_Change()
txtSliderValue.Text = Slider1.Value
End Sub
```

```
Private Sub Slider1_Click()
txtSliderValue.Text = Slider1.Value
End Sub
```

1. Which ProgressBar and Slider property sets the minimum value handled by these controls?
   a. Minimum
   b. Min
   c. MinValue
   d. MinimumValue

2. Which property do you use to change the current value represented by the ProgressBar?
   a. Value
   b. CurrentValue
   c. Val
   d. CurVal

3. Of the following events, which is *not* generated by the Slider to indicate a change in its value?
   a. Change
   b. Scroll
   c. Click
   d. All three events may be generated to indicate a change in value.

4. Which Slider property determines the minimum change affected by dragging the slider's handle?
   a. MinChange
   b. SmallChange
   c. LargeChange
   d. MaxChange

5. How do you get the progress bar to display the percentage value numerically?
   a. By setting its **Percent** property to a percentage
   b. By setting its **DisplayPercent** property to **True**
   c. By setting its **Text** property to the percentage you want to display
   d. You cannot. The ProgressBar displays only a graphic approximation.

Add toolbar buttons in SuperPad for Copy, Cut, Paste, Bold, Italics, and Underline, and implement the corresponding functionality.

CHAPTER 9

PRINTING

The "paperless office" has been a dream of computer manufacturers for years, but it's not likely to become reality. Business needs hard copies of certain documents as a permanent, legal record. People (some people) still write letters, and books are still being published. Chances are that your programs will also need printed output.

Adding print capabilities to a program has traditionally been one of programming's more tedious and most difficult tasks. But printer support is an intrinsic part of Visual Basic and is simple to learn. Its simplicity belies the complexities of the work that Visual Basic is doing behind the scenes to manage your print job.

INTRODUCING PRINTING

The key to printing from Visual Basic is learning how to use the `Printer` class, the `Printer` object, the Printers collection, and the printer itself. Sound confusing? Don't worry, each one is quite distinct from the other in spite of the similarity of their names.

The Printers Collection

When your VB project starts, it automatically creates the Printers collection. The Printers collection consists of a collection of `Printer` objects, one `Printer` object for each printer that is connected to your computer.

To see this for yourself, make sure that you have at least two printers available within your Windows environment. If not, add some. Follow your Windows documentation to add printers. Don't worry if you don't have the specified printer actually connected; Windows won't care. Windows is just installing a *driver* program that will convert standard printer commands into commands that the specified printer can understand. (Be sure to delete the extra printers when you finish these exercises, though, to avoid confusion.)

Figure 9-1 shows a typical Printers window. The first icon in the Printers window lets you add additional printers (well, printer drivers) to the system. The second icon is an HP InkJet printer, and the third is the computer's fax modem. In case you're wondering how a fax modem can be a printer, the software driver for the modem looks like a printer driver to Windows, and you can select the fax modem "printer" to send any printable document via facsimile. If you have a fax modem, your Visual Basic programs will be able to do the same thing.

Now that you know about the Printers collection, take a look at it. Start a new project and enter the code in Listing 9-1.

Figure 9-1
The Windows 95
Printers window

Listing 9-1 Viewing the Printers collection

```
Private Sub Form_Load()
Dim MyPrinter As Printer
For Each MyPrinter In Printers
    Debug.Print MyPrinter.DeviceName
Next MyPrinter
End Sub
```

As you can see, the program creates an object variable, `MyPrinter`, based on the `Printer` class. The `For Each...Next` loop assigns each `Printer` object in the Printers collection to that variable and displays the `DeviceName` property in the Debug window. On the computer shown in Figure 9-1, the Debug window would contain

```
HP DeskJet 520 Printer
WINFAX
```

The Port *Property*

Several printers of the same type may be connected to a computer, especially on networked computers. The `Port` property of the `Printer` object offers the only way to identify a printer uniquely. Although Windows 95 and Windows NT strongly discourage you from writing directly to a port rather than through a driver, you may need to know the port number so you can be sure which printer will be used for a job. Change the code from Listing 9-1 to that of Listing 9-2 (**changes are in bold**).

Listing 9-2 Uniquely identifying a printer

```
Private Sub Form_Load()
Dim MyPrinter As Printer
For Each MyPrinter In Printers
    Debug.Print MyPrinter.DeviceName; " On "; MyPrinter.Port
Next MyPrinter
End Sub
```

The output will change. On the example computer, it now looks like this:

```
HP DeskJet 520 Printer On LPT1:
WINFAX On COM2:
```

The Print Job

Before you get too involved in trying to print, it is important to understand the concept of the print job. Whether you are printing text or graphics or a mixture of both, the printing assignments that you give through Visual Basic are organized into print jobs. Visual Basic buffers the information you send to the printer in memory until your program signals that the print job has ended. Then the Windows Print Manager takes over. It waits until any earlier print jobs complete, then it sends your print job to the computer as a unit.

This idea is critical to the operation of a printer in a multitasking system such as Windows. It is the only way the computer can keep print jobs from different programs separated. If not for print jobs, the printed output of two different operations could get jumbled together. Consider the effect of having a love letter mixed in with a business contract!

The point to understand here is that printing is a two-step process. You begin the process by using the print output methods (coming up soon) for the `Printer` object that you want to receive your print job. There is no need to specify where the print job begins; Visual Basic handles that automatically. When you use the first print output methods, VB starts the print job for you. After that, all further printer output will be buffered for you until you tell Visual Basic to end it.

The `EndDoc` *Method*

How do you end it? There are two ways. You can explicitly use the `EndDoc` method or you can exit from the program. Exiting from a program with a print job pending automatically calls the `EndDoc` method. It's kind of clumsy, but it will get the job printed.

The `NewPage` *Method and the* `Page` *Property*

If your print job requires more lines of text on a page than will fit, the `Printer` object automatically adds a new page and the `Printer` object's `Page` property will be incremented by 1.

Rather than let the `Printer` object determine your page breaks, you can print multipage documents completely under your control. The `NewPage` method closes out the current page and increments the `Page` property. You will have to count lines or otherwise determine when you are about to reach the end of the page to control this, however. Lesson 6 covers this in detail.

The Default Printer and the `Printer` Object

One of the printers connected to your computer is designated as the default printer, which means that it will receive all print jobs that are not specifically sent to another printer. Visual Basic's `Printer` object initially points to the default printer.

The `TrackDefault` *Property*

If you start a program running and then change the default printer, the VB program will point to the new default printer. On occasion, you may not want that behavior. Perhaps, for example, you are sending a fax with Word and want to print hard copy from your VB program. You sure don't want the VB output to go to the fax, too!

The `TrackDefault` property offers the solution. The `TrackDefault` property is a Boolean quantity. When it is set to `True`, VB's `Printer` object always points to the default printer. Set it to `False` and VB's `Printer` object will not change when the default printer changes. You won't need this often, but when you do, you will love it! The syntax is

```
Printer.TrackDefault = False
```

Or, if you have set it to **False** and want to change it back

```
Printer.TrackDefault = True
```

Changing the Printer

What if you want to print to another printer? Preferably, you will let the user choose the printer. If you want to change the printer in code, though, remember that Visual Basic prints to a **Printer** object rather than to a physical device. All you need to do is change the device that the object references. The following code will print to each of your printers in succession.

```
Private Sub Form_Load()
Dim MyPrinter As Printer
Printer.TrackDefault = False
For Each MyPrinter In Printers
    Set Printer = MyPrinter
    Printer.Print "Printing to " & Printer.DeviceName
    Printer.EndDoc
Next
Printer.TrackDefault = True
End Sub
```

The Print **Method**

You have been using the **Print** method almost from the first page of this book. How many times have you typed **Debug.Print**? Actually, there are four possible recipients of the **Print** method's efforts. The syntax for the **Print** method is

```
object.Print outputlist
```

where

- **object** is any one of the Debug window, a form, a picture box on a form, or the **Printer** object.

- **outputlist** is an optional expression or list of expressions to be printed. If **outputlist** is omitted, the **Print** method prints a blank line.

Try it out, using the code in Listing 9-3.

Listing 9-3 The Print method and the Printer object

```
Private Sub Form_Load()

Dim A As Integer, B As Double, S As String
    A = 20
    B = 3.14159
    S = "This is a test"
```

continued on next page

continued from previous page

```
        Printer.Print A
        Printer.Print B
        Printer.Print S
        Printer.Print "And the test has ended"
        Printer.EndDoc

End Sub
```

This will print

```
 20
 3.14159
This is a test
And the test has ended
```

on your printer. Note that the **Printer** object interpreted the variables correctly. **Printer.Print A** did not print the letter **A** on your page.

Formatting the Output

You don't always want to print each variable on a separate line, nor do you always want to print right at the left edge of the page. And you don't have to. Visual Basic offers several ways to position your printed output.

For starters, you can use *concatenation*, which you learned in Chapter 4, Subroutines, Functions, and the Visual Basic 5 Language. The **&** symbol works as well on the printer as it did in a text box. After all, you are printing strings either way. You could write

```
Printer.Print A & " " & B & " " & S
```

and the printer will print

```
20 3.14159 This is a test.
```

Concatenation works with any two string expressions.

Another technique is to use either a comma or a semicolon between variable names at the end of a line. Add a semicolon to the end of each of the **Printer.Print** lines from Listing 9-3. Run the program and see what happens. Replace the semicolon with a comma and run it again. Here's what the symbols do:

Symbol	Action
;	Does not use a linefeed. The next variable or string literal is printed in the next print position.
,	Moves to the next print zone.

Print zones are spaced 14 fixed-width print positions apart. Chances are that you are printing with *proportional fonts*, in which a *w* takes more space than an *i*. If you use print zones or spaces to align text, be sure you leave enough space.

Two functions help you position your text: the `Spc(n)` function and the `Tab(n)` function. As you might guess, `Spc(n)` moves n spaces to the right and `Tab(n)` moves to column n. You can also use TAB by itself to move to the next print zone. It is easier to see than it is to describe. (If you want to save paper, use `Debug.Print` instead of `Printer.Print` for the following demonstration.) Enter the code in Listing 9-4 and try it out.

Listing 9-4 Using `Tab()` and `Spc()`

```
Private Sub Form_Load()
Dim A As Integer, B As Long, S As String
A = 20
B = 3.14159
Debug.Print A; Tab; B
Debug.Print A, B
Debug.Print A; Spc(20); B
End Sub
```

In the early days of printing, all characters took up exactly the same space on a line. It was common to refer to a printer as an 80-column printer, which meant that there were 80 character spaces across the page. Publishers and printers, meanwhile, used proportional fonts, where the actual space a character takes on a page depends on the character. The letter *W* takes up more than one fixed-width column, whereas the letter *I* takes less. Proportional fonts are prettier to look at and easier to read, but they make life hard for programmers, especially when they are trying to print columnar data. If the exact print position is important, be sure to test extensively before releasing a program. This issue is covered in more depth later in this chapter.

1. In the code

   ```
   Dim MyPrinter As Printer
   ```

   `MyPrinter` is
   a. A Hewlett-Packard InkJet
   b. The printer connected to LPT1
   c. The default printer
   d. An object based on the `Printer` class

2. How do you tell Windows to start a print job?
   a. `Printer.StartJob`
   b. `Printer.Print`
   c. `Set PrinterJob as New PrintJob`
   d. Use any of the printer output methods.

3. How do you end a print job?
   a. `Printer.EndJob`
   b. `Printer.EndDoc`
   c. `Printer.Quit`
   d. Windows knows when the job ends.

4. How does Visual Basic set the default printer?
   a. With the `TrackDefault` property
   b. With the `Printer.Change` method
   c. The default printer is set by Windows.
   d. None of the above

5. The line _____ will send `sData` to the printer.
   a. `Printer.Print sData`
   b. `Printer.Show sData`
   c. `sData.Print`
   d. `Printer.Text = sData`

USING FONTS

Typesetters argue that different styles of print are *typefaces* and that a *font* is a collection of all of the characters in a typeface of any single *size*. Typesetters are, of course, correct; they are experts their own field. Sometime in the early days of computers, however, the term *font* came to mean typeface, and the name has stuck. So, at least while you are working with computers, fonts refer to typefaces.

This lesson teaches you how to work with different fonts in printing. You don't have to settle for your printer's default fonts. In fact, you don't have to settle for your *printer's* fonts at all!

Fonts, Fonts, and More Fonts

Early computers and printers offered little in the way of fonts. They didn't really have the capability of displaying and printing anything finer than 5 × 7 dot-matrix letters and numbers, which are quite crude compared to today's standards. The EGA display and 9-pin printers brought some improvements. The SVGA display and lower-cost laser and InkJet printers have brought a revolution.

Windows supports TrueType fonts, which *are* the revolution. TrueType fonts are *scaleable*, which means that the font can be displayed (and printed) in any desired size. (Well, there *are* limits.) Windows itself comes with a good variety of TrueType fonts, and if you want more they are available from other vendors at low cost, and from the Internet at no cost. TrueType fonts means that Windows can use the same typefaces to display a document as to print it. From the viewpoint of printing, it means that you can print in almost any typeface you want.

Most TrueType fonts are proportional fonts, which means that each character takes up a different (proportional) amount of space. Windows supports some fixed-width fonts, which are easier to display and require fewer resources. Compare the differences between the main text in this book and the listings. The listings are printed in a fixed-width typeface, whereas the balance of the book is printed in a proportional font.

The effect of all this is that you get a wide choice of fonts and font sizes to use in your printing projects. Start a new project, the Font Demo project, or load the completed project from the CD that comes with this book. Add a label and three Command buttons to the form. Set the properties according to Table 9-1.

Table 9-1 The Font Demo project's first controls

Object	Property	Value
Form	Name	frmFontDemo
	Caption	Font Demo
Label	Name	Label1
	Caption	Fixed Tests
CommandButton	Name	cmdFixed
	Caption	Fixed Pitch
CommandButton	Name	cmdProportional
	Caption	Proportional
CommandButton	Name	cmdPrint
	Caption	Click to Print

The layout of the form is shown in Figure 9-2.

Listing 9-5 shows the code for the two Command buttons.

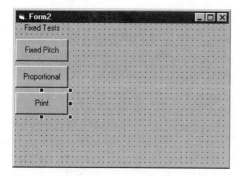

Figure 9-2
The Font Demo
form at design time

Listing 9-5 Code for `cmdFixed` and `cmdProportional`

```
Private Sub cmdFixed_Click()
    Printer.Print ;
    With Printer
        .Font.Name = "Courier"
        .Font.Size = 12
        .Font.Bold = False
        .Font.Italic = False
        .Font.Underline = False
    End With
    Printer.Print "Fixed"
    Printer.Print "WWWWWWWWWWWWWWWWWWWW"     ' 20 of them
    Printer.Print Tab; "^"
    Printer.Print "iiiiiiiiiiiiiiiiiiii"     ' 20 of them
    Printer.Print Tab; "^"
End Sub

Private Sub cmdProportional_Click()
    Printer.Print ;
    With Printer
        .Font.Name = "Times"
        .Font.Size = 12
        .Font.Bold = False
        .Font.Italic = False
        .Font.Underline = False
    End With
    Printer.Print "Proportional"
    Printer.Print "WWWWWWWWWWWWWWWWWWWW"     ' 20 of them
    Printer.Print Tab; "^"
    Printer.Print "iiiiiiiiiiiiiiiiiiii"     ' 20 of them
    Printer.Print Tab; "^"

End Sub


Private Sub cmdPrint_Click()
    Printer.EndDoc
End Sub
```

A Look at the Code

The code in Listing 9-5 introduces several new concepts. The first thing to notice is that the first line of each procedure is **Printer.Print ;**. It isn't necessary to start a print job explicitly, but one of the tricky vagaries of the **Printer** object is that when you want to change a font, you have to start by getting the **Printer** object's attention with **Printer.Print**. (The semicolon keeps the printer in the same row on the page.)

The **With...End With** structure shows that **Font** is a property of the **Printer** object. Use **With...End With** to change several of the **Font** property's attributes at once. If you want to change only one, for example if all you need to do is make the font bold, use `Printer.Font.Bold = True`. In the code for this program, you are setting five different properties; the `With...End With` structure is more efficient.

Even though `Font` is a property, it also *has* properties. Table 9-2 lists the font's properties.

Table 9-2 The attributes of the `Font` property

Attribute	Type	Definition
Name	String	Selects the font to use. Examples are Times (for Times New Roman) and Arial.
Size	Number	Sets the point size of the font. See note below.
Bold	Boolean	Turns bold print on or off.
Italic	Boolean	Turns italic on or off.
Underline	Boolean	Turns underline on or off.
Strikethrough	Boolean	Turns strikethrough on or off.
Weight	Number	Another way to handle bold. Numbers less than 550 are set to 400, which is normal weight. Numbers greater than 550 are set to 700, which is bold.

The `cmdPrint` button ends the print job with `EndDoc`.

Running the Program

When you run the Font Demo program, click on `cmdFixed`, then on `cmdProportional`, and finally on `cmdPrint`. The program demonstrates the proportional font problem by printing 20 Ws and 20 is in a fixed-width font and a proportional font. Under each row of letters, the program prints a carat at the beginning of the second print zone.

Notice that the carat is under letter number 15 for both letters in the fixed-width font. Then look at the proportional font, and you will have a good idea of what the problem is. Twenty *W*s certainly take up a lot more room than 20 *i*'s!

When you are setting fonts to sizes lower than 8 points, you have to get tricky. First set the font size, then set the font name, then set the size again. Windows will most likely not use the font you selected, but substitute a similar font that is easier to read in the smaller size. The font "Small Font" was created for just this purpose.

More Fonts

Now to improve the project. Add the objects listed in Table 9-3 to the form.

Table 9-3 Additional objects for Font Demo

Object	Property	Value
Label	Name	Label2
	Caption	Available Fonts
Label	Name	Label3
	Caption	Selected Tests
Label	Name	Label4
	Caption	Size
Label	Name	Label5
	Caption	Attributes
CommandButton	Name	cmdArial
	Caption	Arial
CommandButton	Name	cmdTimes
	Caption	Times New Roman
CommandButton	Name	cmdWingDings
	Caption	WingDings
CommandButton	Name	cmdSelected
	Caption	Click to Accept Selected Font
ListBox	Name	lstFontName
	Sorted	True
ListBox	Name	lstFontSize
CheckBox	Name	chkBold
	Caption	Bold
	Font	MS SansSerif Bold
CheckBox	Name	chkItalic
	Caption	Italic
	Font	MS SansSerif Italic
CheckBox	Name	chkUnderline
	Caption	Underline
	Font	MS SansSerif Underlined

Arrange the objects as shown in Figure 9-3.

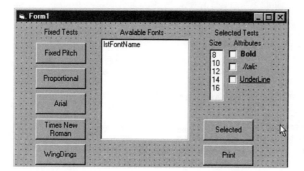

Figure 9-3
The finished
version of
Font Demo

Now add the code from Listing 9-6 to the project.

Listing 9-6 Completing the Font Demo program

```
Option Explicit
Public sFontName As String
Public sngFontPoints As Single
Public bFontBold As Boolean
Public bFontItalic As Boolean
Public bFontUnderLine As Boolean

Private Sub Form_Load()
    Dim j As Integer
    For j = 0 To Printer.FontCount - 1
        lstFontName.AddItem Printer.Fonts(j)
    Next
    lstFontName.ListIndex = 0
    sFontName = lstFontName.List(lstFontName.ListIndex)
End Sub

Private Sub chkBold_Click()
    bFontBold = chkBold
End Sub

Private Sub chkItalic_Click()
    bFontItalic = chkItalic
End Sub

Private Sub chkUnderline_Click()
    bFontUnderLine = chkUnderline
End Sub

Private Sub cmdArial_Click()
    Printer.Print ;
    With Printer
        .Font.Name = "Arial"
```

continued on next page

continued from previous page

```
                .Font.Size = 12
                .Font.Bold = False
                .Font.Italic = False
                .Font.Underline = False
        End With
        Printer.Print "Testing the Arial font"
    End Sub

    Private Sub cmdPrint_Click()
        Printer.EndDoc
    End Sub

    Private Sub cmdRoman_Click()
        Printer.Print ;
        With Printer
            .Font.Name = "Times"
            .Font.Size = 12
            .Font.Bold = False
            .Font.Italic = False
            .Font.Underline = False
        End With
        Printer.Print "Testing Times New Roman"
    End Sub

    Private Sub cmdSelected_Click()
        Printer.Print ;
        With Printer
            .Font.Size = sngFontPoints
            .Font.Name = sFontName
            .Font.Bold = bFontBold
            .Font.Italic = bFontItalic
            .Font.Underline = bFontUnderLine
        End With
        Printer.Print "Printing with " & sFontName; _
            " at "; sngFontPoints; " Point Size"
        Printer.Print "Attributes: Bold = "; bFontBold; _
            " Italic = "; bFontItalic; " Underline = "; bFontUnderLine
    End Sub

    Private Sub cmdWingDings_Click()
        Printer.Print ;
        With Printer
            .Font.Name = "WingDings"
            .Font.Size = 12
            .Font.Bold = False
            .Font.Italic = False
            .Font.Underline = False
        End With
        Printer.Print "Testing WingDings:"
    End Sub

    Private Sub lstFontName_Click()
```

```
        sFontName = lstFontName.List(lstFontName.ListIndex)
End Sub

Private Sub lstFontSize_Click()
        sngFontPoints = lstFontSize.List(lstFontSize.ListIndex)
End Sub
```

A Look at the New Code

The Declarations section declares five formwide variables for font attributes.

The first **For...Next** loop in the **Form_Load** procedure reads the available fonts from the **Printer** object and fills **lstFontNames** with them. The second loop fills **lstFontSize** with the numbers **8, 10, 12, 14,** and **16**. Both list boxes have their **ListIndex** property set to **0** and a default value is assigned to **sFontName** and **sngFontSize**. The default value prevents an error if you attempt to print without having designated a font or a font size.

Visual Basic really makes your work easy here. You don't need to be concerned with what fonts are installed on a given system. VB reads and lists them for you.

The code in the **Click** events of all except the **cmdSelected** Command button prints a brief message to the print job identifying the font that is selected by the button. The **Click** event for **cmdSelected** is more complicated because it has more work to do. It builds a message that includes the font name, size, and attributes and prints it to the print job.

The **Click** events for the list boxes set the appropriate variable for font name and font size. The **Click** events for the check boxes set the variables for font attributes in the same way.

Running the Program

When you run the program this time, click once on each of the buttons on the Fixed Tests side of the form. Then select a font and one or more attributes and click on Selected. Select fonts and attributes several times, clicking on Selected after each set of choices. Finally, close the print job by clicking on Print.

The running program is shown in Figure 9-4.

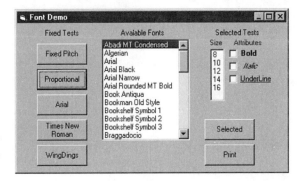

Figure 9-4
The running Fonts
demo program

This time you get a more varied printout. Some of it may be surprising. Not all the fonts give you letters! The Symbols and WingDings fonts let you do some pretty interesting things, especially when you change font sizes to go with them.

1. Because TrueType fonts are _____, they can be printed and displayed in any reasonable size.
   a. Scaleable
   b. Resizable
   c. Proportional
   d. Portable

2. Proportional fonts give a different amount of _____ to different characters.
   a. Ink
   b. Space
   c. Points
   d. Tabs

3. Which command makes the printer's font 16 points?
   a. `Printer.Font.16`
   b. `Set Font.Size = 16`
   c. `Printer.Font.Size = 16`
   d. `Let FontSize = 16`

4. Which of the following is *not* a valid attribute for a font?
   a. `Size`
   b. `Bold`
   c. `UnderLine`
   d. `Color`

5. Font is a(n) _____ of the `Printer` object.
   a. Class
   b. Property
   c. Subobject
   d. Array

LESSON 3

THE PRINTER AND THE COMMONDIALOG

The best way to handle printers, as with many other features of the computer, is to let your user have control. It may be that on Monday Jane User wants to send her print output to a laser printer, on Wednesday she wants to send it to a dot-matrix printer, and on Friday she prefers her fax. In Chapter 8, Discovering the CommonDialog and Windows 95 Controls, you learned about the Windows Common|Dialog control and used it for file management. Now it is time to use the printer control features of the Common-Dialog control.

The Printer Common Dialog Boxes

The CommonDialog adds two dialog boxes to your arsenal. They are the Print Setup dialog box and the Print dialog box. Use the Common|Dialog control to add the user interface to let your users change printer settings in SuperPad. Load SuperPad as you left it in Chapter 8. New code added in this lesson demonstrates the two printer Common Dialog boxes and improves the printer functions in SuperPad.

The Print Setup Dialog Box

The Print Setup dialog box is shown in Figure 9-5.

From the Print Setup dialog box, the user can select the default printer, set the printer orientation, and select the paper size and the source of the paper (if there is more than one paper tray for the printer). By clicking on the Properties button, the user can also set the printer's properties.

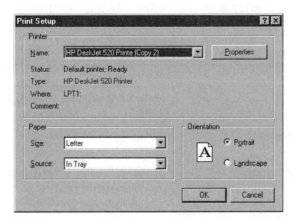

Figure 9-5
The Print Setup
dialog box

Different printers have different capabilities. The Print Setup dialog box will, for the most part, reflect those capabilities.

The key to the appearance and function of the common dialog is in the **Flags** property. In the code of Listing 9-7, the **Flags** property is set to show the Printer Setup dialog box. Setting the **PrinterDefault** property to **True** allows you to print to the selected printer with the **Print** method, and the printer that you select in the Printer Setup dialog box becomes the default printer.

Listing 9-7 Displaying the Print Setup dialog box

```
Private Sub mnuFilePrintSetup_Click()
'..Set Flags to show the print setup dialog
CommonDialog1.Flags = cdlPDPrintSetup
'..Set Selected printer = default printer
CommonDialog1.PrinterDefault = True
'   Show the dialog
CommonDialog1.ShowPrinter
End Sub
```

The last line in the listing calls the Print dialog's only method, **ShowPrinter**.

The Printer Setup dialog box does not return the name of the selected printer, nor does it inform you in any way that the user has changed the printer. You can detect this quite easily with code, however, by storing **Printer.DeviceName** in a variable before calling the dialog box and comparing it with **Printer.DeviceName** after the dialog box is exited.

The Print Dialog Box

Now that Jane User can select which printer to use, it is time to allow her to specify how the printed output should be handled. Opening the Print dialog box is a matter of calling the **ShowPrinter** method without setting the **Flag** property to **cdlPDPrintSetup**. That does not mean that you won't set any flags, though. The Print dialog box is extremely flexible. You can allow (or disallow) a large array of features. Table 9-4 lists the flags and their meaning.

Table 9-4 The Printer dialog flags

Flag	Description
cdlPDAllPages	Returns or sets the state of the All Pages option button.
cdlPDPageNums	Returns or sets the state of the Pages option button.
cdlPDNoPageNums	Disables the Pages option button and the associated edit control.

Flag	Description
cdlPDSelection	Returns or sets the state of the Selection option button. If neither cdlPDPageNums nor cdlPDSelection is specified, the All option button is in the selected state.
cdlPDNoSelection	Disables the Selection option button.
cdlPDPrintToFile	Sets or returns the state of the Print to File check box.
cdlPDDisablePrintToFile	Disables the Print to File check box.
cdlPDHidePrintToFile	Hides the Print to File check box.
cdlPDCollate	Returns or sets the state of the Collate check box.
cdlPDReturnDefault	Returns the default printer's name.
cdlPDUseDevModeCopies	If the printer does not support multiple copies, setting this flag disables the Number of Copies spinner control in the Print dialog box. If the printer does support multiple copies, the requested number of copies is stored in the Copies property.
cdlPDHelpButton	Causes the Print Dialog box to show the Help button.
cdlPDPrintSetup	Causes the system to display the Print Setup dialog box instead of the Print dialog box.
cdlPDNoWarning	Disables the No Default Printer warning message.
cdlPDReturnIC	Returns an information context for the printer selection made in the dialog box. The information is returned in the dialog box's hDC property.
cdlPDReturnDC	Returns a device context for the printer selection made in the dialog box. The information is returned in the dialog box's hDC property. To use more than one flag, which is the usual case, OR together all the flags that you want to use.

The Print dialog box for SuperPad is called by selecting Print from the File menu. The code for mnuFilePrint is shown in Listing 9-8.

Listing 9-8 Bringing up the Print dialog box

```
Private Sub mnuFilePrint_Click()
Dim Cancel As Boolean
Dim Copy As Integer
On Error GoTo ErrorHandler
Cancel = False
CommonDialog1.Flags = cdlPDHidePrintToFile Or _
                      cdlPDNoSelection Or _
                      cdlPDNoPageNums Or _
                      cdlPDCollate
CommonDialog1.CancelError = True
CommonDialog1.PrinterDefault = True
CommonDialog1.Copies = 1
CommonDialog1.ShowPrinter
If Cancel = False Then
    'Add actual print routines here
    For Copy = 1 To CommonDialog1.Copies
        'PrintDocument
    Next Copy
End If
Exit Sub

ErrorHandler:
If Err.Number = cdlCancel Then
    Cancel = True
    Resume Next
End If
End Sub
```

The code in Listing 9-8 creates the Print dialog box shown in Figure 9-6.

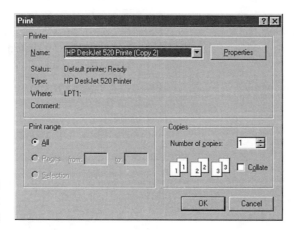

Figure 9-6
SuperPad's Print
dialog box

A Look at the Code

You can see the effects of the code in Figure 9-6. The code that sets the `Flag` property,

```
CommonDialog1.Flags = cdlPDHidePrintToFile Or _
                cdlPDNoSelection Or _
                cdlPDNoPageNums Or _
                cdlPDCollate
```

- Hides the Print to File check box

- Disables the Selection option button

- Disables the Pages option button and the edit boxes for it (Note that this automatically selects the All option button.)

- Enables the Collate check box

Multiple Copies

Rather than rely on the iffy proposition that Jane User's printer driver supports multiple copies, the flag `cdlPDUseDevModeCopies` is not used. Instead, the common dialog's `Copies` property is used in a `For...Next` loop to print the file `Copies` times.

Although most laser and inkjet printers support multiple copies, some of the current crop of dot-matrix printers do not. Because there is no way to be sure what kind of printer Jane User has, the `For...Next` loop offers multiple copies at the expense of speed. That is because each copy is a separate print job. If you use the `cdlPDUseDevModeCopies` flag and do not select Collate, printers that support multiple copies can make multiple copies as a part of the same print job, which is much faster. Printers that do not support multiple copies require that you open the Print dialog box for each copy you want.

Collating Copies

If the Collate check box is selected, each copy of a multipage document will be printed as a unit. For example, if you have a three-page document and print two copies with Collate checked, you will get pages 1,2,3 and pages 1,2,3. With Collate turned off, you would get pages 1,1,2,2,3,3. Collating copies is a great convenience, but it does slow the printing process because each copy becomes a separate print job. The overall job, especially for large documents, may still be faster because if the printer doesn't collate the pages, someone will have to do it by hand.

Print to File

With the Print to File option, you can send the printer output to a file on disk instead of to a printer. You can print the file at a later time. Note that if you later print the file to a different type of printer than the one selected during the Print to File operation, the page breaks and font spacing may be incorrect. The Print to File option is not enabled for SuperPad.

Selection and Pages Options

The Selection option and the Pages option are disabled in SuperPad. Enabling Selection allows you to print only selected text. Enabling Pages allows you to print a specified page or range of pages instead of the entire document. Many users consider these to be important options and you may wish to include them.

Printing

The Print dialog does not print your document. As you can see from the code in Listing 9-8, you are responsible for using the properties to format and control your print job. What the Common Dialog control does for you with the Print dialog box is provide you with a standard, professional user interface for collecting the print job's parameters. The common interface, the same one that most commercial programs use, gives your users a familiar and comfortable way to work with the printer.

1. Where do you change the printer's orientation from Portrait to Landscape?
   a. The Print dialog box
   b. The Print Setup dialog box
   c. The Properties dialog box of Print Setup
   d. It can be changed only by pushing a button on the printer.

2. Where do you change the paper size?
   a. The Print dialog box
   b. The Print Setup dialog box
   c. The Properties dialog box of Print Setup
   d. It can be changed only in code.

3. Where do you change the number of copies to be printed?
   a. The Print dialog box
   b. The Print Setup dialog box
   c. The Properties dialog box of Print Setup
   d. The printer can print only one copy.

4. The `cdlPDUseDevModeCopies` flag:
   a. Disables multiple copies for all printers
   b. Enables multiple copies for all printers
   c. Disables multiple copies for printers that do not have built-in copies support
   d. Creates multiple copies for printers that do not have built-in copies support

5. After the user clicks OK in the Print dialog box:
   a. The common dialog prints the desired materials.
   b. The common dialog prepares the print job, but your code must supply the **EndDoc** method.
   c. Your code must use the common dialog properties to prepare and execute the print job.
   d. Any one of the above, depending on the **Flags** property.

PRINTER CAPABILITIES

You're getting close to being able to write some practical print routines now. However, it's important that you understand something about the printer that your software is going to use and the dimensions of the paper that it is going to print on. You might wonder why this is necessary. After all, if the **Print** method simply sends text to the printer, isn't that enough to get on with, well, printing text? The fact is that, although the **Print** method is all you need to know about how to print text, you can make your software far more intelligent, and therefore produce more professional-looking reports and other printed output by determining the capabilities of the printer itself and taking the time to ensure that, for instance, the user isn't trying to print a report on envelopes.

Printer Driver

There are literally thousands of different makes and models of printers out there. You have no way of knowing in advance which printers the users of your software are going to have installed.

Windows uses a subprogram called a printer driver so that application software doesn't have to concern itself with the intricacies of each printer's software interface. For example, many printers expect to receive instructions of what to print coded in the Postscript printer language. Other printers use their own proprietary languages. Many dot-matrix printers use escape sequences instead of a defined language. The bottom line is that the actual sequence of instructions sent to each printer is different for each printer.

The printer driver translates your software's requests for print output into the low-level commands or character sequences needed to produce the desired effects.

The effect of the printer driver goes much further than this, however. You can also find out quite a lot of information about the capabilities of the printer by using a combination of **Printer** class programming and error handling, using the following **Printer** class properties:

- ColorMode
- Duplex
- Orientation
- PaperBin
- PaperSize
- PrintQuality

Each of these properties can be set to a range of different values, as described in the Visual Basic online Help. However, not all printers support the full range of settings. If you try to set, for example, the **Duplex** property to **vbPRDPVertical**, which indicates double-sided printing with a vertical page turn, on a printer that supports only one-sided printing, an error will occur. The error is code 380 (**Invalid property value**). The fact that an error occurs when you select an invalid property setting may seem inconvenient, but you can use this feature and trap the errors so that you can identify the capabilities of a particular printer.

Error handling is covered in detail in Chapter 10, Error Handling and Debugging. Listing 9-9 provides an example of how to implement this technique. It identifies the paper sizes the default printer supports. This code is on the CD that comes with this book as **Sizes.VBP**.

Listing 9-9 Checking supported paper sizes

```
Private Sub Form_Load()
Dim OldPaperSize As Integer
OldPaperSize = Printer.PaperSize 'Save original paper size
CheckPaperSizeSupported vbPRPSLetter
CheckPaperSizeSupported vbPRPSLetterSmall
CheckPaperSizeSupported vbPRPSTabloid
CheckPaperSizeSupported vbPRPSLedger
CheckPaperSizeSupported vbPRPSLegal
CheckPaperSizeSupported vbPRPSStatement
CheckPaperSizeSupported vbPRPSExecutive
CheckPaperSizeSupported vbPRPSA3
CheckPaperSizeSupported vbPRPSA4
CheckPaperSizeSupported vbPRPSA4Small
CheckPaperSizeSupported vbPRPSA5
CheckPaperSizeSupported vbPRPSB4
CheckPaperSizeSupported vbPRPSB5
CheckPaperSizeSupported vbPRPSFolio
CheckPaperSizeSupported vbPRPSQuarto
CheckPaperSizeSupported vbPRPS10x14
CheckPaperSizeSupported vbPRPS11x17
CheckPaperSizeSupported vbPRPSNote
CheckPaperSizeSupported vbPRPSEnv9
CheckPaperSizeSupported vbPRPSEnv10
CheckPaperSizeSupported vbPRPSEnv11
```

```
CheckPaperSizeSupported vbPRPSEnv12
CheckPaperSizeSupported vbPRPSEnv14
CheckPaperSizeSupported vbPRPSCSheet
CheckPaperSizeSupported vbPRPSDSheet
CheckPaperSizeSupported vbPRPSESheet
CheckPaperSizeSupported vbPRPSEnvDL
CheckPaperSizeSupported vbPRPSEnvC3
CheckPaperSizeSupported vbPRPSEnvC4
CheckPaperSizeSupported vbPRPSEnvC5
CheckPaperSizeSupported vbPRPSEnvC6
CheckPaperSizeSupported vbPRPSEnvC6
CheckPaperSizeSupported vbPRPSEnvB4
CheckPaperSizeSupported vbPRPSEnvB5
CheckPaperSizeSupported vbPRPSEnvB6
CheckPaperSizeSupported vbPRPSEnvItaly
CheckPaperSizeSupported vbPRPSEnvMonarch
CheckPaperSizeSupported vbPRPSEnvPersonal
CheckPaperSizeSupported vbPRPSFanfoldUS
CheckPaperSizeSupported vbPRPSFanfoldStdGerman
CheckPaperSizeSupported vbPRPSFanfoldLglGerman
Printer.PaperSize = OldPaperSize 'restore original paper size
End Sub

Private Sub CheckPaperSizeSupported(PaperSize As Integer)
Dim Supported As Boolean
On Error GoTo ErrorHandler
Supported = True
Printer.PaperSize = PaperSize
If Supported = True Then
    Debug.Print "This printer supports paper size: "; PaperSize
Else
    Debug.Print "This printer does not support paper size: "; PaperSize
End If
Exit Sub

ErrorHandler:
If Err.Number = 380 Then
    Supported = False
    Resume Next
End If
End Sub
```

The code in the **CheckPaperSizeSupported** procedure begins by initializing the **Boolean** variable **Supported** to **True**. The routine then tries to change the paper size. If the change is successful, **Supported** is still **True**. If the change triggers an invalid property error (code 380), the error routine sets **Supported** to **False**. If some other error occurs (which it shouldn't), this example ends the subroutine. In this example, the code prints out each printer constant and whether or not it is supported. It would be a simple exercise to rewrite the routine as a function that returns either **True** or **False**, and then the calling routine could decide what to do if the paper size isn't supported. Note that this code will work only when using the **Printer** variable. When accessed via the Printers collection, **Printer** object properties are read-only.

1. Windows' printer capabilities can make your software:
   a. Complex and unreliable
   b. Into a flight simulator
   c. Far more intelligent
   d. Into a duplex color mode orientation

2. You identify the paper size that the default printer supports with:
   a. `Printer.PaperSize`
   b. `CheckPrinterSizeSupport`
   c. `vbPRPSLetterSmall`
   d. `If Supported = True Then`

3. A simple way to send text to the printer is by using:
   a. `Printer.PaperBin`
   b. `Debug.Print`
   c. `Printer.Print`
   d. `Printer.PrintQuality`

4. To set double-sided printing with a vertical page orientation:
   a. Set the `Simplex` property to `vbVertical`
   b. Set the `Simplex` property to `OldPaperSize`
   c. Set the `Duplex` property to `vbPRPSFanfoldUS`
   d. Set the `Duplex` property to `vbPRDPVertical`

5. When printing under Windows, the VB programmer needs to be aware of:
   a. Literally thousands of different makes and models of printers
   b. Visual Basic printing methods
   c. Postscript language instructions
   d. How to write a printer driver

REVIEW

John: We've been using the `Print` method all along. It's the same way we send output to the Debug window.

Lisa: Printing text seems to be pretty straightforward. I think I'll need to learn more about the graphics methods before I'm comfortable printing out graphics, though.

John: That won't be until Chapter 10, Error Handling and Debugging. It's good to have a preview of the coordinate system, though. I have a feeling that will be pretty important.

Lisa: Do we use the same `ScaleWidth` and `ScaleHeight` properties to position text on the screen?

John: I don't think so. We'll be using `CurrentX` and `CurrentY` instead. But you can still put what you learned about the page's coordinate system to use in working with those properties.

Lisa: I'm not surprised. It was good to see how to implement the Print Setup and Print dialog boxes. Of course, by now we probably could have figured it out. What is coming up later in the chapter?

John: Text printing, printing reports, and the `Format` function, which gives you control over how your variables are output, both on the screen and on the printer.

COMBINING TEXT AND GRAPHICS

Although Visual Basic's graphics methods are covered more fully in Chapter 10, this lesson demonstrates how to add certain graphics features to your printed output. The basic principles outlined in this lesson can be combined with the more advanced features of Chapter 10 to create elaborate printed forms.

The Virtual Page

When you print from a Visual Basic program, you are actually printing to a *virtual page*, a page that exists only in the computer's memory. The physical page does not get printed until you use the `EndDoc` method to send the print job to the printer. Once you grasp this idea, you can change the way you think about printing. The concept that printing begins at the top-left corner of a page and continues in sequential order to the bottom-right corner no longer needs to limit the way you handle your print jobs. Right up to the moment of `Printer.EndDoc`, you can "print" anything you want, anywhere at all on the page!

The Coordinate System

The key to locating printed items on the page is the coordinate system. If you have ever played MineSweeper or located a street on a map of your city, you already understand the coordinate system. The Visual Basic coordinate system for your virtual page sets the origin, that is, the starting point, at the top-left corner of the page. This is the point where X = 0 and Y = 0. (X is the horizontal location and Y is the vertical location)

CurrentX *and* CurrentY

Visual Basic keeps track of the next print location in two variables. The exact location of the next thing to be printed is at `Printer.CurrentX` and `Printer.CurrentY`. You can read this information with your code. Better yet, you can change `CurrentX` and `CurrentY` to move your text and graphics to any point on the virtual page.

ScaleMode

The default measuring system for Visual Basic is *twips*. A twip is 1/20 of a point. (Points are typesetters' measurements. A point is 1/72 of an inch.) There are 1,444 twips in an inch, which allows incredibly precise positioning for your output—much more precise, in fact, than you probably need.

Measuring in twips means that you have to calculate positions in twips. If you want something at 1.25 inches from the left edge of the page, for example, you would need to calculate the position as `Printer.CurrentX = 1.25 * 1444`. No, it isn't hard, but it is extra code and extra work. This is where `ScaleMode` comes into play. You can change the measurements to points, pixels, characters, inches, millimeters, or centimeters. You can even create your own measurement system! Table 9-5 lists the available `ScaleMode` values.

Table 9-5 The `ScaleMode` property

Constant	Meaning
0	User-defined
1	Twips
2	Point
3	Pixel
4	Character
5	Inch
6	Millimeter
7	Centimeter

You can set the `ScaleMode` property for forms and objects on forms in the Properties window, but you must set it with code for the `Printer` object. Try the code in Listing 9-10.

Listing 9-10 Using the `ScaleMode` property

```
Private Sub Form_Load()
    Printer.ScaleMode = 5
    Printer.CurrentX = 1
    Printer.CurrentY = 1
    Printer.Line -(2, 1)
    Printer.EndDoc
End Sub
```

This code starts by setting the printer's `ScaleMode` property to 5, for inches. It then sets the next print position at one inch from the left edge of the page and one inch from the top of the page, and uses the `Line` method to draw a one-inch-long horizontal line. (The `Line` method is covered in more detail later in this lesson.) Try it out and measure the line's length and position on the page.

Hmmm. What happened? If your printer is typical, the line is one inch long, all right, but it isn't in the right place, because most printers can't start printing right at the edge of the paper.

ScaleWidth *and* ScaleHeight

The ScaleWidth and ScaleHeight properties are the *useable* dimensions of your page. Try the code below:

```
Private Sub Form_Load()
    Printer.ScaleMode = 5
    Debug.Print Printer.ScaleWidth
    Debug.Print Printer.ScaleHeight
    End
End Sub
```

With the HP 520 printer, this code displays

```
8
10
```

in the Debug window. You know you have 8 1/2 × 11-inch paper in the printer, but the printable width is 8 inches and the printable height is 10 inches. The difference is the built-in printer margins, that part of the page that the printer cannot use. Change the code from Listing 9-10 to that of Listing 9-11 (changes are in bold).

Listing 9-11 Improved code for drawing a line

```
Option Explicit
Public dXOffSet As Double
Public dYOffSet As Double

Private Sub Form_Load()
    Printer.ScaleMode = 5
    dXOffSet = (Printer.Width / 1444 - Printer.ScaleWidth) / 2
    dYOffSet = (Printer.Height / 1444 - Printer.ScaleHeight) / 2
    Printer.CurrentX = 1 - dXOffSet
    Printer.CurrentY = 1 - dYOffSet
    Printer.Line -(Printer.Currentx + 1, Printer.Currenty)
    Printer.EndDoc
End Sub
```

Run this program and again measure the line's position and length. The line's length, of course, didn't change. The position from the left of the page is now correct, but the position from the top is *still* incorrect! Take a look at the code, in particular the assumptions that it makes.

The two public variables, dXOffSet and dYOffSet, are calculated to be half the difference between the page's actual size and the ScaleWidth and ScaleHeight sizes. (Note that the values of Printer.Width and Printer.Height are still in twips, which is why they are divided by 1,444.) The assumption is that the printer divides that difference equally, which is true for width but apparently false for height.

In fact, most printers need a little more margin on the bottom to grip the paper while it prints. Hewlett-Packard's manual says that the top margin is 0.4 inches, but experimental data shows that even that is incorrect. Change `Printer.CurrentY = 1 - dYOffSet` to `Printer.CurrentY = 0` and run the program again. The line will be printed at the top edge of the printable page. If you measure the distance from the top edge, you now have the Y margin offset for your printer. (On the HP 520, that distance is 5/16 of an inch.)

The problem with this, of course, is that you have no idea what printer the user will be using. If you write all your code based on *your* printer's Y margin offset, your measurements will be wrong more often than not. There is no absolute solution. You could provide your users with a setup section in your code that would save their Y margin offset to the system registry, which is probably the only way to get precision printing. (Using the system registry is covered in Chapter 17, Register Your Programs—Using the Windows Registry.) Fortunately, you rarely have to go to this extreme because most of your print jobs can use less precise vertical positioning. The idea is to get the text and graphics to print correctly relative to each other rather than relative to the top edge of the page.

The Line Method

The most common requirement for mixing text and graphics calls for text to be placed either just above a line or inside a box. Both requirements use the same method, the `Line` method. The correct syntax for the `Line` method is

```
object.Line Step (x1, 1) Step (x2, y2), color, BF
```

where

- ● `object` is an optional expression that evaluates to a form, the `Printer` object, or a picture box. If `object` is omitted, the form with the focus is assumed to be `object`.

- ● `Step` is an optional keyword specifying that the starting point coordinates are relative to the current graphics position given by the `CurrentX` and `CurrentY` properties.

- ● `(x1, y1)` are optional single values indicating the coordinates of the starting point for the line or rectangle. The `ScaleMode` property determines the unit of measure used. If omitted, the line begins at the position indicated by `CurrentX` and `CurrentY`.

- ● `Step` is an optional keyword specifying that the end-point coordinates are relative to the line starting point.

- (x2, y2) are required single values indicating the coordinates of the end point for the line being drawn.

- color is an optional long integer value indicating the RGB color used to draw the line. If color is omitted, the ForeColor property setting is used. You can use the RGB function or QBColor function to specify the color.

- B is an optional parameter. If it is included, it causes a box to be drawn using the coordinates to specify opposite corners of the box.

- F is an optional parameter. If the B option is used, the F option specifies that the box is filled with the same color used to draw the box. You cannot use F without B. If B is used without F, the box is filled with the current FillColor and FillStyle. The default value for FillStyle is transparent.

For output to the printer, the two most common implementations of the **Line** method are shown in Listing 9-12. The code is available as **Lines.VBP** on the CD that comes with this book.

Listing 9-12 Using the Line method with the printer

```
Option Explicit
Public dXOffSet As Double
Public dYOffSet As Double

Private Sub Form_Load()
    Printer.ScaleMode = 5
    dXOffSet = (Printer.Width / 1444 - Printer.ScaleWidth) / 2
    dYOffSet = 5 / 16
    Printer.CurrentX = 1 - dXOffSet
    Printer.CurrentY = 1 - dYOffSet
    Printer.Line -(Printer.CurrentX + 2, Printer.CurrentY)
    Printer.CurrentX = 1 - dXOffSet + 1 / 16
    Printer.CurrentY = Printer.CurrentY - _
        Printer.TextHeight("I")
    Printer.Print "Atop the Line"
    Printer.CurrentX = 1 - dXOffSet
    Printer.CurrentY = 2 - dYOffSet
    Printer.Line -(Printer.CurrentX + 2, _
        Printer.CurrentY + 5 / 16), , B
    Printer.CurrentX = 1 - dXOffSet + 1 / 16
    Printer.CurrentY = Printer.CurrentY - _
        Printer.TextHeight("I")
    Printer.Print "Inside the Box"
    Printer.EndDoc
    End
End Sub
```

A Look at the Lines Program Code

Note that the variable `dYOffSet` is set here for the HP 520 printer. You can adjust it to suit your own printer. There are a couple of new ideas in the code, and two practical uses of the `Line` method.

The line `Printer.Line`

```
(Printer.CurrentX + 2, Printer.CurrentY)
```

draws a two-inch horizontal line. Because the `Line` method changes `CurrentX` and `CurrentY` to the end point of the line that it draws, the following line in the code

```
Printer.CurrentX = 1 - dXOffSet + 1 / 16
```

resets `CurrentX`. Note that it adds 1/16 of an inch to the original `CurrentX` so that the text will begin slightly inset from the start of the line. The tricky part of the code comes next. The `CurrentY` property for text is *the top of the text*. To print text on top of the line, you must move the `CurrentY` position above the line by the height of the characters. Rather than use a constant for this—a technique that fails when the font size changes—the code uses another property of the `Printer` object, the `TextHeight` property.

```
Printer.CurrentY = Printer.CurrentY - Printer.TextHeight("I")
```

`Printer.TextHeight("I")` returns the height of the tallest letter in the font. The code line subtracts that from the existing `CurrentY` to position the text above the line.

Drawing a box on the screen uses more of the parameters of the `Line` method. The code

```
Printer.Line -(Printer.CurrentX + 2, Printer.CurrentY + 5 / 16), , B
```

starts at the printer's current X and Y positions and draws a two-inch box that is 5/16 of an inch high. Note the `, , B` at the end of the line. It is required because the code leaves out the `color` parameter, which precedes the `B` in the syntax of the `Line` method. The following code sets the printer's `CurrentX` and `CurrentY` parameters to position the text inside the box.

To position text inside a box, you must draw the box first. If you do it the other way, the box will cover the text.

Summary

These techniques enable you to reproduce fill-in forms with Visual Basic 5. With care and attention to detail, you can reproduce them almost exactly. Chapter 10, Error Handling and Debugging, shows how to add other graphics, including company logos, to the virtual page.

QUIZ

1. To change the printer's measurements to inches, use the line:
   a. `Printer.ScaleMode = 0`
   b. `Printer.ScaleMode = 2`
   c. `Printer.ScaleMode = 5`
   d. `Printer.ScaleMode = 6`

2. The parameter `Printer.CurrentX` represents:
   a. The next print position relative to the left edge of the page
   b. The next print position relative to the left edge of the printable area
   c. The next print position relative to the top edge of the page
   d. The next print position relative to the top edge of the printable area

3. The code `Printer.Line - (CurrentX + 2, CurrentY)` draws:
   a. A box
   b. A vertical line
   c. A horizontal line
   d. Nothing, because no color is specified

4. When printing text, the `Print` method places the text:
   a. Above the `CurrentY` position
   b. Below the `CurrentY` position
   c. Centered on the `CurrentY` position
   d. None of the above

5. To place text in a box:
   a. You can print the text and the box in any order.
   b. You must print the text first.
   c. You must print the box first.
   d. You must print the box with a color of 0 to make the background transparent.

PRINTING REPORTS FROM VISUAL BASIC

In this lesson, we will concentrate on the type of issues that arise specifically when printing reports. Everything that you have learned so far about printing from Visual Basic still applies. However, some additional techniques will help you print better-looking reports than you might be able to achieve otherwise.

Printing Headers and Footers

Headers and footers often appear in printed reports. Typically, the sort of information that you might include in a header would be:

- Report title
- Date and time
- Column headings (if you are printing a tabular report)

Typical footers may include

- Date and time
- Author
- Page number

Whatever you decide to include in your report headers, the first thing you need to determine is how to structure the report programming so that you can detect when the report needs to print a header. The best way to do this is to write a subroutine that does some basic checking on the CurrentY property before anything is printed. For example, Listing 9-13 checks to see if CurrentY is within an inch of the bottom of the printed page. If it is, then a footer is printed. Once the footer has been printed, it's then necessary to check if the CurrentY is at the top of page, which it will be because you will have advanced to the next page after the footer was printed. In this case, the header is printed. You can put what you like into the subroutines to print the headers and footers, but we have provided you with some simple routines to get you going. The code is on the CD as HeadFoot.VBP.

Listing 9-13 Routines to print headers and footers

```
Private Sub CheckHeaderAndFooter()
If Printer.CurrentY + 1440 > Printer.ScaleHeight Then
    PrintFooter
End If
If Printer.CurrentY = 0 Then
    PrintHeader
End If
End Sub

Private Sub PrintFooter()
Dim Footer As String
' setup the font for the footer
Printer.Print ;
Printer.Font.Name = "Arial"
Printer.Font.Size = 10
Printer.Font.Bold = False
Printer.Font.Italic = False
Printer.Font.Strikethrough = False
```

```
Printer.Font.Underline = False
'Create the text to be printed
Footer = "Page - " & CStr(Printer.Page)
'Print the footer in the center of the page, three quarters of an inch
'from the bottom of the page
Printer.CurrentX = (Printer.ScaleWidth - Printer.TextWidth(Footer)) / 2
Printer.CurrentY = Printer.ScaleHeight - 1080
Printer.Print Footer
'Print a Line across the page, one inch from the bottom
Printer.Line (0, Printer.ScaleHeight - 1440)-(Printer.ScaleWidth, Printer.ScaleHeight⇐
- 1440)
'Advance to the next page
Printer.NewPage
End Sub

Private Sub PrintHeader()
Dim Header As String
'Set the font for the header
Printer.Font.Name = "Arial"
Printer.Font.Size = 10
Printer.Font.Bold = False
Printer.Font.Italic = False
Printer.Font.Strikethrough = False
Printer.Font.Underline = False
'Set the text to be printed
Header = "My application"
'Print the text at the top of the page, in the center
Printer.CurrentX = (Printer.ScaleWidth - Printer.TextWidth(Title)) / 2
Printer.CurrentY = 0
Printer.Print Header
'Print a Line one inch down the page
Printer.Line (0, 1440)-(Printer.ScaleWidth, 1440)
'Set the CurrentX and Y up ready for printing the text to go on this page
Printer.CurrentX = 0
Printer.CurrentY = 1800 '1 and a quarter inches down the page
End Sub
```

Detecting the End of the Page

In Listing 9-13, you need to detect the end of the page about one inch prior to getting there. That's why `CheckHeaderAndFooter` checks that there is at least one inch left. Of course, the `CurrentY` value is being tested before any printing actually gets done, so you are assured of trapping this condition before it's too late.

If you are about to print into the area that is defined as the footer margin, the program prints the footer. The subroutine that prints the footer makes sure that the end of the page is marked by calling the `NewPage` method. This will cause the printer to throw a new page and move `CurrentX` and `CurrentY` back to `0`.

Finally, the header print subroutine ensures that the `CurrentX` value is reset to `0` (the left of the page) and that `CurrentY` is left at a position below the header. If it didn't do this, the text would end up printing in the space allocated to the header.

1. When printing headers and footers:
   a. Use `Printer.SectionMode = vbPRNTExtra`
   b. Use the same print methods you've learned in previous lessons to output the header/footer information.
   c. It's necessary to adjust the virtual page height to exclude the header (and footer).
   d. All of the above

2. Typically, the sort of information you might include in a header would include:
   a. Report title
   b. Date and time
   c. Column headings
   d. All of the above

3. To check whether you need to print a header or a footer:
   a. Look at the value of `Printer.SectionMode`
   b. Interactively query the user
   c. Check the specifications in your printer manual for the dimensions of the printable section of the page
   d. Look at the value of `Printer.CurrentY`

4. A twip is approximately:
   a. 1/1440th of an inch
   b. 11 1/2 inches
   c. 2 millimeters
   d. None of the above

5. `Printer.NewPage` serves the following function:
   a. Erases the current virtual page without printing it
   b. Forces the print job to be sent to the printer
   c. Advances to the next page
   d. Returns `True` if the print head is at the end of a page

FORMATTING NUMERIC OUTPUT

This lesson and the next explore the `Format` function. This versatile function converts and formats dates, numbers, strings—anything you like. Unlike some of the other formatting functions provided by Visual Basic (such as `Str` and `Val`), `Format` gives you a much greater degree of control over how your data is presented. You can choose from `Format`'s predefined named formats, such as `Currency` or `Fixed`, or insist on finer control by creating your own user-defined format.

The `Format` function returns a string, which you can use for either screen or printer output. This lesson covers `Format`'s options for numeric formatting; Lesson 8 covers date formatting.

The `Format` **Function**

The syntax for `Format` is

```
Format(Expression [, Format [, FirstDayOfWeek [, FirstWeekOfYear]]])
```

The `Format` function always returns a `String` data type. The idea is that you are formatting one of the built-in data types and producing a string formatted in a particular way.

Let's look at each data type in turn that can be formatted using `Format`.

Numeric Formatting

Numbers (whatever their type: integers, longs, singles, doubles, or currencies) can be formatted using the `Format` function. The simplest way to use `Format` is to provide the numeric expression without providing any formatting characters in the second parameter.

For example:

```
Private Sub Form_Load()
Dim MyInteger As Integer
MyInteger = 5
Debug.Print Format(MyInteger)
Debug.Print Str(MyInteger)
End Sub
```

This code outputs

```
5
 5
```

Note that both functions return a number formatted as a string. However, positive values formatted by `Format` do not have a leading space. The `Str` version has an extra space at the beginning. (Recall that this space is the position that would be occupied by a minus sign if the number were negative.)

Named Numeric Formats

One of `Format`'s predefined numeric formats may suffice for your needs. `Format` makes nine different named numeric formats available. These are summarized in Table 9-6.

Table 9-6 Named numeric formats

Format Name	Description
General number	Displays the number without any thousands separators.
Currency	Displays the number depending on the settings for currency formatting currently configured in the control panel.
Fixed	Displays a minimum of one digit to the left and two to the right of the decimal place.
Standard	The same as fixed, except that the number is also formatted with thousands separators.
Percent	Displays the number as a percentage by multiplying it by 100 first. The number is always displayed with two digits to the right of the decimal point and with the trailing % sign.
Scientific	Uses standard scientific notation.
Yes/No	Displays No if the number is zero; otherwise displays Yes.
True/False	Displays False if the number is zero; otherwise displays True.
On/Off	Displays Off if the number is zero; otherwise displays On.

Try out these predefined formats. Enter the example in Listing 9-14. The code is available on the CD that accompanies this book as **Format1.VBP**.

Listing 9-14 The named formats

```
Private Sub Form_Load()
Dim MyInteger As Integer
Dim MySingle As Single
MyInteger = 12345
MySingle = 1.54321E-2
Debug.Print Format(MyInteger, "General Number")
Debug.Print Format(MyInteger, "Currency")
Debug.Print Format(MyInteger, "Fixed")
Debug.Print Format(MyInteger, "Standard")
Debug.Print Format(MySingle, "Percent")
Debug.Print Format(MySingle, "Scientific")
Debug.Print Format(False, "Yes/No")
Debug.Print Format(50, "True/False")
Debug.Print Format(True, "On/Off")
End Sub
```

This code produces the following output:

```
12345
$12,345.00
12345.00
```

```
12,345.00
1.54%
1.54E-02
No
True
On
```

As you can see, these predefined named formats are extremely useful and may suffice for your needs when it comes to formatting numbers for display.

User-Defined Numeric Formats

There are occasions, however, when these named formats will not suffice and you require more control over your number formats. In these situations, you may use a combination of a series of special formatting characters to control exactly how the `Format` function formats your numbers. These formatting characters are summarized in Table 9-7.

Table 9-7 Characters for user-defined formatting

Character	Name	Description
0	Digit placeholder	Forces `Format` to display a zero or a digit if the number passed contains a digit in that position. If the number passed contains more digits to the right of the decimal point than are specified in the format string, the number is rounded to as many decimal places as there are 0s in the format string.
#	Digit placeholder	Works in a similar way to 0 except that if the number does not contain a digit in the position specified by the format string, `Format` will display nothing in that character position.
.	Decimal point position	Fixes the position of the decimal point. Depending on your locale settings, `Format` may display a comma instead of a decimal point.
%	Percentage	The number passed to `Format` is multiplied by 100 and the % sign is displayed at the position given in the format string.

continued on next page

continued from previous page

Character	Name	Description
,	Thousands separator	If the number is large enough to extend to the left of the decimal point past the position of this character in the format string, a comma will be displayed as a thousands separator. The actual character displayed as the thousands separator depends on your locale settings in the control panel. In some locales a decimal point is displayed instead of a comma.
E-, E+, e-, e+	Scientific	Causes Format to display the number in scientific format. The use of lowercase or uppercase E determines whether the exponent character will be displayed with a lower- or uppercase E. The – sign indicates that numbers with a negative exponent will be displayed with a negative sign next to the exponent. Numbers with a positive exponent will be displayed with a space. The + sign indicates that numbers displayed with a positive exponent will be displayed with a plus sign next to the exponent.
\	Literal character display	To display a literal character, just precede it with a \ (backslash).

For example, type in Listing 9-15. The code is available on the CD as `Format2.VBP`.

Listing 9-15 User-defined formats

```
Private Sub Form_Load()
Dim MySingle As Single
Dim MyInteger As Integer
Dim MyCurrency As Currency
MySingle = 0.23
MyInteger = 123
MyCurrency = 123456.78
Debug.Print Format(MyInteger, "00000")
```

```
Debug.Print Format(MyInteger, "#####")
Debug.Print Format(MySingle, "###%")
Debug.Print Format(MyCurrency, "###,###,##0.00")
Debug.Print Format(0, "###,###,##0.00")
Debug.Print Format(MyCurrency, "\$###,###,##0.00")
End Sub
```

This code outputs

```
00123
123
23%
123,456.78
0.00
$123,456.78
```

Note the backslash in Listing 9-15. It allows the computer to interpret the next character literally instead of as a format character.

As you can see, the range of options is extremely flexible. Experiment with the **Format** function yourself with the numeric formatting characters so that you are satisfied that you understand how they can be used.

1. The **Format** function:
    a. Is used to initialize the virtual page
    b. Always returns a number
    c. Provides less control than the **Str** function
    d. Provides a great degree of control over how your data is presented

2. Which of the following types of numbers can be used with the **Format** function?
    a. Integer
    b. Currency
    c. Single
    d. All of the above

3. Which of the following is *not* a named numeric format?
    a. Yes/No
    b. Percent
    c. Dollars
    d. Standard

4. What is the output of the following code?
    ```
    Debug.Print Format(1.02,"True/False")
    ```
    a. **True**
    b. **1.02**
    c. **1**
    d. **<1>**

5. What is the output of the following code?

```
Debug.Print Format(123.45,"###,###%")
```

   a. 012,345
   b. 12,345%
   c. 123.45%
   d. 123%

FORMATTING DATES FOR OUTPUT

The **Format** function has a number of predefined formats for displaying dates and times as well as numbers.

Named Date Formats

The named date formats are summarized in Table 9-8.

Table 9-8 The named date formats

Format Name	Description
General Date	This is the most flexible date/time format. If the Date expression passed has only an integer portion, only the date is displayed. Similarly, if it has only a decimal portion, only the time is displayed. The format of the date and time displayed depends on your system's locale settings.
Long Date	This format will display a date in the format specified by your system locale's long date setting.
Medium Date	This format will display a date in the format specified by your system locale's medium date setting.
Short Date	This format will display a date in the format specified by your system's short date setting.
Long Time	This format will display a time only in your system locale's long time format.
Medium Time	This format displays the time in 12-hour format using only hours and minutes and the AM/PM indicator.
Short Time	This format displays the time in 24-hour format.

Try the examples in Listing 9-16 to see how these formats work. You could even try changing your locale settings in the control panel to see how this affects the displayed dates and times. The code is available on the CD as `Format`.

Listing 9-16 Named date format examples

```
Private Sub Form_Load()
Debug.Print Format(Now, "General Date")
Debug.Print Format(Now, "Long Date")
Debug.Print Format(Now, "Medium Date")
Debug.Print Format(Now, "Short Date")
Debug.Print Format(Now, "Long Time")
Debug.Print Format(Now, "Medium Time")
Debug.Print Format(Now, "Short Time")
End Sub
```

The output on your system is

```
3/12/96 9:52:04 AM
Tuesday, March 12, 1996
12-Mar-96
3/12/96
9:52:04 AM
09:52 AM
09:52
```

User-Defined Date/Time Formatting Characters

If one of the above built-in formatting types is insufficient for your needs, `Format` has a range of date and time formatting characters that you can use to build up your own date and time formats. These are summarized in Table 9-9.

Table 9-9 Characters for user-defined date formatting

Character	Description
:	Time separator.
/	Date separator.
c	Displays date and time information only.
d	Displays the day of the month as a number (1-31).
dd	Displays the day of the month with a leading zero (01-31).
ddd	Displays the day of the week as an abbreviated name (Sun-Sat).
dddd	Displays the day of the week as a full name (Sunday-Saturday).

continued on next page

continued from previous page

Character	Description
ddddd	Displays the date according to your locale's short date settings.
dddddd	Displays the date according to your locale's long date settings.
w	Displays the day of the week as a number (1-7), starting at the day specified in FirstDayOfWeek (defaults to Sunday).
ww	Displays a number representing the week of the year (1-53).
m	Displays the month as a number without a leading zero (1-12). If m immediately follows h or hh, Format displays the minute rather than the month.
mm	Displays the month as a number with a leading zero (01-12). If m immediately follows h or hh, Format displays the minute rather than the month.
mmm	Displays the abbreviated name of the month (Jan-Dec).
mmmm	Displays the full name of the month (January-December).
q	Displays the quarter of the year as a number (1-4).
y	Displays the day of the year as a number (1-366).
yy	Displays the year as a two-digit number (00-99).
yyyy	Displays the year as a four-digit number (100-9999).
h	Displays the hour as a number without leading zeros (0-23).
hh	Displays the hour as a number with leading zeros (00-23).
n	Displays the minute as a number without leading zeros (059).
nn	Displays the minute as a number with leading zeros (00-59).
s	Displays the second as a number without leading zeros (059).
ss	Displays the second as a number with leading zeros (00-59).
ttttt	Displays a complete time depending on your system's locale settings.
AM/PM	Displays the time in 12-hour format, using the text AM or PM.
am/pm	Displays the time in 12-hour format, using the text am or pm.
A/P	Displays the time in 12-hour format, using the text A or P.
a/p	Displays the time in 12-hour format, using the text a or p.
AMPM	Displays the time in 12-hour format, using your locale's AM or PM text setting.

The range of different formats available is quite broad, but Listing 9-17 gives you some examples to get you going. The code is on the CD as `Format4.VBP`.

Listing 9-17 User-defined date format examples

```
Private Sub Form_Load()
Debug.Print Format(Now, "dddd  d mmmm yyyy")
Debug.Print Format(Now, "AM/PM")
Debug.Print Format(Now, "hh:mm:ss")
Debug.Print Format(Now, "ttttt")
End Sub
```

The output of this program, of course, depends on the current date and time. It will look something like the following:

```
Tuesday  12 March 1996
AM
09:58:41
9:58:41 AM
```

Experiment some more yourself with these settings.

1. How can you display the current time in the format `hh:mm:ss`?
   a. `Debug.Print Format(Now, "hh:mm:ss")`
   b. `Debug.Print Format(Now, "Short Time")`
   c. `Debug.Print Format(Now, "Medium Time")`
   d. `Debug.Print Now`

2. What is the output from the following program?

   ```
   Dim SomeDate As Date
   SomeDate = "Dec 31, 1999"
   Debug.Print Format(SomeDate, "Short Date")
   ```

   a. The last day of 1999 in a short format, suitable for the country and control panel settings
   b. `12/31/99`
   c. `12-31-99`
   d. `99DEC31`

3. Which code fragment displays the current day of the week?
   a. `Debug.Print Format(Now,"Weekday")`
   b. `Debug.Print Format(Now,"dddd")`
   c. `Debug.Print Format(Weekday)`
   d. None of the above

4. Assume the following declaration:

```
Dim LastDay As Date
LastDay = "Dec 31 1999 23:59:59"
```

How would you format this date to produce the following output?

`23:59:59 12/31/1999`

a. `Format(LastDay,"Long Date")`
b. `Format(Lastday,"hh:mm:ss mm/dd/yyyy")`
c. `Format(LastDay,"q")`
d. `Format(LastDay,"hh:mm:ss mm/dd/yy")`

5. Using the same variable as in question 4, how would you format the following date output?

`1999:12:31:23:59:59`

a. `Format(LastDay,"Condensed")`
b. `Format(LastDay,"yyyy:mm:dd:hh:mm:ss")`
c. `Format(LastDay,"General Date")`
d. `Format(LastDay,"Short Date:Short Time")`

Implement print functionality in SuperPad. Include a footer with the date, centered, in the format December 31, 1999.

CHAPTER 10

ERROR HANDLING AND DEBUGGING

LESSON 1

ERRORS IN VISUAL BASIC 5 PROGRAMS

Errors? There are *errors* in my program? Impossible! Unfortunately, errors creep (sometimes gallop!) into programs. Often they show up where you least expect them, in that really simple piece of code. This chapter explains what kinds of errors there are, how to deal with them, and how to avoid them. Noble goals indeed.

Types of Errors

It may seem like there are more, but only three kinds of errors show up in Visual Basic programs.

Syntax Errors

They can be *very* taxing, but syntax errors are not taxes. *Syntax* is defined as the rules for making meaningful phrases out of words. In programming, it's pretty much the same thing. As clever as your computer may seem, it has a rigid set of rules about how and when things must be done. You can violate syntax in speech or writing and still convey some meaning, but your computer won't even try to understand you if you key something in incorrectly.

First, deliberately create a few syntax errors so you can get an idea of what they are and how Visual Basic 5 responds to them. Start a new project and enter the following code in the **Form_Load** event:

```
Private Sub Form_Load()
Dim i As Integer

If i = 0

End Sub
```

It's hard to miss Visual Basic's reaction when you hit ENTER after that zero! The message box jumps right out and tells you all about it: **Compile Error: Expected: Then or GoTo**. Just to make sure you know *where* your problem is, it even paints the line red! The error, of course, is that **If** requires either **Then** or **GoTo** in order to make sense.

Now delete the offending line and put a Command button on your form. Put the following code in the **Click** event:

```
Private Sub Command1_Click()
Dim i As Integer
For i = 1 To 3

Debug.Print i
End Sub
```

Run the program and click on the Command1 button. The **For...Next** loop is incomplete without the **Next**. Visual Basic can't detect this one as easily because **Next** is not expected to be on the same line as **For**.

You can generate hundreds of syntax errors like these. Ideally, you will never forget a **Then** or a **Next**, but until you are perfect, just grin and bear it. Your program won't make it out the door with syntax errors, and you are the only one who knows about them.

Runtime Errors

Runtime errors are more insidious; they may or may not show up the first time you click on Run. Runtime errors are errors that appear only when you run your program, and often only when a certain sequence of events takes place. Change the code in the **Click** event of Command1 to the following:

```
Private Sub Command1_Click()

Dim A As String, B As Integer
A = "a"
B = A

End Sub
```

Now what happens when you click on the Command1 button? This runtime error does not appear until you click that button, but it shows up the first time you do. Replace that code with the following for a less obvious runtime error:

```
Private Sub Command1_Click()

Dim i As Integer, j As Integer
j = 6
For i = 6 To 0 Step -1

Debug.Print j / i
Next

End Sub
```

This code actually runs—for a while. You probably would never write this code into a program because you know that division by zero is not allowed. And that is exactly what happens when the loop steps down to zero. What is probable, though, is that a variable you *expect* to be nonzero somehow *becomes* zero. It can happen. Worse yet, it can happen months after you release the program to your customer. When it happens in a running program, outside the development environment, the program displays a message box and then shuts down with no chance for recovery.

Obviously, runtime errors are dangerous to your well-being. Most of this chapter is about how to deal with them.

Logic Errors

Some runtime errors, including the examples above, are caused by *logic errors*, which are really *thinking* errors. A thinking Visual Basic programmer, for example, would not attempt to assign a string value to an integer. (It is legal in C and C++, but that's a different book.) Having a variable unexpectedly become zero is a bit different; even the best programmers can't anticipate everything that might happen.

Logic errors do not necessarily cause runtime errors. Sometimes a logic error may "just" cause data corruption or generate incorrect results. The only way to avoid logic errors is to plan your program carefully before you begin writing code.

How Visual Basic 5 Helps You Avoid Errors

Microsoft added several new features to Visual Basic 5 that can help you avoid the most common errors. Take a look at them before you move on. Click on the Tools menu and select Options. The five check boxes on the left of the Code Settings frame help you detect and prevent errors in your code. Figure 10-1 shows the Editor tab with all five of the check boxes selected.

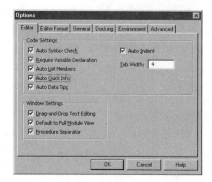

Figure 10-1
The Code Settings
options

Auto Syntax Check

The automatic syntax check is on by default. It was the syntax checker that warned you about the missing **Then** in the first example in this chapter. The only mystery about automatic syntax checking is why Visual Basic lets you turn it off. In a word, don't.

Require Variable Declaration

One of the most common sources of runtime errors is mistyped variable names. For example, you may have something like the following:

```
Private Sub Form_Load()

Dim iNumber As Integer
iNumber = 47
Debug.Print iNmber

End Sub
```

With Require Variable Declaration disabled, this code runs just fine, but **iNmber** shows as zero in the Immediate window. That is, after all, the value of **iNumber** because it was never declared.

If Require Variable Declaration is disabled in your Code Settings frame, enable it now. That simple option places Option Explicit in the General Declarations section of every part of your program. That requires that all variables must be declared, and it detects typing errors like this. With Option Explicit enabled, Visual Basic 5 provides you with a warning, as shown in Figure 10-2.

Figure 10-2
The error message
for undefined
variables

Auto List Members

The Auto List Members option tells Visual Basic to help you complete a statement as you are writing it. If the feature is disabled in your IDE, enable it and enter the following code:

```
Private Sub Form_Load()

Dim iNumber As

End Sub
```

As soon as you press the space bar after **As**, you see the drop-down list shown in Figure 10-3.

As you continue typing, the word **Integer** appears in the drop-down menu. Press (ENTER) when the integer is highlighted, and VB 5 completes the statement for you.

You might or might not consider Auto List Members a desirable feature. You have to wait a moment before the drop-down box appears, which may be an annoyance. On the other hand, this feature reduces the number of errors your typing skills inject into your program, which is, of course, a benefit. Remember that you can always change the setting.

Auto Quick Info

Quick Info provides you with a pop-up box that tells you the correct syntax for any function you use in your code. Visual Basic 5 is loaded with functions you can call. Even as brilliant as you are, it is not likely that you will remember the correct syntax for all of them. Figure 10-4 shows the Quick Info popup.

Like Auto List Members, Auto Quick Info adds a brief delay to your programming. You may prefer to bring up Quick Info only when you really need it; it is always only a keystroke away. You can view Quick Info by pressing (CTRL)-(I) while the cursor is on the function name.

Auto Data Tips

The Auto Data Tips option helps during the debugging and testing stages of your program. Take a look at Auto Data Tips at work. If Auto Data Tips is not enabled, enable it first. (Enabled means there is a checkmark in the check box.) Then enter the following code:

```
Private Sub Form_Load()

Dim dAngle As Double, dSine As Double
dAngle = 90 * 3.14159 / 180
dSine = Sin(dAngle)

End Sub
```

Figure 10-3
The Auto List
Members drop
down box

Figure 10-4
The Quick Info
popup

Place the cursor on the line **dSine = Sin(dAngle)** and press F9 to set a breakpoint there; then run the program. When the program enters the Break mode, place your mouse pointer over the variable **dAngle**. A text box pops up and shows you the current value of the variable. Now place the mouse pointer over **dSine**. Its value is zero because it has not yet been assigned a value. If you press F8 and place the mouse pointer over **dSine** again, the variable's new value appears.

You can see that Auto Data Tips can be most helpful for finding unexpected values. Later in this chapter, you will see some other useful ways to uncover them.

1. Syntax errors are detected:
   a. At design time
   b. At runtime
   c. Only when specific conditions are met
   d. When your program crashes

2. What type of error allows a variable to assume an unexpected value?
   a. A runtime error
   b. A syntax error
   c. A logic error
   d. It can never happen.

3. What Visual Basic 5 feature helps you complete a statement that you have begun typing?
   a. Auto Data Tips
   b. Auto Syntax Check
   c. Auto List Members
   d. Auto Quick Info

4. What Visual Basic 5 feature helps you with the syntax of a function call?
   a. Auto Data Tips
   b. Auto Syntax Check
   c. Auto List Members
   d. Auto Quick Info

5. What Visual Basic 5 feature lets you examine the value of a variable during break time?
   a. Auto Data Tips
   b. Auto Syntax Check
   c. Auto List Members
   d. Auto Quick Info

ERROR HANDLERS

Whaddaya mean, *error handlers*? I don't need no stinking error handlers! The fact is, though, that Visual Basic makes errors, and it does it on purpose! Remember the error that the common dialog generates when you cancel a save? It isn't really an error, but it is a convenient mechanism that VB 5 uses to signal that the save is canceled.

Realistically, all programs generate errors, some on purpose, but most unexpectedly. Being ready for the unexpected separates a great program from an okay program, and a great programmer from an ordinary programmer. This lesson explains how to expect the unexpected.

What Happens When an Error Occurs

Visual Basic 5 provides a rich tapestry of error-handling power. You can, and *should*, draw upon it to handle any errors that may crop up in your program. Take a look at the object that makes it all possible.

The `err` *Object*

VB 5 contains a built-in object for error handling. The `err` object has six properties and two methods. When an error occurs, VB 5 sets the `err` object's properties to reflect the nature of the error. You can determine the exact error by reading those properties. Most programmers use two of the `err` object's properties: `Number` and `Description`. As you hone your skills, the others will become useful as well.

The `Number` property contains the number of the last error. VB 5 has reserved error numbers 1 through 1,000 for its own use, although it does not yet use all of them. Additionally, error numbers above 31,000 are reserved. You can use numbers between 1,000 and 31,000 to create your own error numbers.

The `Description` property contains a text string that describes the error. The description is most useful to programmers while they are testing a program. Your program's users are likely to be confused by some of the cryptic messages in `err.description`.

The `Raise` statement lets you generate errors on purpose. Why would you want to do that? So you can see how your program responds to the error, of course.

The `Error` *Function*

The `Error` function returns the error message that corresponds to a specific error number. If you do not supply a number, it returns a message corresponding to the last error that occurred. The error message is the `Description` property of the `err` object. If no error has occurred, the `Error` function returns an empty string.

The Error Handler

Your program should anticipate errors. Actually, the best programmers attempt to *prevent* errors by allowing only valid inputs and by disabling menu options and buttons that are not valid at a specific time. For example, Microsoft Word does not let you use Save or Save As if there is no file to be saved. Nevertheless, some things sneak past us and some things are impossible to prevent, like the Cancel error in the CommonDialog File controls. So you must prepare for errors, and the way to do that is to include error handlers in your code. Take a look at the special statements and functions that Visual Basic provides so you can do just that.

On Error

The `On Error` statement is a *conditional branching* statement, like `If...Then`. It says "If there is an error, here is where to go." There are several choices about where to go.

The `GoTo line` statement causes program execution to branch to a line number or label in the same procedure. Line number is a misnomer, because it must also be a label. (A label is a word or number followed by a colon. See the code in Listing 10-1 for an example.)

The `GoTo 0` statement turns off error trapping in your subroutine or function. If there is no `On Error GoTo` statement in your subroutine or function, this is the default condition. This doesn't mean that the computer does not respond to errors, but that your `On Error GoTo` statement has been turned off and Visual Basic's default error handling is turned on. In some cases, the default error handling might be okay, but in many cases it displays a message and then unceremoniously dumps you from the program. Not at all nice.

The `On Error` statement affects only the subroutine or function in which it appears. When `End Sub` is executed, the error trapping that was effective for that subroutine is turned off. It is said to "go out of scope."

Resume

If the `On Error` statement is anything other than `On Error GoTo 0`, there must be a `Resume` statement. The `Resume` statement tells Visual Basic what to do after it has noticed and dealt with the error. The choices are simple.

 The `Resume` statement tells Visual Basic to continue execution on the same line that caused the error in the first place. If you are clever, your program has fixed the error condition before it resumes. If not, it generates an *infinite loop*. Your program goes 'round in circles like a dog chasing its tail!

● The `Resume Next` statement tells the program to continue execution on the next line. That may seem reckless, but sometimes it is exactly the right thing to do.

● The `Resume Line` statement sends the program off to another line number or label.

Try It Out

Enough of this talk. It's time to try out some code to see how error handlers work. Create a new directory called Goofs. Create a new project in Visual Basic or copy `Goofs.vbp` from the CD that comes with the book.

The project needs two Command buttons and a text box on the form, but there is nothing special here, so you can leave them with their default names and labels. See Figure 10-5.

Add code to the project as shown in Listing 10-1.

Listing 10-1 The Code for `Goofs.vbp`

```
Option Explicit

Private Sub Form_Activate()

' Clear the label
Label1.Caption = ""
' Clear the textbox
Text1.Text = ""
' set the focus on the textbox
Text1.SetFocus

End Sub

Private Sub Text1_GotFocus()

Text1.SelStart = 0
Text1.SelLength = Len(Text1.Text)
```

continued on next page

Figure 10-5
The Goof project

continued from previous page

```
      End Sub

      Private Sub Command1_Click()

      Dim iNum1 As Integer, iNum2 As Integer
      On Error GoTo Error_Handler
      iNum2 = 22
      iNum1 = Val(Text1.Text)
      Label1.Caption = iNum2 / iNum1

      Exit_Command1_Click:
      Text1.SetFocus
      Exit Sub

      Error_Handler:
      MsgBox "Error Number " & Err & vbCrLf & Error, 48, "Whoops!"
      Resume Exit_Command1_Click

      End Sub

      Private Sub Command2_Click()

      Dim iError As Integer
      On Error GoTo Error_Handler
      iError = Int(Val(Text1.Text))
      Err.Raise iError

      Exit_Command2_Click:
      Text1.SetFocus
      Exit Sub

      Error_Handler:
      MsgBox "Error Number " & Err & vbCrLf & Err.Description, 48, "Whoops!"
      Resume Exit_Command2_Click

      End Sub
```

Running Goof

Now run the program. Start by clicking on both Command buttons without entering anything into the text box. Then enter various numbers, clicking on Command1 and Command2 to see the results. Try numbers that are beyond the correct range for integers, too.

Note that many of the error messages you get from Command2 say the same thing: `Application-defined` or `object-defined error`. That is because Microsoft has not yet assigned a meaning to that specific error number.

A Look at the Code

Notice that the initialization code for this project is in the form's `Activate` event instead of the `Load` event. The main reason is that the `SetFocus` method does not work until the form has been loaded and **Text1** exists. The **Activate** event clears the text box and the label and sets the focus in the text box. (Real tough stuff!)

Take a look at the **GotFocus** event of **Text1**. The code sets the beginning position for text selection at the beginning of any text that is in the text box. Then it sets the length of the selection the same as the length of the string. In other words, it selects all the text that is in the text box whenever the text box receives focus. That way you can simply type new numbers in the text box without having to erase the old ones manually.

The code that is most interesting here is that for Command1 and Command2. Command1's **Click** event contains a typical **On Error** statement: **On Error GoTo Error_Handler**. The label **Error_Handler:** appears at the end of the procedure. In this case, it simply displays a message box and sends program flow off to the label **Exit_Command1_Click**. A more sophisticated error handler might use a **Select-Case** statement to deal with specific errors. For example, an effort to open a file can generate error numbers 52 through 76. A well-written error handler would deal with many of them specifically.

Instead of displaying the **Error** string **Disk not ready** for error 71, for example, you might display a less cryptic message that suggests that your user should insert a disk in the drive. The error strings you get from the **err** object are not very informative to people who are not computer geeks. Error 6, for example, simply states **Overflow**. You know that that means you entered a value that is outside of the maximum range for the variable type, but you should *tell* your user. Replace the error handler code for Command1 with the code in Listing 10-2 and try the program again.

Listing 10-2 An improved error handler

```
Select Case Err
Case 6
MsgBox "Values must be between +32767 and -32768", 48, "Please Note:"
Case 11
MsgBox "Division by 0 is not allowed", 48, "Please Note:"
Case Else
MsgBox "Error Number " & Err & vbCrLf & Error, 48, "Sorry."
End Select
```

True, it seems like a lot of work to deal with every possible error, and it is. It also makes the difference between a program that is frustrating to use and one that your users are happy to double-click through.

The **Exit_Command1_Click:** label and code are necessary to keep the program from running into the error handler when there are no errors.

The code for Command2 uses the **Raise** method to generate an error in the program. The error handler is different, too; it uses **Err.Description** instead of the **Error** function. The effect is the same.

1. _____ is the Visual Basic error object.
   a. `err`
   b. `Error`
   c. `VB_Err`
   d. `ErrorObj`

2. What does the following line do?.

   ```
   On Error Goto 0
   ```

   a. It jumps program execution to line 0 if an error occurs.
   b. It jumps program execution to line 0.
   c. It is a case of a syntax error.
   d. It disables error handling.

3. In the following code, which one of the following is *not* true?

   ```
   MyDay()
   {
           On Error GoTo First_Exit
           On Error GoTo Second_Exit
           A = C/D
   ```

   a. You cannot have two error handlers in the same procedure.
   b. The second error handler is the active error handler when `A=C/D` is
      executed.
   c. The error handler `First_Exit` is the first active error handler.
   d. If the statement `A=C/D` fails, program execution transfers to `Second_Exit`.

4. Error handlers go out of scope when:
   a. Program flow exits the procedure containing the error handler.
   b. Never, if you declare a global handler.
   c. The form in which the handler is declared is unloaded.
   d. You receive the message `On Error GoTo -1`.

5. To display error messages, use the error object's:
   a. `Description` property
   b. `ErrorMessage` property
   c. `Tag` property
   d. `ErrorString` property

DEBUGGING: THE NOBLE ART

You've written your program and it works. Okay, it works *most* of the time. Or worse yet, it doesn't work most of the time, even though you know the code is perfect. What to do?

Now comes the part of programming that separates the programmers from the dabblers: the noble (and sometimes not so noble) art of debugging. It is a form of puzzle solving that explains why programmers are known to stay up all night and consume anything at all that contains caffeine.

What's All This Business About a Bug, Anyhow?

The story goes that one of the earliest computers—built with electromagnetic switches called relays in the days before transistors—failed one day. The technicians labored until they found the cause: A moth had become trapped between a pair of relay contacts. Since that day, any failure in computer hardware or software is called a bug. There is some debate about the veracity of the story, although the grand lady of computing, Admiral Grace Hopper, swears it is true, and if you search the Internet, you can find a picture of the moth.

Visual Basic 5's Debugging Tools

Visual Basic 5 has a wealth of tools to help us debug and test our programs. You'll learn how to use them in this lesson. Open the View menu and select Toolbars. From the Toolbars popup, select Debug. The Debug toolbar appears, as shown in Figure 10-6.

You can quickly open any of the toolbars by right-clicking on any other toolbar or on the menu bar. A popup window offers you access to all the available toolbars.

Take a quick look at each of the items on the Debug toolbar; then you can do a couple of exercises so you can practice using them.

Start

The first three buttons are called VCR buttons because they look and behave exactly like the buttons on your VCR. The first button is the Start button, which starts your program running.

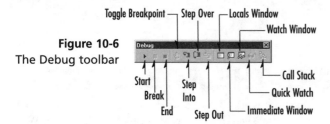

Figure 10-6
The Debug toolbar

Break

The second button is the Break button. It acts like the pause button on a VCR. The program stops running when you click it. You can view and work in the Immediate window, the Code window, and all the other Visual Basic windows while your program is paused. The Break button is also a good way to get out of an infinite loop condition. You can also break your program by pressing CTRL-BREAK, which is helpful if you don't have the Debug toolbar open.

While your program is in Break mode, the Start button becomes a Continue button that you can use to restart the program.

End

The End button stops the running program. In VCR terms, it is a stop and rewind button, because you cannot pick up where you left off after you click on End.

Set Breakpoints

Now you are getting to the real goodies! A *breakpoint* is a spot in the code where the program automatically goes into Break mode. That means that if you are having problems, you can run your program to a given point and then stop it and check and even change the values of your variables. It is a great way to watch the progress of a program as it executes.

To set a breakpoint, put your cursor on the line where you want to stop the program and click on the Set Breakpoint button, or press F9. To clear single breakpoint, put the cursor on the line containing the breakpoint and click on Set Breakpoint or press F9. On the Debug menu is an item that allows you to clear *all* your breakpoints at the same time.

Baby Steps

Once your program has hit a breakpoint, the fun really begins. Now you can make the program continue for a single step at a time or for a whole group of steps. There are four step commands, shown in Table 10-1.

Table 10-1 The Step commands

Command	Action	Shortcut
Step Into	Single-steps: Each time you click on Step Into, the program executes a single line of code and stops again. It is a wonderful way to watch the flow of a program, one step at a time. Between steps, you can check the values of the variables in the program, and even change them.	F8
Step Over	A great convenience when the program branches to a procedure or to a function that you already know works. Rather than single-stepping your way through the procedure, you click on Step Over. The program branches to the procedure, carries out the instructions there, and returns to the next line. It is especially nice when the procedure contains a lengthy For...Next loop. If the current line of the program is not a function or procedure call, Step Over acts the same as Step Into.	SHIFT-F8
Step Out	Handy if you happen to forget to use Step Over or if you have seen all the execution necessary in a function. When you click on Step Out, the program completes execution of all the code in the current function and stops at the line following the function call.	None
Run to Cursor	Lets you skip through part of your code. Imagine, for example, that you need to see what is happening in a function that also contains a lengthy For...Next loop. Single-stepping through the loop takes forever and accomplishes almost nothing. After you have run through the loop once, put your cursor on the line after the loop and click on Run To Cursor. The program completes the loop and stops where the cursor is waiting.	None

Watch This

Now that you have all these ways to stop your program, single-step through your program, and skip over parts of your program, what good is it all? Just what can you do with it? Simply put, you can use the rest of your debugging features to test and validate your program's operation. You can *watch* what is happening through several windows that Visual Basic makes available to you.

It's time to put your knowledge of the Debug tools to work. Create a new directory called Debug Demo, then open a new project in Visual Basic or load **debugging.vbp** from the CD that comes with this book. The components of the project are described in Table 10-2.

Table 10-2 Controls for the debugging.vbp project

Control	Property	Value
Form	Name	frmDebug
	Caption	Debug Demo
Label	AutoSize	True
	Caption	X
Label	Autosize	True
	Caption	Y
Label	AutoSize	True
	Caption	Y
Label	AutoSize	True
	Caption	Select Operation
OptionButton	Name	optOperation
	Caption	&Add X + Y
	Index	0
Value	True	
OptionButton	Name	optOperation
	Caption	&Subtract X – Y
	Index	1
OptionButton	Name	optOperation
	Caption	&Multiply X * Y
	Index	2
OptionButton	Name	optOperation
	Caption	&Divide X/Y
	Index	3

Control	Property	Value
OptionButton	Name	optOperation
	Caption	&Raise X ^ Y
	Index	4
OptionButton	Name	optOperation
	Caption	Yth Roo&t of X
	Index	5
CommandButton	Name	cmdCalculate
	Caption	&Calculate
CommandButton	Name	cmdQuit
	Caption	E&xit

Arrange the controls as shown in Figure 10-7.
Listing 10-3 shows the code for this project.

Figure 10-7
The Debug Demo
form

Listing 10-3 The Debug Demo project

```
Option Explicit
Public iOperation As Integer

Private Sub subRoot()

    lblAnswer = txtOpX ^ (1 / txtOpY)

End Sub

Private Sub subRaise()

Dim iCounter As Integer
Dim dCumulator As Double
dCumulator = 1
For iCounter = 1 To txtOpY
    dCumulator = txtOpX * dCumulator
Next iCounter
lblAnswer = dCumulator
```

continued on next page

continued from previous page

```
    End Sub

    Private Sub subAdd()

    lblAnswer = txtOpX + txtOpY

    End Sub

    Private Sub subDivide()

    lblAnswer = txtOpX / txtOpY

    End Sub

    Private Sub subMultiply()

    lblAnswer = txtOpX * txtOpY

    End Sub

    Private Sub subSubtract()

    lblAnswer = txtOpX - txtOpY

    End Sub

    Private Sub cmdCalculate_Click()

    Select Case iOperation
        Case 0: subAdd
        Case 1: subSubtract
        Case 2: subMultiply
        Case 3: subDivide
        Case 4: subRaise
        Case 5: subRoot
    End Select

    End Sub

    Private Sub cmdQuit_Click()

    Unload Me
    End

    End Sub

    Private Sub optOperation_Click(Index As Integer)

    iOperation = Index

    End Sub

    Private Sub txtOpX_GotFocus()
```

```
txtOpX.SelStart = 0
txtOpX.SelLength = Len(txtOpX)

End Sub

Private Sub txtOpY_GotFocus()

txtOpY.SelStart = 0
txtOpY.SelLength = Len(txtOpY)

End Sub
```

You should be aware that there is at least one serious flaw in this code (this is a *debugging* lesson!). The flaw is a logic error, and one that causes some consternation. Take a brief look at the code so you can get an idea of what is happening before you explore the debugging process.

What It Does

The program is a crude calculator. It handles only two numbers at a time, without accumulation, and it lacks the sophistication of a real calculator.

Enter the operands into the text boxes, select an operation from the Option button array, and press the Calculate command button. The result appears in `lblAnswer`.

When you click on an Option button, the global variable `iOperation` is set to the value of the `optOperation` index. The `Select-Case` structure in `cmdCalculate`'s `Click` event uses `iOperation` to select a procedure that performs the selected operation. One of the operations has a bug in it, and the procedure for raising a number to a power uses a `For...Next` loop to multiply X by itself Y times when the code `X^Y` would have done the job in a single step. This example uses that to demonstrate the value of Step Over and Step Out.

Running and Debugging the Debug Demo Program

If you do not have the Debug toolbar showing, right-click on the menu bar and select Debug now. Click on the Run button to run the program. Move everything around so that you have full access to the program window, the Debug toolbar, and the Immediate window that pops up every time you run a program in the IDE. Your screen should look something like Figure 10-8.

When you select the Debug toolbar or the Immediate window to move them, the program window may disappear. The (ALT)-(TAB) combination lets you bring it back.

Now type a **2** in the X text box and a **3** in the Y text box. The Add X + Y option is on by default, so click on Calculate to perform the calculation.

What's this? 2 + 3 does *not* equal 23! (If you think it does, you are reading the wrong book.) It's time for some debugging, but first check out the other operations, just to evaluate how wide ranging the debugging process needs to be. Select each of the other

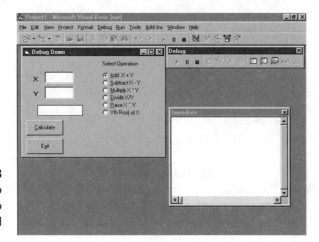

Figure 10-8
The Debug Demo
program ready to
be tested

operations in turn and click on `cmdCalculate` after each one. Hmmm, *they* seem to be working okay. But what is the bug in the addition routine?

Click on Break. The program window disappears, but don't worry about that. It is typical behavior and you don't need it for the moment. You need the Immediate window.

The Immediate Window

The Immediate window shows up every time you run your program from the IDE. You've been using it all along to receive information from your programs to help you in debugging. It is the window that gets the results from a `Debug.Print` operation. What you may not know is that you can also type commands into it while your program is in Break mode. You can use the Immediate window to check on the values of your variables or even to change them.

Select the Immediate window now by clicking on the window. To check on your values, enter **? `txtOpX`** and press ENTER. Okay, it shows you the 2 that you know is in there, so the X value has not changed. Try the Y value by entering **? `txtOptY`** and pressing ENTER. Well, it seems to be okay, too. Try **? `txtOpX + txtOpY`**. Darn! There's that 23 again! Try **? `txtOpY + txtOpX`**. Interesting, now the answer is 32. Change one of the variables. Type **`txtOpX = 3`** in the Edit window and press ENTER. Now move your cursor back to the line **? `txtOpX + txtOpY`** and press ENTER again. This time you get 33! There's a clue here somewhere. See if you can figure it out before you read the next paragraph.

Yep! You got it! The operands in the expression are *strings*, not numbers, and the plus sign *concatenates* the strings. Visual Basic is clever enough with all the other operations to convert the strings into numbers because there is no way to subtract or multiply strings. But when the arguments are strings, the plus sign performs concatenation, just like the ampersand (&) does. Fixing this is going to take some serious work!

Click on the Stop button and bring up the Code window. In the Declarations section of General, add the line:

```
Public dOpX As Double, dOpY As Double
```

to create some numeric variables to use.

Now the program must convert the string values of **txtOpX** and **txtOpY** into doubles and replace every instance of **txtOpX** and **txtOpY** that involves a calculation with **dOpX** and **dOpY**. The process is simple enough, but tedious. After you read through the description of how to do this in your own projects, the example shows you a shortcut for this project.

Under the Edit menu, select Replace, or press CTRL-H to bring up the Replace window. The Replace window is shown in Figure 10-9.

Enter **txtOpX** in the Find What box and *dOpX* in the Replace With box, then click on Find Next. (Do *not* click on Replace All! That really makes you have to work hard!) Replace each instance of **txtOpX** where it is used in a calculation with **dOpX**. When the Replace routine gets to the **Click** event of **txtOpX**, click on Find Next to skip each instance of **txtOpX** in that procedure. Repeat the same process to replace **txtOpY** with **dOpY** for the calculations.

Now go to the **Click** event for **cmdCalculate** and add the following code just before the **Select** statement:

```
dOpX = Val(txtOpX)
dOpY = Val(txtOpY)
```

That wasn't all that bad, was it? Now for the shortcut. If you do not want to make the changes by hand, open the Project menu and select Remove **frmDebug.frm**. Open the Project menu again and select Add File. Find the file **frmDebug2.frm** on the CD that came with the book and add it to your project. Open the Project menu again. Select Project 1 Properties and change the Startup Object to **frmDebug2**.

All done. Run the program again and try the same two numbers. This time 3 + 2 really does equal 5. Much better. Now, back to the debugging tools. You've seen how to use the Immediate window to check a variables value, but there is another, more automatic way. You can set up *watches* to keep an eye on your variables for you!

The Watch Window

The Watch window shows you the value of your program variables. Stop your program and click on the Watch Window icon on the Debug toolbar or select it on the Debug menu. Close the Immediate window for now so the screen doesn't get too cluttered, and drag and size the Watch window so it is out of the way of your program.

Now select Add Watch and type **dOpY** in the Expression box and select All Procedures in the Context frame. Click on OK and the variable is added to your Watch window. Figure 10-10 shows the way it looks.

Figure 10-9
The Replace
window

Add **d0pY** to the Watch window, too, and click on Run to start the program. Enter some numbers and do a calculation. Nothing happened? Yep, that's the way it works. Click on Break. *There* are the watches, plain as day.

Now add some power to the watch. Put your mouse pointer on **d0pY** and right-click. Select Edit Watch from the popup that appears. In the Edit Watch window, click on Break When Value Changes, then click on OK. Now press [F5] to continue your program, and enter **22** for X and **66** for Y. Select the Raise X ^ Y option this time and then click on Calculate.

What happened? The Watch Manager noticed the change in **d0pY** and the program entered Break mode.

While you are in Break mode, take a moment to explore some of the other debugging features.

Quick Watch

You are not watching the variable **iOperation**, but you may be curious about its value just the same. Click on the variable name and then click on Quick Watch on the Debug toolbar. The Quick Watch window shown in Figure 10-11 comes up.

Figure 10-10
Adding a variable
to the Watch
window

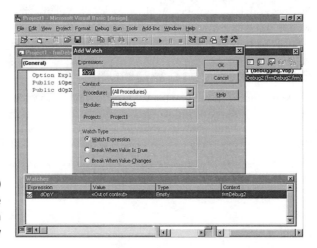

Figure 10-11
The Quick Watch
window

Pretty slick! But Visual Basic 5 is even slicker than that. Close the Quick Watch window and just hold the mouse pointer over the variable name **dOpY** for a second. There is the value right before your eyes! Now it's time to explore the single-step operation.

Single-step through the program by pressing F8 repeatedly. Each time you press F8, Visual Basic executes the next command in your program. Watch it work its way through the **Select-Case** structure until it gets to **Case 4:**, when it jumps to the call to **subRaise**. Press F8 again and watch the program *jump* to the new procedure.

It is interesting to watch the **For...Next** loop operate for a while. For that, use the Locals window.

The Locals Window

Click on the Locals Window icon on the Debug toolbar. The new window covers up the Watch window, but don't worry about it because **dOpX** and **dOpY** are not going to change. The Locals window creates a watch on all the *local* variables—those that are declared in the current procedure. The first item in the window even tells you what procedure you are in. The Locals window is shown in Figure 10-12.

Continue pressing F8 for a while and watch the values change. The **iCounter** value increases by 1 each time, while **dCumulator** increases exponentially. Remember, though, that **dOpY = 66**. You probably don't want to sit there pressing F8 66 times—it would get terribly boring. In a moment you will see the quick way out, but first you need a brief side trip.

Don't Blow Your Stack!

Sometimes you find yourself single-stepped into a procedure without really being sure of how you got there. Never fear, Visual Basic can even tell you that. Click on Call Stack and watch what happens. Figure 10-13 shows the Call Stack window. It lists the current procedure on top, followed by the calling routines. In this simple demo program, there is only a single calling routine; in more complex programs, the stack might contain several other procedures or functions.

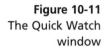

Figure 10-12
The Locals window

Figure 10-13
The Call Stack
window

Now for the quick escape from the 66-step loop. Click on the Step Out icon on the Debug toolbar. Visual Basic completes the loop and returns you to the **End Select** statement back in the **cmdCalculate_Click** procedure.

One more demonstration before you finish. Change the number in **txtOpY** again and click on the Calculate button. Single-step to the call to **subRaise**, but do not press F8 to branch to that procedure. Instead, click on the Step Over icon on the Debug toolbar. Program flow drops to the **End Select** statement. Click on Continue and note that the calculation has been done. Visual Basic ran the **subRaise** procedure without stopping there.

But Wait—There's More!

Click on Break and open the Watch window if it is not visible. Select the first item in the Watch window by clicking on the Eyeglass icon next to the variable name. Remove the item from the Watch window by pressing DEL. Delete all items in the Watch window in the same way and close the Watch window.

Now place your cursor on the statement **Select Case iOperation** and click on Toggle Breakpoint on the Debug toolbar. Note what happens in the Code window.

Click on Continue (or press F5). When the program's screen comes back up, click on Calculate. The program enters Break mode on the line where you inserted the breakpoint. Now move the cursor to the **End Select** statement. Open the Debug menu and click on Run To Cursor. The program runs through all the steps before that line and enters Break mode again. Click on Continue to complete the operation.

Enter new values for both X and Y. Pick a different operation if you wish, and click on Calculate again. When the program hits the breakpoint, place your cursor on **End Select** and click on Set Next Statement on the Debug menu. The current statement marker jumps to the **End Select** statement. Click on Continue and note that the program skipped all the steps between **Select Case iOperation** and **End Select** and the calculation did not get done.

The **Set Next** statement is a convenient way to skip over statements that you do not want to execute. It may seem frivolous to you at the moment, but it will become invaluable as you gain more programming practice.

When you close the project, do not save the changes you have made. The project is used again later in this chapter, and you want the old, defective version.

1. To cause the program to enter the Break mode when it reaches a certain line:
   a. Put an error in the code on that line.
   b. Put the word **Break** on that line.
   c. Set a breakpoint on that line.
   d. Click on the Break button when the program reaches that line.

2. To run a procedure without stopping in it while you are single-stepping through a program:
   a. Click on Step Into.
   b. Click on Step Over.
   c. Click on Step Out.
   d. Click on SkipMe.

3. To view the value of variable **d0pX** while you are in Break mode, you can
   a. Use Quick Watch.
   b. Type **? d0pX** in the Immediate window.
   c. Hold the mouse pointer over the variable name for a second.
   d. All the above

4. To view all the variables that are declared in a procedure, you can use
   a. The Immediate window
   b. The Locals window
   c. Call Stack
   d. Step Into

5. To skip over a portion of code in the current procedure, use
   a. Run to Cursor
   b. Step Into
   c. Step Out
   d. Step Over

REVIEW

John: Wow, there is a lot to debugging!

Lisa: That's right. But the tools are there to help. I like that single-stepping idea.

John: Yeah, it's interesting to watch how the program jumps from place to place to do its work.

Lisa: I like the way you can change values in the Immediate window, too. I'll bet that comes in handy.

John: It will all come in handy. I think there's more to programming than I suspected when I started this!

Lisa: A whole lot more. Let's get back to work.

DEBUGGER BUGS

Bugs in the Debugger? Not really, but there are some things that will surprise you if you are not aware of them. For example, imagine that you are building a mission-critical application and you think you have it working. Before you ship it out the door, you decide to walk through the application using the debugger one last time. After several hours of testing, you click on a button and nothing happens. What's going on? An event procedure should have been fired! You end the debug session and click on the button to make sure the code is still there; it is. You try again with the debugger and the same thing happens. What's going on? A few hours and a call to tech support later, you learn that there is nothing wrong with your code; an event was lost while in Debug mode! Visual Basic is an event-driven programming environment and, in some instances, using the debugger and Break mode can alter the way your application behaves, causing lost events, timing problems, or lost Windows messages. There are not many cases where the debugger changes behavior, but you need to be aware of them. Take a look.

KeyDown

Load **debugging.vbp** again if you closed it between lessons. Add the code **Debug.Print "Keydown Event Fired"** in the **txtOpX KeyDown** event and add the code **Debug.Print "KeyUp Event Fired"** to the **txtOpX KeyUp** event.

Run the program and enter a few characters in the **txtOpX** text box. As you might expect, the two phrases appear in the Immediate window for each keystroke.

Now break the program and put a breakpoint on the line **Debug.Print "Keydown Event Fired"**. Run the program again and watch what happens. For one thing, the **KeyUp** event is never fired. Because of the break in **KeyDown**, the computer's **KeyUp** event takes place *outside the program*. As a result, the text box's **KeyUp** event is not fired. Another event that is skipped is the **KeyPress** event, which normally would have followed the **KeyDown** event. As a result, the keyboard character never gets placed in the text box.

If you must test something that takes place in the **KeyDown** event, use **Debug.Print** to display values rather than setting breakpoints.

MouseDown

Delete the code form **txtOpX**'s **KeyDown** and **KeyUp** events. Be sure to toggle the breakpoint off, too. Select **cmdCalculate** in the Code window. Place **Debug.Print "MouseDown fired."** in the **cmdCalculate MouseDown** event and **Debug.Print "MouseUp fired."** in the **cmdCalculate MouseUp** event.

You know what's going to happen, don't you? Run the program, enter some numbers for X and Y, and click on Calculate. Just as it should, the program dutifully reports both events in the Immediate window. Place a breakpoint in the **MouseDown** event and try again with some new numbers. The break in **MouseDown** prevents all the Command button's subsequent events from being fired. Not only did the program miss the **MouseUp** event, it missed the **Click** event, too; the calculation was never performed.

Use **Debug.Print** statements to monitor changes in the **MouseDown** event.

Focusing on Focus

There is no major problem with breaks in the **GotFocus** and **LostFocus** events in Visual Basic 5, although there was a problem in Visual Basic 4. You *can* have a problem with infinite loops, though, if you use the **LostFocus** event to set focus back to the same control or the **GotFocus** event to set focus back to the previous control.

The Moving Mouse

Putting breakpoints in **MouseMove** events won't cause any lost events either. It makes it awfully hard to do anything with the mouse, however! Try to avoid it, especially for controls that take up a lot of space on your form.

Expect the Unexpected

You have a powerful instrument in the Visual Basic debugging tools. You can walk through programs a step at a time or skip through (or past) several steps or whole procedures. You can break out of programs when a variable changes, or when a **Boolean** variable assumes a **True** condition, or when the program reaches a certain line. And you can dynamically display variable values in the Immediate window while the program runs full speed. A wealth of tools, indeed.

On the other hand, in some cases the debugger causes problems with event sequences and timing. If you suspect the debugger is causing you problems (that is, missing events) use a **Debug.Print** statement to prove that the event is being fired.

Beware, too, of background events that might cause your program to change expected program flow. A **Timer** event is a classic example of something that can send your program off in an unanticipated direction during debugging.

In short, expect the unexpected while debugging. Use your knowledge of event-driven programming to help you understand why the program is behaving in such a strange way. And, as always, when in doubt, read the instructions.

1. The best way to debug events in a **KeyDown** event (not **KeyUp**) is:
   a. **Debug.Print**
   b. The debugger
   c. **MsgBox**
   d. To print error statements

2. In some cases, using the debugger can throw off application timing and cause lost:
   a. Events
   b. Variables
   c. Code
   d. Properties

3. Which of the following events do *not* cause debugger problems?
   a. `MouseDown` and `MouseUp`
   b. `KeyDown` and `KeyUp`
   c. `GotFocus` and `LostFocus`
   d. `Command_Click` and `Command_Dbl_Click`

4. If you set a breakpoint in the `MouseMove` event, using the debugger:
   a. Causes lost events
   b. Produces flaky results
   c. Might be hard because moving the mouse always causes the program to enter Break mode
   d. Works well

5. Use the _____ when you suspect lost events during a debug session.
   a. `Debug` object
   b. Break points
   c. `Watch` expression
   d. `err` object

HOW TO WRITE CODE THAT IS EASY TO MAINTAIN

In Lesson 4, you learned how to solve problems by using the debugging tools and about some of the problems the debugging tools introduce into the debugging process. This lesson looks at a different kind of debugging problem. Not problems caused by the debugging tools but problems caused by bad coding techniques. (We are not talking about *you*; after all, you have perfect coding techniques.)

Coding is a lot like maintaining a tool shed or a garage. Everyone knows somebody who has an immaculate garage. The floor is clean and everything is either hung on pegboard or neatly stowed in a toolbox or drawer. If you want to find a bolt or a hammer or a saw—no problem! Then there is the other garage. You know, the one most of us own. The tools are there, alright; scattered on the floor, dropped behind a cabinet, thrown in heaps and haphazardly stowed wherever it was convenient when they were last used. Find a hammer? Not in your lifetime! You get the point. Writing well-organized code makes maintaining and debugging it easier, like finding tools in a well-organized garage.

One of the main benefits of object-oriented programming is the organization of code into classes so that everything that affects a specific piece of data is all in the same place. To appreciate the benefits of well-organized code, it will be helpful to see an example of really *bad* coding technique.

Spaghetti Code

Before Visual Basic, programmers used languages like C, FORTRAN, COBOL, and assembly language. (They are all still in use, and they all have their place and purpose. Try not to get involved in the "religious wars" over which is the best programming language.) In all these languages, programmers have to write many lines of code to accomplish tasks that a Visual Basic programmer does easily. In fact, just creating a simple form, something Visual Basic programmers don't even have to do, takes a few hundred lines of carefully crafted code.

With all that code to write, some programmers fell into the habit of writing inline code instead of using more structured programming. It is not unusual to find programs so loaded with branching and conditional branching statements that it is impossible to follow the program flow. No, the programmers were not *taught* to do that, but they fell into the habit and it was hard to break. It was also hard to maintain that code.

You can read about coding problems in the news. The "year 2000 problem" is made worse by this kind of coding technique. A recent news item described a team of programmers who were searching through more than 25,000 lines of code looking for references to dates. To make it worse, they reported that there were dozens of different variable names all representing dates, not including the ubiquitous names `temp` and `tmp`! Imagine how much easier it would have been if object-oriented programming had existed when the original code was written. There would have been a few classes to change—maybe only one. The job would have been done in a few hours by a single programmer.

Code like this, that seems to have no clear beginning, no clear end, and no clear path, is called *spaghetti code*. Program flow is as clear as the path through a bowl of spaghetti.

Sadly, you can write spaghetti code in Visual Basic, too. This example gives you an idea of what NOT to do. After you have seen that, you can learn what to do.

Create a new directory called Spagh. Start a new project, also called Spagh. The project requires only a single form and a single Command button. The properties are shown in Table 10-3.

Table 10-3 Object and property settings for project Spagh

Object	Property	Setting
Form	Caption	Debug Spaghetti
	Height	3435
	Name	frmSpagh
	Width	5070

continued on next page

continued from previous page

Object	Property	Setting
CommandButton	Caption	Start
	Height	915
	Left	1185
	Name	cmdStart
	Top	885
	Width	2205

Enter the code from Listing 10-4 in the **Command_Click** event.

Listing 10-4 Spaghetti code

```
Private Sub cmdStart_Click()
Dim A As Integer, I As String, DN As Integer

GoTo I_V

S_T:
If DN > 1 Then GoTo G_N
DN = 2
GoTo I_V

T1:
If A > 5 Then GoTo I_V
Exit Sub

G_N:
Randomize
A = Int((10 * Rnd) + 1)
DN = 0
GoTo T1

Init_Var:
A = 0
I = "one"
DN = 2
GoTo S_T

End Sub
```

Set a breakpoint on the line **GoTo Init_Var** and run the program. Click on the Start button and then press F8 repeatedly until you finally exit from the procedure. Wasn't that fun? Were you able to follow the sequence of steps? The application jumps around the code until variable **A** contains an integer greater than **5**. The variable is set using Visual Basic's random number generator, **Rnd**.

This application is a very brief and simple example of code that is hard to maintain. There are no comments, the variable names are meaningless, the logic is poor, and the organization is worse. Imagine a program like SuperPad written in code like this! Decide to make one change and you have a lifetime career.

Writing Clear and Maintainable Code

It doesn't have to be that way. You can write code that you or any other programmer can modify and maintain with minimum effort. The following list of hints and tips makes your code look professional and your programming life a lot easier.

1. Find a naming convention and stick with it. Use a convention that tells you the type of object represented by a variable name. For example, start all form names with the three-letter code `frm`. Start all text box names with the three-letter code `txt` and Command buttons with `cmd`. There is a long list of naming conventions in the `VB Books On Line` file that comes on the CD with Visual Basic 5. Use that or devise your own, but be consistent.

2. Use meaningful names for variables. For example, you have little trouble deciding what `curCar_Payment` represents. Compare that with something like `CP`, which might represent the same thing, or perhaps it means *current price,* or perhaps, well, who knows what it means?

3. Comment your code! Comment your code! Comment your code! Comments make it easier for you and others to maintain your code. You may find yourself making changes to code you wrote over a year ago. What is perfectly clear when you write it can become obscure over a period of time.

4. Organize your code into classes, procedures, and functions. If the functions and procedures become too long, consider breaking them into smaller functions and procedures. Consider placing your procedures and functions on separate code modules, just as classes are in class modules. Even then, organize: Put collections of procedures and functions that deal with financial calculations in one code module, those that handle strings in another.

5. Avoid `GoTo` as much as possible. When you must use it, in error handlers, for example, make the `GoTo` label names meaningful. Don't even consider using numbers as `GoTo` labels.

6. Use space to separate your code into logical groupings. For example, separate all of a `For...Next` loop from the other code in a procedure so you can see where it begins and ends. Most programmers like to use indentation to group their code. That is usually a good technique if the code lines aren't too long and there aren't too many levels of indentation. In fact, it is our preferred grouping method. The code in this book is grouped using blank lines because of typesetting considerations.

Now it's time to rewrite the Spagh program, this time using good coding techniques. Create a directory named GoodCode and start a project with the same name. Table 10-4 lists the objects in the project.

Table 10-4 Object and property settings for project GoodCode

Object	Property	Setting
Form	Caption	Spaghetti Code Redone— Good Coding Techniques
	Height	3435
	Name	frmGood
	Width	5070
CommandButton	Caption	Start
	Height	915
	Left	1185
	Name	cmdStart
	Top	885
	Width	2205

The code for `GoodCode.vbp` is in Listing 10-5.

Listing 10-5 The code for the GoodCode project

```
Private Sub cmdStart_Click()

Dim iRandom_Value As Integer
'Initialize variables
iRandom_Value = 10

'Repeat until we generate a value less then or equal
'to five.

While iRandom_Value > 5
'Call function GetNew
iRandom_Value = GetNew
Wend

End Sub

Public Function GetNew() As Integer

'Generate a random number
Randomize
GetNew = Int((10 * Rnd) + 1)

End Function
```

Compare the code in GoodCode to the code from the Spagh project. Which would you rather meet in a dark alley?

1. _____ code is a nickname for hard-to-maintain, unorganized code.
   a. Spaghetti
   b. Noodle
   c. Good
   d. Excellent

2. Writing easy-to-maintain code means taking advantage of Visual Basic's _____ features.
   a. Procedure
   b. Forms
   c. Object-oriented
   d. Function

3. _____ your code to make it more readable and easier to maintain.
   a. Save
   b. Comment
   c. Uncomment
   d. Debug

4. What is the best name for a string variable that holds a bank name?
   a. `BankName`
   b. `x`
   c. `Bank`
   d. `sBankName`

5. Avoid using the following statement except with error handlers:
   a. `GoTo`
   b. `Jump`
   c. `BPT`
   d. `Stop`

LESSON 6

ADVANCED DEBUGGING TECHNIQUES

There's more? You have already learned a lot of debugging techniques in this chapter. This lesson looks at a few more concepts that make debugging even easier. To prepare for the lesson, load the `debugging.vbp` project again.

Fixing Code in Break Mode

As you test your projects, you often wind up in Break mode because of an error. To see this at work, open the Code window for the debugging project and change the code in the `subAdd` procedure by adding an `e` in the variable name `txtOpX`. Make the line read `lblAnswer = textOpX + txtOpY`. Check the Declarations section and if the line `Option Explicit` is not there, type it in.

Now run the program. Enter numbers for X and Y, select `Add X + Y`, and click on Calculate. The program enters Break mode with a message box, as shown in Figure 10-14.

Click on OK to close the message box. Visual Basic opens the Code window, with the procedure name highlighted and the error selected as shown in Figure 10-15.

The good news is that you can edit the variable name while you are in the Break mode. There is no need to exit, edit, and restart the program. Click the mouse on the letter `e` in the variable name and delete it, then click on the Continue button or press F5 to continue the program.

You can make a lot of changes in the Edit mode, but once in a while you make one that does not allow a simple continue. In that case, Visual Basic warns you that the program must be reset.

Getting Error Numbers and Descriptions

Back in the "bad old days," when your program generated an error, it delivered a cryptic message. Often all you got was an error number. The next step was to pick up the programmers' manual and look it up, and often the message from the book was no more meaningful than the number! With Visual Basic, you get a better shot at figuring out exactly what the error means. Recall that the message box shown in Figure 10-14 offers two buttons, OK and Help. Put the error back into the `subAdd` procedure and run the program again. This time click on the Help button.

Pretty clear, isn't it? The last paragraph:

Explicitly declare the variable, or change the spelling of the variable to match that of the intended variable.

tells you exactly how to fix the problem.

You can even learn about specific errors without actually generating one in your program. In the Immediate window, type `Error 10` and press ENTER. Bingo! Up pops the message box for the error, along with that handy Help button. Too bad it can't find out logic errors, too.

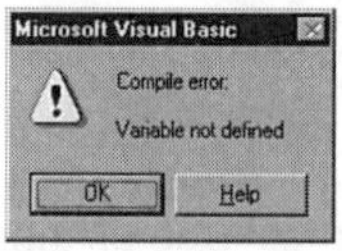

Figure 10-14 `Variable not defined` error

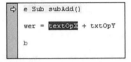

Figure 10-15
The error is selected
for editing

Testing Procedures and Functions

During development, you can test procedures, code segments, and functions using the debugger. From the Break mode, you can enter the name of a function or procedure in the Immediate window and press ENTER to run it.

If your debugging project is not running, start it. Enter numbers for X and Y and then press CTRL-BREAK to enter Break mode. Click in the Immediate window and type **subMultiply** and press ENTER. Use ALT-TAB to get back to the program's window and there is your answer, displayed in the proper place.

You can also type Visual Basic commands and function calls in the Immediate window. Enter the Break mode and type **MsgBox "Testing", vbOKCancel, "Gee!"** in the Immediate window and press ENTER.

Use the Immediate pane to test your own functions and procedures or to experiment with the functions and procedures that come with Visual Basic.

Conditional Compilation

You learned how to use the **Debug.Print** statement in code to help monitor applications and get information without using the debugger. A part of Visual Basic called the *compiler* converts Visual Basic *source code* (what you write) into *executable code* that the computer can read and understand. When the compiler creates an executable for the application, the **Debug** statements are ignored. When the program is run from a compiled executable, there is no Immediate window and **Debug.Print** has no effect.

Sometimes you might want to use special routines or lines of code such as message boxes to help provide even more information during debugging. You might also want to give your users an executable with debugging code for user testing. You cannot use **Debug.Print** statements because they are deactivated when running from an executable. You can use *conditional compilation* statements.

Conditional compilation statements work similarly to Visual Basic **If...Then** blocks, except they are *compiler* **If...Then** blocks. The format for conditional compilation statements is:

```
# If conditional directive Then
        Visual Basic Code
# End If
```

The compiler uses the conditional directive to determine if the Visual Basic code in the **#If...#End If** block is included in the running application. If the conditional directive is **True**, the statement is included in the executable code. The conditional directive is a constant defined by you in code or a compilation flag to include or exclude the code block. The following is an example:

```
#Const Debug_Flag = True
```

```
#If Debug_Flag Then
    MsgBox "Debug App"
#End If
```

If the constant **Debug_Flag** is set to **True**, the statement

```
MsgBox "Debug App
```

is included in the application. If the flag is set to **False**, the code is not included. Give it a try. Place the example code in a **CommandButton** click event and toggle the value of the constant **Debug_Flag** from **True** to **False**. Conditional compilation is a very powerful tool that has been used by C programmers for years.

Break On...

You can control when Visual Basic enters the Break mode. Open the Tools menu and select Options. Select the General tab. The General tab is shown in Figure 10-16.

The choices are

- **Break on All Errors:** Any error causes the project to enter Break mode, whether or not an error handler is active and whether or not the code is in a class module.

- **Break in Class Module:** Any unhandled error produced in a class module causes the project to enter Break mode at the line of code in the class module that produced the error.

- **Break on Unhandled Errors:** If an error handler is active, the error is trapped without entering Break mode. If there is no active error handler, the error causes the project to enter Break mode. An unhandled error in a class module, however, causes the project to enter Break mode on the line of code that invoked the offending procedure of the class.

Figure 10-16
The General Tab

While you are learning, Break on All Errors is probably the safest. By now, though, Break on Unhandled Errors would be a good choice. These settings are not part of your project, but are set as a default condition that is active in all your VB projects until you change it.

Another Break On choice is available. Recall that you can select two different Break conditions in the Add Watch window:

- Break When Value Is `True`: Breaks when a variable becomes `True`, which can also be defined as `Not Zero`.

- Break When Value Changes: Lets you keep a check on a variable's value. If you have a variable that seems to become something other than you expected mysteriously, this is the way to find it.

These settings are valid only for the individual Watch items. They are not persistent—when you remove the Watch, the setting is gone.

Coming Attractions

Now that you know how to handle errors, you can go back and add error handlers to your code. As an exercise, change the form in **debugging.vbp** to **frmDebug2** and add error handlers to the program. Possible errors include division by zero in two places and overflow errors in several. Remember that overflow (underflow?) can occur when numbers get too small, too!

Chapter 11, Graphics, looks at some of Visual Basic 5's graphics capabilities.

1. When can you fix code while in Break mode?
   a. Never.
   b. Sometimes.
   c. Always.
   d. You can fix variables but not properties.

2. The Visual Basic environment can be set up to enter Break mode:
   a. Every five minutes
   b. Every 10 lines of execution
   c. When an error occurs
   d. When you press F5

3. Entering `Error 34` in the Immediate window and pressing ENTER:
   a. Produces an error
   b. Displays the associated error message for error 34
   c. Sets the variable `Error` to `34`
   d. Does nothing

4. Use _____ when you need to create executable code in different environments or to include `Debug` statements in executables that can easily be removed later.
   a. `Debug.Print`
   b. Conditional compilation
   c. Comments
   d. `Print` statements

5. _____ can be used to display the values of variables or to halt when a variable reaches a value.
   a. Breakpoints
   b. The Immediate window
   c. Conditional compilation
   d. Watch points

GRAPHICS

What is the first thing that comes to mind when you think about graphics? Drawing shapes like circles, lines, or squares? Or do you think of a computer animation application, or perhaps a picture displayed in an application? In this chapter, you will learn how to use graphics in Visual Basic to draw shapes and display pictures. You will develop a simple drawing application and create an application that performs animation. You will learn how to include pictures in your applications, add shapes at design time, and create graphics at runtime, using Visual Basic code and methods. But first, here is a discussion of coordinates.

UNDERSTANDING COORDINATES

Sitting at the heart of all of VB 5's visual elements (forms, controls, and so on) is something called a *coordinate system*. The first thing to understand is what it is and why it's there at all.

Start by drawing a picture of a house on a piece of paper. Make it a simple line drawing, a standard house, with a roof, chimney, four windows, and a door. You'll probably draw something like Figure 11-1.

You thought that was easy. The truth is that you just performed a very complex task. Try doing it again, but this time, write a program in Visual Basic to draw the house rather than using a pencil and paper. Not as easy a task after all, is it?

What made the task appear simple at first was that you made some very important assumptions before you carried it out. One of those assumptions was how big a piece of paper you were going to use. You assumed that you would use a small piece of paper in relation to the real size of the object, for example. It wouldn't have made sense to use a house-sized piece of paper! That meant you had to use some sort of scale to which your drawing would adhere. Again, it wouldn't have made sense to draw two different windows to different scales. You could have ended up with something that looks like Figure 11-2.

Figure 11-1
Line drawing of a house

Figure 11-2
Effect of incorrect
scaling

Another thing you assumed was how big your drawing was going to be in relation to the size of the paper you were using. After all, if you made it too big, half of your drawing would have ended up on the table and not on the paper at all. Similarly, if you made it too small, the picture would look out of proportion to the piece of paper on which it was drawn.

One final assumption you made was which way was up, down, left, and right, as shown in Figure 11-3. Pretty useful when drawing a house, particularly if you're going to give your drawing to a builder and tell him or her to build it for you.

Now you're beginning to understand why a coordinate system is needed.

Your Computer's Screen and the Screen **Object**

The place to start understanding Visual Basic's coordinate system is your computer's screen itself. Your computer's screen is made up of a large grid of very small dots. Each dot is called a *pixel* (taken from the words "picture element"). Just how many pixels there are physically across and down your computer's screen depends on the hardware in your computer. There are a number of different resolutions available, anything from 640 pixels across and 480 down, to 1280 across and 1024 down. There are even higher resolutions available at a price.

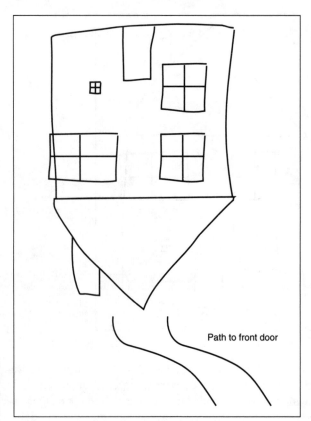

Figure 11-3
It's important to
know which way
is up!

You can find out about your computer's screen characteristics by using Visual Basic's built-in **Screen** object. You learned in Chapter 7, Classes, about some objects that Visual Basic provides by default. One example is the Printer object. The **Screen** object is another, which represents your computer's physical screen.

You can use the **Screen** object to find out the resolution of your computer's screen by querying the **Screen** object's **Width** and **Height** properties. For instance, you could set the width and height of a form to half the width and height of the screen with the following code:

```
Private Sub Form_Load ()
Form1.Width = Screen.Width / 2
Form1.Height = Screen.Height / 2
End Sub
```

You can use the information to position the form in the same relative position on the screen, again independent of the physical size of the screen. The following code centers a form on a screen:

```
Private Sub Form_Load ()                    <
    Form1.Width = Screen.Width / 2
    Form1.Height = Screen.Height / 2
    Form1.Top = (Screen.Height - Form1.Height) / 2
    Form1.Left = (Screen.Width - Form1.Width) / 2
End Sub
```

You could actually do this in one statement using the form's **Move** method, but the above "broken down" version helps to explain the concept of coordinates.

Device-Independent Measurement

Knowing and being able to use information about the physical size of the screen is only part of the picture, however. What you really need is a measurement system that is fully device-independent. In other words, you need a way to tell how big an inch is regardless of the physical size of the screen.

Luckily, Visual Basic comes to the rescue with the *twip*. That's not a typo. A twip is a unit of measurement that is approximately a 567th of a centimeter (or a 1440th of an inch, depending on how old you are!). The name comes from typesetting terms; it means a twentieth of a point. In typography, there are 72 points in an inch. You may already be familiar with the term *point*. It is common in computers. The print on your screen is probably 10 points high. A twip is a tiny unit of measurement, much smaller than one pixel on your screen. But, because it is a device-independent measurement, it has the same size regardless of whether your screen has 640 pixels across or 1280.

To see twips in action, size a form to be two inches square:

```
Private Sub Form_Load ()
    Form1.Width = 2880     '1440 twips per inch
    Form1.Height = 2880    'regardless of physical size of screen
End Sub
```

If the number of twips per inch is always the same regardless of the screen resolution, this must mean that the number of twips per pixel changes with different screen resolutions. After all, two inches requires a different number of pixels in different screen resolutions. This information is available, again, through the **Screen** object. You can use the **TwipsPerPixelX** and **Y** properties to determine just how many twips one physical screen pixel represents.

```
Private Sub Form_Load
    Debug.Print Screen.TwipsPerPixelX
    Debug.Print Screen.TwipsPerPixelY
End Sub
```

TwipsPerPixelX gives the number of twips per pixel across the screen, whereas **TwipsPerPixelY** gives the number per pixel down the screen.

Screen Origin

Remember we said it is important to know which way is up, down, left, and right? Well, Visual Basic allows you to determine the direction and distance on a form by placing the origin of the x and y axes (that's the point where x and y are both zero) at the top-left corner of the form. So assume you want to draw a line from the top-left corner diagonally down the screen so that the end point is one inch to the right and two inches down the form. You could simply write

```
Form1.Line (0,0) - (1440, 2880)
```

The coordinates that are given (0,0) and (1440,2880) are scaled in twips. The first number in each parentheses is the x position (the horizontal axis), and the second relates to the y position (the vertical axis). Therefore, the start position of the line (0,0) relates to the top-left corner of the form, while the end position of the line (1440,2880) relates to a point one inch to the right on the x axis and two inches down on the y axis. The **Line** method draws a line between these two points, as shown in Figure 11-4. To display the line, place this statement in the **Click** event subroutine for Form1, and then click the mouse button on the form.

Using Other Coordinate Systems

Using twips is all well and good, but it gets rather tedious converting all of your measurements to and from the actual scale you want. Here's how to get Visual Basic to do some of the work.

One of the properties of a form (ignored up to now) is the **ScaleMode** property. If you look at its possible values, you find that you can set the scaling to inches, centimeters, and millimeters, as well as to some other types of **ScaleModes**, as shown in Table 11-1.

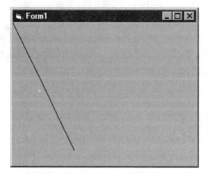

Figure 11-4
Using coordinates
to draw a line

Table 11-1 ScaleMode property settings

Value	Description
0	User-defined
1	Twip
2	Point
3	Pixel
4	Character
5	Inch
6	Millimeter
7	Centimeter

Try setting the ScaleMode for Form1 to inches, but don't forget that you are only changing the ScaleMode for this one form, not for all of the forms in your project. Tell Visual Basic to draw a line as before. Because you're now using inches as your ScaleMode, you don't have to convert inches to twips. So the line method now reads

```
Form1.Line (0, 0) - (1, 2)
```

That's much simpler!

The user-defined ScaleMode property (value 0) allows you to define your own coordinate system. You can set the ScaleMode property to 0 and then create your own coordinate system by setting the ScaleWidth, ScaleHeight, ScaleLeft, and ScaleTop properties.

Spend a little time experimenting with the other ScaleModes. You may find them useful in your own graphics programs.

1. A dot on a computer screen is referred to as a:
   a. Pixie
   b. Twip
   c. Dot
   d. Pixel

2. In order to find out information about your computer's display (monitor), use the Visual Basic _____ object.
   a. Screen
   b. Monitor
   c. Display
   d. CRT

3. The default Visual Basic `ScaleMode` is:
   a. Inches
   b. Millimeters
   c. Twips
   d. User-defined

4. The code

```
Form1.Line (0,0) - (1440, 2880)
```

   a. Draws a line starting at coordinates (0,0) to coordinates (1440,2880)
   b. Draws a dot
   c. Draws a line starting at (0,1440) to (0,2880)
   d. Draws a line starting at (1440,2880) to (0,0)

5. What does the following code do? (Note that the `Move` method moves a form.)

```
Form1.Move (Screen.Width - Width)/ 2, (Screen.Height - Height) / 2
```

   a. Moves the form off the screen
   b. Centers the form on the screen
   c. No way to know without knowing the values of `Height` and `Width`
   d. Places the form in the top-right corner of the screen

USING GRAPHICAL CONTROLS

In the last lesson, you learned about the coordinate system. Now take a look at the simplest way to add graphical shapes to your Visual Basic program. It uses some special custom controls referred to as the *graphical controls*.

Graphical Controls

The graphical controls that come with Visual Basic 4, shown on the tool bar in Figure 11-5, are the

● Shape control

● Line control

● Image control

● Label control

The graphical controls allow you to create graphics at design time. Better yet, they require fewer Windows resources than the average custom control. The graphical controls are known as *light* controls because, unlike other custom controls, they are not true windows. The advantage of a light control is it takes up fewer system resources, but with the good news comes a few restrictions. For example, the graphical controls

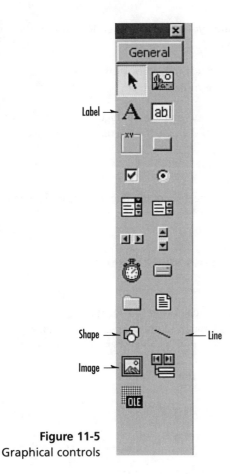

Label

Shape

Image

Line

Figure 11-5
Graphical controls

cannot receive focus at runtime, they cannot act as a container control, and they cannot appear on top of other controls unless they are inside a container such as a PictureBox control. Examine each of the graphical controls except for the Image control and the Label control. You will learn more about the Image control later, and you have already made wide use of the Label control in previous applications.

Line Control

The Line control allows you to draw lines on your forms at design time. Use the Line control for special visual effects. Consider using the Line control to place borders around controls instead of using a Panel or Frame control. Try out the Line control. Start a new project with a single form. To draw a line using the Line control, perform the following steps:

1. Click on the Line control on the Visual Basic toolbar shown in Figure 11-5. The mouse cursor changes into a crosshair.

2. Select a point on the form to start your line, and then left-mouse click, holding the mouse button down.

3. Drag the cursor, while holding the left mouse button down, to the line's ending point, and then release the mouse button.

Congratulations, you have just created a line, as shown in Figure 11-6. Press F4 and take a brief look at some of the properties of the Line control that you may need from time to time.

BorderStyle

Use the **BorderStyle** property to change the style of the line. For example, you can change the line from being solid to being dashed or dotted.

BorderWidth

Increasing the **BorderWidth** property increases the thickness of your line.

X1, X2, Y1, Y2

The **X** and **Y** properties are (you guessed it) the coordinates for the starting and end points of your line. This comes in handy if you happen to draw the line a little cockeyed. If **X1** and **X2** are the same, the line is horizontal; if **Y1** and **Y2** are the same, the line is vertical.

You can change the **X** and **Y** properties or the border width property in your program to create animation.

Shape Control

The Shape control, shown in Figure 11-5, allows you to create the following shapes at design time:

- Oval
- Circle
- Square

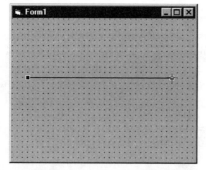

Figure 11-6
Creating a line
using the Line
control

- Rectangle
- Rounded Rectangle
- Rounded Square

Create a new project with a single form. Don't worry about saving the project since you are only adding Shape controls to a form to experiment with them. Adding a Shape control is similar to adding a Line control. When you click on the Shape control, the mouse cursor changes to a crosshair. As with the Line control, place the crosshair on the form where you want the corner of the shape to begin, and then, while holding down the left mouse button, drag the cursor until you have the correct size. Then release the mouse button. Set the following properties for your form, and add the six Shape controls. When you draw a Shape, the default shape is a rectangle. Add six Shape controls to the form. Don't worry about the size of your shapes; just make sure they all fit on the form. Set the properties for the form and for each Shape control, as shown in Table 11-2.

Table 11-2 Object and property settings for Shape control demo

Object	Property	Setting
Form	Height	3480
	Name	frmShape
	Width	5295
Shape1	Shape	0 - Rectangle
Shape2	Shape	1 - Square
Shape3	Shape	2 - Oval
Shape4	Shape	3 - Circle
Shape5	Shape	4 - Rounded Rectangle
Shape6	Shape	5 - Rounded Square

Figure 11-7 shows a form similar to the one you have just created.

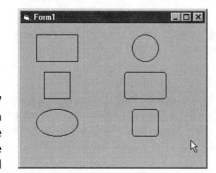

Figure 11-7
Form with each possible shape using the Shape control

Take a look at the properties of the Shape control.

BorderWidth, BorderColor

The Shape control has a **BorderWidth** property, similar to the Line control. It was increased on each of the shapes on the form in this project, from 1 to 3, shown in Figure 11-7, to add line thickness. Of course, the border can be drawn in any color you wish.

BorderStyle

The **BorderStyle** property has the same meanings for the Shape control that it had for the Line control. The **BorderWidth** property affects how well **BorderStyles** other than solid work. For best results, use **BorderWidth** = 1 for **BorderStyles** other than solid.

Style

The **Style** property of the Shape control determines the shape of the control. It can be set to any of the six shapes displayed on the form shown in Figure 11-7.

FillStyle

The Shape control can be displayed as an outline, as you did in the exercise, or it can have any of eight different *fill styles*. Actually, you were using the *transparent* fill style in the exercise.

FillColor

If you use a **FillStyle** other than **1** (transparent), then the fill pattern is displayed in the **FillColor**. By default, that color is black, but it is easily changed.

BackStyle, BackColor

The Shape control can be either transparent, which is the default, or solid. If it is solid, the color of the shape is set by the **BackColor** property. If the **BackStyle** is transparent, then the **BackColor** property has no effect.

DrawMode

The **DrawMode** property is used to create special effects, but its effects are rather unpredictable. Perhaps the less said about it the better! The **DrawMode** property affects how Visual Basic combines the **Pen Color**, which is the **BorderColor**, with the background color. The default **DrawMode** is **Copy Pen**, which ignores the background color. Even Microsoft declines to predict the results of changes in the **DrawMode** property. The only way to tell what happens is to experiment.

The Shape and Line controls are powerful custom controls that allow you to add graphics to your applications at design time. Experiment with the two controls. Try using a rounded rectangle for looks instead of a frame control to group buttons or text boxes together. In the next lesson, you will learn how to draw shapes using coding methods instead of custom controls. Experiment also with the **BackStyle** and **FillStyle** properties of the Shape control.

1. Which one of the following custom controls is not a light graphical control?
   a. PictureBox
   b. Image
   c. Line
   d. Shape

2. To increase the thickness of the line drawn, set the following property on the Shape and Line control:
   a. `BorderStyle`
   b. `LineThickness`
   c. `BorderWidth`
   d. `LineWidth`

3. Modifying the _____ property changes a line from solid to dotted or dashed.
   a. `LineStyle`
   b. `BorderStyle`
   c. `LineFill`
   d. `BorderType`

4. The following shape cannot be created with the Shape control:
   a. Oval
   b. Rectangle
   c. Diamond
   d. Rounded square

5. The default `DrawMode` property is:
   a. `Mask Pen`
   b. `Invert`
   c. `Copy Pen`
   d. `Merge Pen`

USING GRAPHICAL METHODS

In the last lesson, you learned to use the graphical custom controls. In this lesson, you will learn how to create graphical images using Visual Basic commands called *graphical methods*. Use the graphical methods when the custom controls would require too much work, or the graphical effects you require cannot be done with the custom controls.

Remember when you got your first box of crayons or paint brush set? Well this section is similar to that experience. You will learn how to use various methods in Visual Basic to create your own graphics and drawings. The fundamentals of drawing that you learned as a kid are similar to the fundamentals of computer drawing. To program with graphical methods requires a general understanding of the coordinate system which was covered in Lesson 1. Then you need tools to draw with and something to draw on. With Visual Basic, you can create graphics using graphical methods by drawing on a form, a picture box, or the Printer object. As for the drawing tools, in this lesson you will examine the following graphical methods:

● Cls

● Pset

● Line

Graphical Methods

Let's examine all the graphical methods and use them in an application.

Cls

The **Cls** method is like a chalkboard eraser. Invoking the method on a Form, PictureBox, or Image control erases all graphics or text on the form or in the control. The syntax for the **Cls** method is as follows:

```
object.Cls
```

Pset

The **PSet** method is used to set a specific point on a form or picture box to a specified color. The syntax is as follows:

```
object.PSet (x,y) [color]
```

where

● (x,y) are coordinates.

● color is an optional parameter that specifies the color of the point.

Line

The **Line** method is used to draw lines on an object and can be used to create many different shapes. **Line** has the following syntax:

```
[Object].Line [Step][(x1,y1)] [-] [Step][(x2,y2)], [color], [BF]
```

where

- **step** is an optional keyword to specify the starting point relative to the current x and y coordinates.

- **x1, y1** are optional parameters indicating the starting point of the line (otherwise, the current x and y position is used).

- **x2, y2** are required and are the end point for the line.

- **color** sets the color of the line.

- **B** is used to draw a box using the coordinates.

- **F** specifies that the box be filled in with the same color the box was drawn in.

That's a lot! A few examples are in order to help clarify the issue. Start a new project. Set the form's **WindowState** to **Maximized** and add the following code to **Form_Click**:

```
Private Sub Form_Click()
' Set ScaleMode to inches
Form1.ScaleMode = 5
' Draw a one inch horizontal line
Form1.Line (0.5, 0.5)-(1.5, 0.5)
' Draw a one inch vertical line down from the end of the first line
Form1.Line -(1.5, 1.5)
' Change form's forecolor property
Form1.ForeColor = QBColor(1)
' Draw a box
Form1.Line (2, 2)-(2.5, 2.5), , B
' Draw another box, using line color
Form1.Line (3, 3)-(3.5, 3.5), QBColor(2), B
' Draw a filled box, using line color
Form1.Line (3, 2)-(3.5, 2.5), QBColor(3), BF
End Sub
```

The remarks explain what each of the **Line** method statements is doing when you click on the form.

Chalkboard

Now create an application using some of the commands you have just learned. For your first graphics method application, you will create a chalkboard. Using your mouse, you can draw pictures on the chalkboard. If you don't like the picture, you can erase the board. The drawing area for the chalkboard is a picture box. Start a new Visual Basic project called chalkbrd. Add the controls and set the properties as shown in Table 11-3.

Table 11-3 Object and property settings for project chalkbrd

Object	Property	Setting
Form	Caption	Chalkboard
	Height	3930
	Name	frmDraw
	Width	5295
PictureBox	BackColor	&H00FFFFFF&
	DrawWidth	2
	Height	2295
	Left	90
	Name	Picture1
	ScaleMode	3 - Pixel
	Top	60
	Width	4965
TextBox	Height	285
	Left	1155
	Name	txtWidth
	Top	2430
	Width	885
CommandButton	Caption	Change Draw Width
	Height	480
	Left	705
	Name	cmdWidth
	Top	2880
	Width	1755
Label	Caption	DrawWidth
	Height	255
	Left	225
	Name	lblWidth
	Top	2475
	Width	900

Object	Property	Setting
CommandButton	Caption	Clear the Board
	Height	480
	Left	2865
Name	cmdClear	
	Top	2880
	Width	1755

The completed project is on the CD that comes with this book.

Now give the user a way to change the line width by setting the `DrawWidth` property. Add the following code to the click event of the Command button, `cmdWidth`, to change the `DrawWidth` property of the picture box.

```
Private Sub cmdWidth_Click()
    '
    'If valid number change the width of the point
    If IsNumeric(txtWidth.Text) Then
        Picture1.DrawWidth = Val(txtWidth)
    End If
End Sub
```

Now add the code to perform the actual drawing in the picture box. To draw the line while the mouse is moving, use the **PSet** command and the **MouseMove** event. A flag that prevents points from being drawn while a mouse button is down allows the mouse to move without drawing. Define the following variable in the form's general declaration section:

```
Dim bDrawFlag As Boolean
```

Set the variable **DrawFlag** to **True** when a mouse button is clicked over the picture box in the mouse down event, as shown in the following code:

```
Private Sub Picture1_MouseDown(Button As Integer, Shift As Integer, X As Single, ⇐
Y As Single)
    'set flag to start drawing
    bDrawFlag = True
End Sub
```

To stop drawing when the user releases the mouse button, set the variable **DrawFlag** to **False** in the picture box's mouse up event as follows:

```
Private Sub Picture1_MouseUp(Button As Integer, Shift As Integer, X As Single, ⇐
Y As Single)
    'Set flag to Stop Drawing
    bDrawFlag = False
End Sub
```

Use the **PSet** method and the current x and y coordinates to draw a line as the user moves the mouse by adding the following code to the picture box's **MouseMove** event:

```
Private Sub Picture1_MouseMove(Button As Integer, Shift As Integer, X As Single, ⇐
Y As Single)
    'Only draw if the mouse button is being
    'held down.
    '
    If bDrawFlag = True Then
        Picture1.PSet (X, Y)
    End If
End Sub
```

Add the following code to the click event of the Command button, **cmdClear**, to clear the picture box:

```
Private Sub cmdClear_Click()
    Picture1.Cls
End Sub
```

To finish the application, add the following code in the form's load event:

```
Private Sub Form_Load()
    bDrawFlag = False
    txtWidth = Picture1.DrawWidth
End Sub
```

You are now ready to test the application. Start the application, click in the picture box, and hold down the right or left mouse button. Move the mouse around. What happens? Change the **DrawWidth** property using the text box and the Command button, shown in Figure 11-8. What do you think? Just like a real chalkboard (except for the "artist")!

You have now created your first application using graphical methods. In the next lesson, you will use graphical methods to create various shapes.

Figure 11-8
Chalkboard
application

1. The Shape control and the _____ control do not support graphical methods.
   a. Form
   b. Image
   c. PictureBox
   d. Printer Object

2. A PictureBox control has the following line of code in the form activate event:

   `Picture1.Cls`

   The code does one of the following:
   a. Closes a picture box named Picture1
   b. Clears (erases) the contents of the PictureBox control for Picture1
   c. Initializes the picture box Picture1 for graphical methods
   d. Will not work; it should be `Picture1.Cls(x1,y1)`

3. The graphical method `Pset` does the following:
   a. Sets a specific point on a form or picture box to a specified color
   b. Draws a line
   c. Clears the picture box or form
   d. Sets the mouse cursor to a point on the form

4. The following line of code

   `Picture1.Line -(100,200),,B`

   a. Will not work because the statement is missing a set of coordinates
   b. Draws a line from the current x and current y position to the coordinates (100,200)
   c. Draws a box
   d. Draws a bold line from the current x and current y position to the coordinates (100,200)

5. The function to test for a valid number used in the Chalkboard application is:
   a. `IsNumeric()`
   b. `Number()`
   c. `Val()`
   d. `ValNumeric()`

DRAWING SHAPES

You will build on the different graphics methods you learned in the last lesson to create various shapes like squares and rectangles, and use a new method that allows you to create circles. This is an interactive lesson with a lot of code samples, so start up Visual Basic and get going. Create a new project so you can use it to test graphical methods code. Name the project TstShape, and add a form, three text boxes, a picture box, and three labels. Set the properties as shown in Table 11-4. The completed project is on the CD that comes with this book.

Table 11-4 Object and property settings for project TstShape

Object	Property	Setting
Form	Caption	Test Shapes
	Height	4545
	Name	frmTestShapes
	Width	6810
PictureBox	BackColor	&H00FFFFFF&
	DrawWidth	2
	Height	2685
	Left	1800
	Name	Picture1
	ScaleMode	3 - Pixel
	Top	90
	Width	4590
TextBox	Height	285
	Left	820
	Name	txtX
	Top	180
	Width	900
TextBox	Height	285
	Left	820
	Name	txtY
	Top	540
	Width	900

Object	Property	Setting
TextBox	Height	285
	Left	820
	Name	txtSize
	Top	930
	Width	900
Label	Caption	X coord
	Height	285
	Left	180
	Name	lblX
	Top	210
	Width	630
Label	Caption	Y coord
	Height	285
	Left	180
	Name	lblY
	Top	585
	Width	675
Label	Caption	Size
	Height	285
	Left	315
	Name	lblSize
	Top	945
	Width	375

Your test application is now complete. Well, almost. You have to write some code to draw various shapes. Start with a box.

Drawing Boxes

Think about how you would draw a box if you had a pencil, paper, and a ruler. You would draw one side of the box, draw another side starting where the line just finished, and continue on around until your box is drawn. You can use the same drawing technique using the **Line** method. The following code draws a box that starts at coordinates (100,100) and measures 200 pixels on each side:

```
Picture1.Line (100,100) - Step (200,0)
Picture1.Line - Step(0,200)
Picture1.Line -Step(-200,0)
Picture1.Line -Step(0,-200)
```

Take a look at the code. The first line uses the keyword **Step**. As a matter of fact, **Step** is used in all the code lines with the **Line** method. **Step** allows you to use a relative position instead of figuring out exact coordinates for each ending point. Relative coordinates means that the coordinates you use are based on the current x and y position of the cursor. For example, using exact coordinates, the first line of code could be rewritten without the **Step** keyword as

```
Picture1.Line1 (100,100) - (300,100)
```

Using the keyword **Step** prevents you from having to figure out the ending coordinates. For example:

```
Picture1.Line (100,100) - Step (200,0)
```

The **Step** command adds 200 units to the x position of **100** and 0 units to the y position of **100**. The line still ends at (300,100), but all you did was give the width of the line instead of the exact coordinates using relative position. Notice that you can leave the first set of coordinates out of the **Line** method, and the line starts using the current x and y coordinates.

 You can set the current x and y coordinates of a form or PictureBox control by setting the **CurrentX** and **CurrentY** properties.

Now add a Command button to draw a box in your application. Add the Command button, and set the properties as shown in Table 11-5.

Table 11-5 Box Command button property settings for project TstShape

Object	Property	Setting
CommandButton	Caption	Box
	Height	555
	Left	2400
Name	c	dBox
	Top	3150
	Width	1470

Add the following code shown in Listing 11-1 to the Command button click event.

Listing 11-1 Draw Box Command button click event code

```
Private Sub cmdBox_Click()
Dim iX As Integer, iY As Integer, iSize As Integer
Dim lColorValue As Long

    If (IsNumeric(txtX) And IsNumeric(txtY) _
      And IsNumeric(txtSize)) Then
        iX = Val(txtX)
        iY = Val(txtY)
        iSize = Val(txtSize)
        '
        'Get the Color
        '
        lColorValue = GetColor
        'Draw the Box
        Picture1.Line (iX, iY)-Step((iX + iSize), (iY + iSize)), lColorValue, BF
    End If

End Sub
```

Examine the code you used to create a box:

```
'Draw the Box
 Picture1.Line (X, Y)-Step((X + Size), (Y + Size)), , B
```

Instead of using the **Line** method four times to draw each line of the box, you used the special option *B*, to create boxes of the given size and starting points. The **IsNumeric** function is used to validate that the points in the text boxes are numeric. Run the application and enter an x coordinate, a y coordinate, and the size, and then click the Box Command button. The box drawn by the code is shown in Figure 11-9.

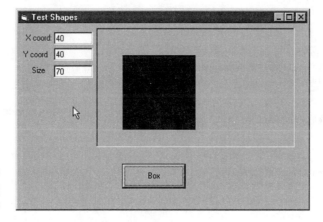

Figure 11-9
Box drawn using
graphical methods

Drawing Triangles

Think about how you would draw a triangle. Do you think you could put it into code? Unfortunately the **Line** method does not have a draw triangle switch. To draw shapes like triangles, stars, or octagons requires you to write the functions and subroutine that allow you to create these various shapes. Add a Command button and set the properties as shown in Table 11-6.

Table 11-6 Triangle Command button property settings for project TstShape

Object	Property	Setting
CommandButton	Caption	Triangle
	Height	555
	Left	2400
	Name	cmdTriangle
	Top	3150
	Width	1470

Add the code to draw a triangle, as shown in Listing 11-2.

Listing 11-2 Code to draw a triangle

```
Private Sub cmdTriangle_Click()
Dim iX As Integer, iY As Integer, iSize As Integer

    If (IsNumeric(txtX) And IsNumeric(txtY)) Then
        iX = Val(txtX)
        iY = Val(txtY)
        iSize = Val(txtSize)
        '
        'Get the X and Y coordinates to draw
        'the triangle. Set the starting
        'coordinates.
        '
        Picture1.CurrentX = iX
        Picture1.CurrentY = iY

        'Draw Right Triangle
        '
        Picture1.Line -(iX + iSize, ((iY + iSize) / 2))   'Hypotenuse
        Picture1.Line -(iX, ((iY + iSize) / 2)) ' Bottom
        Picture1.Line -(iX, iY) 'Straight line up - back

    End If

End Sub
```

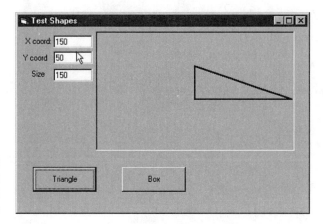

Figure 11-10
Triangle drawn
using graphical
methods

Run the application and enter 150 for the x coordinate, 50 for the y coordinate, and 150 for the size, and then click the Triangle button. A right-angle triangle appears in your drawing area, as shown in Figure 11-10.

Drawing Circles

The `Circle` method allows you to draw circles, arcs, and ellipses. It has the following format:

```
[object].Circle [Step](x,y), radius, [color], [start], [end], [aspect]
```

where radius is a required field and specifies the length of the radius of the circular shape. `Color` is an optional field used to set the background color of the circular shape. The start and end variables are used to create arcs and ellipses. The aspect parameter is the aspect ratio of the circular shape and defaults to 1.0 for a perfect circle. Add a Command button to draw circles, and set the properties as shown in Table 11-7.

Table 11-7 Circle Command button property settings for project TstShape

Object	Property	Setting
CommandButton	Caption	Circle
	Height	555
	Left	4455
	Name	cmdCircle
	Top	3150
	Width	1470

Add the code in Listing 11-3 to the Command button's click event.

Listing 11-3 Adding a button to draw circles

```
Private Sub cmdCircle_Click()
Dim iX As Integer, iY As Integer, iSize As Integer
Dim lColorValue As Long

    If (IsNumeric(txtX) And IsNumeric(txtY) _
      And IsNumeric(txtSize)) Then
        iX = Val(txtX)
        iY = Val(txtY)
        iSize = Val(txtSize)
        '
        '
        'Get the Color
        '
        lColorValue = GetColor
        '
        'Set the Fill color on the Picture box
        If chkFillColor = vbChecked Then
            Picture1.FillColor = lColorValue
            Picture1.FillStyle = vbSolid
        Else
            Picture1.FillStyle = vbTransparent
        End If
        '
        'Draw the Circle
        Picture1.Circle (iX, iY), iSize, lColorValue
    End If

End Sub
```

In the code, the **Size** parameter is used to create the radius of the circle. Try the circle function. Run the application, enter some parameters, and click the Circle Command button. A perfect circle displays in the drawing area of the application, as shown in Figure 11-11.

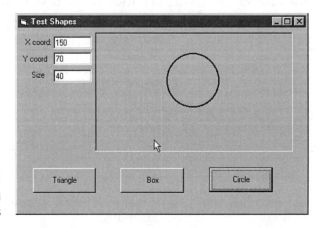

Figure 11-11
Circle drawn using
graphical methods

You now have all the tools required to create complex shapes with Visual Basic. Try to draw other shapes not covered in this lesson, like ellipses, arcs, polygons, and stars. In the next lesson, you will learn how to spice up the looks of your graphical applications using colors.

1. Executing the following code

   ```
   Picture1.Line (100,100) - (250,150)
   ```

   is equivalent to:
   a. `Picture1.PSet (250,150)`
   b. `Picture1.Line (100,100) - Step (150,0)`
   c. `Picture1.Line (100,100) - Step(150,50)`
   d. `Picture1.Line (100,100) + Step(150,50)`

2. The code:

   ```
   Picture1.Line (100,100) - Step(50,50), , B
   ```

   a. Draws a triangle
   b. Draws a box
   c. Draws a circle
   d. Draws a line

3. The code:

   ```
   Picture1.Line - (50, 25)
   Picture1.Line - (0, 25)
   Picture1.Line - (0,0)
   ```

   a. Draws a triangle
   b. Draws a series of lines
   c. Draws a semicircle
   d. Draws two lines

4. To draw a circle, use the:
   a. `Circle` property
   b. `Pset`
   c. `Ellipse` method
   d. `Circle` method

5. What does the aspect parameter value of **1.0** do when using the `Circle` method?
   a. Creates an ellipse
   b. Creates a semicircle
   c. Creates an arc
   d. Creates a perfect circle

REVIEW

John: I really like doing graphics with Visual Basic, but I'm not so sure I'll spend too much time learning about coordinates or graphical methods.

Lisa: Why is that?

John: I think that, for most of the things I need to do, I can get away with just using the Shape or Line custom controls.

Lisa: I'm not so sure it's wise to skip over the coordinates system. Understanding the Visual Basic coordinates system is not only very important in using graphical methods, but it can be used in automatic form resizing and placement. Besides, the coordinate system takes us back to basic geometry with x and y coordinates and is not too difficult to understand.

John: You have a point, no pun intended, but when would I use graphical methods?

Lisa: Anytime you need to draw some complex picture, like a map of a country.

John: You can do that with Visual Basic?

Lisa: Sure, given the right x and y coordinates and the proper data points.

John: I'll bet I could use graphical methods to create my own graphs and charts, that is, if I could just add some color to my drawings.

Lisa: Sure you could create your own graphs and charts. But I think Visual Basic has a graph custom control. You can add colors using graphical methods which are explained in the next lesson.

John: You were reading ahead again?

Lisa: No. This time I just checked the Table of Contents for this chapter!

John: Well, what are we waiting for? Time to learn about colors!

COLORS

In this lesson, you will examine several different ways to add colors to your applications. Visual Basic supports 256 colors on properly configured computer systems. Colors in Visual Basic are represented by a long integer (4 bytes), as shown in Figure 11-12.

The high byte is set to **0**; and the next three bytes contain the amount of red, green, and blue associated with the color. Colors are represented by hexadecimal numbers in the control and form properties, and they can be set directly using a hex number. For example, the hex number for the color red shown in Figure 11-12 is **&H000000FF&**. Note that the arrangement of digits in the hexadecimal numbers is the reverse of what you might expect. It is **00BBGGRR**.

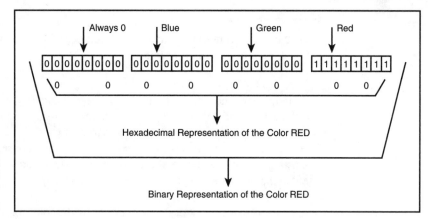

Figure 11-12
Visual Basic byte
color
representation

Setting Colors on Forms and Controls Using Properties

Throughout this book, you have changed the colors of forms and controls such as the PictureBox and the Label by setting certain properties at design or runtime. Properties of forms and controls can be set by selecting the property in the Properties window and assigning a hex number to the property, or by clicking on the property and selecting from the color palette displayed. Here is a quick review of some of the properties you can use to change the colors of a form or control.

BackColor

The **BackColor** property determines the background color of the form or control. You have used this property several times throughout this book to change the background color of a form.

BorderColor

BorderColor is the color used to paint the border of a control.

ForeColor

ForeColor is used to create the graphics or text drawn on an object such as a form or control.

FillColor

FillColor is the color used to fill the inside of boxes created with the **Line** method and circular shapes created with the **Circle** method.

Color Functions

Visual Basic offers two functions that return valid color numbers to set colors of objects during runtime. They are the **RGB** function and the **QBColor** function.

RGB

The **RGB** function is used to return a valid number that represents a color value. The syntax of the **RGB** function is as follows:

```
RGB (red, green, blue)
```

where red, green, and blue are numbers between 0 and 255; and where 0 represents *none* of the color and 255 represents the maximum possible amount of the color. These numbers correspond to the binary numbers in the byte color representation shown in Figure 11-12, but notice that the three colors are listed in *reverse order*. That is not particularly significant to you unless you choose to use the hexadecimal number for a color instead of the simpler **RGB** representations. Recall that a Byte type variable can hold numbers between 0 and 255.

To create a color using **RGB** you need to specify the color component values for your color. A value of **0** excludes the color and a value of **255** uses the maximum amount of the color. Here are some examples of using the **RGB** function to return some well known RGB color numbers:

```
Black = RGB(0,0,0)
Red = RGB(255,0,0)
Yellow = RGB(255,255,0)
```

It may seem odd using red, green, and blue as the primary colors, when you learned in grade school to use red, yellow, and blue. The reason for the difference is that video displays are working with *transmitted* light instead of the reflected light from your water color paints.

QBColor

Trying to get the correct color value using the **RGB** function may be difficult, even when trying to use standard colors. Visual Basic provides a function called **QBColor** that allows you to select the color by name instead of toggling different **RGB** values to create the correct color number.

The function gets its name from a previous version of Microsoft Quick Basic. You can use the **QBColor** function to return an RGB color value based on a color constant value. **QBColor** has the following syntax:

```
QBColor(color)
```

where the color parameter is one of the constant values listed in Table 11-8.

Table 11-8   QBColor constants

Number	Color
0	Black
1	Blue

Number	Color
2	Green
3	Cyan
4	Red
5	Magenta
6	Yellow
7	White
8	Gray
9	Light blue
10	Light green
11	Light cyan
12	Light red
13	Light magenta
14	Light yellow
15	Bright white

Visual Basic Constants

Visual Basic also has predefined constants specifying RGB number values for a few standard colors. You can use these values, shown in Table 11-9, to set the color of an object instead of using either the **RGB** or **QBColor** functions.

Table 11-9 Visual Basic color constant values

Constant	Description
vbBlack	Black
vbRed	Red
vbGreen	Green
vbYellow	Yellow
vbBlue	Blue
vbMagenta	Magenta
vbCyan	Cyan
vbWhite	White

It is safer to use the QBColors than the RGB colors because almost any computer that runs your programs responds correctly to them. The RGB colors do not show up correctly on computers that are not set up for 256 color displays. It may seem odd that, in this day of SVGA monitors, someone would not have it set up to handle 256 colors, but it happens.

Now, add some color to the TestShape project by adding code that fills the circles and boxes drawn with a selected color using the **QBColor** function. Add a combo list box and a check box to the form, **frmTestShape**, and set the properties as shown in Table 11-10.

Table 11-10 Color objects and properties for project TstShape

Object	Property	Setting
ComboBox	Height	315
	Left	105
	Name	cmbColor
	Style	2 - Dropdown List
	Top	1485
	Width	1530
CheckBox	Caption	Fill Color
	Height	255
	Left	135
	Name	chkFillColor
	Top	1980
	Value	0 - UnChecked
	Width	1140

In the form **frmTestShape** load event, add the code shown in Listing 11-4 to load the possible **QBColor** codes into the ComboBox.

Listing 11-4 Loading possible QBColors into a combo box during form load

```
Private Sub Form_Load()
    cmbColor.AddItem "Black"
    cmbColor.AddItem "Blue"
    cmbColor.AddItem "Green"
    cmbColor.AddItem "Cyan"
    cmbColor.AddItem "Red"
    cmbColor.AddItem "Magenta"
    cmbColor.AddItem "Yellow"
    cmbColor.AddItem "White"
    cmbColor.AddItem "Grey"
    cmbColor.AddItem "Light Blue"
    cmbColor.AddItem "Light Green"
    cmbColor.AddItem "Light Cyan"
    cmbColor.AddItem "Light Red"
    cmbColor.AddItem "Light Magenta"
    cmbColor.AddItem "Light Yellow"
```

```
        cmbColor.AddItem "Bright White"
        cmbColor.ListIndex = 0

End Sub
```

Add a new function to **frmTestShape** that uses the color in the combo box to get an **RGB** value using the **QBColor** function. Add the following function, shown in Listing 11-5, to **frmTestShape**.

Listing 11-5 GetColor function

```
Public Function GetColor() As Long
Dim sColor As String, lColorValue As Long
'
'Return the proper Color code
'for the color selected in the list.
'
 sColor = cmbColor
 Select Case sColor
    Case "Black"
        lColorValue = QBColor(0)
    Case "Blue"
        lColorValue = QBColor(1)
    Case "Green"
        lColorValue = QBColor(2)
    Case "Cyan"
        lColorValue = QBColor(3)
    Case "Red"
        lColorValue = QBColor(4)
    Case "Magenta"
        lColorValue = QBColor(5)
    Case "Yellow"
        lColorValue = QBColor(6)
    Case "White"
        lColorValue = QBColor(7)
    Case "Grey"
        lColorValue = QBColor(8)
    Case "Light Blue"
        lColorValue = QBColor(9)
    Case "Light Green"
        lColorValue = QBColor(10)
    Case "Light Cyan"
        lColorValue = QBColor(11)
    Case "Light Red"
        lColorValue = QBColor(12)
    Case "Light Magenta"
        lColorValue = QBColor(13)
    Case "Light Yellow"
        lColorValue = QBColor(14)
    Case "Bright White"
        lColorValue = QBColor(15)
  End Select
  GetColor = lColorValue
End Function
```

Now that you have created a mechanism to select different colors, add the code that fills the boxes and circles with the selected color. Add the code shown in Listing 11-6 to the click event of the Circle Command button. The new code is shown in bold.

Listing 11-6 Circle Command button click event with color-changing code

```
Private Sub cmdCircle_Click()
Dim iX As Integer, iY As Integer, iSize As Integer
Dim lColorValue As Long

    If (IsNumeric(txtX) And IsNumeric(txtY) _
      And IsNumeric(txtSize)) Then
        iX = Val(txtX)
        iY = Val(txtY)
        iSize = Val(txtSize)
        '
        '
        'Get the Color
        '
        lColorValue = GetColor
        '
        'Set the Fill color on the Picture box
        If chkFillColor = vbChecked Then
            Picture1.FillColor = lColorValue
            Picture1.FillStyle = vbSolid
        Else
            Picture1.FillStyle = vbTransparent
        End If
        '
        'Draw the Circle
        Picture1.Circle (iX, iY), Size, lColorValue
    End If

End Sub
```

For the Box Command button click event, add the code shown in Listing 11-7.

Listing 11-7 Box Command button click event with color-changing code

```
Private Sub cmBox_Click()
Dim iX As iInteger, iY As Integer, iSize As Integer
Dim iColorValue As Long
    If (IsNumeric(txtX) And IsNumeric(txtY) _
      And IsNumeric(txtSize)) Then
        iX = Val(txtX)
        iY = Val(txtY)
        iSize = Val(txtSize)
        '
        'Get the Color
        '
        lColorValue = GetColor
```

```
        'Draw the Box
        Picture1.Line (iX, iY)-Step((iX + iSize), (iY + iSize)), lColorValue, BF
    End If

End Sub
```

Now you are ready to test the application. Select a color from the combo box, enter coordinates and size, and click the Box Command button. What happens? A box is drawn and filled with the selected color. To create the color effect, the **Line** method used to draw the box was modified to specify a color using the color parameter, and the **F** option was added to fill the box with the same color used to draw the box. Now try to create a circle. What happened? The circle does not fill with the selected color. In order to fill a circle, you must set the **FillStyle** and **FillColor** properties of the object on which you are drawing the circle, in this case, the picture box. Check the check box Fill Style, and try again. Figure 11-13 shows a filled circle.

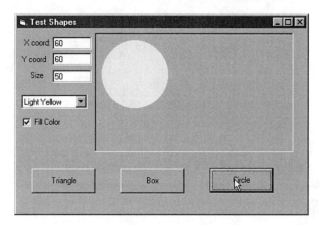

Figure 11-13
Circle filled with a selected color

The Graphics methods also work with the **Printer** object. **Printer.Line (0,0)-(1444,2888)** has the same effect on the printer as it did on the form. Of course, if you don't have a color printer, the colors are rendered as grey scales.

1. Colors are represented in Visual Basic by a:
   a. String variable
   b. Integer variable
   c. Decimal variable
   d. Long integer

2. RGB stands for:
   a. Red Green Blue
   b. Raster Graphical Bits
   c. Red Green Black
   d. Real Graphical Bits

3. The `FillColor` property is the:
   a. Background color in forms and text boxes
   b. Color used to fill shapes created with `Line` and `Circle` methods
   c. Foreground color for custom controls
   d. Value which combines with the background property to blend special colors when using graphical methods

4. Which of the following will not change the background color of a form named `Form1`?
   a. `Form1.BackColor = QBColor(12)`
   b. `Form1.BackColor = vbRed`
   c. `Form1.BackColor = RGB(0,0,255)`
   d. `Form1.BackColor = QBColor(12)`

5. What will the following line of code do?

   ```
   Picture1.Circle (50,50),,vbRed
   ```

   a. Draw a circle with a red outline
   b. Draw a circle filled with red
   c. Nothing, because the statement is missing parameters
   d. Draw a circle with a red outline and red fill

PICTURE CONTROL VERSUS IMAGE CONTROL

Nothing adds as much flair to an application as a well-placed picture or company logo displayed on a form or splash screen. Everyone loves pictures, and Visual Basic provides you with two custom controls that allow you to display pictures and images in your applications. They are

 PictureBox

 Image

The PictureBox and Image controls, shown in Figure 11-14, allow you to load pictures into your application at design time or runtime. Before you examine the two controls, review the types of picture files available.

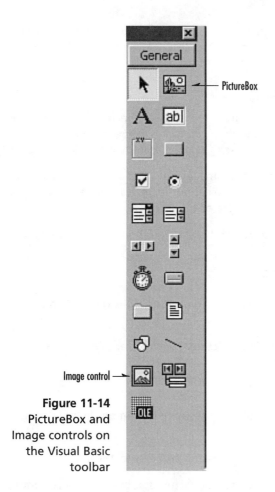

PictureBox

Image control →

Figure 11-14
PictureBox and
Image controls on
the Visual Basic
toolbar

Picture Files

The *bitmap* is a picture file with a `.BMP` file extension in which the image is stored with a pixel representation; each bit represents a pixel. An *icon* is a bitmap that is usually used to represent pictures on buttons, minimized windows, or the graphical representation of the application in a windows folder. Icons have an `.ICO` extension and have a size of 32 by 32 pixels.

A *metafile* stores the picture as a collection of graphical objects such as lines, circles, and squares instead of pixels. Metafiles have a `.WMF` file extension and are usually smaller than bitmaps. *GIF* and *JPG* files are industry standard file formats for pictures, either of which is suitable for Internet applications.

Where can you find pictures for your applications? Visual Basic comes with several icons, metafiles, and bitmaps. These files can be found off of the Visual Basic home directory (`C:\VB`) in the subdirectories metafiles, bitmaps, and icons. You can also download images from electronic bulletin boards, purchase clip art pictures, scan pictures into a PC, or create your own pictures using tools like Microsoft Paintbrush or an icon editor. There is also a wide assortment of images in all formats available for download to be found on the Internet.

Loading a Picture

Take a short walk through the steps required to a load a picture into a PictureBox control or an Image control. Start Visual Basic and create a new project. Don't worry about saving the project. The examples here are to help you learn how to load pictures.

1. Place a PictureBox control and an Image control, shown in Figure 11-14, onto the form. Make the PictureBox about an inch square and make the Image control about twice the size of the PictureBox.

2. Click on the PictureBox control, and press F4 to bring up the control's properties window.

3. Set the AutoSize property to True.

4. Scroll to the Picture property and click on the ... button. A file dialog box is displayed.

5. Use the file dialog box to find a picture. For this example, go to the Visual Basic icons folder.

6. Go into the folder labeled Misc.

7. Select the file misc39a.ico and click the Open button on the file dialog box.

8. Select the Image control. Set its Stretch property to True.

9. Using the same steps you used for the PictureBox, load Misc39b.ico into the Image control.

The picture is now loaded in your PictureBox. You should see the firecracker icon in the PictureBox control, and the exploded firecracker in the Image control, as shown in Figure 11-15.

Sometimes you may want to load your pictures at runtime instead of design time, for instance, if you are trying to keep the size of your executable file small. (Pictures loaded at design time become part of the application size; thus, a large picture can substantially increase the size of your executable.)

To Load a Picture at Runtime

Use the loadpicture command that has the following syntax:

`LoadPicture(image file)`

where *image file* is the name and path name of the picture to load in the control.

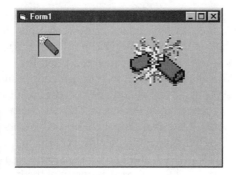

Figure 11-15
Firecracker icon
displayed in a
picture box

The code in Listing 11-8 loads the Visual Basic icon `misc39a.ico` into the Image control.

Listing 11-8 Loading an icon at runtime

```
Private Sub Form_Load()
Dim IconPath As String

    IconPath = App.Path & "\icons\misc\misc39b.ico"
    Image1.Picture = LoadPicture(IconPath)

End Sub
```

If you want to share the same image between two controls, you do not need to reload the picture. Instead, you can use the picture properties, as follows:

```
Image1.Picture = Picture1.Picture
```

Sharing images between controls conserves Windows resources. When you no longer need a picture, unload it to free up the resources by using the `LoadPicture` command as follows:

```
Image1.Picture = LoadPicture("")   'Clear out picture
```

Differences Between Image and PictureBox Controls

You may be asking yourself, why have two controls to display pictures? After all, they seem to perform the same function. They both *are* used to display pictures. But the two controls have different features which distinguish them from each other. For one thing, the Image control, as mentioned earlier, is a lightweight control. This means it is not a window, so it uses substantially fewer resources than a PictureBox control. However, you cannot use the Image control to contain other controls; you have to use the PictureBox. If you want to use the graphical methods you learned earlier, such as `Line`, `Circle`, or `Pset`, you have to use the PictureBox control. Finally, if you want to transfer pictures in a DDE exchange, you must use the PictureBox control.

So when should you use the Image control? If you want to display pictures or use pictures as buttons, then use the Image control. Another difference between the Image control and the PictureBox is how the control responds to pictures that are larger or smaller than the Image control or PictureBox control. The PictureBox has a property called `AutoSize`. When `AutoSize` is set to `True`, the control automatically resizes the control to display the picture. Image controls do not have an `AutoSize` property because they are automatically resized to fit the image. There is one last important difference between the two controls. The Image control can be used to stretch an image (i.e., make it larger or smaller). To stretch an image, set the `Stretch` property on the Image control to `True`. Picture boxes cannot stretch images! Experiment with the `AutoSize` property of the PictureBox control and the `Stretch` property of the Image control.

1. Visual Basic provides two controls to display pictures, the PictureBox and the _____ control.
   a. Shape
   b. Image
   c. TextBox
   d. Photo

2. A _____ stores images with a pixel representation.
   a. Bitmap
   b. Metafile
   c. Icon
   d. GraphicRaster

3. To add a picture to a PictureBox or Image control at runtime, use the:
   a. `PictureLoad` property
   b. `AddPicture` method
   c. `LoadPicture` method
   d. `AddPicture` property

4. Which one of the following is not a characteristic of the Image control?
   a. Displays pictures
   b. `Stretch` property
   c. Considered a Windows light control
   d. `AutoSize` property

5. Which of the following is not a characteristic of the PictureBox control?
   a. Displays pictures
   b. Can be used to stretch an image
   c. Automatically resizes to fit the size of the picture
   d. Has graphical methods like `Pset` and `Line`

SIMPLE ANIMATION

In this lesson, you will learn about *animation*, which is making objects on the screen appear as if they are moving. You will develop a simple animation program to help you understand several graphical methods and techniques. The example is based on the old bouncing-ball animation. Instead of a ball moving from side to side and up and down, the application uses a smiley face icon; as the icon moves, the facial expressions of the icon change. Before you get started, take a look at the method that is used to move the icon. The **Move** method has the following syntax:

```
object.Move left, [top], [width], [height]
```

where

● **Left** is the only required parameter and indicates the direction you wish to move the object.

● **Top** is the up or down direction to move the object.

● **Width** and **Height** values allow you to change the size of the object.

Here's how to use the **Move** method to move an object using *absolute movement* or *relative movement*. Using absolute movement, you specify the destination x and y coordinates to move the object inside of its container. For example, the following code moves the object to the coordinates (50,20):

```
Image1.Move 50,20
```

Relative movement specifies how far to move the object relative to its current position. For example the following code moves the Image control 50 units to the left and 20 units up:

```
Image1.Move Image1.Left - 50, Image1.Top - 20
```

Notice that the code uses the current position of the Image control to determine the destination coordinates. To move left using relative position, subtract from the object's left property; to move right, add; to go up, subtract from the object's top property; and to move down, add.

The Animation Program

Now for a quick look at how the animation program works. An Image control displays an icon, in this case, the smiley face icon. The form acts as the container for the Image control to move around. For simplicity, the Image control only goes from side to side. The image itself changes appearance as it moves across the screen. Do this by changing the icon each time the Image control is moved.

Start by creating a new project called Animate that has a single form and a Timer control. The Timer control is the control that looks like a stopwatch on the toolbar. The timer control is covered in detail in Chapter 14, Advanced Features. For now you only need to understand that the Timer control periodically runs the code required to move the images across the screen. Set the properties as shown in Table 11-11. The completed project is on the CD that comes with this book.

Table 11-11 Form and Timer control property settings for project Animate

Object	Property	Setting
Form	Caption	Simple Animation
	Height	4545
	Name	frmAnimation
	Top	1485
	Width	1530
Timer	Enabled	True
	Interval	250
	Name	Timer1

In order to scroll through a series of icons, create an Image control array with four Image controls in the array (0-3). Only the first Image control in the array requires additional properties set. The others only need the picture property. Set the picture properties for each image in the image array accordingly. The images to use are the face01.ico, face02.ico, and face03.ico files located in VB\GRAPHICS\ICONS\MISC. Set the Image control properties as shown in Table 11-12.

Table 11-12 Image control array property settings for project Animate

Object	Property	Setting
Image1(0)	Height	480
	Left	75
	Picture	face01.ico
	Top	645
	Width	480
Image1(1)	Height	480
	Left	75
	Picture	face01.ico
	Top	1290
	Width	480

Object	Property	Setting
Image1(2)	Height	480
	Left	75
	Picture	face02.ico
	Top	1890
	Width	480
Image1(3)	Height	480
	Left	75
	Picture	face03.ico
	Top	2475
	Width	480

The completed form with the images is shown in Figure 11-16.

Declare the following variables and constants in the form's general declaration section:

```
Dim iImageIndex As Integer, iDirection As Integer
Const ImageRight = 1
Const ImageLeft = 2
```

The variable **ImageIndex** is used to toggle through the Image control array and display each image in the control array. The Direction variable determines the direction the Image control is moving and is set to one of the constants: **ImageRight** or **ImageLeft**. Add the code in Listing 11-9 to the form load event to initialize the **ImageIndex** and **Direction** variables.

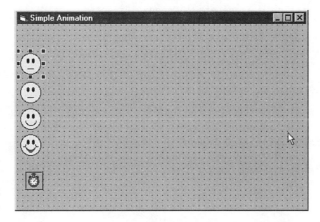

Figure 11-16
Animation form
with icons at
design time

Listing 11-9 Form load event initialization code

```
Private Sub Form_Load()
    '
    'Set up the Image control array
    '
    iImageIndex = 1
    '
    'Start in the right iDirection
    '
    iDirection = ImageRight
    '
    '
    Slider1.Value = Timer1.Interval
End Sub
```

Now to add the code that actually performs the animation. In the Timer control's timer event, add the code shown in Listing 11-10.

Listing 11-10 The Timer control's timer event code to perform animation

```
Private Sub Timer1_Timer()
    '
    'Move the Graphic
    '
    If iDirection = ImageRight Then
        'Move the Image 75 twips to the right
        'don't move the image up
        '
        Image1(0).Move Image1(0).Left + 75
        '
        'Check to see if the image is of the edge of the form
        '
        If Image1(0).Left >= (frmAnimation.Width − Image1(0).Width) Then
            iDirection = ImageLeft ' Change iDirection
        End If
    ElseIf iDirection = ImageLeft Then
        'Move the Image 75 twips to the left
        'don't move the image up
        '
        Image1(0).Move Image1(0).Left − 75
        '
        'Check to see if the image is off the edge of the
        ' form
        If Image1(0).Left <= 0 Then
            '
            'Change the iDirection
            '
            iDirection = ImageRight
        End If
    End If
    '
```

```
'Change the picture to give us that
'stop motion picture animation
'
Image1(0).Picture = Image1(iImageIndex).Picture
'
' Bump to the next frame
iImageIndex = iImageIndex + 1
'
'Check to see if we have exceeded
'The max number of images
If iImageIndex = 4 Then
    iImageIndex = 1 'Reset
End If

End Sub
```

For the finishing touch, add a Windows 95 control to allow the user to control the speed of the smiley face as it bounces across the screen. Add a Slider control, and set the properties as shown in Table 11-13.

Table 11-13 Slider control property settings for project Animate

Object	Property	Setting
Slider	Height	375
	Max	100
	Min	5
	Name	Slider1
	Top	3360
	Width	4575

In the form load event, add the following code:

```
Slider1.Value = Timer1.Interval
```

In the slider scroll event, add the following code:

```
Private Sub Slider1_Scroll()
    Timer1.Interval = Slider1.Value
End Sub
```

Run the application, shown in Figure 11-17. The smiley face is moving across the screen, changing facial expressions along the way. You have created a simple animation application! To change the speed of the smiley face's movement, adjust the **Interval** property of the Timer control by using the slider control. As an exercise, enhance the application to include up and down movement. Before you show off the application, don't forget the quiz!

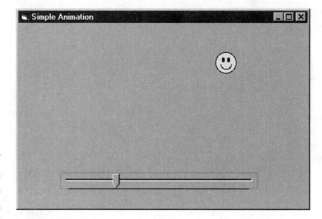

Figure 11-17
Animation
application in
action

1. The following line of code

```
Image1.Move 50,20
```

is an example of:
a. Relative movement
b. Absolute movement
c. Direct movement
d. Coordinate movement

2. What does the following code do?

```
Image1.Move Image1.Left - 50, Image1.Top - 20
```

a. Moves a form to the right 50 units and down 20 units
b. Moves an Image control to the right 50 units and up 20 units
c. Moves an Image control to the left 50 units and up 20 units
d. Moves an Image control to the right 50 units and down 20 units

3. The following code

```
Image1.Move Image1.Left - 50, Image1.Top - 20
```

is an example of:
a. Relative movement
b. Absolute movement
c. Direct movement
d. Coordinate movement

4. The following code

```
If Image1(0).Left >= (frmAnimation.Width - Image1(0).Width) Then
```

is used to determine:
a. If the image is at the top of the form
b. If the image is off the left edge of the form
c. If the image is off the bottom of the form
d. If the image is off the right edge of the form

5. In order to make the smiley face in your program change expressions, you used:
a. A control array of Image controls
b. A control array of PictureBox controls
c. Separate Image controls
d. Separate PictureBox controls

MISCELLANEOUS GRAPHICS ISSUES

In this lesson, you will take a close look at the effect of the **AutoRedraw** property. You will learn how to print high resolution graphics from a picture control to the printer, and you will also examine a custom control that is included in all of the editions of Visual Basic except for the standard edition. The Graph custom control allows you to display graphs and charts in your applications.

AutoRedraw

Run the chalkboard application you created during Lesson 3. Draw a line or a picture on the chalkboard, and then bring up the debug window. Overlay the chalkboard application with the debug window. Now, close the debug window; notice your drawing's gone! Next, set the **AutoRedraw** property on the picture box to **True**, and try the same experiment. The drawing is still there! So what is the **AutoRedraw** property up to? When a window is overlaid with another window and then redisplayed, Microsoft Windows automatically redraws the window and all of the controls. But Windows does not redraw the graphics you created with graphical methods unless the **AutoRedraw** property for the form or picture box is set to **True**. When the **AutoRedraw** property is set to **True**, Windows applies the graphical methods to your form or picture box and to a copy of the form or picture box in memory. If another window overlays your graphics, then Windows uses the copy of the image in memory to re-create the graphics.

PictureBox

The default value for the `AutoRedraw` property is `False`. You may be thinking to yourself, no problem. I'll just set `AutoRedraw` to `True` all the time and then I won't have to worry about graphical methods being erased. However, remember that setting `AutoRedraw` to `True` causes Windows to keep a copy of the image in memory. This increases the application's consumption of memory. Only set `AutoRedraw` to `True` when you are using graphical methods; otherwise, your forms and controls are repainted normally by Windows. If possible, minimize the amount of memory `AutoRedraw` eats up by using a picture box instead of a form. The amount of memory required to maintain a picture box is normally less than the amount required to maintain the entire form or screen. If you are working on a system without a lot of memory, consider redrawing the graphics yourself instead of using the `AutoRedraw` property.

Hard Copy

When you want to print your pictures to paper, Visual Basic comes to the rescue. Not only will VB 5 send the bitmap from a picture box to the printer, but you can locate it anywhere you want on the page, and you can scale it to any size you want. The latter is important, as you will see.

When you program for businesses, they like to see their logo on the forms, and they also like it on their printed output. It is not hard to scan a logo into the computer using a full page scanner or a hand scanner. The images you get, though, are often far too large to use on printed pages. Graphics programs can reduce images in almost any format, but the reduced image tends to get pretty ugly. Parts that were once round grow jagged edges, and angled lines look more like staircases than straight lines. The solution is the `PaintPicture` method.

The `PaintPicture` *Method*

The syntax of `PaintPicture` is enough to frighten almost anyone. It is

```
object.PaintPicture picture, x1, y1, width1, height1, x2, y2, width2, height2, opcode
```

where

- `object` is an optional object expression that evaluates to a Form, a PictureBox, or a Printer. If object is omitted, the Form with the focus is assumed to be object.

- `Picture` is the source of the graphic to be drawn onto the object. This must be the `Picture` property of a Form or a PictureBox.

- `x1, y1` are single-precision values indicating the destination coordinates (x-axis and y-axis) on the object for the picture to be drawn. The `ScaleMode` property of the object determines the unit of measure used.

- `width1` is an optional single-precision value indicating the destination width of the picture. The `ScaleMode` property of the object determines the unit of measure used. If the destination width is larger or smaller than the source width (width2), the picture is stretched or compressed to fit. If it is omitted, the source width is used.

- `height1` is an optional single-precision value indicating the destination height of the picture. The `ScaleMode` property of the object determines the unit of measure used. If the destination height is larger or smaller than the source height (height2), the picture is stretched or compressed to fit. If it is omitted, the source height is used.

- `x2, y2` are optional single-precision values indicating the coordinates (x-axis and y-axis) of a clipping region within the picture. The `ScaleMode` property of object determines the unit of measure used. If omitted, 0 is assumed.

- `width2` is an optional single-precision value indicating the source width of a clipping region within the picture. The `ScaleMode` property of object determines the unit of measure used. If omitted, the entire source width is used.

- `height2` is an optional single-precision value indicating the source height of a clipping region within the picture. The `ScaleMode` property of object determines the unit of measure used. If omitted, the entire source height is used.

- `opcode` is an optional long value or code that is used only with bitmaps. It defines a bit-wise operation that is performed on the picture as it's drawn on object.

If you use negative numbers for the destination height, your picture prints upside down. If you use negative numbers for width, your picture prints as a mirror image.

It seems a bit overwhelming, doesn't it? Fortunately, you can leave out most of the parameters and still get exactly the results you want.

Time to put together a little demo program. Assume that John and Lisa have started their own programming business, named *Mythical Programming Company*. They paid a graphic artist to create a logo, which is on the CD with the name **Mythical.GIF**. Now they want to use that logo when they print their invoices.

Start a new project called PixLogo. The completed project is on the CD that accompanies this book. Place a picture box, two command buttons, and an array of three option buttons on the form. The properties are shown in Table 11-14.

Table 11-14 Properties for the PixLogo project

Object	Property	Value
Form	Name	frmPixLogo
PictureBox	Name	pixLogo
	AutoSize	True
	Picture	Mythical.GIF
Command Button	Name	cmdPrint
	Caption	Print
Command Button	Name	cmdDone
	Caption	Done
Option Button	Name	optScale
	Index	0
	Caption	Full
	Value	True
Option Button	Name	optScale
	Index	1
	Caption	Half
Option Button	Name	optScale
	Index	2
	Caption	Quarter

The layout of the form is shown in Figure 11-18. Now add the code from Listing 11-11.

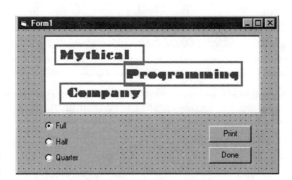

Figure 11-18
The PixLogo Project

Listing 11-11 The code for PixLogo

```
Option Explicit

Private Sub cmdDone_Click()
'    Finished -- Close the print job and exit
     Printer.EndDoc
     End
End Sub

Private Sub cmdPrint_Click()
 Static lPrintY As Long
     '    Paint the picture to the correct scale
     '    and reset the picture's currency so
     '    the next picture will not overprint it
     If optScale(0) Then
     '    Full scale
         Printer.PaintPicture pixLogo.Picture, 0, lPrintY
         lPrintY = lPrintY + pixLogo.Height + 722
     ElseIf optScale(1) Then
     '    half scale
         Printer.PaintPicture pixLogo.Picture, _
             0, lPrintY, pixLogo.Picture.Width / 2, _
             pixLogo.Picture.Height / 2
         lPrintY = lPrintY + pixLogo.Height / 2 + 722
     Else
     '    neither of above, must be quarter scale
         Printer.PaintPicture pixLogo.Picture, 0, _
             lPrintY, pixLogo.Picture.Width / 4, _
             pixLogo.Picture.Height / 4
         lPrintY = lPrintY + pixLogo.Height / 4 + 722
     End If
End Sub
```

A Look at the Code

There is nothing spectacular here. To save paper (and time), the logo can be printed repeatedly on the same sheet of paper. To keep them from all being printed in the same place, a static variable is used in **cmdPrint**'s click event. Each time a logo is printed, 722 twips (0.5 inches) are added to the variable.

The code for full scale printing,

```
Printer.PaintPicture pixLogo.Picture, 0, lPrintY
```

uses only the picture and the X1 and Y1 coordinates for printing the logo. The code for half-scale and quarter-scale printing also requires **Width1** and **Height1**. In this case, the program simply divides the actual picture's width and height by the correct factor. So the code for half scale is

```
Printer.PaintPicture pixLogo.Picture, _
         0, lPrintY, pixLogo.Picture.Width / 2, _
         pixLogo.Picture.Height / 2
```

and the code for quarter scale divides the picture's dimensions by four.

Note that none of the **PaintPicture** routines includes the **EndDoc** method, which is in **cmdDone**'s click event instead.

Running the Program

When you run the program, have it print one copy of the logo at full scale, one at half scale, and one at quarter scale, and then click Done. It takes a while before the program finishes processing the print job and sends it to the printer; high resolution graphics take a lot more "thinking time" than text.

The Graph Control

Say you have an application that is tracking several data points, and you would like to create a chart to graphically display them. You could use OLE and Microsoft Excel to create a chart and display the data in your program, or if you have the Professional or Enterprise edition of Visual Basic, you can use the special Graph custom control. The Graph custom control, shown in Figure 11-19, allows you to create different types of

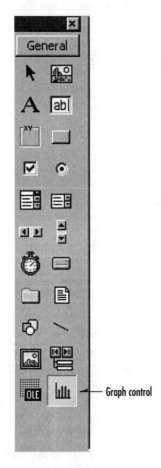

Figure 11-19
Graph custom control on the Visual Basic toolbar

Graph control

graphs such as pie charts, bar charts, Gantt charts, 3D charts, and area graphs. You can access these features and define the graph by setting property values. First, we'll provide a brief review of some of the important Graph control properties, and then a simple application to exercise the Graph control.

If you do not find the Graph control in your toolbox, remember that it is a *custom control*. Click on Components under the Project menu and find and check Pinnacle *BPS* Graph control. This adds the Graph control to your toolbox.

ThisPoint *Property*

In order to build a chart or graph with data, you must treat each data item as a point in the graph or chart. To modify a specific data item in the graph or chart, you must point to the data point on the graph using the `ThisPoint` property. Setting the `ThisPoint` property identifies a specific point in the graph so you can add or modify data for that point.

AutoInc *Property*

The graph control has a feature called the `AutoInc` property that allows you to automatically increment to the next data point in the graph when adding data. Set the `AutoInc` property to `On` (`1`) when adding several data points to a graph. When the `AutoInc` property is set to `On`, the `ThisPoint` value is automatically incremented by one when a data point is added.

GraphData *Property*

To add data to the graph, once you have set the `ThisPoint` property, set the `GraphData` property to your data. The data is added to the Graph control at the location pointed to by the `ThisPoint` property.

GraphType *Property*

The `GraphType` property determines the type of graph displayed, for example, pie charts or bar charts. Valid `GraphType` values and descriptions are shown in Table 11-15.

Table 11-15 Graph type values

Value	Description
0	None
1	2D pie
2	3D pie
3	(Default) 2D bar
4	3D bar
5	Gantt
6	Line

continued on next page

continued from previous page

Value	Description
7	Log
8	Area
9	Scatter
10	Polar
11	HLC

LabelText *Property*

Use the `LabelText` property to assign specialized labels to each data point on the graph.

Using the Properties Together

The properties that were just reviewed are used together to graph data points. The simplest way to add data points to a graph is to set the `ThisPoint` property to the starting point and then set the `AutoInc` property to `On`. With `AutoInc` set to `On`, each time a data value is assigned to the `GraphData` property, the `ThisPoint` property is automatically incremented.

Using the Graph Control

Start a new Visual Basic project with a single form, a combo box, three command buttons, and a Graph control. Set the properties as shown in Table 11-16.

Table 11-16 Object property settings for project Graph

Object	Property	Setting
Form	Caption	Example of the Graph control
	Name	frmGraph
ComboBox	Height	315
	Left	960
	Name	cmbType
	Style	2 - Dropdown List
Graph	DrawMode	2 - Draw
	GraphType	3 - 2D Bar
	Name	Graph1
Command Button	Name	cmdChange
	Caption	Change 1

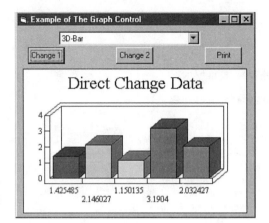

Figure 11-20
The Graph project
in action

Object	Property	Setting
Command Button	Name	cmdChange2
	Caption	Change 2
Command Button	Name	cmdPrint
	Caption	Print

See Figure 11-20 for the layout of the form.

ComboBox

Now add the code in Listing 11-12 to the project.

Listing 11-12 Code for the Graph project

```
Option Explicit

Private Sub cmbType_Click()
    Dim sSelectedGraph As String
    sSelectedGraph = cmbType.Text
    '
    ' Change the graph to the type selected
    Select Case sSelectedGraph
        Case "3D-Bar"
            Graph1.GraphType = gphBar3D
        Case "2D-Bar"
            Graph1.GraphType = gphBar2D
        Case "2D-Pie"
            Graph1.GraphType = gphPie2D
        Case "3D-Pie"
            Graph1.GraphType = gphPie3D
```

continued on next page

continued from previous page

```
            Case "Line"
                Graph1.GraphType = gphLine
            Case "Area"
                Graph1.GraphType = gphArea
            Case Else
                Graph1.GraphType = gphLine
        End Select
        Graph1.DrawMode = 2 'Redraw the Graph
End Sub

Private Sub cmdChange_Click()
    '   Directly change graph data values
    '   by writing them to the points
    Dim iX As Integer, snglNew(5) As Single
    '   Set number of graph points
    Graph1.NumPoints = 5
    Graph1.ThisPoint = 1            'Start at the first data point
    Graph1.AutoInc = 1              'Set Auto Increment to One to move
    For iX = 1 To 5
    '   Set the data point to graph
        snglNew(iX) = Rnd(1) * iX + 1
        Graph1.GraphData = snglNew(iX)
    Next iX
    Graph1.ThisPoint = 1            'Start at the first data point
    Graph1.AutoInc = 1              'Set Auto Increment to One to move
    For iX = 1 To 5
        Graph1.LabelText = snglNew(iX)
    Next
    Graph1.GraphTitle = "Direct Change Data"
    Graph1.DrawMode = 2 'Redraw the Graph
End Sub

Private Sub cmdChange2_Click()
    '   Change graph values using the QuickData string
    '   String data items must be tab delimited
    Dim iX As Integer, snglNew(10) As Single, sData As String
    For iX = 1 To 10
    '   Set the data point to graph
        snglNew(iX) = Rnd(1) * iX + 1
        '   The first data item gets no tab
        If iX <> 1 Then sData = sData & vbTab
        '   Add data to the string
        sData = sData & CStr(snglNew(iX))
    Next iX
    Graph1.QuickData = sData
    '   Display labels
    Graph1.GraphTitle = "Using QuickData"
        For iX = 1 To 10
        Graph1.LabelText = snglNew(iX)
    Next
    Graph1.DrawMode = 2 'Redraw the Graph
End Sub
```

```
Private Sub cmdPrint_Click()
    '    The following line does not work
    '
    '    Graph1.DrawMode = 5
    '
    '    although the docs say it will.
    '    Must use PaintPicture method instead
    '    Must include Width1 and Height1 parameters to
    '    get a graph printed
    Printer.PaintPicture Graph1.Picture, 0, 0, 2888, 2888
    Printer.EndDoc
End Sub

Private Sub Form_Load()
Dim iX As Integer
    '
    'Add 5 data points to the graph
    'Make the difference between each point 2.
    '
    'Turn the Auto increment property on
    Graph1.AutoInc = 1
    For iX = 1 To 9 Step 2
        Graph1.GraphData = iX 'Set the data point to graph
    Next iX
    '
    'Add a Title to the graph
    '
    Graph1.GraphTitle = "VB Interactive Course"
    '
    'Add a label to each data point
    '
    Graph1.ThisPoint = 1           'Start at the first data point
    Graph1.AutoInc = 1             'Set Auto Increment to One to move
                                   'to the next data point after a label is
                                   'added
    Graph1.LabelText = "One"
    Graph1.LabelText = "Two"
    Graph1.LabelText = "Three"
    Graph1.LabelText = "Four"
    Graph1.LabelText = "Five"
    '
    'Add some different graph selections to the ComboBox control
    '
    cmbType.AddItem "2D-Bar"
    cmbType.AddItem "3D-Bar"
    cmbType.AddItem "2D-Pie"
    cmbType.AddItem "3D-Pie"
    cmbType.AddItem "Line"
    cmbType.AddItem "Area"
    cmbType.ListIndex = 0
End Sub
```

A Look at the Code

The `Form_Load` event initially sets up the graph to have five data points, assigns values to the data points, assigns a title, and creates the labels. The `autoincrement` property must be `On` (=1), or all of the data will be assigned to the same point. (Not much of a graph then!)

The code in `cmbType_Click` sets the *type* of graph, and it redraws the graph with `Graph1.DrawMode = 2`. There are several types of graphs that were not included because they are more suited to scientific applications than business graphing. If you need one of the other types, it can be added in.

It's pretty easy to set up the Graph control for a single set of data, but some programmers have experienced problems *changing* the data once it is graphed. There's no good reason for that. The code in `cmdChange` and `cmdChange1` shows two different ways to change the data.

In `cmdChange`, the data is assigned directly to the data points on the graph. The data for this routine is generated randomly and stored in an array. (The array data is later used to set the labels for each data point.) Note the line `Graph1.NumPoints = 5`. If the number of data points on the graph is reduced, you must tell the Graph control how many data points to use for the new data. If you don't, the data from the previous graph is used. You have to set `numPoints` to `5` here because the code in `cmdChange1` changes the number of points to `10`. Note also that the line `Graph1.DrawMode = 2` is necessary or the graph won't change at all.

The code in `cmdChange1` uses the `QuickData` property to change the graph. `QuickData` uses a *tab delimited string* (a string containing the data points, with the data points separated or *delimited*, by tab characters). The line `Graph1.QuickData = sData` assigns the newly created string to the Graph control's `QuickData` property. Each data point's value is saved in an array to facilitate labeling the data points with their values.

The most interesting code in this program is in the click event for `cmdPrint`. According to the documentation, including the Help files, setting the Graph control's `DrawMode` property to five causes it to print a hard copy of the graph. The problem is, it is broken. Fortunately, the graph is a *picture*, so there is a workaround for the problem. The code in `cmdPrint's` click event shows the workaround: Use the `PaintPicture` method. You *must* include `Width1` and `Height1`, or the graph still doesn't print. The advantage of the `PaintPicture` method, of course, is that it lets you print the graph anywhere on the page and in whatever size you choose.

Running the Program

Try the program out. You should be able to view and print six different styles of graph. Once more, you can add the other styles as needed.

More About the Graph Control

This simple exercise barely touches the capabilities of the Graph control. You can add tick marks to the graph's axes, add a label to the y axis, control the colors and line thickness, save the graph as a bitmap, and include many other refinements. One of the more interesting is to include more than one data set. Change the code in **cmdChange1** as shown in Listing 11-13. (Changes in bold.)

Listing 11-13 Adding a second data set

```
'    Change graph values using the QuickData string
'       String data items must be tab delimited
    Dim iX As Integer, snglNew(10) As Single, sData As String
    For iX = 1 To 10
'       Set the data point to graph
        snglNew(iX) = Rnd(1) * iX + 1
'          The first data item gets no tab
        If iX <> 1 Then sData = sData & vbTab
'          Add data to the string
        sData = sData & CStr(snglNew(iX))
    Next iX
'      add a second data set
    sData = sData & vbCrLf
    For iX = 1 To 10
'       Set the data point to graph
        snglNew(iX) = Rnd(1) * iX + 1
'          The first data item gets no tab
        If iX <> 1 Then sData = sData & vbTab
'          Add data to the string
        sData = sData & CStr(snglNew(iX))
    Next iX
    Graph1.QuickData = sData
'      Display labels
    Graph1.GraphTitle = "Using QuickData"
        For iX = 1 To 10
            Graph1.LabelText = snglNew(iX)
    Next
    Graph1.DrawMode = 2 'Redraw the Graph
End Sub
```

One of the things this change points out is that some graph styles don't work too well with multiple data sets. The Line, Area, and 2D Bar graphs are pretty clear. The rest generate more confusion than light. That is always the case with graphics. They add a lot of pizzazz to a project when they are used correctly, but they can also obscure the very information you are trying to present.

Summary

Now you have the tools to dress up your programs with slick looking graphics. You can draw pictures, use and print high resolution graphics, and put well-designed graphs in your project. In the next lesson you will learn to use disk files so you can save that data you have been generating, and call it up and use it again.

1. A box is drawn using graphical methods on a form. Another application overlays the form and is then minimized. The box on the form is missing. Why?
   a. It's a Windows screen paint problem.
   b. The form's `AutoRedraw` property is `True`.
   c. The form's `DrawMode` property is `manual`.
   d. The form's `AutoRedraw` property is `False`.

2. The line of code

   ```
   Graph1.ThisPoint = 3
   ```

   a. Sets the current point of the graph to **3**
   b. Sets the value of the current point to **3**
   c. Adds a new point with the value of **3**
   d. Sets the graph auto increment counter

3. To change a graph from a pie chart to a bar chart, set the:
   a. `GraphStyle` property
   b. `GraphStyle` method
   c. `GraphData` property
   d. `GraphType` property

4. After the following code executes

   ```
   Graph1.ThisPoint = 1
   Graph1.AutoInc = 1
   Graph1.GraphData = 3
   Graph1.GraphData = 5
   ```

   a. Two points are added to the graph with data values of **3** and **5**.
   b. Two points are added to the graph with values of **0** and **1**.
   c. One point is added to the graph with a value of **3**.
   d. One point is added to the graph with a value of **5**.

5. The property to add data to a graph is:
   a. `ThisPoint`
   b. `GraphData`
   c. `Value`
   d. `Data`

CHAPTER 12

FILES

T his chapter shows how to use Visual Basic's File controls to let your users browse through files on their systems. It also shows how to perform various file input and output operations. It explains the different terms used to describe the file system and the different types of file input and output access methods. Best of all, it puts all this knowledge to work by showing you how to create several applications. For instance, it shows you how to develop a file-browsing application and an object-oriented notepad application. Get started by reviewing the Windows 95 file system.

USING THE FILE SYSTEM CONTROLS

This lesson explains how to use the file system controls provided by Visual Basic 5 to let your user easily navigate the file system. The file system controls consist of

- DriveListBox

- DirListBox

- FileListBox

The File controls are shown in Figure 12-1.

The best way to learn about these controls is to create an application that uses them. Create a new project called Browse. Add the objects and set the properties shown in Table 12-1.

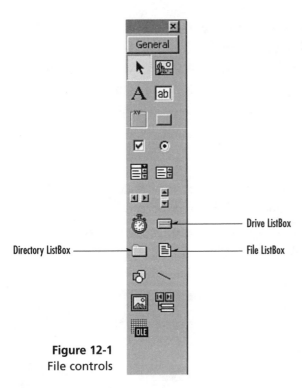

Figure 12-1
File controls

Table 12-1 Browse project object and property settings

Object	Property	Setting
Form	BackColor	&H0FFFFFF&
	BorderStyle	1 - Fixed Single
	Caption	File Browser
	Height	5010
	Icon	face02.ico
	Name	frmBrowse
	Width	6810
DriveListBox	Height	315
	Left	1560
	Name	drvBrowse
	Top	120
	Width	2295
DirListBox	Height	2055
	Left	1560
	Name	dirBrowse
	Top	480
	Width	2295
FileListBox	Height	1620
	Left	1560
	Name	filBrowse
	Top	2640
	Width	2295

DriveListBox

The DriveListBox control is a drop-down list box used to present a list of available computer drives. No code is required to get the list or to determine which drives are on the computer. The DriveListBox control gets the drive information for you from the operating system. Let's add some code to the DriveListBox **Change** event.

```
Private Sub drvBrowse_Change()
  MsgBox "The following drive has been selected: " _
  & drvBrowse.Drive
End Sub
```

Run the application. The drive letter displayed in the list box is your current drive. Select a new drive by clicking on the list box and changing the drive. The message box in Figure 12-2 appears.

Selecting a different drive from the list box does not change your current directory, it only changes the **Drive** property for the DirListBox control. The new drive information could be used to change your current working directory using code or to provide information to other controls. Remove the code you added to the DriveListBox **Change** event. (The code was used for demonstration purposes only and is not part of the application.)

DirListBox

The DirListBox control works a lot like the DriveListBox control. The DirListBox control displays a list of the current directories and subdirectories for the current drive. (Remember that a directory and folder are the same thing. Visual Basic 5 uses the same name for the control as Visual Basic 3 and Visual Basic 4 do.)

Run the project. The top folder in the list box is your current folder (the Visual Basic folder) and is contained on your current drive. Select a new folder by double-clicking on any folder. Notice how the control automatically updates the list box for you to represent the newly selected folder and subfolders.

FileListBox

Files are displayed using the FileListBox control. The FileListBox control displays all the files in the current drive and folder. The FileListBox control has properties that allow you to set up search criteria to limit or expand the file names displayed in the list box. The **Pattern** property provides a filter to set up file-specific search criteria. For instance, if you want to see all the files in a folder, use the default ***.*** setting of the property. Suppose you want to see only files with an **EXE** extension. The following code limits the files displayed, in the list box to only those files with an **EXE** extension:

```
File1.Pattern = "*.EXE"
```

The search criteria for a FileListBox control can be further fine-tuned to exclude or include files with specific file attributes. Table 12-2 contains a list of properties associated with file attributes. Setting any of the properties to **True** includes the file type as part of the file search criteria. Setting the property to **False** prevents the file type from being displayed, even if it matches the search criteria set in the **Pattern** property.

Figure 12-2
Message box with
selected drive

Table 12-2 File control properties and file attributes

Property	Description
ReadOnly	Read-only files
Archive	Files with Archive attribute
Normal	All files without system or hidden attributes
System	System files
Hidden	Hidden files

Run the application. If you change the drive, the DirListBox control does not display the folders for the new drive. If you change the DirListBox control, the FileListBox control does not display the files in the new directory. The File controls are not working together! The next lesson demonstrates how to synchronize them.

1. The best way to display only a list box of folders is to:
   a. Write code to scan a drive and populate the list box.
   b. Use the CommonDialog custom control.
   c. Read an initialization file of the folder structure and populate a list box.
   d. Use the DirListBox custom control.

2. How would you view only files with a .DOC file extension with a FileListBox control?
   a. Set the Filter property to *.DOC.
   b. Set the Pattern property to *.DOC.
   c. This cannot be done.
   d. Set the FileFilter property to "*.DOC".

3. Which of the following is not a file attribute that can be controlled by setting properties in the FileListBox control?
   a. Hidden
   b. Visible
   c. Normal
   d. Archive

4. To get the string value of the current drive in a DriveListBox control, you would get the value from the
   a. Text property
   b. Drive property
   c. String property
   d. Value property

5. To view folders, use the
    a. DirListBox control
    b. DriveListBox control
    c. FolderListBox control
    d. None of the above

MAKING THE FILE SYSTEM CONTROLS WORK TOGETHER

You have created a form with DriveListBox, DirListBox, and FileListBox controls. If you run the application, you quickly find that these are not very useful, because they show file information for the current drive and folder only. Each control should provide information for the next control in the hierarchy list. In other words, the DriveListBox control should provide information to the DirListBox control and the DirListBox control should provide information to the FileListBox control.

Figure 12-3 shows the chain reaction scenario where changes in one control trickle down immediately to the next control in the chain.

Chaining the DriveListBox Control to the DirListBox Control

The Visual Basic 5 event-driven programming model makes it possible to create a chain reaction among the **File** controls, automatically updating any lower control in the hierarchy if an upper-level control is changed. The first chain reaction is the DriveListBox control providing drive information to the DirListBox control. To chain the DirListBox control to the DriveListBox control, add the code shown in Listing 12-1 to the DriveListBox **Change** event.

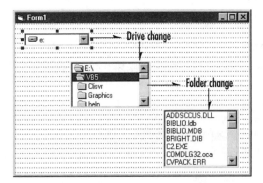

Figure 12-3
Control chain
reaction

Listing 12-1 Setting the directory list box drive

```
Private Sub drvBrowse_Change()
  'Set the directory list box to the new drive
  dirBrowse.Path = drvBrowse.Drive
End Sub
```

Chaining the DirListBox Control to the FileListBox Control

When you click on a new folder in the DirListBox control, or when the folder in the box changes because the drive changed, the change needs to be relayed to the file list box. Add the code shown in Listing 12-2 to the DirListBox **Change** event.

Listing 12-2 Setting the file list box

```
Private Sub dirBrowse_Change()
  'If the folder changes - update the file list box
  filBrowse.Path = dirBrowse.Path
End Sub
```

Rounding Out the File Browser

To finish the File Browser project, add three labels to the form and set the properties for the labels shown in Table 12-3.

Table 12-3 File browser label property settings

Object	Property	Setting
Label	Caption	Select a Drive
	Height	255
	Left	120
	Name	lblDrive
	Width	1335
Label	Caption	Select a Folder
	Height	255
	Left	120
	Name	lblFolder
	Width	1335
Label	Caption	Files
	Height	255

continued on next page

continued from previous page

Object	Property	Setting
	Left	870
	Name	lblFile
	Width	600

Add a frame and five check boxes inside the frame and set the properties shown in Table 12-4.

Table 12-4 Frame and check box property settings

Object	Property	Setting
Frame	Caption	Select File Attributes
	Height	1650
	Left	3930
	Name	frmAttributes
	Width	2295
CheckBox	Caption	Read Only
	Height	195
	Name	chkRead
	Left	90
	Top	285
	Value	1-Checked
	Width	1350
CheckBox	Caption	Archive
	Height	195
	Name	chkArchive
	Left	90
	Top	510
	Value	1-Checked
	Width	1350
CheckBox	Caption	Normal
	Height	195
	Name	chkNormal
	Left	90
	Top	780

Object	Property	Setting
	Value	1-Checked
	Width	1350
CheckBox	Caption	System
	Height	195
	Name	chkSystem
	Left	90
	Top	1035
	Value	0-UnChecked
	Width	1350
CheckBox	Caption	Hidden
	Height	195
	Name	chkHidden
	Left	90
	Top	1305
	Value	0-UnChecked
	Width	1350

Add a label and text box and set the properties shown in Table 12-5.

Table 12-5 Text box and label property settings

Object	Property	Setting
Label	Caption	Search Filter
	Height	225
	Name	lblFilter
	Top	1800
	Width	990
TextBox	Height	330
	Name	txtFilter
	Text	*.*
	Top	1770
	Width	1260

The form is completed, as shown in Figure 12-4.

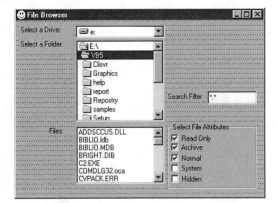

Figure 12-4
Completed File
Browser form

Time to add code! The CheckBox controls added to the form control the type of files viewed in the FileListBox control. Each check box is named for a corresponding property on the List Box control. The text box added to the project sets the **Pattern** property for the FileListBox control. By using the check boxes and the text box, you can use the application to view different file types and to use filter criteria. Add the code in Listing 12-3 to the corresponding check boxes.

Listing 12-3 Setting search criteria

```
Private Sub chkRead_Click()
  'Set search criteria to disable or enable
  'viewing of Read Only Files
  '
  If chkRead.Value = Checked Then
 filBrowse.ReadOnly = True
  Else
 filBrowse.ReadOnly = False
  End If
End Sub

Private Sub chkSystem_Click()
  'Set search criteria to disable or enable
  'viewing of System Files
  '
  If chkSystem.Value = Checked Then
 filBrowse.System = True
  Else
 filBrowse.System = False
  End If
End Sub

Private Sub chkArchive_Click()
  'Set search criteria to disable or enable
  'viewing of Archive Files
```

```
    '
    If chkArchive.Value = Checked Then
  filBrowse.Archive = True
    Else
  filBrowse.Archive = False
    End If
End Sub

Private Sub chkHidden_Click()
    'Set search criteria to disable or enable
    'viewing of Hidden Files
    '
    If chkHidden.Value = Checked Then
  filBrowse.Hidden = True
    Else
  filBrowse.Hidden = False
    End If
End Sub

Private Sub chkNormal_Click()
    'Set search criteria to disable or enable
    'viewing of Normal Files
    '
    If chkNormal.Value = Checked Then
  filBrowse.Normal = True
    Else
  filBrowse.Normal = False
    End If
End Sub
```

Add the following code to the text box **Change** event:

```
Private Sub txtFilter_Change()
    '
    'Assign search criteria to the file list box control
    '
    filBrowse.Pattern = txtFilter.Text
End Sub
```

The running application should resemble Figure 12-5. Test the File Browser application by selecting different drives and folders. Notice how the FileListBox control changes when you click on a folder. Insert a disk in your floppy drive and select the floppy drive in the DriveListBox. The folder and FileListBox control automatically update to reflect the files and folders on the floppy disk. Use the check boxes to view different file types. Modify the search filter criteria in the text box to view only certain files or extensions. Notice that the browser application serves the same purpose as the CommonDialog control used in Chapter 8, Discovering the CommonDialog and Windows 95 Controls.

Figure 12-5
File Browser
application

You have now learned how to use the File system controls to browse the Windows file system. The next lesson begins the process of opening, reading, and closing a file.

QUIZ

1. A DriveListBox control supplies information to a DirListBox control. In what event should code be placed to tie the controls together?
   a. `Click`
   b. `Dbl_Click`
   c. `Change`
   d. `Validate`

2. A DriveListBox control supplies information to a DirListBox control when a new drive is selected. What property on the DirListBox control should be set to reflect the change in the DriveListBox control?
   a. `CurrentDrive`
   b. `Drive`
   c. `Path`
   d. `Text`

3. Setting the `Archive` property to `False` on a FileListBox control:
   a. Archives the files in the folder
   b. Removes all files with the `Archive` bit set from the FileListBox control
   c. Displays all files with the `Archive` bit set in the FileListBox control
   d. Does nothing

4. If the `Pattern` property of a file list control is set to `*.EXE`, what will be displayed in the FileListBox control?
   a. All the files in the current folder
   b. All the files on the drive with a file extension of `*.EXE`
   c. All the files in the current folder, except those with a file extension of `*.EXE`
   d. All the files in the current folder with an extension of `*.EXE`

5. What control can be used instead of the File controls to present the user with a window to allow the user to browse the file system to select a file to open in an application?
   a. Data Access control
   b. Grid control
   c. File Explorer control
   d. CommonDialog control

OPENING, READING, AND CLOSING A FILE

Using the File custom controls allows you to create applications to browse through the file system. The next logical step is file input/output, or file I/O. This term is used to represent the many different input and output operations that can be performed on a file, such as reading from the file or writing to the file. Accessing data via file I/O is like reading a book.

File I/O follows the same sequence of events. The first step is to locate the file you want to use. In the first part of this chapter, you learned how to locate files, using the File control; in Chapter 8 you learned to use the CommonDialog control. Once the file has been located, the next step is to open the file. File I/O operations such as reading or writing can be done only on an open file. When you are done with the file, you close it. Let's take a look at some of the basic file I/O commands.

Opening a File

The **Open** command opens a file in Visual Basic 5. The **Open** command is covered in more detail in Lesson 4, Sequential and Random Access Files. For the time being, assume that a sequential file is nothing more than a file that consists of ASCII characters. The **Open** statement has the following syntax:

```
Open pathname For Input As [#]filenumber
```

where

- `pathname` is the full path and file name of the file to open.

- `Input` specifies to open the file for reading.

- `filenumber` is an integer number between 1 and 511. The `Open` command allocates a buffer to perform the file I/O and determines the type of access to use with the buffer. A *buffer* is a block of memory the computer sets aside for input and output operations. The file number is used to identify the open file to other file I/O commands. For example, assume you want to open a file named VB.TXT in C:\VB using the file number 1. The code required to perform this task looks like the following:

```
Open "C:\VB\VB.TXT" For Input As #1
```

If you do not specify the path of the file, Visual Basic will assume that the file you are opening is in the current directory, usually the directory from which your application is executing.

```
Open "VB.TXT" For Input As #1
```

You can open more than one file at a time. However, you must use different file numbers for each open file. For instance, you might want to open a file called VB.TXT and copy the contents to another file, called BACKUP.TXT. If you try to use a file number currently in use by another file, an error occurs. Keeping track of file numbers can be a problem if you have to write applications that require using many different files simultaneously. Fortunately, Visual Basic provides a function called FreeFile that returns an available file number. The FreeFile syntax is as follows:

```
FreeFile[(rangenumber)]
```

where **rangenumber** is an optional parameter. If **rangenumber = 0** (the default), FreeFile returns file numbers between 1 and 255. If **rangenumber = 1**, FreeFile returns file numbers between 256 and 511.

The code below shows how to use FreeFile.

```
Dim iFileNum As Integer
iFileNum = FreeFile
Open "TEST.TXT" For Input As #FileNum
```

You must save the file number in a variable so you can read from the file, write to it, or close it. A line such as Open "TEST.TXT" For Input As #FreeFile would leave you with an orphan file that you could not use for anything.

Closing a File

When you are finished with the open file, you must execute code that will *close* the file. Closing the file releases the file buffer and returns the file number to the unused pool. It also flushes the buffer so that all new data for the file is saved. The Close statement has the following syntax:

```
Close [filenumberlist]
```

where **filenumberlist** is a list of file numbers to close. If no file number list is provided, then all open files are closed.

The following code example closes an open file with the file number 1:

```
Close #1
```

Determining the Size of the File

Before you attempt to read a file, it is a good idea to know when to stop. Attempting to read past the end of a file will generate an error. Reading less than an entire file may also prove troublesome, depending on your program's needs.

Visual Basic has two functions that you can use to determine how much to read and when to stop reading.

● LOF returns the size in bytes of an open file.

● EOF returns True when the end of the file is reached.

The syntax for LOF is as follows:

```
FileSize = LOF(filenumber)
```

where **filenumber** is the file number of the open file for which you want to obtain the size in bytes.

To determine when you have reached the end of a file, use the EOF function, which has the following format:

```
EOF(filenumber)
```

where **filenumber** is the file number of the open file. The EOF function returns True when the end of the file is reached.

Reading a File

Reading a file means extracting the characters that are in the file into a memory buffer. To a read a file, you must

● Determine how many characters to read.

● Provide variables to receive the data.

Visual Basic 5 provides several functions and statements to read a sequential file. They are

● Input

● Input #

● Line Input t #

Input

The **Input** function has the following syntax:

```
Input(number, [#]filenumber)
```

where

●   number is the number of characters to read.

●   filenumber is the file number of the open file to read.

The Input function is used to read any number of bytes from a file into a Visual Basic variable. For instance, the following example uses the Input function to read 10 characters into the string variable LastName:

```
LastName = Input(10, #1)
```

Input

The Input # statement provides an easy way to read a list of numbers or strings from a file and assign them to variables. The syntax for the Input # function is

```
Input #filenumber, varlist
```

where

●   filenumber is the file number of the open file to read.

●   varlist is a list of variables to receive the data.

Assume a file contains the following: Mark, Wednesday. Using the Input function, Mark and Wednesday could be read into local variables Name and DayOfWeek.

```
Input #1, Name, DayOfWeek
```

Line Input

The Line Input # statement reads a single line of data at a time. The statement will read all the characters until it encounters a carriage return-linefeed sequence and returns all the data up to the carriage return. The syntax for Line Input # is

```
Line Input #filenumber, varname
```

where

●   filenumber is the file number of the open file.

●   varname is the variable to hold the line of data.

For example:

```
Line Input #1, OneLine
```

Sequential Read Example

The example program puts it all together and uses Open, Close, and all three input commands to read a sequential file. It reads the seq.txt file located on the CD that comes with the book. To read the text file, make sure `seq.txt` is located in the same directory as the project files. The general format of the `seq.txt` file is as follows:

`Name, DayOfWeek.`

Each line contains two comma-delimited variables and ends with a carriage return-linefeed.

The application opens the text file, reads the entire file, and displays it in a picture box. To experiment with the different formats of the `Input` command, the application can read the file using any of the methods covered so far: `Input`, `Input #`, or `Line Input #`.

Creating a New Project called Seq

The new project Seq consists of a single form, a Command button, a picture box, a Frame control, and three Option buttons. The completed project is on the CD that comes with this book. Set the properties for each of the controls as shown in Table 12-6.

Table 12-6 Form `frmSequential` objects and property settings

Object	Property	Setting
Form	Caption	Sequential Read
	Height	3810
	Name	frmSequential
	Width	6855
OptionButton	Caption	Input
	Height	195
	Name	optInput
	Left	90
	Top	240
	Value	True
	Width	990
OptionButton	Caption	Input #
	Height	195
	Name	optInNum
	Left	120
	Top	525
	Value	False
	Width	990

continued on next page

continued from previous page

Object	Property	Setting
OptionButton	Caption	Input Line #
	Height	195
	Name	optLine
	Left	1230
	Top	240
	Value	False
	Width	1245
PictureBox	Height	195
	Name	Picture1
	Left	180
	Top	195
	Width	6630
CommandButton	Caption	Test Sequential Read Method
	Height	705
	Name	cmdInput
	Left	240
	Top	2640
	width	2520
Frame	Caption	Read Method
	Height	810
	Name	Frame1
	Left	3885
	Top	2565
	Width	2610

The Option buttons are used to determine which sequential **Read** command to use to read the text file. Complete the project by adding the code shown in Listing 12-4 to the **Click** event of the Command button.

Listing 12-4 Sequential I/O read code in Command button **Click** event

```
Private Sub cmdInput_Click()
Dim Read_Buffer As String  ' Buffer to read the file
Dim File_Length As Integer ' Integer to store file size

    On Error GoTo File_Error ' Set up the error handler
```

```
    ' Clear the Picture Box
    Picture1.Cls
    '
    ' Open the text file seq.txt
    '
    Open App.Path & "\seq.txt" For Input As #1 ' Open the file
    File_Length = LOF(1) ' Get the size of the file
    If optInput.Value = True Then
        Picture1.Print "Input Command" ' Display Command in Picture Box
        ' Input Command
        ' Read the entire file into the string
        Read_Buffer = Input(File_Length, #1)
        ' Display the contents of the file in the picture box
        Picture1.Print Read_Buffer

    ElseIf optInNum.Value = True Then
        Picture1.Print "Input # Command" ' Display Command in Picture Box
        ' Input # Command
        ' Read the entire file into the strings - Note use of EOF
        Do While Not EOF(1)
            Input #1, Read_Buffer
            ' Display the contents of the file in the picture box
            Picture1.Print Read_Buffer
        Loop
    Else
        Picture1.Print "Line Input # Command" ' Display Command in Picture Box
        '
        ' Line Input # Command
        ' Read the entire file into the strings - Note use of EOF
        Do While Not EOF(1)
            Line Input #1, Read_Buffer
            ' Display the contents of the file in the picture box
            Picture1.Print Read_Buffer
        Loop
    End If

    Close #1 ' Close the File
Exit_Input:
    Exit Sub ' Exit

' Basic Error Handler
File_Error:
    MsgBox Err.Description, vbCritical, "File Error"
    Resume Exit_Input
End Sub
```

The best way to see how each of the commands differs from the others is to use the Debug mode.

● Open the Tools menu and select Options. Be sure that Auto Data Tips is checked.

● Set a breakpoint on the line

```
Open App.Path & "\seq.txt" For Input As #1 'Open the file
```

● Press F5 or click on the Start button to start the program. The first option, Input, is already selected.

● Click on the Command button.

● When the program reaches the breakpoint, single-step through the rest of the `cmdInput_Click` function. Hold the cursor on each of the variables before and after the program has assigned it a value. Figure 12-6 shows what this looks like.

● Repeat the single-step process for each of the Read options.

The two dark vertical bars you see between items in **Read_Buffer** during the **Input** function are the **CR-LF** characters that delimit (separate) the items in the text file. They are referred to as the "unprintable characters."

Note that the **Input #** statement reads the name and the day in two separate operations, whereas the **Line Input #** statement reads the entire line at once. The **Input #** statement reads single data items, up to the delimiter, whereas **Line Input #** reads the entire line, up to the **CR-LF**.

You can read more than one variable with **Input #** by changing the **varlist** parameter. The new line for **Seq.VBP** would look like this:

```
Input #1, Name, DayOfWeek
```

You also must change the following line to

```
Picture1.Print Name, DayOfWeek
```

Try it.

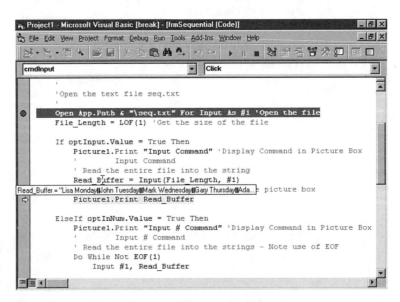

Figure 12-6
Single-stepping through Seq.VBP

Summary

This lesson demonstrated how to open and read a sequential data file. You learned how to

● Open a sequential ASCII file.

● Read data from the file using three different techniques.

● Close the file.

The next lesson covers random access files and files that store data in binary format.

1. What does the following code do?

```
Open "Quiz.txt" For Input As #23
```

   a. Opens the file `Quiz.txt` to write characters to
   b. Opens a file called `#23` with an identifier of `Quiz.txt`
   c. Opens the file `Quiz.txt` with file number `23` for reading
   d. Opens the file called `Quiz.txt` and writes the number `23` to the file

2. The `FreeFile` function:
   a. Frees all open files by closing them
   b. Returns a free file number
   c. Deletes a file
   d. Creates a new file and places it in the Windows 95 free file pool

3. To read a list from a file, use the following function:
   a. `Input`
   b. `Input #`
   c. `Line Input #`
   d. `List Input#`

4. When you are done with a file, execute the _____ command to free the I/O buffer, release the file number, and close the file.
   a. `Terminate`
   b. `FileClose`
   c. `Close`
   d. `ReturnHandle`

5. What does the following code do?

```
Do While Not EOF(1)
    Line Input #1, Read_Buffer
Loop
```

a. Reads an open file a line at a time until the end of the file is reached

b. Reads an open file a character at a time until the end of the file is reached

c. Reads an open file one line at a time until an error occurs when it reads beyond the end of the file

d. Reads an open file one character at a time until an error occurs when it reads beyond the end of the file

REVIEW

John: I was already quite familiar with the overall file hierarchy. I actually installed a hard drive on my PC once, and of course I created my own folders and files.

Lisa: You're right, but the review was good, especially because it led into the Visual Basic File controls.

John: Yeah, I thought the File controls were pretty cool. They really do a lot for you without requiring a lot of code. For the type of projects I have in mind, I still think I'll use the CommonDialog control, discussed in Chapter 8 instead.

Lisa: Planning some projects to allow users to select files?

John: Yes, I'd actually like to create a file to track my baseball cards. I'm not sure how I'd do this with a sequential file.

Lisa: I'm not so sure a sequential file would be the right file type for a baseball card tracking program. Sequential files are text files—for instance, an application initialization file. But if we continue on, I'm willing to bet we will learn about a file type that handles record-type data.

John: Then what are we waiting for?

SEQUENTIAL AND RANDOM ACCESS FILES

A file is nothing more than a group of related bytes, bunched together and stored on a drive. A file can contain ASCII text characters, fixed-length records, or binary data. When designing an application to read and write data to a file, you must take into consideration the type of data your application expects to read and write. With Visual Basic, you select the data type when you open a file by setting the access mode of the file.

The possible file access modes are:

- Sequential
- Random
- Binary

The examples you have completed so far used sequential file access functions and statements. In this lesson, you will learn about sequential access files, random access files, and binary files.

Sequential Access

Sequential file access is used for data files comprising ASCII text characters. Figure 12-7 represents an example of an ASCII sequential text file—an application initialization file. This figure shows how the file would look if you were to open it with a file Text Editor such as Notepad and how the data in the file is stored. Each box in the drawing represents one byte of data in the disk file. To parse the initialization file, use the `Line Input #` statement, reading a line at a time until you find the correct parameter. Use sequential access when reading and writing files that contain ASCII characters.

But what if you have a non-ASCII file with a fixed-length record?

Random Access

A *fixed-length record* is a data structure that always has the same length. That is, each record takes up exactly the same number of bytes in the disk file. The record may have a single data member or it may have several members. Table 12-7 represents a data structure called `EmployeeName`. If you fill the data structure with data and write the structure to a file, you have a fixed-length record file. For instance, the first 15 bytes in the file would always contain the value of the field named `First`, the next 15 bytes would always contain the value of the field named `Last,` and the last 2 bytes would contain the value of the field named `Count`.

Figure 12-7
Sequential file
example

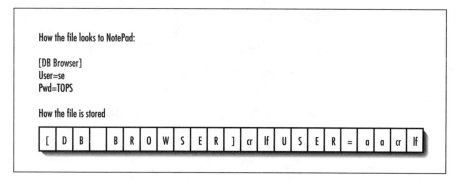

Table 12-7 `EmployeeName` data structure

Name	Size
First	15 bytes
Last	15 bytes
Count	2 bytes
Total record length	32 bytes

What happens if you want to put a 4-byte name in the `First` field, rather than a 15-byte name? Because the record is of fixed length, you would use a *fill character* for the remaining 11 bytes. A fill character is a character selected to pad or fill fields in fixed-length records when the data is not large enough to fill the field. In this example, the `First` and `Last` fields use a space for a fill character so that when the `First` and `Last` fields are displayed, the fill character is not seen. What happens if you have a last name that is longer than 15 characters and try to write it to the `Last` field? Because the record is fixed length, the `Last` field cannot be larger than 15 characters; any characters past the 15th character would be dropped (truncated).

The file access mode for fixed-length records is the *random access* mode. Random access allows you to take advantage of fixed-length records by retrieving records by record number rather than one character at a time. A sequential access CD player requires you to listen to songs 1 and 2 before you can listen to song 3. A random access CD player allows you to listen to song 3 while skipping the other songs. Random access mode works by using the fixed-length record size and the file size to skip over records, compute the correct record offset, and go to the record you specify.

For example, if 100 names were written to a file using the `EmployeeName` structure defined in Table 12-7, the file opened in random access mode would be able to read the 50th name in the file by specifying record number 50. Instead of reading character by character, the `Read` command would seek to the 50th record and read it. File access mode is specified in the `Open` statement. Take another look at the syntax for the `Open` statement. This time the command contains the `FileMode` parameter.

```
Open pathname [For FileMode] As [#]filenumber [Len=length]
```

where

- `pathname` is the full file name.

- `FileMode` can be `Input` for sequential access, `Random` for random access, and `Binary` for binary access.

- `Len` is the length for sequential access or the record length for random access.

The code shown in Listing 12-5 opens a file named `Random.dat` in random mode containing the data structure in Table 12-7.

Listing 12-5 Opening the file `Random.dat` in random access mode

```
Type Name
   First * 15 string
   Last * 15 string
   Count Integer
End Type

Dim Record Size as Integer
RecordSize = Len(Name)
Open "Random.dat" For Random As #1 Len = 32
```

This code creates a user-defined type (UDT) for the record `Name`. UDTs are similar to arrays, except that the elements can be of different data types. The one in the code contains two strings and an integer. Note the use of fixed-length strings for `First` and `Last`.

To read a random access file, use the `Get` statement. The `Get` statement has the following syntax:

```
Get [#]filenumber, [recnumber], varname
```

where

- **filenumber is the file number of the open file to read.**

- **recnumber is the record number to read.**

- **varname is the storage variable for the record being read.**

The following code example retrieves the 50th record from an open file:

```
Get #1, 50, HoldRecord
```

If you leave off the record number, `Get` returns the next record. Closing a random file uses the same syntax as the sequential file `Close` command.

Random Access Project, Part I

Begin a new project that uses random access to read a fixed-length record. This is a two-part project. This part shows how to add the code to read a fixed-length record and how to step through the file when a user clicks a Next or Previous button. The next part shows how to add the code that creates a random access file. Create a new project called Random. Add the objects and set the properties shown in Table 12-8. The completed project is on the CD that comes with this book.

Table 12-8 Objects, properties, and settings for form `frmRandom`

Object	Property	Setting
Form	Caption	Random File - Reading and Writing
	Height	2970
	Name	frmRandom
	Width	4425
CommandButton	Caption	<<
	Height	330
	Name	cmdPrevious
	Left	330
	Top	2100
	Width	1380
CommandButton	Caption	>>
	Height	330
	Name	cmdNext
	Left	2475
	Top	2100
	Width	1380
Label	Caption	First
	Height	345
	Left	615
	Name	label1
	Top	195
	Width	705
Label	Caption	Last
	Height	345
	Left	615
	Name	label2
	Top	825
	Width	705
Label	Caption	Count
	Height	345
	Left	615

Object	Property	Setting
	Name	label3
	Top	1455
	Width	705
TextBox	Height	360
	Left	1455
	Name	txtFirst
	Top	210
	Width	1995
TextBox	Height	360
	Left	1455
	Name	txtLast
	Top	810
	Width	1995
TextBox	Height	360
	Left	1455
	Name	txtCount
	Top	1455
	Width	1995

The completed form is shown in Figure 12-8.

The project uses the record structure **EmployeeName**, shown in Table 12-7. Insert a new module called **random.bas** in the project and add the following record structure definition in the Declarations section of the module:

```
Type EmployeeName ' Define user-defined type.
    First As String * 15
    Last As String * 15
    Count As Integer
End Type
```

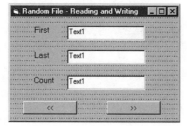

Figure 12-8
Project Random
form frmRandom

Add the code to read a record from an open random file and place data from the record into the text boxes on the form. Add a new procedure to the form. Name the procedure `GetRecord` and add the code shown in Listing 12-6.

Listing 12-6 `GetRecord` procedure

```
Public Sub GetRecord(RecNum As Integer)
'
'Read the specified record from the file and display on the form
'
Dim RecBuf As EmployeeName

    'Read the first record and place in the form
    Get #1, RecNum, RecBuf
    txtFirst = RecBuf.First
    txtLast = RecBuf.Last
    txtCount = RecBuf.Count
End Sub
```

Now add the code to manage stepping through the file. The two Command buttons allow the user to step through the file one record at a time. The Command button with the caption >> moves to the next record in the file until the end of the file is reached. The Command button with the caption << moves to the previous record in the file until the beginning of the file is reached. Add the code shown in Listing 12-7 to the `Click` event of the Command button `cmdNext`.

Listing 12-7 `cmdNext Click` event code

```
Private Sub cmdNext_Click()
    'Get the next record in the file
    '
    If CurrentRec <> MaxRec Then
        '
        'Increment the record Number
        CurrentRec = CurrentRec + 1

        'Retrieve and display
        GetRecord (CurrentRec)
    Else
        MsgBox "End of file. No next record."
    End If

End Sub
```

In the `Click` event of the Command button `cmdPrevious`, add the code shown in Listing 12-8.

Listing 12-8 `cmdPrevious Click` event code

```
Private Sub cmdPrevious_Click()
    'Get the previous record in the file
    '
```

```
If CurrentRec > 1 Then
    '
    'Decrement the record Number
    CurrentRec = CurrentRec - 1

    'Retrieve and display
    GetRecord (CurrentRec)
Else
    MsgBox "Start of file. No previous record."
End If

End Sub
```

You may have noticed the two new variables in Listing 12-7 and Listing 12-8, **CurrentRec** and **MaxRec**. The variable **CurrentRec** is used to determine which record number in the file is currently being displayed. The **MaxRec** variable is used to determine how many records are in the file so the program does not try to read past the end of the file. Add the two variables to the Declarations section of the form, as shown below.

```
Dim CurrentRec As Integer 'Current Record
Dim MaxRec As Integer 'Max Record
```

Writing

It is time to round out your file I/O skills by learning how to write to a file. First, consider an example to help you understand the decisions you must make when writing to files.

You decide to go on a diet and want to write down everything you eat. You purchase a nice blue notebook with 200 pages. The first day of your diet, you open the notebook and begin to write on the very first page. The day slowly passes by; at the end of the day, you have filled up half a page with your meals for the day. The next day, when you write your first meal in the notebook, you decide to start the day's meal at the end of the previous day's meals, using the same sheet of paper instead of starting on a new sheet. At lunch time, you begin to enter your meal and realize that you made an error entering the morning meal. You erase the entry (because you made it in pencil) and add the correction.

The decisions and actions you take when writing your diet diary are very similar to the decisions and actions you make when writing to a file in sequential access mode. The first time you write to a newly opened file, the data is placed at the beginning of the file. If you open a file with existing data, you must decide if you want to write new data after the existing data, like writing a new day's meals at the end of the existing day, or if you want to write over existing data, like erasing the mistake in the diet log and writing a new entry.

Writing to Sequential Files

How do you write to a sequential file? Once again, reexamine the **Open** command. Take a look at the full syntax for the **Open** command for sequential access.

```
Open pathname For [Input Output Append] As [#]filenumber [Len=length]
```

In Lesson 2, you learned how to use the **Input** option to read a sequential file. The **Output** and **Append** options are used to open a file for writing. The **Append** option differs from the **Output** option in that any data written to the file is appended to the end of the file. If a file that does not exist is opened with **Output** or **Append**, a new file is created. Existing files opened with the **Output** option are overwritten. The command to write to a sequential file is the **Print #** command, which has the following syntax:

```
Print #filenumber, [outputlist]
```

where

- **filenumber** is the file number of the open file to which to write.

- **outputlist** is a list of strings or a variable to write to the text file. Use a space or semicolon to separate multiple items.

The following example uses the **Print #** statement to write a variable to a file.

```
Dim strCount as String

strCount = "one two three four five"
Print #1, strCount
```

The **Print #** statement makes writing to a sequential file very simple and is similar to other commands you have used, like the **Debug.Print** statement. The results go out to a file instead of to a screen or a printer.

Writing to Random Files

Once a file has been opened for random access, use the **Put** command to write fixed-length records to the file. The **Put** statement has the following syntax:

```
Put [#]filenumber, [recnumber], varname
```

where

- **filenumber** is the file number of the open file to write.

- **recnumber** is the offset to write the fixed-length record (**recnumber** starts with the number 1).

- **varname** is the variable to write to the file.

To write a record at the end of the file, set the **recnumber** parameter to one more than the last record. The following example shows how to write a record at the end of the file by setting the **recnumber** parameter to one more than the last record (for this example, assume the last record is number 10):

```
Put #1, (10+1), MyRec
```

Random Access Project, Part II

Now that you know how to write data to a random file, it's time to finish the random access project. So far, you have added the code required to read and scroll through a file of fixed-length records, but you don't have a file to read. Add the code shown in Listing 12-9 to the **Form_Load** event.

Listing 12-9 Form `frmRandom` Load event

```
Dim MyRecord As EmployeeName    'Declare the fixed length record
Dim FileName As String    'Filename and path
Dim RecNum As Integer      'Record Number Counter

    On Error GoTo rand_err
    '
    'Set up filename
    FileName = App.Path & "\random.txt"

    ' Open sample file for random access.
    Open FileName For Random As #1 Len = Len(MyRecord)

    'Write some records to the file
    '
    MyRecord.First = "John"
    For RecNum = 1 To 8
        MyRecord.Last = "Doe" & Str$(RecNum)
        MyRecord.Count = Str$(RecNum)
        '
        'Write the record to the file
        Put #1, RecNum, MyRecord

    Next RecNum
    '
    'Determine the number of records in the file
    '
    MaxRec = LOF(1) / Len(MyRecord)

    'Read the first record and place in the form
    GetRecord (1)

    'Initialize the Current Record
    CurrentRec = 1

rand_exit:
Exit Sub

'Error handler
rand_err:
    MsgBox Err.Description, vbCritical, "File I/O Error"
    Resume rand_exit
End Sub
```

This code is for the sake of example. A functional program would allow the user to enter the data to be saved to the file.

What the Code Does

Listing 12-10 shows the correct method of opening the data file.

Listing 12-10 Creating and opening the file `random.txt`

```
'Set up filename
    FileName = App.Path & "\random.txt"

    ' Open sample file for random access.
    Open FileName For Random As #1 Len = Len(MyRecord)
```

If the file does not already exist, the **Open** statement creates a new file.

The code in Listing 12-11 shows how to write records to a random access file.

Listing 12-11 Writing random records to file `random.txt`

```
MyRecord.First = "John"
    For RecNum = 1 To 8
        MyRecord.Last = "Doe" & Str$(RecNum)
        MyRecord.Count = Str$(RecNum)
        '
        'Write the record to the file
        Put #1, RecNum, MyRecord

    Next RecNum
```

To make the example simple, this code artificially generates eight different **John Doe** entries. It adds **RecNum** to the end of each last name to make them all different.

Random access files let you change the data stored in any record simply by writing directly to the record. Changing a sequential file requires storing the data from the entire file in an array, changing the data in the array, and writing the file back to disk. Clearly, if your data may change, it is preferable to use random access files.

To manage the scrolling through the file using the Next and Previous Command buttons, the value of the form variables **CurrentRec** and **MaxRec** must be set. The following code uses the **LOF** function to determine the size of the open file and divides by the size of the fixed-length record to get the number of records in the file.

```
'Determine the number of records in the file
    '
    MaxRec = LOF(1) / Len(MyRecord)
```

To set the value of the current record, set the variable to the record number. The example below sets it to the first record.

```
CurrentRec = 1
```

You are now ready to test the application. Run the Random application. Use the Next and Previous Command buttons to scroll through the different records in the file. The running Random application is shown in Figure 12-9.

Figure 12-9
Running the
Random
application

You have now learned the commands to read and write a file! The next lesson explains binary access files.

QUIZ

1. _____ access is used to read or write ASCII text files.
   a. Sequential
   b. Text mode
   c. Binary
   d. Random

2. The ___ command is used to read random access files.
   a. **Read**
   b. **Write**
   c. **Get**
   d. **Input**

3. Reading or writing a fixed-length record is an example of _____ file access.
   a. Sequential
   b. Normal
   c. Random
   d. Read_Write

4. **Open "C":\VB.TXT" For Random as #1 Len=20**
   a. Opens the file **C:\VB.TXT** in random access mode with a fixed-length record size of 20.
   b. The syntax is incorrect.
   c. Opens the file **C\VB.TXT** in binary mode.
   d. Opens the file **C\VB.TXT** with 20 records in random access mode.

5. To write a record past the last record in a random access mode file:
   a. Use **Seek** to go to the end of the file and the **Print** command.
   b. Use the **Put** command, where the record number is one more than the current total in the file.
   c. Use the **Put** command with the last record number in the file.
   d. Use the **Print** command.

BINARY FILE ACCESS

Random access files are convenient and easy, but they do have their drawbacks. This lesson explains the ins and outs of binary file access. Many programmers avoid binary access because it is a bit complicated. But the advantages of binary access make it worth considering when you must deal with large amounts of data.

Why Use Binary Access?

Random access records are fixed-length records. Consider the record structure in Listing 12-12.

Listing 12-12 Fixed-length customer record

```
Type Customer
     ID As Integer
     FirstName As String * 20
     LastName As String * 20
     Title As String * 15
     Address As String * 30
     City As String * 20
     State As String * 2
     ZipCode As String * 11
     Phone As String * 13
End Type
```

This data structure requires 137 bytes of disk space for each record. The string for `FirstName` is always 20 characters long, whether the customer's first name is Ed or Rumpelstiltskin. The customer who lives at 1 D St. requires as much space for the address as the customer who lives at 27898 Wilkinshire Boulevard. In other words, random access records take a lot of disk space.

Binary access files do not use fixed-length records, which is their strength and their weakness. Look at the type declaration in Listing 12-13.

Listing 12-13 A `Customer` type for binary files

```
Type Customer
     ID As Integer
     FirstName As String
     LastName As String
     Title As String
     Address As String
     City As String
     State As String
     ZipCode As String
     Phone As String
End Type
```

Note that the strings are no longer declared as having a fixed length. Each record now requires exactly as many bytes as there are characters in the strings, plus 2 bytes for the integer variable. It is this economy of space that makes binary files attractive.

Reading a Binary Access File

You read a binary access file the same way you read a random access file, with the `Get` statement. As a reminder, the syntax of `Get` is

```
Get [#]filenumber, [recnumber], varname
```

The difference is that `recnumber` for binary access is really the number of the first byte of the variable in the file. How do you know what that number is? For the first variable, it is obviously 1. Once that variable has been read, you can find exactly where you are in the file by using the `Seek` function. The syntax is

```
Seek(Filenum)
```

where `Filenum` is the number of the open file. The function returns the file position, that is, the number of the first byte of the next variable in the file.

Writing a Binary Access File

Write to a binary access file with the `Put` statement. As a refresher, the syntax is

```
Put [#]filenumber, [recnumber], varname
```

For binary access files, `recnumber` is the byte position where you want to write the file. If you leave `recnumber` out, the data will be written at the current file position. The statement without `recnumber` would look like

```
Put #1, , varname
```

A Programming Example

Start a new project in Visual Basic. Name the project **fBinary.vbp**. Place the objects in Table 12-9 on the form. The completed project is on the CD that comes with this book. This project is rather complicated, so you might want to copy it from the CD rather than type it in. If so, because the program writes data to disk, you must copy it to your hard disk. (Follow the explanations of the code!)

Table 12-9 Starting the Binary project

Object	Property	Value
Form	Name	Form1
	Caption	Binary Files
	Height	3855
	Width	6600
PictureBox	Name	Picture1

continued on next page

continued from previous page

Object	Property	Value
	Enabled	False
	Height	3195
	Width	6315
	Left	120
	Top	60

Draw 11 text boxes inside the picture box. Set their properties according to Table 12-10.

Table 12-10 Adding text boxes to Picture1

Object	Property	Value
TextBox	Name	txtFirst
	Top	345
	Left	300
	Width	2055
	Height	285
	TabIndex	0
	Text	(None)
TextBox	Name	txtLast
	Top	345
	Left	2400
	Width	2155
	Height	285
	TabIndex	1
	Text	(None)
TextBox	Name	txtRecNum
	Top	60
	Left	4980
	Width	735
	Height	285
	Text	(None)
	TabStop	False
	Locked	True

Object	Property	Value
TextBox	Name	txtTitle
	Top	960
	Left	300
	Width	2055
	Height	285
	TabIndex	2
	Text	(none)
TextBox	Name	txtPay
	Top	960
	Left	2460
	Width	2055
	Height	285
	TabIndex	3
	Text	(none)
TextBox	Name	txtAddress
	Top	1515
	Left	300
	Width	4215
	Height	285
	TabIndex	4
	Text	(none)
TextBox	Name	txtCity
	Top	2115
	Left	300
	Width	2355
	Height	285
	TabIndex	5
	Text	(none)
TextBox	Name	txtState
	Top	2155

continued on next page

continued from previous page

Object	Property	Value
	Left	2700
	Width	375
	Height	285
	MaxLength	2
	TabIndex	6
	Text	(none)
TextBox	Name	txtZip
	Top	2115
	Left	3120
	Width	1395
	Height	285
	TabIndex	7
	Text	(none)
TextBox	Name	txtPhone
	Top	2700
	Left	300
	Width	2235
	Height	285
	TabIndex	8
	Text	(none)
TextBox	Name	txtID
	Top	2700
	Left	3780
	Width	2235
	Height	285
	TabIndex	9
	Text	(none)

Add labels for each text box. Rather than using a table to place the labels, use Figure 12-10 as a guide.

From Figure 12-10, you can see that you also need to add eight Command buttons. Use Table 12-11 to place the Command buttons.

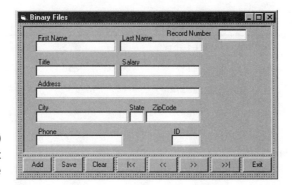

Figure 12-10
The Binary project at design time

Table 12-11 The Command buttons for Binary

Object	Property	Value
CommandButton	Name	cmdAdd
	Caption	Add
	Height	375
	Left	120
	TabIndex	10
	Top	3360
	Width	735
CommandButton	Name	cmdSave
	Caption	Save
	Height	375
	Left	925
	TabIndex	11
	Top	3360
	Width	735
CommandButton	Name	cmdClear
	Caption	Clear
	Height	375
	Left	1730
	TabIndex	12
	Top	3360
	Width	735
CommandButton	Name	cmdFirst
	Caption	|<<

continued on next page

continued from previous page

Object	Property	Value
	Height	375
	Left	2535
	TabIndex	13
	Top	3360
	Width	735
CommandButton	Name	cmdPrev
	Caption	<<
	Height	375
	Left	3340
	TabIndex	14
	Top	3360
	Width	735
CommandButton	Name	cmdNext
	Caption	>>
	Height	375
	Left	4145
	TabIndex	15
	Top	3360
	Width	735
CommandButton	Name	cmdLast
	Caption	>>|
	Height	375
	Left	4980
	TabIndex	16
	Top	3360
	Width	735
CommandButton	Name	cmdQuit
	Caption	Exit
	Height	375
	Left	5760
	TabIndex	17
	Top	3360
	Width	735

Take a deep breath, then add a module to the project. Use the Properties window to name the module **Binary**. Add the declarations in Listing 12-14 to the Declarations section of the module.

Listing 12-14 Global declarations for Binary

```
Option Explicit
Public udtPlayer As Player
Public arrRecPos() As Long

Type Player
    ID As Integer
    FirstName As String
    LastName As String
    Title As String
    Salary As Currency
    Address As String
    City As String
    State As String
    ZipCode As String
    Phone As String
End Type
```

The declarations create a user-defined data type, **Player,** as a template for the data. They also declare a global variable of type **Player** and set up a dynamic array for storing the file positions of each record. Unlike random access files, binary access files do not store records in fixed-length blocks. To move to anything other than the next record, the program must keep track of the byte position of each record in the file.

Add a procedure to the module and enter the code from Listing 12-15.

Listing 12-15 The **FillText** procedure

```
Public Sub FillText()
    With udtPlayer
        Form1.txtID = .ID
        Form1.txtFirst = .FirstName
        Form1.txtLast = .LastName
        Form1.txtTitle = .Title
        Form1.txtPay = .Salary
        Form1.txtAddress = .Address
        Form1.txtCity = .City
        Form1.txtState = .State
        Form1.txtZip = .ZipCode
        Form1.txtPhone = .Phone
    End With
End Sub
```

When the program reads a record from the file, this procedure is used to copy data from the record into the text boxes. Because this procedure is in a module, each text box must be referenced to its parent form. (The code would be more efficient if it used a second **With...End With** nested inside the first one.)

Checking for Valid Data

Often certain parts of a record may be allowed to be empty, whereas other parts are *required fields*. That means that a record that does not have data in those fields is invalid and should not be saved to disk. This program does not allow data to be saved unless there is a first name, a last name, and a salary.

Add a new function to the module and enter the code from Listing 12-16.

Listing 12-16 The `CheckValidData` function

```
Public Function CheckValidData() As Boolean
    CheckValidData = True
    If Form1.txtFirst = "" Or _
        Form1.txtLast = "" _
        Or Form1.txtPay = "" Then
        CheckValidData = False
        MsgBox "Empty data", vbOKOnly, "Note!"
    End If
End Function
```

This function is an example of how to handle required fields. If any of the three required fields is empty, a message box warns the user, and the **Save** operation (the procedure that calls this function) is aborted. A more sophisticated example would point out which field needs to be fixed.

That is all the code for the module. Close the module's Code window and open the Code window for **Form1**.

Opening the File

The code in Listing 12-17 is in three parts. The first part is the formwide variable declarations. The second part is the **Form_Load** procedure. It opens the data file when the form is loaded. The third part is the **Form_Unload** procedure, which closes the file before unloading the form.

Listing 12-17 The declarations and the `Form_Load` procedure

```
Option Explicit
Public lFileLen As Long
Public iRecNum As Integer
Public lFilePos As Long

Private Sub Form_Load()
Dim sFileName As String
'   Build the filename
    sFileName = App.Path & "\Player.dat"
'   open the file
    Open sFileName For Binary As #1
'   get length of file
    lFileLen = LOF(1)
End Sub
```

```
Private Sub Form_Unload(Cancel As Integer)
    Close #1
End Sub
```

The formwide variables are used to keep track of the file's length, the file position, and the record number. All three change as data is added to the file.

The first thing the code in **Form_Load** does is build the string for the file name. Note that it uses **App.Path**; the data file **Player.dat** must be in the same directory as the executable file. The **Open** statement opens the file for binary access. Finally, the **LOF()** function returns the file length to the variable **lFileLen**. This is used to determine when the **Read** operation reaches the end of the file.

The **Form_Unload** event explicitly closes the file. Always remember the three steps for file handling:

1. Open the file.

2. Manipulate the file (read or write or both).

3. Close the file.

When you write data to a file, it is *buffered* in memory until a large enough block of data has been prepared to make writing to that disk efficient. If you do not close the file, the data that is buffered in memory will be lost.

Reading the File

The data from the file is read by the **Form_Activate** procedure. The code for **Form_Activate** is in Listing 12-18.

Listing 12-18 Reading the file

```
Private Sub Form_Activate()
    '   initialize to starting position
    iRecNum = 0
    lFilePos = 1
    '   read in the data file to get position information
    '   and number of records
    Do
        Get #1, lFilePos, udtPlayer
        iRecNum = iRecNum + 1
        '   add position to array
        ReDim Preserve arrRecPos(iRecNum)
        arrRecPos(iRecNum) = lFilePos
        '   get file position for next record
        lFilePos = Seek(1)
    Loop Until lFilePos >= LOF(1)
    '   display next blank record number
'   disable data entry
    Picture1.Enabled = False
    '   enable/disable command buttons
    cmdSave.Enabled = False
```

continued on next page

continued from previous page

```
            cmdClear.Enabled = False
            cmdNext.Enabled = True
            cmdPrev.Enabled = True
            cmdFirst = True
    End Sub
```

The reading begins at file position (byte) 1. After the data has been read, the file position is stored in the dynamic array so it can be found again. The array index for each record is the record number of that record. The line `ReDim Preserve arrRecPos(iRecNum)` adds a new element to the array for each record that is read. Note the use of `Redim Preserve` to save the existing array data.

Once the old file position has been saved, the current file position is saved in `lFilePos` by calling the `Seek` function. The loop checks to be sure that `lFilePos` is less than the length of the file. If it is not, the program has finished reading.

Once all the records have been read in, the program sets you up to view them. `Picture1` is disabled to prevent typing new data into the text boxes, and the Navigation buttons `cmdFirst`, `cmdNext`, `cmdPrev`, and `cmdLast` are enabled.

Because you need at least those Navigation buttons to be operational before you can view the file, they are next. The code for all four Navigation buttons is in Listing 12-19.

Listing 12-19 The Navigation buttons

```
Private Sub cmdFirst_Click()
'    Goes to first record
'    disable data entry
    Picture1.Enabled = False
'    enable/disable command buttons
    cmdSave.Enabled = False
    cmdClear.Enabled = False
    cmdNext.Enabled = True
    cmdPrev.Enabled = True
'    First record
    iRecNum = 1
    lFilePos = 1
    Get #1, lFilePos, udtPlayer
    txtRecNum = iRecNum
'    Fill in the textboxes from the udt
    Call FillText
'    cmdNext is logical focus
    cmdNext.SetFocus
End Sub

Private Sub cmdLast_Click()
'    disable data entry
    Picture1.Enabled = False
'    enable disable command buttons
    cmdSave.Enabled = False
    cmdClear.Enabled = False
    cmdNext.Enabled = True
```

```
        cmdPrev.Enabled = True
        '    find last file position
        lFilePos = arrRecPos(UBound(arrRecPos))
        Get #1, lFilePos, udtPlayer
        '    get record number
        iRecNum = UBound(arrRecPos)
        txtRecNum = iRecNum
        '    fill in the textboxes
        Call FillText
        '    cmdPrev is logical focus
        cmdPrev.SetFocus
End Sub

Private Sub cmdNext_Click()
        '    test for last record
        If Val(txtRecNum) + 1 > UBound(arrRecPos) Then
            MsgBox "This is the last record", vbOKOnly, "End of File"
            cmdPrev.SetFocus
            Exit Sub
        End If
        '    get file position
        lFilePos = arrRecPos(Val(txtRecNum) + 1)
        Get #1, lFilePos, udtPlayer
        iRecNum = iRecNum + 1
        txtRecNum = iRecNum
        '    Fill in the textboxes
        Call FillText
        cmdNext.SetFocus
End Sub

Private Sub cmdPrev_Click()
        '    text for first record
        If Val(txtRecNum) - 1 < 1 Then
            MsgBox "This is the first record", vbOKOnly, "Beginning of File"
            cmdNext.SetFocus
            Exit Sub
        End If
        '    get file position
        lFilePos = arrRecPos(Val(txtRecNum) - 1)
        Get #1, lFilePos, udtPlayer
        iRecNum = iRecNum - 1
        txtRecNum = iRecNum
        '    fill in the textboxes
        Call FillText
        cmdPrev.SetFocus
End Sub
```

With the exception of **cmdFirst**, the Navigation buttons use the array to find the file position of the record. Of course, **cmdFirst** need only read from byte 1 of the file. The **cmdNext** code checks to be sure it is not going beyond the last record, and **cmdPrev** checks to be sure it does not go beyond record number one.

Adding Data

While you are reading the existing data, you cannot edit the fields. The text boxes are disabled by the simple trick of putting them all in a picture box and disabling the picture box. Data in the records cannot be changed in this program, because new data may overwrite the next record with variable-length fields. The program will let you add new data only at the end of the file.

Adding data begins with the Add button, which clears all the text boxes and moves the file position to the end of the file. It also enables the picture box so you can enter text into the text boxes and enables the Save and Clear buttons so you can save your changes or clear the text boxes. The code for **cmdAdd**, **cmdClear**, and **cmdSave** is in Listing 12-20.

Listing 12-20 Adding data and writing to the file

```
Private Sub cmdAdd_Click()
'    Prepare to add a new record
     '    Clear all textboxes
     cmdClear = True
End Sub

Private Sub cmdClear_Click()
'    Clears all text boxes
     txtID = ""
     txtFirst = ""
     txtLast = ""
     txtTitle = ""
     txtPay = ""
     txtAddress = ""
     txtCity = ""
     txtState = ""
     txtZip = ""
     txtPhone = ""
     iRecNum = UBound(arrRecPos)
     txtRecNum = iRecNum
     '    enable data entry
     Picture1.Enabled = True
     '    enable/disable command buttons
     cmdSave.Enabled = True
     cmdClear.Enabled = True
     cmdNext.Enabled = False
     cmdPrev.Enabled = False
     txtFirst.SetFocus
End Sub

Private Sub cmdSave_Click()
     '    Check to be sure the key data is filled in
     If CheckValidData = False Then Exit Sub
     '    Put data from textboxes into udt
     With udtPlayer
```

```
        .ID = Val(txtID & "")
        .FirstName = txtFirst
        .LastName = txtLast
        .Title = txtTitle
        .Salary = Val(txtPay)
        .Address = txtAddress
        .City = txtCity
        .State = txtState
        .ZipCode = txtZip
        .Phone = txtPhone
    End With
'       Calculate File Postion
        lFilePos = lFileLen + 1
'   Save it to disk
    Put #1, lFileLen + 1, udtPlayer
'   update record number
    iRecNum = UBound(arrRecPos) + 1
'   Add the record position to array
    ReDim Preserve arrRecPos(iRecNum)
    arrRecPos(iRecNum) = lFilePos
'       update record number
    txtRecNum = iRecNum + 1
'   Clear textboxes for next new entry
    cmdClear = True
'       update file length
    lFileLen = LOF(1)
End Sub
```

Note that `cmdAdd` calls on `cmdClear` to do all its work. You can "click" a Command button in code by setting it to `True`, as in `cmdClear = True`. It's a convenient way to avoid writing the same code twice. The main reason for having two buttons that do the same thing is to avoid confusing the user. Add and Clear have two, apparently different, meanings.

The code in `cmdSave` calls the `CheckValidData` function to assure that the required fields are filled in. If they are, it next copies data from the text boxes into the UDT to prepare it for saving. The file position is calculated as 1 byte past the end of the file. Finally, it writes the data to the end of the file with

```
Put #1, lFileLen + 1, udtPlayer
```

To finish off the process, `cmdSave` puts a reference to the new data in the array and recalculates `lFileLen` and `iRecNum`.

And Now, the Rest of the Code

The balance of the code adds restrictions to some of the text boxes so that only certain keystrokes will be recognized. The code is in Listing 12-21.

Listing 12-21 The rest of the code

```
Private Sub txtPay_KeyPress(KeyAscii As Integer)
    '   only numbers and backspace and decimal point allowed
    If KeyAscii <> Asc(".") And KeyAscii <> 8 And _
        (KeyAscii < Asc("0") Or KeyAscii > Asc("9")) _
    Then KeyAscii = 0
End Sub

Private Sub txtState_KeyPress(KeyAscii As Integer)
    '   only letters and backspace allowed
    If KeyAscii <> 8 And (UCase(Chr(KeyAscii)) < "A" Or _
        UCase(Chr(KeyAscii)) > "Z") Then KeyAscii = 0
End Sub


Private Sub txtState_LostFocus()
    txtState = UCase(txtState)
End Sub
```

The code for **txtPay** allows only numbers, a decimal point, and the backspace key (**KeyAscii = 8**). All other keystrokes are converted to **KeyAscii = 0**.

The code for **txtState** allows only letters and the backspace key. When the text box loses focus, the letters are converted to uppercase letters.

Running the Program

You've studied all the code, so running Binary should be simple. When the program starts, it reads in the data from **Player.dat**. If the file does not exist, it is created.

Scan through the records with the Navigation buttons, then add a couple of records. Be sure to try adding a record with one of the required fields empty.

Summary

Use Notepad to view the way the data is actually stored in **Player.dat**. Notice that the plain ASCII data is still readable, but the text is interspersed with some unrecognizable characters. When you store numeric data in binary form, you cannot read it with an ordinary text viewer. There is a minor benefit from this—the average snoop will not be able to learn Freddy Kruger's salary just by viewing the file!

In fact, one of the major space savings with binary access is in the storage of numeric data. Saving an integer like 32333 in text requires 5 bytes of storage. Saving the same number in binary requires only 2 bytes. It doesn't sound like much, but with a large collection of data, the savings in disk space can be significant.

The price to pay is the inconvenience in changing data. It's easy enough to add to the end, but to change something in the middle means that you have to read *all* the data into an array or a temporary disk file and then rewrite it all, one record at a time, inserting the changed record in place of the original. Perhaps that is why so many programmers avoid binary access files.

1. Records saved in binary access files are:
   a. Fixed length
   b. Variable length
   c. Completely unreadable
   d. Encrypted

2. If file #1 is a binary access file, what is the code `Get #1,20, udtRecord` reading?
   a. 20 bytes of data from `udtRecord`
   b. A single record beginning at byte 1
   c. A single record beginning at byte 20
   d. The 20th record in the file

3. The variable `iNumber` is declared as an integer. If it is assigned the value `23,456`, how much disk space will it take in a binary access file?
   a. 6 bytes
   b. 5 bytes
   c. 8 bytes
   d. 2 bytes

4. What is the main advantage of using binary access files?
   a. They save space on the disk.
   b. They are easier to use than random access.
   c. They make you look smart.
   d. The files are more secure.

5. What is the main disadvantage of using binary access files?
   a. The files take too much disk space.
   b. It is difficult to edit data in existing records.
   c. `Put` and `Get` are too confusing to use.
   d. All of the above.

A NOTEPAD APPLICATION

In this lesson, you will create a simple application that can create, read, or write text files: a notepad application. So why write another notepad application when Windows already comes with a notepad application and you have seen notepad applications elsewhere (like SuperPad)? Well, the important part of this notepad application is the object-oriented approach taken for file I/O to create the notepad, using a `File` class.

Figure 12-11 shows the design for the **File** class. The **File** class consists of three private properties: **FileHandle**, **fMode**, and **Status**. The file handle stores the file number returned from **FreeFile** and used in file I/O commands. The **fMode** property stores the file access mode to use when opening the file (that is, read or write). The **Status** property stores the current error status of the **File** object. The class also has two public properties: **FileName** and **Mode**. The **FileName** member is the path and name of the file. The **Mode** property is a public property that allows you to set the private variable **fMode** to read or write. The class has four methods: **OpenFile**, **CloseFile**, **ReadAll**, and **WriteAll**. The **OpenFile** method is used to open a file, and **CloseFile** is used to close a file. The **ReadAll** method reads the entire contents of the file, and the **WriteAll** method writes a string to a file.

Create a new project called Notepad. The completed project is on the CD that accompanies this book.

Before you set any form properties, insert a class module by selecting Add Class Module on the Project menu. Use the Properties window to name the class **File**.

Now add the private and public properties shown in Figure 12-11. In the Declarations section of the class module, add the following variables and constants:

```
Private FileHandle As Integer 'Private File Number
Private Status As Integer 'Error Flag - True = OK
Private fMode As Integer ' Mode to Open the file
Public FileName As String 'File Name

'
'File Mode Constants
'
Const FInput = 0 'Input Sequential Mode
Const FOutput = 1 'Output Sequential Mode
```

Next add the **Mode** property, which allows users to set the private property **fMode**. To create the public property, add the **Get** and **Set** property procedures, shown in Listing 12-22.

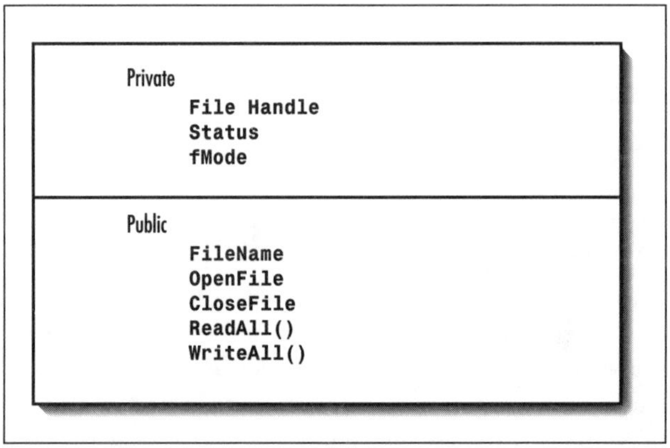

```
Private
        File Handle
        Status
        fMode

Public
        FileName
        OpenFile
        CloseFile
        ReadAll()
        WriteAll()
```

Figure 12-11
File class

Listing 12-22 Public property procedures for the property `Mode`

```
Public Property Get Mode() As String
    'Return the current value of mode
    If fMode = FInput Then
        Mode = "read"
    Else
        Mode = "write"
    End If
End Property

Public Property Let Mode(vNewValue As String)
    'set the mode
    If vNewValue = "read" Then
        fMode = FInput
    Else
        fMode = FOutput
    End If
End Property
```

The class properties have been added. It's time to create the class methods. There are four procedures in the class module that create the four methods. Start with the `OpenFile` procedure.

OpenFile **Method**

The `OpenFile` method opens the file contained in the public member `FileName`. The file handle, a private member, contains the next available file number, returned from the `FreeFile` function. A simple error-handling routine is installed that sets the private member status to `False` if an error occurs. Other member methods will not execute during an error condition. The application using the file object does not have to check for file errors because errors are handled in the object. Add a new procedure called `OpenFile` to the class module and add the code shown in Listing 12-23.

Listing 12-23 `OpenFile` method

```
Public Sub OpenFile()
    'Set up the error handler
    On Error GoTo Open_Error
    '
    ' Get a free file handle and store in private area
    FileHandle = FreeFile
    '
    'Open the file in Sequential Mode
    '
    '  Check the status of the private property and
    '  open the file for input or output.
    '
    Select Case fMode
        Case FOutput
            Open FileName For Output As #FileHandle
        Case Else
```

continued on next page

continued from previous page

```
              Open FileName For Input As #FileHandle
    End Select
    'Set the Status property for other member functions
    Status = True
Exit_Open:
    Exit Sub


'
'Error Handler
'
Open_Error:
    MsgBox "OpenF()- Error opening file. " _
        & Err.Description
    'Set the Status property to failure
    Status = False
    Resume Exit_Open

End Sub
```

CloseFile **Method**

The CloseFile method closes the open file and resets the private properties of the class. Create the method by adding a procedure named CloseFile to the class and then adding the code shown in Listing 12-24.

Listing 12-24 CloseFile method

```
Public Sub CloseFile()
    '
    'Close the FileHandle and set to 0
    '
    Close #FileHandle
    FileHandle = 0 'Reset the file handle
    Status = False 'Reset the Status
End Sub
```

ReadAll **Method**

The ReadAll method takes a single parameter, TextBuffer, and reads the entire file into the string. Add the ReadAll procedure to the class module and add the code shown in Listing 12-25.

Listing 12-25 ReadAll method

```
Public Sub ReadAll(TextBuffer As String)
Dim OneLine As String

    '
    'Check Private member for errors and exit if False
    If Status = False Then GoTo Exit_Read
    '
```

```
     'Setup the error handler
     On Error GoTo Read_Error
         '
     'Read data into
     'the OneLine variable and
     'store in the TextBuffer
     'until the end of the File
         '
     While Not (EOF(FileHandle))
         Line Input #FileHandle, OneLine
         TextBuffer = TextBuffer + OneLine + Chr(13) + Chr(10)
     Wend
     Status = True
Exit_Read:
     Exit Sub
         '
     ' Error Handler
         '
Read_Error:
     MsgBox "ReadAll()- Error reading file. " _
         & Err.Description
     Status = False   'Set the status property to error condition
     Resume Exit_Read

End Sub '
```

WriteAll **Method**

The **WriteAll** method writes the **TextBuffer** passed into the method to the open file. Add the **WriteAll** procedure to the class module and add the code shown in Listing 12-26.

Listing 12-26 WriteAll method

```
Public Sub WriteAll(TextBuffer As String)
   If Status = False Then GoTo Write_Error
   On Error GoTo Write_Error
      '
   'Write the String
      '
   Print #FileHandle, TextBuffer
   Status = True
Exit_Write:
   Exit Sub
'
'Add some simple Error Handling code
'
Write_Error:
   MsgBox "WriteAll()- Error writing text to file. " _
   & Err.Description
   Status = False
   Resume Exit_Write

End Sub
```

The `File` class is now complete. Add the objects to the form and set the properties as shown in Table 12-12.

Table 12-12 Objects, properties, and settings for Notepad application

Object	Property	Setting
Form	Caption	NotePad
	ClipControls	False
	Height	4560
	Top	1395
	Width	5730
TextBox	Height	3210
	Left	60
	MultiLine	True
	Name	txtBuffer
	ScrollBars	3 – Both
	Top	15
	Width	5490
CommonDialog	DialogTitle	Select Text File
	Filter	Text (*.txt)|*.txt
	Left	0
	Name	cmdlgFile
	Top	3225
CommandButton	Caption	&Open
	Height	465
	Left	105
	Name	cmdOpen
	Top	3360
	Width	1290
CommandButton	Caption	&New
	Height	465
	Left	1500
	Name	cmdNew
	Top	3360
	Width	1290

Object	Property	Setting
CommandButton	Caption	&Save
	Height	465
	Left	2865
	Name	cmdSave
	Top	3360
	Width	1290
CommandButton	Caption	E&xit
	Height	465
	Left	4230
	Name	cmdExit
	Top	3360
	Width	1290

Add the menu items shown in Table 12-13.

Table 12-13 Menu properties for `frmNotePad`

Caption	Name
&File	mnuFile
&New	mnuNew
&Open	mnuOpen
&Save	mnuSave
sep1	–
E&xit	mnuExit

Add the following code to the `Form_Terminate` event:

```
Private Sub Form_Terminate()
    End
End Sub
```

Now add the code shown in Listing 12-27 to the `cmdOpen_Click` event.

Listing 12-27 Open button click event code

```
Private Sub cmdOpen_Click()
Dim ReadBuffer As String

    On Error GoTo Open_Cancel
    cmdlgFile.ShowOpen
    If cmdlgFile.FileName <> "" Then
        'Clear Buffer
        txtBuffer.Text = ""
        'Create a File Object
        Set MyFile = New File
        'Set the FileName
        MyFile.FileName = cmdlgFile.FileName
        'Set the Mode to read
        MyFile.Mode = "read"
        'Open the File
        MyFile.OpenFile
        'Read the file into a buffer
        MyFile.ReadAll ReadBuffer
        'Close the file
        MyFile.CloseFile
        'Place the file contents in the textbox
        txtBuffer.Text = ReadBuffer
        '
        'Enable the Save button
        '
        cmdSave.Enabled = True
        mnuSave.Enabled = True
        'Release the object
        Set MyFile = Nothing
    End If
Open_Exit:
    Exit Sub

Open_Cancel:          'Assume Cancel was pressed
    Resume Open_Exit
End Sub
```

Add the code shown in Listing 12-28 to the **cmdNew_Click** event.

Listing 12-28 New button click event code

```
Private Sub cmdNew_Click()

    On Error GoTo New_Cancel 'Enable the error handler
    txtBuffer.Text = ""         'Clear the text
    cmdlgFile.FileName = "NewFile" 'Set Default Name
    cmdlgFile.ShowOpen  'Show the File Window
    cmdSave.Enabled = True 'Enable command buttons
    mnuSave.Enabled = True '
New_Exit:
    Exit Sub
    '
```

```
    'Error Handler
New_Cancel:
    cmdlgFile.FileName = ""
    Resume New_Exit

End Sub
```

The code in Listing 12-29 is for the `cmdSave_Click` event.

Listing 12-29 Save button `Click` event code

```
Private Sub cmdSave_Click()
    '
    'Check if File Name is Valid
    '
    If cmdlgFile.FileName <> "" Then
        'Create a File Object
        Set MyFile = New File

        'Set the FileName
        MyFile.FileName = cmdlgFile.FileName

        'Set the Mode to write
        MyFile.Mode = "write"

        'Open the File
        MyFile.OpenFile

        'Write the buffer to the file
        MyFile.WriteAll txtBuffer

        'Close the file
        MyFile.CloseFile
        MsgBox "File " & MyFile.FileName & " saved.", _
            MB_ICONINFORMATION, "File Saved"
        '
        'Release the Object
        '
        Set MyFile = Nothing
    End If
End Sub
```

The `cmdExit_Click` event is shown in Listing 12-30.

Listing 12-30 Exit button `Click` event code

```
Private Sub cmdExit_Click()
    Unload Me
End Sub
```

The code for the menus is shown in Listing 12-31. Each menu item calls the corresponding Command button. For example, the code for **mnuNew_Click** calls the procedure **cmdNew_Click**. The line **Call cmdNew_Click** is equivalent to **cmdNew = True**, which you learned in the last lesson.

Listing 12-31 Menu items `Click` event code

```
Private Sub cmdExit_Click()
  Unload Me
End Sub

Private Sub mnuNew_Click()
  Call cmdNew_Click
End Sub

Private Sub mnuOpen_Click()
  Call cmdOpen_Click
End Sub

Private Sub mnuSave_Click()
  Call cmdSave_Click
End Sub

Private Sub mnuExit_Click()
  Call cmdExit_Click
End Sub
```

Run the application. Press the New button, enter a file name, and press OK. Enter text in the text box, as shown in Figure 12-12. Press the Save button or use the menu selection to save the text to the file. Press the Open button and select the file you have just created. The text you saved will appear in the text box. To cut and paste text, highlight the text and use the Windows shortcut keys CTRL-X to cut, CTRL-C to copy, and CTRL-V to paste.

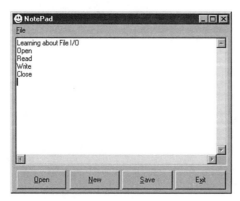

Figure 12-12
NotePad
application

The `File` class is a base template you can use to build a more complex `File` class with more members and methods to shield you from the many different file I/O access modes. The `File` class can be modified to work with binary and random files as well as sequential files. Use the quiz below to see how well you understand the code you have just written.

The following questions are based on the code you have just completed.

1. What does the following line of code do?

   ```
   Set MyFile = New File
   ```

   a. Opens a file
   b. Creates a `File` object using the `File` class
   c. Sets the value of `MyFile` to the value of `New File`
   d. Creates a new `File` class

2. `MyFile.OpenFile` is an example of:
   a. Using the `File` object's method `OpenFile`
   b. Referencing the `File` object's property `OpenFile`
   c. Referencing the `File` object's member `OpenFile`
   d. Invalid syntax

3. What is wrong with the following code?

   ```
   Set MyFile = New File
   MyFile.FileName = cmdlgFile.FileName
   MyFile.Mode = "read"
   MyFile.OpenFile
   MyFile.WriteAll txtBuffer
   Set MyFile = Nothing
   MyFile.CloseFile
   ```

   a. There is nothing wrong with the code.
   b. `MyFile.Mode = "read"` should be `Set MyFile.Mode = "read"`.
   c. The object tries to execute the `CloseFile` method after `MyFile` has been set to nothing.
   d. `MyFile.FileName = cmdlgFile.FileName` is incorrect; use the `Name` property on `cmdlgFile` instead.

4. If you wanted to change the name of the class from `File` to `MyFile`, you would:
   a. Change the public member `FileName` to `MyFile`.
   b. Change the class property `Name` to `MyFile`.
   c. Change the project name to `MyFile`.
   d. Change the class `ClassName` property to `MyFile`.

5. The following code:

```
Select Case Mode
  Case FOutput
     Open FileName For Output As #FileHandle
  Case Else
     Open FileName For Input As #FileHandle
  End Select
```

a. Opens two files, one for input and one for output.
b. Opens a single file, based on the value of **Mode**.
c. Will cause an error by opening two files with the same file number.
d. Opens a file for output; if the file exists, it will open it for input.

USING FILES IN DEVELOPMENT TIME VERSUS STAND-ALONE APPLICATIONS

This lesson examines real-world file paths. It explains the difference between using files during development time and in a distributed, stand-alone application. It also explains how to create applications that work in network environments, where the application may be installed in one location and be referenced by several different client PCs.

Begin by setting up an example to use throughout the lesson. Create a new application named Do Whatever that reads and writes files.

Figure 12-13 shows the runtime file configuration for the application. The application uses an initialization file that is located in the application's folder, DO WHATEVER. The DO WHATEVER folder in turn has two subfolders: read and write.

Figure 12-14 shows the file structure you created to save the DoWhatever Visual Basic project. For testing purposes, the two folders, read and write, have been included. Now you have a problem: The application is expected to run with the disk and file configuration in Figure 12-13, but during design and testing, the disk and file configuration will look like Figure 12-14. What is the best way to handle this problem?

Figure 12-13
DO WHATEVER
runtime file
structure

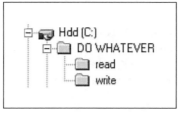

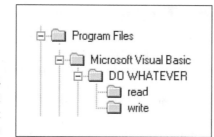

Figure 12-14
DO WHATEVER
Visual Basic project
file structure

Furthermore, let's say the application Do Whatever becomes a big success, so much so that your boss tells you to put it on the network so the whole company can use it. You keep the same file and disk structure as Figure 12-13. Figure 12-15 shows the new problem. PC 1 has mapped the DO WHATEVER C:\ drive to drive G: and PC 2 has mapped the DO WHATEVER C:\ drive to drive F:. A *mapped drive* is a drive that a computer has connected to by way of a network. Each mapped drive on a computer is assigned a local drive letter. When PC 1 wants to read from the host computer's drive C:\, it "knows" it locally as G:\. PC 2, on the other hand, has mapped the same drive as drive F:\. How will Do Whatever know the correct drive letter to use to read and write files? To answer these questions, take a look at file access from the start of the application development to completion.

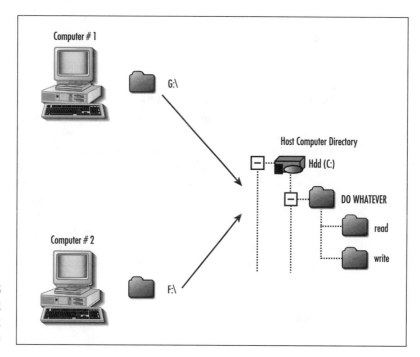

Figure 12-15
DO WHATEVER
network
configuration

Development Time

Development time is the period when you are creating forms and coding your application. As you begin to create the DOWHATEVER application, you create one or two forms and some simple code to open and read the initialization file. Before you save the project, you test the existing code by running the application from Visual Basic. The application wants to open the initialization file in the execution directory of the application. Where is the application running from? Because you have not saved the project, the application is running from the Visual Basic directory. The application cannot read the initialization file, because it's in the wrong directory. What do you do? You write the following line of code:

```
Open "C:\PROGRAM FILES\MICRTOSOFT VISUAL BASIC\DO WHATEVER\DO_WHATEVER.INI for Input⇐
as #Filenum
```

To get around the problem of the application's initialization file location, the file's location and name is *hardcoded*. Hardcoding is a term used to signify that the code is not flexible and relies on some set parameters. In this case, the initialization file cannot be opened unless the file is located in the folder C:\PROGRAM FILES\MICROSOFT VISUAL BASIC\DO WHATEVER\. You are happy with your test results and you save the project to the C:\PROGRAM FILES\MICROSOFT VISUAL BASIC\DO WHATEVER\ folder, shown in Figure 12-13. What happens when you create a stand-alone application that is to be distributed to many users via a network drive? If the user does not have the file `DoWhatever.ini` in the directory C:\PROGRAM FILES\MICROSOFT VISUAL BASIC\DO WHATEVER\, the file open will fail. Hardcoding a path can create problems, because you have to make sure that the hardcoded path exists on the machine that executes your application. Now consider a stand-alone application and a better method than hardcoding to obtain the correct path.

Stand-alone Application

A Visual Basic stand-alone application is an application created with Visual Basic that has been compiled, debugged, and tested and is ready to be distributed to others. Perhaps the application will be installed on a network drive for many different users to access or on several individual PCs. You cannot make assumptions about the drive and directory structure your distributed application will have. So how do you code to handle an unknown drive number or path without modifying the application initialization file? Visual Basic's **App** object has a property called **Path** that contains the current path the application is running from. Listing 12-32 shows how to use the **App** object to build valid paths. The example in Listing 12-32 creates a path to the read and write directories with the **SafePath** function and will work at design time, runtime, and in a stand-alone application.

Listing 12-32 Using the Visual Basic App object

```
Dim ReadFolder as String, WriteFolder as String

ReadFolder = SafePath(App.Path, "read")
WriteFolder = SafePath(App.Path, "write")

Function SafePath(ByVal Path as String, ByVal File As String)
'When given a path and a directory or file, SafePath returns
'a fully-qualified filename.
'Adds a trailing \ to Path if necessary

   If Right$(Path, 1) = "\" Then
      SafePath = Path & File
   Else
      SafePath = Path & "\" & File
   End If

End Function
```

The important lesson in this is to do as little hardcoding as possible. Use the **App** object at every phase of development instead of hardcoding path values. You never know where your application will be installed.

Chapter 13, Data Access, examines database access, database design, and report writing using Visual Basic.

1. If you start a new project with a single form and run the application before you save the project, the application runs from the _____ home directory.
   a. Visual Basic
   b. Windows Temp
   c. Swap Space
   d. User

2. *Hardcoding* is:
   a. A difficult program to write
   b. Slang for someone who is always coding
   c. `strName = App.Path`
   d. `MyPath = "C:\VB"`

3. The object to use to get the current path an application is executing from is:
   a. `Dir`
   b. `Screen`
   c. `App`
   d. `Debug`

4. If a PC connects to a drive on a network and assigns the drive a local letter of F:, the drive referred to has a _____ drive.
   a. Mapped
   b. Disk
   c. System
   d. Offset

5. _____ is a completed application, compiled and ready to be distributed.
   a. Design time
   b. Runtime
   c. Execute time
   d. Stand-alone

DATA ACCESS

This chapter introduces data access. Data access describes the different methods available to store, retrieve, add, delete, and update information in a database. The chapter provides an introduction to databases, database design, and the Open Database Connectivity standard (ODBC). Finally, the chapter describes how to create classy-looking custom reports from database files.

Visual Basic is a convenient way to create *front-end* programs for database access. Front-end programs insulate the ordinary user from the complexities of database management systems (DBMS) and protect the data from accidental (or malicious) deletion and alteration.

WHAT IS A DATABASE?

You have probably heard the term *database* used before. In very general terms, a database is an object that stores information and provides methods for managing the data, adding new information, or editing or retrieving existing information. A database can be a single file or a complex, full-scale client/server relational database management system. There are many different types of databases and access methods. Examples include x-base, ISAM, relational databases, and object databases. Each of the different types of databases mentioned has different internal database structures and query languages. The database and access methods we will concern ourselves with are in the database that ships with Visual Basic 5, the Microsoft Access database and the Jet database engine. The methods and techniques you learn with Visual Basic using the Access database and the Jet engine can be applied to many of the databases described above through the magic of ODBC. Before you get into the details of the Access database and the Jet database engine, consider an everyday example of a database, a loose-leaf recipe book.

A recipe book contains information for many different recipes and is organized into different categories like meat, poultry, fish, bread, or desserts to speed up the search for specific recipes. The main food categories in a recipe book can be broken down further into subcategories. For example, the dessert recipes can be broken into subcategories such as ice cream, cakes, and pies. Recipes in each subcategory are ordered alphabetically to make recipe searches easier. If you wanted to make an apple pie, you could quickly go to the dessert category, look in the pie subcategory, and search for recipes that start with the letter A. Using categories in a recipe book makes finding a recipe much faster than scanning through every recipe in the book. Some recipe books provide a table of contents where you can look up apple pie and quickly get the page number. You can also add new recipes to the book or change existing recipes in the book by writing in new ingredients. If you find a recipe you do not like, you can remove it from the book. A database is much the same. It provides the means to retrieve existing data quickly, to add new data, and to remove data. A database lets you go a step or two further than any type of book, though. Consider trying to list all of the recipes that use salt as an ingredient. With a cookbook, that would be a major chore. With a database and a program, it is child's play.

Visual Basic comes with built-in support for the Microsoft Access database program and for the database files that are created by Access. You can distribute database files with your VB programs and your users do not need to have Access on their computers to use the files. (Actually, that is true of all of the different database files that Visual Basic supports.)

Access Database

The Access database is a relational database shared by Visual Basic 5 and Microsoft Access. A relational database is a database that structures the data by breaking them into logical objects that have relationships between them. Using relationships reduces the amount of redundant data and makes comprehension easier. Relational databases also provide mechanisms to correctly maintain the relationships between objects; this function is called *referential integrity*. Referential integrity assures, for example, that if you substitute Equal for sugar in one part of a recipe, the same substitution is made throughout the recipe.

Relational databases support the SQL language to manipulate and retrieve data. The Access database consists of a single file, with a file extension of MDB, to store the many different parts of the database. The Jet database engine is a set of dynamic link libraries used to manage the Access database. Jet provides the application developer with a database object interface to simplify database manipulation.

Database Terms

SQL

SQL stands for Structured Query Language. Most books tell you that SQL is pronounced Sequel, but most database programmers just say Ess Cue Ell. SQL is a language that allows you to perform operations like retrieving data, sorting data, adding new data, deleting data, or updating data in relational databases.

Tables

Tables are the storage areas for specific types of information. A table is made up of columns, which describe each attribute of an item stored in the table, and of rows, which are individual records in the database. Columns have names, data types, and sizes. A single record in a table is made up of one row containing all of the columns in the table. A table named Authors is shown in Figure 13-1.

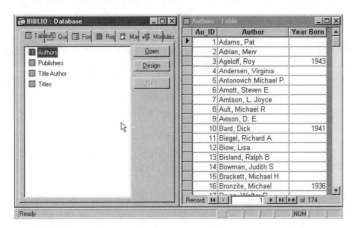

Figure 13-1
Authors table in
BIBLIO.MDB

A good way to visualize a table is to think of a telephone book. The listings in the white pages have three columns, Name, Address, and Phone Number. Each line in the book is equivalent to a row in the database; it is a single record.

Primary Key

Primary key is a database term used to signify the column or columns that uniquely identify a single row in a table. In Figure 13-1, the AU_ID column is the primary key of the Authors table.

Foreign Key

Foreign key is a database term that refers to a column in a secondary table that is related to a column in a primary table.

Indexes

The idea of an index is similar to the categories and subcategories contained in the recipe book example. An index is built on table columns and is used to speed up the retrieval of data from an executing query. Indexes are used to order (sort) the data in specific ways. In the phone book database, one could have a Last Name index (like the real phone book is ordered) and a Phone Number index, which would make it easy to, say, count all the numbers in a given exchange.

Queries

A query is an SQL statement used to retrieve rows of information from one or more tables. A query can also have search criteria to limit the amount of data returned from the tables. For example, you could create a query to return only cake recipes.

RecordSets

A RecordSet is a Microsoft Access Jet database object that represents the data in a table or a query. You can use a RecordSet to view, update, or delete data in a table or query.

Relational Database Example

Figure 13-2 shows an example of two database tables, one called Employee and the other called Skills. The employee table has information about a particular person who works for a company. The skills table has information about the job skills that are important to the company. The company president decides that they would like to be able to review each employee and the employee's job skills. He asks you to create a database that will allow him to view that information. Well, how do you do that? First, take a look at solving the problem with a non-relational method, by creating a single table that contains the employee information and the employee skills information in a single table.

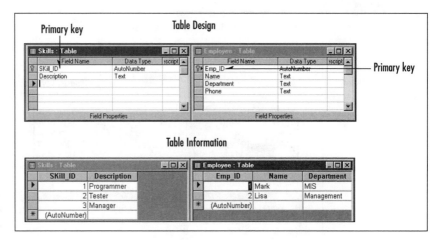

Figure 13-2
Employee and Skills
tables

Figure 13-3 shows the new table. But what if an employee has more than one skill? You would have to repeat all of the employee information to show each employee skill. For example, if Fred has three skills, you must repeat his ID, name, department and phone number three times. That doesn't seem very efficient, does it?

Now look at how it could be done using a relational database model. Look at the tables from a relational viewpoint. First examine the relationship between employees and job skills: A single employee can have more than one job skill. The employee could be a programmer and a tester. What about the skills? A single skill can belong to more than one employee; for example, there could be more than one programmer. The relationship between the employee and skills is said to be a *many-to-many* relationship since a single employee can have more the one job skill and a single job skill can be possessed by more than one employee. To solve our problem, let's create another table that establishes *one-to-many* relationships with the employee and skills tables, called the Employee Skills table, shown in Figure 13-4.

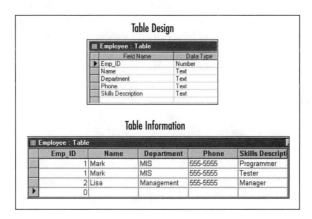

Figure 13-3
Employee and Skills
tables combined

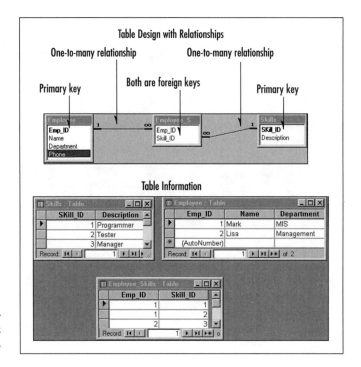

Figure 13-4
Employee Skills
table

The employee skills table contains two fields: the employee_id and the skill_id. To add a skill to an employee, you add one entry to the employee skills table. You do not repeat all the information in the employee table or the skills table: Only the primary keys of each table are repeated. To find all the skills for a single employee, you start with the employee table and find the primary key of the specific employee. You then use the employee_id and search the employee skills table for all entries with the specific employee_id. You then use each of the skill_ids to retrieve the specific skill.

One of the biggest advantages of organizing data this way is that it avoids duplication of data. Not only does that save disk space, but it helps avoid errors. For example, are Fred Prinznettle and fred Prinznettle the same person?

Note that the primary keys of the employee table and the skills table become foreign keys to the employee skills table.

The process of using information from many tables in a relational database is called *joining* the tables. You could join the three tables to find all the employees who were programmers or testers. You could display a single column from one table or several columns from multiple tables. From this, you can begin to see the flexibility and power of relational databases.

Lesson 5, which discusses database design, covers relationships more fully. The next lesson introduces the Visual Basic Data control that uses the Jet engine to connect to databases. But first it's time for a quiz.

1. An Access database is a _____ shared by Visual Basic 5 and Microsoft Access.
   a. Relational database
   b. Flat file
   c. Client/server database
   d. X-base database

2. _____ is a database mechanism to correctly maintain the relationship between objects.
   a. Index
   b. Table
   c. Referential integrity
   d. RecordSet

3. _____ are blueprints and holding areas for specific types of information.
   a. Indexes
   b. Databases
   c. Primary Keys
   d. Tables

4. A(n) _____ is built on table columns and is used to speed up data retrieval from an executing query.
   a. Primary key
   b. Index
   c. SQL
   d. RecordSet

5. A consumer can belong to many banks. Banks can have more than one consumer. This type of relationship is a _____.
   a. One-to-one
   b. Many-to-many
   c. Many-to-one
   d. Master detail

LESSON 2

USING THE DATA CONTROL

In this lesson, you will begin to create database applications using Visual Basic. You may be wondering how complex the code must be for database applications. The programming can be tricky, but luckily for you, Visual Basic provides a custom control called the Data control that allows you to create database applications without writing a single line of code.

The Data control icon is shown in Figure 13-5.

Data Control

The best way to understand the Data control and how it works is to write a single form application that uses the Data control. Since you have not yet learned how to design and create your own database, this program uses the example database that comes with Visual Basic, BIBLIO.MDB. BIBLIO.MDB is located in the Visual Basic home directory and is an Access database that contains information on database books. The database contains several tables and SQL queries. For an example, you will use only the Authors table, which has the structure shown in Table 13-1.

Table 13-1 Authors table in BIBLO.MDB

Column	Data Type	Description
Au_ID	Long Integer	Primary key
Author	Text	Author's name
Year Born	Integer	Year author was born

Now start a new project named Authors, add a Data control, and set the properties for the objects as shown in Table 13-2. The completed project is on the CD that accompanies this book.

— Data control

Figure 13-5
Data control on the
Visual Basic toolbox

Table 13-2 Object and properties settings for Authors project

Object	Property	Setting
Form	Caption	Authors Table
	Height	2910
	Width	5100
Data control	Align	2—Align Bottom
	Caption	Authors
	Name	datAuthors

How do you tie a database to the Data control on the form? First, you need to determine the type of database you are going to use. Click on the Data control, bring up the Properties window for the Data control, and find the **Connect** property.

Connect *Property*

The **Connect** property can be set at design time or at runtime. It tells the Data control the type of database being used. For our application, set the **Connect** property to **Access**. Notice the many different options that are displayed as possible choices for the **Connect** property. The **Connect** property allows you to use the Data control to access many different databases without learning new query grammar or languages. Table 13-3 lists the options.

Table 13-3 Data connection types for the Data control

Database	Version
dBase	III
	IV
	5.0
Excel	3.0
	4.0
	8.0
FoxPro	2.5
	2.6
	3.0
Lotus	WK1
	WK3
	WK4

continued on next page

continued from previous page

Database	Version
Paradox	3.x
	4.x
	5.x
Text	

DatabaseName *Property*

Next, find the `DatabaseName` property and set the property value to the path and file name of the database BIBLIO.MDB located in the Visual Basic home directory. For instance, if your Visual Basic home directory is `C:\VB5`, then set the `DatabaseName` property to `C:\VB5\BIBLIO.MDB`. The property sets the name and location of the data source and can be set at design time or runtime.

The following examples use very little code and the path to the database is *hardcoded* in the `DatabaseName` property. The application will not run if BIBLIO.MDB is not located in the expected location. Setting the `DatabaseName` property in this manner makes things very convenient at design time, but it is a bad practice unless balanced by code in the `form_load` event that resets the database path to reflect the directory structure on the user's machine.

RecordsetType *Property*

The `RecordsetType` property determines the type of database recordset object the custom control uses to access the data in the database. There are three recordset possibilities:

- The `Table` type recordset creates an editable recordset based on a single table.

- A `Dynaset` recordset can be used with multiple or single table queries, and the recordset can be edited

- A `Snapshot` recordset can be used with multiple or single table queries, but the recordset cannot be edited. A snapshot contains a fixed copy of the data at the moment the snapshot was created.

For this application, set the `RecordsetType` property to `0—Table`.

RecordSource *Property*

Click on the `RecordSource` property. A list of tables and queries in the BIBLIO.MDB database will be displayed. The `RecordSource` property is the table or query used by the Data control to create a recordset object. Set the `RecordSource` property to `Authors`.

BOF Action *and* EOF Action *Properties*

The BOF Action property controls what happens when you move to the beginning of the recordset—to the first record. The EOF Action property controls what happens when you reach the end of the recordset.

For BOF, you get two choices:

● MoveFirst keeps the Data control pointing to the first record.

● BOF moves beyond the first record. Of course, there is no record before the first record. The action causes the Data control to execute the Validation event on the first record, and then disables the Move Previous button on the Data control.

MoveFirst is the most logical setting, and it is the default for the Data control. For EOF, you get three choices:

● MoveLast keeps the Data control pointing to the last record. This is the default mode.

● EOF moves the Data control beyond the last record. This triggers the Data control's Validation event on the last record, and then disables the Move Next button on the Data control.

● AddNew adds a new record to the recordset. It sounds good, but a user can unknowingly add a huge number of empty records to the recordset that way.

ReadOnly *Property*

Setting the ReadOnly property to True prevents changing the RecordSet or the underlying database table(s). Attempting to update the RecordSet raises an error. It is as easy to use a SnapShot type of RecordSet, which is automatically read-only. Because the SnapShot is a fixed copy that cannot be updated, it creates less processor overhead, and your program runs slightly faster.

Navigating the Recordset with the Data Control

A recordset created with the Data control can be navigated without writing any code by using the arrow buttons on the Data control. Figure 13-6 shows the Data control and the action taken when the navigation arrows in the Data control are pressed.

Figure 13-6
Data control
navigation

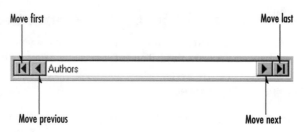

Run the Authors application and press on the Data control navigation arrows. What happens? Nothing. So far you have created a recordset on the Authors table, but you have not told Visual Basic what information in the Authors table to display and where to display the information. To display information in the recordset, you must *bind* a control to a column in the recordset. Binding a control associates a column in the recordset with the control. When the application runs, the data in the selected row is displayed automatically in the bound control. The following standard Visual Basic controls can be bound to a database column:

- TextBox
- ListBox
- CheckBox
- ComboBox
- ImageControl
- Label
- PictureBox

How do you bind a control to a database column? To find out, add a TextBox to frmAuthors and set the properties as shown in Table 13-4.

Table 13-4 Property settings for TextBox `txtAu_ID`

Object	Property	Setting
TextBox	Height	330
	Left	840
	Name	txtAu_ID
	Top	465
	Width	1305

To bind the TextBox control to a database column:

1. Click on the TextBox and bring up the Properties window.

2. Click on the DataSource property in the Properties window, and a list of Data controls on the form will be displayed.

3. Set the DataField property to datAuthors. This binds the control to the recordset of the selected Data control, in this case, the Authors table recordset.

4. Click on the DataSource property. A list of columns defined in the table or query specified in the RecordSource property of the Data control is displayed.

5. Set the DataField property to Au_ID. The TextBox control, txtAu_ID, is bound to the Author's table, column Au_ID.

Run the application. What happens now? The TextBox has a number in it. This is the Au_ID of the first record in the recordset.

Press the Data controls navigation bars. See the information in the TextBox change. Let's finish the project. Add the following controls to the form and set the properties as shown in Table 13-5.

Table 13-5 Objects and property settings for Authors project

Object	Property	Setting
Label1	Caption	Id
	Height	255
	Left	90
	Name	lblAu_ID
	Top	465
	Width	710
Label2	Caption	Name
	Height	255
	Left	90
	Name	lblName
	Top	945
	Width	710
Label3	Caption	Year Born
	Height	255

continued on next page

continued from previous page

Object	Property	Setting
	Left	90
	Name	lblBorn
	Top	1425
Text1	DataSource	datAuthors
	DataField	Author
	Height	330
	Left	840
	Name	txtAuthor
	Top	945
	Width	3420
Text2	DataSource	datAuthors
	DataField	Year Born
	Height	330
	Left	840
	Name	txtYearBorn
	Top	1425
	Width	1050

Run the project, as shown in Figure 13-7.

Use the navigation controls to step through the different records in the database. Congratulations. You have just created an application to navigate the Authors table without writing a single line of code. The next lesson explains how to manipulate the data in the database with code and how to quickly generate database entry forms. But first, it's time for a quiz.

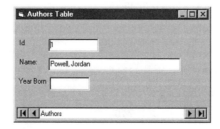

Figure 13-7
Author application

1. The _____ property, set at design time or runtime, tells the Data control the type of database being used.
   a. `Database`
   b. `RecordSource`
   c. `Connect`
   d. `DatabaseName`

2. The _____ property sets the name and location of the data source.
   a. `Database`
   b. `RecordSource`
   c. `Connect`
   d. `DatabaseName`

3. Which one of the following is not a valid `RecordsetType` setting?
   a. `Dynaset`
   b. `QueryDef`
   c. `SnapShot`
   d. `Table`

4. The _____ property is the table or query used by the Data control to create a recordset object.
   a. `Database`
   b. `DatabaseName`
   c. `Connect`
   d. `RecordSource`

5. Which one of the following cannot be bound to a Data control?
   a. `TextBox`
   b. `ListBox`
   c. `CheckBox`
   d. `CommandButton`

LESSON 3

ACCESSING DATA WITH CODE

In the last lesson you learned how to use the Data control to create database applications without writing any code, but sooner or later you need to perform functions that are not provided by the Data control. For example, the Data control does not provide a search facility. Imagine searching through several thousand records looking for a specific one. Not to worry. You can write code to manipulate the recordset in the Data control to perform this type of function.

To learn how to manipulate the database recordset using code, start a new project. The following examples use an Access database that comes with Visual Basic, BIBLIO.MDB. The table for the following example is the Publishers table, which has the format shown in Table 13-6.

Table 13-6 Publishers table in BIBLIO.MDB

Column	Data Type	Description
PubID	Long integer	Primary key used to uniquely define a Publisher
Name	Text	Publisher's name
CompanyName	Text	Name of the company
Address	Text	Publisher's address
City	Text	Publisher's city
State	Text	Publisher's state
Zip	Text	Publisher's zip code
Telephone	Text	Publisher's telephone number
Fax	Text	Publisher's fax number
Comments	Text	Free form description area

An Easier Way

Visual Basic 5 provides a quick and easy way to create forms based on database tables. It is part of the VB Application Wizard you saw in Chapter 1, What's All That Stuff on My Screen? Before you can use the Application Wizard, it must be available as an Add-In. To check this, open the Add-Ins menu. If the Application Wizard is not in the list of Add-Ins, select Add-In Manager. The window for the Add-In Manager is shown in Figure 13-8.

If there is no checkmark in the box next to the Application Wizard, click in the check box, and then click on OK.

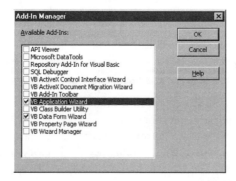

Figure 13-8
Add-In Manager

Building the Form

Once the Application Wizard Add-In is available, you are ready to go. Although the completed program is on the CD that accompanies this book, you should follow these steps instead of simply loading it from the disk. Just try—it's fun!

1. Select the Application Wizard from the Add-Ins menu.

2. On the opening screen, select Single Document Interface and then click on Next.

3. To simplify the program, click on Clear All on the Menus screen and then click on Next.

4. The next screen is the Resources screen. You don't want a resource file for this project, so just click on Next.

5. You also don't want Internet connectivity. Click on Next.

6. You do not want to include any of the Standard Forms. So be sure they are all cleared and then click on Next.

7. Finally. The Data Access Forms screen is the one you have been looking for. Select the Yes option button, and then use the Browse button to find and select BIBLIO.MDB as your database. Then click on Next. The Data Access Forms screen is shown in Figure 13-9.

On the Select Tables screen, be sure that Tables is selected. Double-click on Publishers; then click on Next. The Select Tables screen is shown in Figure 13-10.

The Finish screen appears. Enter **Publishers** in the text box, and then click on Finish.

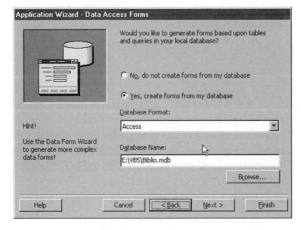

Figure 13-9
The Wizard's Data
Access screen

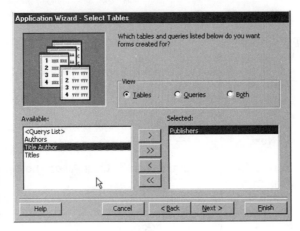

Figure 13-10
The Wizard's Select
Tables screen

Now sit back and watch while Visual Basic 5 builds your application. Pretty spectacular, right? But there are probably some things you will want to change, at least for this project.

Making Some Changes

Chances are that Visual Basic has left your last project intact. (The way around this is to select Application Wizard from the New Project selection of the Files menu.) You don't need the original, blank project. Select it in the Project Explorer, and click on Remove Project from the Files menu.

The Application Wizard creates a more elaborate application than you need. Before you make the changes, run the application as it is. It opens with a Main form, complete with a toolbar and one menu item, the View menu.

The toolbar doesn't work yet. From Chapter 1, What's All That Stuff on My Screen?, you know that you need to write the code to make it work. In fact, that is superfluous for this project, as is all the Main form. From the View menu, you can select Publishers to open the data form that is the main subject of this lesson. Actually, you can open as many copies of the data form as your computer's memory will allow.

There is nothing on frmMain that this project needs. It adds an extra layer between your user and the data form. Select frmMain in the Project Explorer. Right-click anywhere in the Project Explorer and select Remove frmMain. While you are there, remove frmDataGrid and Module1, too.

Because you removed frmGrid, cmdGrid no longer has any work to do. Delete cmdGrid from your form and delete the code for cmdGrid_Click from the Code window. The form looks a little strange with the missing Command button, but leave it alone for now. This example adds another button a bit later.

Yes, you have "broken" the program. If you try to run it now, it will protest mightily. Time to fix it. Select Publishers Properties from the Project menu and change the Startup Object to frmPublishers. Click on OK, and it is all fixed.

Manipulating the Recordset with Code

Examine the code generated by the Application Wizard. The Data control on the form is named Data1 and has a recordset based on the table Publishers. (Remember, a recordset is an object that represents the records in a database table or query.) In the last lesson, you learned that hardcoding the path and name is not the best thing to do. Remove the **DatabaseName** property and the **RecordSource** property from the **Data1** Properties window, and add the code in Listing 13-1 to the **Form_Activate** procedure.

Listing 13-1 New `Form_Activate` procedure

```
Private Sub Form_Activate()
    Data1.DatabaseName = App.Path & "\Biblio.mdb"
    Data1.RecordSource = "Publishers"
    Data1.Refresh
End Sub
```

Now the path to the database name is the same as the path to the application. At design time, that is still the path to Visual Basic 5. Were you to distribute this program, the Setup program must copy the MDB file into the application's subdirectory.

The projects on the CD that comes with this book will probably refer to directories that do not match the ones on your computer. That is most likely when there is a Data control in the project. Please adjust the **DatabaseName** property to match your computer before you try to run the projects.

Note the line:

```
Data1.Refresh
```

The **Refresh** method reads the recordset into the Data control. Use it when you make changes to the Data control's **DatabaseName** or **RecordSource** properties. If you leave it out of **Form_Activate**, you will get a form full of empty TextBoxes.

Add Button

In design mode, double-click the button labeled Add. The code in the button click event is

```
Private Sub cmdAdd_Click()
    Data1.Recordset.AddNew
End Sub
```

The **AddNew** method creates a new record in the recordset. When the **AddNew** method is invoked, all of the bound controls are cleared and an empty record is placed in the recordset. One thing missing is that when you click on Add, the focus remains with the button. Change the code to look like this:

```
Private Sub cmdAdd_Click()
    Data1.Recordset.AddNew
```

continued on next page

continued from previous page

```
        txtFields(0).SetFocus
End Sub
```

When you click on Add, you can enter data into the bound TextBoxes and save the new record by using the **Update** method or by moving to a different record with one of the navigation buttons on the Data control.

Update Button

The code behind the Update button is

```
Private Sub cmdUpdate_Click()
    Data1.UpdateRecord
    Data1.Recordset.Bookmark = Data1.Recordset.LastModified
End Sub
```

The **UpdateRecord** method saves the values of the current bound controls. When you change a record or add a record, the Data control sets a Bookmark named **LastModified**. Bookmarks are placeholders that allow you to quickly jump to selected (or *bookmarked*) records. The line

```
Data1.Recordset.Bookmark = Data1.Recordset.LastModified
```

takes you back to the last record that you added. Without it, the **Update** method takes you back to the first record.

Delete Button

The code in the click event of the Delete button is

```
Private Sub cmdDelete_Click()
    'this may produce an error if you delete the last
    'record or the only record in the recordset
    Data1.Recordset.Delete
    Data1.Recordset.MoveNext
End Sub
```

Note the comments that Visual Basic added to the event. How can you handle this? Add an error handler, of course—except that Data control errors are not generated by Visual Basic, so the normal On Error GoTo in the **cmdDelete_Click** event won't do you a lot of good. Instead, the Data control has its own error handling event. The Application Wizard has already put some code into the event:

```
Private Sub Data1_Error(DataErr As Integer, Response As Integer)
    'This is where you would put error handling code
    'If you want to ignore errors, comment out the next line
    'If you want to trap them, add code here to handle them
    MsgBox "Data error event hit err:" & Error$(DataErr)
    Response = 0   'throw away the error
End Sub
```

As it turns out, the Publishers table is linked to other tables in BIBLIO.MDB by referential integrity, so deletions are not allowed on anything except new entries you might add.

Now, back to the Delete button. The `Delete` method deletes the current record in the recordset object. Then the current record no longer exists, so the `MoveNext` method is used to move to the next record. The `MoveNext` method is the same as clicking the > arrow on the navigation bar of the Data control. Other recordset methods that perform the same functions as the Data control navigation bar are `MovePrevious`, `MoveLast`, and `MoveFirst`.

Refresh Button

The code in the click event of the Refresh button is

```
Private Sub cmdRefresh_Click()
    'this is really only needed for multi user apps
    Data1.Refresh
End Sub
```

The `Refresh` method rebuilds the current recordset. The `Refresh` method can be used in multi-user environments to update the recordset a user is working on, with new records and changes made by other users. Using it in a single-user environment doesn't accomplish much unless you are fond of the hourglass icon.

Adding Search Capability

Let's add the capability to search for a publisher by name in the publishers data entry form created by the Data Form Designer. (In database lingo, a search is a query.) Change the following properties on the frmPublishers form. Then add the objects and set the properties shown in Table 13-7.

Table 13-7 Objects and settings on frmPublishers

Object	Property	Setting
frmPub	Height	4875
TextBox	Height	310
	Left	300
	Name	txtSearch
	Top	3720
	Width	3435
	Text	(none)
CommandButton	Caption	&Find
	Height	300
	Name	cmdFind
	Top	3300
	Width	975

Note The position numbers in the table are meant to give the form a uniform appearance. If you are using a different screen resolution than the test computer, adjust the position and sizes of the new controls until you like the way your form looks.

Add the code shown in Listing 13-2 to the click event of the Command button.

Listing 13-2 Command button Find Click event code

```
Private Sub cmdFind_Click()
'
'Find the Publisher whose name matches
'the value in the TextBox
'
' Note: When searching Text fields you
' must put string values in single quotes.
' Example: Name = 'Waite Group Press'
'   NOT Name = Waite Group Press
'
Data1.Recordset.FindFirst "Name = '" & txtSearch & "'"

End Sub
```

To find a record using a recordset, you can use the following find methods:

- **FindFirst**—Finds the first record that meets the search criteria
- **FindLast**—Finds the last record that meets the search criteria
- **FindNext**—Finds the next record that meets the search criteria
- **FindPrevious**—Finds the previous record that meets the search criteria

If the recordset type is **Table**, you can also use the **Seek** method to find records. The code added to the find button performs the **FindFirst** method. How does our search function work? When the user enters a publisher's name in the text box and clicks the Find button, the **FindFirst** method uses the text in the **txtSearch** text box as its search criteria and scans the recordset, searching the column Name for a match. If the text in the text box matches a publisher's name in the recordset, the corresponding record is returned. Save the application as Publish. Now, start the Publish application and give the search function a try. Enter the following in the text box, shown in Figure 13-11.

Click the Find button. What happens? The Waite Group Press record becomes the current record. You can improve the application by adding buttons to perform the other Find methods like **FindNext** or **FindLast**. You may want to add query capabilities on other fields in the database, like the city or state columns.

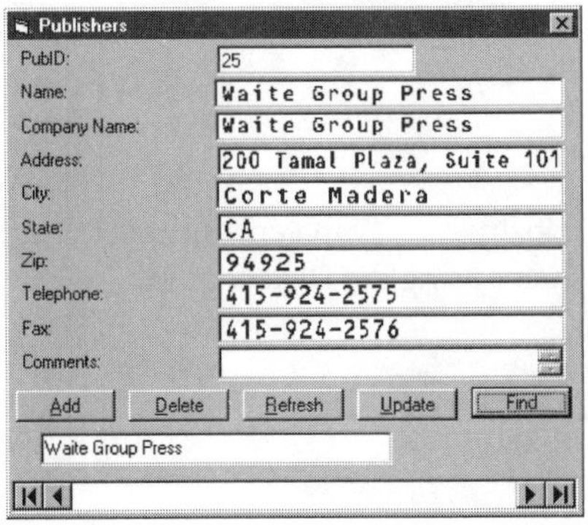

Figure 13-11
The Publishers
Project with Find

The Find button is less than perfect. Unless you know the exact name of the publisher, it will find nothing. And if it doesn't find the publisher you entered, it doesn't tell you about it. Change the code as follows (note that changes are indicated in bold):

```
Private Sub cmdFind_Click()
    '
    'Find the Publisher whose name matches
    'the value in the TextBox
    '
    ' Note: When searching Text fields you
    ' must put string values in single quotes.
    ' Example: Name = 'Waite Group Press'
    '   NOT Name = Waite Group Press
    '
    Data1.Recordset.FindFirst "Name LIKE '*" & txtSearch & "*'"
    Screen.MousePointer = vbDefault
    If Data1.Recordset.NoMatch Then
        MsgBox txtSearch & " Not Found", vbOKOnly, "Sorry."
    End If
End Sub
```

The first change is the use of the **LIKE** keyword in the **FindFirst** search criteria. With the **LIKE** keyword and the wildcard character *****, you can search for names that *contain* the search term that you enter rather than match it exactly. If you enter **ait** into **txtSearch**, **FindFirst** will now look for ***ait***, which means any name containing the letters ait.

The next lesson introduces some special database bound controls to add to your arsenal of database tools.

1. The Visual Basic Add-In _____ can generate a data entry form to manipulate a database table or query using the Data control.
   a. Table Wizard
   b. Form Wizard
   c. Data Form Designer
   d. Data Manager

2. The recordset method _____ creates a new record in a recordset.
   a. `AddNew`
   b. `Insert`
   c. `InsertNew`
   d. `Update`

3. To remove a record from a recordset use the _____ method.
   a. `Delete`
   b. `Remove`
   c. `Kill`
   d. `RemoveCurrent`

4. Use the _____ method of a recordset to rebuild the recordset.
   a. `Rebuild`
   b. `Run`
   c. `Search`
   d. `Refresh`

5. Which one of the following is *not* a valid method for finding a record using a recordset?
   a. `FindFirst`
   b. `FindAll`
   c. `FindNext`
   d. `FindLast`

Exercise

Using the BIBLIO.MDB database and the Data control, create an application using the Authors table that allows you to add, update, or delete entries in the Authors table. Do not use the Data Form Designer.

USING THE BOUND CONTROLS

The applications you have created so far in this chapter have used the standard Visual Basic controls in conjunction with the Data control to display and manipulate the data in RecordSets. Quickly review the standard controls that can be bound to a column in a recordset to display data:

- TextBox
- ListBox
- CheckBox
- ComboBox
- ImageControl
- Label
- Picture Box

If the Data Bound controls do not appear in your Toolbox, right-click on the Toolbox and select Components. The Data Bound controls are Microsoft Data Bound Grid, Microsoft Data Bound List and Microsoft FlexGrid. In the interest of creating smaller programs, select only those that you need for a project.

You have bound a TextBox control to a database field to display the data in the record-set, but you could have easily used a label control in cases where you did not want the user to be able to modify the data fields. The CheckBox control can have the value `True` or `False`; it should only be used for database Boolean fields. The PictureBox and Image controls are used to display graphical data from the database: bitmaps, icons, and metafiles. Visual Basic provides three other special Data Bound custom controls:

- Data Bound ListBox
- Data Bound ComboBox
- Data Bound grid
- MSFlexGrid

The three special Data Bound controls shown in Figure 13-12 are tightly integrated with the Data control to offer you more flexibility and functionality. Let's examine how to use these new controls.

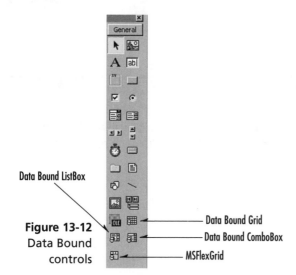

Data Bound ListBox

Figure 13-12
Data Bound
controls

Data Bound Grid

Data Bound ComboBox

MSFlexGrid

Data Bound ListBox and Data Bound ComboBox

The Data Bound ListBox and Data Bound ComboBox are very similar to the standard ListBox and ComboBox. However, there are some key features that make these two controls a better choice for database applications.

- The controls automatically fill up with a selected field from the recordset. The normal ListBox and ComboBox must be populated with the recordset using the AddItem method.

- The controls can pass a value to a second Data control, making these two Data controls ideal for lookup tables when entering foreign key information from another table.

Filling a ComboBox with the Results from a Query

Let's look at the first key feature by filling a ComboBox with publisher names from the Publishers table. Start a new Visual Basic project called LookUp. The completed project is on the CD that comes with this book. Add the objects and set the properties for the LookUp project, as shown in Table 13-8.

Table 13-8 Object and property settings for LookUp project

Object	Property	Setting
Form	Caption	Publisher Look Up
	Height	3480
	Name	frmLook
	Width	6195
DataControl	Connect	Access
	Database	BIBLIO.MDB
	Height	300
	Left	90
	Name	datPublisher
	RecordsetType	2 – SnapShot
	RecordSource	Select Name from Publishers
	Top	90
	Visible	False
	Width	2280
DBCombo	Height	315
	Left	315
	Name	dbcPublisher
	Style	2 – Dropdown List
	Top	1050
	Width	3255

The Data control above is tied to the SQL query `Select Name from Publishers`. The query returns a single column from the Publishers table Name. It's time to set the two properties that will fill the Data Bound ComboBox with the query information. Set the RowSource property of the Data Bound ComboBox to the Data control `datPublisher`. The `RowSource` property specifies the recordset to use to fill the ListBox. Set the `ListField` property to `Name`. The `ListField` property specifies the field from the recordset that is displayed in the combo ListBox.

Run the application and click on the ComboBox shown in Figure 13-13 to see the publisher names in the Publishers table. The list is automatically populated with information. Close the ComboBox and type the letter "W" in the TextBox portion of the ComboBox. The TextBox automatically fills with *Waite Group Press*.

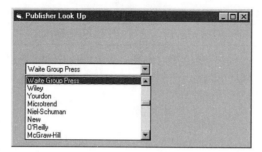

Figure 13-13
Data Bound
ComboBox
displaying a list of
publishers

Styles of the DBComboBox

The DBComboBox has three different styles which affect the way the control looks and behaves on the form.

- *Dropdown combo*: Includes a text box and a dropdown list. The list drops down when the user clicks on the dropdown arrow. Clicking on one of the items in the list copies it to the TextBox portion of the DBCombo. The user can also type in an entry that is not in the list.

- *Simple combo*: Includes a text box and a list which doesn't drop down. This must be resized so that the user can see the list. Clicking on one of the items in the list copies it to the TextBox portion of the DBCombo. The user can also type in an entry that is not in the list. Typing in the text box also causes the list to scroll to the first matching entry.

- *Dropdown list*: Includes a text box and a dropdown list. The list drops down when the user clicks on the dropdown arrow. Clicking on one of the items in the list copies it to the TextBox portion of the DBCombo. Typing in the text box also causes the list to scroll to the first matching entry. The user cannot type in an entry that is not in the list.

Note that these are the same styles that are available for the ComboBox control you used in Chapter 5, Controls. Choosing the correct style is important for making your programs behave the way you want. Change the `Style` property of the DBCombo and experiment with all three styles until you are satisfied that you understand the differences.

Passing a Value to Another Data Control

Why would you want to pass a value from a Data Bound ListBox or Data Bound ComboBox to another Data control?

To help find the answer, examine Table 13-9, the Titles table, which contains the titles of database books. If you were creating a data entry screen for the Titles table, how would you display the foreign keys coming from other tables such as PubID from the Publishers table? After all, the `PubID` field is a system identity field used to uniquely identify a publisher and has no meaning outside of our database. In a data entry screen for the Titles table, you would want to display the publisher's name and, when the record was saved, store the field PubID in the Titles table. The Data Bound ListBox and Data Bound ComboBox allow you to do this by passing a value back to another Data control.

Table 13-9 Partial column listing of the Title table in `BIBLIO.MDB`

Column	Data Type	Description
Title	TextBook	Title
Year Published	Integer	Year the book was published
ISBN	Text	Primary key, uniquely identifies a book
PubID	Long Integer	Foreign key to the Publishers table

Save the LookUp project, and start a new project called Titles. Instead of using the Application Wizard, create a data entry screen the old-fashioned way—by hand. The project uses seven TextBoxes, a DBComboBox, eight Labels, two Data controls, and five Command buttons. Use Table 13-10 and Figure 13-14 as guides for positioning and naming the controls.

Table 13-10 The Titles project

Object	Property	Value
Form	Name	frmTitle
	Caption	"Titles"
	Height	3270
	Left	1980
	Top	2400
	Width	5520
Data control	Name	datPublishers
	Caption	"Data2"
	Connect	"Access"
	DatabaseName	C:\VB5\BIBLIO.MDB
	RecordsetType	2 - Snapshot
	RecordSource	"Select PubID, Name from Publishers"
	Top	375
	Visible	0 'False

continued on next page

continued from previous page

Object	Property	Value
CommandButton	Name	cmdClose
	Caption	"&Close"
	Height	300
	Left	4440
	TabIndex	19
	Top	2610
	Width	975
CommandButton	Name	cmdUpdate
	Caption	"&Update"
	Height	300
	Left	3360
	TabIndex	18
	Top	2610
	Width	975
CommandButton	Name	cmdRefresh
	Caption	"&Refresh"
	Height	300
	Left	2280
	TabIndex	17
	Top	2610
	Width	975
CommandButton	Name	cmdDelete
	Caption	"&Delete"
	Height	300
	Left	1200
	TabIndex	16
	Top	2610
	Width	975
CommandButton	Name	cmdAdd
	Caption	"&Add"
	Height	300
	Left	120

Object	Property	Value
	TabIndex	15
	Top	2610
	Width	975
Data control	Name	Data1
	Align	2 'Align Bottom
	Connect	"Access"
	DatabaseName	C:\VB5\BIBLIO.MDB
	Height	345
	Left	0
	ReadOnly	0 'False
	RecordsetType	1 'Dynaset
	RecordSource	"Titles"
	Top	2925
	Width	5520
TextBox	Name	txtComments
	DataField	"Comments"
	DataSource	"Data1"
	Height	310
	Left	2040
	MultiLine	1 'True
	ScrollBars	2 'Vertical
	TabIndex	14
	Top	2270
	Width	3375
TextBox	Name	txtSubject
	DataField	"Subject"
	DataSource	"Data1"
	Height	285
	Left	2040
	MaxLength	50
	TabIndex	12
	Top	1954
	Width	3375

continued on next page

continued from previous page

Object	Property	Value
TextBox	Name	txtNotes
	DataField	"Notes"
	DataSource	"Data1"
	Height	285
	Left	2040
	MaxLength	50
	TabIndex	10
	Top	1640
	Width	3375
TextBox	Name	txtDescription
	DataField	"Description"
	DataSource	"Data1"
	Height	285
	Left	2040
	MaxLength	50
	TabIndex	8
	Top	1326
	Width	3375
TextBox	Name	txtISBN
	DataField	"ISBN"
	DataSource	"Data1"
	Height	285
	Left	2040
	MaxLength	20
	TabIndex	5
	Top	668
	Width	3375
TextBox	Name	txtYearPub
	DataField	"Year Published"
	DataSource	"Data1"
	Height	285
	Left	2040
	TabIndex	3

Object	Property	Value
	Top	354
	Width	1935
TextBox	Name	txtTitle
	DataField	"Title"
	DataSource	"Data1"
	Height	285
	Left	2040
	MaxLength	255
	TabIndex	1
	Top	40
	Width	3375
DBCombo	Name	dbcPublishers
	DataField	"PubID"
	DataSource	"Data1"
	Height	315
	Left	2040
	TabIndex	20
	Top	982
	Width	3360
	Style	2
	ListField	"Name"
	BoundColumn	"PubID"
	Text	"dbcPublishers"

Use Figure 13-14 to place the labels and enter their captions.

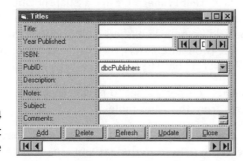

Figure 13-14
The Titles project at design time

Fortunately, for all of the controls on frmTitles, there is surprisingly little code. Add the code in Listing 13-3 to the project.

Listing 13-3 Code for the Titles project

```
Private Sub cmdAdd_Click()
    Data1.Recordset.AddNew
End Sub

Private Sub cmdDelete_Click()
    Data1.Recordset.Delete
    Data1.Recordset.MoveNext
End Sub

Private Sub cmdRefresh_Click()
    Data1.Refresh
End Sub

Private Sub cmdUpdate_Click()
    Data1.UpdateRecord
    Data1.Recordset.Bookmark = Data1.Recordset.LastModified
End Sub

Private Sub cmdClose_Click()
    Unload Me
End Sub

Private Sub Data1_Error(DataErr As Integer, Response As Integer)
    MsgBox "Data error event hit err:" & Error$(DataErr)
    Response = 0   'throw away the error
End Sub

Private Sub Data1_Reposition()
    Screen.MousePointer = vbDefault
    On Error Resume Next
    Data1.Caption = "Record: " & (Data1.Recordset.AbsolutePosition + 1)
End Sub
```

The keys to the operation of this project lie in the two Data controls and the DBComboBox. The Data control **Data1** creates a Dynaset from the Titles table of BIBLIO.MDB. Each of the text boxes on the form draws its data from one of the fields in the table. The Data **datPublishers** creates a Snapshot from the query **"Select PubID, Name from Publishers"**. The snapshot contains only two fields, the **PubID** field and the **Name** field from the Publishers table of BIBLIO.MDB.

Now that there are two Data controls, each with its own RecordSet, the bulk of the work is done by the DBCombo. The steps below explain how it works.

1. The **DataSource** property is set to **Data1**. That binds the DBCombo to the RecordSource from the Titles table.

2. The **RowSource** property is set to **datPublishers**. That means that the list will be filled with data from the **datPublishers** Data control.

3. The `ListField` property is set to `Name`, which means that the `Name` field from the snapshot will display in the DBCombo list.

4. The `BoundColumn` property is set to `PubID`. This is the `PubID` field from the `RowSource` RecordSet, the recordset of `PubId` and `Name` from `datPublishers`.

5. The `DataField` property is set to `PubID`. This is the `PubID` column from the `DataSource` RecordSet, the RecordSet of `Data1`.

Steps four and five link the two RecordSets together. The **PubID** field in the Publishers table is the primary key of that table. It is a foreign key in the Titles. That means it is a reference to the record in the Publishers table that has the same **PubID** value. (That is what referential databases are all about.)

Now that the two RecordSets are linked together in the DBCombo, when you scroll through the list of titles, the correct publisher's name is shown in the DBCombo. The **PubID** from the Titles table is passed to the DBCombo and it instantly scrolls to the correct record.

Better yet, if you add a new record, you can now select a publisher from the DBCombo list and the correct **PubID** is passed back to the Titles table.

Try it out. Run the program. After you have stepped through a few titles, click on Add and add in the information from this book. Be sure to select the correct publisher. The running program is shown in Figure 13-15.

The Data Bound Grid Control

The Data Bound grid allows you to quickly display data from a table or query in a spreadsheet fashion and even to update the data in the grid. The Data Bound grid ties directly to the Data control so the information in the recordset is automatically loaded into the grid. The Data Bound grid is one of the easiest Data Bound controls to use. Getting the Data Bound grid up and running only requires setting the grid **DataSource** property. Save the Titles project, and start a new project called DBGrid. Add the objects and set the properties for the DBGrid project as shown in Table 13-11.

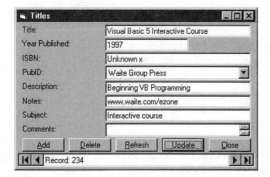

Figure 13-15
The Titles project at runtime

Table 13-11 Object and property settings for DBGrid project

Object	Property	Setting
Form	Caption	Testing Data Bound Grid
	Height	4410
	Name	frmGrid
	Width	8895
DataControl	Connect	Access
	Database	BIBLIO.MDB
	Height	300
	Left	75
	Name	datTitles
	RecordsetType	1 - Dynaset
	RecordSource	Titles
	Top	285
	Visible	False
	Width	2025
Data Bound Grid	DataSource	datTitles
	Height	2610
	Left	210
	Name	dbgTitles
	Top	975
	Width	8455

Run the application, shown in Figure 13-16. Scroll the grid and resize the columns. Try modifying a record. The Data Bound grid makes displaying information easy. You can add any of the same Command buttons for the DBGrid that you used with other data forms. The **AddNew** and **Delete** methods don't really care how you are displaying the data.

You can add a touch of sophistication to this project. Add the following code:

```
Private Sub DBGrid1_HeadClick(ByVal ColIndex As Integer)
    datTitles.RecordSource = "Select * From Titles Order By [" & _
        DBGrid1.Columns(ColIndex).DataField & "]"
    datTitles.Refresh
End Sub
```

When you click on one of the column headers, the RecordSet will be sorted on that field. The **RecordSource** is set to the string **"Select * From Titles Order By ["** **& DBGrid1.Columns(ColIndex).DataField & "]"**, which is an SQL query. SQL will be discussed in the next lesson.

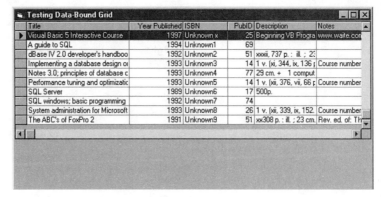

Figure 13-16
Data Bound grid
displaying
information from
BIBLIO.MDB

The DBGrid control example is deceptively simple. Actually, there are many properties, events, and methods to be used with the DBGrid, and many complications can develop from its use. But the brand new MSFlexGrid control can do all of the same things, and it offers greater flexibility in the process.

The MSFlexGrid Control

The MSFlexGrid control is one of the most versatile controls in your database arsenal. (It is also quite useful in applications that are not database-oriented.) MSFlexGrid does everything that the Data Bound grid can do, and then some. An important difference is that when the MSFlexGrid is bound to a Data control, it is read-only. The control adds a collection of capabilities in data management and appearance that will keep you amazed and pleased for a long time to come. This section contains two projects, and it is only an introduction.

Introduction to MSFlexGrid

Start a new project named flxGrid.VBP. Put an MSFlexGrid, a Data control and five Command buttons on the form. Set the properties according to Table 13-12. The completed project is on the CD that comes with this book.

Table 13-12 The flxGrid project

Object	Property	Value
Form	Name	frmFlexGrid
	Caption	FlexGrid One
	Height	3945
	ClientWidth	5595
CommandButton	Name	Command5
	Caption	"BackColor"

continued on next page

continued from previous page

Object	Property	Value
	Height	555
	Left	4440
	Top	3360
	Width	1035
CommandButton	Name	Command3
	Caption	"ForeColor"
	Height	555
	Left	3360
	Top	3360
	Width	1035
CommandButton	Name	Command4
	Caption	"Font"
	Height	555
	Left	2280
	Top	3360
	Width	1035
CommandButton	Name	Command2
	Caption	"Grid Lines Fixed"
	Height	555
	Left	1200
	Top	3360
	Width	1035
CommandButton	Name	Command1
	Caption	"Grid Lines"
	Height	555
	Left	120
	Top	3360
	Width	1035
Data control	Name	datAuthors
	Connect	"Access"
	DatabaseName	"C:\VB5\BIBLIO.MDB"

Object	Property	Value
	RecordSource	"Authors"
	Visible	0 'False
MSFlexGrid	Name	MSFlexGrid1
	DataSource	datAuthors
	Height	3075
	Left	120
	Top	60
	Width	5295
	AllowBigSelection	0 'False
	GridLines	0
	GridLinesFixed	0
	AllowUserResizing	1

This project shows you what some of the property settings mean and how they affect the overall appearance of the MSFlexGrid. Add the code from Listing 13-4.

Listing 13-4 The code for the FlexGrid project

```
Private Sub Command1_Click()
    If MSFlexGrid1.GridLines < 3 Then
        MSFlexGrid1.GridLines = MSFlexGrid1.GridLines + 1
    Else
        MSFlexGrid1.GridLines = 0
    End If
End Sub

Private Sub Command2_Click()
    If MSFlexGrid1.GridLinesFixed < 3 Then
        MSFlexGrid1.GridLinesFixed = MSFlexGrid1.GridLinesFixed + 1
    Else
        MSFlexGrid1.GridLinesFixed = 0
    End If
End Sub

Private Sub Command3_Click()
    Static iClicks As Integer
    Select Case iClicks
        Case 0: MSFlexGrid1.CellForeColor = &HFF&
        Case 1: MSFlexGrid1.CellForeColor = &HFF00&
        Case 2: MSFlexGrid1.CellForeColor = &HFF0000
        Case 3
            MSFlexGrid1.CellForeColor = 1
            iClicks = -1
    End Select
```

continued on next page

continued from previous page

```
        iClicks = iClicks + 1
    End Sub

    Private Sub Command4_Click()
        Static iClicks As Integer
        Select Case iClicks
            Case 0: MSFlexGrid1.CellFontBold = 1
            Case 1: MSFlexGrid1.CellFontItalic = 1
            Case 2: MSFlexGrid1.CellFontBold = 0
            Case 3
                MSFlexGrid1.CellFontItalic = 0
                iClicks = -1
        End Select
        iClicks = iClicks + 1
    End Sub

    Private Sub Command5_Click()
        Static iClicks As Integer
        Select Case iClicks
            Case 0: MSFlexGrid1.CellBackColor = &HFF&
            Case 1: MSFlexGrid1.CellBackColor = &HFF00&
            Case 2: MSFlexGrid1.CellBackColor = &HFF0000
            Case 3
                MSFlexGrid1.CellBackColor = &HFFFFFF
                iClicks = -1
        End Select
        iClicks = iClicks + 1
    End Sub
```

Command1 and Command2 show you the meaning of the GridLines and FixedGridLines properties. They step through the four choices for each one, giving you a live chance to see the effects of changing the properties. Command3 cycles you through four choices of ForeColor which, you may recall, is the color of the text. Command5 does the same for BackColor. There is an anomaly in the ForeColor and BackColor properties: Setting them to 0 does *not* give you black. Instead it gives you the system colors. To get black, set the color to 1. Command4 gives you a selection of font effects.

Run the program and click each of the buttons several times. As you do, watch the effects and take note of the ones you like. Note that you can resize the cells so that you can read all of the text in them. The running program is shown in Figure 13-17.

And Now for Something Completely Different

When you were learning about the ideas behind the relational databases, you considered an employee skills database. Recall that Mark had more than one skill. If you were to view that database with a DBGrid control, Mark's name would be listed once for each skill he had. That isn't bad, but it would be nice to find a way to *merge* the rows so that Mark's name appeared in a larger block beside his group of skills. Well, guess what the MSFlexGrid can do? You've got it!

Figure 13-17
The MSFlexGrid in
action

Start a new project named flxMerge.prj. The finished project is on the CD that comes with this book. Place an MSFlexGrid control, a Data control, and a check box on the form. Use Table 13-13 to position and name the objects.

Table 13-13 Objects for the flxMerge.prj project

Object	Name	Property
Form	Name	frmMerge
	Caption	"Skills"
	Height	3195
	Width	6870
CheckBox	Name	chkMerge
	Caption	"Merge Cells"
	Height	255
	Left	5640
	Top	120
	Width	1215
Data control	Name	Data datSkills
	Connect	"Access"
	DatabaseName	""
	RecordSource	""
	Visible	'False
MSFlexGrid	Name	flxSkills
	DataSource	datSkills
	Height	2535

continued on next page

continued from previous page

Object	Name	Property
	Left	180
	Top	120
	Width	5415
	MergeCells	1

Now add the code from Listing 13-5 to the Code window.

Listing 13-5 Code for flxMerge

```
Option Explicit

Private Sub Form_Load()
    Dim sSQL As String
    datSkills.DatabaseName = App.Path & "\SKILLS.MDB"
    sSQL = "SELECT DISTINCTROW Employees.Name, "
    sSQL = sSQL & "Employees.Department, Skills.Skill "
    sSQL = sSQL & "FROM ([Emp Skills] "
    sSQL = sSQL & "INNER JOIN Employees "
    sSQL = sSQL & "ON [Emp Skills].EmpID = Employees.EmpID) "
    sSQL = sSQL & "INNER JOIN Skills "
    sSQL = sSQL & "ON [Emp Skills].SkillID = Skills.SkillID "
    sSQL = sSQL & "ORDER BY Employees.Department;"
    datSkills.RecordSource = sSQL
    datSkills.Refresh
    DoInitialSettings
'    flxSkills.Refresh
End Sub

Sub DoInitialSettings()
    Dim i As Integer
    flxSkills.Row = 0
    For i = 0 To flxSkills.Cols - 1
        flxSkills.Col = i
        flxSkills.CellFontSize = 8
        flxSkills.CellAlignment = 1
        ' Allow merge on all Columns
        flxSkills.MergeCol(i) = True
    Next i
    flxSkills.ColWidth(1) = 1.5 * 1444
    flxSkills.ColWidth(2) = 1.5 * 1444
    flxSkills.MergeCells = 0
End Sub

Private Sub chkMerge_Click()
    flxSkills.MergeCells = chkMerge
End Sub
```

A Look at the Code

The **Form_Load** procedure sets the **DatabaseName** property of the Data control to the SKILLS.MDB database that is included on the CD. It then builds an SQL query that returns the employee names and departments from one table and the employee skills from another, based on the information in yet a third table. The SQL query looks like this:

```
SELECT DISTINCTROW Employees.Name, Employees.Department, Skills.Skill FROM ([Emp
Skills] INNER JOIN Employees ON [Emp Skills].EmpID = Employees.EmpID) INNER JOIN
Skills ON [Emp Skills].SkillID = Skills.SkillID ORDER BY Employees.Department;
```

Don't get too excited by this complicated-looking query. The SQL query language is covered in the next lesson.

Once the query is built, the **Form_Load** procedure assigns it to the **RecordSource** property of the Data control, and then it refreshes the Data control so that it returns the selected RecordSet.

The MSFlexGrid control's **DataSource** property is **datMerge**, the Data control on the form. When the Data control is refreshed, the MSFlexGrid expands to accommodate the RecordSet's three fields, and the **Form_Load** procedure calls the **DoInitialSettings** procedure.

The key to the behavior of the MSFlexGrid is to set the control's properties *before* you do anything fancy. The **DoInitialSettings** procedure does that. It starts by making row **0** the active row. The **For...Next** loop then cycles through all of the columns in the MSFlexGrid and sets the properties for each column in the grid. The **CellAlignment** property has 10 options, from **0** through **9**. Try all of them to select the one that you like best.

The feature that this demonstration emphasizes is the **MergeCells** property. Before a column's cells can merge, its **MergeCol** property must be set to **True**. This is also done in the **For...Next** loop. Finally, the **MergeCells** property is set to **0**, which disables the **MergeCells** action.

Run the program now. The initial screen is shown in Figure 13-18.

Note that several of the employees are listed more than once in the Name column because they have more than one skill. Click on the Merge Cells check box. Pretty neat, isn't it? The screen with **MergeCells = 1** is shown in Figure 13-19.

The code for the CheckBox simply sets the **MergeCells** property to match the value of the check box, either **0** or **1**.

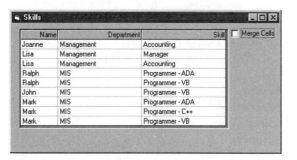

Figure 13-18
The flxMerge screen at runtime—
MergeCells = 0

Skills

Name	Department	Skill	☑ Merge Cells
Joanne	Management	Accounting	
Lisa	Management	Manager	
		Accounting	
Ralph	MIS	Programmer - ADA	
John	MIS	Programmer - VB	
		Programmer - ADA	
Mark		Programmer - C++	
		Programmer - VB	

Figure 13-19
The flxMerge
screen—
`MergeCells = 1`

More About MSFlexGrid

The MSFlexGrid control has many more properties, many of them not available at design time. The `CellPicture` property allows you to add a picture to any cell in the grid. You can have text in the same cell with a picture, or you can have the picture alone. You can use the MSFlexGrid in unbound mode and fill the cells using the `AddItem` method. And you can use SQL queries to get around the read-only restriction, but that's in the next lesson.

1. Which of the following is *not* a special Data Bound custom control provided with Visual Basic?
   a. Data Bound ListBox
   b. Data Bound ComboBox
   c. Data Bound grid
   d. Data Bound Command button

2. To automatically populate a Data Bound ComboBox, you must:
   a. Set the `RowSource` property of the Data Bound ComboBox to a properly configured Datacontrol.
   b. Set the `DataSource` property of the Data Bound ComboBox to a properly configured Data control.
   c. Use the `AddItem` method of the Data Bound ComboBox.
   d. Set the `RecordSource` property of the Data Bound ComboBox to a properly configured Data control.

3. When passing a value from a Data Bound ComboBox to another Data control, the value for the properties `DataField` and _____ must be the same, but from different RecordSets.
   a. `DataSource`
   b. `RecordSource`
   c. `BoundColumn`
   d. `Database`

4. What Data control property should you set with the following SQL statement to return the Name column from the Publishers table into a Data Bound ListBox?

`Select Name from Publishers _____.`

a. `Database`
b. `RecordSource`
c. `DataField`
d. `SQLStatement`

5. The _____ allows you to quickly display data in a table or query in a spreadsheet fashion.
   a. Data Bound grid
   b. Data Bound spreadsheet
   c. Data Bound ListBox
   d. Data Bound TextBox

REVIEW

John: I have heard so much about databases, and all I really knew about a database was that it stored data. I now have a good understanding about the different objects and terms found in a database such as tables, indexes, and queries.

Lisa: I was just happy to finally learn what SQL was. I see the word in all the different want ads.

John: Looking for a job as a database programmer?

Lisa: Not yet, but maybe after I finish this lesson.

John: Visual Basic's Data control really makes programming a database simple. I can create entire Access database applications without knowing SQL. Just set a few properties and use some methods.

Lisa: You're right about the Data control, but what about the Application Wizard for creating quick data entry screens? I like the fact that it automatically binds all of the controls to the different columns and builds a working form for you.

John: I liked the Application Wizard, but my favorite bound control is the Data Bound MSFlexGrid. I have so many applications in mind where I can take advantage of the Data Bound MSFlexGrid. The best thing about Data Bound is how easy it is to fill the grid with data.

Lisa: You're right. Now I'm looking forward to learning more about SQL.

John: You're in luck. Read on.

MANAGING YOUR DATA WITH SQL

The early days of computer database programming were a nightmare. There were a dozen different database management programs, and each one had its own language and its own techniques for retrieving data. Programmers became expert in one or another of the languages, or they became jack-of-all-trades programmers, subject to interference from all of the different techniques they had to remember. Relational database systems, for all of their advantages, performed poorly because of the extra work required to maintain relationships.

The first commercial SQL product was released by IBM in 1981. It was quickly followed by products from Oracle and several other vendors. A *standard* was proposed to the American National Standards Institute (ANSI) in 1988, which had the effect of stabilizing the SQL language. Currently there are over 70 DBMS products that use SQL. There are slight differences, true, but a programmer who knows SQL can adapt readily. This chapter serves as your introduction to SQL.

SQL is built around two concepts: Data Definition Language (DDL), which is used for creating databases, and Data Manipulation Language (DML), which is used for retrieving and editing data. DDL is available in the Professional and Enterprise editions of Visual Basic, but is not covered in this book.

Data Manipulation Language (DML) is built around a few statements and operations. It is really a simple language, although it can create very complex "sentences." This lesson takes you from the simplest of SQL statements into more elaborate (and, thus, more selective) statements. Each new statement is introduced in its simplest form. Then, modifying *clauses* are added to refine the statement.

Trying Out the Examples

The project to try out the SQL examples is deliberately simple. Start a new project named SQL.vbp. Maximize the form and add a Data control, a DBGrid and a Command button. Use Table 13-14 as a guide.

Table 13-14 Objects for SQL.vbp

Object	Property	Value
Form	Name	frmSQL
	Caption	"SQL Demo"
	WindowState	2 'Maximized
CommandButton	Name	cmdQuit
	Caption	"E&xit"

Object	Property	Value
	Height	435
	Left	180
	Top	5880
	Width	1095
Data control	Name	Data1
	Connect	"Access"
	DatabaseName	"C:\VB5\BIBLIO.MDB"
	RecordSource	""
	Visible	0 'False
DBGrid	Name	dbgSQL
	Height	5535
	Left	120
	Top	120
	Width	9315

Now add the code from Listing 13-6.

Listing 13-6 Code for the SQL demo project

```
Option Explicit
Public sSQL As String

Private Sub cmdQuit_Click()
    Unload Me
End Sub

Private Sub Form_Load()
    BuildSQL
    Data1.RecordSource = sSQL
    Data1.Refresh
End Sub

Public Sub BuildSQL()
    sSQL = "SELECT *"
    sSQL = sSQL & " FROM Publishers"
End Sub
```

The secret of this project is the **BuildSQL** procedure. You will have to revise this procedure to try out each new SQL statement. The procedure builds the **sSQL** string using concatenation. For each change, you have to rewrite the code in this function, and you must follow specific guidelines to avoid errors. For example, the second SQL statement is

```
SELECT Publishers.[Company Name], Publishers.State
FROM Publishers;
```

To build the **sSQL** string from this statement, change the procedure to

```
Public Sub BuildSQL()
    ssQL = "SELECT Publishers.[Company Name], Publishers.State"
    ssQL = ssQL & " FROM Publishers;"
End Sub
```

Add **sSQL** = " in front of the first line of the SQL statement, and add **sSQL** = **sSQL** & " in front of all of the other statements.

Note the space between the quotation mark and the first character in the line that adds the second string to the first. It is *very important* that you add that space as the first character of every line except the first. If you do not, the concatenated statement will be wrong because the words on separate lines will be smashed together to form a single, indecipherable word. The Code window including this new version of the **BuildSQL** procedure is shown in Figure 13-20.

The running program is shown in Figure 13-21.

Figure 13-20
The Code window
with the second
SQL statement

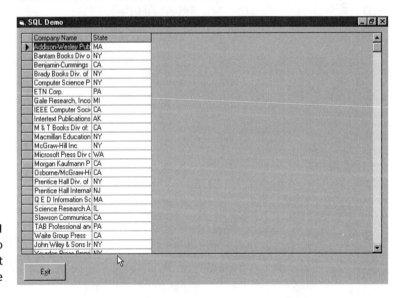

Figure 13-21
The SQL demo
program at
runtime

The Select **Statement**

The Select statement *returns* selected data to a recordset. You've seen several examples of the Select statement already. In its simplest form it looks like

```
SELECT * FROM Publishers
```

If you make that statement the RecordSource of a Data control, it returns all of the fields from all of the records from the Publishers table. The * is a wildcard that tells SQL to select every field in the table. The FROM clause defines the table.

Narrowing the Field

What if you don't *want* all of the fields? Suppose you only want Company Name and State? You would modify the Select statement to read

```
SELECT Publishers.[Company Name], Publishers.State
FROM Publishers;
```

There are two items of interest in this new statement. The first is the list of fields to select. Like any list in programming, the items in the list are separated (delimited) by commas. Note that each field is qualified by the table name; that is, the State field is listed as Publishers.State. You could have used State in this query because the query is based on a single table, but it is a good idea to reference the table name in all of your queries so you can avoid the mistake of not referencing it when you should.

The second new idea is the use of square brackets around the Company Name field. These are required because of the space in the field's name. Some programmers avoid the space by using the underline character, as in Company_Name, but SQL provides you with a tool for resolving spaces in the field name, and the brackets do improve readability. If you get to design your own tables, the choice is yours. You may use spaces or underbars. Note that Company Name and Company_Name are not the same.

The WHERE **Clause: Becoming More Selective**

What happens if you only want the names of publishers from California? The WHERE clause lets you be as selective as you wish. The query for California publishers looks like this:

```
SELECT Publishers.[Company Name], Publishers.State
FROM Publishers
WHERE Publishers.State="CA";
```

The runtime screen is shown in Figure 13-22.

You must handle queries with the WHERE clause a bit differently. The line

```
WHERE Publishers.State="CA"
```

requires special handling in the VB code. Change it to read:

```
sSQL = sSQL & " WHERE Publishers.State=" & Chr(34) & CA" & Chr(34)
```

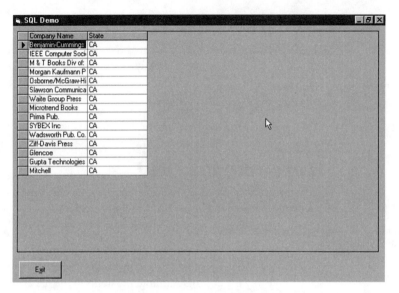

Figure 13-22
Publishers from
California

The string **CA** must be *delimited* before it is sent to the database in an SQL statement. Different data types require different delimiters. The requirements are listed below.

- *String*: Quotation marks. Example:

  ```
  sSQL = sSQL &  Chr(34) & sVar & Chr(34)
  ```

- *String*: Single Quotation marks—"'" or Chr(39). Example:

  ```
  sSQL = sSQL &"'" & sVar & "'"
  ```

- *Date*: Pound Sign—"#" or Chr(35). Example:

  ```
  sSQL = sSQL & "#" & datVar & "#"
  ```

- *Number*: No delimiter. Example:

  ```
  sSQL = sSQL & nVar
  ```

The first string example uses **Chr(34)** instead of a quotation mark because we have to pass a quote symbol to the SQL engine, but we don't want VB to think we're ending the string literal. Therefore, we use an alternate way of specifying the quote symbol, **CHR(34)**.

The **WHERE** clause specifies the Selection Criteria for the query. You can refine the **WHERE** clause with other qualifiers. For example:

```
SELECT Publishers.[Company Name], Publishers.State
FROM Publishers
WHERE (((Publishers.State)="CA")) OR (((Publishers.State)="NY"));
```

selects publishers from California or New York.

Putting Things in Order

The query that returns California and New York publishers might display them in almost any order. Access displays them in the order in which they were entered, but some database engines do not guarantee an order without the ORDER BY clause. The result is that publishers from both states are intermixed. You can have them sorted, if you want, by adding the ORDER BY clause.

```
SELECT Publishers.[Company Name], Publishers.State
FROM Publishers
WHERE (((Publishers.State)="CA")) OR (((Publishers.State)="NY"))
ORDER BY Publishers.State;
```

By default, ORDER BY sorts in ascending order. Add DESC to the end if you want them in descending order. Refine it one more step with

```
SELECT Publishers.[Company Name], Publishers.State
FROM Publishers
WHERE (((Publishers.State)="CA")) OR (((Publishers.State)="NY"))
ORDER BY Publishers.State, Publishers.[Company Name] ;
```

This sorts the publishers alphabetically as well. The first item in the ORDER BY list is the priority item. That is, the data is sorted first by State and then by [Company Name]. If you reverse the order, the query returns a list that is sorted first on [Company Name], with the State field sorted second.

Change the ORDER BY clause to

```
ORDER BY Publishers.State DESC, Publishers.[Company Name] ;
```

and the states will be sorted into descending order.

Using a Variable in a Statement

Database front-end programs often have to make a selection based on user input. Add two more controls to frmSQL to see how this is done. You will need a TextBox and a Command button. Use Table 13-15 to set the properties.

Table 13-15 Adding user-defined selection

Object	Property	Value
TextBox	Name	txtVariable
	Height	315
	Left	3060
	Text	"NJ"

continued on next page

continued from previous page

Object	Property	Value
	Top	5940
	Width	675
CommandButton	Name	cmdGo
	Caption	"GO"
	Height	435
	Left	4320
	Top	5880
	Width	1155

Add the following code in **cmdGo_Click**:

```
Private Sub cmdGo_Click()
    sSQL = "SELECT Publishers.[Company Name], Publishers.State"
    sSQL = sSQL & " From Publishers"
    sSQL = sSQL & " Where Publishers.State = "
    sSQL = sSQL & Chr(34) & txtVariable & Chr(34)
    Data1.RecordSource = sSQL
    Data1.Refresh
End Sub
```

Type any two-letter state abbreviation in the text box and click on GO. The DBGrid is updated to list the publishers from that state. (There are some states that will not return anything. Guess why?)

The runtime screen is shown in Figure 13-23.

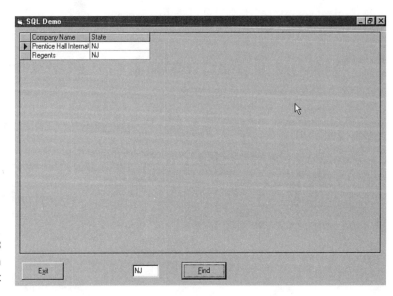

Figure 13-23
Selection based on user input

Queries on More Than One Table

The key word in "relational database" is *relational*. It means, as you know, that tables are related to each other via a key. You might guess that you can create queries to select items from more than one table, and you would be correct. In fact, you saw just that when you worked with the MSFlexGrid's MergeCells property. The following query:

```
SELECT Publishers.[Company Name], Titles.[Year Published]
FROM Publishers
INNER JOIN Titles ON Publishers.PubID = Titles.PubID
ORDER BY Publishers.[Company Name], Titles.[Year Published] DESC;
```

returns a sorted list of the publishers and the years in which they have published books. (BIBLIO.MDB is *terribly* out of date.) What makes it all work is the INNER JOIN, which links the key in Publishers with the foreign key in Titles.

What About Duplicates?

Sometimes a query returns duplicate records. The INNER JOIN query above is an example. If a publisher has more than one book for a given year, then each one will get its own record in the RecordSet. If all you wanted to know was whether a publisher has published a book in a specific year, you must add a predicate to the query. The query would change to

```
SELECT DISTINCT Publishers.[Company Name], Titles.[Year Published]
FROM Publishers
INNER JOIN Titles ON Publishers.PubID = Titles.PubID
ORDER BY Publishers.[Company Name], Titles.[Year Published] DESC;
```

The DISTINCT predicate assures that only records that are different from one another will be returned.

Aggregate Queries

Sometimes you need to know details about a database that cannot be found using a standard SELECT query. For example, you might want to know how many titles each publisher has produced. That calls for an *aggregation* of the data, a grouping and counting. Queries that do this are called, not surprisingly, aggregate queries.

The following query solves the problem:

```
SELECT DISTINCTROW Publishers.Name,
Count(Titles.Title) AS Count,
Titles.[Year Published]
FROM Publishers
INNER JOIN Titles ON Publishers.PubID = Titles.PubID
GROUP BY Publishers.Name, Titles.[Year Published];
```

The SQL statement has a few new wrinkles. The second item in the select list is Count(Titles.Title) AS Count. Count is one of the aggregate functions. As you might expect, it counts all of the records that meet the criteria, which in this case is all of the titles. There is no field in the database that includes the count, so an *alias* must be created for it—something to call it in the RecordSet the query generates. That alias is created by the **AS** clause. The column in the grid is titled Number. Finally, the **GROUP BY** clause combines all records that have identical values into a single record in the RecordSet. It isn't likely that this particular recordset will return identical records, but every item that is returned from an aggregate query *must* have an aggregate function. Table 13-16 lists the aggregate functions.

Table 13-16 The aggregate functions

Function	Action
GROUP BY	Combines all identical records into a single record. Each row in the result table will be unique on whatever this clause is. It also defines the summing level of the aggregate functions.
SUM	Finds the total of the values in a field.
AVG	Finds the average of the values in a field.
MIN	Finds the lowest value in a field.
MAX	Finds the highest value in a field.
COUNT	Finds the number of values in a field.
STDev	Finds the standard deviation of the values in a field.
VAR	Finds the variance of the values in a field.
FIRST	Returns the first record.
LAST	Returns the last record.
EXPRESSION	Creates a calculated field.

Computer books often go out of print. Generally, a five-year-old book is out of date because most of the information it contains is no longer meaningful. Change the SQL query to

```
SELECT DISTINCTROW Publishers.Name,
Count(Titles.Title) AS Count
FROM Publishers INNER JOIN Titles
ON Publishers.PubID = Titles.PubID
WHERE (((Titles.[Year Published])>1991))
GROUP BY Publishers.Name;
```

This **WHERE** clause is no different from the **WHERE** clause in a regular **SELECT** query.

The aggregate function lets you gather or create an aggregation of useless data, too. Avoid the temptation. Your user doesn't really need to know the average or the standard deviation of the year of publication.

More SQL

SQL is a simple language that provides database programmers with tremendous power to manipulate databases and tables. Because the Data control does not support them, this book does not include **Action** statements that can create new tables, delete tables, add new records to a table or delete records from a table. The Data control also does not support the Data Definition Language (DDL) that lets you create a whole new database.

If you want to expand your knowledge of database programming after you have completed this course, read *Visual Basic 5 Database How-To* from Waite Group Press, or point your Web browser to **www.mcp.com/waite** for a list of the latest and best books in the field.

Use the following SQL statement for questions 1 and 2:

```
SELECT Publishers.[Company Name], Publishers.State
FROM Publishers
WHERE (((Publishers.State)="CA")) OR (((Publishers.State)="NY"))
ORDER BY Publishers.State;
```

1. This query will return:
   a. All of the records in the Publishers table
   b. Only the records where **State = CA**
   c. Only the records where **State = NY**
   d. All of the records where **State = CA or State = NY**

2. The **ORDER BY** clause:
   a. Places orders for books in the Titles list
   b. Sorts the RecordSet into alphabetical order on the publishers.name field
   c. Sorts the RecordSet into alphabetical order on the publishers.state field
   d. None of the above

3. To use user-supplied data in a **SELECT** statement:
   a. Delimit it with quotation marks
   b. Delimit it with the pound sign
   c. Delimit it with single quotes
   d. No delimiters are needed

4. The line

   ```
   INNER JOIN Titles ON Publishers.PubID = Titles.PubID
   ```

   a. Links two tables together on the **PubID** field
   b. Adds the **PubID** field to the Titles table
   c. Merges the Publishers table and the Titles table into a single table
   d. Contains a syntax error and will not work

5. The line

```
SELECT DISTINCTROW Publishers.Name, Count(Titles.Title) AS Count
```

    a. Counts the number of publishers
    b. Counts the number of titles
    c. Eliminates duplicate titles
    d. Contains a syntax error and will not work

CREATING REPORTS

Imagine you have developed a great Visual Basic database application that stores information about all your customers, invoices, and orders. How do you get the information out of the database and onto a sheet of paper so you can mail your customers their invoices for the month? The answer is to use a *report*. Visual Basic allows you to create professional looking reports using a report writer called Crystal Reports Pro. Crystal Reports Pro can create customized reports, form letters, mailing lists, invoices, summary sheets, and orders. You can use Crystal Reports Pro to generate reports from many different databases.

Report Designer

From the Visual Basic menu, select Add-Ins and then select the Report Designer. The Crystal Reports Pro Report Designer, shown in Figure 13-24, is displayed.

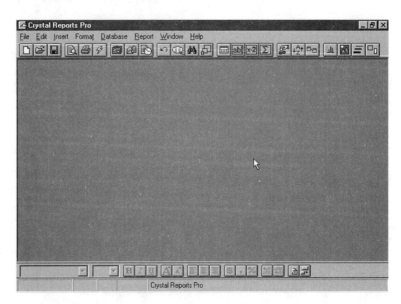

Figure 13-24
Crystal Reports Pro
Report Designer

Design a report that prints out some selected fields from the query All Titles in the database BIBLIO.MDB. To design the report, perform the following steps:

1. From the Report Designer menu, select File and then New. The Create New Report dialog box, shown in Figure 13-25, is displayed. Click on the Standard icon.

2. The window that appears is the Create Report Expert. It will help you build exactly the report you want. The window is shown in Figure 13-26.

3. Click on the Data File icon. A file selection window opens. Select the BIBLIO.MDB file for this report and click on the Add button. This report does not use any other databases, so click on the Done button. Now use the Delete button to remove all except the Publishers table from the Tables tab of the Create Report Expert.

4. Click on the Fields tab to select the fields for the report. Use the Add button to add Name, Address, City, State, and Zip to the report. With Zip highlighted in the Report Fields list, change the column heading to Zipcode. This is shown in Figure 13-27.

Figure 13-25
Create New Report
dialog box

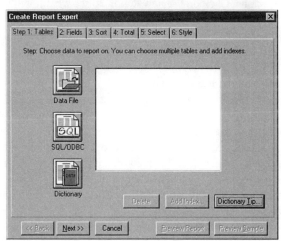

Figure 13-26
Create Report
Expert window

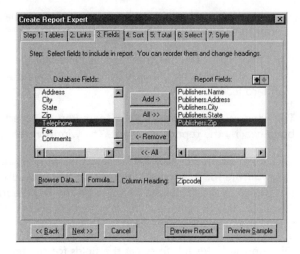

Figure 13-27
Selecting the
report fields

5. Click on the Sort tab and use the Add button to select Publishers.State as the *Group Field* for the report. The report will gather the publishers into groups using this field as the key.

6. Click on the Total tab and use the Add button to select Publishers.Name as the *Total Field.* In the ComboBox beneath the list, select Count. The report will now count how many of the publishers are in each of the states.

7. Click on the Style tab. Enter Publishers in the Title text box and select Executive, Trailing Break for the report's style. (Experiment with the different styles to decide which you like best.)

You are done. Click on Preview Report to see what it will look like. Hmmmm, a little hard to see. Select Zoom from the Report menu. Much better. The finished report is shown in Figure 13-28.

The first thing you might notice is that the first item in the report is missing a state. That happens because that publisher's record has a **NULL** in its State field. Nulls are sorted to the top of the list when you sort in ascending order.

The next thing to notice is that the text box for the count of states is far too large. The number is placed far to the right of the state's name. Not to worry. You can adjust it easily. Click in the text box to select it, just as you do in Visual Basic. When you see the resizing handles, resize the text box so it is about 1/2 inch wide. Notice that all of the count text boxes below the one you are resizing are also resized.

Also, since the state is listed at the bottom of each group, you don't really need to list it beside the name of each publisher. Click in one of the State fields. All of the other State fields are selected, too. Press Delete and watch them all disappear.

Of course, now that the State field is no longer displayed, it would be nice if the State-Count combination were at the top of each group instead of at the bottom. Select Report

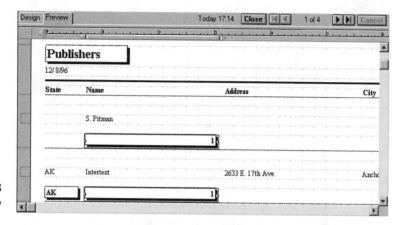

Figure 13-28
The report preview

Style Expert from the Format menu and change the style to Executive Leading Break. Isn't that better? Sure it is, but the style expert changed some things you had already adjusted. (Sigh.) For one thing, there is a State field at the bottom of each grouping and another at the top. For another, the text boxes have all been resized again.

Select the bottom State text box and delete it. Resize the State text box at the top of the group to a more comfortable size. Also resize the Count text box, then drag it to the top and place it alongside the State text box.

Now add a page number. Click on the Design tab. Note the difference in the appearance of the report. The Design View does not include the report's data. There is just a template for each section. Use the scroll bar to find the Page Footer section. Click in that section. Select Text Field from the Insert menu, and type the word Page in the Edit box. When you accept the text you have entered, a small box appears, attached to your mouse pointer. Move the box to the Page Footer section and click it into place. Next, select Special Field from the Insert menu. Select Page Number field from the pop-up menu that appears. Click the Page Number field into place just to the right of your Page text box.

You have one change to make before you save the report, but your report is essentially done. Open the File menu. Note that the item Save Data With Report is checked. If you leave that checkmark, the report will always show the data that was available when the report was created. In other words, it will not show any changes that are made to the database. Click on the selection to remove the checkmark.

Now save the file as Pub1.rpt, and it is ready to be included in a Visual Basic project. Save the file in the same directory where you have the BIBLIO.MDB file.

Crystal Custom Control

Crystal Reports Pro supplies a Visual Basic custom control that allows you to access your reports. You can create a database application that allows users to print various reports or set report criteria dynamically. The Crystal custom control is shown in Figure 13-29.

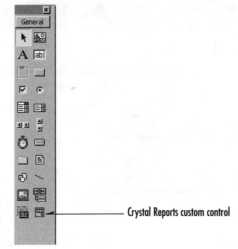

Figure 13-29
Crystal Reports
custom control

Crystal Reports custom control

The Crystal custom control is visible at design time, but is invisible at runtime. Examine some of the Crystal custom control properties before you use the report you saved in an earlier application.

ReportFileName

The **ReportFileName** property is the path and name of the report to print. You can set the property at design time or at runtime. For instance, you could present a list box of reports in your application and set the **ReportFileName** property based on the list selection.

Destination

The **Destination** property tells Crystal Reports where to print the report, and has four possible values:

- 0—To Window
- 1—To Printer
- 2—To File
- 3—To MAPI (for email)

When the **Destination** property is set to **0—To Window**, the output of the report is printed to the screen as a Print Preview. The **1—To Printer** option prints the report to the default printer. The **2—To File** prints the report output to a file specified in the **PrintFileName** property. Several file formats are supported, such as comma-separated and text format; the file type is set using the **PrintFileType** property. Finally, the **3—To MAPI** option prints the report to an e-mail message.

Action

The `Action` property is set at runtime to print the report. The following code prints a report:

```
Report1.Action = 1
```

The only value the `Action` property can be assigned is `1`. The property is not available at design time and is `Write-only` at runtime.

CopiesToPrinter

Set the `CopiesToPrinter` property to the number of copies to send to the printer.

Using the Crystal Control in an Application

Now it is time to use the report you created earlier, Pub1.rpt, in an application. Open the Publish project you created in Lesson 4. Save the project as RPublish. The RPublish application allows us to scroll through the Publishers table in the BIBLIO.MDB database and print a report displaying the publisher's name and state. Add the objects and set the properties for the RPublish project as shown in Table 13-17.

Table 13-17 Objects and property settings for the Rpublish project

Object	Property	Setting
CrystalReport	CopiesToPrinter	1
	Destination	0—To Window
	Left	4230
	Name	rptPublishers
	ReportFileName	Publish.rpt
	ReportSource	0—Report File
	Top	0
CommandButton	Caption	&Print
	Height	300
	Left	3795
	Name	cmdPrint
	Top	3675
	Width	975

Add the following code to the click event of the Command button `cmdPrint`:

```
Private Sub cmdPrint_Click()
    'Print the report
    rptPublishers.Action = 1
End Sub
```

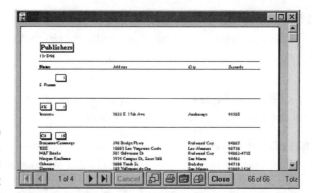

Figure 13-30
RPublish
application and
Report Publish.rpt

Run the application. Click on the Command button labeled Print. The report you designed earlier, Publish.rpt, is executed, as shown in Figure 13-30.

You can now develop reports that print out database information and incorporate these reports into your applications. Experiment with the Crystal Reports custom control. In the next lesson, you will learn how to design your own databases.

1. You can print information in a database to a printer by creating a:
   a. Query
   b. RecordSet
   c. Snapshot
   d. Report

2. The add-in used to create a report is the:
   a. `Form Designer`
   b. `Report Designer`
   c. `Query/Report/Form Builder`
   d. `Report Builder`

3. To modify a report to display the names in descending order using the Report Designer, select the _____ menu option.
   a. Record Sort Order
   b. Order By
   c. Ascending Order
   d. Order Items

4. Which one of the following is not a correct setting for the Crystal custom control destination property?
   a. `To Window`
   b. `To Printer`
   c. `To File`
   d. `To Form`

5. To execute a saved report from a Visual Basic application, use the:
   a. `Action` method of the Crystal control
   b. `Action` property of the Crystal control
   c. `Print` method of the Crystal control
   d. `Print` property of the Crystal control

EXERCISE

Modify the Rpublish application to write the report to a file, printer or the window. Add a screen that allows you to change the output of the report at runtime.

LESSON 7

DESIGNING A DATABASE

You now have the skills to manipulate data in a database with Visual Basic. To further enhance your database abilities, this lesson covers some basic concepts of database design. A well designed database makes programming and tuning the application much easier. In this lesson, you learn a simple design methodology for relational databases and a standard relational database technique called *normalization*.

The lesson also examines *logical database design* issues. A logical database design is typically a block diagram of entities and relationships referred to as an E-R diagram. Relational databases use the term *entities* to represent an object in the logical design, and *attributes* to represent the properties of the entity. For example, the tables in BIB-LIO.MDB are entities, and the fields in each table are the attributes of each entity.

Logical design is creating all the entities in a database and establishing relationships between the entities. Logical design does not take into account the type of database or the system on which the database will reside. *Physical database design* is taking the logical database design and creating a database and database objects to represent the entities and relationships in the logical database design. In the physical database design, each entity becomes a table, and the attributes of the entity become the columns of the table.

Database Design Goal

Before you begin the process of designing a database, it is important to understand some of the goals. The design goals for logical database design are to

- Establish database purpose
- Support all queries
- Produce all reports
- Be able to perform all calculations
- Process all transactions
- Enforce restrictions and defaults

Database Design Process

Where do you start the database design process?

Retrieving Information and Analyzing Information

The first step in designing a database is to talk to the people who will use it. Gather all the information to be represented in your database. Gather all the reports generated by hand that you expect to generate with the database. Add in the new reports that the users want. Gather any information sheets and any available information on the data and their characteristics. This is an important step because it will answer the following questions: What is in the database, and why is it in the database?

Break Down Information into Separate Entities

Get a piece of paper or a special database design tool and break down the collected data items collected into separate entities. An entity is a distinct object in the database. Each entity becomes its own table. For example in the BIBLIO.MDB database, entities are the Publishers, Authors, and Titles tables.

Assign Attributes to Each Entity

Once you have created separate entities for each object, assign attributes to each entity. An attribute is a property or characteristic of the object, such as its name, address, or amount. Each attribute becomes a field in the table.

Identify a Unique Identifier for Each Entity

A row in a relational database needs to be uniquely identified so you can retrieve that row and only that row. Select one or more attributes that uniquely identify a single row in the entity. This unique identifier is referred to as the primary key. For example, if you live in the United States, your Social Security number is an attribute that uniquely identifies you to the IRS at tax time. So your Social Security number is your primary key in the IRS database.

Establish Relationships Among the Entities

Determine the types of relationships that exist among your entities. There are three types of relationships in relational database design:

● One-to-one

● One-to-many

● Many-to-many

One-to-One

A one-to-one relationship is one in which each row in one table is represented by a single row in another table.

One-to-Many

A one-to-many relationship is one in which a row in one table may be represented by many rows in another table.

Many-to-Many

A many-to-many relationship is one in which a row from one entity may be represented by one or many rows in another table, and a row from the second table may be represented by one or many rows in the first table. Many-to-many relationships should not exist in a relational database design because many-to-many relationships cannot be properly joined to represent a single row correctly. To resolve the problem, create another table that has a many-to-one relationship with the first table and a many-to-one relationship with the second table. For example, the TitlesAuthors table in the BIBLIO.MDB database is a table created to solve the problem of the many-to-many relationship between Authors and Titles.

Normalize the Logical Design

Once you have established relationships for your logical design, it is time to *normalize* the design. Normalization involves a set of rules used to test the soundness of your database design. Each rule is applied to the logical database design, and then the logical design is said to be in rule# form, where rule# is first, second, ... fifth. There are five normalization rules. For most database designs and for the methodology used in this book, you will apply only the first three rules, leaving the database in Third Normal Form. Normalization will not fix inaccuracies or missing data items in your logical design. However, normalization will help point out possible problems with a logical database design. The following are the first three rules of normalization:

First Normal Form

No columns (attributes) may be multivalued columns or repeating groups. In other words, each column in a row can have only one value.

Second Normal Form

When the primary key consists of more than one column (attribute), all of the non-primary key columns (attributes) must depend on the entire primary key and not a part of the key. Note that a primary key that is made up of more than one attribute is called a *composite* key.

Recall the BIBLIO.MDB database. It contains a table named Authors, a table named Titles, and a table named TitlesAuthors which links the two together. If you attempt to combine Authors and Titles into a single table, then the only key for uniquely identifying a row is a composite key made up of `Au_ID` and `ISBN`. But the information about the author, the fields `Author` and `Year Born`, depend only on `Au_ID`, which is only part of the primary key. The combined table would be in First Normal Form, but not in Second Normal Form. Splitting the table into two, even at the cost of adding a third table to link them, is more efficient. Note that the two attributes of the Authors table are entered only once. Note that, in a First Normal Form, if an author had more than one title, the same data about the author would be repeated for each title.

Third Normal Form

Non-key attributes must not depend on other non-key attributes. Consider the Titles table, as an example. Imagine that someone added the publisher's phone number to that table. The primary key of the table is `ISBN`, but the publisher's phone number is dependent on `PubID` and not on `ISBN`. The table would be in Second Normal Form.

Design Exercise

Design a simple database using the methodology described in this lesson, starting from the beginning.

Retrieving Information and Analyzing Information

For this exercise, you have been given the task of creating a simple database for a local school. The following reports are required:

- A list of the students and their local addresses
- A list of the students and the teachers they have
- A list of teachers and the students they teach
- A list of the teacher's names and the subjects they teach

During the fact-finding mission, you find the following:

- Several students have the same first and last name. There are two John Smiths and a pair of twins named Billy and Bobby Johnson.

- Each student has a unique student ID number assigned by the school.

- No teachers have the same first and last name, but no teachers have ID numbers. There is a temptation to use the teachers' last names as the key, but the possibility exists that new teachers might be hired. A single duplicate last name would ruin the whole system.

- The most subjects taught by a single current teacher is two, but the most subjects any teacher has ever taught at the school is three.

Break Down Information into Separate Entities

Study the information gathered and think for a few minutes about the types of entities (objects) you need in your school database to provide the types of reports and requirements defined in the analysis stage. Remember, entities become tables in your physical database design. Jot down the separate entities you have come up with on a sheet of paper, and go to the next step.

Assign Attributes to Each Entity

Assign attributes to each of the entities on your paper. Remember, attributes are like object properties and, in the physical database design, are the columns to your tables.

Identify a Unique Identifier for Each Entity

Assign the primary key status to one or more attributes in each entity. Remember, the primary key must uniquely identify each entry. For example, for any value of the primary key in the Authors table in BIBLIO.MDB, only a single author is returned. If the entity does not have a unique identifier, then create an identity attribute for the entity. Identity attributes (contrived columns or counters in the physical database) are system-generated numbers used to uniquely identify a record. Let's take a look at the entity design created so far for our exercise. Your design should be similar. Don't worry if you have more attributes or entities than shown in Figure 13-31. For the exercise, the smallest number of attributes were used, and some attributes have been added to help you understand normalization.

The primary key selected for the Students entity is the unique student number Student ID. For the Teachers entity, the primary key is a contrived key since the teachers had no unique identifier. Notice the attributes in each entity. The non-key attributes of the Students entity are Name and Address. The non-key attributes of the Teachers entity are `Name`, `Subject1`, `Subject2`, and `Subject3`. The attributes `Subject1`, `Subject2`, and `Subject3` will hold the different subjects taught by a teacher. Three subject fields were selected, since the maximum number of subjects ever taught by a teacher is three. At this time, there is nothing to establish relationships between the Teachers and Students tables.

Establish Relationships Between the Entities

The next step is to determine the relationships between the tables.

The relationship can be created with a third table that establishes the connections between the two. For example, teacher A teaches students B and C. The new table is shown in Figure 13-32.

Normalize

Begin to apply the rules of normalization to your design.

First Normal Form

Look at the logical database design shown in Figure 13-32, and make sure that no attributes are multivalued columns (repeating groups). Wait a minute—look at the Teachers table. `Subject1`, `Subject2`, and `Subject3` are repeating groups. The design does not meet First Normal Form. So fix the logical design by removing the subject attributes, and then create another table called Subject, plus a table called Teacher/Subject to link the Subject table to the Teachers table. Now your logical design is said to be in First Normal Form. This new design is better because it might not always be true that no teacher teaches more than three courses. With this design, adding extra courses for a teacher is a matter of adding a record. Remember that it is always easier to add records than it is to add fields.

Figure 13-31
The Teachers and
Students tables

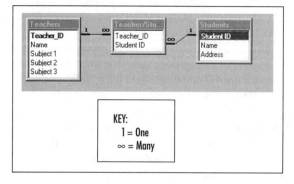

Figure 13-32
Connecting the
tables

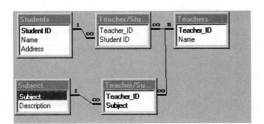

Figure 13-33
Normalized logical
database design

Second Normal Form

The second rule of normalization is applied to only entities that have composite primary keys (a primary key with more than one attribute). The only entities that meet this requirement are Teacher/Student and the new link table, Teacher/Subject. Because both tables are link tables, there are no non-key fields that do not depend on the primary key, so our database is already in Second Normal Form.

Third Normal Form

The third and final rule says all non-key attributes must not depend on other non-key attributes. Study the logical design. What do you think? No problems, right? Now your logical design, as shown in Figure 13-33, is in Third Normal Form. The logical design process is complete.

It is rare that a design is carried beyond Third Normal Form. There's such a thing as going too far. Using this design in a Visual Basic program will involve a lot of **INNER JOIN** clauses in **SQL** statements. Adding a higher level of normalization only increases the complexity of data retrieval.

You can use this design methodology to create your own databases. Once you have a working logical design, use a tool like Microsoft Access or the Visual Basic Data Manager to create the database and tables. Each entity becomes a table and each attribute becomes a column. Where you have key relationships, set up referential integrity to maintain the relationships correctly.

1. Which one of the following is not one of the primary goals of database design discussed earlier?
   a. Support all queries.
   b. Produce all reports.
   c. Create small tables.
   d. Be able to perform all calculations.

2. The first step in the database design process discussed in this section is:
   a. Retrieving information and analyzing information
   b. Breaking down information into separate entities
   c. Normalization
   d. Assigning attributes to each entity

3. A _____ relationship is one in which a row in one entity is represented by many rows in another entity.
   a. One-to-one
   b. One-to-many
   c. Many-to-many
   d. Primary

4. Allowing no columns (attributes) that are multivalued columns repeating groups is the rule for:
   a. Third Normal Form
   b. Second Normal Form
   c. Normalization
   d. First Normal Form

5. When converting the logical design into the physical design, each entity becomes a:
   a. Column
   b. Table
   c. Attribute
   d. Database

UNDERSTANDING ODBC

It is important to understand why ODBC is needed and the problem that it solves.

Assume that you own a small business that sells computer design solutions. Actually, your business sells the best computer design solutions in the world, and that is where your problems begin. All of your employees speak only English. So far, that hasn't been a problem because all of your customers speak only English. But one day, you receive a call from a huge company whose computer employees speak only Spanish. The English-speaking vice president asks you to design a very expensive computer system using input from employees who speak only Spanish. You quickly put out want ads for computer designers who can speak English and Spanish. After a lot of interviews and many days of searching, you find the correct bilingual people to do the job. But then, a few days later, you receive calls from a large German company and a large Japanese company who also want you to design computer systems and who are short on English-speaking individuals. Again, you put out the want ads and begin your search. Several weeks later you have found the right bilingual designers to perform the jobs but, in the meantime, you have been approached by Italian- and French-speaking companies for similar services.

You think to yourself, "There must be a better way." The company cannot continue to locate and hire bilingual designers every time a new job from a different foreign-speaking country comes along. You find a translator program that lets you write English or any other language and translates your text into any language. Using the translator program, you can communicate with any company, regardless of the language, and they can communicate with you—the problem is solved. So how does this story translate (no pun intended) to ODBC?

In the dark ages of programming before ODBC, there existed many different database products (just like today). Database application developers began to develop products that met their customers' needs, and many times these applications used a database. There were financial applications, industrial applications, and customized business applications, all using databases. As these applications grew in popularity, the demand for the applications from other customers became great, and the application developers were excited to expand their markets. However, there *was* one problem. Each application used a specific database product and would not work with other database products. Many times, customers who wanted the application were using a different database and refused to switch. To make the application work with a new database often required rewriting all the database code.

Just like the company in the previous story that had to hire specialized people to support a different language, the application developers had to hire new programmers to support new databases and rewrite code. The code rewrites were expensive, and the number of database products vast, so trying to support all the database products with a single application was close to impossible. In the world of database applications, a language translator of sorts called ODBC now solves the application developer's problem of creating applications capable of supporting many databases.

ODBC

ODBC stands for open database connectivity. ODBC is not really a translator, but an open standard that provides a common set of API (application interface) calls for manipulating databases. The ODBC APIs are implemented through Windows DLLs (dynamic linked libraries). Application developers can write applications that make ODBC calls and will work with many databases instead of writing programs specifically for a particular database. Some of the advantages of ODBC are as follows:

- A single application developer database interface to databases
- An open standard supported by many development tools
- The ability to access data from more than one type of database using the same application
- Applications isolated from network or backend databases
- The use of SQL promoted

ODBC Concepts

ODBC provides the developer with many benefits, but how does it work? To quickly understand the ins and outs of ODBC, take a look at an example that defines some important terms.

Figure 13-34 depicts a single table called Authors in a Microsoft SQL Server database called Pubs. Here's how you would use ODBC to retrieve all the data rows from the Authors table located on the Microsoft SQL Server. The SQL command to retrieve the records is familiar:

```
Select * From Authors
```

The first step to using ODBC is to set up an ODBC data source.

ODBC Data Source

An ODBC data source is a name that references a particular ODBC database and is used by applications to specify the database. The data source is also referred to as a *DSN*, for *data source name*. You must setup a DSN for a database before applications can use ODBC to retrieve information from that database. The DSN is used by ODBC to look up specific database information in the **ODBC.INI** file or the Windows registry, such as the type of database, the location of the database, and the ODBC driver used. An ODBC data source is added by using the ODBC option that is located in the Windows control panel shown in Figure 13-35.

To add an ODBC source:

1. **Double-click the ODBC icon shown in Figure 13-35. The ODBC Data Source Administrator shown in Figure 13-36 appears.**

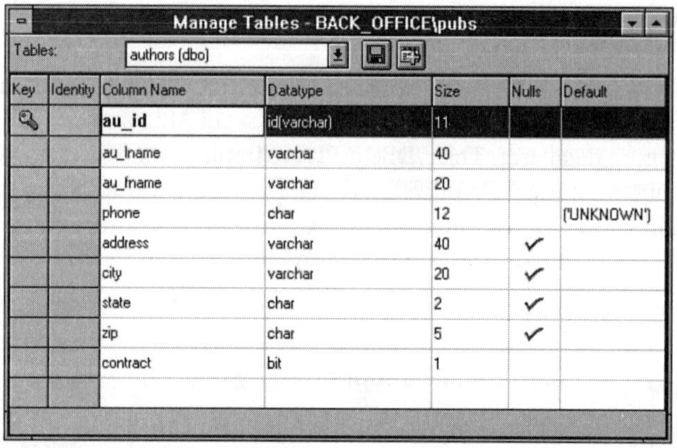

Key	Identity	Column Name	Datatype	Size	Nulls	Default
		au_id	id(varchar)	11		
		au_lname	varchar	40		
		au_fname	varchar	20		
		phone	char	12		('UNKNOWN')
		address	varchar	40	✓	
		city	varchar	20	✓	
		state	char	2	✓	
		zip	char	5	✓	
		contract	bit	1		

Figure 13-34 Microsoft SQL Server database Pubs

Figure 13-35
ODBC driver
manager in the
Windows control
panel

2. Click the Add button. The Create New Data Source dialog box shown in Figure 13-37 appears. The Create New Data Source dialog box displays all the installed *ODBC drivers* on your PC. An ODBC driver is a dynamic link library that processes ODBC function calls from the application and translates them to the native database language. The driver also receives information from the database and translates the information to an ODBC format if required. For this example, select the SQL Server ODBC driver installed on your PC. If you do not have the SQL Server driver, then select any installed driver. If you do not have any installed ODBC drivers, refer to your Visual Basic documentation about installing ODBC drivers.

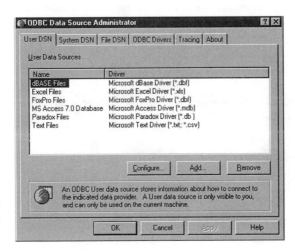

Figure 13-36
ODBC Data Source
Administrator

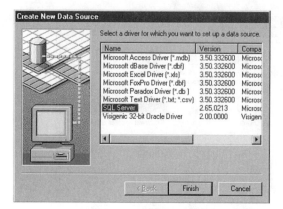

Figure 13-37
Create New Data
Source dialog box

Once you have selected an ODBC driver, click the OK button. The ODBC
SQL Server Setup dialog box shown in Figure 13-38 appears.

3. Fill in the Data Source Name text box. Remember, you will use this name
   in your applications to refer to the database you are accessing. You can
   use any name you desire, but you should use a descriptive name that
   gives you information on the type of database or the database server the
   DSN represents. For our example, use SqlSrvPubs for the Data Source
   Name. SqlSrvPubs represents our SQL Server database name Pubs, along
   with the prefix SqlSrv to represent a Microsoft SQL Server database.

4. The Description text box provides more information about the database.
   In the Description text box, enter: Interactive VB ODBC example.

5. The Server text box is for the name of the server the database resides on.
   For this example, use local, which signifies a copy of Microsoft SQL Server
   for an NT workstation running on the same PC as the Visual Basic program that uses the DSN.

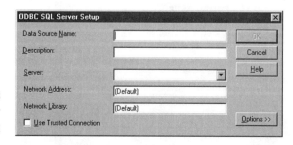

Figure 13-38
ODBC SQL Server
Setup dialog box

6. The Network Address and the Network Library text boxes are optional parameters depending on the type of database. The Network Address is the address of the database server, and the Network Library is the specific network dynamic linked library to use to communicate with the server. If the database were a Client/Server database system on a TCP/IP network, you would set the Network Address with the TCP/IP address of the server and the port number of the database server. For example:

```
Network Address: 101.200.200.201,4096
```

If the network protocol changes from TCP/IP to IPX, the only change required for the application using ODBC is to change the Network Address and Network Library from TCP/IP to IPX. No changes in the application code are required. For this example, just use the defaults.

7. Click the OK button to add the ODBC data source.

Now that you have added an ODBC data source, it's time to examine how to use the ODBC data source with Visual Basic.

ODBC and the Jet Database Engine

Visual Basic provides a multitude of options for accessing databases with ODBC. This section examines briefly how the Jet database can be used with ODBC to provide you with the same data access object you are already familiar with. Figure 13-39 shows how the Jet database engine fits into the ODBC picture. Jet provides the Visual Basic developer with the same set of database objects you have been using with the Access database. The database object model provides a much simpler and easier approach that requires less code than calling the ODBC API directly. The Jet database engine uses ODBC to provide the Visual Basic developer with transparent access to many different databases.

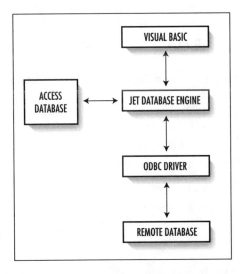

Figure 13-39
Jet and ODBC

Putting It All Together

This lesson has touched on what ODBC is and how it fits into the Jet database engine. Now try creating a project that uses the ODBC data source, **SqlSrvPubs**, created earlier, to bring back all the data in the Authors table located in the Pubs database. Do not worry if you do not have access to a Microsoft SQL Server. You will not be able to do this project, but as the purpose of this exercise is to show how you can use an ODBC data source with the standard Data control, just read through the steps anyway.

If you do have SQL Server, start a new project and add a Data Bound grid and a single Data control. Set the properties as shown in Table 13-18.

Table 13-18 Objects and property settings for ODBC exercise

Object	Property	Setting
Form	Height	5295
	Name	frmOdbc
	Width	6810
Data control	Height	435
	Left	255
	Name	datOdbc
	RecordSource	Select * from Authors
	Top	345
	Width	6045
DBGrid	DataSource	datOdbc
	Height	3510
	Left	330
	Name	dbgOdbc
	Top	975
	Width	61501

Notice that setting up the Data Bound grid with the Data control does not seem any different from when you used the Access database. Make the one property modification that tells the Data control to use the ODBC data source you created earlier. To use your ODBC data source, you must modify the **Connect** property of the Data control. The correct ODBC **Connect** property string format is as follows:

```
ODBC;DATBASE=Database Name;UID=User Id;PWD=Password;DSN=Data Source Name
```

You can set the **Connect** property to the entire string or to parts of the string. Setting the **Connect** property to **ODBC** displays several dialog boxes at runtime that allow the user to select a data source and to enter login information for the database. For this exercise, set the **Connect** property to the data source you created earlier, and specify the Pubs database on Microsoft SQL Server. Set the **Connect** property as follows:

```
ODBC;DATABASE=pubs;DSN=SqlSrvPubs
```

Run the project. The ODBC logon dialog box is displayed. If you have access to a Microsoft SQL Server, enter your user ID and password and click the OK button. Otherwise, click the Cancel button. You can see that using ODBC with Visual Basic and the Jet database engine is very similar to using Jet with Access. This lesson has covered the very basics of using Jet with ODBC. Be forewarned that using Jet and ODBC requires a good understanding of the ODBC database and of Jet to get the best possible performance.

That's it for this chapter. The next chapter covers a wide variety of topics, ranging from calling procedures in dynamic link libraries to using DDE. Before you close the book, though, let's not forget the quiz.

1. An _____ is a name that references a particular ODBC database and is used by applications to specify the database.
    a. ODBC driver
    b. ODBC administrator
    c. ODBC data source
    d. ODBC Driver Manager

2. When adding an ODBC data source via the ODBC SQL Server Setup dialog box, the _____ text box provides the name of the server the database resides on.
    a. Server
    b. Description
    c. Network
    d. Data source

3. Which one of the following is *not* true?
    a. You can access an ODBC data source using the Jet database engine.
    b. Microsoft SQL Server is an example of an ODBC database.
    c. The database object model provided by Jet is much simpler than calling the ODBC API directly.
    d. Microsoft Access is an example of a Visual Basic ODBC database.

4. To use ODBC with the Data control requires setting the _____ to **ODBC**.
    a. **Connect** property
    b. **RecordSource** property
    c. **DataBase** property
    d. **Options** property

5. What will the following line do when set to the **Connect** property of a Data control?

```
ODBC;DATBASE=Pubs;UID=sa;DSN=Finance
```

a. Nothing. The **Connect** property cannot accept strings.
b. Tell the Data control that the database is an ODBC database called Pubs located at the Finance Data Source Name, with a user ID of sa.
c. Tell the Data control that the database is an ODBC database called Finance located at the Pubs Data Source Name, with a user ID of sa.
d. Tell the Data control that the database is an ODBC database called Finance located at the sa Data Source Name, with a user ID of Pubs.

CHAPTER 14

ADVANCED FEATURES

This chapter covers many different topics: calling functions in dynamic link libraries, DDE implementation, and creating setup programs to distribute your applications. It teaches you how to use functions in dynamic link libraries to increase your application's performance time or to perform operations that are not normally part of Visual Basic. It shows how to use Visual Basic's Timer control to perform background processing.

Wonder what it means to be multitasking? This chapter gives you the answer as you examine Visual Basic and the Windows architecture. It teaches you how to create applications that can communicate with each other using DDE.

Finally, it teaches you how to create an executable, to distribute your applications, and to optimize the code you write.

USING THE WINDOWS API

Dynamic link libraries, commonly referred to as DLLs, are code libraries that contain functions and procedures. The word *dynamic* is a reference to the fact that, unlike traditional code libraries that are linked into your application during compile time, DLLs are loaded while the application is executing. When the application calls a function in a DLL, the DLL is loaded into memory and the function executes and returns information to the application, just like a standard compiled function call. DLLs were created to help reduce the size of Windows applications by providing a common set of functions and procedures. Visual Basic 5 gives you the ability to create your own DLLs with Visual Basic. In this section, you will examine the more traditional DLLs that are written in other programming languages such as C or C++. You will examine a particular set of DLLs (User, GDI, and Kernel) that contain Windows functions and procedures commonly referred to as the Windows API (application programming interface) functions. The great news for the Visual Basic programmer is that you can call Windows API functions and procedures easily from Visual Basic. Suddenly, you have hundreds of functions and procedures already written, sitting on your PC just waiting to be used! Using the Windows API, you can perform tasks that normally cannot be done in Visual Basic, or have improved processing speed over standard Visual Basic programming methods.

Using Non-Visual Basic Dynamic Link Libraries

To call a routine in a DLL from Visual Basic, perform the following steps:

1. Declare the function or procedure.

2. Call the function or procedure.

DLL functions and procedures are external, not part of a module, class, or form, but part of another file. The operative word here is *library*. The library is set up so all Windows applications can call on it and use its functions and procedures. By following the steps listed above, you can take advantage of the functions in procedures in the DLL. Let's walk through the example shown in Figure 14-1.

Figure 14-1 shows one of the Windows API DLLs, **USER32.DLL**. Three of the many functions contained in **USER32.DLL** are listed in Figure 14-1. Notice how the Visual Basic application shown in Figure 14-1 is using the **SendMessage** function that is located outside of the Visual Basic application. Let's see what is required for the Visual Basic application to call an API function. The first step is to tell Visual Basic where the function or procedure can be found. Use the **Declare** statement, which has the following syntax:

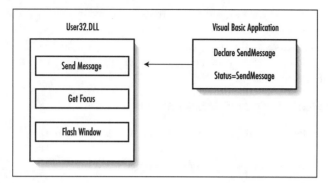

Figure 14-1
Visual Basic
application calling
a DLL function

● **Procedures**

```
Declare Sub name Lib "libname" [Alias "aliasname"][([arglist])]
```

● **Functions**

```
Declare Function name Lib "libname" [Alias "aliasname" ]
[([arglist])][As type]
```

where **name** is the function or procedure to call and **libname** is the DLL library name where the function is located.

Alias is an optional entry. When present, it indicates that the function being called by **name** has another name, **aliasname**, within the DLL. It is used when the name in the DLL is the same as a VB keyword or when you have already used that name for another purpose in your program.

The Visual Basic code to declare the function **SendMessage** is

```
Declare Function SendMessage Lib "user32" _
    (ByVal hWnd As Long, ByVal wMsg As Long, _
    ByVal wParam As Long, lParam As Any) As Long
```

Once you have declared an external procedure, you can use the function in your Visual Basic programs just as you would with any other function.

By Value or By Reference

In order to use DLLs effectively, you need to understand what is meant by passing *by value* or passing *by reference*. When a parameter is passed by value, the actual value of the parameter is passed to the function or procedure. If a parameter is passed by reference, the address of the parameter is passed to the function, not the value.

The example shown in Figure 14-2 may help explain the difference. Figure 14-2 depicts a chunk of memory that starts at address **0000** and goes to address **FFFF**. (Addresses are traditionally given in base 16, or hexadecimal form.) At address **9100** is a variable called **MyVal** which contains the string **"Hello"**. In the example, the function **MyFunc** is called with the variable **MyVal**. When **MyVal** is passed by value, the string **"Hello"** is passed to the function. When `MyVal` is passed by reference, the address of `MyVal`, 9100, is passed to the function. By default, Visual Basic passes parameters by reference. In many cases a DLL requires the value of the parameter and not the address.

To pass the value of the parameter, use the `ByVal` keyword in the `Declare` statement. For example:

Passing by Value

```
Declare Function MyFunc Lib "MyStuff" (ByVal MyVal as String)
```

Passing by Reference

```
Declare Function MyFunc Lib "MyStuff" (MyVal as String)
```

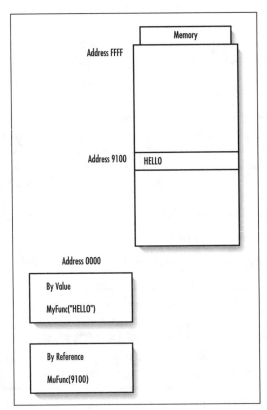

Figure 14-2
Memory map of
variable `MyVal`

hWnd **and** hDC **Properties**

Many of the Windows API calls require a Windows *handle*, which uniquely identifies a window or device context handle. If you want to use a Windows API call to modify a form or control, use the hWnd property. The hWnd property contains the Windows handle for the form or control. The property hDC gives you the device context handles of a form, PictureBox , or printer object. A handle is always declared as a long integer data type.

Converting Data Types

Calling a DLL is very similar to calling a regular procedure or function, except for setting up the parameters. Earlier you learned that DLLs not created by Visual Basic were written in other programming languages, like C and C++. Visual Basic data types are different from C or C++ data types, however, so you need to use caution when calling a DLL and make sure the data types for the parameters are correct. Table 14-1 helps you convert C language declarations into the proper Visual Basic declarations. The table is important because reference materials for some DLLs show only the C++ declarations. When you run into that, use the table to substitute the correct VB variable types for the C variable types in the declaration.

Table 14-1 DLL data conversion

C	Visual Basic
BOOL	ByVal *variable* As Boolean
INT32-bit	ByVal *variable* As Long
Float	ByVal *variable* As Single
Double	ByVal *variable* As Double
Pointer to a string	ByVal *variable* As String
Pointer to a Long	ByVal *variable* As Long
NULL Pointer	vbNullString
Void Pointer	*variable* As Any
Char	ByVal *variable* As String

Finding a List Item

You are ready to write an application that calls a DLL. This example calls a Windows API function called SendMessage. SendMessage allows you to send messages to controls to change the control's appearance or to get information back from the control. For instance, you can use SendMessage to add a horizontal scroll bar to a list box control. This example uses Send Message to search a list box and return the index value of the search string. Code that uses the Windows API to search a list box for a string runs much faster than the following Visual Basic code that searches a list box:

```
For iX = 1 to List1.ListCount -1
    If List1.ListIndex(iX) = "Fifty" Then
        Exit For
    End If
Next iX
```

Start a new project named test_dll. Add a form, and then add a list box, a text box, and a Command button to the form. Set the properties as shown in Table 14-2.

Table 14-2 Object and properties settings for project test_dll

Object	Property	Setting
Form	Name	frmMain
	Caption	"Test DLL"
	Height	4050
	Width	4095
TextBox	Name	txtSearch
	Height	285
	Left	2160
	Top	420
	Width	1695
CommandButton	Name	cmdQuit
	Caption	"E&xit"
	Height	315
	Left	2220
	Top	3360
	Width	1725
ListBox	Name	lstData
	Height	3600
	Left	150
	Sorted	-1 'True
	Top	120
	Width	1785

Object	Property	Setting
VB.Label	Name	Label1
	Caption	"Enter search text:"
	Height	225
	Left	2160
	Top	240
	Width	1665

Add the code shown in Listing 14-1 to the **Form_Load** event.

Listing 14-1 Code to fill `ListBox` in `Form_Load` event

```
Private Sub Form_Load()      '
    'Fill The List Box
    '
    List1.AddItem "One"
    List1.AddItem "Two"
    List1.AddItem "Three"
    List1.AddItem "Four"
    List1.AddItem "Five"
    List1.AddItem "Six"
    List1.AddItem "Seven"
    List1.AddItem "Eight"
    List1.AddItem "Nine"
    List1.AddItem "Ten"
End Sub
```

Add the following line to the **Form_Activate** event:

```
Private Sub Form_Activate()
    '   Set the focus in the TextBox
    txtSearch.SetFocus
End Sub
```

The first step in using a dynamic link library is to declare the function. Visual Basic comes with a utility that allows you to cut and paste Windows API declarations and constants called the API Text Viewer. The API Text Viewer is shown in Figure 14-3. The API Text Viewer is accessible through an add-in in Visual Basic 5. Its use is covered more fully in Chapter 18, Visual Basic 5 Communications.

The API Text Viewer lets you copy the declarations for all of the API functions, procedures, and constants so you can paste them directly into the Code window of your VB application. This can be a great time saver.

Create a new module for the sample project. Name the module **TestDLL.bas**. Use the API viewer to copy and paste the definition, or type the following code in the module's general declaration section:

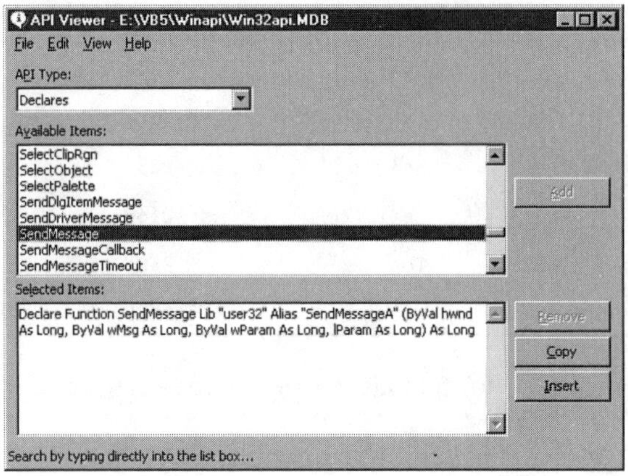

Figure 14-3
Windows API Text
Viewer

```
Option Explicit
Declare Function SendMessage Lib "user32" _
    Alias "SendMessageA" _
        (ByVal hwnd As Long, _
         ByVal wMsg As Long, _
         ByVal wParam As Long, _
         ByVal lParam As Any) As Long
'    Message for ListBox
Public Const LB_FINDSTRING = &H18F
```

If you pasted the declaration into the program, it was pasted as a single, very long string in the Code window. Improve readability by adding line continuation characters. It is worth the extra time! There is a catch in the pasted-in code too. The last parameter in the API Text Viewer version is **lParam As Long**. The parameter sent to **SendMessage** when you are searching for a string, however, is a *string*. The declaration must be changed to allow for that. It should read, as it does above, **lParam As Any**. (It's these little tricks that keep programming interesting.) Now the DLL function is declared. Add the code in Listing 14-2 to the change event for the TextBox.Command button. It is the code that calls the API function.

Listing 14-2 Calling API function in `Text_Change` event Command button

```
Private Sub txtSearch_Change()
    Dim sTempStr        As String
    Dim lResult         As Long
    '    If nothing in list then don't search
    If lstData.ListCount < 1 Then Exit Sub
    '    Save the text contents to a temporary string
    sTempStr = txtSearch.Text
    If Len(sTempStr) = 0 Then
    '    There is no text or it is blank
    '    Set ListIndex to first item in list
```

```
            lstData.ListIndex = 0
      Else
      '     There is text so send the message to look for it
      '     and reposition to the list to the matching entry
            lstData.ListIndex = SendMessage((lstData.hwnd), _
                  LB_FINDSTRING, -1, sTempStr)
      End If
End Sub
```

You're now ready to try out the application. Run the application and enter any part of one of the text strings that shows in the ListBox.TextBox. What happens? The list box cursor moves to the number you enter. The running application is shown in Figure 14-4.

You now have a basic understanding of how to call a DLL and the Windows API. There are many reference books available to help you determine which API functions to use. Calling DLLs and the Windows API can enhance your program greatly!

Figure 14-4
Application TestDLL

1. DLL stands for:
   a. Data Linked List
   b. Dynamic Link Library
   c. Windows API
   d. Dynamic Linked List

2. To use a non-Visual Basic created DLL, you must first _____ the function or procedure.
   a. Call
   b. Pass by reference
   c. Declare
   d. Execute

3. Passing the address of a variable is called passing:
   a. By value
   b. By memory
   c. By variable
   d. By reference

4. To use many of Windows API routines requires a Windows handle, which can be obtained from the _____ property of most forms or controls.
   a. `WindowHandle`
   b. `hWnd`
   c. `APIHandle`
   d. `hAPI`

5. _____ is a Visual Basic utility that allows you to get Windows API declarations easily.
   a. Windows API Text Viewer
   b. DLL Viewer
   c. Help Compiler
   d. Debugger

TIMER CONTROL

Throughout this book, we have been covering user event-driven programming, where events are triggered as a result of a user action. What if you wanted to check every 10 minutes to see if a file existed, or your application was required to take some action every few seconds without any user input?

The Timer control in Visual Basic 5 keeps track of time intervals and fires a `Timer` event whenever a certain amount of time has elapsed. Timer controls can be used for background processing or to take some sort of action at regular intervals. Before you jump into the specifics of the control, consider how timers are used in everyday life.

Timers are found everywhere in the real world. The most obvious example is an alarm clock. You set your alarm clock to wake you up at a specified time. Another good example is a VCR. Assume you can actually figure out how to program your VCR and you set it to record a half-hour TV show at 8:00 p.m. on one channel, and then record another half-hour TV show at 10:00 p.m. on a different channel. So what happens? At 8:00 p.m., an event is triggered to start recording a TV show on the specified channel. Somehow, the VCR checks to see if the recording interval of a half hour has elapsed, and if so, it stops recording. When 10:00 p.m. arrives, the whole process starts over.

Using Timer Controls

To understand the Timer control, create a new project that displays the current time in a status bar at the bottom of the form. Start a new project called timerapp. Add the Timer control shown in Figure 14-5 to the form.

It's no mistake that the icon looks like a stopwatch!

Now take a look at the two most important Timer control properties: **Enabled** and **Interval**.

Enabled **Property**

The **Enabled** property has two possible settings, **True** or **False**. If the **Enabled** property has a value of **True**, the timer is operational and counting down the time interval. If the property is set to **False**, the timer is not operational and is not counting down any time interval.

Interval **Property**

The **Interval** property is the number of milliseconds between **Timer** events. Let's say we want to do some task every 10 seconds. A millisecond is one thousandth of a second. Setting the **Interval** property to represent a 10-second time period, we divide 10 seconds by .001 to get 10,000. A value of **1000** would be every one second and a value of **500** every half second. The minimum value for a timer interval is **0** and the maximum value is **65,536**, which is just over a minute. You can set the **Interval** property and the **Enabled** property at design time or at runtime.

You want the time in the status bar to update every second, so using the formula above to compute the interval value, set the value of the **Interval** property to **1000** (1/.001 = 1000) and set the **Enabled** property to **True**.

Add the objects shown in Table 14-3 and set the properties.

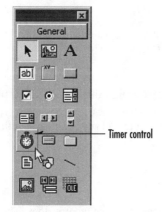

— Timer control

Figure 14-5
Timer control on the Visual Basic toolbar

Table 14-3 Application timerapp objects and property settings

Object	Property	Setting
Form	Caption	Example of Background Processing
	Height	2790
	Name	frmTimer
	Width	6390
Timer	Enabled	True
	Interval	100
	Left	15
	Name	Timer1
	Top	45
StatusBar	Height	615
	Name	StatusBar1

Add three panels to the status bar, and then place the following code into form frmTimer's load event:

```
Private Sub Form_Load()
    StatusBar1.Panels(1).Text = "Grey"
    StatusBar1.Panels(2).Text = Date$
    StatusBar1.Panels(3).Text = Time$
End Sub
```

The code sets the text of each of the three panels on the StatusBar control. The first panel of the status bar represents the current background color, the second panel displays the date, and the third panel displays the time. The line

```
StatusBar1.Panels(2).Text = Date$
```

uses the **Date$** function to return a string value of the current date, and it displays the date in the second panel of the status bar. The line

```
StatusBar1.Panels(3).Text = Time$
```

uses the **Time$** function to return a string value of the current time, and it displays the time in the third panel of the status bar.

Add the following line of code in the **Timer** event subroutine:

```
Private Sub Timer1_Timer()
    StatusBar1.Panels(2).Text = Date$
    StatusBar1.Panels(3).Text = Time$
End Sub
```

OK, it's time to run the application to see what it does. The application looks like Figure 14-6.

Figure 14-6
Application
timerapp
displaying date
and time

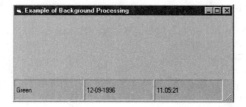

Notice when the application is running that the time in the third panel is being updated every second. What's happening? The timer interval counts down and executes the code in the **Timer** event. Change the **Interval** property to **5000**, and run the program again. Now the time is being updated at five-second intervals instead of one-second intervals.

As it turns out, displaying the date and time in the StatusBar control can be done without a timer control by setting the **Style** property of the panel. Take a look at a more complex problem.

Background Processing

The Timer control is limited in that the maximum interval allowed is 65,535 milliseconds. What do you do if you need to load a file into a database at 10-minute intervals or you want to do some other background task while the user is idle? Simple. Just keep an internal count of the number of time intervals that have passed. Modify the current project to change the background color of the form every 10 seconds. Reset the **Interval** property setting to **1000** so that it fires the **Timer** event every second. Add the following to the declarations in the form frmTimer module:

```
Dim iTimeToChange as Integer
```

The **iTimeToChange** variable is used to keep track of the number of intervals that have passed since the last time the background color of the form was changed. Add the following code to the form's load event:

```
Private Sub Form_Load()
    StatusBar1.Panels(1).Text = "Grey"
    StatusBar1.Panels(2).Text = Date$
    StatusBar1.Panels(3).Text = Time$
    iTimeToChange = 0
End Sub
```

Next, add the code shown in Listing 14-3 to the **Timer** event.

Listing 14-3 Timer event code

```
Private Sub Timer1_Timer()
    StatusBar1.Panels(3).Text = Time$
    iTimeToChange = iTimeToChange + 1
    If iTimeToChange = 10 Then
        '
        ' Case Statement to check the Text in the first panel and
        ' then change the  background color based on the
        ' current color
        '
        Select Case StatusBar1.Panels(1)
        Case "Red"
            Me.BackColor = RGB(0, 255, 0)
            StatusBar1.Panels(1) = "Green"
        Case "Green"
            Me.BackColor = RGB(0, 0, 255)
            StatusBar1.Panels(1) = "Blue"
        Case Else
            Me.BackColor = RGB(255, 0, 0)
            StatusBar1.Panels(1) = "Red"
        End Select
        iTimeToChange = 0 'Reset the Back color counter
    End If

End Sub
```

The following lines:

```
iTimeToChange = iTimeToChange + 1
If iTimeToChange = 10 Then
```

increment the **iTimeToChange** variable and check to see if the variable is equal to 10. They change the background color every 10 intervals, in this case every 10 seconds. If you set the timer **Interval** to **60000**, or 60 seconds, the background color would change every 10 minutes.

Run the application. Notice how the time changes in the status bar every second and how the background color only changes every 10 seconds.

Now that you are an expert with the Timer control, it is time (no pun intended) to bring up a few limitations of the control:

1. Even though the timer **Interval** property is measured in milliseconds, the system only generates 18 clock ticks per second, so the actual precision of a timer interval is no more than 1/18th of a second, which is a little over 55.5 milliseconds.

2. If your application is performing intensive computing like querying a database, accessing a network, or performing file input or output, your application may not get the **Timer** events as often as the **Interval** property specifies. Also, the interval is not guaranteed to fire the event exactly on time. If you need precision timing, use the **GetSystemTime** API function.

3. Using a small timer interval can slow system performance because the `Timer` events are continuously triggered. Do not use a small interval unless you really need one.

Despite the Timer control's limitations, it is a very useful control for taking action at specific intervals. You, the programmer, must take its limitations into account and set the `Interval` property accordingly, based on your application's needs.

1. The Timer control's `Interval` property is measured in:
   a. Seconds
   b. Minutes
   c. Milliseconds
   d. 1/18ths of a second

2. To disable a Timer control, do the following:
   a. Set the `Start` property to `Off`.
   b. Set the `Run` property to `False`.
   c. You cannot disable a timer.
   d. Set the `Enable` property to `False`.

3. The true precision of the Timer control is:
   a. 1 millisecond
   b. 1/18th of a second
   c. 1/10th of a second
   d. 1/100th of a second

4. If I have a Timer control on a form named Timer1, what event procedure is called when the timer interval counts down?
   a. `Timer1_Timer`
   b. `Timer1_Click`
   c. `Timer1_Activate`
   d. `Timer1_Run`

5. I want to write a buffer to a file every 18.5 seconds. To what value would I have to set the `Interval` property of a Timer control to accomplish this?
   a. `18.5`
   b. `185`
   c. `1850`
   d. `18500`

UNDERSTANDING THE ARCHITECTURE

You have almost made it to the end of the book, and by now you should have a good grasp of the things Visual Basic can do. This lesson briefly examines some key Windows and Visual Basic architecture issues in order to enhance your abilities as a programmer. Start by considering the different types of multitasking environments available to the Visual Basic programmer.

Cooperative Multitasking Versus Preemptive Multitasking

In order to help you understand the different types of multitasking, imagine you work at a day-care center and are in charge of three seven-year-old children. It's recess time, so you take the children outside to play. The three children want to ride bicycles; the problem is that you only have one bicycle, so the children have to share. You tell the children to share the bicycle and just take turns so that everyone gets to ride. You have some work to do so you leave the children. They begin to ride the bike, sharing and taking turns. But it's not too long before one child decides that the other kids have ridden the bike longer then they should have and decides to forget sharing and keep the bike.

The example of the children voluntarily sharing the bicycle is the premise of *cooperative multitasking*. Applications execute and share the computer's processor with the other applications. It is up to the applications to decide when to give up the system processor and allow another application to run. Like the child who decided not to give up the bicycle, there are many applications that perform tasks such as file I/O and database access that do not free up the processor. Windows 3.x is an example of a cooperative multitasking operating system.

Now back to our story. The two children who are not getting a chance to ride the bike run in to tell you that the third child refuses to share. You grab your work and an alarm clock and head outside to enforce the shared bike policy. You tell the three children that they each get to ride the bike for 10 minutes. You use the alarm clock to let them know their turn is over. You decide to stay outside with the children to make sure they relinquish the bike every 10 minutes. You are now operating on the same premise as *preemptive multitasking*. With preemptive multitasking the operating system allows each application to execute for a certain amount of time. If the application does not give up the processor voluntarily, then when the time slice expires, the operating system gives the processor to another application. This is a simplistic explanation, for there are other factors like task priority and interrupts that this book does not go into. Windows 95 and Windows NT are examples of preemptive multitasking systems.

Single or Multithread

What does it mean when someone says they have a single-threaded application, and what the heck is a *thread*? A thread is simply executing code. Every application in a Windows environment has at least a single thread of execution. An application is said to be multithreaded when it can create more then one thread of execution. For instance, suppose you have a database application and you have a query that executes for a long time. Your application also needs to allow your user to edit some data in another table. If your application is multithreaded, you can start your query by creating a thread to perform the query and then, while the query thread is executing, begin to edit the table using another thread. Multitasking preemptive operating systems allocate separate time slices to each thread (i.e., the query thread and the edit table thread). In Windows 3.x, applications can only be single threaded. Windows 95 and Windows NT allow applications to use multiple threads, which can all run at the same time.

Visual Basic Applications

Let's examine briefly the architecture of a Visual Basic application. Visual Basic 5 applications will run only in a 32-bit Windows environment like Windows 95 or Windows NT. When you compile a Visual Basic project, Visual Basic produces an executable file composed of *P-code* rather than machine instructions that can be directly executed by the system processor. P-code stands for *pseudo-code*. It is an intermediate step between the instructions in your Visual Basic project and the low-level *native code* or *machine code* that your microprocessor actually executes. At runtime, **VBRUN500.DLL** converts the P-code into native code. If you have the Professional or Enterprise editions of Visual Basic, you can compile directly into native code. Compiling to native code is covered in Lesson 6.

Take a look at some important limitations of a Visual Basic application.

Stack Size

The program stack is a limited area of memory used to store various types of information in a running application. The stack stores return addresses of calling functions and procedures, arguments, and local variables in procedures, and is used in many other ways. The stack has a limited amount of space available to your application; 32-bit Visual Basic applications have a stack size of 1MB.

Maximum Number of Controls per Form

There is a limit of 254 controls on a single form. You can get around this limitation by using control arrays, which count as only one control.

Form, Class, and Module Limitations

A Visual Basic module cannot exceed 64K in code. If the 64K limit is exceeded, you will get a error during compilation. To fix the error, remove some of the code in the module and place it in another module. The maximum number of lines of code in a form, class, or module is 65,534 lines.

Data Limitations

A data segment is an area of memory allocated to an application to store data. In a Visual Basic application, each form, class, and module is allocated a 64K data segment. This segment stores all static local variables, module level fixed strings, module level variables other than arrays, and variable length strings. Arrays and variable length strings are treated differently. Each variable length string is allocated its own data segment. Variable length strings can have up to four gigabytes of characters. There is no limit to the size of arrays, which are limited only by the amount of available memory. Array indexes, however, must be in the range of -2147483648 to +2147483648.

Summary

You should have a general understanding of some key features and terms of the Visual Basic and Windows architectures. Understanding the terms and concepts will come in handy, especially in the next section when you learn about programming with idle loops. Before you continue, don't forget to take the quiz.

1. _____ is when applications are required to voluntarily yield so other applications can execute.
   a. Preemptive multitasking
   b. Context switch
   c. Program fork
   d. Cooperative multitasking

2. Applications created with Visual Basic are:
   a. Single-threaded
   b. Multithreaded
   c. Multiprocess
   d. Cooperative-threaded

3. A Visual Basic application that is compiled as P-code requires the:
   a. **VBRUN500.DLL**
   b. **VB50032.DLL**
   c. **VBRUN5.DLL**
   d. **VB500RUN.DLL**

4. The maximum size of a form, class or module is:
   a. 1MB
   b. Unlimited
   c. 64K
   d. 32K

5. The maximum number of controls allowed on a single form is:
   a. 254
   b. Unlimited
   c. 64
   d. 1,024

IDLE TIME

In this lesson, you will build on the concepts of preemptive and cooperative multitasking by introducing the concept of *idle time*. To understand idle time, think about a word processing application. You create a new document, and suddenly you get writer's block and can't think of anything to write. You just sit there being idle. Well you're not the only one being idle; because you're not doing anything, the word processing application is also doing nothing.

Application idle time is the time when nothing is happening in the application between events. For some applications you might want to use this idle time by creating a background process using a Timer control, as described in Lesson 2. Other applications may present you with a different problem. For instance, you probably wouldn't want a process performing iterations that would tie up the application for an extended period of time. In a preemptive multitasking system like Windows 95 or Windows NT, you could still use your PC while the application performs the iterations thanks to the preemptive time slice, but you would not be able to interact with the application. On a cooperative multitasking system like Windows 3.1, a process performing a large number of iterations not only locks up the executing application, but the PC as well, since there is no time for any other process to run. What happens if you accidentally started the process and wanted to stop it? You would have to let the process complete or kill the application, which sounds severe! Happily, there is a way to momentarily halt your application and return control to the operating system to allow other applications the chance to run and allow other events in your application to be processed. This technique is called an idle loop.

Idle Loops

To create an idle loop, use the Visual Basic command **DoEvents**.

DoEvents returns control momentarily to the operating system so that other events can be processed. **DoEvents** has the following syntax:

DoEvents

With preemptive multitasking systems like Windows 95 or Windows NT, use **DoEvents** in any case where you need to allow your application to process events during a long process. For instance, in the case of a process performing a lot of iterations or calculations in a loop, you can use **DoEvents** to provide a way to give the user a chance to cancel the operation. In the past, programmers have been very creative in the use of **DoEvents** and idle loops. For example, idle loops make sure graphics and status bars are being updated correctly. Try an experiment with **DoEvents** and idle loops. Create a new project called idleloop. Add the objects and set the properties shown in Table 14-4.

Table 14-4 Application `idleloop` objects and property settings

Object	Property	Setting
Form	Caption	Testing Idle Loops
	Height	2985
	Left	1920
	Name	frmIdle
	Top	2010
	Width	5235
CommandButton	Caption	Start
	Height	585
	Left	1665
	Name	cmdStart
	Top	1770
	Width	1620
TextBox	Height	435
	Left	1350
	Name	txtCount
	Top	960
	Width	2400

Add the code in Listing 14-4 to the `click` event of the Command button.

Listing 14-4 Start button `Click` event

```
Private Sub cmdStart_Click()
Dim iLoopCount As Integer, iCounter As Integer

  iCounter = 0
  Me.MousePointer = Hourglass
  For iLoopCount = 0 To 500
    'Increment the Counter value
    iCounter = iCounter + 1
    'Display the count in the TextBox
    txtCount = Str$(iCounter)
```

```
    Next iLoopCount
    Me.MousePointer = Default
End Sub
```

When the user clicks the Command button labeled Start, the `Counter` variable in the `Click` event procedure is incremented by 1, and the value is displayed in the text box until the variable `LoopCount` exceeds `500`. Run the application and click the Start button.

What happened? The text box did not display every value, only the final value `501`. Why? The repaint event for the text box was not allowed to process during the loop, so only the final result was displayed. Now add a `DoEvents` after the line of code `txtCount = Str$(iCounter)`:

```
For iLoopCount = 0 To 500
    'Increment the Counter value
    iCounter = iCounter + 1
    'Display the count in the TextBox
    txtCount = Str$(iCounter)
    DoEvents
  Next iLoopCount
```

Run the application and click the Start button. See the difference? `DoEvents` halts execution in the loop and transfers control to the operating system. This allows other events and messages in the application to be processed, so you see the numbers incrementing in the text box.

If you are having problems with screen repaints—for instance, if a status bar display is not being updated or a text box is not displaying incremental values—consider using the `Refresh` method of the control or form instead of `DoEvents`. In the example above, remove the `DoEvents` statement and put the following code in its place:

```
txtCount.Refresh
```

Now run the application. This gives the same results, but uses the correct method. Since there are better ways to refresh displays, use `DoEvents` to allow your user to exit the counter loop in the application. Modify the code in the command `Click` event as shown in Listing 14-5.

Listing 14-5 New Start button `Click` event

```
Private Sub cmdStart_Click()
Static iLoopCount As Integer 'Save Value
Dim iCounter As Integer
Const Max_Loop = 1500
  iCounter = 0
  '
  'Check if already processing
  ' (i.e. Caption on button says Cancel)
  ' If so set iLoopCount to the max
  ' Reset the Caption on the button
  ' and Exit
  If cmdStart.Caption = "Cancel" Then
```

continued on next page

continued from previous page

```
        iLoopCount = Max_Loop
        cmdStart.Caption = "Start"
        Exit Sub
    Else
        cmdStart.Caption = "Cancel"
    End If
    Me.MousePointer = Hourglass
    For iLoopCount = 0 To Max_Loop
        'Allow events to be processed
        DoEvents
        'Increment the Counter value
        iCounter = iCounter + 1
        'Display the count in the TextBox
        txtCount = Str$(iCounter)
        'Repaint
        txtCount.Refresh
    Next iLoopCount
    Me.MousePointer = Default
    cmdStart.Caption = "Start"
End Sub
```

The procedure was modified so the **iLoopCount** variable is static, and a **DoEvents** was added in the loop to allow the process to be interrupted. If the **Caption** property of the CommandButton reads **Start**, the process is started and the **Caption** property is set to **Cancel**. If the **Caption** property is set to **Cancel**, the routine variable **iLoopCount** is set to the maximum value in the loop, which terminates the loop on the next iteration and resets the **Caption** property to **Start**. Run the application and click the Start button. Now click the Cancel button to stop processing. Figure 14-7 shows the program at runtime.

You have now written an idle loop that allows you to interrupt a lengthy process. Remember, if you are having trouble with screen repaints, use the **Refresh** method of the form or control. Use Timer controls for background processing and **DoEvents** to interrupt lengthy tasks. Avoid using **DoEvents** with global data, and remember that **DoEvents** will not return control to your application when performing blocking I/O instructions, like a file read or a database query.

Figure 14-7
Idleloop
application

1. The Visual Basic command to return control momentarily to Windows to allow other events to be processed is called:
   a. `Switch`
   b. `Sleep`
   c. `DoEvents`
   d. `ProcessEvents`

2. To make sure forms or controls repaint correctly, use the _____ method of the object.
   a. `Refresh`
   b. `Repaint`
   c. `DoRepaint`
   d. `Draw`

3. The following code is an example of an(a):
```
For iLoopCount = 0 To Max_Loop
'Allow events to be processed
DoEvents
'Increment the Counter value
iCounter = iCounter + 1
'Display the count in the TextBox
txtCount = Str$(iCounter)
'Repaint
txtCount.Refresh
Next iLoopCount
```

   a. Iteration loop
   b. Event loop
   c. Real-time loop
   d. Idle loop

4. An idle loop can be used to allow:
   a. Database retrievals
   b. File I/O processing
   c. Users to cancel lengthy processes
   d. Background processing

5. Idle loops are beneficial in:
   a. Cooperative multitasking environments
   b. Cooperative and preemptive multitasking environments
   c. Preemptive multitasking environments
   d. Only background processing

REVIEW

John: I sure was surprised to learn how easy it is to use the Windows API.

Lisa: You're right, but not only can you use the Windows API, but any other DLL. All you have to do is include the **Declare** statement and then call the function or procedure. I'm really going to use the ListBox search routine we wrote earlier in my applications.

John: I have several application needs that are going to require some background processing, so I expect to make heavy use of the Timer control. I was surprised how easy it is to use a Timer control to create processes that need to occur every few minutes without user intervention.

Lisa: I agree. So, are you finally clear on cooperative multitasking versus preemptive multitasking?

John: After reading Lesson 3, I'm very clear. Not to mention that I learned Visual Basic has a few limitations I was not aware of, like a maximum of 254 controls on a form.

Lisa: I already knew that. I was surprised to see that I could still use idle loops effectively in a preemptive multitasking environment.

John: We sure are covering a lot of useful information in this chapter! What's next?

Lisa: DDE.

John: What's DDE?

Lisa: Read on.

DDE

DDE stands for *dynamic data exchange* and is a form of interprocess communications supported by the Windows operating system. Interprocess communication is two or more applications exchanging data with each other. OLE (object-linking and embedding) is another form of interprocess communications. OLE is covered in the next chapter's lessons. OLE is the preferred method of Microsoft Windows interprocess communication. However, OLE is not supported by all Windows applications, so DDE is still very important.

Source and Destination

Data exchange in DDE is referred to as a *conversation* between a source application and a destination application. As an analogy, say you have a friend you would like to call. You dial the phone number and, if your friend is there, he or she picks up the phone and begins to talk. The two of you are now engaging in a conversation. When the conversation is complete, you both hang up the phone. DDE is similar; an application makes a call to another application. If the other application is available and can establish the link, then the DDE conversation can begin. The application that initiates the DDE exchange is called the *destination*, while the application responding to the request is called the *source*. Applications can be both DDE sources and destinations.

Figure 14-8 shows a DDE example where Microsoft Excel is the source application and is sending data from spreadsheet cells to text boxes in a Visual Basic application.

Establishing DDE Links

Establishing DDE links between a Visual Basic application and another application requires setting properties on controls or forms to establish the link and exchange the data. A form is the only Visual Basic object that can act as a DDE source. TextBox, Label, and PictureBox custom controls can be DDE destinations. To set up a form to be a DDE source requires setting the following properties in order:

To set up a DDE destination on a TextBox, PictureBox, or Label control, set the following properties in order:

- `LinkTopic`
- `LinkItem`
- `LinkMode`
- `LinkTimeout`

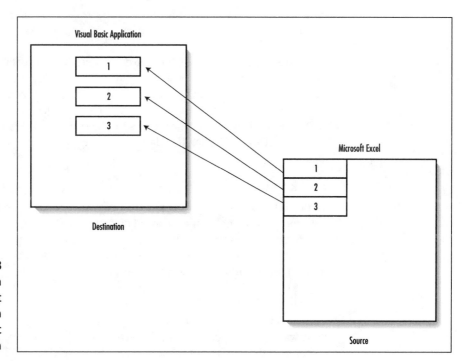

Figure 14-8
DDE conversation with a Microsoft Excel source and a Visual Basic destination

LinkTopic

In a destination control, the `LinkTopic` property has the following format: **application|topic**, where **application** is the name of the source application the destination wants to converse with, and **topic** is the topic of the conversation. For example, to start a DDE conversation with Microsoft Excel using the spreadsheet **DDE.xls**, the `LinkTopic` property would be set as follows:

```
LinkTopic = "Excel|c:\spreadsheets\[DDE.xls]Chart1"
```

In a source application, `LinkTopic` is set to the topic that can respond to a DDE conversation, for example, a form name.

```
LinkTopic = Form1
```

LinkMode

The `LinkMode` property specifies the type of DDE link to be established between a source application and a destination application.

For a DDE source, a form, the `LinkMode` property can be set to **None** or **Source**. **None** is the default value for both the source and the destination. When a DDE source's `LinkMode` is set to **None**, no applications can start a DDE conversation with the source topic (form). Also, if the `LinkMode` property is set to **None** at design time, then the property cannot be modified at runtime. However, if the property is set to **Source**, then the `LinkMode` property can be toggled between **Source** and **None** at runtime. Setting the `LinkMode` property to **Source** allows the form to be a topic of DDE conversation with other applications.

For destination controls, `LinkMode` determines how the data is exchanged between the source application and the destination control. Valid settings are **None**, **Automatic**, **Manual**, or **Notify**. In **Automatic** mode, if the data in the source changes, the destination control automatically receives the data. In **Manual** mode, the destination control only receives data when it asks for the data. In **Notify** mode, the destination control receives notification that data has changed, but then must manually ask for the data.

LinkItem

The `LinkItem` property only applies to a destination, like a text box, label, or picture box, and is the item that is exchanged during the DDE conversation. For example, in a DDE conversation between two Visual Basic applications, the `LinkItem` property could be **Text1** or, if the source application is a spreadsheet, the `LinkItem` property could be **R1C1**, the coordinates of a spreadsheet cell.

LinkTimeout

The `LinkTimeout` property applies only to destinations, and is the amount of time Visual Basic waits for a response in a DDE conversation before raising an error. If there is no response within the `LinkTimeout` period, an error is raised. This prevents VB from getting hung up waiting for a response that might never come. The value of `LinkTimeout` is measured in tenths of a second. The default value is **50** (5 seconds).

Events and Methods

LinkOpen *Event*

The `LinkOpen` event occurs when a DDE link is established.

LinkNotify *Event*

`LinkNotify` is triggered when a DDE conversation is in Notify link mode, and the data in the source changes.

LinkError *Event*

The `LinkError` event is triggered if an error occurs during a DDE conversation.

LinkClose *Event*

The `LinkClose` event occurs when the DDE link is broken.

LinkRequest *Method*

The `LinkRequest` method is invoked by a destination control to retrieve data from a source in Manual or Notify link modes.

LinkPoke *Method*

The `LinkPoke` method allows the destination control to send data to the source application.

LinkSend *Method*

The `LinkSend` method is used to transfer the contents of a picture box from the source to the destination.

DDE Application

To test DDE, you are going to create two projects, one for the DDE source and another for the DDE destination. Creating and testing the applications requires running two instances of Visual Basic. Start with the source project. Create a new project named VBSrc. It is important that you name the project before running the application because the DDE destination application must use the Visual Basic project name or executable name to establish a DDE link. Add a single form to the project, add the objects, and set the properties as shown in Table 14-5.

Table 14-5 Application VBSrc objects and property settings

Object	Property	Setting
Form	Caption	Source DDE
	Height	2175
	LinkMode	1 - Source
	LinkTopic	frmSource
	Name	frmSource
	Width	3930
TextBox	Height	300
	Left	675
	Name	txtItem
	Text	""
	Top	540
	Width	2175

The DDE source application is complete, with no code! Run the project from Visual Basic and leave it running. Start a new instance of Visual Basic to create the DDE destination project. Start a new project named VbDest with a single form. Add the objects and set the properties, as shown in Table 14-6.

Table 14-6 Application VbDest objects and property settings

Object	Property	Setting
Form	Caption	Destination Application
	Height	2175
	LinkMode	0 - None
	Name	frmDest
	Width	4665
TextBox	Height	330
	Left	1560
	Name	txtReceive
	Text	""
	Top	450
	Width	2505

Object	Property	Setting
Frame	Caption	Link Mode
	Height	1110
	Left	195
	Name	Frame1
	Top	345
	Width	1230
OptionButton	Caption	Manual
	Height	315
	Left	90
	Name	optManual
	Top	240
	Width	1020
OptionButton	Caption	Automatic
	Height	315
	Left	90
	Name	optAutomatic
	Top	465
	Width	1020
OptionButton	Caption	Notify
	Height	315
	Left	90
	Name	optNotify
	Top	975
	Width	1020
CommandButton	Caption	Conversation
	Height	465
	Left	1530
	Name	cmdConversation
	Top	990
	Width	1185

continued on next page

continued from previous page

Object	Property	Setting
CommandButton	Caption	Get Data
	Height	465
	Left	2760
	Name	cmdGetData
	Top	990
	Width	1185

Add the code shown in Listing 14-6 to the `Click` event of the Command button `cmdConversation`.

Listing 14-6 Command button `cmdConversation` `Click` event

```
Private Sub cmdConversation_Click()
  '
  'Start DDE conversation
  '
  cmdGetData.Enabled = False
  ' Set DDE link to None
  txtReceive.LinkMode = vbLinkNone
  'Establish Topic to Source
  txtReceive.LinkTopic = "VBSrc|frmSource"
  'Establish the item of conversation
  txtReceive.LinkItem = "txtItem"
  'Set Timeout to 10 seconds
  txtReceive.LinkTimeout = 100
  '
  'Determine the type of link
  '
  If optManual.Value = True Then
    cmdGetData.Enabled = True
    txtReceive.LinkMode = vbLinkManual
  ElseIf optAutomatic.Value = True Then
    txtReceive.LinkMode = vbLinkAutomatic
  ElseIf optNotify.Value = True Then
    txtReceive.LinkMode = vbLinkNotify
  End If

End Sub
```

Add the code shown in Listing 14-7 to the `Click` event of the `cmdGetData` Command button.

Listing 14-7 Command button `cmdGetData` `Click` event

```
Private Sub cmdGetData_Click()
  'Get data from the source
  txtReceive.LinkRequest
End Sub
```

Figure 14-9
DDE test
applications

Add the code shown in Listing 14-8 to the **LinkNotify** event of the **txtReceive** TextBox.

Listing 14-8 TextBox **txtReceive LinkNotify** event

```
Private Sub txtReceive_LinkNotify()
  MsgBox "Link Notify Event Received"
  cmdGetData.Enabled = True
End Sub
```

Run the destination application from Visual Basic. You should now have both applications running. To test the applications, select a conversation mode by using the radio buttons on the destination application. Once you have selected a mode, press the Command button Conversation. Switch to the source application and enter text. If you have established a DDE automatic link, when you enter text in the text box of the source application, you will see the text appear in the destination application's TextBox control. For Manual and Notify modes you must click the button Get Data to retrieve the data from the source. Try the different modes. Remember, after you select a new mode with the radio buttons, you must click the Conversation button to establish the new DDE mode. The two applications are shown in Figure 14-9.

1. DDE stands for:
    a. Destination to Destination Exchange
    b. Destination Data Exchange
    c. Dynamic Destination Exchange
    d. Dynamic Data Exchange

2. The _____ initiates the DDE exchange.
    a. Source application
    b. Destination application
    c. LinkMode application
    d. Initiator application

3. The _____ property specifies the type of DDE link established between two applications.
   a. `LinkMode`
   b. `LinkItem`
   c. `LinkType`
   d. `LinkSource`

4. Which one of the following is not a valid `LinkMode` property setting for a destination?
   a. `None`
   b. `Manual`
   c. `All`
   d. `Notify`

5. The ____ occurs when a DDE link is established.
   a. `LinkNotify` event
   b. `LinkRequest` event
   c. `LinkOpen` event
   d. `LinkError` event

CREATING AN EXECUTABLE

You have written many different applications while working with this book. In this lesson you will learn the various options available to create an *executable* for your applications. Creating an executable file allows you and your user to run your applications from the Windows environment without having to be in Visual Basic.

Generating an Executable

What happens when you generate an executable for an application? Visual Basic builds a Windows file that can run outside of the Visual Basic design environment by compiling the forms and code in the project. The file created has an `.EXE` extension and is called an executable file. The executable file can be run from the Windows desktop by clicking on its icon or by running the executable from the Run task bar in Windows.

Compiling NotePad.EXE

To create an executable for the NotePad application, perform the following steps:

1. Open the NotePad project from the Chapter 12 files.

2. Select Make EXE File from the File menu.

3. The Make Project dialog box, in Figure 14-10, appears. The default name for the executable is the same as the Visual Basic project name. If you want to use another name for your executable file, modify the text in the FileName text box. For this exercise, do not change it.

4. Click the Options button to bring up the dialog box shown in Figure 14-11.

5. Use the Project Properties dialog box to customize your executable file.

Let's examine some of the options found on the EXE Options dialog box.

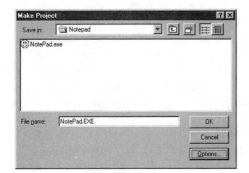

Figure 14-10
Make Project
dialog box

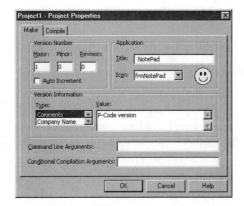

Figure 14-11
Project Properties
dialog box

Version Number

The options in the Version Number are used to assign version release numbers to your executable files. An example might be NotePad Version 3.1.2, where 3 is the major revision number, 1 the minor revision number, and 2 the revision number of the project. If the Auto Increment check box is selected, the Revision number is increased every time you create an executable file for the project. Increment the Major revision number when the application goes through a large number of changes or you add major new functionality. The Minor revision number is for small changes and bug fixes to the application.

Application

The frame labeled Application contains a Title text box and drop-down combo box to add an icon to the executable file. The Title text box is the name of the executable file to create; it has the same effect as the FileName option on the Make EXE dialog box. The Icon drop-down combo box allows you to choose an icon to assign the application. The list of icons is taken from the icons assigned to forms in the project. In the example, the form frmNotePad has the smiley face icon assigned to it. Selecting the icon in the drop-down list box assigns it to the executable file.

Version Information

The version information frame allows you to enter values for various types of information. The Type list box contains the following values:

- Comments
- Company Name
- File Description
- Legal Copyright
- Legal Trademarks
- Product Name

Click on Comments and add P-Code version to the Value box. Then click on Company Name and add Interactive VB5 to the Value box. These values will become part of the executable file's properties. You can see them in Windows Explorer by right-clicking on the file icon and selecting Properties.

Now, finish making the EXE file.

6. After you have set the values on the EXE Options dialog box, click the OK button and return to the Make EXE dialog box.

7. Click the OK button in the Make EXE dialog box. Visual Basic begins to compile the application. It's not very exciting to watch—all there is is the Hourglass icon and the blinking of your hard disk activity light.

You can use the Windows Explorer to verify that the executable file has been created by going to the appropriate folder and searching for a **NotePad.EXE** file.

Find the executable file you just created and execute the application by double-clicking the file.

Compiling NativePad.EXE

By default, Visual Basic 5 compiles its executables to P-code, but you can also compile to native code. Programs compiled into native code run faster than programs compiled into P-code because they don't need to be interpreted.

Repeat steps one through five. Change the file name from **NotePad** to **NativePad**. In the Project Properties window, change the comment to **Native code version**. Then click on the Compile tab and select Compile to Native Code. Select Optimize for Small Code and click the OK button. The Compile tab is shown in Figure 14-12.

After you click OK, click the OK button on the Make Project dialog. The compiler has to work harder to compile native code, so the process is not as fast.

When it is all done, use Windows Explorer to view both files. The **NativePad.EXE** file is slightly larger than the **NotePad.EXE** because some of the things that were done by DLL files in NotePad are now built in to NativePad. If you run the two programs side by side, you will not notice a lot of difference in their speed. Why not? Mainly because it is a small program that doesn't really *do* much. If it were a large program filled with number-crunching and data access, you would see a big difference.

You can also create an executable file from the command line. This comes in handy if you use batch programs to recompile several projects at once.

To create an executable from the command line, go to a DOS window and enter the following:

```
vb /make project_name [exename] [switches]
```

where

- project_name is the name of the Visual Basic project to build the executable.

- exename is an optional parameter if you want to select a different file name for the executable.

- switches are any compile switches to use while creating the executable file for the project.

See the help file for more information.

Now you can create executables for all of your applications and run them in the Windows environment without having to be in Visual Basic. What do you do if you want to give your application to someone else? That's covered in the next lesson.

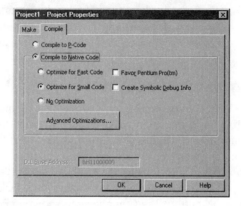

Figure 14-12
The Compile tab

1. When you create an executable application for Visual Basic the file created can be:
   a. Executed outside the Visual Basic design environment
   b. Executed from the Visual Basic design environment
   c. A text file
   d. A database file

2. The option _____ on the EXE Options dialog box allows you to assign release numbers to an executable.
   a. Release Number
   b. Version Number
   c. Application Number
   d. EXE Number

3. The option _____ on the EXE Options dialog box allows you to name the executable file.
   a. Release Number
   b. Name
   c. Title
   d. Information

4. The following DOS command line:

   `vb /make NotePad`

   a. Searches for the file **NotePad**
   b. Displays information about the file **NotePad**
   c. Removes the file **NotePad**
   d. Creates an executable file using the Visual Basic project NotePad

USING THE SETUP WIZARD

In the last lesson, you learned how to create executable files for your Visual Basic projects. This lesson teaches you how to distribute your application to other users. Unfortunately, this may not be as easy as creating an executable file, copying the executable file to a disk, and then running your application from another PC. When Visual Basic creates a P-code executable file, the P-code requires the file **VBRUN500.DLL** to interpret the P-code. Even if the **.EXE** file were truly compiled and did not require the **VBRUN500.DLL**, your application still might not be able to run. Any OCXs and DLLs you used must be on the end user's PC or the application will not be able to execute properly. The OCXs and DLLs can also require a lot of storage space to distribute on your application's floppy disks.

To distribute your application, you will need to install the application **.EXE** file, **VBRUN500.DLL**, and any **.OCX** and **.DLL** files that your project uses.

Fortunately, Visual Basic comes with a utility to allow you to create distribution floppies for your applications with ease. The utility is called the *Setup Wizard*. The Setup Wizard performs the following functions:

- Creates a setup program

- Builds the executable file

- Compresses files (EXEs, DLLs, OCXs, and so on)

- Determines the number of disks required to distribute your application

- Copies all the files required for distribution to blank floppy disk

- Optionally copies the necessary files to hard disk for network distribution or makes *Disk Image files* that make it easy to make many copies of your distribution disks.

The Setup Wizard is an application distributed with Visual Basic and is not invoked from the Visual Basic design environment. You will find it in the Visual Basic 5 program group on the Startup menu.

Walking Through the Setup Wizard

The Setup Wizard guides you through the steps required to create a program to distribute your application by asking you questions about your application and by examining your project file. This exercise will walk you through each step of the Setup Wizard. Start the Setup Wizard.

1. Figure 14-13 shows the Setup Wizard. The first question is the name and location of the project you want to distribute. You can use the Browse button shown in Figure 14-13 to select a project, or you can enter the path and project name in the Project File box. Check the Rebuild Project's EXE option if you want the Setup Wizard to recompile your application and generate a new executable; otherwise, the Setup Wizard will use the existing EXE file. Select the NotePad project that you just compiled, `NotePad.vbp`, which was originally created in Chapter 12, Files. Other options that you may need from time to time are

   - *Generate Dependency File*: Generates a file that contains dependency information and includes it in the setup. Dependency files are used for any object of an .OCX, .DLL, or .EXE, ActiveX component, or a project that could be used as a component in other projects. The dependency file is included with your setup program.

   - *Create Internet Download Setup*: Allows you to create an Internet download setup for only ActiveX Control projects, ActiveX EXE, and ActiveX DLL projects that have public classes, including projects that contain `UserDocuments`. If you have the Learning Edition of Visual Basic, you will not see this choice.

   - *Generate Dependency File Only*: Generates a dependency file with the same name as your project and a `.dep` extension, and places it in the same directory as your project.

   - *Create a Setup Program:* Select this, and click the Next button. The Setup Wizard will move to the next step in the distribution process.

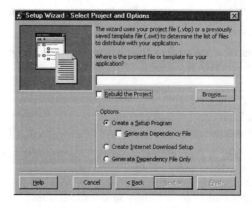

Figure 14-13
Application Setup
Wizard—step 1

2. The next window offers you a choice of distribution media. You can choose

   ● *Floppy Disk* if you just want to make a single set of distribution disks.

   ● *Single Directory* for distribution over a network or by compact disk.

   ● *Disk Directories*, which creates an *image* of floppy disk distribution files. You can copy the disk images to floppy to make multiple copies of the distribution set.

If you have a couple of floppy disks on hand, select Floppy Disk. If not, select Disk Directories. The Distribution Method dialog is shown in Figure 14-14. When you have made your selection, click on Next.

3. If you selected Floppy Disk distribution, the dialog in Figure 14-15 lets you select the disk drive and the disk size for the distribution disks. Make the selections that match your system, and click on Next.

   While you were answering questions, the Setup Wizard has been busy analyzing your VBP file and its components. Among other things, it has checked your project for its use of ActiveX components. The dialog box in Figure 14-16 reports the ActiveX components that were found and allows you to add any that were missed. NotePad does not use any ActiveX components. Click on Next.

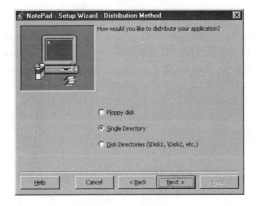

Figure 14-14
The Distribution
method dialog

Figure 14-15
Choosing the floppy disk

Figure 14-16
The Setup Wizard's ActiveX component dialog box

5. The Setup Wizard also detects *dependencies*, which are the .DLL and .OCX files that your project requires beyond the ones that are always included. The Confirm Dependencies dialog in Figure 14-17 lists the dependencies that were found. You can remove any file from the list, but be aware that your distributed program probably will not run if the file is not already on the target platform (your user's computer, that is). You can get more information by clicking on the File Details button. (Surprise!) Click on Next when you are done.

6. The next dialog is the File Summary dialog. It is a list of the standard .DLL and .OCX files that must be distributed with your application. The dialog is shown in Figure 14-18.

If there are additional files that your application needs—Help files, database files, or any others—use the Add button to include them as well. The Summary Details button tells you how many files must be distributed, and totals their size.

7. Finished! The only choice left on the dialog shown in Figure 14-19 is whether or not to save a *template* for your project. The template simplifies the creation of another set of setup disks if you make changes in your project. You won't need them for this one. Click on Finish.

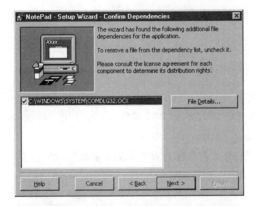

Figure 14-17
The Dependency
dialog box

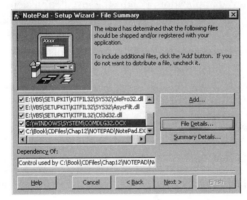

Figure 14-18
The File Summary
Wizard

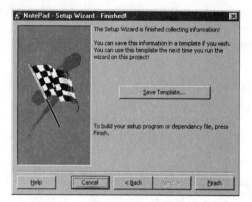

Figure 14-19
Finished!

8. The Setup Wizard then sets about collecting and compressing the files for your very own `Setup.exe` program. The files are all compressed and packed into as small a space as possible. The compressed set of files for `NOTEPAD.EXE` only take about two megs of disk space.

Testing the Distribution Floppies

Try out the distribution floppy(ies) you just created by placing the first floppy disk in the drive and running **SETUP.EXE**. The setup application created by the Setup Wizard installs the NotePad application. Follow the installation steps and install the application on your PC. If possible, find a PC that has never had Visual Basic installed. One of the hardest parts of creating an application for distribution is to make sure that all the DLLs, OCXs, and other files are all in the right places. Installing on a PC that lacks Visual Basic or the application you're testing helps you locate the missing files so you can add them to the setup process. Once you have installed the application, make sure you test it. The Setup Wizard is a good utility to speed up application development!

1. The Visual Basic application to help you distribute your applications is called the:
   a. Application Distribution program
   b. Setup Wizard
   c. Distribution Wizard
   d. Setup program

2. Can you use hard drives or network drives as application distribution media?
   a. Yes
   b. No
   c. Network drive only
   d. Local hard drives only

3. The Visual Basic Setup Wizard performs all the following except:
   a. Creating a setup program
   b. Building the executable file
   c. Compressing files
   d. Creating a printable setup error and status report

4. What is the default media format for floppy disk distribution?
   a. 1.44MB
   b. 640K
   c. 1.22MB
   d. 320K

5. Running the **SETUP.EXE** for the NotePad application created by the Setup Wizard:
   a. Executes the Setup Wizard
   b. Executes a program to install the NotePad application
   c. Executes the NotePad application
   d. Executes Visual Basic

APPLICATION OPTIMIZATION

Optimizing is the process of tweaking your code so that it runs better or faster, or uses less memory. One aspect of optimization is to make your program *seem* to run faster even though it doesn't. This lesson introduces optimization, but you should keep in mind that optimization is an ongoing process that should begin before you write the first line of code.

Optimization Goals

If you compile a project to native code, the Compile tab on the Project Properties dialog box offers a choice of optimization techniques: Optimize for Small Code and Optimize for Fast Code. (There are a couple of specialized check boxes, too, but they require machine code techniques that are meaningless at the Visual Basic code level.) The suggestion is that you can have one or the other, and that is essentially true. But many of the techniques that generate small code also enhance a program's speed, if only because they create better organized programs.

Getting Started: The Appearance of Speed

If your programs are going to be used by other people, one of the first things you want to do is make them at least *appear* to load faster. How many times have you sat in front of your computer, drumming your fingers and waiting for that doggone program to load? The first thing to do is add a splash screen, that fancy little gizmo that pops up and keeps your mind occupied for a while until the real program loads.

Even the splash screen can be optimized.

● Keep it simple. The fewer controls, the better. If it has a picture, use an Image control instead of a PictureBox (more on that later).

● Use the Show method in the form load event. Use code like this:

```
Sub Form_Load ()
'    Make it paint
     Show
'    Give it a chance to paint
     DoEvents
'    Load the main form
     Load frmMain
'    Get rid of this memory hog
     Unload Me
'    Bring up frmMain
     frmMain.Show
End Sub
```

When a form is loaded, all of the code in the load event is executed before the form is shown. The **Show** method forces the form to be painted before the event is completed, and the **DoEvents** gives the processor the time to do the paint job. The splash form stays on the screen until **frmMain** has been completely loaded. Once that is done, there is no need for it, and it is unloaded to free the memory that it used. As a final act, it invokes the **Show** method on **frmMain**. Since **frmMain** is already loaded, the **Show** method brings it up instantly.

More Appearance Issues

If your project has more than one modeless form, consider loading all of them at start-up while your user is enjoying the splash screen. You *will* take a memory hit for this, but it may be worth it. To switch from **frmMain** to **frmSecondChoice** requires only:

```
frmSecondChoice.Show
frmMain.Hide
```

and the form snaps onto the screen. It can be impressive!

If there is data that you know your application will need, preload it. Get it into memory while your splash screen is still up. It will add a slight delay to your startup time, but the data will *be there* when you need it. No need to wait for that slow, slow hard drive. (Remember when you thought it was fast?)

Loading the forms and data may seem to take an uncomfortably long time. So add a progress bar to your splash screen. It really does create enough distraction to keep your user's mind occupied.

Get rid of everything you don't need. There's no way to write a program that doesn't use any DLL files or any OLE files. Actually, it would be a pretty dull program if you could! But Visual Basic includes some controls by default that you may not be using. And you may have added some custom controls to your project that you never used, but never deleted, either. If a custom control is on the toolbar, it will be included in your project, and it will be loaded into memory along with the ones you *are* using. Open the Components dialog before you compile your program and un-select everything that VB will allow. Do the same with the References dialog. For example, by default VB always includes OLE Automation in your project references. It adds a considerable overhead that you may not need. (If it is actually in use, you won't be allowed to delete it.)

Optimizing Display Speed

Because Windows is so graphical, the display speed contributes to the perceived speed of your application. Keep the following in mind:

- Turn off `ClipControls` unless you are using graphical methods.

- If you can spare the memory, set `AutoRedraw` to `True` for complicated forms.

- Use the Image control instead of a PictureBox control. The Image control is always faster.

- Make controls invisible when you are resizing or moving them with code. When you resize a control, Windows must erase it from the screen, repaint the background where it was, and *repaint* it at its new size. When you move a control, Windows must erase it from the screen, repaint the background where it was, and *repaint* it in its new location. Both take time. Making the control invisible reduces the number of repaints and improves the speed greatly.

- If you have to move a lot of controls, put them in a picture box and set its `Visible` property to `False`. Then you can move the picture box, or move the controls within the picture box. When you make the picture box visible again, one repaint does the whole job.

Optimizing Real Speed

Following just a few rules can enhance your program's actual operating speed. Unless you are doing major calculations, the improvement might not be apparent. More than likely, the video speed of the computer, network delays and disk I/O will affect the program's speed more than anything you can do in code. Still, try the following:

● Avoid variant variables. This is important from a size viewpoint, too. Be sure that you Dim every variable in your program. You might have noticed Option Explicit throughout your reading of this book. That simple declaration *forces* all variables to be declared. While you are declaring them, give them a type.

● Use integers where you can, using long integers as a second choice.

● Use Double in preference to Currency for calculations.

● Use variables rather than properties. Using a property in an expression always triggers an event. For example, to align an array of text boxes with another text box:

```
For i = 0 to 10
   txtData(1).Left = txtOther.Left
Next i
```

is slow, while

```
iLeft = txtOther.Left
For i = 0 to 10
   txtData(1).Left = txtOther.Left
Next i
```

is much faster.

● Use For...Each rather than For...Next where applicable.

● Use With...End With to resolve object references.

● Reduce what you do inside your loops.

Optimizing Size

● Avoid variants. (Heard that before?)

● Reclaim memory space used by global arrays and strings that are no longer needed. Use code like sString = "" to reclaim string space. And use Erase arrLongArray to get rid of the space used up by an array.

● Unload forms you no longer need. Hiding a form only makes it invisible.

● If you no longer need a picture, get rid of it with Image1.Picture = Loadpicture() or Set Image1.Picture = Nothing.

● Use Image controls instead of PictureBox when you can. Image controls are *lightweight* controls that use far fewer resources.

● Share your picture. If you need the same picture in several different places, don't load it into each place. Using the following code requires that the picture only be in memory once. That saves loading time *and* memory.

```
pixStored = LoadPicture("C:\Windows\Arches.BMP")
Image1.Picture = pixStored
Picture1.Picture = pixStored
```

● Use RLE or WMF pictures instead of bitmaps.

● Take out the trash. Chances are your program has been through a lot of false tries. You have added controls to a form, then changed your mind and removed them. If you added code to their events, did you get rid of that, too? When you delete a control, its code moves from its normal position into the General section of the code, where your user-defined procedures and functions are placed. While you are at it, get rid of those variables you added and never used. Take out the trash!

Summary of Optimization

This lesson provides a beginning look at optimization. As your skills and knowledge improve, you will find more optimizing techniques. The important thing to remember about optimization is that you must begin optimizing with the first line of code, not after it is all written.

1. Putting the Show method in the Form_Load procedure:
   a. Raises a fatal error
   b. Has no effect on the program
   c. Causes the form to be painted, but all of the controls are transparent
   d. Causes the form to be painted before the rest of the load procedure runs

2. If loading data and forms at startup seems to take too long, one trick you can use is to:
   a. Use a Timer control to load them in the background
   b. Add a progress bar to the form
   c. Add an OLE server to store the data
   d. None of the above

3. Avoiding the use of variant variables:
   a. Improves speed
   b. Improves program size
   c. Both a and b are correct
   d. None of the above

4. Use `With...End With` to resolve object references to improve:
   a. Speed
   b. Size
   c. Both speed and size
   d. Apparent speed

5. Which of the following code fragments is best for putting the same picture into several controls?
   a.
   ```
   Picture1.Picture = "C:\Windows\Arches.bmp"
   Image1.Picture = "C:\Windows\Arches.bmp"
   ```

   b.
   ```
   pixStore = LoadPicture()
   Picture1.Picture = pixStore
   Image1.Picture = "pixStore
   ```

   c.
   ```
   pixStore = LoadPicture("C:\Windows\Arches.bmp")
   Picture1.Picture = pixStore
   Image1.Picture = "pixStore
   ```

   d.
   ```
   Image1.Picture = "C:\Windows\Arches.bmp"
   Picture1.Picture = Image1
   ```

INTERFACING WITH EXCEL AND OTHER PROGRAMS

This chapter introduces a new method of designing and building applications with Visual Basic: using OLE. Using object-oriented techniques and OLE, you can build your own software components. This chapter examines the different features of OLE. It explains how to create applications that use the Visual Basic OLE container control to link and embed documents from Microsoft Word and Microsoft Excel. It explains OLE automation and how to create OLE client and server applications. This chapter also provides a review of Visual Basic's system objects and a simple methodology to help design OLE objects.

WHAT IS OLE?

You have just written a really good application, maybe a slick notepad or text editor. You are showing the application off, and someone asks, "Can you do spell checking?" You think to yourself, "Spell checking? No way! It would take longer to write a spell checker than it took to develop the entire application!" The moral of this story is that people expect more from their applications today.

But all is not lost. A few years ago, Microsoft and several other ISVs (Integrated System Vendors) created an open specification that allows applications to communicate with one another. The specification also defines a programming interface to use another application's objects, including that spell checker. Application developers can use objects from existing applications to enhance their own applications, rather than reinventing the wheel. And now OLE has been extended with ActiveX technology so that it works with intranet and Internet applications. Reusable components mean faster application development and higher quality applications. The open standard created by Microsoft and the ISVs is *OLE* (Object Linking and Embedding). Microsoft has been preaching the virtues of OLE to developers with the claim that OLE is a major technology in today's applications.

In its infancy OLE represented the ability to link and embed documents from one application to another. However, OLE has grown into several standards for interprocess communication, object storage, and object reuse. Before you start looking at all of the major technologies that make up OLE, study a few OLE terms to make the discussion more meaningful.

- *Compound Documents*: Documents that contain data from more than one application

- *OLE Object*: Data that is stored or linked in a compound document, for example, a spreadsheet, a Word document, or a sound file

- *Container/Controller/Client Application:* An application that can create and manage OLE objects

- *Server/Object Application:* An application that creates OLE objects

- *Visual Editing:* Objects that activate in place and can be edited without manually switching to another application

- *ActiveX:* An extension of OLE technology that extends OLE to Internet and intranet applications

OLE allows you to display and use data from other applications and to edit data from the applications that created them. And OLE enables you to include functionality and objects found in other applications. Consider some of the different ways OLE is used.

Custom Controls

Did you know that with Visual Basic you have been using OLE all along? In Visual Basic Version 3, the custom controls (like the Data Bound list box) are called VBXs. Visual Basic 5 uses the OLE custom control known as an OCX (OLE Custom Control) instead. Even though VB 5 OCX controls look and act like the corresponding VB 3 VBX controls, they are actually very different. VBXs are tied to the 16-bit architecture of Windows 3.x, and cannot take advantage of the advances in 32-bit Windows. VBXs are fast and use Windows messaging for communication. However, VBXs are not portable to 32 bits and have limited application support. The OCX, however, is based on OLE technology. OCXs communicate via OLE interfaces, 32-bit, and can work with any OLE enabled application. OCXs are as fast as VBXs because they are implemented as an in-process OLE server, meaning that the OCX and the application share the same address space so that communications is not across applications, but within the same application.

OLE Automation

OLE automation is a standard that allows applications to expose their objects and methods so that other applications can use them. Examples include Microsoft Word's spell checker and Excel's calculating abilities. Sound confusing? OLE automation is covered in detail in Lesson 3, and Lesson 5 uses OLE automation to integrate Microsoft Word's spell checker into the Notepad application developed in Chapter 12, Files.

Object Linking and Embedding

The next stop in your tour of OLE technology is *object linking and embedding*. Object linking and embedding allows you to create applications that are document centered. You can work with data from several applications without having to exit your application. Object linking and embedding allows you to work with applications with which you are already familiar.

What is the main difference between a linked object and an embedded object? Figure 15-1 shows an example of a linked object.

When an object is linked, the container application contains a pointer or *reference* to the object, not the actual data. If the object is modified, the application that created the object saves the data. Linking a document is useful when you want to share the same data across many users or with different applications. If the linked object is changed by one application, other applications linking to the object will have the changed data. Note that to link an Excel chart, Excel must be running and accessible from both computers.

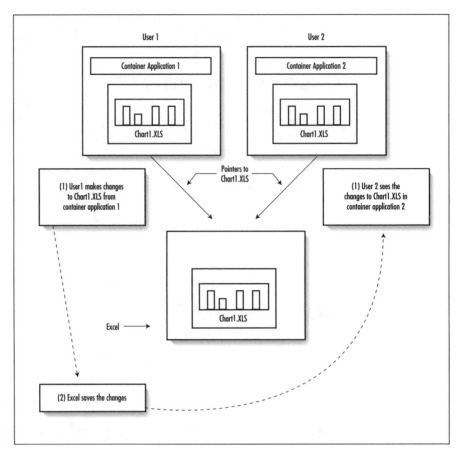

Figure 15-1
Linked object

Figure 15-2 shows an embedded object. With an embedded object, the data exists within the container application. When the object is first created, the object's data is copied into the container application, and no other applications have access to the data. If an application modifies an embedded document, other applications do not see the changes. Embedded objects travel with the container applications. Use embedded objects when you want to display and edit data that was created in another application, but you want to maintain the data from within your application without opening the application that created the data.

Embedded or linked, the objects you access with OLE are accessed by way of a *server*. The server for an Excel chart, for example, is Excel. Your user must have Excel in order to use the embedded chart.

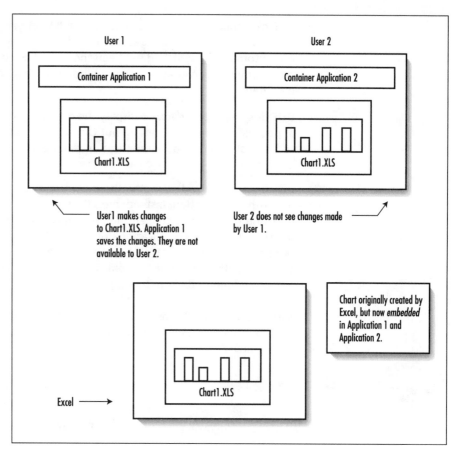

Figure 15-2
Embedded object

Visual Editing

Visual editing allows you to edit an OLE object without having to switch to the application that created the object. *Embedded* objects support visual editing, while *linked* objects do not support it.

What About DDE?

So what about DDE (Dynamic Data Exchange)? After all, DDE allows you to share data between two applications and is a form of interprocess communication. When do you use DDE over OLE, or vice versa?

Both OLE and DDE provide a method of direct interprocess communication and allow you to display data from other applications and use functions from other applications. However, the abilities of the two technologies are very different. (OLE is the most able technology.) Here is a comparison.

● DDE exchanges data via a conversation (link) between two applications. While data is being exchanged between the two applications, control is not automatically switched between them. In OLE, control actually transfers to the OLE server application temporarily while the data is being modified.

● DDE does not permit you to display the data from one application as it appears in another application, but OLE allows data from one application to be displayed in another application *as it appears* in the original application.

● DDE does not provide a method to modify the data from one application in another application. Instead, modifications must be done by sending data and commands between the two applications. OLE provides an interface to another application's objects and methods that can be used programmatically to control the objects. Also, OLE allows the user to edit and modify the data directly from your application using the application menus and methods from the application that created the object.

In general, always use OLE instead of DDE; use DDE only in cases where OLE is not yet supported by the application. You should now have a better understanding of OLE and its capabilities.

1. Which of the following is *not* part of OLE technology?
   a. OCX
   b. OLE automation
   c. Embedding documents
   d. OLE DDE exchange

2. _____ is the equivalent of the VBX it replaced.
   a. OLE server
   b. OCX
   c. OLE automation
   d. OLE container

3. A(n) _____ document can be shared by many applications. Modifications are saved by the application that created the object, and the changes are reflected in the other applications.
   a. Linked
   b. Embedded
   c. OLE automation
   d. Container

4. An embedded document is created from **CHART1.XLS**. Application 1 modifies the chart significantly. Application 2 then creates an embedded document from **CHART1.XLS**. The chart displayed in application 1 is:
   a. Different than the chart display in application 2.
   b. The same as the chart displayed in application 2.
   c. Invalid because application 2 cannot use **CHART1.XLS** after application 1 saved the modification.
   d. The same, once application 2 does an OLE refresh.

5. Which one of the following is *not* a characteristic of OLE but of DDE?
   a. Documents displayed in the same view as the creating application
   b. Programmatic interface to an application's objects and methods
   c. Ability to edit the document from the container application
   d. No automatic switching from one application to another during data modifications

USING THE OLE CONTAINER CONTROL

This lesson demonstrates how to use the OLE container control provided by Visual Basic 5 to integrate object and linking capabilities into your applications. The OLE container control is shown in Figure 15-3.

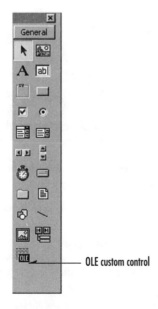

— OLE custom control

Figure 15-3
OLE custom control

The OLE container control allows you to link or embed objects from other applications by providing a place to insert objects into your Visual Basic application or display objects you create at runtime. Here are some of the OLE container control properties you will be using.

Class

The `Class` property is used to set or return the class of an embedded object. For example, the class of the embedded Excel chart shown in Figure 15-2 is Excel.Chart.5. The class name *identifies* the object you are embedding.

Object

The `Object` property is used to access the methods or properties of an embedded object. It is a read-only property and is not visible in the Properties window.

OLEType

The `OLEType` property is only available at runtime and can be used to determine whether the container control is empty or contains a linked or embedded object. Because it is a runtime-only property, it does not appear in the Properties window.

OLETypeAllowed

`OLETypeAllowed` can be set at runtime or design time and determines the type of object the container control can contain: linked, embedded, or either.

Using the OLE Control to Link and Embed Data

This project helps you learn how to use the OLE container for visual editing and linking and embedding documents. The following examples use Microsoft Excel Version 7 and Microsoft Word Version 7. If you do not have these applications, you will still be able to use the OLE container control using whatever OLE objects are available on your PC. (Don't worry if you're not sure what OLE objects are on your PC.)

Start a new project named learnole. The learnole application will consist of a single form with two OLE container controls and a few command buttons, labels, and text boxes. The objects in the OLE containers of the learnole application are

- An embedded Excel chart to demonstrate embedded documents, visual editing, and in-place activation

- A linked Word document to demonstrate the differences between linking and embedding

To keep things simple and fast, all of the OLE container control's objects will be inserted at design time instead of at runtime. Set the following properties on the form and objects, as shown in Table 15-1.

Table 15-1 Object and property settings for project learnole

Object	Property	Setting
Form	Caption	VB 5 Interactive Course Learn OLE
	Height	6345
	Name	frmLearnOLE
	Width	6810
Lable1	Caption	Class
	Height	315
	Left	1740
	Name	lblClass
	Top	5400
	Width	60
ComboBox	Height	315
	Left	720
	Name	cmbOLE
	Style	2 - Dropdown List
	Width	1680
TextBox	Height	315
	Left	3195
	Name	txtClass
	Top	5520
	Width	2640

Add the following menu items, as shown in Table 15-2.

Table 15-2 Menu for `frmLearnOLE`

Menu Name	Caption
mnuFile	&File
mnuEdit	&Edit

Add an OLE container control to the form. The Insert Object dialog box, shown in Figure 15-4, will appear.

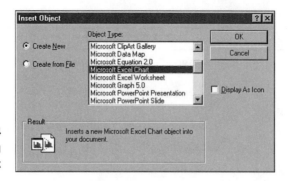

Figure 15-4
Insert Object dialog
box

The Insert Object dialog box appears every time you add an OLE control, and is used to insert embedded or linked objects in the container control at design time. Select an object to place in the container control from the list of available objects. If it is available on your PC, select Microsoft Excel Chart. Check the Create New option in the Insert Object dialog box and click the OK button. You have just created an embedded object in the OLE container control. Set the properties for the OLE control as shown in Table 15-3.

Table 15-3 Property settings for OLE control with embedded Excel chart

Object	Property	Setting
OLE	Height	2550
	Left	885
	Name	OLE_Embed
	Top	570
	Width	5340

Add another OLE container control to the application. This time, select the option Create From File on the Insert Object dialog box. If you have Microsoft Word, select the file that comes with this book, learnole.doc, or select any document on your PC. After you have selected the file, check the box Link to link the document instead of embedding the document. Set the properties for the OLE control as shown in Table 15-4.

Table 15-4 Property settings for OLE control with linked Word document

Object	Property	Setting
OLE	Height	1980
	Left	930
	Name	OLE_Link

Object	Property	Setting
	Top	3405
	Width	5190

Add the code shown in Listing 15-1 to the form load event.

Listing 15-1 `frmLearnOLE FormLoad` event code

```
Private Sub Form_Load()
    '
    'Add The Following the Combo Box
    '
    cmbOLE.AddItem "Link"
    cmbOLE.AddItem "Embed"
    cmbOLE.ListIndex = 0
End Sub
```

Add the code in Listing 15-2 to the `Click` event of the ComboBox to display the `Class` of the selected OLE container control.

Listing 15-2 `cmbOLE` ComboBox `Click` event code

```
Private Sub cmbOLE_Click()
    '
    'Display the Object class in the
    'text box - toggle value with the
    'Combo box
    '
    If cmbOLE.Text = "Link" Then
        txtClass.Text = OLE_Link.Class
    Else
        txtClass.Text = OLE_Embed.Class
    End If
End Sub
```

Now run the application. First, select Embed in the drop combo box list. Notice the format of the `Class` property, displayed in the text box control for the selected OLE control. Now, activate the embedded object, the Excel spreadsheet, by double-clicking on the OLE container control. What happened? You have activated the object in the container and invoked visual editing. A border appears around the container control signifying that the control has been activated and that the menu options for the learnole application have been replaced with Excel's menu options, shown in Figure 15-5.

You can use the menu options in your application as if you were using Excel instead of your application. Try it. Use the menu options to change the chart from 2D to 3D by selecting the Format menu option and then selecting Chart Type. Try some of the other Chart Type options, too.

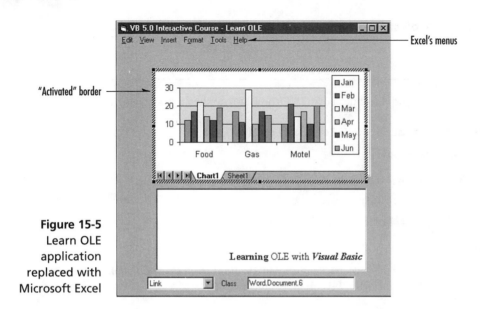

"Activated" border

Excel's menus

Figure 15-5
Learn OLE
application
replaced with
Microsoft Excel

To see the difference between embedded and linked documents, double-click on the OLE container control that holds the Word document. What happens? Microsoft Word is activated and becomes the active window. You can modify the linked document using Microsoft Word. To see this in action, change some text to bold and add something. Then save the changes in Word and exit from Word. What is displayed in the OLE container control after you changed the information? The changed information appears in the OLE container control, of course.

How would you save information in the embedded worksheet? Since the worksheet is embedded, Visual Basic code must be used to save the data to a file and to read the data back at application startup. Do this with the OLE container control methods **SaveToFile** and **ReadFromFile**.

This lesson clearly demonstrates the difference between linked and embedded documents. It also shows the one weakness in OLE linking and embedding: When you activate an OLE document, the OLE container (program) must be loaded before you can edit the document. The very perceptible delay makes your application seem sluggish. You can improve the appearance of speed by using the **Shell** function to load the OLE server for linked documents while your splash screen is showing. The code

```
Dim dWordID As Double
    dWordID = Shell("C:\MSOFFICE\WINWORD\WINWORD.EXE", vbMinimizedNoFocus)
```

loads Word, but leaves it minimized and keeps the focus in your application.

1. The OLE container control allows you to:
   a. Easily link and embed OLE documents
   b. Turn your application into an OLE server
   c. Contain OLE applications like Microsoft Word and Excel
   d. Perform visual editing on a linked document

2. The correct way to represent an Excel Version 5 chart in the **Class** property of an OLE container control is:
   a. 5.Chart.Excel
   b. Excel.Chart.5
   c. Microsoft.Excel5.Chart
   d. Excel5.Chart

3. A(n) ____ document supports visual editing.
   a. Linked
   b. Stored
   c. OLE automation
   d. Embedded

4. When an OLE embedded document is activated, the ____ take(s) the appearance of the object creating application.
   a. Form
   b. Menu
   c. Buttons
   d. Text boxes

5. Use the new methods of the OLE container control to work on an object instead of the ____ property.
   a. **Work**
   b. **SourceDoc**
   c. **Action**
   d. **LinkItem**

Write a program that uses two OLE container controls. Select an OLE object such as a Microsoft Word document or an Excel spreadsheet and link the object to one OLE container control and embed the object in the other control. Run the program and experiment with the differences between a linked and an embedded object. Write the code required to save the embedded object.

WHAT IS OLE AUTOMATION?

This lesson examines OLE automation. To gain an understanding of what OLE automation is all about, consider the concept of exposed objects.

Exposed Objects

Look to your bank for a good example of exposed objects. As a bank customer, you can go into the lobby of the bank to do your banking, depositing or withdrawing money and checking your account balance. Before computers, that was the only way you could do your banking. Now computers have revolutionized banking; you can use an automatic teller to handle most of your banking chores.

If you think about your bank account as an *object* and the functions you perform, withdrawing and depositing money, as the *methods* of the bank account object, then what did the bank do with the ATM? It provided its customers with a *programmable interface* to execute the methods of the bank account object.

Thinking in OLE programming terms, the bank account is an object with methods, and the ATM is a controlling application that has access to some of the bank account methods. The object (bank account) and methods (deposit) which the bank gives the ATM access to are called *exposed objects*. Exposed objects are objects that exist in one application and are made available to other applications.

Try one more example to make sure that you understand the idea of exposed objects.

Figure 15-6 shows a cartoon figure of a word processor application. The application is holding out two objects, a document object and a drawing object. A third object, the file object, is hidden inside of the word processor with Off Limits and No Trespassing signs. The document and drawing objects are *public* objects. A public object is an object that can be used by outside applications. The file object, which is hidden in Figure 15-6, is a *private* object. A private object is not exposed and cannot be used by outside applications.

Building with Components

Now you know what an exposed object is, but what use is it? Think about another real world example—a car. A car is a great object that helps you get to and from your favorite places. It also gets you to the dentist, but you can forgive that, can't you?

Once again, think in terms of objects and pieces, or *components,* this time in terms of a car. A car is built from many different parts and components. A car manufacturer selects many different parts and integrates them to build a car. When you buy the car, you have the capability to modify some of the components that make up your car. You may not like the tires the manufacturer used, so you can swap them for a set of different tires, perhaps a set of racing tires. The point is, in the real world many different objects are built from existing objects to create other objects.

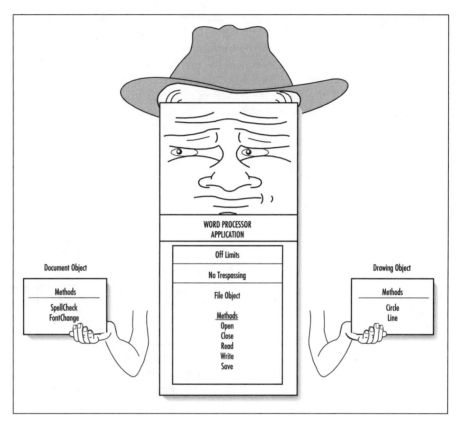

Figure 15-6
Word processor with exposed objects

Using OLE, programmers can build software applications in the same way a manufacturer builds a car. The programmer can integrate software components from existing applications into totally new programs. The developer makes component choices, like selecting a spell-checking component for text editing applications or a graphing component for number-crunching applications. The OLE components that developers so easily integrate into applications are exposed objects from other applications, and the technology that allows an application to create and manipulate these exposed objects is *OLE automation*.

OLE Automation

OLE automation allows you to integrate functionality into your application that you may not be capable of writing or may not want to write. Figure 15-7 shows an example of an application using an existing spreadsheet and word processor spell checker via OLE automation. Controlling applications, sometimes referred to as *OLE clients*, use the exposed objects to perform tasks, like creating new objects, getting existing objects, setting object properties, or using object methods. In Figure 15-7, the controlling application uses an existing spreadsheet to compute a total for two numbers and uses the word processor's spell checker to spell check a comment's text box. The object's application shown in Figure 15-7, sometimes referred to as an *OLE server*, exposes objects and methods to be used by other applications.

OLE servers can be applications in their own right, like Microsoft Word and Microsoft Excel, or they may exist only to support client applications. OLE automation allows programmers to use existing code from any OLE server without having to rewrite the code. The use of OLE components follows the object-oriented approach of reusable code, data encapsulation, and easy integration. Visual Basic can be used to create OLE controlling/client applications or, in the Professional and Enterprise editions, OLE object application/servers. This chapter explains how to create both using Visual Basic.

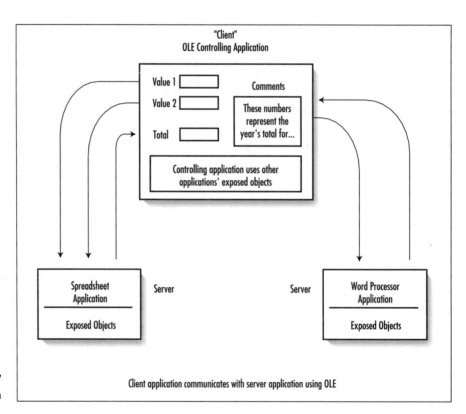

Figure 15-7
OLE automation

Client application communicates with server application using OLE

1. _____ exist in one application and are made available to other applications.
   a. Private objects
   b. Private properties
   c. OLE properties
   d. Exposed objects

2. An advantage to using objects is that you can create applications:
   a. Using existing software components
   b. Writing existing objects over again
   c. With Visual Basic, writing the application from scratch
   d. Using DLLs instead of objects

3. _____ allow(s) the developer to manipulate objects exposed by other applications.
   a. Linked documents
   b. Embedded documents
   c. OLE automation
   d. Object classes

4. An OLE controlling application is also referred to as a(n):
   a. OLE server
   b. Linked document
   c. Embedded document
   d. OLE client

5. An OLE object application is also referred to as a(n):
   a. OLE server
   b. Linked document
   c. Embedded document
   d. OLE client

OBJECT HIERARCHY AND THE OBJECT BROWSER

Before you start using OLE automation in your Visual Basic programs, you must first understand the *object hierarchy* of the application objects you want to use. The object hierarchy is like a road map. If you wanted to go from your home town to a city called Visual Basic City several hundred miles away, you would get out a road map to find the correct highways and roads to take. The road map also provides the names of cities and towns along the way where you can stop for meals or lodging.

The object hierarchy of an application provides you with the exposed objects available to your application and with the route to take to get the correct object. In other words, it is a road map of the object. The hierarchy for Excel is shown in Figure 15-8.

The Legend key shows that the Workbook is part of a collection. The hierarchy also shows the member objects of an Excel Workbook. If you expand the Worksheet object, the Range object appears. The hierarchy of the Range object is shown in Figure 15-9.

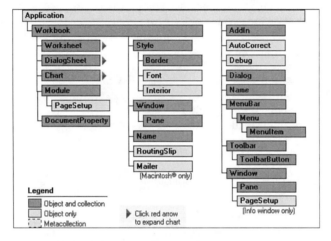

Figure 15-8
The hierarchy of
Microsoft Excel

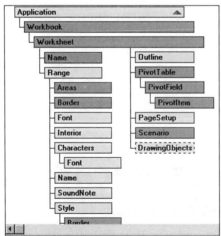

Figure 15-9
The hierarchy of
the Range object

Here's how you figure out the hierarchy diagram in Figure 15-9:

- The Parent object, Application, is at the top of the hierarchy.

- According to the key, the Workbook object is an *object* and a *collection*. When that is the case, the name of the collection is the plural of the name of the object. Then the hierarchy so far is Application.Worksheets.Worksheet.

- The Range object is an object of Worksheet. Thus, the hierarchy of the Range object so far is Application.Worksheets.Worksheet.Range.

And now you know why people draw hierarchy diagrams instead of trying to describe them in words!

The last concept you need to understand about the object hierarchy is the concept of *dependent* objects. A dependent object is an object in the hierarchy that cannot be created or accessed by itself but is created by using a method of the object on which it is dependent. In Figure 15-9, the Range object is a dependent object of the Worksheet object. You cannot access or create an Excel Range object; instead, you must create a Worksheet object and then use the Range method to create a Range object. The object hierarchy may seem a bit complex at first, but Visual Basic 5 provides you with a tool to access and navigate the hierarchy, called the Object Browser.

Using the Object Browser

The Object Browser allows you to view exposed objects from other applications as well as classes from object libraries and procedures contained in your Visual Basic project. The following examples use the Object Browser to browse Microsoft Excel's object hierarchy. If you do not have Excel, don't worry. Select any available object and follow through the various exercises. The goal of this section is to teach you how to use the Object Browser to integrate exposed application objects into your applications. First, add Excel to your References profile.

1. Select the Project menu from the Visual Basic menu bar.

2. Select References.

The References dialog box, shown in Figure 15-10, now appears.

3. If you have Microsoft Excel Version 5 or greater, you should see a check box titled Microsoft Excel 5.0 Object Library. Check the check box if it is not already checked, and click the OK button.

Now you are ready to use the Object Browser to explore Excel's object hierarchy. Click the Object Browser button on the Visual Basic toolbar. The icon is shown in Figure 15-11.

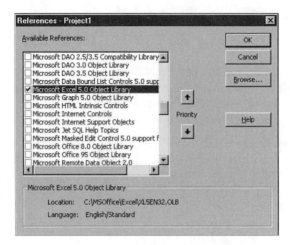

Figure 15-10
Visual Basic
References
dialog box

Figure 15-11
Object Browser
button on the
Visual Basic
menu bar

Object Browser

If the Object Browser is missing from your toolbar, you can use the Customize option to place it there. You can also open the Object Browser with F2 or from the View menu.

The Object Browser, shown in Figure 15-12, appears.
To view Excel's object module, do the following:

1. Select Excel-Microsoft Excel 5.0 Object Library from the Project/Library drop-down list box.

2. Scroll through the Classes list box and find the Range object.

3. Click on the Range object. The methods and properties for the object are displayed in the Members of list box. The key to the icons in the list box is shown in Figure 15-13.

4. Click on the Object Browser's Help button to view the hierarchy of the Range object, or

5. Scroll through the Members list and select the member of the property for which you need help. Then click on the Object Browser's Help button to bring up detailed help information on the selected method, property, or object.

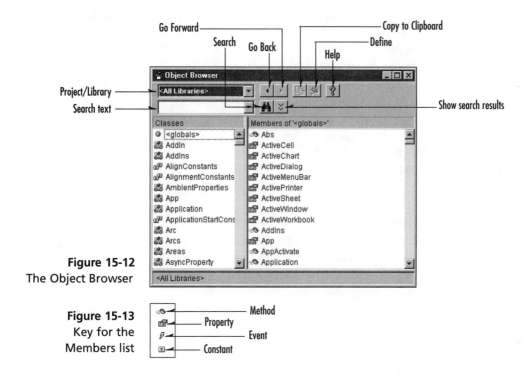

Figure 15-12
The Object Browser

Figure 15-13
Key for the
Members list

The help file for objects offers more help than you might think. Figure 15-14 shows the help screen for the Range object. The hierarchy is shown at the top. Each item in the hierarchy is a hyperlink that will take you to the help file for that part of the hierarchy. The last item in the hierarchy diagram is labeled Multiple Objects. Clicking on that link opens a list of the member objects of the Range object, as shown in Figure 15-14.

1. _____ is like a road map that describes objects exposed by applications.
   a. The object map
   b. The object file
   c. The Object Browser
   d. The object hierarchy

2. _____ is a container for other objects. An example is the Microsoft Excel object **Charts**.
   a. An OLE group
   b. An OLE set
   c. A collection object
   d. An object hierarchy

3. _____ cannot be created or accessed by itself, but is created using a method of another object.
   a. A dependent object
   b. A public object
   c. A group object
   d. An independent object

4. _____ allows you to view exposed objects from other applications.
   a. The Object Browser
   b. The Project Viewer
   c. The Object Viewer
   d. The Class Wizard

5. To view or browse an object's properties and methods, you must make sure the object is:
   a. Added to the Visual Basic toolbar
   b. Selected in the References dialog box
   c. Selected in the Project dialog box
   d. Selected in the OLE dialog box

Figure 15-14
The member objects of the Range object

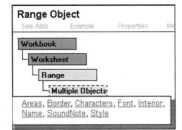

REVIEW

Lisa: I sure was surprised to see all the different things you can do with OLE. I thought OLE was only good for linking and embedding documents. With VB 5, the custom controls (OCXs) use OLE technology.

John: You're right. In the previous version of Visual Basic, I used OLE in limited cases, for instance, using an OLE custom control to embed or link Microsoft Word or Excel objects. By the way, speaking of the OLE custom controls, I think they really made some good enhancements to the controls. I especially like the way they provide methods instead of the Action property. I really think I'm ready to get more involved with OLE automation. I already understood the concept of "exposed objects." I do a lot of database programming with Visual Basic using the Data Access Objects. So, the idea of objects, methods, and properties was nothing new. The idea of being able to create my own objects that expose methods and properties is what I really want to be able to do.

Lisa: I think that before this chapter is done, you will get your wish.

John: Are you sure about that?

Lisa: Most definitely. I glanced through the next few lessons, and it looks like we are going to do a lot with OLE automation, including creating our own objects!

John: So now that we have the general understanding of OLE and exposed objects, we are going to get some hands-on coding experience?

Lisa: We sure are, so let's get into the next lesson!

USING OLE AUTOMATION WITH MICROSOFT WORD AND MICROSOFT EXCEL

This lesson shows how to use OLE automation to integrate Microsoft Word and Microsoft Excel into your applications. Using OLE automation requires five steps:

1. Determine the type of object to use.

Before you can use an OLE automation object, you must determine the type of object you wish to use. Use the Object Browser and the Reference dialog box to determine the OLE objects available to you, and pick the one you need to do the job.

2. Declare an object variable for the object.

You must declare a variable to store the object. If you have an object library (type library) in the Reference dialog box for the object, you can define the type of object your application will contain at design time. For instance, if you want to use a Microsoft Project Task object, and you have Microsoft Project's object library checked in the References dialog box, you can define an object variable in the following manner:

```
Dim MyTask As Task
```

You are telling the compiler that the variable **MyTask** will contain a Microsoft Project Task object. If you try to use the variable **MyTask** to hold an Excel Worksheet object, Visual Basic returns a runtime error message. This method of object declaration is known as *early binding* because Visual Basic determines the type of object the variable will hold during compilation.

What do you do if you don't have an object library for the application or if you are not sure of the object type? You can define the variable using the **Object** data type as follows:

```
Dim MyTask as Object
```

Using the **Object** data type is called *late binding*. When it uses late binding, Visual Basic does not know the object type the variable will contain until the object is created at runtime.

Whenever possible, use early binding because it offers efficiencies in speed.

3. Get an existing object or create a new object.

To create a new object, use the command `CreateObject`. The syntax is

```
CreateObject(class)
```

where `class` is the class of the object to create.
The `class` parameter has the format:

```
appname.objecttype
where:
```

`appname` is the application name, and `objecttype` is the object or class to create.
For example:

```
Set wd = CreateObject("Word.Basic")
```

To use an existing object, like a Word document or an Excel spreadsheet, use the command `GetObject`, which has the following syntax:

```
GetObject([pathname][, class])
```

where `pathname` is the full path and file name of the object, and `class` is the type of class or object.
For example:

```
Set wd = GetObject("Word.Basic")
```

4. Use the object's properties and methods.

Once you have an instance of the object, use any of the available properties and methods. For example, using an Excel application object:

```
Xl.Visible = True
```

5. Close the object, if required, and then release the instance of the object.

When you have completed your task and you no longer need the object, you sometimes must close the object with the close method, and you must always release the object by setting the object variable to `Nothing`. For example:

```
Set Xl = Nothing
```

Early Binding and the Following Examples

As stated in step 2 in this lesson, whenever possible, you should use early binding because it offers efficiencies in speed and validates the methods and properties you use for the object during compilation. The following examples use late binding because at this time, using early binding with Microsoft Word requires a special type library file that is not distributed with Visual Basic 5 or Word 6. Currently some bugs exist when trying to use early binding with Excel 5 that require work-arounds. Instead of assuming you have the Word type library, and instead of confusing you with elaborate work-arounds, the following examples use late binding. Remember to use early binding in your projects whenever possible.

The first project uses OLE automation by integrating Microsoft Word's spell checker into a previous application, the Notepad application developed in Chapter 12, Files. Microsoft Word has a very simple object model that has only a single object, the `Basic` object. All methods and commands for Word are part of the `Basic` object. This project adds a single routine to the Notepad application. That routine uses Word.Basic to check the spelling of the text in the Notepad, making spelling corrections and then replacing the text in Notepad with the corrected text.

Start by creating a new project. Right-click on Form1 in the Project Explorer and remove the form from the project. Right-click in the Project Explorer window again, and use Add File to add `frmNotePad` from the Notepad project in Chapter 12, Files. Then add `File.cls` from the same directory. Now open the Project menu and select Project Properties. Change the Startup form to `frmNotePad`. Finally, use `SaveAs` to save the project, the form, and the class to a new directory. Name the project SpellPad. (And now you know one way to reuse objects you have already created!)

Add the menu option shown in Table 15-5 to `frmNotePad`.

Table 15-5 Menu properties for `frmNotePad`

Caption	Name
&Tools	mnuTools
&Spelling	mnuSpelling

Add the code shown in Listing 15-3 to `mnuSpelling_Click`.

Listing 15-3 `mnuSpelling_Click` event code

```
Private Sub mnuSpelling_Click()
Dim objWord As Object       ' Generic Object Type

  On Error GoTo Word_Error
  If txtBuffer.Text = "" Then
    MsgBox "Notepad is empty - need text to check spelling.", _
        MB_ICONSTOP, "Empty NotePad"
    Exit Sub
  End If
  '
  'Check all of the Text in the NotePad Text box
  'Create Word object and assign it to object variable
  '
  Set objWord = CreateObject("Word.Basic")
  '
  'Use WordBasic functions as methods of the object
  objWord.FileNewDefault      'Create a New File in Word

  objWord.startofdocument     'Move to the start of the document
```

continued on next page

continued from previous page

```
    objWord.Insert txtBuffer.Text 'Insert the notepad text
    objWord.EditSelectAll        'Select all of the text
    On Error Resume Next   'Ignore Word's message box
    objWord.ToolsSpelling        'Invoke the Spell Checker
    On Error GoTo Word_Error
    objWord.startofdocument       'Go to the start of the document
    objWord.EditSelectAll        'Select all of the text
    objWord.editcut          'Cut the text to the clip board
    '
    'place the text back in the notepad
    'from the clipboard
    '
    txtBuffer.Text = Clipboard.GetText(vbCFText)
    '
    objWord.FileClose 2      'Close the file without saving
    Set objWord = Nothing     'Release the object
EndWordDemo:
  Exit Sub
'
'Error handler
'
Word_Error:
  MsgBox Error$(Err)
  If Not (wd Is Nothing) Then
    '
    'Close Word and release the Object Variable
    objWord.FileClose 2
    Set objWord = Nothing
  End If
  Resume EndWordDemo

End Sub
```

Test the spell-checking feature with the SpellPad application. Enter some text in the SpellPad and select the Spelling option under the Tools menu. What happens? Microsoft Word starts up, and all of the text in the notepad is selected and placed in a Word document. Word then checks the spelling of the text, prompting you for any changes, as shown in Figure 15-15. When all of the text has been spell-checked, the corrected text in the Word document is cut to the clipboard and pasted back into the Notepad. Then Microsoft Word is closed (without saving the document), and the object variable is released. OLE automation rules!

Where Is the Word Basic Object?

If you spent any time at all looking for the Basic object or for Microsoft Word with the Object Browser, you discovered that it is not there. How do you learn what objects and methods are in it? Well, if you want to use Word.Basic. Open Macros in Word's Tools menu and select Word Commands. There they are, dozens of them—*hundreds* of them! The simplest way to get them in the right order to do what you want to do is to record a macro in Word and copy it into your code window. Add your object reference and it is done. (You probably will need to tweak it a little.)

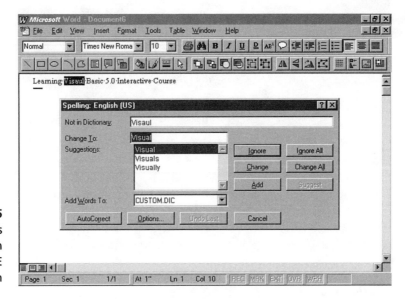

Figure 15-15
Microsoft Word's
spell checker in
action via OLE
automation

Using Microsoft Excel

The next project uses OLE automation with Microsoft Excel. It creates a simple application that makes a new Excel worksheet, and then adds four values to the worksheet using the Range object. From those four values, it creates an Excel chart, makes the chart 3D, and rotates it. So you can see OLE automation at work; the project makes Excel visible while it manipulates the Excel objects via OLE automation. (Ordinarily Excel would be left invisible.) After the chart is created and rotated, the program calls the Windows API *Sleep* and "sleeps" for five seconds so you can view the chart. Finally, the program closes Excel without saving the worksheet or the chart, and sets the object to **Nothing**.

Begin by creating a new project named **ExcelOLE**, with a single form and a single command button. Set the properties for the form and command button according to Table 15-6.

Table 15-6 Objects and properties settings for ExcelOLE

Object	Property	Setting
Form	Caption	OLE Automation with Excel
	Height	3435
	Name	frmExcelOLE
	Width	5425

continued on next page

continued from previous page

Object	Property	Setting
CommandButton	Caption	Control Excel
	Height	990
	Left	1320
	Name	cmdControlExcel
	Top	945
	Width	2535

Add the code shown in Listing 15-4 to the click event of the command button.

Listing 15-4 Command button `click` event code to control Excel via OLE automation

```
Private Sub cmdControlExcel_Click()
Dim Xl As Object
Dim XlChart As Object
    On Error GoTo OLE_ERROR
    'Create Excel object
    Set Xl = CreateObject("Excel.Application")
    '
    'Normally when using OLE Excel is invisible.
    'For demonstration purposes let's
    'toggle the visible property to True
    'so you can see the different events
    'taking place.
    Xl.Visible = True

    'Add an Excel Workbook
    Xl.Workbooks.Add

    'Put values into some cells using the Range object
    Xl.Range("a1").Value = 3
    Xl.Range("a2").Value = 2
    Xl.Range("a3").Value = 1
    Xl.Range("a4").Value = 5
    '
    'Select the data in the cells
    '
    Xl.Range("A1:A4").Select

    'Create a new chart
    Set XlChart = Xl.Charts.Add()

    'make the chart 3D Column
    xlchart.Type = -4100 'xl constant for 3D Column chart

    'rotate the chart
```

```
    For i = 35 To 175 Step 10
        xlchart.rotation = i
    Next

    '
    'Sleep for 5 seconds (Using the Sleep API) - so you can see
    'the chart created via OLE Automation.
    '
    Sleep (5000)

    'Close the Workbook without saving - could save if we wanted.
    '
    ' Note: Passing the parameter False suppresses the message box
    ' that asks if the spreadsheet is to be saved.
    '
    Xl.Workbooks(1).Close (False)
    '
    'Close Microsoft Excel with the Quit Method
    '
    Xl.Application.Quit
    '
    'Release the the object Variable
    '
    Set Xl = Nothing

EndDemo:
    Exit Sub
'
'Error handler
'
OLE_ERROR:
    MsgBox Error$(Err)
    If Not (Xl Is Nothing) Then
        '
        'Close Excel and release the Object Variable
        Set Xl = Nothing
    End If
    Resume EndDemo
End Sub
```

Add a module to the project. Name it **ExcelOLE.bas** and add the following Windows API declaration in the declarations section of the module:

```
Declare Sub Sleep Lib "kernel32" (ByVal dwMilliseconds As Long)
```

Run the application, and click the Control Excel button. What happens? Excel begins to run and becomes visible when your program sets the **Application.Visible** property to **True**. Four values are added to cells in a worksheet. The four cells are selected, and a new chart, shown in Figure 15-16, is created from the values in the four cells. Excel then exits without saving any of the changes.

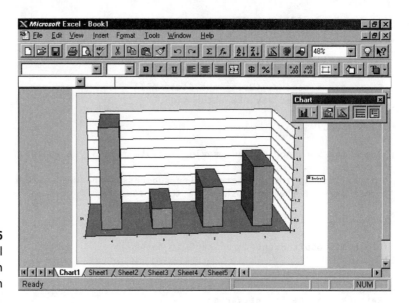

Figure 15-16
Microsoft Excel
chart created with
OLE automation

You may be wondering what object methods to use to perform a certain function. Here's a useful tip: If you are using Microsoft Word or Microsoft Excel, use their macro recorders to generate Visual Basic for Applications code. Start the macro recorder, perform the functions you want to do in the application, and then stop the macro recorder. You have now generated Visual Basic for Applications code. You can then copy the code into your Visual Basic applications!

1. A(n) _____ defines the type of objects and methods exposed by an application.
   a. Include file
   b. Header file
   c. Type library
   d. Declaration file

2. What does the following code do?
```
Dim wd as Object
    Set wd = CreateObject("Word.Basic")
```

   a. Creates a Word Basic object.
   b. Nothing, because **CreateObject** is not a valid Visual Basic function.
   c. Creates a wd object.
   d. The syntax for the **CreateObject** is incorrect.

3. To release an OLE automation object:
   a. Set the object to zero.
   b. Close the object.
   c. Set the object's reference to **Nothing**.
   d. Set the object to **Empty**.

4. If you have an Excel application object variable **XL**, what does the following code do?

   XL.Workbooks.Add

   a. Executes an Excel macro called Add
   b. Adds an Excel workbook
   c. Reads the workbook collection
   d. Adds an Application object to the workbook

5. What function can be used to get an existing object?
   a. **CreateObject**
   b. **GetObject**
   c. **New**
   d. **FindObject**

EXPOSING YOUR OWN CLASSES: CREATING OLE SERVERS

In the last few lessons, you learned how to use exposed objects from other applications. Up to this point, you have used your Visual Basic programs as a controlling application. Building class modules and using object-oriented programming is valuable, but wouldn't it be great if you could create applications that exposed objects? Think of how easy it would be to reuse code! Maybe you wrote a great database security application, and you want to include the same functionality in a new application. If you can expose the objects in your security application, you can check database security from other applications without rewriting the code.

Visual Basic 5 provides you with the capability to expose your classes and create OLE servers! This capability is found in the Visual Basic Professional and Enterprise editions. If you own the Standard edition, you will not be able to create OLE servers, but the ability to create OLE servers is so important that you should read through and understand this section anyway.

Important: For this programming exercise to work properly, it is important that you follow the steps in the exact order in which they are written.

The VBCalc Project: An Out-of-Process OLE Server

Start a new project, or load **VBCalc.VBP** from the CD files that come with this book. When the New Project dialog box appears, select ActiveX EXE. The project opens with a Class module and no forms. Open the Properties window, name the class **clsCalculator**, and set the **Instancing** property to **5 - Multiuse**. This setting makes the class **Public**, which exposes it for use by other programs and allows several programs to use it at the same time. If you change the setting to **3 - Single Use**, then each program that wants to use it must run a separate instance of **VBCalc**. If you change the setting to **1-Private**, then no programs can use the class except **VBCalc**.

If you use the files from the CD, they must be copied to your hard disk first because this project must write to the project's directory.

Open the Project menu and select Properties. Set the Project Properties according to Table 15-7.

Table 15-7 Project property settings for VBCalc

Tab	Property	Value
General	Project Type	ActiveX EXE
	Startup Object	(None)
	Project Name	VBCalc
	Project Description	4
	Function	Calculator
	Upgrade ActiveX Controls	Checked
Make	Title	VBCalc
	Type	Comments
	Value	Four Function Calculator OLE Demo
Compile	Compile to Native Code	Checked
	Optimize for Fast Code	Checked

On the Tools menu, select Options. Set the Options according to Table 15-8.

Table 15-8 Option settings for VBCalc

Tab	Setting	Value
Editor	Autolist Members	Checked
	Default to Full ModuleView	Checked
General	Compile on Demand	Checked
Environment	Prompt to Save Changes	Checked

Add the code in Listing 15-5 to the declarations section of clsCalculator.

Listing 15-5 Public property declarations for clsCalculator

```
Option Explicit
Public Result As Double ' Class Property - Result
Public Enum CalcShowMode
    CalcModal = vbModal
    CalcModeless = vbModeless
End Enum
```

Add the Public procedures in Listing 15-6 to clsCalculator. These are the methods for the class.

Listing 15-6 Methods for clsCalculator

```
Public Sub Add(x As Double, y As Double)
    If IsNumeric(x) And IsNumeric(y) Then
        Result = x + y
    End If
End Sub

Public Sub Multiply(x As Double, y As Double)
    If IsNumeric(x) And IsNumeric(y) Then
        Result = x * y
    End If
End Sub

Public Sub Subtract(x As Double, y As Double)
    If IsNumeric(x) And IsNumeric(y) Then
        Result = x - y
    End If
End Sub

Public Sub Divide(x As Double, y As Double)
    On Error GoTo err_Divide
    If IsNumeric(x) And IsNumeric(y) Then
        Result = x / y
    End If
exit_Divide:
    Exit Sub
err_Divide:
```

continued on next page

continued from previous page

```
        Result = 0
        Resume exit_Divide
End Sub
```

VBCalc is an *out-of-process server*. In other words, it is an .EXE file that is capable of running on its own, just like Word and Excel. Unlike those applications, however, it does not have a user interface. The following steps show that it is possible for an out-of-process server to display either modal or modeless forms, if needed.

First, select Add Form on the Project menu. Select Form from the dialog box that opens. Add a Command button to the form. Press F4 to open the Properties window, and set the form's properties according to Table 15-9.

Table 15-9 Properties for `frmVBCalc`

Object	Property	Value
Form	Name	frmVBCalc
	Caption	VBCalc Modal
	Left	0
	Top	0
	Height	930
	Width	2670
	MaxButton	False
	MinButton	False
CommandButton	Name	cmdQuit
	Caption	Exit
	Height	375
	Left	540
	Top	60
	Width	1515

Add the following lines of code to `cmdQuit_Click`:

```
Private Sub cmdQuit_Click()
        Unload Me
End Sub
```

That's all for the form, but now you must add code to `clsCalculator` to show the form. Add the code in Listing 15-7 as a new method for `clsCalculator`.

Listing 15-7 The ShowForm method for clsCalculator

```
Public Sub ShowForm(Optional Modality As _
    CalcShowMode = CalcModal)
    Dim frm As New frmVBCalc
    If Modality = CalcModeless Then
        frm.Caption = "VBCalc - Modeless"
    End If
    frm.Show Modality
End Sub
```

A Look at the Code

The methods of clsCalculator are pretty standard stuff. The code in the **Divide** method contains an error handler that sets Result to zero if a divide error occurs. Division causes more errors than the other simple math functions, so a bit of added safety isn't misplaced.

The **ShowForm** method uses the Enums to determine whether to show the form as a Modal or Modeless form. If the form is shown Modeless, the caption is changed.

Getting Ready to Run

Before you can use an out-of-process server, the system must have a reference to it, a *reference EXE* to help your test program maintain its connection to the server. To create your reference EXE, click Make **VBCalc.Exe**. You need do this only once.

The program must register its public members with the system registry so your test program can find it. Running the EXE of an out-of-process server automatically registers it. You are not running the EXE, however, because debugging is almost impossible then. Instead, select Start With Full Compile from the Start menu, which does the same thing on a temporary basis.

That's it! You now have an OLE server running. Nothing happened? Sure it did; it just doesn't show. You need a test program to be sure it's working OK, a program to exercise the server.

The TestCalc Project

In order to test **VBCalc**, you must start another instance of Visual Basic 5. Before you do, minimize the one that is already running to help avoid confusion. (It can get *very* confusing!) Use the Windows Start menu to open another instance of Visual Basic 5. The new project will be a standard EXE.

On the Project menu, select References. The project description of **VBCalc** appears in the References list twice. Select the one that lists its location as the VBP file. (If you select the EXE file, you will not be able to debug the project.) Click on OK to add the new component to your project and make its methods and properties available to your code.

Open Options from the Tools menu and place a check on AutoList Members so you can see the new objects as you type.

Before you begin, press F2 and look for **clsCalculator** in the Object Browser. It is an example of how you can use the Object Browser to learn about programs that expose their objects for use.

Add seven Command buttons, three text boxes, and three labels to the form. Set the properties according to Table 15-10. (The sizes and positions are not listed in the table. Use Figure 15-17 as a guide, and use the Format menu to size and position the controls.)

Table 15-10 The TestCalc project

Object	Property	Value
Form	Name	frmTestCalc
	Caption	"Test Calculator"
CommandButton	Name	cmdQuit
	Caption	"Exit"
CommandButton	Name	cmdModeless
	Caption	"Modeless"
CommandButton	Name	cmdModal
	Caption	"Modal"
CommandButton	Name	cmdDivide
	Caption	"Divide"
CommandButton	Name	cmdMultiply
	Caption	"Multiply"
CommandButton	Name	cmdSubtract
	Caption	"Subtract"
CommandButton	Name	cmdAdd
	Caption	"Add"
TextBox	Name	txtResult
TextBox	Name	txtY
TextBox	Name	txtX
Label	Name	Label3
	Caption	"="
Label	Name	Label2
	Caption	"Y"
Label	Name	Label1
	Caption	"X"

Open the Form Layout window and move the form to the right of the screen so it will be out of the way at runtime. (Yes, it really matters.)

None of the part placements are critical. Strive for a layout that pleases you. Add the code in Listing 15-8 to project TestCalc.

Listing 15-8 The code for TestCalc

```
Option Explicit
Private x As Double, y As Double
Private Calc As clsCalculator

Private Sub cmdAdd_Click()
    If txtX <> "" And txtY <> "" Then
        x = CDbl(txtX)
        y = CDbl(txtY)
        Calc.Add x, y
        txtResult = Calc.result
    Else
        MsgBox "Must have X and Y Values to do math!", vbOKOnly
    End If
End Sub

Private Sub cmdDivide_Click()
    If txtX <> "" And txtY <> "" Then
        x = CDbl(txtX)
        y = CDbl(txtY)
        If y <> 0 Then
            Calc.Divide x, y
            txtResult = Calc.result
        Else
            MsgBox "Can't divide by 0!", vbOKOnly
        End If
    Else
        MsgBox "Must have X and Y Values to do math!", vbOKOnly
    End If
End Sub

Private Sub cmdModal_Click()
    Calc.ShowForm VBModal
End Sub

Private Sub cmdModeless_Click()
    Calc.ShowForm vbModeLess
End Sub
```

continued on next page

continued from previous page

```
Private Sub cmdMultiply_Click()
    If txtX <> "" And txtY <> "" Then
        x = CDbl(txtX)
        y = CDbl(txtY)
        Calc.Multiply x, y
        txtResult = Calc.result
    Else
        MsgBox "Must have X and Y Values to do math!", vbOKOnly
    End If
End Sub

Private Sub cmdQuit_Click()
    Unload Me
End Sub

Private Sub cmdSubtract_Click()
    If txtX <> "" And txtY <> "" Then
        x = CDbl(txtX)
        y = CDbl(txtY)
        Calc.Subtract x, y
        txtResult = Calc.result
    Else
        MsgBox "Must have X and Y Values to do math!", vbOKOnly
    End If
End Sub

Private Sub Form_Load()
    Set Calc = New clsCalculator
    txtResult = 0
End Sub

Private Sub Form_Unload(Cancel As Integer)
    Set Calc = Nothing
End Sub
```

A Look at the Code

The declarations section early binds **Calc** as an object of type clsCalculator, and **Form_Load** creates an instance of the class. Note that **Form_Unload** releases the object with **Set Calc = Nothing**.

The math function Command buttons check to be sure that there are numbers typed into the X and Y text boxes before the call on clsCalculator's methods. If either fails the test, a **MsgBox** informs the user. The Divide button also checks to prevent division by zero.

Finally, the two ShowForm buttons call the **ShowForm** method of the object, sending appropriate values.

Running TestCalc

Press F5 to run the program. Before you try it out, minimize the VB5 window. The only open window on your screen should be TestCalc. (Windows get lost behind each other a lot in this kind of work. Keep your screen simple to avoid confusion.) Enter some numbers into txtX and txtY and try the different math functions on the numbers. VBCalc performs the calculations and puts the results in the public variable Result. Then TestCalc reads Result from VBCalc and places it into txtResult. You have a running OLE server!

Now click on Modeless. VBCalc creates an instance of **frmVBCalc** and shows it. Prove to yourself that you can continue using TestCalc with the Modeless form showing. The running TestCalc and the Modeless form are shown in Figure 15-17.

Close the Modeless form and click on the Modal button. Looks a lot like the other one, doesn't it? Try running a new math problem with the Modal form still showing. What's this (see Figure 15-18)?

As soon as the running instance of VBCalc displays the Modal form, it becomes "busy" waiting for the form to close. The Windows error message warns you that the server is not responding and, of course, it can't. Click on Switch To and close the Modal form to resume normal operation.

Before you close TestCalc, click on Modeless one more time. Now close TestCalc. Hmmmm, the Modeless form is still there, which shows that the server is running independently of the test program.

Close the Modeless form, and then maximize the Visual Basic instance that is running VBCalc and click on the End button to close the OLE server.

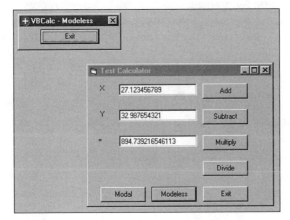

Figure 15-17
Calculating with
TestCalc

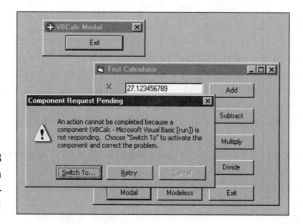

Figure 15-18
Calculating with
the Modal form—
an error!

The Electric KoolAid Acid Test

Well, you can run two programs and have them communicate via OLE. Do you have to start VBCalc every time you need to use it? That wouldn't be good, would it? And, since it has no internal way of closing itself, how do you stop it? (If there weren't good answers to these questions, would they have been asked?) Follow these steps:

1. If you have made changes to VBCalc since you made your reference EXE, compile the program again. If not, just close that instance of Visual Basic.

2. Now maximize the VB instance with TestCalc, open the Project menu, and click on References. There are still two references to the Four Function Calculator, but the one that is checked says [Missing]. Clear that checkmark and check the one that points to the EXE file instead, and click on OK.

3. Now select Make TestCalc.Exe from the File menu. When it is done, close that instance of Visual Basic, too.

4. Use Windows Explorer to find TestCalc.Exe.

5. Double-click on the icon to run the program.

6. Try out the same things you did before. They all work!

Because TestCalc is now referencing the EXE file, it creates an instance of clsCalculator by running the VBCalc program. And as soon as there are no references to clsCalculator, VBCalc is closed. The whole thing is transparent to the user, who never needs to know that VBCalc was opened, used, and then closed.

Summary of Building an Out-of-Process OLE Server

Out-of-process servers are handy for doing complicated, slow chores for another program while still letting the other program function normally. In today's terminology, an out-of-process is called an *ActiveX EXE*. The following steps outline the normal building process for ActiveX EXE files.

1. Decide what features you want your component to have.

2. List the objects you will need to provide these features. (Each object is a separate class.)

3. If your component will have any forms, design them.

4. Add the properties and methods for your classes. This is the *interface* for the component.

5. Compile the ActiveX EXE to create a reference EXE.

6. Start the ActiveX EXE with *Full Compile*.

7. Start a new instance of Visual Basic. Select the VBP version of the new reference so you can debug.

8. Design a test program to exercise all of the features of the ActiveX EXE.

9. When all is working, compile your new ActiveX EXE again. It will now be available for use.

1. For an OLE server, the _____ in the Project Property dialog box identifies the OLE server to the system registry.
   a. Startup form
   b. StartMode check box
   c. Application description
   d. Project name

2. If the class property `Instancing` is set to Private:
   a. Other applications can use the class.
   b. Other applications can use the class, but the class cannot be viewed by the Object Browser.
   c. Other applications can use the class, depending on the setting of the class property `Instancing`.
   d. Other applications cannot use the class.

3. What does the code below do?

```
Dim Calc as Object
Set Calc = New clsCalculator
```

    a. Creates a new instance of the **clsCalculator** object.
    b. Creates a new instance of the application Calculator's class VBCalc.
    c. It is an invalid statement.
    d. Invokes the Calculator method of the object VBCalc.

4. Text entered in the Application Description field of the Options dialog box appears in the References dialog and the:
    a. Help system when you press F1
    b. Object ToolTips
    c. Object Browser
    d. Debugger

5. To test your OLE server:
    a. Run the OLE server from Visual Basic, start a second instance of Visual Basic, and create a test program to use the OLE server's objects.
    b. Run the OLE server from Visual Basic. If it runs with no errors, then you have tested it.
    c. You do not need to test OLE servers. Visual Basic's compiler will catch OLE server problems.
    d. Create a standalone application, test the application, and then create an OLE server based on the standalone application.

USING VISUAL BASIC BUILT-IN OBJECTS

So far you have concentrated on using objects from other applications and creating objects from your own applications. This lesson looks at some often overlooked objects that are a part of Visual Basic. You are already familiar with Visual Basic objects such as forms and controls, but did you know that there are six system objects in Visual Basic? They are

 App

● Clipboard

● Debug

● Err

Printer

Screen

You have already used several system objects. This lesson uses your new perspective on objects to take another look at each Visual Basic object and at how to integrate the object into your Visual Basic applications. For an added bonus to this chapter, use the Object Browser to look at each of the objects in this lesson as you proceed, and try to imagine uses for some of the ones not mentioned here.

Forms and Controls

You have already covered the use of forms and controls. They are mentioned here as a reminder that they are Visual Basic objects. You have already seen that you can create forms and controls dynamically with the **Set** and **New** keywords. The Forms collection object is a collection of all the forms in a project. There is always a risk, when programs use many forms, that a form will be left open when the program closes, using valuable memory resources. Some programmers add the following code in the **Form_Unload** event of their main form:

```
For j = Forms.Count - 1 to 0, Step -1
    Unload Forms(j)
Next j
```

App

The **App** object is a system object that was briefly covered in Chapter 12, Files. In that chapter, the **App.Path** property was used to identify the directory the application resided in while running. The **App** object has other properties that can be useful for creating applications. The **PrevInstance** property can be used to determine the number of instances of any application running on a PC. To prevent multiple instances of an application running on the same PC, add the following code to the startup form's **Load** procedure or **Sub Main**:

```
If App. PrevInstance > 1 Then
    MsgBox "Existing startup - the application " & App.Title _
        & "is already running."
    End
End If
```

In the example above, the **App** object property **Title** was used to display the title of the application. The **HelpFile** property of the **App** object can be used to find the path and file name of the help file associated with the application, and the CompanyName and LegalCopyright information are often used on splash screens.

Clipboard

The **Clipboard** object provides the Visual Basic programmer access to the system clipboard. The **Clipboard** object can be used to cut and paste text or graphics between applications. In Lesson 5, you used the **Clipboard** object to cut spell-checked text from a Word document and paste it into your Notepad application. The **Clipboard** object does not contain any properties that can be set from Visual Basic; however, several methods are available. In the spell-checking Notepad example, you used the **GetText** method, which returns a text string from the clipboard. To get a graphic from the clipboard, use the **GetData** method. Graphics or text can be sent to the clipboard by the **SetText** and **SetData** methods. The **GetFormat** method returns the type of data in the clipboard, and the **Clear** method empties the clipboard.

Debug

The **Debug** object is used to print messages to the Debug window. You have used the **Debug** object throughout the book to help debug your applications. The **Debug** object has no properties and only one method, **Print**. **Debug** statements are ignored when an executable is created, but they still increase the size of your executable, so if you want the smallest possible executable, comment out your **Debug** statements.

Err

The **Err** object was covered in some detail in Chapter 10, Error Handling and Debugging. The **Err** object contains information on Visual Basic runtime errors. The error number and a text description of the error can be found by using the **Err** object properties **Number** and **Description**. The **Err** object supports two methods, **Raise** and **Clear**. Use the **Clear** method to clear the properties of the **Err** object. The **Raise** method is used to generate runtime errors and set the **Err** object to a specific error number.

Printer

The **Printer** object was covered in detail in Chapter 9, Printing. The **Printer** object enables you to send output to a system printer. Visual Basic 5 also supplies a collection object called **Printers** that allows you to scan through the available printers on the system. You can even change the default printer by using the **Set** statement with the **Printers** collection.

Screen

The **Screen** object provides you with useful information which allows you to manipulate the forms in your application based on properties of the **Screen** object. The **Screen** object has no methods but several properties. The **ActiveControl** property specifies the control that has focus. The **ActiveForm** property specifies the current active window. You can use the **ActiveForm** property to set properties on the active form.

```
Screen.ActiveForm.MousePointer = DEFAULT
```

The **Height** and **Width** properties are read-only properties that are always measured in twips. Use the **Height** and **Width** properties to resize your forms to fit a screen size or to position the forms on a screen. The following code centers a form on the screen:

```
Public CenterForm (F as Form)
    F.Top = (Screen.Height - Height) / 2 'Set the Top of the form
    F.Left = (Screen.Width - Width) / 2    'Set the horizontal
End Sub
```

1. Which one of the following is not a Visual Basic system object?
   a. **App**
   b. **Screen**
   c. **Debug**
   d. **Error**

2. The _____ object can be used to cut and paste text or graphics between applications.
   a. **Clipboard**
   b. **Screen**
   c. **App**
   d. **Printer**

3. The _____ property of the **App** object can be used to determine the number of instances of any application running on a PC.
   a. **NumOfApps**
   b. **PrevInstance**
   c. **NumInstance**
   d. **PrevApp**

4. The _____ property of the **Screen** object specifies the control that has focus.
   a. **ActiveControl**
   b. **GotFocus**
   c. **ControlFocus**
   d. **CurrentControl**

5. Which one of the following is *not* true about the **Debug** object?
   a. The **Debug** object has no properties.
   b. The **Debug** object has only one method, **Print**.
   c. **Debug** statements are ignored when an executable is created.
   d. **Debug** statements do not increase the size of your executable.

THINKING IN OBJECTS

The first version of Visual Basic introduced event-driven programming to many programmers. Visual Basic 4 introduced object-oriented programming features similar to those used in C++ and Pascal, and made it possible to build applications from OLE components. Visual Basic 5 brings in ActiveX technology that expands VB's object orientation even further.

Throughout this book, you have examined the object-oriented features of Visual Basic 5 and learned how to use them. This lesson examines how these new features will influence the way you program today and in the future.

Future OLE

ActiveX/OLE is one of the most exciting and important features of Visual Basic 5. The familiar custom controls, the VBXs, have now been replaced with ActiveX OCXs. To the Visual Basic programmer, the OCX still acts like the previous custom control, but it has many advances. Draw some controls on a form, set a few properties, add some code, and, whamo, you have a working application! The VBX vendors who port their VBXs to ActiveX OCXs have a whole new marketplace opened up to them. Their OCXs can now be used in other development tools and in applications like Microsoft Access.

But the most important new OLE feature is the ability to create your own OLE servers. Visual Basic 5's Professional and Enterprise editions allow you to create OLE automation servers (EXE) or in-process OLE servers (DLL). Your OLE servers can be used and accessed by any application or development tool that can be an OLE controlling application, even over the Internet!

You can now write fully functional applications that can expose objects. You can create applications that have no functionality of their own, but supply objects and methods for other applications. For instance, you can write a single OLE server to determine security or business rules for a company. Applications can use that server to check user access, permissions, or business rules. If the business rules were to change, only the OLE server code would have to be modified.

Consider the case of building file or database applications where you are performing the same type of task in several different programs. Create a single in-process OLE server that handles all of the generic functions required for file I/O or database access. Once the code is debugged and tuned, you have a new component to use in future applications. Building applications from OLE components results in better, more robust applications that can be created in less time. And the functionality is available to applications outside of Visual Basic!

OLE technology will continue to advance. Microsoft has stated that OLE is a major part of its future operating systems. With the ability to create OLE reusable components easily, expect the market for OLE servers and new Visual Basic add-in tools to explode.

In the marketplace and within your organization, the idea of creating reusable code will become a reality. Remember, OLE is an open standard. Look for more and more products and vendors to support OLE. To see how easily OLE integrates into the Visual Basic environment, add Microsoft Word and Excel to the Visual Basic toolbar.

1. From the Visual Basic menu bar, select Project.

2. Select the option Components.

3. On the Insertable Objects tab, check the boxes marked Microsoft Word 6.0 Document and Microsoft Excel 5.0 Chart.

4. Click the OK button.

Figure 15-19 shows the application objects you have added to the Visual Basic toolbar to create OLE automation objects for your application.

Designing OLE Objects

Creating Visual Basic ActiveX OLE applications requires you to spend more time up front designing the application. Specifically, you must determine which objects will be private and which will be exposed. Here's a quick review of some simple steps you can use when you create an object model for your applications:

1. Determine the objects your application will need.

2. Determine the attributes (properties) and actions (methods) of each object.

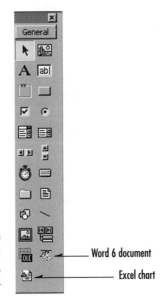

Figure 15-19
Word and Excel objects on the Visual Basic toolbar

Word 6 document

Excel chart

3. Determine any possible object dependencies and create an object hierarchy.

4. Determine the objects that should be exposed to other applications.

Follow this everyday example to get an idea of how to design an object model. The project is to draw the door in Figure 15-20.

1. First determine the objects required for the Door application. Using Figure 15-20 as a guide, the first object will be the Door object. On the Door object, there is a Doorknob object.

2. Next determine the attributes (properties) that will define the Door and any actions (methods) of the Door object. Figure 15-21 shows the properties and methods for the Door and Doorknob objects. The Door object has two properties, both public—Color and Material. The Door has two methods, Open() and Close(). The Doorknob has two properties, HandleStyle and Material. The Doorknob object has a single method, Turn().

3. Make the Doorknob object dependent on the Door object. This means applications cannot create just a Doorknob object; they first must create a Door object and then use it to create a Doorknob object. Figure 15-22 shows the object hierarchy.

4. The last step before you create the class modules is to decide which objects to expose to other applications. In this example, expose both the Door object and the Doorknob object.

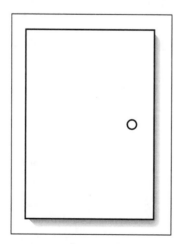

Figure 15-20
Door

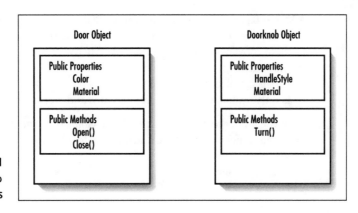

Figure 15-21
Door and Doorknob objects

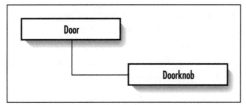

Figure 15-22
Door object hierarchy

Objects, Objects Everywhere

The important thing to remember, whether you are creating standard Visual Basic applications or ActiveX OLE server applications, is to think objects! Use the Visual Basic object-oriented features to create objects within your applications that can easily be integrated into other applications. The use of classes simplifies and speeds up future application development by creating already working, reusable classes. Building OLE components provides reusable code and functionality to any OLE controlling application on your desktop or in your organization. Soon your development environment and toolbar will be covered with reusable objects, and you will be thinking objects, objects everywhere!

1. Visual Basic allows you to create OLE servers:
   a. That can be used only by other Visual Basic applications
   b. That can be used by any OLE controller applications
   c. That can be used by only Microsoft OLE controller applications
   d. That cannot be used by any OLE controller applications, but only by other OLE server applications

2. A Visual Basic OLE custom control (OCX):
   a. Is not tied to a 16-bit architecture and can easily be used by other development tools besides Visual Basic, like Microsoft Access
   b. Can only be used by Visual Basic
   c. Is being replaced by the VBX
   d. Is only available in 32-bit architectures and works only with Visual Basic

3. With the ability to easily create OLE reusable components, expect the market for ___ and new Visual Basic add-in tools to explode.
   a. VBXs
   b. OLE contollers
   c. OLE servers
   d. DDE applications

4. The first step in designing an OLE application is to:
   a. Determine the objects exposed to other applications.
   b. Determine the attributes (properties) and actions (methods) of each object.
   c. Determine any possible object dependencies and create an object hierarchy.
   d. Determine the objects your application will need.

5. Building ____ provides reusable code and functionality to any OLE controlling application on your desktop or in your organization.
   a. Visual Basic applications
   b. OLE components
   c. VBX components
   d. A class

CHAPTER 16

ROLL YOUR OWN: CREATING YOUR OWN ACTIVEX CONTROLS

Visual Basic 5 has two types of controls, *intrinsic controls* and *ActiveX controls*. Intrinsic controls are the controls that appear on the toolbar when you start Visual Basic. ActiveX controls are the custom controls that you can add to the toolbar from the Components dialog box of the Project menu.

Throughout this book you have been using custom controls. For example, you learned how to use the CommonDialog control, which is a custom control supplied by Microsoft. If you look in the WINDOWS\SYSTEM directory, there is a file named `ComDlg32.0CX`, which is the control's file. If you have the Professional or Enterprise edition of Visual Basic 5, you can create your own ActiveX controls. (Before the release of Visual Basic 5, Microsoft made the ActiveX designer available for Internet download under the name `Control Creation Edition`. If you do not have the Professional or Enterprise edition of VB, the CCE will still give you this capability. (The CCE is currently available at `http://www.microsoft.com/vbasic`.)

This chapter takes you step-by-step through the creation of a new ActiveX control.

WHAT IS ACTIVEX?

What is ActiveX? is a question that is asked again and again, and it receives a bewildering array of answers. Visual Basic can create an out-of-process server (EXE file) that is an ActiveX file. Visual Basic can create an in-process server (DLL file) that is an ActiveX file. Visual Basic can create an Internet-accessible file (.VBD file) that is an ActiveX Document. ActiveX documents can be considered Visual Basic programs for Internet pages.

ActiveX controls are what used to be known in Visual Basic (and other) circles as OLE controls. They have been extended, however, to add features that were not available in previous OLE versions, including intranet and Internet support.

Creating the NewBtn Project

Start a new project in Visual Basic. Select ActiveX Control from the New Project dialog box. The New Project dialog box is shown in Figure 16-1.

1. Open the Project Explorer window. Building and testing the control requires a lot of switching between windows, and the Project Explorer window is the easiest way to switch.

2. Open the Properties window.

3. Open the ToolBox.

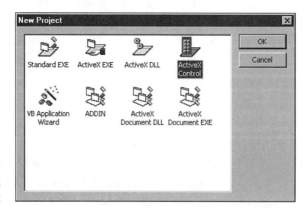

Figure 16-1
Starting an ActiveX
Control project

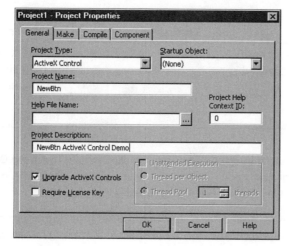

Figure 16-2
The Project
Properties pages

4. Select Options from the Tools menu. Select Require Variable Declaration on the Editor Tab to help avoid typing errors. Select the Environment tab, and check Prompt to Save Changes to remind you to save changes to the project before you run it. Click on OK when you are done.

5. Now select Properties from the Project menu. Fill in the entries on the General tab according to Table 16-1.

The Properties pages are shown in Figure 16-2.

Table 16-1 Settings for the Project Properties pages

Item	Setting	Comment
Project Type	ActiveX Control	The project will be compiled as an OCX file.
Startup Object	(none)	OCX files do not run by themselves.
Project Name	NewBtn1	This is the name that will be used for the control's Type Library file.
Project Description	NewBtn1	ActiveX Control Demo: This is what the developers see when they add your control to their projects.
Upgrade ActiveX Controls Checked		Allows ActiveX controls to be updated when changes are made.

continued on next page

continued from previous page

Item	Setting	Comment
Require License Key Unchecked		License Keys are used when you distribute a control. Even if you plan to use a key, leave this blank until the majority of the work is done.

7. Switch to the Compile tab, select Compile to Native Code, and Optimize for Fast Code. Click on OK when you are done. This option will improve your control's operating speed.

8. Visual Basic adds a User Control Designer to the project. Its default name is UserControl1. Set the properties according to Table 16-2.

Table 16-2 The SButton User Control

Object	Property	Value
UserControl	Name	SButton
	BackColor	&H00FF8080&
	Height	405
	Width	1605

These become the default properties for the new control.

 Select Save Project from the File menu. It will save three files: NewBtn.vbp, which is the project file; SBtn.ctl, which is the user control; and SBtn.ctx, which includes the binary information for the control—bitmaps and so on.

Figure 16-3 shows the project to this point.
Not very impressive yet, is it? Just hang in there.

This chapter uses the same project throughout, building a user control from beginning to end. A partially completed project is available on the CD that comes with this book in the **Lessons1_4** folder, an intermediate level in the **Lessons5_6** folder, and the totally completed project in the **Lessons7_8** folder. For maximum learning, follow the steps in the chapter and use the included files only as reference material.

Adding the TestBtn Project

You can't add a form to the NewBtn project so you can test the project. OCX files cannot run by themselves. Recall that the startup object for the project was (none). Fortunately,

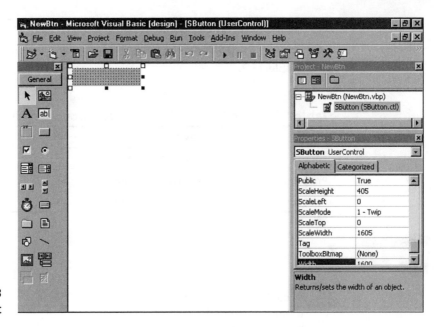

Figure 16-3
The NewBtn project

Visual Basic allows you to load two or more projects at design time so you can test in-process components.

- Select Add Project from the File menu. Do *not* select Open Project or New Project. Either choice will close your control project, and you are not finished with it.

- Select Standard Exe from the New Project dialog box.

Visual Basic adds a new project to the existing project. Your project is now a *Project Group* and the EXE project becomes the startup object for the group. Note that the Project Explorer's title bar has changed to reflect the new condition. Project1 is shown in bold type in the Project Explorer to indicate that it is the startup object for the Project Group. The Project Explorer is shown in Figure 16-4, showing the new group and the new project that has been added to the group.

Figure 16-4
The Project Explorer window with a Project Group

● Rename Form1 as NewBtnDemo and change its caption to Control Demo.

● Select Save Project Group from the File menu. Use the names in Table 16-3.

Table 16-3 The NewBtnDemo Project Group file names

Object	Save As
Form	NewBtnDemo.frm
Project	NewBtnDemo.vbp
Project Group	NewBtnDemo.vbg

1. Visual Basic custom controls are known as:
   a. Intrinsic controls
   b. Private controls
   c. ActiveX controls
   d. DLLs

2. The startup object for an ActiveX control is listed as (none). Why?
   a. ActiveX controls only run out-of-process.
   b. ActiveX controls cannot run by themselves.
   c. ActiveX controls run invisibly.
   d. ActiveX controls only run from Internet browser windows.

3. What will developers see when they add your new control to their projects?
   a. The project description from the Project Properties dialog box
   b. The project name from the Project Properties dialog box
   c. The words *ActiveX Control*
   d. The name of the startup object

4. When you add a new project to an existing project, Visual Basic:
   a. Closes the existing project
   b. Displays an error message
   c. Opens a second instance of Visual Basic
   d. Creates a project group

5. Why add an EXE project to a User Control project?
   a. So you can compile the OCX file
   b. Because you can
   c. To test the control
   d. So you can see what the control looks like on a form

RUNNING THE CONTROL AT DESIGN TIME

Controls are different from other programmable objects because some of the code in controls executes when the designer places the control on her form at design time. In order to debug the design-time behavior of a new control, you must be able to execute the control's code while the test form is still in the design mode. That is one of the reasons you need a project group containing an EXE project as you design your control.

Adding Code to the Resize Event

The **Resize** event is one of the events that is fired at design time as well as runtime. You can see it happening in the Debug window.

- Double-click on SButton in the Project Explorer window to make the Control Designer window the active window.

- Double-click on the control to open its Code window.

- Add the following code to the Resize event:

```
Private Sub UserControl_Resize()
    Static iCtl As Integer
    iCtl = iCtl + 1
    Debug.Print "Resize " & iCtl
End Sub
```

- If the SButton Designer window is not showing, bring it to the top again by double-clicking on SButton in the Project Explorer.

- Double-click the close button on the SButton Designer window.

  As soon as the Designer window closes, the icon for SButton is activated in the Toolbox. Figure 16-5 shows the icon and the Tooltips display showing the control's name.

- Open the Immediate window and arrange the windows on your screen so you can see the Immediate window and the Control Demo form.

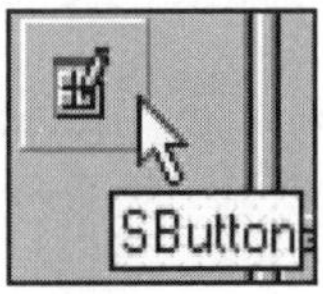

Figure 16-5
SButton in the
toolbox

● Double-click on the SButton icon to place an instance of the new control on the form.

The Immediate window notes the event by displaying

`Resize 1`

● Use the resize handles to resize SButton on the form. Each time you do, the message shows up again.

● Grab SButton with your mouse and move the control. You didn't resize it, and the `Resize` event was not fired.

● Double-click on Width in the Properties window and enter a new width. Watch the Immediate window. Did the event fire?

● Double-click on the SButton control to open the Code window. Note that the control has four default events. These four events are intrinsic for every control you create. Other events must be specifically coded.

● Take a look at the Properties window for the SButton control. The properties listed there are the properties that are intrinsic to every control you create. Other properties must be explicitly coded.

Back to Design Mode

What happens when you switch back to design mode for your control? Try it.

● Double-click on SButton in the Project Explorer.

● Arrange your windows so you can view the Control Designer, the form, and the Immediate window at the same time. Figure 16-6 shows one possible arrangement.

When the Control Designer is enabled, the icon for the new control is disabled, and the control on the form is disabled and filled with hashmarks to show that it is disabled.

● Resize the control on the form. Did the `Resize` event fire? The control is disabled, so no events are fired.

● Resize the control on the Control Designer. Again no `Resize` event is triggered.

● Double-click the Close button on the SButton Designer window.

Closing the Design window enables the control on the form again. Note that the `Resize` event is fired and the hashmarking is gone. Now try another approach.

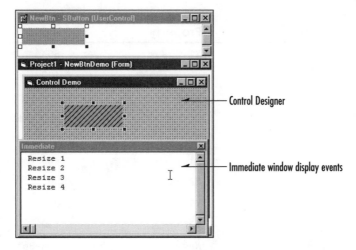

Figure 16-6
Control Designer,
Form, and
Immediate
windows

- Control Designer
- Immediate window display events

⬤ Reopen the Design window.

⬤ Right-click on the form.

⬤ Select Update User Controls from the pop-up that appears.

The control on the form is updated to match the properties of the control, and the Design window is closed automatically.

⬤ Select the SButton control on the form and delete it.

⬤ Double-click on the SButton icon to place a default-sized SButton on the form. *Do not resize it.*

⬤ Open the Control Designer again.

⬤ Add four Line objects to give the new button control a 3D appearance. Set the properties according to Table 16-4.

Table 16-4 Properties for the Line objects

Object	Property	Value
Line	Name	LineRight
	BorderColor	&H00808080&
	BorderWidth	2
	X1	1560
	X2	1560

continued on next page

continued from previous page

Object	Property	Value
	Y1	60
	Y2	400
Line	Name	LineLeft
	BorderColor	&H00E0E0E0&
	BorderWidth	2
	X1	20
	X2	20
	Y1	0
	Y2	400
Line	Name	LineBottom
	BorderColor	&H00808080&
	BorderWidth	2
	X1	40
	X2	1560
	Y1	405
	Y2	405
Line	Name	LineTop
	BorderColor	&H00E0E0E0&
	BorderWidth	2
	X1	0
	X2	1560
	Y1	20
	Y2	20

The **X1**, **X2**, **Y1**, and **Y2** values in Table 16-4 are based on the size of SButton at 1605 by 405 twips. The values make allowances for the border of SButton, and were determined experimentally. If you must adjust these settings, use the SButton control on NewButtonDemo.frm as a guide.

●   Right-click on the form and select Update User Controls to validate the position of the lines on the SButton control.

● When the lines are positioned to suit your taste, click on the Run button or press ⌊F5⌋ to run the NewBtnDemo program.

● Close the program and resize the SButton control on the form.

Hmmmm. Seems to be something wrong here! The control resizes, but the lines stay where they are. Can you explain why? (Hint: The hardcoded positions and dimensions may have something to do with it.)

1. Why must you add an EXE file to the Control Designer project?
   a. So there will be a control group
   b. It makes the project more complicated.
   c. Because you can
   d. You need an EXE file to test the control during development.

2. Unlike EXE projects, controls have behavior at:
   a. Runtime
   b. Design time
   c. Conception
   d. Planning stages

3. By default, Visual Basic makes _____ available without adding extra code.
   a. Some events
   b. Some properties
   c. Both a and b above
   d. None of the above

4. When the Control Design window is open:
   a. The Control icon on the ToolBox is disabled.
   b. The control on the form is filled with hashmarks.
   c. The **Resize** event is not fired.
   d. All of the above

5. Components added to a control:
   a. Automatically move when the control is resized
   b. Do not automatically move when the control is resized
   c. Disappear when you close the Control Designer
   d. None of the above

THE KEY EVENTS OF A USER CONTROL OBJECT

Several key events mark the life cycle of a user control. It is important to understand when these events occur and what they do. This lesson explores the lifetime of a user control at design time and at runtime.

The Key Events

Recall that the control has different behavior at design time than at runtime. Each set of behaviors is considered a different lifetime. You can see the sequence of events in a control's lifetime by adding a few lines of code.

- Click on SButton in the Project Explorer, and then click on the View Code icon.

- Add the code in Listing 16-1.

Listing 16-1 Code to observe the lifetime of a control

```
Private Sub UserControl_Initialize()
    Debug.Print "Initialize"
End Sub

Private Sub UserControl_InitProperties()
    Debug.Print "Init Properties"
End Sub

Private Sub UserControl_ReadProperties(PropBag As PropertyBag)
    Debug.Print "Read Properties"
End Sub

Private Sub UserControl_Resize()
    Static iCtl As Integer
    iCtl = iCtl + 1
    Debug.Print "Resize " & iCtl
End Sub

Private Sub UserControl_Terminate()
    Debug.Print "Terminate"
End Sub

Private Sub UserControl_WriteProperties(PropBag As PropertyBag)
        Debug.Print "Write Properties"
End Sub
```

The code shown in the **Resize** event is already there from Lesson 2.

- Be sure that the Immediate window is visible on your screen.
- Close the Control Design window to update SButton.

As soon as you close the Control Design window, messages appear in the Immediate window:

```
Initialize
Read Properties
Resize 1
```

When you close the Control Design window, the copy of the control on the form is destroyed and re-created, triggering the **Initialize** event, the **Read Properties** event, and the **Resize** event you already expected. (Because the original copy of SButton was created before you added code to the **Terminate** event, that event was not fired when the original control was destroyed.)

- Press [F5] or click on the Run icon to start running NewBtnDemo.

The **Debug.Print** statements put the following messages into the Immediate window:

```
Write Properties
Terminate
Initialize
Read Properties
Resize 1
```

The first two messages indicate that the design-time copy of SButton has been destroyed. The **Terminate** event fires first, followed by the **Write Properties** event. The **Write-Properties** event saves the properties of SButton in the *Property Bag*, which is (Guess?) where Visual Basic saves properties.

When the program begins to run, a new instance of SButton is created. The first event is the **Initialize** event, just as with the class for any object. The **Read Properties** event reads all of the properties from the Property Bag and reestablishes the properties that were set for the control at design time. Of course, among those properties are those that control the size of SButton, so the **Resize** event is fired.

- Click the Close button to end the program.

Again, a series of events is fired, and the Immediate window reflects this with new messages.

```
Terminate
Initialize
Read Properties
Resize 1
```

The **Terminate** event occurs when the runtime instance of SButton is destroyed. The last three events are the now familiar creation of the control on the design-time form.

- Move the SButton control to the top left corner of the form. (Exactly where is not important, just as long as it's out of the way.)

- Double-click on the SButton icon on the toolbox to put a new instance of SButton on the form.

You guessed it—more events to mark the creation of another instance of the control.

```
Initialize
Init Properties
Resize 1
```

- Run the NewBtnDemo program again.

Now there are two instances of the control. Both have their properties saved, and both design-time copies must be destroyed, so there are two **Property Write** messages and two **Terminate** messages. Then, of course, two new instances are created for the runtime form, with the familiar events.

The Lifetime of a Control

By understanding the sequence of events in the lifetime of a control, you can decide which of its events to use to make its behavior reflect your intentions. The following describes the events:

- The **Initialize** event occurs every time the control is created, either at design time or at runtime. It is the first event in the lifetime of the control.

- The **InitProperties** event occurs the first time an instance of the control is created. When the control is placed on the form, it reads the control's initial default properties.

- The **ReadProperties** event occurs on all future instantiations of the control. It reads the control's properties from the Property Bag.

- The **Resize** event is fired every time an instance of the control is created and every time the control is resized. Resizing the control at runtime fires the event as well.

- The **Paint** event occurs whenever the form (or other container object) tells the control to draw itself.

● The `WriteProperties` event occurs when a design-time instance of the control is destroyed if any of the property values have been changed. This event saves all the properties in the Property Bag.

● The `Terminate` event occurs when the control is about to be destroyed.

It is your responsibility to put the proper code in these events to handle the creation, resizing, and destruction of all of a user control's components. But that's another lesson.

1. What is the first event that occurs when a control is placed on a form?
   a. `Initialize`
   b. `ReadProperties`
   c. `Resize`
   d. `Terminate`

2. If you close the Design window after making changes to a control, what happens?
   a. Nothing
   b. Copies of the control on a form are destroyed and replaced with the new version.
   c. Copies of the control on a form must be manually changed for the new version.
   d. The properties of copies of the control on a form are simply updated.

3. A user control's properties are saved in:
   a. The Properties window
   b. Nonvolatile memory
   c. The Property Bag
   d. A properties array

4. The `WriteProperties` event only occurs when:
   a. A runtime instance is created.
   b. A runtime instance is destroyed.
   c. A design-time instance is created.
   d. A design-time instance is destroyed.

5. When is the `Resize` event fired?
   a. When the control is created
   b. When the control is manually resized
   c. When the control is resized by code
   d. All of the above

DRAWING THE CONTROL

You can create your control's appearance with the Graphics methods such as the **Line** method, or you can add intrinsic Visual Basic controls and Visual Basic ActiveX controls to your new control. It doesn't serve the purpose of this simple demonstration control, but you can add TextBoxes, ListBoxes, and any other VB control to a custom control.

Controls added to a user control are called *constituent controls*. In Lesson 2, you added four Line controls to SButton as constituent controls. This lesson builds on your new knowledge of a user control's events to make the lines behave correctly. It also adds a few new components to the SButton control.

Controlling the Shadow Lines

One of your discoveries in Lesson 2 was that resizing the control after you added the lines left the lines exactly where you originally placed them. If you made the control smaller, the bottom and right-hand lines disappeared. If you made it larger, the same two lines just hung there in the center of the control, and the other two lines were too short.

Since the problem occurs when you resize the control, it seems reasonable that the corrections must belong in the **Resize** event.

 Delete the Debug.Print statement from the Resize event, and add the new code in Listing 16-2.

Listing 16-2 Resizing the shadow lines

```
Private Sub UserControl_Resize()
    '    Adjust the length of LineLeft
    LineLeft.Y2 = ScaleHeight
    '    Adjust the length of LineTop
    '    Allow for border
    LineTop.X2 = ScaleWidth - 40
    '    Adjust size and position of LineRight
    '    Allow for border
    LineRight.X1 = ScaleWidth - 20
    LineRight.X2 = ScaleWidth - 20
    LineRight.Y2 = ScaleHeight
    '    Adjust size and position of LineBottom
    '    Allow for border
    LineBottom.X2 = ScaleWidth - 40
    LineBottom.Y1 = ScaleHeight - 20
    LineBottom.Y2 = ScaleHeight - 20
End Sub
```

- Close the Design window or right-click on the NewBtnDemo form and select Update User Controls.

- Resize one of the controls.

When you resize the control now, the shadow lines follow along. If the lines are not to your liking, refer to the Note in Lesson 2. A bit of experimentation is worth a ream of instructions!

Adding a Caption

No self-respecting button can be captionless! You can add a caption to SButton in two different ways. The **Print** method is available for user controls. It could be used to place a caption in the button, but it requires more work to center the caption than it is worth. This lesson does it the easy way, with a Label control.

- Reopen the Control Design window.

- Draw a Label control onto the SButton control. Size it to fill the entire control and set the properties according to Table 16-5.

Table 16-5 Adding a caption

Object	Property	Value
Label	Name	lblCaption
	Alignment	Center
	AutoSize	True
	Font	MS San Serif – Bold
	ForeColor	White
	BackStyle	Transparent
	Caption	(none)
	WordWrap	True

By setting the **BackStyle** property to **Transparent**, you allow all of the control to show through. Making the **AutoSize** property **True** simplifies centering the caption in SButton. Still, you have to work at it, and you have to make the Label's **Caption** property a property of the SButton control.

- Bring SButton's Code window to the front.

- Select Add Procedure from the Tools menu.

- Enter Caption for the name.

- Click on Property and Public, and then click OK.

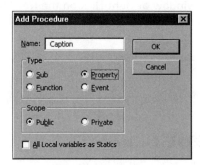

Figure 16-7
Adding the Caption
property

The Add Procedure dialog box is shown in Figure 16-7.

● Add the code in Listing 16-3 to the Property Get and Property Let procedures. Note the changes in the data types.

Listing 16-3 Setting and getting the caption

```
Public Property Get Caption() As String
    Caption = lblCaption.Caption
End Property

Public Property Let Caption(sNewCaption As String)
    lblCaption.Caption = sNewCaption
End Property
```

It is vital that you change the data types for **Property Get** and **Property Let** to **As String**. Note, too, that the parameter name in **Property Let** has been changed, and that **ByVal** has been removed.

● Close the Control Design window to update SButton on the form.

● Select one of the SButton controls on the form. (Note that SButton now has a Caption property.)

● Enter a caption in the Caption property for the two SButton controls on your form.

● Press F5 or click on the Run button to run the program.

What's this? You entered a caption, but when you ran the form the new caption disappeared! What's going on here?

It's (Not) in the Bag!

Think about the lifetime of a user control. When you run the program, the design-time instance of the control is destroyed and a new instance is created. The new instance gets its properties from the **ReadProperties** event! And **ReadProperties** gets its values from the Property Bag. But you have not saved the properties in the Bag, and you have not read them from the Bag. You need more code.

● If the program is still running, close it.

● Add the code in Listing 16-4.

Listing 16-4 Saving and restoring the properties

```
Private Sub UserControl_WriteProperties(PropBag As PropertyBag)
    PropBag.WriteProperty "Caption", Caption, Extender.Name
End Sub

Private Sub UserControl_ReadProperties(PropBag As PropertyBag)
    Caption = PropBag.ReadProperty("Caption", Extender.Name)
End Sub

Private Sub UserControl_InitProperties()
    Caption = Extender.Name
End Sub
```

The lesson here is that for each property you add to your control you must use **WriteProperties** to save it to the Property Bag and **ReadProperties** to get it back. The **InitProperties** procedure is used to provide a default **Caption** property to the control. Remember that **InitProperties** is only fired once, when a developer first places the control on a form. It is this procedure that sets the initial appearance of your control.

The code in Listing 16-4 uses **Extender.Name** as the control's default name. What is this **Extender** object? Take another look at the Properties window of SButton1 (the one on the form). With the exception of the new **Caption** property that you added, the properties in the window are **Extender** properties. They are properties that are automatically provided for the control by the **Extender** object, an object that is automatically supplied for User Controls. There is no point in adding properties that are already provided as **Extender** properties as they will be superseded by the **Extender** and will not be available to developers who use the control.

The third parameter in the line:

```
PropBag.WriteProperty "Caption", Caption, Extender.Name
```

uses the **Extender.Name** property as a default if the developer has not set a **Caption** property. And the reference to **Extender.Name** in

```
Caption = PropBag.ReadProperty("Caption", Extender.Name)
```

uses it as a default if there is no caption in the Property Bag.

The caption still has one more problem. (Well, several more, but one at a time!) If you resize one of the controls on your form, you will see that the caption stays in its old position. Not nice!

Everything in Its Place

There's a clue in that last sentence. Where would you put the code to center the caption? Right! The Resize event is the perfect place. Add the following line of code to the Resize event, just before End Sub:

```
lblCaption.Move (ScaleWidth - lblCaption.Width) / 2, _
     (ScaleHeight - lblCaption.Height) / 2
```

This is standard centering code. `ScaleWidth` and `ScaleHeight` are the internal dimensions of the control.

Other properties of `Caption` that you may want to offer to developers include the font size, weight, and color. All in good time, gentle reader.

1. VB intrinsic controls and ActiveX controls added to a user control are called:
   a. Extrinsic controls
   b. Constituent controls
   c. Add-ins
   d. ActiveX extension controls

2. The correct procedure for positioning controls with a user control is:
   a. `Read` properties
   b. `Init` properties
   c. `Initialize`
   d. `Resize`

3. Adding properties to a user control requires:
   a. `Property Get` and `Property Let` procedure
   b. Public variables
   c. OLE communications
   d. Any of the above

4. When you add properties to a control, you must store them in the:
   a. Properties window
   b. Properties page
   c. Property Bag
   d. Form's code section

5. The default properties supplied to every new user control are properties of:
   a. The `Extender` object
   b. The containing form
   c. `VBRUN500.DLL`
   d. The `Intrinsic` object

THE INS AND OUTS OF EVENTS

You already know that Windows is an event-oriented operating system and that Visual Basic is an event-driven language. But in Lesson 2 you saw that the user control has only four events available to you when you place it on a form, and not very useful events at that.

The User Control's Events

Take a look at the code module for SButton. Click on the down arrow on the right of the Procedures box. In the control itself, it seems, you have a multitude of events! The Procedures drop-down list is shown in Figure 16-8.

If you want to have access to an event, you must somehow send that event back to your program. User controls handle events differently because they have to be able to react to some events themselves before they pass the event back to the program that is using the control.

Extender *Events*

The four events that are automatically provided for every control are `Extender` events. These events are invisible to your control. You can't put code into their event procedures, so there is no need to bother with them at all. The mechanism of these events is already handled by Visual Basic.

Events Received by a User Control

The events listed in the Procedures drop-down list shown in Figure 16-8 are events that are received by your user control. They offer you the chance to do something with the

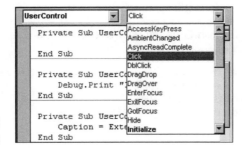

Figure 16-8
`UserControl` events

control. For example, when you click on a Command button, its appearance changes to indicate that it has received the click.

Try it out.

● Add the following declaration to the Declarations section of the user control:

```
Option Explicit
Private lBackColor As Long
```

● Add the following code to the user control:

```
Private Sub UserControl_MouseDown(Button As Integer, Shift As
Integer, X As Single, Y As Single)
    ' Save the original BackColor
    lBackColor = BackColor
    ' Change the BackColor property
    BackColor = &HFFFFFF - BackColor
End Sub

Private Sub UserControl_MouseUp(Button As Integer, Shift As
Integer, X As Single, Y As Single)
    ' Restore the BackColor to original color
    BackColor = lBackColor
End Sub
```

The code provides a place to store the original **BackColor** property because you want to restore the color to its original value when the user releases the mouse button. When the **MouseDown** event is fired, the **BackColor** property is saved, then a calculation replaces it with a new value. When the **MouseUp** event is fired, the color is restored. Try it out.

● Bring the NewBtnDemo from the top and invoke Update User Controls.

● Press [F5] or click on the Run button to start the program.

● Click on one of the SButton controls on the form.

The color changes, as advertised. But what happens if you click on the Caption of the control? Try it. No color change? You have just exposed the fact that you have more to do. Events on constituent controls are not passed to the user control container object. Back to work.

● If NewBtnDemo is still running, click on the Stop button to close it.

● Bring the SButton Code window to the front, and add the following code to the code for lblCaption:

```
Private Sub lblCaption_MouseDown(Button As Integer, Shift As
Integer, X As Single, Y As Single)
    lBackColor = BackColor
    BackColor = &HFFFFFF - BackColor
End Sub
```

```
Private Sub lblCaption_MouseUp(Button As Integer, Shift As
Integer, X As Single, Y As Single)
    BackColor = lBackColor
End Sub
```

Look familiar? It is the same code you put in the **UserControl** events. Now try it out again. Be sure to invoke Update User Controls first.

Much better! The only thing missing is code to change the shadow lines. You can add it now. The code in **UserControl_MouseDown** and **lblCaption_MouseDown** is exactly the same, and the code in **UserControl_MouseUp** and **lblCaption_MouseUp** is the same. This is the perfect place for some private procedures.

- Close the running NewBtnDemo.

- Select Add Procedure from the Tools menu.

- Name the new procedure BtnDown, and set it as a Private Sub.

- Cut the code from lblCaption_MouseDown and paste it into the new procedure.

- Select Add Procedure from the Tools Menu.

- Name the new procedure BtnUp, and set it as a Private Sub.

- Cut the code from lblCaption_MouseUp and paste it into the new procedure.

The new code is shown in Listing 16-5. (Pay careful attention to where each section of code is found.)

Listing 16-5 Color change on MouseDown and MouseUp

```
Option Explicit
Private lBackColor As Long
Const lHighLight = &HE0E0E0
Const Lshadow = &H808080

Private Sub UserControl_MouseDown(Button As Integer, Shift As Integer, X As Single, ⇐
Y As Single)
    BtnDown
End Sub

Private Sub UserControl_MouseUp(Button As Integer, Shift As Integer, X As Single, ⇐
Y As Single)
    BtnUp
End Sub

Private Sub lblCaption_MouseDown(Button As Integer, Shift As Integer, X As Single, ⇐
Y As Single)
    BtnDown
```

continued on next page

continued from previous page

```
End Sub

Private Sub lblCaption_MouseUp(Button As Integer, Shift As Integer, X As Single, ⇐
Y As Single)
    BtnUp
End Sub

Private Sub BtnDown()
    lBackColor = BackColor
    LineLeft.BorderColor = lShadow
    LineTop.BorderColor = lShadow
    LineRight.BorderColor = lHighLight
    LineBottom.BorderColor = lHighLight
    BackColor = &HFFFFFF - BackColor
End Sub

Private Sub BtnUp()
    BackColor = lBackColor
    LineLeft.BorderColor = lHighLight
    LineTop.BorderColor = lHighLight
    LineRight.BorderColor = lShadow
    LineBottom.BorderColor = lShadow
End Sub
```

Using procedures for the internal events simplifies changes. For example, examine the code that changes the **BackColor** property in the **MouseDown** event:

```
BackColor = &HFFFFFF - BackColor
```

This is only one possible method for changing the color. If you would like to experiment, try something like

```
BackColor = BackColor * 1.1
```

Now, to get back to the modification:

- Bring the NewBtnDemo form to the front and invoke Update User Controls.

- Press F5 or click on the Run button to run the program.

Now the BackColor and the shadow lines of SButton change color when you click on the control. But now that the internal effects have been covered, how do you get the SButton to send events to the form that contains it?

Raising Events in the Container

At this point, the control's events are still localized to the control. Clicking on SButton changes the appearance of the control, but has no effect at all in the NewBtnDemo program. The user control must *raise an event* to signal the container form (or other container object, for that matter) that an event should be handled. Raising events is not inherent; you must do it explicitly. Here's how.

● Close the running NewBtnDemo.

● Bring the user control Code window to the front.

● Select Add Procedure from the Tools menu.

● Name the procedure Click, and select Event. The Add Procedure dialog box adds a new declaration, shown here in bold:

```
Option Explicit
Private lBackColor As Long
Const lHighLight = &HEOEOEO
Const Lshadow = &H808080
Public Event Click()
```

● Add the following code to the Click events of SButton and lblCaption.

```
Private Sub UserControl_Click()
    RaiseEvent Click
End Sub

Private Sub lblCaption_Click()
    RaiseEvent Click
End Sub
```

This code adds a **Click** event to the SButton control. The two steps to passing events back to the containing form are

1. Declare the event.

2. Use the RaiseEvents statement to raise the event.

Simple enough. Now to test the new event.

● Bring the NewBtnDemo form to the front and invoke Update User Controls to make the new event available.

● Open the form's Code window.

Note that the SButton controls now have a **Click** event.

● Add the following code:

```
Private Sub SButton1_Click()
    Debug.Print "Thanks for clicking " & SButton1.Caption
End Sub

Private Sub SButton2_Click()
    Debug.Print "Thanks for clicking " & SButton2.Caption
End Sub
```

● Press F5 or click on the Run button to run the program.

Now, when you click on either of the SButton controls, you receive a polite thank you.

1. If you want the developer to have access to an event:
   a. It happens automatically.
   b. User control events are not available to the container form.
   c. You must send the event back to the container form.
   d. You must make it an **Effector** event.

2. Events received by a user control:
   a. Are sent directly to the control's container object
   b. Can be used to do things within the control
   c. Affect the control's appearance
   d. None of the above

3. Events on constituent controls are:
   a. Passed directly to the user control
   b. Passed directly to the user control's container form
   c. Private to the constituent control
   d. Public events that are accessible from anywhere

4. The first thing you must do to send user control events to the container form is:
   a. Nothing. It happens automatically.
   b. Nothing. It can't be done.
   c. Declare the event.
   d. Raise the event.

5. Which of the following would you use to send the **Click** event to the container form?
   a. Nothing. It happens automatically.
   b. **SendEvent Click**
   c. **DoEvents Click**
   d. **RaiseEvent Click**

GIVE YOUR CONTROL A PROPERTY PAGE

If you have purchased a custom control, or if you have used some of the ActiveX controls that come with Visual Basic 5, you have seen the classy-looking Property pages that let you add properties to the control the same way you set Project properties in Visual Basic. Your own user controls can have a Property page, too.

Adding a Property Page

It's really pretty easy to add a Property page if you're a programmer. Property pages are a lot like Visual Basic forms.

● Bring the Control Designer to the front by selecting it in the Project Explorer and clicking on the View Object icon.

● Select Add Property Page from the Project menu and select Property Page from the opening dialog box.

The resulting screen is the Property Page designer. It looks a lot like the Control Designer, a form with no title bar.

● Add a Label and a TextBox to the page. Use Figure 16-9 as a guide to placement.

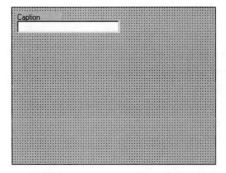

Figure 16-9
The Property page under development

Set the properties according to Table 16-6.

Table 16-6 Properties for the Property page

Object	Property	Value
PropertyPage	Name	NewBtnGeneral
	Caption	"General"
	TextBoxName	txtCaption
	Height	285
	Left	120
	Top	300
	Width	2415
Label	Name	Label1
	Caption	"Caption"
	Height	195
	Left	120
	Top	120
	Width	1035

- Open the Code window for the Property page by double-clicking on the page or selecting the View Code icon from the Project Explorer.

- Add the code in Listing 16-6. Pay close attention to the procedure names so you get the code in the right place.

Listing 16-6 Code for the Property page

```
Private Sub PropertyPage_SelectionChanged()
    ' Display the caption of the first control in the
    txtCaption = SelectedControls(0).Caption
End Sub

Private Sub PropertyPage_ApplyChanges()
    ' Use a generic object variable
    Dim objControl As Variant
    For Each objControl In SelectedControls
        objControl.Caption = txtCaption
    Next
End Sub

Private Sub txtCaption_Change()
    ' Set the Property Page's Changed variable to true
    Changed = True
End Sub
```

What's Going On?

Because it's possible to have more than one control selected at a time, the Property page has a collection named SelectedControls. The TextBox will display the caption of the first control in that collection. The `Selection_Changed` procedure is fired when you open the Property page and when you add more controls to the selection after the Property page is already open. The code in `Selection_Changed` displays the `Caption` property of the first of the selected controls in `txtCaption`.

It's also possible, after you have the page open, to select controls other than SButton controls. Changes made on this Property page can affect all of the controls that are selected. Each control is an object, of course, but there is no way to control what kind of object a developer might select once this Property page is open. The declaration `Dim objControl As Variant` avoids generating an error when something other than an SButton control is selected. The rest of the code in the `ApplyChanges` procedure loops through the `SelectedControls` collection and applies the text in `txtCaption` to all of them. (Normally you would not want to do that, but this is a demonstration.)

The code in the `txtCaption_Change` procedure sets a module-wide variable that lets the Property page know that one of its properties (in fact, its only property) has changed. When `Changed = True`, the Apply button is enabled.

Now, back to work.

Connecting the Property Page

Property pages do not automatically become a part of your control. In order for your new Property page to be available to your control, you must *connect* it.

- Click the Close button to close the Property Page Code window. Also close the Property Page Designer window.

- Bring the SButton designer window to the front.

- Select Property Pages from the Properties window.

- Select NewBtnGeneral from the Connect Property Pages dialog box shown in Figure 16-10. (Resist the temptation to select the others for a while yet.)

- Close the dialog box by clicking on OK.

- Bring the NewBtnDemo form to the front and invoke Update User Controls.

- Select one of the SButton controls on the form. Note that the Properties window now shows (Custom) as the first item in the list.

- Resize both the SButton controls on the form. Make one 2500 twips wide and 500 twips high, and make the other a 1000-twip square.

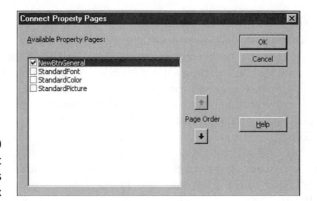

Figure 16-10
The Connect
Property Pages
dialog box

- Select one of the SButton controls, and then select Custom from the Properties window (or right-click on the selected control and select Properties from the c=Context menu).

- Change the caption in txtCaption to "Smile!" and note that the Apply button is enabled.

- Click on Apply. (Do *not* click on OK. It works, but it also affects the next part of this experiment.) You may have to drag the Properties window around to see that the new caption is now displayed.

- Press and hold CTRL, and click on the second sButton control. Note that both controls are now selected.

- Change the Caption to "Hello, My Friend!" and click OK.

Both captions are now the same, but they have a decidedly different appearance. That appearance was set when you chose **AutoSize** and **MultiLine** for **lblCaption**. The Label control cannot be sized to be larger than its original container. When the caption in the label is too large to fit the width of the label, it adds another line. Thus, you now have a button control with a centered **MultiLine Caption** property.

Experiment with a few different controls—labels and command buttons, for example—to see the effect of multiple selections on your new Property page.

Using a Standard Property Page

What about those other Property pages? To use StandardColor you must have a property in your user control that uses a color. That original background color is getting pretty boring, isn't it? Add a **BackColor** property to the control. Forgot how?

- Bring the SButton code window to the front.

- Select Add Procedure from the Tools menu.

● Enter BackColor as the name and click on Property and Public; then click OK.

● Add the code in Listing 16-7. Note the changes that were made in the procedure declarations.

Listing 16-7 The BackColor property

```
Public Property Get BackColor() As OLE_COLOR
    BackColor = UserControl.BackColor
End Property

Public Property Let BackColor(ByVal NewColor _
        As OLE_COLOR)
    UserControl.BackColor = NewColor
    PropertyChanged "BackColor"
End Property
```

When you added the Caption property, you had to make some changes in the user control's code. The same is true here.

● Change the code as shown in Listing 16-8. (Changes are shown in bold.)

Listing 16-8 Adding the BackColor property

```
Private Sub UserControl_InitProperties()
    On Error Resume Next
    Caption = Extender.Name
    BackColor = RGB(192, 192, 192)
End Sub

Private Sub UserControl_ReadProperties(PropBag As PropertyBag)
    Caption = PropBag.ReadProperty("Caption", Extender.Name)
    BackColor = PropBag.ReadProperty("BackColor", RGB(192, 192, 192))
End Sub

Private Sub UserControl_WriteProperties(PropBag As PropertyBag)
    PropBag.WriteProperty "Caption", Caption, Extender.Name
    PropBag.WriteProperty "BackColor", BackColor, RGB(192, 192, 192)
End Sub
```

The value in InitProperties is the default gray that Visual Basic uses for all button controls. Note that it is set as the default color in ReadProperties and WriteProperties as well. If you prefer the hexadecimal colors to RGB colors (which *look* the same but are just different ways of expressing the same thing), use &HC0C0C0&.

● Bring the NewBtnDemo form to the top and invoke Update User Controls.

● Delete the existing controls from the form and double-click on the SButton icon on the ToolBox to place a new SButton control on the form.

● Use the Properties window to change the BackColor property of the control.

Now that you have a color property, you can use the Standard Colors Property page.

● Bring the SButton design window to the top by selecting it in the Project Explorer and clicking on the View Object icon.

● Select Property Pages from the Properties window.

● Select Standard Colors from the Connect Property Pages dialog box.

● Bring the NewBtnDemo form to the front and invoke Update User Controls.

● Right-click on the SButton control and select Properties.

● Click on the Color tab.

The Color Selection dialog box opens. If you want more choices, select Custom Color and click on Edit Custom Colors. The result is shown in Figure 16-11.

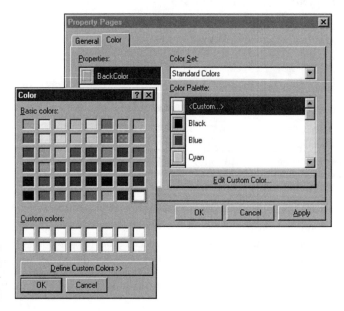

Figure 16-11
The Color selection dialog box with Edit Custom Color selected

Other logical color properties you might include are the colors for the shadow lines and ForeColor for the font in `lblCaption`. You can also add StandardFont and StandardPicture Property pages to allow you to select the font and the font styles for `lblCaption` and to add a picture to the SButton control. Of course, for each item you add to the Property page, you must add a property in the control, with all of its code.

There must be an easier way, and there is. The next lesson introduces a wonderful wizard.

1. Building a Property page is a lot like:
   a. Building a form
   b. Building a control
   c. Using OLE containers
   d. None of the above

2. The Property page keeps a list of:
   a. All the controls on the form that contains your custom control
   b. All the instances of your custom control
   c. All the selected controls on the form that contains your custom control
   d. All its own controls

3. After the Property page is built, it must still be:
   a. Configured
   b. Connected
   c. Contained
   d. Constrained

4. Changes made on a Property page will affect:
   a. Only controls for which the Property page was designed
   b. All controls on the containing form
   c. All selected controls on the containing form
   d. None of the controls on the containing form

5. To use the StandardColor Property page:
   a. Select it from the Connect Property Pages dialog box.
   b. You must add a color property to the user control.
   c. Both a and b above
   d. None of the above

THE CONTROL INTERFACE WIZARD

As you've seen, adding events and properties to a user control is not difficult, but it is detailed. You must remember to put a line or two of code into several different procedures. Make one mistake and your control doesn't work.

This lesson introduces the ActiveX Control Interface Wizard. Try it—you'll like it.

Running the Wizard

The ActiveX Control Interface Wizard is found on the Add-Ins menu. If it is missing from yours, select the Add-In Manager, and add it to the list of selected Add-Ins.

As of this writing, the ActiveX Control Interface Wizard will not run if you have added events to the control.

⬤ **Delete the following code from SButton before you attempt to run the Wizard:**

```
Public Event Click()

Private Sub lblCaption_Click()
    RaiseEvent Click
End Sub
```

Before you can run the Wizard, you must close the NewBtnDemo form and Code windows and open the Control Design window. The second screen of the Wizard is shown in Figure 16-12. (The first screen is just an introduction.)

If you do not delete the events you have added, the Wizard fails and then does not even try to load. You must exit and restart VB5.

⬤ **Select the ActiveX Control Interface Wizard from the Add-Ins menu.**

The Select Interface Members dialog box provides a list of standard properties, events, and methods for selection. You can select individual items from the Available Names list and click on > to move them to the Selected Names list. You can also click on >> to move the entire list of Available Names to the Selected Names list. Be careful here, as some of the offerings are not suitable for SButton. Caption and BackColor are already selected because you created those properties manually.

⬤ **Select the items in Table 16-7.**

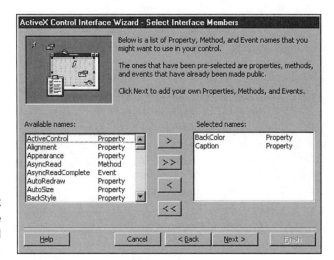

Figure 16-12
Starting the
ActiveX Control
Interface Wizard1

Table 16-7 Properties and events for SButton

Name	Type
Click	Event
DblClick	Event
Enabled	Property
FontBold	Property
FontItalic	Property
FontName	Property
FontSize	Property
ForeColor	Property
Picture	Property

 Click on Next.

The Create Custom Interface Members dialog box opens. The dialog box is shown in Figure 16-13.

If you want to add an interface element that is not part of the standard list, this is where you add it. There are no custom interface elements for this project.

 Click on Next.

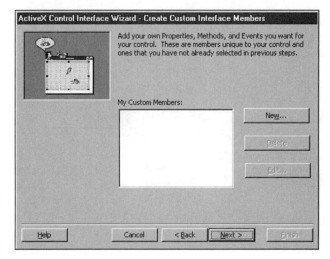

Figure 16-13
The Create
Custom Interface
dialog box

Mapping

The Set Mapping dialog box opens (shown in Figure 16-14).

The Set Mapping dialog box allows you to *map* specific properties, events, or methods to the user control or to a specific constituent component of the control. Mapping means connecting the property, event, or method to a specific component of the control. For example, you already have mapped the **BackColor** property to the user control, and the **Caption** property to **lblCaption**. Properties and events that are not mapped are added to the user control and all of the constituent components.

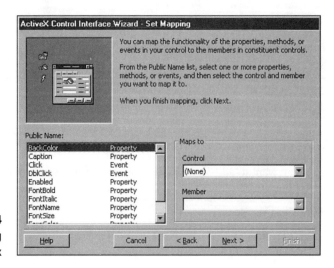

Figure 16-14
The Set Mapping
dialog box

To map the **Enabled** property:

● Click on Enabled in the Public Name list.

● Open the Control drop-down list and select UserControl.

● Map the elements according to Table 16-8.

Table 16-8 Map properties for SButton

Element	Map to
BackColor	UserControl
Caption	lblCaption
Font	lblCaption
FontBold	lblCaption
FontItalic	lblCaption
FontName	lblCaption
FontSize	lblCaption
ForeColor	lblCaption
Picture	UserControl

The **Caption** and **BackColor** properties are mapped by the code you have already written. Do not map them again. The **Click** and **DblClick** events must be available to all parts of the control and should not be mapped.

● Click on Next.

The Set Attributes dialog box shown in Figure 16-15 opens. This dialog box allows you to set the attributes of the unmarked elements. You can also add descriptions which will help the developer using your control.

Properties can be made **Read Only**, **Read/Write**, **Write Only**, or **Not Available**. Note that you can set these attributes to be different for runtime and design time.

● Click on Next.

Finished—Or Are You?

The Finished! dialog box opens. It gives you the option to view a summary report, which gives some advice about what to do next. For the first few times you use the Wizard, you will probably want to see the summary.

● Click on Finish.

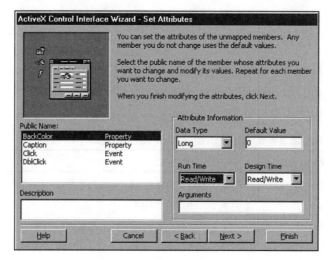

Figure 16-15
The Set Attributes
dialog box

After a slight delay while the Wizard writes some code, you are shown the summary report. If you elect to save the report, it is saved to the current directory as **ctlwiz.txt**. You can then open the text file with NotePad and print it if you want hard copy.

The ActiveX Control Interface Wizard adds a lot of code to the control. Unfortunately, some of it needs to be changed and some of it is incomplete. If you follow the instructions in the summary report, SButton will not work. The code in Listing 16-9 is the declarations section after the Wizard has modified it.

Listing 16-9 The modified declarations section

```
Option Explicit
Private lBackColor As Long
Const lHighLight = &HEOEOEO
Const lShadow = &H808080
'Event Declarations:
Event Click()
Event DblClick()
```

The Wizard has added declarations for the two events. So far, so good. But it has also made the changes in Listing 16-10, some of which are not so good.

Listing 16-10 Some other changes from the Wizard

```
Private Sub UserControl_InitProperties()
'    Caption = Extender.Name
'    BackColor = RGB(192, 192, 192)
End Sub

Private Sub UserControl_ReadProperties(PropBag As PropertyBag)
    UserControl.BackColor = PropBag.ReadProperty("BackColor", &HFF8080)
    lblCaption.Caption = PropBag.ReadProperty("Caption", "")
    lblCaption.FontUnderline = PropBag.ReadProperty("FontUnderline", 0)
```

```
    lblCaption.FontStrikethru = PropBag.ReadProperty("FontStrikethru", 0)
    lblCaption.FontSize = PropBag.ReadProperty("FontSize", 0)
    lblCaption.FontName = PropBag.ReadProperty("FontName", "")
    lblCaption.FontItalic = PropBag.ReadProperty("FontItalic", 0)
    lblCaption.FontBold = PropBag.ReadProperty("FontBold", 0)
    Set Font = PropBag.ReadProperty("Font")
    Set Picture = PropBag.ReadProperty("Picture")
    UserControl.Enabled = PropBag.ReadProperty("Enabled", True)
    lblCaption.ForeColor = PropBag.ReadProperty("ForeColor", &HFFFFFF)
'     Caption = PropBag.ReadProperty("Caption", Extender.Name)
'     BackColor = PropBag.ReadProperty("BackColor", RGB(192, 192, 192))
End Sub

Private Sub UserControl_WriteProperties(PropBag As PropertyBag)
    Call PropBag.WriteProperty("BackColor", _
      UserControl.BackColor, &HFF8080)
    Call PropBag.WriteProperty("Caption", _
      lblCaption.Caption, "")
    Call PropBag.WriteProperty("FontUnderline", _
      lblCaption.FontUnderline, 0)
    Call PropBag.WriteProperty("FontStrikethru", _
      lblCaption.FontStrikethru, 0)
    Call PropBag.WriteProperty("FontSize", _
      lblCaption.FontSize, 0)
    Call PropBag.WriteProperty("FontName", _
      lblCaption.FontName, "")
    Call PropBag.WriteProperty("FontItalic", _
      lblCaption.FontItalic, 0)
    Call PropBag.WriteProperty("FontBold", _
      lblCaption.FontBold, 0)
    Call PropBag.WriteProperty("Font", Font)
    Call PropBag.WriteProperty("Picture", Picture, Nothing)
    Call PropBag.WriteProperty("Enabled", _
      UserControl.Enabled, True)
    Call PropBag.WriteProperty("ForeColor", _
      lblCaption.ForeColor, &HFFFFFF)
'     PropBag.WriteProperty "Caption", Caption, Extender.Name
'     PropBag.WriteProperty "BackColor", BackColor, RGB(192, 192, 192)
End Sub
```

As you can see, ole' Wiz has *remmed out* the entire `InitProperties` procedure. (Remming out means that the section has been converted into remarks, or comments, which are ignored when the program is compiled.) Leave that alone, at least for now. There are more important things to handle.

In `ReadProperties`, for example, the lines:

```
'     Caption = PropBag.ReadProperty("Caption", Extender.Name)
'     BackColor = PropBag.ReadProperty("BackColor", RGB(192, 192, 192))
```

have been replaced with

```
UserControl.BackColor = PropBag.ReadProperty("BackColor", &HFF8080)
lblCaption.Caption = PropBag.ReadProperty("Caption", "")
```

The **BackColor** value is not at all what you want, and the default caption is an empty string!

 Change the new lines to read

```
UserControl.BackColor = PropBag.ReadProperty("BackColor", ⇐
&HCOCOCO)
    lblCaption.Caption = PropBag.ReadProperty("Caption", ⇐
Extender.Name)
```

You will find a similar change in **WriteProperties**. The original lines:

```
'   PropBag.WriteProperty "Caption", Caption, Extender.Name
'   PropBag.WriteProperty "BackColor", BackColor, RGB(192, 192, 192)
```

have been replaced with

```
Call PropBag.WriteProperty("BackColor", _
   UserControl.BackColor, &HFF8080)
Call PropBag.WriteProperty("Caption", _
   lblCaption.Caption, "")
```

 Change the new lines to read

```
Call PropBag.WriteProperty("BackColor", _
        UserControl.BackColor, &HCOCOCO)
    Call PropBag.WriteProperty("Caption", _
        lblCaption.Caption, Extender.Name)
```

As you scroll through the code, you can see the **Property Get** and **Property Let** code that the Wizard added for each of the new properties. It also remmed out the original **Caption** property procedures and added its own. What it *hasn't* done is make the events work.

 Add the following code:

```
Private Sub lblCaption_Click()
    RaiseEvent Click
End Sub

Private Sub lblCaption_DblClick()
    RaiseEvent DblClick
End Sub

Private Sub UserControl_Click()
    RaiseEvent Click
End Sub

Private Sub UserControl_DblClick()
    RaiseEvent DblClick
End Sub
```

One more disaster lurks in the code. The Wizard has created code to handle the font for the caption, but it has made one critical error and one critical omission. Look in `ReadProperties` and you will see

```
lblCaption.FontSize = PropBag.ReadProperty("FontSize", 0)
lblCaption.FontName = PropBag.ReadProperty("FontName", "")
```

And in WriteProperties:

```
Call PropBag.WriteProperty("FontSize", _
     lblCaption.FontSize, 0)
   Call PropBag.WriteProperty("FontName", _
     lblCaption.FontName, "")
```

A `FontSize` of `0` is too small to see. Worse yet, it generates an error. And an empty string for the `FontName` property does the same.

● Change the code to read (changes in bold)

```
lblCaption.FontSize = PropBag.ReadProperty("FontSize", 8)
     lblCaption.FontName = PropBag.ReadProperty("FontName", ⇐
"MS Sans Serif")

     Call PropBag.WriteProperty("FontSize", _
       lblCaption.FontSize, 8)
     Call PropBag.WriteProperty("FontName", _
       lblCaption.FontName, " MS Sans Serif ")
```

The changes provide a default value for the `FontSize` property and the `FontName` property. The defaults are consistent, with standard Visual Basic defaults.

● Delete all of the remmed-out code, just to make it prettier.

● Delete any `Debug.Print` statements that remain.

● Open the user Control Design window.

● Select Property Pages and check all four choices.

Congratulations! You just created a new control. Now it's time to test the new control.

● Click the Close button of the Control Design window to update the control.

● Open NewBtnDemo.

Take a look at the Properties window now. Your control gives you a totally new access to the properties of a push-button control. Unlike the Command button, SButton has a BackColor property that *works*. You can even put a picture on it!

● Select Picture from the Properties window.

● Select a metafile picture from the VB5 Graphics directory.

Pretty sharp! Use metafile pictures unless you need something else. Metafiles will stretch to fill SButton. With all of the other available types, you must size the button to fit the picture.

What Hath Wiz Wrought?

The ActiveX Interface Wizard takes a lot of the drudgery out of control creation. None of what it does for you is difficult, but there is so much of it! Each new property requires a line or two of code in **PropertyGet** and **PropertyLet** and another line in **WriteProperties**, **ReadProperties**, and maybe **InitProperties**. Events and methods must be declared and code written to activate them. Nothing difficult, but nonetheless, a lot of code means plenty of opportunity to make a mistake. The Wizard does most of the work for you. What it misses is not hard to detect and is easy to fix, now that you know the mechanics.

This project made you work a little harder than normal. The time to invoke the Wizard is when you have decided on the features of your control. Do not add any code or properties to the control until the Wizard has done its work. As you saw above, if you do, it will undo some of your work.

Once the Wizard finishes, check the default properties it assigned and adjust them to fit your needs.

The hardest part about creating user controls is deciding what functions and features to include before you begin. Control creation should not be a "Topsy" project. (Remember Topsy? She "just grew.")

1. The ActiveX Control Interface Wizard is found on the:
   a. Project menu
   b. File menu
   c. New Project dialog box
   d. Add-Ins menu

2. The ActiveX Control Interface Wizard lets you add _____ to a user control.
   a. Properties
   b. Methods
   c. Events
   d. All of the above

3. Mapping a property to a specific component of a user control:
   a. Reserves that property for the specific component
   b. Connects the property to all components but gives the specific component priority
   c. Disconnects the property from the specific component and connects it to all other components
   d. Creates a bitmap of the specified component

4. How does the ActiveX Control Interface Wizard handle events?
   a. It adds the declaration for an event but does not write the code.
   b. It adds the declaration for an event and writes the necessary code.
   c. It does not do anything with events except remind you to write them.
   d. It writes the code for the event, but you must add the declaration.

5. The ActiveX Control Interface Wizard lets you make properties:
   a. Read only at runtime and design time
   b. Read only at design time and read/write at runtime
   c. Read/write at design time and read only at runtime
   d. Any of the above

COMPILING AND DISTRIBUTING YOUR CONTROL

Now that you have a user control all designed and tested, it's time to make it into a real OCX file and consider how to distribute it.

A Last Refinement

If you compile SButton now, developers who want to use it will see the standard user control icon on the ToolBox. It's pretty enough, but ToolBox icons should be unique. In other words, each control you make should have a different icon. Take a look at the Property window with the control builder on the screen. The ToolBox **Bitmap** property allows you to select a bitmap for the job.

Here's where your artistic talents get their greatest challenge! The ToolBox Bitmap must be 16 × 15 pixels. That's pretty darned small! If you try to draw a 16 × 15 bitmap in Windows Paint, you'll discover how small. There isn't much you can do with it. On the Visual Basic 5 CD is the **ImageEdit** program. **ImageEdit** gives you a much better canvas for your design but does not have text. Still, some people come up with some pretty creative designs. (**ImageEdit** also makes icons.)

There is a bitmap included with the files for this lesson. It is named, with great originality, **SBtn.bmp**.

- Bring the Control Design window to the front.

- Click on ToolBox Bitmap in the Properties window.

- Select `SBtn.bmp` from the CD files, or select one of the bitmaps in the Visual Basic Graphics directory.

- Close the Control Design window to update the control.

Now SButton has its own icon in the ToolBox.

Making the OCX File

Now it is complete, and it is time to make the OCX file.

- Click on NewBtn in the Project Explorer to select the project.

- Select Make SButton.ocx from the File menu.

- Enter SButton.ocx as a file name in the Make Project dialog box.

That does it. Not only does Visual Basic build your OCX file, but it registers it in the system registry so that other programs can use it. First, though, you need to test it again in the current program.

Test Number One—Testing SButton in the Original NewBtnDemo Program

If you run NewBtnDemo at this point, it will still use the user control that is part of the same project group because that is the connection it has made. To verify the OCX, you must first remove `NewBtn.vbp` from the project group.

- Click on `NewBtn.vbp` in the Project Explorer to select it.

- Select Remove Project from the File menu.

Visual Basic will complain that the project is referenced from another project. That is, of course, because NewBtnDemo contains a reference to it.

- Click on Yes to remove the project.

When NewBtn.vbp is removed, Visual Basic looks for the OCX file in the system registry. If it exists, it is the reference that was set in the NewBtnDemo project. If it does not exist, the reference was removed and the instances of the control disappear from the form.

● Select the SButton icon and draw another copy of SButton on the form.

● Change the properties of the new SButton using the Property Pages. It doesn't matter what you change, just change *something* (or maybe everything).

● Press F5 or click on the Run button to run the project.

When you are satisfied that the control is working, exit from the NewBtnDemo program. It's time to try the new control with a brand new project.

● Select New Project from the File menu and start a Standard EXE project.

The first thing you may notice is that the SButton icon is gone from the ToolBox. And after all that work! Never fear.

● Select Components from the Project menu.

● If SButton.ocx does not appear on the Controls tab, use the browse button to add it to the list.

● Check the control and click on OK.

Normal installation of the OCX would put it in the Windows/System directory. Because this is an experimental control (do not market any programs that use it unless you add a lot of error trapping!), it is not in the expected place, which explains having to browse for it.

● Once the control is in the ToolBox, add a few instances of it to Form1.

● Write some code to show that the control is working. If you can't think of any, try the code in Listing 16-11.

Listing 16-11 Testing SButton

```
Option Explicit

Private Sub SButton1_Click()
    MsgBox "This is SButton1"
End Sub

Private Sub SButton2_Click()
MsgBox "This is SButton2"
End Sub
```

Run the program and verify the SButton works as advertised.

Distribution

You can use the Setup Wizard to create distribution copies of your ActiveX controls.

- Use the Windows Start button to select and run the Setup Wizard.

- Use the Browse... button to select NewBtn.vbp.

- Remove the checkmark from Rebuild the Project.

- Click on Next.

- Select your distribution media (Floppy disk, Single Directory, or Disk Directories).

- If you selected Single Directory or Disk Directories, select a directory for the file(s) on your hard disk drive.

- Click on Next.

- The project does not use any local ActiveX components. Click on Next.

- The project does use STDOLE2.TLB. Click on Next.

- Click on Next to accept the File Summary.

- Click on Finish.

After it analyzes the code for a while, the Setup Wizard creates your distribution files. Note that OCX controls created with Visual Basic require VBRUN500.DLL. If you are distributing only to VB5 developers, you can omit that file and cut your distribution package by almost a meg.

Another approach to distribution is to distribute the source code instead of the compiled OCX. This can be useful for in-house distribution in particular. For wider distribution, it raises licensing problems because there is nothing to stop another developer from marketing the program as his or her own.

Licensing

If you develop a control for commercial distribution, then you've spent hundreds of hours building, debugging and testing the control. The world already has enough buggy custom controls, so you spend enough time to make your control really robust. (Robust in computerese means it doesn't break and it works with anything else a developer may choose to use with it.) The one thing you don't want is for the first developer who purchases your control to "improve" it, making a control project of his own that is nothing more than your control with a trivial addition. You market your control as Gadget.OCX, and he markets his as IGadget.OCX (for "improved" gadget). Worse yet, he undercuts your price by half!

It could happen, but not if you take advantage of the licensing support that is available in Visual Basic. When you add licensing support to a control, VB compiles a *license key* into the program and adds a `.vbl` file to the distribution set. When your competitor creates the distribution set for IGadget, your license file is not (and cannot effectively be) included. Developers who buy his knockoff product will get a product that refuses to work.

To add licensing to your OCX:

1. Select Project Properties on the Project menu.

2. Check Require License Key on the General tab.

3. Click OK.

That's all it takes to protect your control from piracy.

What About Shareware Distribution?

Shareware distribution is one of the most popular ways small-scale programmers distribute their products. Developers like it too because they can have the "try before you buy" advantage. But how do you keep the developer from distributing programs that use your control and making money without paying you for your work?

There are five basic techniques you can use.

The Honor System

You can just trust people to pay for the software if they use it commercially. As strange as it seems, several topnotch developers use it. A few that come to mind are MacAfee's fine antivirus products, the various incarnations of the WinZip file compression/expansion program, and the Paint Shop Pro graphics manipulation program.

CrippleWare

Some developers leave a few key features out of their shareware distribution product. When someone sends in a check, a fully working copy is sent by snail mail or email. It's an effective technique, but many developers will not consider crippleware programs.

Nags

If a shareware product pops up an opening screen that reminds you to buy it, the screen is called a *nag*. It's unlikely that a developer would want to market a program that displays your nag, but she does have a fully working copy for evaluation purposes.

Product Support

The idea of product support goes along with trust in the list of possibilities, because it still relies on trust. If your control requires a lot of documentation, an offer of printed docs may elicit a few checks. Add in free product updates and (maybe) telephone support and you have an even better chance. (But be prepared for some really stupid questions at 3:00 A.M.)

Expiration

If you look hard enough, you can find an OCX for sale that will include an expiration date or a usage meter. After a month of use, or a certain number of uses, the program stops working.

Versioning Issues

Now that you have your control in distribution, the suggestions start rolling in. "Gee, it would be neat if it could delp a glunder!" everyone says. After a few hundred such requests, you study the issue and decide that glunder delping is a really good addition. Better yet, you figure out a really simple way to do it.

You sit down at your computer, and a few dozen hours later, your control delps glunders with the best of them! You recompile the control and announce that Gadget.OCX now has a new feature. Jim D. Veloper buys your upgraded control and adds it to his next project. He is delighted to have a control that does so much and does it so well.

Until he distributes his program, that is. Sue User buys a copy and installs it on the same computer that uses an earlier version of Gadget.OCX. The new program works great, but the earlier program is now broken. Jim D. now has a most upset customer, and so do you.

How do you prevent this common problem?

- Never remove any functioning parts of the control. You can add all you want.

- Don't remove any properties. If you want to stop using a property, you can mark it as hidden in the Procedure Attributes dialog box. You can remove it from `WriteProperties`, but never remove it from `ReadProperties` or it will break every program that uses a previous version.

- Don't change procedure attributes for events or methods.

- On the Make tab of the Project Properties dialog box, check Auto Increment. Each new compilation of the OCX will have a higher version number. `Setup.exe` will not replace an OCX with one that has a lower version number. (It seems to ignore dates.)

- Test, test, test.

Summary

This chapter has introduced control creation, but it is far from an exhaustive study of the subject. Using the techniques in this chapter and the knowledge of programming you have learned in this book, you can write useful controls for your own projects. With experience, you can produce robust, marketable controls.

1. The ToolBox bitmap must be:
   a. 16 × 15 pixels
   b. 32 × 32 pixels
   c. 64 × 64 pixels
   d. The size does not matter.

2. Making the OCX file:
   a. Creates a distributable OCX
   b. Compiles and registers the OCX
   c. Creates a new project
   d. Compiles the OCX and the EXE files together

3. Once it is compiled, the OCX file:
   a. Is ready to use
   b. Only needs to be tested with the original test program
   c. Should be tested with the original test program and other test programs, as well
   d. Does not need testing

4. To distribute your OCX file:
   a. Copy only the OCX to a floppy disk and pass it around
   b. Copy the OCX and **VBRUN500.DLL** to a floppy disk and pass it around
   c. Run the Make OCX file option from the File menu
   d. Use the Setup Wizard

5. The Require License Key option:
   a. Registers your OCX with a driver's license number
   b. Compiles a license key into the OCX and adds a **.vbl** file to the distribution set
   c. Requires a user to enter a license number each time he or she uses your control
   d. Adds a nag screen to your project

CHAPTER 17

REGISTER YOUR PROGRAMS: USING THE WINDOWS REGISTRY

Jim User has resized and moved the window for your program to suit his preferences. After spending an hour using the program's many useful features, Jim closes the program and goes about his business. Later in the day, he needs one more session with your program, but when he starts the program again, it pops right up—full screen again! Grumbling inwardly, he resizes and moves it again before he uses its better features. Jim likes your program, but after a few weeks of resizing and moving it every day, he begins to comment, "Gee, that program is a pain to use!" and his perceptions begin to shift.

Jim would really appreciate a program that *remembers* its size and position when he closes it and opens at his preferred size and position. It would make his perception of your work much more favorable.

Earlier versions of Windows stored program information in initialization (`.INI`) files. Some programs used their own `.INI` files and others used `WIN.INI` or `SYSTEM.INI`. Windows 95 and Windows NT can use initialization files, but Microsoft recommends that you store initialization information in a database called *the system registry*.

You can view the registry with Regedit. Regedit shows the registry in tree format, something like Explorer. Start it by selecting Run from the Windows 95 Start menu, entering **Regedit** on the command line and clicking OK. Figure 17-1 shows what you see.

Do not, under any circumstances, actually *edit* exisiting items in the system registry with Regedit unless you have had specific training. You can really mess things up by deleting or changing something you shouldn't.

Click on the + sign next to **HKEY_LOCAL_MACHINE** to expand that branch, then on the + sign next to Software, on the + sign next to Microsoft, the + sign next to Internet Explorer, and then click on Main. You will see something like Figure 17-2. (Mileage will vary: The registry reflects *your* computer setup. This illustration is only a *typical* view of the registry.)

What we have just done is called *expanding the registry*. Throughout this chapter we will use standard directory path notation to refer to a registry entry. The Internet Explorer entry that we just opened would be referred to as **HKEY_LOCAL_MACHINE\Software\Internet Explorer\Main**.

The information on the right side of the screen shows the configuration setup for MIE on my computer. We won't even try to go into what it all means. The point is that installed software keeps track of things like window state, window position, paths for other features, and user settings by storing them in the registry. Your software can do the same thing.

Look again at Figure 17-1. The collapsed registry tree shows six main roots for the registry. Table 17-1 lists these main roots and explains a little about their purpose.

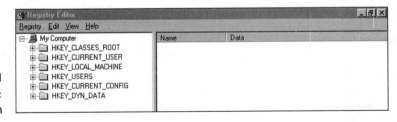

Figure 17-1
The Regedit opening screen

Figure 17-2
Regedit with
HKEY_LOCAL_MACHINE/
Software/ Internet
Explorer/Main
expanded

Table 17-1 The meaning of registry roots

Key	Meaning
HKEY_CLASSES_ROOT	The file name extensions key that tells Windows what application to associate with a file extension. If your application uses a specific extension, it should be added to this key.
HKEY_CURRENT_USER	User-specific data. Used to store configuration infomation for each user. Each user can have his or her own preferences.
HKEY_LOCAL_MACHINE	Computer-specific data. Data stored here is used by all instances of your application and all users get the same data.
HKEY_USERS	Used by Windows to store data about all of the users.
HKEY_CURRENT_CONFIG	Display and printer configuration information.
HKEY_DYN_DATA	Dynamic data, including performance statistics.

Under the roots are *Registry Keys*. Your application stores its data in a subkey under the software key. Microsoft recommends the following set of subkeys:

```
HKEY_LOCAL_MACHINE
    Software
        Company Name
            ProductName
                Version
```

The added subkeys are shown in **bold** print. This type of structure is normally shown the same way we show a path, like this: `HKEY_LOCAL_MACHINE\Software\YourCo\YourApp\1.0`.

Each subkey can have a number of *values* associated with it. The values appear in the right hand pane of the Regedit window, and your program can read those values to determine the paths and the default settings to use when it starts.

USING THE REGISTRY WITH BUILT-IN VB COMMANDS

Visual Basic and the Registry

Visual Basic makes it easy to store your application information in the registry. Visual Basic applications automatically create a registry entry when they are installed. You will find it in `HKEY_CURRENT_USER\Software\VB` and `VBA Program Settings\appname\section\key`. Your first exercise in working with the registry uses the four commands described next.

The GetSetting *Function*

This returns a key setting value from an application's Windows registry entry. Syntax:

```
GetSetting(appname, section, key[, default])
```

where

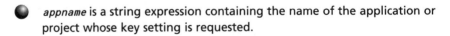

- *appname* is a string expression containing the name of the application or project whose key setting is requested.

- *section* is a string expression containing the name of the section where the key setting is found.

- *key* is a string expression containing the name of the key setting to return.

- *default* is an expression containing the value to return if no value is set in the key setting. If omitted, default is assumed to be a zero-length string ("").

The SaveSetting *Statement*

This saves or creates an application entry in the Windows registry entry.
Syntax:

```
SaveSetting(appname, section, key, setting)
```

where

- *appname* is a string expression containing the name of the application or project to which the setting applies.

- *section* is a string expression containing the name of the section where the key setting is being saved.

- *key* is a string expression containing the name of the key setting being saved.

- *setting* is an expression containing the value that key is being set to.

The DeleteSetting *Statement*

This deletes a section or key setting from the Windows registry entry.
Syntax:

```
DeleteSetting(appname, section[, key])
```

where

- *appname* is a string expression containing the name of the application or project to which the section or key setting applies.

- *section* is a string expression containing the name of the section where the key setting is being deleted. If only *appname* and *section* are provided, the specified section is deleted, along with all related key settings.

- *key* is a string expression containing the name of the key setting being deleted.

The GetAllSettings *Function*

This returns a list of key settings and their respective values from an application's Windows registry entry.

Syntax:

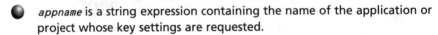

GetAllSettings(*appname, section*)

where

- *appname* is a string expression containing the name of the application or project whose key settings are requested.

- *section* is a string expression containing the name of the section whose key settings are requested. GetAllSettings returns a variant whose content is a two-dimensional array of strings containing all the key settings in the specified section and their corresponding values.

Your First Registry Entries

The idea of this project is to have your program save settings when it exits and use them the next time it loads. The Address Book program from Chapter 2, Object-Oriented Programming, will serve as your experimental platform. You can easily adapt these steps to any of your own applications. Load the Address Book project file. (The version of Address Book that is modified for this project is on the CD in the Chap16 folder.) Add a command button, position it near **cmdSave**, and set the properties as shown in Table 17-2:

Table 17-2 Properties for RegClear command button

Name	Property
Caption	RegClear
Name	cmdRegClear

You will not use this command button in projects that you plan to distribute. The Setup Wizard creates an uninstall file that clears your registry entries when the program is removed from a computer. Since you are not creating setup disks for this project, you need some way of removing your experimental registry entries. Add the following code:

In Declarations, enter

```
Option Explicit
Public bDeleted As Boolean
```

The rest of the code is in Listing 17-1.

Listing 17-1 The code for your first registry manipulation

```
Private Sub Form_Unload(Cancel As Integer)
' Save the form's size and position if bDeleted is false
If bDeleted = True Then Exit Sub
```

```
SaveSetting "AddBook", "Startup", "Left", frmAddressBook.Left
SaveSetting "AddBook", "Startup", "Top", frmAddressBook.Top
SaveSetting "AddBook", "Startup", "Width", frmAddressBook.Width
SaveSetting "AddBook", "Startup", "Height", frmAddressBook.Height
End Sub

Private Sub cmdRegClear_Click()
' Clear the registry and set bDeleted to True
' If there is no registry entry to clear this generates
' an error that we will want to ignore.
On Error Resume Next
DeleteSetting "AddBook"
bDeleted = True
End Sub

Private Sub Form_Load()
'   Reads the registry and sets the form size and position
'   to the settings used in the previous Lesson
Dim iLeft As Integer, iTop As Integer
Dim iWidth As Integer, iHeight As Integer
bDeleted = False
iLeft = Val(GetSetting("AddBook", "Startup", "Left", "0"))
iTop = Val(GetSetting("AddBook", "Startup", "Top", "0"))
iWidth = Val(GetSetting("AddBook", "Startup", "Width", "6500"))
iHeight = Val(GetSetting("AddBook", "Startup", "Height", "4500"))
frmAddressBook.Move iLeft, iTop, iWidth, iHeight
End Sub
```

The variable **bDeleted** is a global variable used as a flag to indicate whether or not to save the settings. You don't want to save the registry entries again if you have cleaned out the entries from the registry by clicking on **cmdRegClear**.

The **Form_Load** event reads the four values from the registry and uses the move method to position and size the form according to the previous settings. What happens the first time you run the program? There are no previous keys or key values to read. Look at the following line of code:

```
iWidth = Val(GetSetting("AddBook", "Startup", "Width", "6500"))
```

The last parameter is the default setting, the string that is returned when there is no registry value to read. The form width is set to 6500 twips when there is no registry key value read.

The code

```
SaveSetting "AddBook", "Startup", "Width", frmAddressBook.Width
```

saves the **"Width"** and the form's width from **frmAddressBook.Width** in **HKEY_CURRENT_USER\Software\VB** and **VBA Program Settings\AddBook\Startup**.

Testing the Program

Press F5 to run the program. Move the form and resize it, and then exit from the program. Then press F5 to run the program again. It should resume running in exactly the same location and at exactly the same size as when you quit the program.

Summary

In this lesson, you have seen how to save data to the system registry and how to retrieve that data using statements and functions from Visual Basic.

In the next lesson, we will use the API to save settings to `HKEY_LOCAL_MACHINE` and `HKEY_CURRENT_USER`.

1. Microsoft recommends that you store program information in the:
    a. `win.ini` file
    b. `system.ini` file
    c. `apname.ini` file
    d. System registry

2. What program should be used for viewing the registry?
    a. Notepad
    b. Write
    c. Regedit
    d. Word

3. The statements and functions that are built in to Visual Basic allow you to store program data in the _____ key of the registry.
    a. `HKEY_CURRENT_USER\Software\VB` and `VBA Program Settings\`
    b. `HKEY_LOCAL_MACHINE\Software\VB` and `VBA Program Settings\`
    c. `HKEY_CURRENT_CONFIG\Software\VB` and `VBA Program Settings\`
    d. Any of the root keys can be used

4. What is the purpose of the default parameter of the `GetSetting` function?
    a. It is written to the registry if no value is there.
    b. It is the value that is returned when there is no value in the registry.
    c. It is reserved by Microsoft for future use.
    d. It is a zero-length string.

5. Which of the statements below is correct?
    a. `SaveSetting (MyApp\Name\Screen.Width = "1000")`
    b. `SaveSetting ("MyApp", "Screen", "Width", 1000)`
    c. `SaveSetting "MyApp", "Screen", "Width", 1000`
    d. `SaveSetting ("MyApp\Screen\Width", 1000)`

USING THE REGISTRY API

The built-in VB registry settings are convenient but limited. By using the Windows APIs, you can save your data in a more powerful way.

Create a new directory, named **Registry Program**. Start a new project, or load **RegAPI.vbp** from the CD that comes with this book. Add a command button to the main form and make five copies of it as a control array. Set the properties according to Table 17-3.

Table 17-3 The property values for the Registry API project

Object	Property	Value
Form	Name	frmRegistry
	Caption	Registry API Project
Command button	Name	Command1
	Index	0
	Caption	Create Key
Command button	Name	Command1
	Index	1
	Caption	Set Key Value
Command button	Name	Command1
	Index	2
	Caption	Query Value
Command button	Name	Command1
	Index	3
	Caption	Delete Value
Command button	Name	Command1
	Index	4
	Caption	Delete Key
Command button	Name	Command1
	Index	5
	Caption	E&xit

You will not use all of these command buttons in the first part of this project. You will add functionality as you move along to demonstrate the flexibility of the registry APIs.

Use Figure 17-3 as a guide for placing the controls on the form.

Now add a frame to your main form, and put two option buttons inside it. The option buttons will be part of a control array. Add a text box and a label to your form, as well. Set the properties for the new controls according to Table 17-4.

Table 17-4 More properties for the RegAPI form

Object	Property	Value
Frame	Name	fraRoot
	Caption	Root
Option Button	Name	optKey
	Index	0
	Caption	HKEY_LOCAL_MACHIN
	Value	True
Option Button	Name	optKey
	Index	1
	Caption	HKEY_CURRENT_USER
	Value	False
TextBox	Name	txtSubKey
	Text	""

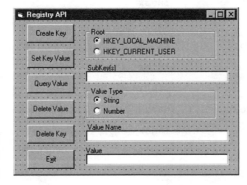

Figure 17-3
The completed
RegAPI form

There are controls on the form that are not yet included in this project. Like the unused command buttons, these are components you will add in a later part of the overall project for this chapter.

Add a module to the project by opening the Project menu and selecting Add Module. With the module Code window active, press F4 and name the module RegAPI. You can use this module in other programs as well, which will be a big time saver.

Using the API Text Viewer

The Visual Basic 5 Professional and Enterprise editions come with a program called *API Text Viewer* that you can use to view information about the Windows API. Better yet, you can copy and paste the declarations from the API Text Viewer into your programs, which can save hours of debugging time. Click on Start and select Visual Basic 5, then select API Text Viewer from the pop-up that appears. The program's opening screen is shown in Figure 17-4.

When the program opens, open the File menu and select Load Text File.

The API Text Viewer offers to convert the text file to a database. It is really better if you do that, but if you elect to do it now, go have a cup of coffee while it does the conversion— it takes awhile.

Switch the API Type to Constants. Search through the list box for `Public Const ERROR_SUCCESS = 0&.` When you find it, click on it to select it, and then click on the Add button. In the same way, select and add all of the constants in the following list:

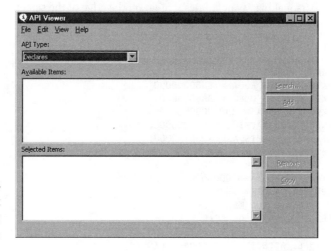

Figure 17-4
The API Text
Viewer's opening
screen

```
Public Const ERROR_SUCCESS = O&
Public Const HKEY_CLASSES_ROOT = &H80000000
Public Const HKEY_CURRENT_USER = &H80000001
Public Const HKEY_DYN_DATA = &H80000006
Public Const HKEY_LOCAL_MACHINE = &H80000002
 Public Const STANDARD_RIGHTS_ALL = &H1F0000
Public Const KEY_QUERY_VALUE = &H1
Public Const KEY_CREATE_LINK = &H20
Public Const SYNCHRONIZE = &H100000
Public Const KEY_SET_VALUE = &H2
Public Const KEY_CREATE_SUB_KEY = &H4
Public Const KEY_ENUMERATE_SUB_KEYS = &H8
Public Const KEY_NOTIFY = &H10
Public Const KEY_ALL_ACCESS = ((STANDARD_RIGHTS_ALL Or _
 KEY_QUERY_VALUE Or KEY_SET_VALUE Or KEY_CREATE_SUB_KEY _
 Or KEY_ENUMERATE_SUB_KEYS Or KEY_NOTIFY Or KEY_CREATE_LINK) _
 And (Not SYNCHRONIZE))
Public Const REG_DWORD = 4
Public Const REG_OPTION_NON_VOLATILE = 0
Public Const REG_SZ = 1
```

Now switch the API Type to Declares, and select and add the following declarations:

```
RegCreateKeyEx
RegCloseKey
```

Finally press COPY to copy the declarations to the clipboard. Now go back to your project and paste them all into the declarations section of the RegAPI module. Put the cursor on the line following Option Explicit, and select Paste from the Edit menu, or press [SHIFT]-[INSERT]. This creates some very long lines in your declarations section. I have a personal bias against lines that go off the edge of the screen, so my declaration section looks like this:

```
Option Explicit

Public Const ERROR_SUCCESS = O&
Public Const HKEY_CLASSES_ROOT = &H80000000
Public Const HKEY_CURRENT_USER = &H80000001
Public Const HKEY_DYN_DATA = &H80000006
Public Const HKEY_LOCAL_MACHINE = &H80000002
Public Const STANDARD_RIGHTS_ALL = &H1F0000
Public Const KEY_QUERY_VALUE = &H1
Public Const KEY_CREATE_LINK = &H20
Public Const SYNCHRONIZE = &H100000
Public Const KEY_SET_VALUE = &H2
Public Const KEY_CREATE_SUB_KEY = &H4
Public Const KEY_ENUMERATE_SUB_KEYS = &H8
Public Const KEY_NOTIFY = &H10
Public Const KEY_ALL_ACCESS = ((STANDARD_RIGHTS_ALL Or _
 KEY_QUERY_VALUE Or KEY_SET_VALUE Or KEY_CREATE_SUB_KEY _
 Or KEY_ENUMERATE_SUB_KEYS Or KEY_NOTIFY Or KEY_CREATE_LINK) _
 And (Not SYNCHRONIZE))
Public Const REG_DWORD = 4
Public Const REG_OPTION_NON_VOLATILE = 0
```

```
Public Const REG_SZ = 1

Declare Function RegCreateKeyEx Lib "advapi32.dll" _
 Alias "RegCreateKeyExA" _
 (ByVal hKey As Long, ByVal lpSubKey As String, _
 ByVal Reserved As Long, ByVal lpClass As String, _
 ByVal dwOptions As Long, ByVal samDesired As Long, _
 lpSecurityAttributes As Any, _
 phkResult As Long, lpdwDisposition As Long) As Long

Declare Function RegCloseKey Lib "advapi32.dll" _
 (ByVal hKey As Long) As Long
```

Never fear. It *does* look intimidating, but it isn't really all that hard to work with. There is one change you must make to **RegCreateKey**. As it is pasted from the API Text Viewer, it contains the line:

```
lpSecurityAttributes As SECURITY_ATTRIBUTES,
```

This line should be changed to read

```
lpSecurityAttributes As Any,
```

In the program you will send a **0&** (long) to the API as a signal to use the default security attributes for your registry entries; if you do not make this change, you will have to work extra hard to accomplish the same thing.

Adding the Code

Now it is time to add some code to the form events. Double-click on one of the command buttons and add the code shown in Listing 17-2:

Listing 17-2 The code for the form

```
Private Sub Command1_Click(Index As Integer)
' Decodes command button array

Dim sType As String

' Selects command action

Select Case Index
Case 0 ' Create new key
If optKey(0) Then
 CreateNewKey HKEY_LOCAL_MACHINE, "\SOFTWARE\" & txtSubKey
 Else
 CreateNewKey HKEY_CURRENT_USER, "\SOFTWARE\" & txtSubKey
End If

Case 1  ' Create new value or set value
If optKey(0) Then
 SetNewValue HKEY_LOCAL_MACHINE, _
 "\SOFTWARE\" & txtSubKey, _
```

continued on next page

continued from previous page

```
     sType, _
     txtValueName, _
     txtValue
Else
  SetNewValue HKEY_CURRENT_USER, _
  "\SOFTWARE\" & txtSubKey, _
  sType, _
  txtValueName, _
  txtValue
End If

Case 2 ' Read a value
Case 3 ' Delete value
Case 4 ' Delete Key

Case 5 ' Quit
Form_Unload (0)

End Select

End Sub
And in Form_Unload add the following:
Private Sub Form_Unload(Cancel As Integer)

Unload Me

End
End Sub
```

Close the form Code window, and open the Code window for **RegAPI.Bas.**

Insert a procedure named **CreateNewKey**, and add the code shown in Listing 17-3:

Listing 17-3 The CreateNewKey sub

```
Public Sub CreateNewKey(lRoot As Long, sSubKey As String)

' Creates a new key in registry
' Parameters:
' lRoot is one of HKEY_CURRENT_USER or HKEY_LOCAL_MACHINE
' sSubKey is the subkey name (requires leading \)

Dim lResult As Long, hKeyHandle As Long, sMsg As String, lType As Long
Dim lValue As Long

' error checks

If Len(sSubKey) = 0 Then
  sMsg = "Bad input to create key" & vbCrLf
  sMsg = sMsg & "Key = " & sSubKey
  MsgBox sMsg
  GoTo Exit_subCreateKey
```

```
End If

' Create the key

lResult = RegCreateKeyEx _
 (lRoot, _
 sSubKey, _
 0&, _
 vbNullString, _
 REG_OPTION_NON_VOLATILE, _
 KEY_ALL_ACCESS, _
 0&, _
 hKeyHandle, _
 lResult)

' check to be sure function created a key
If lResult <> ERROR_SUCCESS Then
 sMsg = "Could not create key"
 MsgBox sMsg
 GoTo Exit_subCreateKey
End If

' Key was created, now close it

lResult = RegCloseKey(hKeyHandle)
If lResult <> ERROR_SUCCESS Then
 sMsg = "Could not close key"
 MsgBox sMsg
 GoTo Exit_subCreateKey
End If

Exit_subCreateKey:
Exit Sub

Error_subCreateKey:
MsgBox Error
Resume Exit_subCreateKey
End Sub
```

A Look at the Code

This is getting pretty involved! Take a look at the code before you get lost. Start with the code for the form. The command buttons are part of an array. When you click on one of them, the only way to know which button was clicked is to look at the array index. That is the purpose of the Select-Case structure. The code

```
If optKey(0) Then
    CreateNewKey HKEY_LOCAL_MACHINE, "\SOFTWARE\" & txtSubKey
Else
    CreateNewKey HKEY_CURRENT_USER, "\SOFTWARE\" & txtSubKey
End If
```

reads the value of the **optKey** option buttons and sends the correct key and subkey information to the **CreateNewKey** sub, which is part of the **RegAPI.Bas** module. At this time, the only other command button that does anything is the Exit button, which switches to **Form_Unload**.

The work is done in the **RegAPI.Bas** module's **CreateNewKey** sub. The code starts with an error check. A message box warns if there is no subkey specified. Then the following code creates the key.

```
lResult = RegCreateKeyEx _
(lRoot, _
sSubKey, _
0&, _
vbNullString, _
REG_OPTION_NON_VOLATILE, _
KEY_ALL_ACCESS, _
0&, _
hKeyHandle, _
lResult)
```

Microsoft defined the third parameter as **lpReserved**, which means that they may find a use for it in the future. Meanwhile, it must be a long integer 0.

The next parameter is a constant, **vbNullString**, provided by Visual Basic for use when calling external procedures where the external procedure requires a string whose value is zero.

The parameter **REG_OPTION_NON_VOLATILE** allows you to save the new subkey to the registry. Changing it to **REG_OPTION_ VOLATILE** creates a subkey that would not last beyond the first computer shutdown. The **KEY_ALL_ACCESS** parameter gives the code permission to read, write, and modify the key. The **0&** that follows is the signal to use the default security structure.

The handle of the key you have created appears in **hKeyHandle**, and **lResult** can be used to determine whether we have created a new key or opened an existing one. You don't really care, so you can use a variable that will be changed almost immediately. Note that the function's return value is stored in **lResult**, which overwrites the new/old key value. If successful, **lResult** holds the constant **ERROR_SUCCESS**.

The balance of the code in this section is error trapping, which you learned about in Chapter 10, Error Handling and Debugging.

Running the Program

Press F5 to run the program. Select the **HKEY_LOCAL_MACHINE** option and enter **VB Interactive** in the SubKeys textbox. When you click on Create Key, the new key is added to the registry. Before you take a look at it, change the SubKeys textbox to read VB Interactive\1.0 and click on Create Key one more time.

Now you can take a look at your results. Start the Regedit program and select **HKEY_LOCAL_MACHINE**. Expand the SOFTWARE key and you will find VB Interactive with a plus sign beside it. Expand that subkey and you find 1.0 as a branch beneath it.

Summary

You have seen how to add registry keys and subkeys using the Win32 API. Using the API is more work, but it provides greater flexibility because you can add keys and subkeys to any of the root keys in the registry.

In the next section, you will add values to the subkeys we have created.

1. The easiest way to get API constants, declarations and types correctly inserted in your programs is to use:
   a. Regedit
   b. Access
   c. Word
   d. The API Text Viewer

2. New keys are placed into the registry using:
   a. `RegCreateKeyEx`
   b. `RegInsertKeyEx`
   c. `RegOpenKeyA`
   d. `RegMakeKeyEx`

3. The parameter `REG_OPTION_NON_VOLATILE` tells Windows to:
   a. Erase the key when the program is terminated.
   b. Erase the key when the computer is turned off.
   c. Save the key to the registry.
   d. None of the above

4. The parameter `KEY_ALL_ACCESS` tells Windows:
   a. To let everybody access Windows without a password
   b. To add a password to the registry files
   c. To require the keylock to be on before registry access is allowed
   d. To allow read, write, modify, add, and delete privileges of accessing the registry

5. If `RegCreateKeyEx` is successful, it will return:
   a. `ERROR_OK`
   b. `ERROR_SUCCESS`
   c. `ERROR_NONE`
   d. `Result`

ADDING VALUES TO SUBKEYS

Now that you have created a subkey, it is time to make it do something useful—store some data. Of course, this means more APIs, but that is the source of your power.

The New Controls

Add another frame to the form, and place two option buttons inside. Add two textboxes and two labels to the form. Again, use Figure 17-3 as a guide to placement. Set the properties for the New controls according to Table 17-5.

Table 17-5 Properties for the New controls

Object	Property	Value
Frame	Name	fraType
	Caption	Value Type
Option Button	Name	optType
	Index	0
	Caption	String
	Value	True
Option Button	Name	optType
	Index	1
	Caption	Number
	Value	False
Label	Name	Label2
	Caption	Value Name
Label	Name	Label3
	Caption	Value
TextBox	Name	txtValueName
	Text	""
TextBox	Name	txtValue
	Text	""

Adding the Code

Open the API Text Viewer and find `RegSetValueEx` in the Declares section. Copy the declaration into the declaration section of `RegAPI.Bas`, as shown in Listing 17-4.

Listing 17-4 The declaration of `RegSetValueEx`

```
Declare Function RegSetValueEx Lib "advapi32.dll" _
Alias "RegSetValueExA" _
(ByVal hKey As Long, ByVal lpValueName As String, _
ByVal Reserved As Long, ByVal dwType As Long, _
lpData As Any, ByVal cbData As Long) As Long
```

Next, open the Code window for the form and add the code shown in Listing 17-5 to the beginning of `Command1_Click`:

Listing 17-5 Additions to `Command_Click`

```
Dim sType As String     (Existing Code)

If optType(0) Then
 sType = "String"
Else
 sType = "Number"
End If


' Selects command action (Existing Code)
In the Select-Case section find Case 1 and add the following:
Case 1  ' Create new value or set value
If optKey(0) Then
 SetNewValue HKEY_LOCAL_MACHINE, _
 "\SOFTWARE\" & txtSubKey, _
 sType, _
 txtValueName, _
 txtValue
Else
 SetNewValue HKEY_CURRENT_USER, _
 "\SOFTWARE\" & txtSubKey, _
 sType, _
 txtValueName, _
 txtValue
End If
```

Close the form's Code window, and open the Code window for `RegAPI.Bas`. Add a new procedure named `SetNewValue`, and then enter the code from Listing 17-6 in `SetNewValue`:

Listing 17-6 The `SetNewValue` sub

```
Public Sub SetNewValue(lRoot As Long, sSubKey As String, _
 sType As String, sValueName As String, sValue As String)
' Sets or changes values in subkeys
```

continued on next page

continued from previous page

```
' Parameters:
' lRoot is one of HKEY_CURRENT_USER or HKEY_LOCAL_MACHINE
' (Could be modified for other roots)
' sSubKey is the subkey name (requires leading \)
' sValue is string version of value to save

 Dim lResult As Long, hKeyHandle As Long, sMsg As String
Dim lValue As Long, lType As Long

' make sure that data has been passed to
' create the key

If Len(sValue) = 0 Then
 sMsg = "Bad input to creat value" & vbCrLf
 sMsg = sMsg & "Value = " & sValue
 MsgBox sMsg
 GoTo Exit_SetNewValue
End If

' If the key\subkey does not exist it will be created
' If it does exist it will be opened

lResult = RegCreateKeyEx _
 (lRoot, _
 sSubKey, _
 0&, _
 vbNullString, _
 REG_OPTION_NON_VOLATILE, _
 KEY_ALL_ACCESS, _
 0&, _
 hKeyHandle, _
 lResult)

If lResult <> ERROR_SUCCESS Then
 sMsg = "Could not open key"
 MsgBox sMsg
 GoTo Exit_SetNewValue
End If

Select Case sType
Case "String"
 lType = REG_SZ
 sValue = sValue & Chr$(0)
 lResult = RegSetValueEx _
 (hKeyHandle, _
 sValueName, _
 0&, _
 lType, _
 ByVal sValue, _
 Len(sValue))

Case "Number"
```

```
lType = REG_DWORD
lValue = Val(sValue)
lResult = RegSetValueEx _
(hKeyHandle, _
sValueName, _
0&, _
lType, _
lValue, _
4)

Case Else
 sMsg = "Bad input to create value" & vbCrLf
 sMsg = sMsg & "Type = " & sType
 MsgBox sMsg
 lResult = RegCloseKey(hKeyHandle)
 GoTo Exit_SetNewValue
End Select

If lResult <> ERROR_SUCCESS Then
 sMsg = "Could not set value"
 MsgBox sMsg
 GoTo Exit_SetNewValue
Else
 lResult = RegCloseKey(hKeyHandle)
End If

lResult = RegCloseKey(hKeyHandle)

Exit_SetNewValue:
Exit Sub

Error_SetNewValue:
MsgBox Error
Resume Exit_SetNewValue
End Sub
```

A Look at the New Code

The **SetNewValue** sub uses **RegCreateKeyEx** to open the key. If the key does not exist, **RegCreateKeyEx** creates it. The program provides for two different types of values: strings and long integers. Both are inserted under the subkey, but the insertion is done differently, so there are two different calls to **RegSetValueEx**.

The code that does the work is inside the select-case structure. Strings sent to API functions must be null-terminated. The last line in the following code adds the null as **Chr$(0)**:

```
Select Case sType
Stype will be one of "String" or "Number"
Case "String"
 lType = REG_SZ
REG_SZ represents a null-terminated string.
```

continued on next page

continued from previous page

```
                sValue = sValue & Chr$(0)

    lResult = RegSetValueEx _
     (hKeyHandle, _
     sValueName, _
     0&, _
     lType, _
     ByVal sValue, _
     Len(sValue))

    Case "Number"
     lType = REG_DWORD
```

REG_DWORD is a 4-byte number—in other words, a long integer.

```
    lValue = Val(sValue)
    lResult = RegSetValueEx _
     (hKeyHandle, _
     sValueName, _
     0&, _
     lType, _
     lValue, _
     4)
```

Note the difference between this section and the string section above. The value changes from a string variable (**sValue**) to a long integer variable (**lValue**). Note also that **sValue** is sent **ByVal**. The other difference is in the final parameter, which is the size of the value.

```
    Case Else
     sMsg = "Bad input to create value" & vbCrLf
     sMsg = sMsg & "Type = " & sType
     MsgBox sMsg
     GoTo Exit_SetNewValue
    End Select
```

The **Case Else** handles improper data types. The rest of the program prevents this from happening, but if you reuse the module in another program, you need this protection.

The rest of the code is typical error trapping.

Running The Code

When you ran the previous section, you created two subkeys, VB Interactive and VB Interactive\1.0. Press F5 to run the program again. Select HKEY_LOCAL_MACHINE for the root and String for the value type. Enter VB Interactive\1.0 in the SubKeys textbox, and test in the Value Name text box. Enter your name in the Value text box and click on Set Key Value.

Change the value type to Number and the value name to Numeric. Enter a whole number in the Value textbox, and once more click on Set Key Value. The SubKeys textbox should still read VB Interactive\1.0. Run Regedit again so you can verify that the data has been written. (If you still had Regedit running from the last lesson, you need to refresh the display: Close the subkey that is open, and click on one of the other subkeys. Then reopen the VB Interactive\1.0 subkey.)

Both of your values have been saved in the registry under the subkey.

Summary

Now you can create new subkeys and store named values in them. The same routine that stores a value can be used to change the value. Now, wouldn't it be nice to be able to recover those values? That is what you will do in the next lesson.

1. The API function `RegSetValueEx` will:
   a. Create a named value and assign it a value
   b. Change an existing value
   c. Both a and b
   d. None of the above

2. If the value's *type* is `REG_SZ`, the function expects you to write a _____ to the registry.
   a. Null
   b. Long integer
   c. Double-precision value
   d. Null-terminated string

3. What is the size of a long integer?
   a. 4 bytes
   b. 6 bytes
   c. 8 bytes
   d. 16 bytes

4. How is the null termination added to a string for the API?
   a. `sValue = sValue & NullString`
   b. `sValue = sValue & VBNull`
   c. `sValue = sValue & Chr$(0)`
   d. `sValue = sValue & 0&`

5. What is the best way to open the registry key for `RegSetValueEx`?
   a. `RegOpenKeyEx`
   b. `RegCreateKeyEx`
   c. `RegGetKeyEx`
   d. `RegFindKeyEx`

READING REGISTRY VALUES

Now it is time to read values back from the registry. The API that you use for this needs some modification to handle three different chores: learning the type and size of the value that is stored, reading string values, and reading long integer values.

You'll be happy to know that there are no new controls in this lesson. In fact, you have all of the controls you need. All you have to do now is add functionality.

Adding Code to Command_Click

Open the form's Code window and add the code from Listing 17-7 to the Command_Click event for Command1:

Listing 17-7 New code for the Command_Click event

```
Case 2 ' Read a value
If optKey(0) Then
 txtValue = ReadRegValue(HKEY_LOCAL_MACHINE, _
 "SOFTWARE\" & txtSubKey, txtValueName)
Else
 txtValue = ReadRegValue(HKEY_CURRENT_USER, _
 "SOFTWARE\" & txtSubKey, txtValueName)
End If
```

Adding New Code to RegAPI.Bas

Close the form Code window and open the Code window for RegAPI.Bas. Now open the API Text Viewer again, select RegQueryValueEx, and paste *three copies* of it into the declaration section of RegAPI.Bas. To make your new function flexible enough to handle everything you want to do, you will create three new variations of RegQueryValueEx: one to determine the details of the value you want to read, one to read strings, and one to read numbers.

Convert the first copy of RegQueryValueEx to look like this:

```
Declare Function RegQueryValueExNULL Lib "advapi32.dll" _
 Alias "RegQueryValueExA" _
 (ByVal hKey As Long, ByVal lpValueName As String, _
 ByVal lpReserved As Long, lpType As Long, _
 ByVal lpData As Long, lpcbData As Long) As Long
```

This is the version we will use to figure out if the value is a string or a long integer.

Convert the second copy to look like this:

```
Declare Function RegQueryValueExLONG Lib "advapi32.dll" _
 Alias "RegQueryValueExA" _
 (ByVal hKey As Long, ByVal lpValueName As String, _
```

```
ByVal lpReserved As Long, lpType As Long, _
lpData As Long, lpcbData As Long) As Long
```

This is the version we will use to read long integers.
Convert the third copy to look like this:

```
Declare Function RegQueryValueExSTRING Lib "advapi32.dll" _
Alias "RegQueryValueExA" _
(ByVal hKey As Long, ByVal lpValueName As String, _
ByVal lpReserved As Long, lpType As Long, _
ByVal lpData As String, lpcbData As Long) As Long
```

This is the version we will use for reading strings.
Now add a new function named `ReadRegValue` to `RegAPI.Bas`.
Add the code from Listing 17-8:

Listing 17-8 The `ReadRegValue` function

```
Function ReadRegValue(lRoot As Long, sSubKey As String, _
sValueName As String) As String
' Reads registry values
' Parameters:
' lRoot is one of HKEY_CURRENT_USER or
' HKEY_LOCAL_MACHINE
' sSubKey is the subkey name (no leading \)
' Returns: String value of registry value

Dim lResult As Long, hKeyHandle As Long
Dim sMsg As String, lType As Long, lValue As Long
Dim lcch As Long, lrc As Long, sValue As String

On Error GoTo Error_ReadRegValue

' Open key

lResult = RegOpenKeyEx(lRoot, sSubKey, 0, KEY_QUERY_VALUE, hKeyHandle)
If lResult <> ERROR_SUCCESS Then
 sMsg = "Could not open key"
 MsgBox sMsg
 GoTo Exit_ReadRegValue
End If

' Determine the size and type of the data to be read
lrc = RegQueryValueExNULL _
 (hKeyHandle, _
 sValueName, _
 0&, _
 lType, _
 0&, _
 lcch)

Select Case lType
Case REG_SZ
```

continued on next page

continued from previous page

```
    sValue = String(lcch, 0)
    lrc = RegQueryValueExSTRING(hKeyHandle, sValueName, _
   0&, lType, sValue, lcch)
    ReadRegValue = Left(sValue, lcch - 1)

Case REG_DWORD
 lrc = RegQueryValueExLONG(hKeyHandle, sValueName, _
 0&, lType, lValue, lcch)
 If lrc = ERROR_SUCCESS Then ReadRegValue = Str(lValue)

Case Else
lrc = -1

End Select

If lrc <> ERROR_SUCCESS Then
 sMsg = "Could not read Key"
 MsgBox sMsg
 lResult = RegCloseKey(hKeyHandle)
 GoTo Exit_ReadRegValue
End If

lResult = RegCloseKey(hKeyHandle)

Exit_ReadRegValue:
Exit Function

Error_ReadRegValue:
MsgBox Error
Resume Exit_ReadRegValue

End Function
```

By replacing the `lpValue` parameter with `0&`, you ask `RegQueryValueExNULL` to return the type of the stored value in `lType` and the size of the data in `lcch`. The variable `lType` then determines whether the program calls `RegQueryValueExSTRING` or `RegQueryValueExLONG`. A long integer value is converted to a string value before it is returned to `Command_Click` event. Strings returned from the API are null-terminated strings. The line

```
ReadRegValue = Left(sValue, lcch - 1)
```

removes the null.

Running the Program

You already have values stored in the registry. Run the program and Select **HKEY_LOCAL_MACHINE** for the root. Enter **VB Interactive\1.0** in the SubKeys textbox and **Test** in the Value Name textbox, and click the Query Value button. The text value you stored in the registry appears in the Value text box.

Change the Value Name to Numeric, and click on the Query Value button again. The number you saved will now be displayed in the Value text box.

Summary

Now you're getting somewhere! You can create keys and subkeys, you can write named data into those keys and subkeys, and you can read that data back. True, this program only displays the data, but you already know other ways to use it.

What remains is to be able to delete values and delete subkeys. In the next lesson you will learn to do both.

1. Replacing the **lpValue** parameter in **RegQueryValueEx** with **0&** causes the function to:
   a. Fail
   b. Return the constant **REG_KEY_EXISTS** or **REG_KEY_NOT_FOUND**
   c. Return the size and type of the key
   d. Return the key no matter what type it is

2. In **RegQueryValueEx**, what are the main differences between fetching a long integer and fetching a string?
   a. The parameters **lType** and **lpcbData**
   b. The words **LONG** and **STRING** in the name
   c. The handle of the key value
   d. All of the above

3. What is the purpose of the line **ReadRegValue = Left(sValue, lcch - 1)**?
   a. It removes **lcch** from the string.
   b. It converts the string into a left-justified string.
   c. It removes the terminating **Null** from the string.
   d. It removes training spaces from the string.

4. What is the purpose of the line **ReadRegValue = Str(lValue)**?
   a. It converts the string into a long integer.
   b. It converts the long integer into a string.
   c. It does nothing; there is a syntax error in the line.
   d. It removes trailing spaces.

5. The function **RegQueryValueEx** needs the handle of the key in order to return its value. Where does it get that handle?
   a. It is generated by the function call itself.
   b. It scans through the entire registry looking for the value name.
   c. It comes from **RegCloseKey**.
   d. It comes from **RegOpenKey**.

DELETING VALUES AND SUBKEYS

You guessed it! More APIs, but simple ones this time.

Adding Code to `Command_Click`

Open the form's Code window. You are going to be adding the code for the remaining two command buttons, indexes 3 and 4, as shown in Listing 17-9.

Listing 17-9 The remaining code for `Command_Click`

```
Case 3 ' Delete value
If optKey(0) Then
 DeleteRegValue HKEY_LOCAL_MACHINE, _
 "SOFTWARE\" & txtSubKey, txtValueName
Else
 DeleteRegValue HKEY_CURRENT_USER, _
 "SOFTWARE\" & txtSubKey, txtValueName
End If
txtValueName = ""
txtValue = ""

Case 4 ' Delete Key
If optKey(0) Then
 DeleteRegKey HKEY_LOCAL_MACHINE, _
 "SOFTWARE\" & txtSubKey
Else
 DeleteRegKey HKEY_CURRENT_USER, _
 "SOFTWARE\" & txtSubKey
End If
txtValueName = ""
txtValue = ""
txtSubKey = ""
```

Both of these routines use **optKey** to determine the registry root to use and call the appropriate routine from **RegAPI.Bas** to accomplish their tasks.

The New Code For RegAPI.Bas

Close the form's Code window and open the Code window for **RegAPI.Bas**. Open the API Text Viewer and select **RegDeleteValue** and **RegDeleteKey**. Copy them, and paste them into the declarations section of **RegAPI.Bas**, as shown in Listing 17-10.

Listing 17-10 Declarations for `RegDeleteValue` and `RegDeleteKey`

```
Declare Function RegDeleteValue Lib "advapi32.dll" _
 Alias "RegDeleteValueA" _
 (ByVal hKey As Long, ByVal lpValueName As String) As Long

Declare Function RegDeleteKey Lib "advapi32.dll" _
 Alias "RegDeleteKeyA" _
 (ByVal hKey As Long, ByVal lpSubKey As String) As Long
```

Create a new subkey in **RegAPI.Bas** named **DeleteRegValue**. Place the code from Listing 17-11 in it.

Listing 17-11 The code for `DeleteRegValue`

```
Sub DeleteRegValue(lRoot As Long, sSubKey As String, sValueName As String)
' Deletes a value from the regisry
' Parameters:
' lRoot is one of HKEY_CURRENT_USER or HKEY_LOCAL_MACHINE
' sSubKey is the subkey name (requires leading \)
' sValueName is the name of the value to delete

Dim lResult As Long, hKeyHandle As Long, sMsg As String

On Error GoTo Error_DeleteRegValue

' Open key

lResult = RegOpenKeyEx(lRoot, sSubKey, 0, KEY_SET_VALUE, hKeyHandle)
If lResult <> ERROR_SUCCESS Then
 sMsg = "Could not open key"
 MsgBox sMsg
 GoTo Exit_DeleteRegValue
End If

lResult = RegDeleteValue(hKeyHandle, sValueName)

If lResult <> ERROR_SUCCESS Then
 sMsg = "Could not delete key value"
 MsgBox sMsg
 lResult = RegCloseKey(hKeyHandle)
 GoTo Exit_DeleteRegValue
End If

lResult = lResult = RegCloseKey(hKeyHandle)

Exit_DeleteRegValue:
Exit Sub

Error_DeleteRegValue:
MsgBox Error
Resume Exit_DeleteRegValue

End Sub
```

Create another new subkey named `DeleteRegKey` and put the code from Listing 17-12 in it.

Listing 17-12 The code for `DeleteRegKey`

```
Sub DeleteRegKey(lRoot As Long, sSubKey As String)
' Deletes key from registry
' Parameters: lRoot is one of HKEY_CURRENT_USER or
' HKEY_LOCAL_MACHINE
' sSubKey is the subkey name (requires leading \)

Dim lResult As Long, hKeyHandle As Long
Dim sMsg As String

On Error GoTo Error_DeleteRegKey

' Open key

lResult = RegOpenKeyEx(lRoot, sSubKey, 0, KEY_QUERY_VALUE, hKeyHandle)

If lResult <> ERROR_SUCCESS Then
 sMsg = "Could not open key"
 MsgBox sMsg
 GoTo Exit_DeleteRegKey
End If

lResult = RegDeleteKey(lRoot, sSubKey)
If lResult <> ERROR_SUCCESS Then
 sMsg = "Could not delete key"
 MsgBox sMsg
 GoTo Exit_DeleteRegKey
End If

Exit_DeleteRegKey:
Exit Sub

Error_DeleteRegKey:
MsgBox Error
Resume Error_DeleteRegKey

End Sub
```

A Look at the Code

There is nothing spectacular in either of these routines. Both start by opening the key, and both then call their respective API functions. If there is any difference, it is that after deleting a value, the key must be closed. Note that the access parameter for the functions is `KEY_SET_VALUE`.

Both `RegDeleteValue` and `RegDeleteKey` require the handle of the target registry key. The handle is provided by the `RegOpenKey` function.

The function `RegDeleteValue` deletes a single value from the registry key, which is then closed by the function `RegCloseKey`. To remove several values from the key, `RegDeleteValue` must be called once for each value.

The function `RegDeleteKey` removes the entire key from the registry. There is no need to close the key afterward; it no longer exists, and `RegCloseKey` would return an error.

Running the Program

When you run the program, you can try out both operations. Enter **VB Interactive\1.0** in the SubKeys textbox, **Test** in the Value Name textbox, and click the Delete Value button. Use Regedit to verify that the text value has been removed. Close Regedit before the next step.

Change the SubKeys textbox to read **VB Interactive**, click the Delete Key button, and run Regedit again to verify that the entire key is gone.

Summary

In this lesson, you completed your exploration of the registry APIs. While the program itself did nothing with the registry subkeys and values that it stored, you have already seen some of the things you can do with that data. Other possibilities include registration information, version information, encrypted passwords, serial numbers, and pallets.

The `RegAPI.Bas` module can be included in other programs, simplifying your future registry access.

1. You can remove values from the registry by using the API function:
   a. `RegDeleteKey`
   b. `RegSetValue,` with nulls in the value position
   c. `RegExit`
   d. `RegDeleteValue`

2. The `RegDeleteKey` function:
   a. Will fail if there are values in the subkey being removed
   b. Will remove the subkey, but leave the values behind as "orphans"
   c. Will remove the subkey and all of its values
   d. Will leave nulls where there used to be values

3. How many values can you remove with `RegDeleteValue`?
   a. Only one at a time
   b. As many as you list in the parameters
   c. All of them at once
   d. No more than two at a time

4. What is the correct access parameter to use for deleting registry values?
   a. `ERROR_SUCCES`
   b. `HKEY_CURRENT_CONFIG`
   c. `KEY_SET_VALUE`
   d. `KEY_NOTIFY`

5. Using the API functions seems like a lot more work than using the Visual Basic built in functions and statements. Why bother?
   a. It makes you look smart.
   b. The API functions allow you to give your values names; the built-in functions and statements don't.
   c. The API functions allow you to use any of the registry keys.
   d. The API functions are faster.

Modify SuperPad to use either the **RegAPI.BAS** module or Visual Basic's built-in registry commands to store the size and placement of the main form.

REVIEW

Lisa: This is nice! Now our programs can really look professional!

John: You bet. I really like that API registry module. We can use that in a lot of our programming, and we never have to go through writing all that code again.

Lisa: I know. I guess that's what they are talking about when you hear "Reusable code" all the time.

CHAPTER 18

VISUAL BASIC 5 COMMUNICATIONS

*C*ommunications! It is one of the bywords of modern computing. If you don't have a modem and an Internet account, you are considered impoverished. And it's an ever-expanding field. More and more business software is Internet-ready.

This chapter introduces some of the communications abilities in Visual Basic 5. All the lessons in this chapter require a modem, and some require an Internet account.

THE MSComm CONTROL

In the days of MS-DOS and Windows 3.x, connection to the serial port or a modem was a matter of sending and reading data from hardware addresses called *ports*. Windows 95 strongly discourages direct port access, which is often a source of system problems. Instead, with Windows 95 and Windows NT computers, accessing input/output (I/O) ports is handled through *drivers*. The result is greater stability for the operating system, but it also has created problems for people with a need for I/O operations because they could no longer get direct access to the ports.

The MSComm control provides serial communications for Visual Basic programs by providing access to the serial ports. This lesson unravels some of the intricacies of using the MSComm control to talk to your modem.

Start a new project and add the MSComm control to the toolbox. Press (CTRL)-(T) or select Components from the Project menu and select Microsoft MSComm Control 5.0. Click on OK. The icon for the MSComm control is shown in Figure 18-1. The completed project is on the CD that comes with this book.

Double-click on the MSComm icon to place the MSComm control on the form. It has no visible interface, so it doesn't matter where you put it. Add three Command buttons and a text box to the form. Set the properties according to Table 18-1.

Table 18-1 Properties for MSComm Project 1

Object	Property	Value
Form	Name	frmComm_1
	Caption	"Comm 1"
	Height	4725
	Width	7650
Command Button	Name	cmdQuit
	Caption	"E&xit"
	Height	315
	Left	5940
	TabIndex	2
	Top	540
	Width	1455
CommandButton	Name	cmdStop
	Caption	"Stop"

Object	Property	Value
	Height	315
	Left	180
	TabIndex	1
	Top	540
	Width	1455
CommandButton	Name	cmdStart
	Caption	"Start"
	Height	315
	Left	180
	TabIndex	0
	Top	60
	Width	1455
TextBox	Name	txtInData
	Height	3615
	Left	60
	MultiLine	-1 'True
	ScrollBars	2 'Vertical
	TabIndex	3
	Top	1020
	Width	7515
MSComm	Name	MSComm1
	DTREnable	-1 'True

Click on Save Project in the File menu and save the project as Comm_1.prj. The design-time form is shown in Figure 18-2.

MSComm Properties

The MSComm control has a bewildering array of properties. They are needed to set up the modem, for handshaking between the computer and the modem, and for transferring data to and from the modem.

Figure 18-1
The MSComm
control in the
toolbox

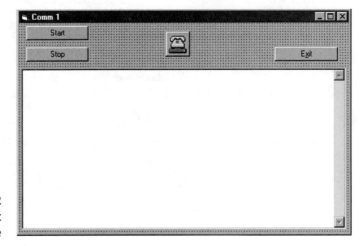

Figure 18-2
frmComm_1 at
design time

Modem Setup

If you and Joe User decided to set up two-way radio communications, and you purchased an FM transceiver while Joe purchased an AM transceiver, there would not be a lot of communications. The same is true of computer serial communications. Before a serial port can start communicating, it must be set up so that the port's properties match those of the data source. With the exception of the **CommPort** property, the parameters listed in Table 18-2 must be the same on both ends for communication to take place.

Table 18-2 Setup property parameters

Parameter	Settings	Meaning
CommPort	1 through 16	Selects the Com port to use. You must set the CommPort property to match the port you plan to use before you do anything else.
Baud rate	110 through 28,800	The number of data bits being transferred per second. If you are connecting to a modem, the number cannot exceed the maximum BPS rate of the modem.
Parity	O, E, N, M, S	An error-checking mechanism based on whether the number of ones in a byte is odd or even. Usually set to N because modems have better error correcting built into them.
Data bits	4 through 8	An integer representing the number of bits to send as a complete unit.
Stop bits	1, 1.5, 2	An extra bit that is sent with each byte to indicate the end of the byte.

The settings are put together in a comma-delimited string. A typical setting would look like this:

```
MSComm1.Settings = "14400,N,8,1"
```

This setup string means 14,400 baud, no parity, 8-bit data, and one-stop bit. This is typical for modem communications.

If you are communicating via modem, set your baud rate at the highest rate available for your modem. When it connects with another modem, the two modems determine the fastest baud rate they can use together. If you are connecting a serial port directly to another computer or to another device with a serial interface, the two must have the same baud rate settings.

The settings are not sent to the modem, actually, but to an integrated circuit called a UART. The UART handles the conversion of data from parallel (8 bits at a time) format to serial (1 bit at a time) format. It also handles the baud rate, parity, and stop bits.

Other properties are involved in setup, too. Much of the time you can use the default values, but there may be times when a change is needed. These properties are listed in Table 18-3.

Table 18-3 Other setup properties

Property	Settings	Meaning
inBufferSize	0 to 65535	Sets or returns the size of the input buffer. This is the number of consecutive bytes that can be received and stored before the computer reads the input data. If the buffer overflows, an overflow error is generated and some of the data will be lost. Default size is 1024 (1K) bytes. If this overflows, increase the size.
outBufferSize	0 to 65535	Sets or returns the size of the output buffer. This is the number of bytes stored in the transmit buffer. If the computer attempts to send more data when this buffer is full, an overflow error is generated and some of the data will be lost. Default size is 512 bytes. If this overflows, increase the size.
DTREnable	True or False	If DTREnable is set to True, the computer signals the modem that it is ready to communicate by making the data terminal ready (DTR) line high when the port is opened. Some serial devices require this, but the default setting is False because most do not.

continued on next page

continued from previous page

Property	Settings	Meaning
RTSEnable	True or False	If RTSEnable is True, the computer will make the request to send (RTS) line high to request permission from the modem before it transmits data. The computer will not send data until the clear to send (CTS) line goes high in response. Some serial devices require this, but the default setting is False because most do not.
NullDiscard	True or False	Determines whether Nulls are sent to the modem. The default value is True.
EOFEnable	True or False	Determines whether MSComm looks for the end of file (EOF) character. If this is set to True, an EOF character terminates data reception. The default value is False.

Most of these properties can usually be left set to their default values. Do not change them unless you have a specific requirement. There are a couple of other properties that fit in this classification. They are used with event-driven communications, and are covered in a later lesson.

Handshaking

Communication with a modem requires a lot of back-and-forth between the computer and the modem. Each must be sure that the other is ready before data transfer can take place. The chatter between the modem and the computer—exclusive of actual data transfer—is called *handshaking*. The handshaking signals are listed in Table 18-4.

Table 18-4 Handshaking signals

Signal	MSComm1	Purpose/Meaning
None	HandShaking	Establishes the handshaking protocol that will be used for data transfers. The default is None. Other choices are comXOnXOff, which is a form of software handshaking; comRTS, which is hardware handshaking; and comRTSXOnXOff, which uses both.
DTR	None	Data terminal ready signal sent from the computer to the modem to indicate that the computer is ready to establish communication. This is automatic when the DTREnable property is set to True.

Signal	MSComm1	Purpose/Meaning
DSR	DSRHolding	Data set ready is a signal from the modem to the computer indicating that the modem is ready for communications. If DSRHolding is True, communications can be started.
RTS	None	A request to send signal is sent from the computer to the modem before the computer sends output data. This is automatic when the RTSEnable property is set to True.
CTS	CTS	A holding clear to send is a signal sent from the modem to the computer in response to RTS. If CTSHolding is True, data can be transmitted.
CD	CDHolding	When the modem is connected to another modem, there is a steady *carrier* signal between them, and the modem makes the carrier-detect (CD) signal high. If CDHolding is True, there is a carrier and the CD line is high.
Break	Break	Some communications programs require that a break signal be sent at specific times. Setting Break to True sends the break signal; setting it to False ends the break signal.
InBufferCount		Returns the number of bytes in the input buffer.
OutBufferCount		Returns the number of bytes in the output buffer.

Data Transfer

Once the modem is set up and handshaking has been determined, you are ready for data transfers to take place. (Finally!) And, after all that work, it's a relief to know how simple it is to send and receive data. Use

```
MSComm1.Output = DataString
```

to send data and

```
MSComm1.InputLen = 0
InputString = MSComm1.Input
```

to receive it.

The `InputLen` property tells the MSComm control how many bytes to read from the input buffer. Setting it to 0 tells it to read all the data that is in the buffer.

Your First Comm Program

It's time to put it all to work now. There's nothing like experience to simplify the complex. Open the Code window and add a declaration to the General Declarations section:

```
Option Explicit
Private bQuit As Boolean
```

Add the following code to the `Click` event of `cmdStop`:

```
Private Sub cmdStop_Click()
    bQuit = True
End Sub
```

Add the following code to the `Click` event of `cmdQuit`:

```
Private Sub cmdQuit_Click()
    Unload Me
    End
End Sub
```

Add the code in Listing 18-1 to the `Click` event of `cmdStart`.

Listing 18-1 Making it work

```
Private Sub cmdStart_Click()
    '   Buffer for input data
    Dim InString As String
    ' Initialize quit command
    bQuit = False
    ' Initialize Com Port
    txtInData = vbCrLf & txtInData & _
      "Opening Com port" & vbCrLf & vbCrLf
    ' Move insertion point to end of text
    txtInData.SelStart = Len(txtInData)
    ' Set Com port to the one in YOUR computer
    MSComm1.CommPort = 2
    ' Send settings: Set Baud rate to the fastest that
    ' YOUR modem can handle. Settings here are
    ' 14400 baud, no parity, 8 data, and 1 stop bit.
    MSComm1.Settings = "14400,N,8,1"
    ' Tell the control to read entire buffer when Input
    ' is used.
    MSComm1.InputLen = 0
    ' Open the port.
    MSComm1.PortOpen = True
    ' Send the attention command to the modem.
    MSComm1.Output = "AT" & vbCrLf
    ' Wait for data to come back to the serial port.
```

```
        Do While Not bQuit
            If MSComm1.InBufferCount Then
                InString = InString & MSComm1.Input
                If InStr(InString, vbCrLf) Then
                    txtInData = txtInData & InString
                    txtInData.SelStart = Len(txtInData)
                    If InStr(InString, "OK") Then Exit Do
                    InString = ""
                    DoEvents
                End If
            End If
            DoEvents
            If bQuit Then Exit Do
        Loop
        txtInData = vbCrLf & vbCrLf & txtInData & _
          "Closing Com port" & vbCrLf & vbCrLf
        txtInData.SelStart = Len(txtInData)
        MSComm1.PortOpen = False
End Sub
```

That's it.

What's Going On?

The code displays messages in **txtInData** that let you follow the progress of the program. The line

```
txtInData.SelStart = Len(txtInData)
```

keeps the insertion point at the end of the text box, which means you always see the last data that was inserted.

The first working step is to set up the modem. The lines

```
MSComm1.CommPort = 2
MSComm1.Settings = "14400,N,8,1"
MSComm1.InputLen = 0
MSComm1.PortOpen = True
```

do that. Be sure to set the **CommPort** property to match your computer and the **Baud** portion of the setup string to the highest baud rate your modem supports.

Next you need to send something to your computer that will make the modem respond. The line

```
MSComm1.Output = "AT" & vbCrLf
```

sends the Attention signal to the modem. The signal is part of the Hayes-compatible command set that is recognized by nearly every modem used in personal computers.

Now comes the hard part: reading the data from the modem and displaying it. The code

```
Do While Not bQuit
        If MSComm1.InBufferCount Then
            InString = InString & MSComm1.Input
```

continued on next page

continued from previous page

```
        If InStr(InString, vbCrLf) Then
            txtInData = txtInData & InString
            txtInData.SelStart = Len(txtInData)
            If InStr(InString, "OK") Then Exit Do
            InString = ""
            DoEvents
        End If
    End If
    DoEvents
Loop
```

sets up a `Do` loop for that. Chances are that your modem, by default, echoes the commands you send it back to your computer. If so, it will send back the `"AT" & vbCrLf`. When `InBufferCount` is not zero (there is data in the input buffer), the outer `If...Then` transfers the data from the input buffer to `InString`. Reading the data from `InBuffer` also clears the buffer.

The inner `If...Then` checks for a carriage-return character, which indicates the end of a line of data. When the carriage return is found, the data is copied from `InString` to the text box, and `InString` is cleared. The `DoEvents` gives the computer time to paint the text into the text box.

Hayes-compatible modems respond to every successful command string with `OK`. Once that `OK` is received, no further data will be received. The third `If...Then` looks for `OK` and exits from the loop when it is found.

What if it is not successful? That's why `cmdStop` is there. Clicking on `cmdStop` sets the Boolean variable `bQuit` to `True`, which also exits from the loop. The code *could* check for the word `ERROR`, too, but there may be cases where the modem just doesn't respond. `cmdStop` handles that case, too.

Finally, the code in `cmdStart` closes the Com port.

Running the Program

Press (F5) or click on the Start button to run the program. Click on Start and watch `txtData`. The running program is shown in Figure 18-3.

Viewing the Handshaking

You can get an idea about some of the handshaking signals by adding a new procedure to this program. Select Add Procedure from the Tools menu. Add a `Private` procedure named `ShowStatus`. Add the code in Listing 18-2 to the `ShowStatus` procedure.

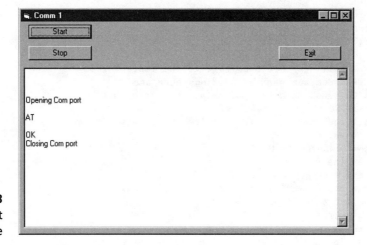

Figure 18-3
prjComm_1 at
runtime

Listing 18-2 The ShowStatus procedure

```
Private Sub ShowStatus()
    Debug.Print "CDHolding " & MSComm1.CDHolding
    Debug.Print "Input Mode " & MSComm1.InputMode
    Debug.Print "CTSHolding " & MSComm1.CTSHolding
    Debug.Print "DSRHolding " & MSComm1.DSRHolding
    Debug.Print "DTREnable " & MSComm1.DTREnable
    Debug.Print "EOFEnable " & MSComm1.EOFEnable
    Debug.Print "Handshaking " & MSComm1.Handshaking
    Debug.Print "RTSEnable " & MSComm1.RTSEnable
End Sub
```

Now change the code in the Click event of cmdStart to that in Listing 18-3 (changes are in bold).

Listing 18-3 Changes to cmdStart_Click

```
Private Sub cmdStart_Click()
    '    Buffer for input data
    Dim InString As String
    ' Initialize quit command
    bQuit = False
    ' Initialize Com Port
    txtInData = vbCrLf & txtInData & _
        "Opening Com port" & vbCrLf & vbCrLf
    ' Move insertion point to end of text
```

continued on next page

continued from previous page

```
    txtInData.SelStart = Len(txtInData)
    ' Set Com port to the one in YOUR computer
    MSComm1.CommPort = 2
    ' Send settings: Set Baud rate to the fastest that
    ' YOUR modem can handle. Settings here are
    ' 14400 baud, no parity, 8 data, and 1 stop bit.
    MSComm1.Settings = "14400,N,8,1"
    ' Tell the control to read entire buffer when Input
    ' is used.
    MSComm1.InputLen = 0
    ' Open the port.
    MSComm1.PortOpen = True
    ' Send the attention command to the modem.
    Debug.Print "After Open"
    ShowStatus
    MSComm1.Output = "AT" & vbCrLf
    ' Wait for data to come back to the serial port.
    Do While Not bQuit
        If MSComm1.InBufferCount Then
            InString = InString & MSComm1.Input
            If InStr(InString, vbCrLf) Then
                txtInData = txtInData & InString
                txtInData.SelStart = Len(txtInData)
                If InStr(InString, "OK") Then Exit Do
                InString = ""
                DoEvents
            End If
        End If
        DoEvents
    Loop
    txtInData = vbCrLf & vbCrLf & txtInData & _
        "Closing Com port" & vbCrLf & vbCrLf
    txtInData.SelStart = Len(txtInData)
    MSComm1.PortOpen = False
    Debug.Print "After Close"
    ShowStatus
End Sub
```

Run the program again. The state of the selected handshaking signals is displayed in the Immediate window.

1. Visual Basic serial communications are provided by the:
   a. MSPort control
   b. MSComm control
   c. Modem
   d. Parallel port

2. The number of data bits transferred in a second is loosely defined as the:
   a. Port number
   b. Parity rate
   c. Data bits
   d. Baud rate

3. Setting `InputLen` to zero tells the MSComm control:
   a. To read all the data in the input buffer
   b. Not to read the data in the input buffer
   c. To stop receiving data
   d. To start receiving data

4. When there is data in the input buffer:
   a. `InputLen` is not zero.
   b. `DTR` is set to `True`.
   c. `RTS` is set to `True`.
   d. `InBufferCount` is not zero.

5. When the modem is connected to another modem, the signal _____ is `True`.
   a. `CDHolding`
   b. `RTSHolding`
   c. `CTSHolding`
   d. `DTREnable`

MORE FROM THE MODEM

It won't take long before just getting your modem to say `OK` gets pretty dull. This lesson uses a different AT command to return the active configuration profile and the configuration profiles that are stored in the modem's nonvolatile RAM. (If that means nothing to you, don't worry about it.)

Reading the Profiles

This program uses the same form as the last one, but makes substantial changes to the code, including two new procedures. It's your choice whether to modify the last program, to start a new one, or to read the completed project from the CD that accompanies this book.

All the code for this project is shown in Listing 18-4.

Listing 18-4 Code for `prjComm_2`

```
Option Explicit
Private bQuit As Boolean
```

continued on next page

continued from previous page

```vb
Private Sub cmdQuit_Click()
    Unload Me
    End
End Sub

Private Sub cmdStart_Click()
    ' Initialize quit command
    bQuit = False
    ' Initialize Com Port
    If Not MSComm1.PortOpen Then OpenCom
    ' Request configuration data
    txtInData = txtInData & vbCrLf & "Sending request" & vbCrLf & vbCrLf
    txtInData.SelStart = Len(txtInData)
    ' Send it
    MSComm1.Output = "AT &V" & vbCrLf
    ' Wait for data to come back to the serial port.
    ReadModem
End Sub

Private Sub cmdStop_Click()
    If MSComm1.PortOpen = False Then Exit Sub
    bQuit = True
    txtInData = vbCrLf & txtInData & _
        "Closing Com port" & vbCrLf & vbCrLf
    txtInData.SelStart = Len(txtInData)
    MSComm1.PortOpen = False
    txtInData = vbCrLf & txtInData & _
        "Closed " & vbCrLf & vbCrLf
    txtInData.SelStart = Len(txtInData)
End Sub

Public Sub ReadModem()
    Dim InString As String
    Do
        If MSComm1.InBufferCount Then
            InString = InString & MSComm1.Input
            If InStr(InString, vbCrLf) Then
                txtInData = txtInData & InString
                txtInData.SelStart = Len(txtInData)
                If InStr(InString, "OK") Then Exit Do
                InString = ""
                DoEvents
            End If
        End If
        DoEvents
        If bQuit Then Exit Do
    Loop
End Sub

Public Sub OpenCom()
    txtInData = vbCrLf & txtInData & _
        "Opening Com port" & vbCrLf & vbCrLf
```

```
        txtInData.SelStart = Len(txtInData)
        ' Set Com port to the one in YOUR computer
        MSComm1.CommPort = 2
        ' Send settings: Set Baud rate to the fastest that
        ' YOUR modem can handle
        ' 14400 baud, no parity, 8 data, and 1 stop bit.
        MSComm1.Settings = "14400,N,8,1"
        ' Tell the control to read entire buffer when Input
        ' is used.
        MSComm1.InputLen = 0
        ' Open the port.
        MSComm1.PortOpen = True
End Sub
```

The main difference, aside from the **AT** command, is that this program divides up the work into more logical units. When you click on Start, the code in the **cmdStart_Click** event tests to see if the Com port is already open. (Trying to open an already open port raises an error.) If the port is not open, the program calls the **OpenCom** procedure, which contains all the familiar code to open the Com port.

The command **AT &V** asks the modem to return the current configuration and a listing of all the stored configurations from the modem's nonvolatile RAM (NVRAM). After sending this command to the modem, the program calls the **ReadModem** procedure, which is also familiar code in a new place. When **ReadModem** returns to **cmdStart_Click**, however, there is a change—the Com port is not closed. If you plan to send a *series* of commands to the modem, you don't want to close the Com port after each one. Closing the Com port after each command resets everything back to its default, undoing the changes you've made.

Running prjComm_2

Run the program by pressing F5 or clicking on the Start button. When you click on Start, you should get a screen that looks something like Figure 18-4.

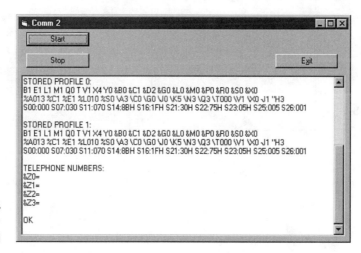

Figure 18-4
After the AT &V
command

What is all that stuff? Something like 50 settings are stored in your modem to set it up for communications. Communications programs and Internet dialers set specific values by sending *setup strings* to the modem. (Values not specifically changed are left with their default values, which are chosen by the modem's manufacturer.) Toward the top of `txtData`, the *current* configuration is listed. The stored profiles are sets of configurations that have been stored in NVRAM. If you send `"AT &Y1"` as a command string, stored profile number 1 will become the active profile.

Getting the correct setup string for an application is tricky. It is the source of more problems in communications than probably any other single issue. Being able to view the current profile can sometimes help you figure out why a modem communication link is not working. Listing and explaining each of the entries in the profile is well beyond the scope of this book. Consult your modem's manual for help.

A Phone Dialer

It doesn't take much to convert this program into a useful phone dialer. Once you can safely send one `AT` command to your modem, you can send *any* `AT` command to your modem. To create the dialer, start by adding a list box to your form and changing the captions on a few of the buttons. Name the list box lstNumbers. Change the caption on the `cmdStart` to Dial and the caption on `cmdStop` to Disconnect. The completed project is on the CD that accompanies this book. Use Figure 18-5 as a guide for laying out the form.

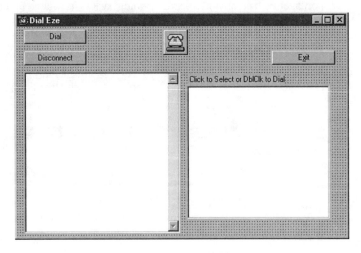

Figure 18-5
The dialer project

Add the following code to the **Form_Load** event:

```
Private Sub Form_Load()
    Dim j As Integer
    ' Put names and numbers into array
    PhoneList(1).Name = "John"
    PhoneList(1).Number = "555-1234"
    PhoneList(2).Name = "Lisa"
    PhoneList(2).Number = "(555) 555-1212"
    PhoneList(3).Name = "Sam"
    PhoneList(3).Number = "555-2345"
    j = 1
    ' Put names into listbox
    Do While PhoneList(j).Name <> ""
        lstNumbers.AddItem PhoneList(j).Name
        j = j + 1
    Loop
End Sub
```

Substitute the names and numbers of your friends for the dummy names and numbers included here. Of course, if you want to make this into a practical dialer, you need a way to add and delete names and numbers. That exercise is left to your imagination.

Now add the following to the **lstNumbers_Click** and **lstNumbers_DblClick** events:

```
Private Sub lstNumbers_Click()
    ' Set index into array
    iIndex = lstNumbers.ListIndex + 1
End Sub

Private Sub lstNumbers_DblClick()
    ' Set index into array
    iIndex = lstNumbers.ListIndex + 1
    ' Dial
    cmdStart_Click
End Subx
```

The **Click** event returns an index into the array of names and numbers. The second does the same, then clicks the Dial button.

Change the code in **cmdStart** to

```
Private Sub cmdStart_Click()
    ' Initialize quit command
    bQuit = False
    ' Check for selection
    If iIndex < 1 Then
        MsgBox "No number selected", vbOKOnly, "Sorry"
        Exit Sub
    End If
```

continued on next page

continued from previous page

```
' Get number
PhoneNumber = PhoneList(iIndex).Number
txtInData = txtInData & "Dialing " & _
   PhoneList(iIndex).Name & vbCrLf
' Initialize Com Port
If Not MSComm1.PortOpen Then OpenCom
' Dial the number
' Use DP for pulse dial
MSComm1.Output = "AT DT " & PhoneNumber & vbCrLf
' Wait for data to come back to the serial port.
ReadModem
End Sub
```

The first new part of the code makes sure that a number has been selected, and displays a message if it hasn't. The next two lines change the display in `txtInDate` to reflect the new functionality of the program. The line that does the work is `MSComm1.Output = "AT DT " & PhoneNumber & vbCrLf`. The `AT` gets the modem's attention. The `D` tells it that it is going to dial a number, and the `T` instructs it to use tone dialing. (If you have a pulse-dial phone, change the `T` to `P`). The phone number can be entered in almost any form: 5551212, 555-1212, and (555) 555-1212 all work. When the modem is dialing, it ignores almost everything but numbers.

Change `Sub ReadModem` to

```
Public Sub ReadModem()
   Dim InString As String
   Do While Not bQuit
      If MSComm1.InBufferCount Then
         InString = InString & MSComm1.Input
         If InStr(InString, vbCrLf) Then
            txtInData = txtInData & InString
            DoEvents
            txtInData.SelStart = Len(txtInData)
            If InStr(InString, "BUSY") Then bQuit = True
            If InStr(InString, "NO") Then bQuit = True
            InString = ""
         End If
      End If
      DoEvents
   Loop
   cmdStop_Click
End Sub
```

There are two possible responses from the modem, `BUSY` and `NO DIALTONE`. If either shows up, `ReadModem` exits the `Do` loop and clicks `cmdStop` to disconnect. Sadly, most modems will not tell you when they get a voice response. (If you have the speaker on the modem turned on, you can usually hear when somebody answers.)

Running the Program

Run the program by pressing F5 or clicking on the Start button. Select a number from the list and click the Dial button. After a few seconds, pick up your handset and click on the Disconnect button. The modem acts like a second phone on the telephone line and reduces the phone's volume.

Have the program dial your own number so you can see the **BUSY** response. If you want to see the **NO DIALTONE** response, unplug the modem from the phone jack before you try to dial a number.

1. If you send **AT &V** to a modem it will:
   a. Disconnect
   b. Dial a stored number
   c. Return its stored profiles
   d. Ignore the command because the command is not valid

2. The modem command **ATDT** tells the modem to:
   a. Dial
   b. Detect a dial tone
   c. Disconnect the telephone
   d. Act as a digital time counter

3. When the modem dials a busy number, it:
   a. Sounds the busy signal over its built-in speaker
   b. Automatically redials
   c. Ignores it
   d. Puts the word **BUSY** in the input buffer

4. The phone number to dial should be entered as:
   a. **5551212**
   b. **555 1212**
   c. **555-1212**
   d. Any of the above will work.

5. If you send **AT &Y1** to a modem, the modem will:
   a. Dial a stored number
   b. Ignore the command because it is an incorrect command
   c. Say **OK**
   d. Disconnect

COMMUNICATIONS WITH MSCOMM

It's all well and good to be able to chat with your modem, but the idea of having a modem is to be able to chat with the rest of the world. This lesson explains how to accomplish that daunting task.

First, a comment. There are dozens of useful communications programs already written and distributed. They are used by hobbyists and businesses for calling computer bulletin board systems (BBS) and text-only Internet services. The best of them can handle ANSI graphics and RIP graphics and provide terminal emulation of a half dozen or so common dumb terminals. They also handle file transfers using any of a dozen different transfer protocols. (A transfer protocol is a set of agreed-upon rules for transferring data.)

The program developed in this lesson does none of that. It is not meant to be a replacement for commercial terminal programs. Translating raw ANSI codes into colors and symbols is a complex and time-consuming task that can only interfere with the main point of the lesson. And handling file transfer protocols like ZModem and HSLink requires purchasing commercial ActiveX controls.

That out of the way, welcome to Chat. Chat lets you use a modem to chat with someone across the miles.

The OnComm Event

The MSComm programs in Lesson 1 and Lesson 2 use *polled* communications. Once the Com port is open, the program sits in a **Do** loop and waits for **InBufferCount** to indicate that there is data to be read. It works, but it also ties up a lot of processor time just waiting for something to happen.

The MSComm control has one event, the **OnComm** event. The **OnComm** event is fired when almost *any* change occurs at the Com port. When a character arrives or is sent, the **OnComm** event is fired. When one of the handshaking lines changes, the **OnComm** event is fired. When an error is raised, the **OnComm** event is fired. And, when the **OnComm** event is fired, the **CommEvent** property returns a numeric code for the event.

The neat thing about **OnComm** is that it doesn't use any processor time until something happens. It is event-driven, just like Command buttons and check boxes. The not-so-neat thing is that all UARTs do not support all the events. The program in this lesson shows you how to use event-driven communications.

1. Start a new project in Visual Basic 5. Set the properties of the form according to Table 18-5. The completed project is on the CD that accompanies this book.

Table 18-5 Properties for `frmChat`

Object	Property	Value
Form	Name	frmChat
	Caption	"Chat"
	Height	4320
	Width	7140
	ControlBox	False
	Icon	Graphics\Icons\Comm\ Phone01.Ico
	MaxButton	False
	StartUpPosition	Windows Default

This is the main form for the program, but you need one more.

2. Add a second form to the project by selecting Add Form from the Project menu or clicking on the Add Form icon on the toolbar. Set its properties according to Table 18-6.

Table 18-6 Properties for `frmSetup`

Object	Property	Value
Form	Name	frmSetup
	BorderStyle	Fixed Single
	Caption	"Set-Up Modem"
	Height	2415
	Width	2970
	ControlBox	False
	MaxButton	False
	MinButton	False

3. Press (CTRL)-(T) or select Components from the Project menu. Find and select Microsoft MSComm 5.0 and Microsoft Windows Common Controls 5.0; then click on OK. Chances are your toolbox must be resized to see all the controls it now holds.

4. Select Properties from the Project menu and set the program's properties according to Table 18-7.

Table 18-7 Project settings

Tab	Property	Value
General	Project Type	Standard EXE
	Startup Object	frmSetup
	Project Name	Chat
Make	Title	Chat
	Icon	frmChat
Compile	Compile to Native Code	Selected
	Optimize for Small Code	Selected

5. Click on OK when you are finished, then save the project to disk.

Don't run the project yet; there is no way except CTRL-BREAK to exit from **frmSetup**, which is the startup form.

6. Make **frmSetup** the active window and add two Command buttons. Set their properties according to Table 18-8.

Table 18-8 **frmSetup** properties

Object	Property	Value
CommandButton	Name	cmdCancel
	Caption	"Cancel"
	Default	False
	Height	375
	Left	480
	TabIndex	1
	Top	1920
	Width	855
CommandButton	Name	cmdOK
	Caption	"OK"
	Default	True
	Height	375
	Left	1440
	TabIndex	0
	Top	1920
	Width	855

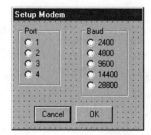

Figure 18-6
frmSetup at design
time

Always be sure, when you have a form that has no Control box, to provide a way out! This form is used to set up the modem. Figure 18-6 shows **frmSetup** at design time so you can use it as a guide for the next several steps.

7. Add two frames to the form.

8. Add four Option buttons to Frame 1.

9. Add five Option buttons to Frame 2.

10. Set the properties according to Table 18-9.

Table 18-9 The frames and Option buttons for frmSetup

Object	Property	Value
Frame	Name	Frame1
	Caption	"Port"
	Height	1335
	Left	120
	Top	120
	ToolTipText	"Select a Baud Rate"
	Width	975
OptionButton	Name	optPort
	Caption	"1"
	Index	0
OptionButton	Name	optPort
	Caption	"2"
	Index	1
OptionButton	Name	optPort
	Caption	"3"
	Index	2

continued on next page

continued from previous page

Object	Property	Value
OptionButton	Name	optPort
	Caption	"4"
	Index	3
Frame	Name	Frame2
	Caption	"Baud"
	Height	1575
	Left	1560
	Top	120
	ToolTipText	"Select a Baud Rate"
	Width	1095
OptionButton	Name	optBaud
	Caption	"2400"
	Index	0
OptionButton	Name	optBaud
	Caption	"4800"
	Index	1
OptionButton	Name	optBaud
	Caption	"9600"
	Index	2
OptionButton	Name	optBaud
	Caption	"14400"
	Index	3
OptionButton	Name	optBaud
	Caption	"28800"
	Index	4

Use the Format menu to size and position the Option buttons within their respective frames.

Obviously, **frmSetup** is used to select the port number and baud rate. Just as obviously, the user will not want to make the selection every time he or she runs the program, so Chat must save the selected port number and baud rate somewhere. In Chapter 17, Register Your Programs: Using the Windows Registry, you learned how to use the Windows Registry to store program configuration data. This lesson uses a different idea—a simple text data file—for the same purpose.

11. Open your favorite text editor and enter three lines of text, pressing ENTER after each line.

0
0
0

(Those are zeros, not letter Os.)

12. Save the file in the directory with `Chat.vbp`. Name it `Chat.Dat`.

The first two numbers are indexes into the Option button control arrays and the third indicates whether the settings have been saved to disk by the program (`0` = `No`.)

13. Add the code from Listing 18-5.

Listing 18-5 Code for `frmSetup`

```
Option Explicit
Private iBaud As Integer, iSet As Integer
Public iPort As Integer, sBaud As String
Private bChanged As Boolean, sDatFile As String

Private Sub Form_Load()
ReadDat
If iSet = 1 Then
    optBaud(iBaud) = True
    optPort(iPort) = True
    sBaud = optBaud(iBaud).Caption
    bChanged = False
    cmdOK_Click
End If
End Sub

Private Sub cmdOK_Click()
If bChanged Then
' Save port and baud data
Open sDatFile For Output As #1
Print #1, iBaud
Print #1, iPort
Print #1, 1
Close #1
bChanged = False
End If
Load frmChat
DoEvents
frmChat.Show
Me.Hide
End Sub

Private Sub Form_Unload(Cancel As Integer)
```

continued on next page

continued from previous page

```
If bChanged Then
' Save port and baud data
Open sDatFile For Output As #1
Print #1, iBaud
Print #1, iPort
Print #1, 1
Close #1
End If
End
End Sub

Private Sub optBaud_Click(Index As Integer)
bChanged = True
iBaud = Index
sBaud = optBaud(Index).Caption
End Sub

Private Sub optPort_Click(Index As Integer)
bChanged = True
iPort = Index
End Sub
```

What the Code Is Doing

The **Form_Load** event opens **Chat.Dat** and reads three values from the data file. The following lines check the data file to see if it is the dummy file or if it has been saved by the program.

```
If iSet = 1 Then
    optBaud(iBaud) = True
    optPort(iPort) = True
    sBaud = optBaud(iBaud).Caption
    bChanged = False
    cmdOK_Click
End If
```

If it has been saved by the program, the code selects the Option button to match the stored baud rate and port number, then calls **cmdOK_Click**. The code in **cmdOK_Click** saves any *changed* data back to the disk file, loads and shows **frmChat**, and hides **frmSetup**.

If the user has changed one or both settings and then decides to cancel the changes, **cmdCancel** reads the original data back from disk and calls **cmdOK_Click**. Note that **cmdCancel** sets **bChanged** to **False** to avoid having to save the data back to the same file it just finished reading.

Figure 18-7 shows **frmChat** at runtime.

Note that there is still no way to exit from the program while **frmSetup** is active. That privilege is reserved for the main form, **frmChat**.

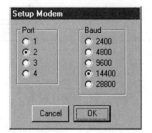

Figure 18-7
frmChat at runtime

Building frmChat

Save and close **frmSetup** and bring the Form view of **frmChat** to the top.

1. Add a toolbar, an image list, and an MSComm control to frmChat.

2. Right-click on the image list and select Properties from the Context menu.

3. Select the images shown in Table 18-10.

Table 18-10 Icons for the image list

Image	Index	Key
Graphic\Icons\Comm\Phone13.Ico	1	Call
Graphic\Icons\Comm\Phone14.Ico	2	Wait
Graphic\Icons\Comm\Phone16.Ico	3	Disconnect
Graphic\Icons\Industry\Wrench.Ico	4	Setup
Graphic\Icons\Traffic\Trffc14.Ico	5	Exit

Click on OK when you are finished.

4. Click on the toolbar and press F4 to open the Properties window.

5. Name the toolbar Tools.

6. Open the Property pages by clicking on Custom in the Properties window.

7. On the General tab, set the image list to ImageList1.

8. Switch to the Buttons tab and add five buttons to the toolbar. Set their properties according to Table 18-11.

Table 18-11 Toolbar buttons

Index	Caption	Key	Image
1	Dial	Dial	1
2	Wait	Wait	2
3	Disconnect	Disconnect	3
4	Setup	Setup	4
5	Exit	Exit	5

Add tooltip text if you like.

9. Set the properties for the MSComm control according to Table 18-12.

Table 18-12 Properties for MSComm1

Object	Property	Value
MSComm Control	Name	MSComm1
	DTREnable	True
	Handshaking	2
	Rthreshold	1
	RTSEnable	True
	Sthreshold	1

10. Click on OK when you are done.

The design-time form up to this point is shown in Figure 18-8.

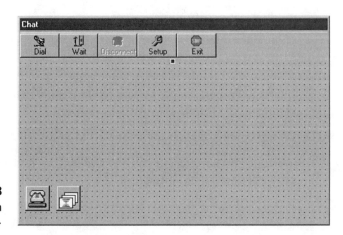

Figure 18-8
frmChat with
ToolBar

11. Open the Code window and add the code from Listing 18-6.

Listing 18-6 Code for ToolBar `Private Sub DialNumber ()`

```
End Sub

Private Sub HangUp ()

End Sub

Private Sub WaitForRing ()

End Sub

Private Sub SetUp ()

End Sub

Private Sub QuitMe ()
If MSComm1.PortOpen Then MSComm1.PortOpen = False
Unload frmSetup
Unload Me
End
End Sub

Private Sub Tools_ButtonClick(ByVal Button As ComctlLib.Button)
Select Case Button
    Case "Dial"
        DialNumber
    Case "Disconnect"
        HangUp
    Case "Wait"
        WaitForRing
    Case "Setup"
        frmSetup.Show
    Case "Exit"
        QuitMe
End Select
End Sub
```

Finally, there is a way to exit from the program! The stubs get filled in later with code to make it all work.

12. Draw two text boxes right on top of the toolbar, one above the other. Set their properties according to Table 18-13.

Table 18-13 Properties for toolbar text boxes

Object	Property	Value
TextBox	Name	txtLabel
	Appearance	Flat
	BackColor	&H80000004&
	BorderStyle	None
	Height	195
	Left	4920
	Locked	True
	TabStop	False
	Text	"Phone Number"
	Top	0
	Width	1935
TextBox	Name	txtNum
	Height	285
	Left	4920
	ToolTipText	"Enter Phone Number"
	Top	240
	Width	2055

13. Add a status bar, a text box, a check box, and a Command button to the form.

14. In the Properties window, name the status bar Status.

15. Set the properties for the text box, the check box, and the Command button according to Table 18-14.

Table 18-14 Properties for txtChat, chkEcho, and cmdClear

Object	Property	Value
TextBox	Name	txtChat
	Height	2895
	Left	120
	MultiLine	True

Object	Property	Value
	ScrollBars	Vertical
	Top	720
	Width	6855
CheckBox	Name	chkEcho
	Caption	"Echo On/Off"
	Height	255
	Left	= 3480
	Top	3720
	Width	1575
CommandButton	Name	cmdClear
	Caption	"Clear"
	Height	255
	Left	5760
	Top	3720
	Width	1215

Almost there! (Really.)

16. Right-click on the status bar and select Properties from the Context menu.

17. On the Panels tab, add five panels. Set their properties according to Table 18-15.

Table 18-15 Properties for the status bar

Index	Key	AutoSize
1Stat	sbrText	sbrSpring
2	sbrCaps	sbrContents
3	sbrNum	sbrContents
4	sbrDate	sbrContents
5	sbrTime	sbrContents

The completed form at design time is shown in Figure 18-9.

Now it's code time. Switch to the Code window and add the code in Listing 18-7.

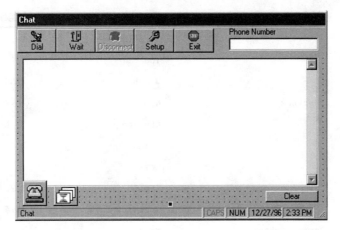

Figure 18-9
frmChat at design
time

Listing 18-7 Startup code for frmChat

```
Option Explicit
Private sSettings As String, iMyPort As Integer
Private Activity As Integer
Private bEcho As Boolean
Private Const Dialing As Integer = 1, Waiting As Integer = 2

Private Sub Form_Activate()
txtNum.SetFocus
OffLine
Status.Panels("Stat").Text = "Off-Line"
End Sub

Private Sub Form_Load()
iMyPort = frmSetup.iPort + 1
sSettings = frmSetup.sBaud & ",N,8,1"
End Sub

Private Sub cmdClear_Click()
txtChat = ""
End Sub

Private Sub chkEcho_Click()
bEcho = chkEcho.Value
End Sub
```

Nothing spectacular here. The **Form_Load** event reads two values from **frmSetup** and uses them to create the settings string for **MSComm1**. Now to fill in the stubs from that initial code. Start with Listing 18-8.

Listing 18-8 Dialing out

```
Private Sub DialNumber()
If txtNum = "" Then
    MsgBox "No number to dial", vbOKOnly, "Sorry."
    Exit Sub
End If
' Clear the chat box
txtChat = ""
If Not MSComm1.PortOpen Then
    OpenCom
    ' Wait for OK
    Do
        DoEvents
    Loop Until InStr(txtChat, "OK")
End If
Status.Panels("Stat").Text = "Dialing"
' dial
MSComm1.Output = "ATDT " & txtNum & vbCrLf
OnLine
Activity = Dialing
txtChat.SetFocus
txtChat.SelStart = Len(txtChat)
End Sub
```

Before the program can dial a number, it must *have* a number. `DialNumber` checks to be sure that something has been entered in `txtNum` and exits if the text box is empty. If the test is passed, `txtChat` is cleared and the status of `PortOpen` is tested. If `PortOpen` is `False`, the `OpenCom` procedure is called, and the code loops until the modem responds with `OK`.

If the `PortOpen` is `True`, or after `OpenCom` has done its job, `MSComm1.Output = "ATDT " & txtNum & vbCrLf` dials the number and calls the `OnLine` procedure.

If you want to receive calls instead of make them, you must take a different tack. Listing 18-9 shows the code from the `WaitForRing` procedure.

Listing 18-9 Waiting for a call

```
Private Sub WaitForRing()
txtChat = ""
If Not MSComm1.PortOpen Then
    OpenCom
' Wait for OK
    Do
        DoEvents
    Loop Until InStr(txtChat, "OK")
End If
' Set autoanswer to one ring
```

continued on next page

continued from previous page

```
MSComm1.Output = "ATS0=1" & vbCrLf
' Wait for OK
Do
      DoEvents
Loop Until InStr(txtChat, "OK")
OnLine
Activity = Waiting
txtChat.SetFocus
txtChat.SelStart = Len(txtChat)
End Sub
```

This procedure, too, must check the **PortOpen** property before it can do anything else. Again, if **PortOpen** is **False**, the **OpenCom** procedure is called and the code waits for **OK** from the modem before it proceeds.

Modems output a Ring Detect signal when they receive ring voltage from the phone line. Unfortunately, all UARTs do not support this signal, so the code in this procedure uses the modem's autoanswer feature instead. The line **MSComm1.Output = "ATS0=1" & vbCrLf** does the job. Setting the modem's S0 register to 1 tells the modem to answer the phone on the first ring. (Be sure not to leave it that way. Callers who get modem negotiation tones when they call you tend to get annoyed!)

Opening the Com Port

The **DialNumber** procedure and the **WaitForRing** procedure call on **OpenCom** if the Com port is not already open. The code is shown in Listing 18-10.

Listing 18-10 Opening the Com port

```
Private Sub OpenCom()
Dim i As Integer
If Not MSComm1.PortOpen Then _
  MSComm1.PortOpen = True
' Reset modem
MSComm1.Output = "ATZ" & vbCrLf
' Setup string sets DCD ON (&C1)
' DTR ON (&D2), Echo ON (E1),
' Speaker ON (M1) and Speaker volume MAX (L3)
MSComm1.Output = "AT&C1&D2E1M1L3" & vbCrLf
End Sub
```

Once the Com port is open, this procedure resets it with **MSComm1.Output = "ATZ" & vbCrLf**. It's always a good idea to reset the modem to factory defaults before you do anything else. Otherwise you may get some unpleasant surprises. The setup string, **AT&C1&D2E1M1L3**, does a number of chores.

1. **&C1** sets the modem's data carrier detect (DCD) signal so it will follow the state of the received signal. If the modem on the other end hangs up, the DCD signal will switch to low (**False**).

2. **&D2** tells the modem how to handle the data terminal ready (DTR) signal.

3. M1 turns the modem's speaker on while a connection is being made and off after the connection has been made. M0 turns the speaker off.

4. L3 sets the modem speaker's volume. Most modems have three acceptable values: L1, which is the softest; L2, which is medium; and L3, which is the loudest. Feel free to change this to suit your ears.

Hanging Up

No matter how much you like the person on the other end, eventually you will want to hang up and go eat lunch! The code in Listing 18-11 shows you how.

Listing 18-11 Hanging up

```
Private Sub HangUp()
If MSComm1.PortOpen Then
    ' Hang up the modem
    MSComm1.Output = "ATHO" & vbCrLf
    ' Turn off autoanswer
    MSComm1.Output = "ATS0=0" & vbCrLf
    ' turn off local echo
    bEcho = False
    chkEcho.Value = False
End If
Activity = 0
Tools.Buttons("Disconnect").Enabled = False
txtNum = ""
Status.Panels("Stat").Text = "Off-Line"
OffLine
End Sub
```

There's nothing special here. ATHO is the command that tells the modem to hang up. Note that the procedure also turns off autoanswer with ATS0=0 and does a few other housekeeping chores.

All three procedures call on either OnLine or OffLine. They are shown in Listing 18-12.

Listing 18-12 Online and offline

```
Private Sub OnLine()
Tools.Buttons("Disconnect").Enabled = True
Tools.Buttons("Dial").Enabled = False
Tools.Buttons("Wait").Enabled = False
Tools.Buttons("Setup").Enabled = False
txtNum.Enabled = False
End Sub

Private Sub OffLine()
Status.Panels("Stat").Text = "Off-Line"
Tools.Buttons("Disconnect").Enabled = False
```

continued on next page

continued from previous page

```
Tools.Buttons("Dial").Enabled = True
Tools.Buttons("Wait").Enabled = True
Tools.Buttons("Setup").Enabled = True
txtNum.Enabled = True
End Sub
```

As you can see, these procedures handle the enabling and disabling of buttons on the toolbar so the user can't crash the program by clicking on the wrong thing. While you are offline, you really don't need to hang up, and while you are online, there is no good reason to dial a number.

Using the OnComm Event

This program happily sits idle while it waits for signals from the UART to tell it something happened. When something does happen, an OnComm event is triggered. The OnComm event for frmChat is shown in Listing 18-13.

Listing 18-13 The OnComm event

```
Private Sub MSComm1_OnComm()
Dim sInBuffer As String
Select Case MSComm1.CommEvent
' Errors
    Case comBreak    ' A Break was received.
        Status.Panels("Stat").Text = "Received Break"
    Case comCDTO     ' CD Timeout.
        Status.Panels("Stat").Text = "CD Timed Out"
    Case comCTSTO    ' CTS Timeout.
        Status.Panels("Stat").Text = "CTS Timed Out"
    Case comDSRTO    ' DSR Timeout.
        Status.Panels("Stat").Text = "BDSR Timed Out"
    Case comFrame    ' Framing Error
        txtChat.SelStart = Len(txtChat.Text)
        txtChat.SelText = vbCrLf & "Framing Error" & vbCrLf
    Case comOverrun ' Data Lost.
        txtChat.SelStart = Len(txtChat)
        txtChat.SelText = vbCrLf & "TX OverRun Error" & vbCrLf
    Case comRxOver   ' Receive buffer overflow.
        txtChat.SelStart = Len(txtChat)
        txtChat.SelText = vbCrLf & "RX OverRun Error" & vbCrLf
    Case comRxParity    ' Parity Error.
        txtChat.SelStart = Len(txtChat)
        txtChat.SelText = vbCrLf & "RX Parity Error" & vbCrLf
    Case comTxFull   ' Transmit buffer full.
        txtChat.SelStart = Len(txtChat)
        txtChat.SelText = vbCrLf & "Trasmit Buffer Full" & vbCrLf
    Case comDCB ' Unexpected error retrieving DCB]
        txtChat.SelStart = Len(txtChat)
        txtChat.SelText = vbCrLf & "DCB Error" & vbCrLf
    ' Events
```

```
    Case comEvCD      ' Change in the CD Line.
        If MSComm1.CDHolding Then
            Status.Panels("Stat").Text = "Connected"
            If Activity = Waiting Then
              MSComm1.Output = _
                "You have connected to Chat." & vbCrLf
                Status.Panels("Stat").Text = "Received call"
            End If
        Else
            HangUp
    End If
    Case comEvDSR      ' Change in the DSR Line.
        If MSComm1.DSRHolding Then
        '   DSRChange
        Else
            Status.Panels("Stat").Text = _
            "Modem Not Ready"
        End If
    Case comEvReceive     ' Received Some Characters
        sInBuffer = MSComm1.Input
        ParseString (sInBuffer)
End Select
End Sub
```

The variable **CommEvent** reports exactly what caused the event to occur. The program uses a **Select Case** structure to respond. Take a look at the code.

Chances are you will never see the error messages in action. Modem technology is good enough these days that overflows and framing errors are rare.

ComEvCD

The real work begins with **ComEvCD**, which is triggered when the carrier detect (CD) signal changes. Recall that the CD signal reports whether or not you are online. The actual status of the CD line is reported by **CDHolding**.

When **CDHolding** is **True**, the modem is connected. Because there are two ways the modem can get connected—placing a call or receiving a call—the **Activity** variable (you've been wondering about that one, haven't you?) determines what to do next. The **If...Then** sends out a welcome message when a call is received, but does nothing when the call is outgoing.

When **CDHolding** is **False**, you have been disconnected, so the code calls the **HangUp** procedure.

ComEvDSR

The **ComEvDSR** event changes when the modem switches between ready and not ready. (The modem is the data set and the computer is the data terminal.) The only change of concern is when **DSRHolding** is **False**, meaning the modem is not available. It's unlikely you will ever see this event, but it must be handled.

ComEvReceive

The event that gets fired the most is **ComEvReceive**, which is fired when the receive buffer has **RThreshold** or more characters. Recall that **RThreshold** is set to 1; the event is fired for every single character received! Each time it is fired, the characters in the receive buffer are read into the string **sInBuffer**.

Unfortunately, you can't just dump the characters into **txtChat**. Some characters are considered "unprintable" characters and leave ugly black lines on the screen. This is true of a linefeed character (**vbLf**), a carriage-return character (**vbCr**), and a backspace character (**vbBack**). To handle this, **sInBuffer** is sent to the **ParseString** procedure.

Handling the Unprintable Characters

The **ParseString** procedure is shown in Listing 18-14.

Listing 18-14 The ParseString procedure

```
Private Sub ParseString(sString As String)
' Deals with "Unprintable Characters"
Dim iPos As Integer, iLen
iLen = Len(txtChat)
txtChat.SelStart = iLen
' Start with Backspace
Do
    iPos = InStr(sString, vbBack)
    If iPos Then
        If iPos = 1 Then ' BS is first character
            txtChat.SelStart = iLen - 1
            ' Back up in the exisiting text
            txtChat.SelLength = 1
            sString = Mid$(sString, iPos + 1)
        Else
            sString = Left$(sString, iPos - 2) & _
                Mid$(sString, iPos + 1)
        End If
    End If
Loop While iPos
' Strip out all linefeed characters
Do
    iPos = InStr(sString, vbLf)
    If iPos Then
        sString = Left$(sString, iPos - 1) & _
            Mid$(sString, iPos + 1)
    End If
Loop While iPos
' Now add linefeed to all carriage returns
iPos = 1
Do
    iPos = InStr(iPos, sString, vbCr)
    If iPos Then
```

```
        sString = Left$(sString, iPos) & _
            vbLf & Mid$(sString, iPos + 1)
        iPos = iPos + 1
    End If
Loop While iPos
' Display the string
txtChat.SelText = sString
txtChat.SelStart = Len(txtChat)
End Sub
```

The `ParseString` procedure runs through the string three times. The first `Do` loop deals with `vbBack`, the backspace character. The only special case is when `vbBack` is the first character in the string, in which case a character must be deleted from those already in `txtChat`. That nifty little trick is done by moving `txtChat.SelStart` back a space. If `vbBack` is not in the first character position, `Left$()` and `Mid$()` concatenate a new string minus one character. Note the code fragment `Left$(sString, iPos - 2)`. The − `2` deletes the preceding character and the backspace character from the string.

The second `Do` loop removes every linefeed character from the string using concatenation.

The third `Do` loop puts all the linefeed characters back. Well, sort of. It adds `vbLf` to the string immediately following every `vbCr` character. The result, of course, is `vbCrLf`, which multiline text boxes like `txtChat` can handle with ease.

Running Chat

Testing Chat is a little different from testing other programs in this book. As a first test, enter your own phone number in `txtNum` and click on Dial. You should see the following messages appear in `txtChat`:

```
ATZ
AT&C1&D2E1M1L3

OK
ATDT 5551211

BUSY
```

Between the `ATDT` and the `BUSY`, you should hear the modem dialing out.

You can do a more thorough calling-out test if you have an account on a bulletin board system. Before you place the call, log on to the BBS and change your defaults so your account is a text-only connection. Figure 18-10 shows a BBS connection that has sent ANSI graphics to Chat.

Hard to read, isn't it? All that strange-looking gibberish is code for colors and ANSI symbols. Figure 18-11 shows the same part of the BBS with graphics turned off.

If you want to do a full test of Chat, you will have to install it on a friend's computer. Compile the program by selecting Make Chat.exe from the File menu. Run the Setup Wizard (see Chapter 14, Advanced Features) and install the program on your friend's computer. At a prearranged time, start Chat and click on Wait. Then have your friend use Chat to call your computer. You should be able to chat back and forth.

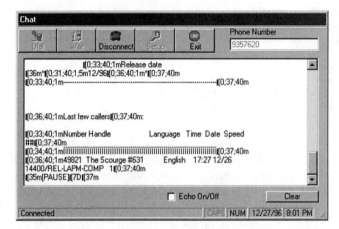

Figure 18-10
Chat connected to an ANSI BBS

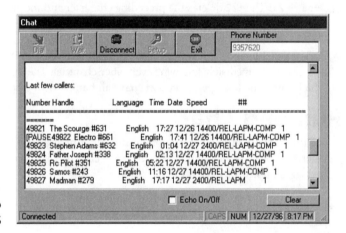

Figure 18-11
Chat connected to a text-only BBS

About Echo

If you type something in Chat and don't see it on your screen, the other computer is not echoing your keystrokes back to your computer. Turn Echo on. If you see double characters, turn Echo off.

1. The MSComm control uses its _____ event to provide event-driven communications.
   a. `GotFocus`
   b. `LostFocus`
   c. `Enabled`
   d. `OnComm`

2. Sending the modem `AT S0=1` tells the modem:
   a. To answer the phone after the first ring
   b. To not answer the phone
   c. To hang up in one second
   d. To go off-hook

3. Sending the modem `ATZ`:
   a. Sets the modem to zero, which disables it
   b. Resets the modem to factory defaults
   c. Tells the modem to pause (snooze) for 15 seconds
   d. Raises an error

4. To turn the modem's speaker on, send it the command:
   a. `S1=1`
   b. `M1`
   c. `M0`
   d. `Z`

5. When the `OnComm` event is fired, the variable _____ reflects what made it fire.
   a. `ComEvCD`
   b. `ComEvDTR`
   c. `CommEvent`
   d. `CommIRQ`

REVIEW

John: I like that control. Now I can use my modem.

Lisa: Yes, and, from what I understood, you can even connect computers together without a modem.

John: That's right, but remember not to look for modem signals when you do that. There won't be a carrier detect, for example.

Lisa: I know that one, but I may have to read up on serial communications a little bit more to figure out which signals are there and which ones are not.

John: Or you could just experiment. I've found that's the easiest way to get answers.

Lisa: You would! But what I really want to do is connect my programs to the Internet. I've been looking at the table of contents again. Guess what's next?

John: I've been peeking, too. I can't wait to get on with it!

CONNECT TO THE WORLD WIDE WEB

The Internet! You can't read a newspaper or watch television without seeing a reference to the Internet. It has become the darling of the press and a buzzword for politicians. It is either the salvation of mankind or its end. Whatever it is, it is real, and it must be a part of every programmer's arsenal.

Although there is much more to the Internet than the World Wide Web, it is the Web that has popularized Internet access. Visual Basic 5 includes the Microsoft WebBrowser control, which makes accessing the World Wide Web as easy as accessing a text file on your disk.

The Microsoft WebBrowser Control

The WebBrowser control is an ActiveX control that lets you add browsing capabilities to your applications. It can be used to browse "live" on the Web or to browse files on your hard drive or on network servers.

It's not that you want to try to create a new Web browser to rival Microsoft's Internet Explorer or Netscape's Navigator. But more and more business software has a need to connect to a specific Web page, perhaps to download the latest sales figures or information about the new products in the company's line. More and more companies are using the Internet (or private intranets) to disseminate information to their employees and customers.

frmMain

The opening form in this project doesn't do much. If you were programming for business, the Web browser would not be the main form in the project. Instead, it would most likely be accessed from a menu. The opening form of this project simulates that.

1. Start a new project named `www.vbp` or load the completed project from the CD that accompanies this book. Set the form's properties according to Table 18-16.

Table 18-16 Properties for `frmMain`

Object	Property	Value
Form	Name	frmMain
	Caption	"Web Viewer"
	Height	3915
	Left	240
	Top	1830
	Width	6630

Recall from Chapter 1, What's All That Stuff on My Screen?, that you can also have the Application Wizard add browsing capabilities to the programs that it creates.

2. Add a second form to the project. Name it `frmBrowser` and set its `WindowState` property to `Maximized`.

3. Bring `frmMain` to the top and select Menu Editor from the Tools menu or press CTRL-E to open the Menu Editor.

4. Create a top-level menu named &File. Add a submenu under File named E&xit.

5. Create a top-level menu named &View. Add a submenu under View named &Web Browser.

The Menu Editor is shown in Figure 18-12.

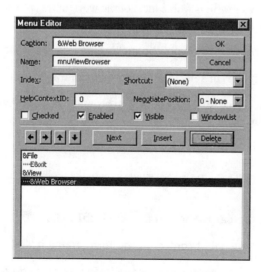

Figure 18-12
Building the menus
for `WWW.vbp`

Add the code in Listing 18-15 to `frmMain`.

Listing 18-15 Code for `frmMain`

```
Option Explicit

Private Sub Form_Unload(Cancel As Integer)
Dim i As Integer
'close all sub forms
For i = Forms.Count - 1 To 1 Step -1
    Unload Forms(i)
Next
End Sub

Private Sub mnuViewBrowser_Click()
Dim frmB As New frmBrowser
frmB.StartingAddress = "http://www.mcp.com/waite/ezone/"
frmB.Show
End Sub

Private Sub mnuFileExit_Click()
'unload the form
Unload Me
End Sub
```

That's all the code you need for `frmMain`. The work is all done in the code for `frmBrowser`. If you were writing a business application, `frmMain` would be more involved, but this is only a demonstration project.

Building `frmBrowser`

The Web browser form is where most of the work in this project is done. It is the container for the WebBrowser control and the controls that support it.

1. Close `frmMain`. You won't be making any further changes to it.

2. Press CTRL-T or select Components from the Project menu.

3. Click on Microsoft Internet Controls and Microsoft Windows Common Controls 5.0.

4. Click on OK.

Microsoft Internet Controls adds a single icon to the toolbox. The icon is shown in Figure 18-13.

5. Add a toolbar to the form. Name it tbToolBar.

6. Add an ImageList control to the form. Name it tlbrImages.

7. Open the Property page for the image list and add the six images in Table 18-17.

Figure 18-13
The WebBrowser
control

Table 18-17 Images for tlbrImages

Index	Name
1	Back
2	Forward
3	Stop
4	Refresh
5	Home
6	Search

You can find the bitmap files for the images on the CD that comes with this book, in the same directory as the **vbp** files for this project.

8. Close the ImageList Property page.

9. Open the Property page for the toolbar.

10. On the General tab, select tlbrImages as the image list for the toolbar.

11. Switch to the Buttons tab and add six buttons. Use Table 18-18 as a guide.

Table 18-18 Toolbar buttons for `frmBrowser`

Index	Caption	Key	Image
1	Back	Back	1
2	Forward	Forward	2
3	Stop	Stop	3
4	Refresh	Refresh	4
5	Home	Home	5
6	Search	Search	6

12. Add a picture box to the form. Draw the box immediately beneath the toolbar. Make it the width of the form and 675 twips in height.

13. Add a Timer control to the form.

14. Draw a label into the picture box.

15. Draw a combo box into the picture box.

Use Figure 18-14 as a guide to placing the Label and PictureBox controls.

16. Set the properties according to Table 18-19.

Table 18-19 Properties for the Address picture box

Object	Property	Value
Timer	Name	timTimer
	Enabled	False
	Interval	5
PictureBox	Name	picAddress
	Align	Align Top
	BorderStyle	None
	Height	675
ComboBox	Name	cboAddress
	Height	315
	Left	45
	Top	300
	Width	3795
Label	Name	lblAddress
	Caption	"&Address:"
	Height	255
	Left	45
	Top	60
	Width	3075

17. Finally, add a WebBrowser control to the form and set its properties according to Table 18-20.

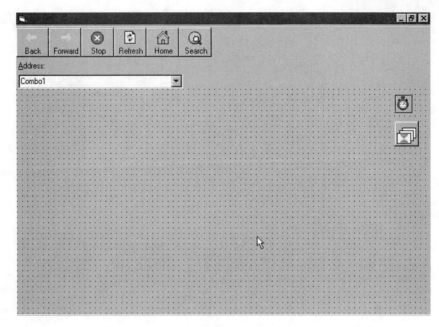

Figure 18-14
frmBrowser at
design time

Table 18-20 Properties for the WebBrowser control

Object	Property	Value
WebBrowser	Name	brwWebBrowser
	Height	3495
	Left	120
	TabIndex	0
	Top	1440
	Width	5400

Figure 18-15 shows frmBrowser with the WebBrowser control added.

The WebBrowser control offers an array of useful methods, properties, and events. To open an Internet site, for example, use the Navigate method, which has the following syntax:

```
object.Navigate url, flags, TargetFrameName, PostData, Headers
```

where

 object is the name you've given to the WebBrowser control.

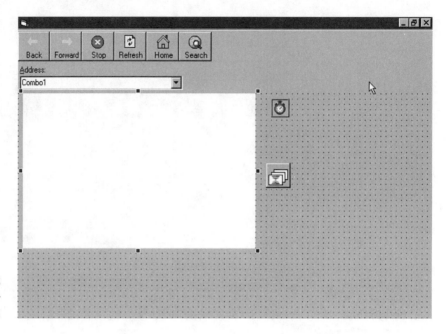

Figure 18-15
The WebBrowser
control

● url is a required string that evaluates to the URL of the resource to display or the full path of the file to display.

● flags is an optional constant or value that specifies whether to add the resource to the history list, whether to read from or write to the cache, and whether to display the resource in a new window. It can be a combination of the values listed in Table 18-21.

● TargetFrameName is an optional string that evaluates to the name of a frame in which to display the resource.

● PostData is optional data to send to the server during the HTTP POST transaction. This parameter is ignored if the URL is not an HTTP URL.

● Headers is an optional value that specifies additional HTTP headers to send to the server. This parameter is ignored if the URL is not an HTTP URL.

Table 18-21 Flags for the Web browser `Navigate` method

Constant	Value	Description
`navOpenInNewWindow`	1	Opens the resource or file in a new window.
`navNoHistory`	2	Does not add to the history list. The new page replaces the current page in the list.
`navNoReadFromCache`	4	Does not read from the disk cache for this navigation.
`navNoWriteToCache`	8	Does not write the results of this navigation to the disk cache.

To navigate to the eZone, for example, the **Navigate** method can be called with the following code:

```
brwWebBrowser.Navigate "http://www.mcp.com/waite/ezone/", navNoReadFromCache
```

The **Flags** parameter is optional. Using **navNoReadFromCache** opens the site and reads the URL from the Internet instead of opening a copy of the page stored in the cache. (The cache is a collection of files on your hard disk drive that Web browsers use to speed access to Web sites you have visited recently.)

A number of the Web browser methods correspond to the toolbar buttons. They require no parameters because the actions they perform are based on the history list and the settings for Internet Explorer. These are listed in Table 18-22.

Table 18-22 Toolbar navigation methods

Method	Syntax	Action
`GoBack`	`object.GoBack`	Jumps back in the history list.
`GoForward`	`object.GoForward`	Jumps forward in the history list.
`GoHome`	`object.GoHome`	Jumps to Internet Explorer's home page.
`GoSearch`	`object.GoSearch`	Navigates to the current search page specified in Internet Explorer and the Internet control panel.
`Quit`	`object.Quit`	Closes the Web browser.
`Refresh`	`object.Refresh`	Reloads the current page.
`Stop`	`object.Stop`	Cancels the current navigation.

The code in Listing 18-16 demonstrates the use of the methods and properties. Enter this code in your program.

Listing 18-16 Code for `frmBrowser`

```
Option Explicit
Public StartingAddress As String
Dim mbDontNavigateNow As Boolean

Private Sub Form_Load()
On Error Resume Next
Me.Show
tbToolBar.Refresh
Form_Resize
cboAddress.Move 50, lblAddress.Top + lblAddress.Height + 15
If Len(StartingAddress) > 0 Then
    cboAddress.Text = StartingAddress
    cboAddress.AddItem cboAddress.Text
    'try to navigate to the starting address
    timTimer.Enabled = True
    brwWebBrowser.Navigate StartingAddress
End If
End Sub

Private Sub Form_Resize()
cboAddress.Width = Me.ScaleWidth - 100
brwWebBrowser.Width = Me.ScaleWidth - 100
brwWebBrowser.Height = Me.ScaleHeight - _
  (picAddress.Top + picAddress.Height) - 100
End Sub

Private Sub brwWebBrowser_DownloadComplete()
On Error Resume Next
Me.Caption = brwWebBrowser.LocationName
End Sub

Private Sub brwWebBrowser_NavigateComplete(ByVal URL As String)
Dim i As Integer
Dim bFound As Boolean
Me.Caption = brwWebBrowser.LocationName
For i = 0 To cboAddress.ListCount - 1
    If cboAddress.List(i) = brwWebBrowser.LocationURL Then
        bFound = True
        Exit For
    End If
Next i
mbDontNavigateNow = True
If bFound Then
    cboAddress.RemoveItem i
End If
cboAddress.AddItem brwWebBrowser.LocationURL, 0
cboAddress.ListIndex = 0
mbDontNavigateNow = False
End Sub
```

```
Private Sub cboAddress_Click()
If mbDontNavigateNow Then Exit Sub
timTimer.Enabled = True
brwWebBrowser.Navigate cboAddress.Text
End Sub

Private Sub cboAddress_KeyPress(KeyAscii As Integer)
On Error Resume Next
If KeyAscii = vbKeyReturn Then
    cboAddress_Click
End If
End Sub

Private Sub Form_Resize()
cboAddress.Width = Me.ScaleWidth - 100
brwWebBrowser.Width = Me.ScaleWidth - 100
brwWebBrowser.Height = Me.ScaleHeight - (picAddress.Top + picAddress.Height) - 100
End Sub

Private Sub timTimer_Timer()
If brwWebBrowser.Busy = False Then
    timTimer.Enabled = False
    Me.Caption = brwWebBrowser.LocationName
Else
    Me.Caption = "Working..."
End If
End Sub

Private Sub tbToolBar_ButtonClick(ByVal Button As Button)
On Error Resume Next
timTimer.Enabled = True
Select Case Button.Key
    Case "Back"
        brwWebBrowser.GoBack
    Case "Forward"
        brwWebBrowser.GoForward
    Case "Refresh"
        brwWebBrowser.Refresh
    Case "Home"
        brwWebBrowser.GoHome
    Case "Search"
        brwWebBrowser.GoSearch
    Case "Stop"
        timTimer.Enabled = False
        brwWebBrowser.Stop
        Me.Caption = brwWebBrowser.LocationName
End Select
End Sub
```

What's Going On?

When the form is loaded, Form_Load starts with a call to the Form_Resize event. The Form_Resize event sets the width of picAddress and the width and height of the Browser window. When control returns to the `Form_Load` event, the combo box is moved to a position relative to its label.

Recall that **mnuViewBrowser** sent the URL to the new **frmBrowser** instance with the code

```
frmB.StartingAddress = "http://www.mcp.com/waite/ezone/"
```

The variable is copied into the combo box and also used as the **URL** parameter for the **Navigate** method. If the user is already connected to the Internet, the WebBrowser control opens the URL. If the user is not connected to the Internet, the browser opens the Connect Dialog box shown in Figure 18-16.

After the connection is made, the timer is enabled and the WebBrowser control navigates to the URL, downloads the page, and displays it. This is shown in Figure 18-17.

The timer checks the **Busy** property every 5 milliseconds while the **Navigate** method is attempting to download the page. When **Busy** is **True**, the timer displays **Working...** as the form's caption. When **Busy** is **False**, the form's caption is changed to **brwBrowser.LocationName**, which is the title of the Web page.

Meanwhile, when the URL is located and loaded, the **NavigateComplete** event is fired. The code here scans through the combo box to see if the URL address is already there. If it is, the code deletes the address and then adds it back in with the **AddItem** method. Sound silly? The idea is to have the current URL as the first one in the list, but not to have it in the list twice.

Finally, the toolbar's **ButtonClick** event handles the rest of the work. The only thing notable here is the **Stop** method. Because the timer is enabled when the **Navigate** method is called, its **Enabled** property must be set to **False**. The **Stop** subroutine must also set the new caption for the form.

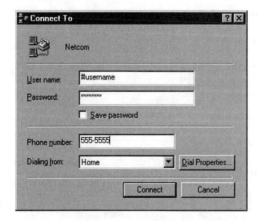

Figure 18-16
Connecting to the Internet

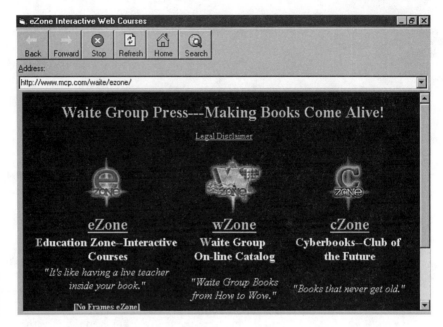

Figure 18-17
Connected to the
eZone!

Running the Program

When the program runs, **frmMain** opens. Selecting Web Browser from the View menu
loads a new instance of **frmBrowser**. That implies, correctly, that you can have several instances running at the same time.

Once the connection is made and the site is connected, you can type other URLs
into the text box portion of **cboAddress**. Pressing [ENTER] or clicking in the combo box
navigates to the new URL.

What's Next?

Programs like this do not replace Microsoft's Internet Explorer or Netscape's Navigator.
They do provide a way for business programs to access specific Internet or intranet Web
pages, an important consideration. The control's **BeforeNavigate** event can be used
to prevent leaving the startup site or to limit site changes to a specific list. There is even
a **ProgressChange** event that you can use to fill a progress bar! Like much of Visual
Basic 5, the main limitation is your own imagination.

1. The WebBrowser control is:
   a. A Visual Basic intrinsic control
   b. An ActiveX control
   c. A Visual Basic add-in
   d. None of the above

2. To open the URL `http://www.mcp.com/waite/ezone/`, use the:
   a. `OpenSite` method
   b. `GoTo` method
   c. `Find` method
   d. `Navigate` method

3. If you add the flag `navNoReadFromCache` to the `Navigate` method, the browser will:
   a. Read the file from the Internet site unless it is stored in the cache directory
   b. Read the file from the cache directory
   c. Read the file from the Internet site even if it is in the cache directory
   d. Raise a `No Cache` error

4. To move back to the previous page, use the:
   a. `GoBack` method
   b. `MovePrev` method
   c. `GoHome` method
   d. `Refresh` method

5. What is the cache?
   a. A `Collection` object continuing your most recently visited Web pages
   b. A directory in which the HTML files from recently visited Web pages are stored
   c. A hidden file containing data about Web sites
   d. None of the above

FILES, FILES, FILES: USING FTP

The World Wide Web generates excitement, but it is far from all there is to the Internet. For one thing, a wealth of files is available for download from *FTP sites*. FTP stands for *file transfer protocol*, the protocol (agreed-upon set of rules) for transferring text and binary files over the Internet.

True, you can find files on the Web, but not all FTP sites are available from the Web. And FTP connections generally run faster because there is less demand for them. Some say they are more reliable, too. FTP also has business uses: Business applications use FTP connections to update distributed database files, sales catalogs, and other business documents.

This lesson explains how to use the Internet Transfer control to establish an FTP connection and download files.

The Internet Transfer Control

The Internet Transfer Control (ITC) implements either FTP or Hypertext Transfer Protocol (HTTP). When the ITC is set up for FTP, it can be used to create an FTP browser or to download files from a public or private FTP site. It can operate with the default Internet settings from the system registry, with a direct (T1) connection to the Internet, or through a proxy server.

Adding the ITC to the Toolbox

Before you can use the ITC, you must add it to your toolbox.

1. Press CTRL-T or select Components from the Project Menu.

2. Select Microsoft Internet Transfer Control 5.0.

3. Click OK.

The ITC icon is shown in Figure 18-18.

The FTP Project

Accessing an FTP site requires navigating to the site, listing directories, changing directories, reading text files, and downloading files. The project in this lesson demonstrates how to add an FTP browser to your programs.

1. Start a new project and add the ITC to your toolbox as described above. The completed project is on the CD that accompanies this book.

2. Press F4 to open the Properties window and set the form's properties according to Table 18-23.

Figure 18-18
The ITC in the
toolbox

Table 18-23 Properties for `frmFTP`

Object	Property	Value
Form	Name	frmFTP
	Caption	"FTP Client"
	Height	6015
	Width	6360
	Icon	Graphics\Icons\Comm\Net10a.ico
	MaxButton	False

For convenience, the form needs to display the FTP host site, the current FTP directory name, and the commands that are sent to the FTP host.

3. Add three text boxes and three labels to the form. Set their properties according to Table 18-24.

Table 18-24 Properties for labels and text boxes on `frmFTP`

Object	Property	Value
TextBox	Name	xtServer
	Height	285
	Left	1440
	Top	240
	Width	4575
TextBox	Name	txtDirectory
	Height	285
	Left	1440
	Locked	True
	TabStop	False
	Top	600
	Width	4575
TextBox	Name	txtCommand
	Height	855
	Left	120
	MultiLine	True
	ScrollBars	Vertical
	Top	5040

Object	Property	Value
	Width	6075
Label	Name	Label1
	AutoSize	True
	Caption	"Working Directory:"
	Left	0
	Top	600
Label	Name	Label2
	AutoSize	True
	Caption	"Host:"
	Left	
	Top	40
Label	Name	lblWhat
	AutoSize	True
	Caption	"lblWhat.Caption"
	Left	0
	Top	0

The form also needs a place to display the files and subdirectories in an active directory.

4. Add a list box to the form. Set its properties according to Table 18-25.

Table 18-25 Properties of lstDir

Object	Property	Value
ListBox	Name	lstDir
	Height	3990
	Left	1440
	Top	960
	Width	4695

The project also requires six Command buttons to send commands to the FTP site.

5. Add six Command buttons to frmFTP. Set their properties according to Table 18-26.

Table 18-26 Properties for the Command buttons

Object	Property	Value
CommandButton	Name	cmdConnect
	Caption	"&Connect"
	Height	495
	Left	120
	Top	1020
	Width	1095
CommandButton	Name	cmdDirectory
	Caption	"Get &Directory"
	Enabled	False
	Height	495
	Left	120
	Top	1668
	Width	1095
CommandButton	Name	cmdReadText
	Caption	"Read Text File"
	Enabled	False
	Height	495
	Left	120
	Top	2316
	Width	1095
Command Button	Name	cmdDownLoad
	Caption	"Download File"
	Enabled	False
	Height	495
	Left	120
	Top	2964
	Width	1095
Command Button	Name	cmdClose
	Caption	"C&lose Connection"
	Enabled	False

Object	Property	Value
	Height	495
	Left	120
	Top	3612
	Width	1095
CommandButton	Name	cmdQuit
	Caption	"E&xit"
	Height	495
	Left	120
	Top	4260
	Width	1095

6. Add the ITC to the form. The control is not visible at runtime, so it does not matter where you place it. Set the control's properties according to Table 18-27.

Table 18-27 Properties for the ITC

Object	Property	Value
Inet	Name	Inet1
	Protocol	2
	URL	(Leave blank)
	UserName	"anonymous"
	Password	(See text)

Anonymous FTP

Public sites that let you download files are *anonymous* FTP sites. That means that you do not have to be registered with the site in order to log on and download files. Instead, logon is with the user name **anonymous**.

The **Password** property for anonymous FTP is your e-mail address. If you are writing a program to call a single, proprietary FTP site, the URL, user name, and password can be saved in the system registry and set programmatically.

The completed form is shown in Figure 18-19.

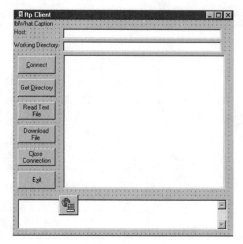

Figure 18-19
The completed
form

The Internet Transfer Control's Methods

The ITC has only a few methods.

The Execute *Method*

Most commands to the FTP site are made using the **Execute** method. The syntax for the **Execute** method is

```
object.Execute url, operation, data, requestHeaders
```

where

● object is the name you gave the ITC.

● url is an optional string that specifies the URL to which the control should connect. If no URL is specified here, the URL specified in the URL property will be used.

● operation is an optional string that specifies the type of operation to be executed. See Table 18-28 for a list of the supported operations.

● data is an optional string that specifies the data for operations. This parameter is not used for FTP.

● requestHeaders is an optional string that specifies additional headers to be sent from the remote server. This parameter is not used for FTP.

Table 18-28 FTP commands

Operation	Description
CD file1	Change directory. Changes to the directory specified in file1.
CDUP	Change to parent directory. Equivalent to "CD.."
CLOSE	Closes the current FTP connection.
DIR file1	Directory. Searches the directory specified in file1. (Wildcards are permitted but they must be recognized by the remote host.) If no file1 is specified, a full directory of the current working directory is returned. Use the GetChunk method to return the directory data.
GET file1 file2	Retrieves the remote file specified in file1 and creates a new local file specified in file2.
RECV file1 file2	Retrieves the remote file specified in file1 and creates a new local file specified in file2. Equivalent to GET.
LS file1	List. Searches the directory specified in file1. (Wildcards are permitted but the remote host dictates the syntax.) Use the GetChunk method to return the file directory data.
PWD	Print working directory. Returns the current directory name. Use the GetChunk method to return the data.
SIZE file1	Returns the size of the directory specified in file1.
QUIT	Terminates the current user.
* DELETE file1	Deletes the file specified in file1.
* MKDIR file1	Make directory. Creates a directory as specified in file1. Success is dependent on user privileges on the remote host.
* PUT file1 file2	Copies a local file specified in file1 to the remote host specified in file2.
* RENAME file1 file2	Renames the remote file named in file1 to the new name specified in file2. Success is dependent on user privileges on the remote host.

continued on next page

continued from previous page

Operation	Description
* RMDIR file1	Remove directory. Removes the remote directory specified in file1. Success is dependent on user privileges on the remote host.
* SEND file1 file2	Copies a local file, specified in file1, to the remote host, specified in file2. Equivalent to PUT.

The commands marked with an asterisk (*) can be executed only if the user has privileges on the FTP host. Anonymous FTP sites will not allow anyone to create directories or to delete files or directories. Anonymous FTP sites also allow uploads only to certain directories.

The ITC uses the **Execute** method to start almost every operation. Uploads and downloads are automatic; all you need to do once they begin is wait until they are done. Listing directories and reading text files are more complicated. Both of these operations require the **GetChunk** method.

The GetChunk *Method*

The syntax for **GetChunk** is

```
object.GetChunk( size [,datatype] )
```

where

● object is the name you gave to the ITC.

● size is a long numeric expression that determines the size of the chunk to be retrieved.

● datatype is an optional integer parameter that specifies the data type of the retrieved chunk. The datatype may be either icString, which returns string data for reading text files, or icByte, which returns the data as a byte array.

The OpenURL *Method*

The **OpenURL** method is used to open and return documents from a site. Its syntax is

```
object.OpenUrl url [,datatype]
```

where

● object is the name you gave the ITC object.

● url is the URL of the document to be retrieved.

● datatype is an optional integer that specifies the type. This is identical to the datatype parameter in GetChunk.

The Cancel *Method*

The only other ITC method that is used by the FTP protocol is the Cancel method. The Cancel method cancels the current operation and closes the connection. The syntax is

```
object.Cancel
```

where **object** is the name you gave to the ITC.

The StateChanged Event

The ITC has only one event, the **StateChanged** event. The control receives reports from the FTP site and reports them as **State** through the **StateChanged** event. The different states are listed in Table 18-29.

Table 18-29 State-changed constants

Constant	Value	Description
icNone	0	No state to report.
icHostResolvingHost	1	The control is looking up the IP address of the specified host computer.
icHostResolved	2	The control successfully found the IP address of the specified host computer.
icConnecting	3	The control is connecting to the host computer.
icConnected	4	The control successfully connected to the host computer.
icRequesting	5	The control is sending a request to the host computer.
icRequestSent	6	The control successfully sent the request.
icReceivingResponse	7	The control is receiving a response from the host computer.
icResponseReceived	8	The control successfully received a response from the host computer.
icDisconnecting	9	The control is disconnecting from the host computer.
icDisconnected	10	The control successfully disconnected from the host computer.
icError	11	An error occurred in communicating with the host computer.
icResponseCompleted	12	The request has been completed and all data has been received.

Programs use the **StateChanged** event to determine what to do and when. Now it's time to look at some code.

Code for StateChanged

The control has a single event, but it is a busy event indeed. Add the code in Listing 18-17 to the **StateChanged** event.

Listing 18-17　The StateChanged event

```vb
Private Sub Inet1_StateChanged(ByVal State As Integer)
'    Fired each time inet control detects a change in state
Dim sMsg As String
On Error GoTo Error_Handler
'    Figure out what to do
Select Case State
    Case icResponseCompleted
    '    All of the preliminaries are done, now get the information
    lblWhat.Caption = "Response Completed "
    '    Display response
    If Inet1.ResponseCode <> 0 Then _
        txtCommand = txtCommand & vbCrLf & Inet1.ResponseCode & _
            ": " & Inet1.ResponseInfo
    txtCommand.SelStart = Len(txtCommand.Text)
    DoEvents
    Select Case iAction
        Case 0, 1, 4: subGetDir '    Make connection, CDUP, or change directory
        Case 2: '    Read text file -- handled in cmdReadText_Click
        Case 3: '    Download a file -- handled in cmdDownLoad_Click
    End Select
    Case icConnecting
        lblWhat.Caption = "Connecting"
        DoEvents
    Case icConnected
        lblWhat.Caption = "Connected"
        DoEvents
    Case icDisconnected
        lblWhat.Caption = "Disconnected"
        DoEvents
    Case icDisconnecting
        lblWhat.Caption = "Disconnecting"
        DoEvents
    Case icHostResolved
        lblWhat.Caption = "Host Resolved"
        DoEvents
    Case icReceivingResponse
        lblWhat.Caption = "Receiving Response "
        DoEvents
    Case icRequesting
        lblWhat.Caption = "Sending Request"
        DoEvents
    Case icRequestSent
        lblWhat.Caption = "Request Sent"
        DoEvents
```

```
    Case icResolvingHost
        lblWhat.Caption = "Resolving Host"
        DoEvents
    Case icError
        sMsg = "Error Code " & Inet1.ResponseCode
        sMsg = sMsg & vbCrLf & Inet1.ResponseInfo
        MsgBox sMsg, vbOKOnly, "Error Response Received"
        DoEvents
        Exit Sub
    Case icResponseReceived
        lblWhat.Caption = "Response Received!"
        '   Display response
        If Inet1.ResponseCode <> 0 Then _
            txtCommand = txtCommand & vbCrLf & Inet1.ResponseCode & _
            ": " & Inet1.ResponseInfo
        txtCommand.SelStart = Len(txtCommand.Text)
        DoEvents
    Case Else   '   Should never get here
        lblWhat.Caption = "Unknown State Received"
        DoEvents
End Select
Ok_Exit:
Exit Sub
Error_Handler:
MsgBox "Error # " & Err & " " & Error, vbOKOnly, "State Changed"
GoTo Ok_Exit
End Sub
```

A lot there, isn't there? Most of it, fortunately, is pretty simple. Skip over `icResponseCompleted` for the moment. The next eight values of **State** are informative responses. Each causes a message to be displayed as `lblWhat.Caption`, providing the user with visual feedback about what is happening.

If **State** equals `icError`, an error message is displayed in a message box. When the user clicks OK in the message box, the procedure is exited.

If **State** equals `icResponseReceived`, the exact response is added to `txtCommand`. The user can scroll back in `txtCommand` to review the commands that were sent to the host and the host's responses to them.

Now take a look at `icResponseCompleted`. When this state is received, decisions must be made to handle the response. Exactly what to do depends on what the program did to generate the response. When it is making a connection or changing directories, the code must explicitly use the **GetChunk** method to process the data. When the program is uploading or downloading a file or reading a text file, the action is handled automatically.

Using GetChunk

Recall that the **GetChunk** method has two parameters, **size** and **datatype**. Because directories are always text, the **datatype** for reading directory contents is **icString**.

1. Create a new Public procedure by selecting Add Procedure from the Tools menu.

2. Name the procedure GetDir.

3. Enter the code from Listing 18-18 into the procedure.

Listing 18-18 The GetDir procedure

```
Public Sub subGetDir()
'    Reads directory or directory name from host
'    called from inet control state changed event
Dim vtData As Variant ' Data variable.
Dim strData As String: strData = ""
Dim bDone As Boolean: bDone = False
' Get first chunk.
vtData = Inet1.GetChunk(1024, icString)
'    continue until no data is in the buffer
Do While Not bDone
    lblWhat.Caption = "Reading DIR "
    DoEvents
    strData = strData & vtData
    ' Get next chunk.
    vtData = Inet1.GetChunk(1024, icString)
    lblWhat.Caption = "Reading DIR "
    DoEvents
    If Len(vtData) = 0 Then
        bDone = True
    End If
Loop
If iAction = intntGetDirName Then
    txtDirectory = strData
ElseIf iAction = intntConnect Then
    lstDir.Clear
    FillDir (strData)
ElseIf iAction = intntChangeDir Then
    lstDir.Clear
    lstDir.AddItem ".."
    FillDir (strData)
End If
lblWhat.Caption = "Directory Done"
End Sub
```

To allow any type of data to be read, **vtData** is declared as a variant. The line **vtData = Inet1.GetChunk(1024, icString)** "gets one chunk" of data from the host and stores it in **vtData**. The string in **vtData** is immediately copied into **strData**. The **Do** loop repeats the same action until there is no data left to be read.

The If...ElseIf...End If structure then decides what to do with the data in sData. If iAction is intntGetDirName, which is the case when the command is PWD, sData is copied into txtDirectory.

If iAction is intntConnect, the command was LS. The list box is cleared and sData is passed to the FillDir procedure that breaks it into its separate parts and adds them to the list.

If iAction is intntChangeDir, the command was also LS, but because the connection is already established, the directory being read is not the root directory. The code adds ".." as the first item in the list, then calls the FillDir procedure.

The FillDir *Procedure*

The FTP site sends its directory as a single, delimited string. The string must be parsed so the directory entries can be displayed in the list box.

1. **Create a new Public procedure by selecting Add Procedure from the Tools menu.**

2. **Name the procedure FillDir.**

3. **Enter the code from Listing 18-19 into the procedure.**

Listing 18-19 The FillDir procedure

```
Sub FillDir(strData As String)
' Parses strData and fills lstDir with
' directory and file names
Dim iCR As Integer
Dim iStart As Integer: iStart = 1
Do
     ' Find vbCrLf
     iCR = InStr(iStart, strData, vbCrLf)
     ' If not found, exit loop
     If iCR = 0 Then Exit Do
     ' Found, add next item to listbox
     lstDir.AddItem Mid(strData, iStart, iCR - iStart)
     ' Skip start position over vbCrLf (2 characters)
     iStart = iCR + 2
Loop
End Sub
```

The string is downloaded with each directory item delimited by a carriage-return linefeed pair, vbCrLf. The code in FillDir Do loops through the string looking for the next vbCrLf and uses AddItem to add each item to the lstDir.

THE REST OF THE GENERAL SECTION

There are three more procedures in the General Declarations section of the code. Create each of the procedures shown in Listing 18-20 and add the code.

Listing 18-20 Controlling the Command buttons

```
Sub subConnected()
cmdDirectory.Enabled = True
cmdDownLoad.Enabled = True
cmdReadText.Enabled = True
cmdClose.Enabled = True
cmdConnect.Enabled = False
End Sub

Sub subDisConnected()
cmdDirectory.Enabled = False
cmdDownLoad.Enabled = False
cmdReadText.Enabled = False
cmdClose.Enabled = False
cmdConnect.Enabled = True
End Sub

Public Sub subBusy(bz As Boolean)
If bz Then
    cmdDirectory.Enabled = False
    cmdDownLoad.Enabled = False
    cmdReadText.Enabled = False
    cmdClose.Enabled = True
    cmdConnect.Enabled = False
Else
    cmdDirectory.Enabled = True
    cmdDownLoad.Enabled = True
    cmdReadText.Enabled = True
    cmdClose.Enabled = True
    cmdConnect.Enabled = False
End If
End Sub
```

These subs enable or disable Command buttons depending on what the program is doing. If you are already connected, for example, you should not be able to press Connect again. While data is being retrieved, only the Close button should be enabled (to disconnect if something goes wrong).

Open the Code window of `frmFTP` and add the code from Listing 18-21.

Listing 18-21 Declarations and form events for `frmFTP`

```
Option Explicit
Public sCommand As String
Public sServer As String
Public iAction As Integer
```

```
' Download Directory Path
Const DownLoadDir As String = "C:\Temp\"
' Activity Constants
Const intntConnect As Integer = 0
Const intntChangeDir As Integer = 1
Const intntGetText As Integer = 2
Const intntGetFile As Integer = 3
Const intntGetDirName As Integer = 4

Private Sub Form_Load()
lblWhat.Caption = "Enter Server Name"
End Sub

Private Sub Form_Unload(Cancel As Integer)
Dim i As Integer
For i = Forms.Count - 1 To 0 Step -1
    Unload Forms(i)
Next
End
End Sub
```

Note the constant **DownLoadDir**. If your computer does not have a C:\Temp directory, either create one or change the path in the constant to match a directory of your choice.

The activity constants are used elsewhere in the program to control the program's response to codes from the **StateChanged** event.

Note the code in the **Unload** event. The **For** loop assures that all the forms are unloaded, avoiding memory leaks.

Making the Connection

The code in Listing 18-22 opens the connection to the FTP site.

Listing 18-22 Code for `txtServer` and `cmdConnect`

```
Private Sub txtServer_KeyPress(KeyAscii As Integer)
If KeyAscii = 13 Then
    sServer = txtServer.Text
    cmdConnect_Click
End If
End Sub

Private Sub txtServer_LostFocus()
sServer = txtServer.Text
End Sub

Private Sub txtServer_Change()
    cmdConnect.Enabled = True
End Sub

Private Sub cmdConnect_Click()
On Error GoTo Error_Handler
```

continued on next page

continued from previous page

```
'    Can't open a non-existent server
If sServer = "" Then
    MsgBox "Must enter server name", vbOKOnly, "Note:"
    Exit Sub
End If
'    OK, open the server and get the directory
With Inet1
    .URL = sServer
    iAction = intntGetDirName
    .Execute , "PWD"
    '    Wait until done before doing anything else
    Do While Inet1.StillExecuting
        DoEvents
    Loop
    iAction = intntConnect
    '    Display command being sent
    txtCommand = txtCommand & vbCrLf & "LS"
    txtCommand.SelStart = Len(txtCommand.Text)
    .Execute , "LS"
    '    Wait until done before doing anything else
    Do While Inet1.StillExecuting
        DoEvents
    Loop
    Call subConnected
End With
Exit_Normal:
    Exit Sub
Error_Handler:
    MsgBox Err & " " & Error, vbOKOnly, "Connect Error"
    Select Case Err
        Case 35761: Inet1.Cancel    ' Timeout
        Case 35764: Inet1.Cancel    ' Still Executing
    End Select
    Resume Exit_Normal
End Sub
```

When a user types a URL into **txtServer** and presses (ENTER) or clicks on the Connect button, the text in **txtServer** is copied into the string **sServer**. If **cmdConnect** is disabled, typing into **txtServer** enables it. (**cmdConnect** is disabled while the program is online.)

The code in **cmdConnect_Click** begins by checking to be sure that the user has entered a URL. If so, the **With...End With** structure copies **sServer** to the URL property and invokes the **Execute** method with the command **PWD**. The **Execute** method opens the connection to the host site and sends it the **PWD** command. From here, the **StateChanged** event takes over for a while.

Note the block of code

```
Do While Inet1.StillExecuting
    DoEvents
Loop
```

This code waits for the **StillExecuting** property to become **False**. Because **StateChanged** depends on the speed of the Internet, the program must wait for the host to catch up after sending it a command.

Once the **PWD** command is completed, the code issues an **LS** command to get the directory listing.

Changing Directories

When you log on to an FTP site, the first directory is called the root directory. (Sound familiar?) Chances are there is not much there for downloading. You must change directories to get to the good stuff. (Hint: Look for the Pub directory.) The program needs a way to select and switch to a new directory.

Add the following code to **lstDir_DblClick**:

```
Private Sub lstDir_DblClick()
    If Right$(lstDir.List(lstDir.ListIndex), 1) = "/" Then cmdDirectory_Click
End Sub
```

Add the code in Listing 18-23 to the **Click** event of **cmdDirectory**.

Listing 18-23 Code for **cmdDirectory**

```
Sub cmdDirectory_Click()
On Error GoTo Error_Handler
'    Change directory on remote computer
Dim sDirectory As String
sDirectory = lstDir.List(lstDir.ListIndex)
'    Test for no directory selected
If sDirectory = "" Then
    MsgBox "No directory selected.", vbOKOnly, "Note:"
    Exit Sub
End If
'    Test for file name selected
If sDirectory <> ".." And Right$(sDirectory, 1) <> "/" Then
    MsgBox "File selected.", vbOKOnly, "Note:"
    Exit Sub
End If
'    OK, there is something selected
iAction = intntChangeDir
If sDirectory = ".." Then
    '    Move up
    '    Display activity
    lblWhat = "Moving to parent directory"
    Call subBusy(True)
    DoEvents
    With Inet1
        .URL = sServer
        '    Display command being sent
        txtCommand = txtCommand & vbCrLf & "CD .."
        txtCommand.SelStart = Len(txtCommand.Text)
        sCommand = "CD .."
```

continued on next page

continued from previous page

```
            .Execute , sCommand
            '   Wait until done before doing anything else
            Do While Inet1.StillExecuting
                DoEvents
            Loop
            '   Display command being sent
            txtCommand = txtCommand & vbCrLf & "PWD"
            txtCommand.SelStart = Len(txtCommand.Text)
            sCommand = "PWD"
            iAction = intntGetDirName
            .Execute , sCommand
            '   Wait until done before doing anything else
            Do While Inet1.StillExecuting
                DoEvents
            Loop
            '   Display command being sent
            txtCommand = txtCommand & vbCrLf & "LS"
            txtCommand.SelStart = Len(txtCommand.Text)
            sCommand = "LS"
            iAction = intntChangeDir
            .Execute , sCommand
            '   Wait until done before doing anything else
            Do While Inet1.StillExecuting
                DoEvents
            Loop
        End With
    '   End of CDUP routine
    Else
        '   Move to new directory
        '   Display activity
        lblWhat = "Moving to " & sDirectory
        Call subBusy(True)
        DoEvents
        With Inet1
            .URL = sServer
            sCommand = "CD " & txtDirectory
            If Right$(sCommand, 1) <> "/" Then
                sCommand = sCommand & "/" & sDirectory
            Else
                sCommand = sCommand & sDirectory
            End If
            '   Display command being sent
            txtCommand = txtCommand & vbCrLf & sCommand
            txtCommand.SelStart = Len(txtCommand.Text)
            iAction = intntChangeDir
            .Execute , sCommand
            '   Wait until done before doing anything else
            Do While Inet1.StillExecuting
                DoEvents
            Loop
            iAction = intntGetDirName
            '   Display command being sent
            txtCommand = txtCommand & vbCrLf & "PWD"
```

```
    txtCommand.SelStart = Len(txtCommand.Text)
    txtCommand = txtCommand & vbCrLf & "PWD"
    txtCommand.SelStart = Len(txtCommand.Text)
    .Execute , "PWD"
    '    Wait until done before doing anything else
    Do While Inet1.StillExecuting
        DoEvents
    Loop
    iAction = intntChangeDir
    '   Display command being sent
    txtCommand = txtCommand & vbCrLf & "LS"
    txtCommand.SelStart = Len(txtCommand.Text)
    .Execute , "LS"
    '    Wait until done before doing anything else
    Do While Inet1.StillExecuting
        DoEvents
    Loop
    End With
'   Directory read
End If
Exit_Normal:
    Call subBusy(False)
    Exit Sub
Error_Handler:
    MsgBox Err & " " & Error, vbOKOnly, "Directory Error"
    Select Case Err
        Case 35761: Inet1.Cancel    ' Timeout
        Case 35764: Inet1.Cancel    ' Still Executing
    End Select
    Resume Exit_Normal
End Sub
```

To change directories, the user first selects a directory and then clicks on the Get Directory button. Double-clicking on the selection in `lstDir` calls `cmdDirectory_Click` automatically. The procedure checks to be sure something has been selected from `cmdDir`, and then checks for a trailing `/` to be sure it is a directory.

Changing directories takes three steps:

1. Change the directory.

2. Get the new directory name.

3. List the directory.

There are two possibilities: selecting a new directory or moving up to a higher-level directory. The code issues either `"CD..."` or `"CD " & txtDirectory`.

Closing the Connection

You can't "break" the Internet, so you can close the connection to a site simply by exiting from the program. If you want to explore another site, though, that means you must start the program all over again, which is not very convenient. It is far better to close the connection the "polite" way.

Add the following code to the **Click** event of **cmdClose**:

```
Private Sub cmdClose_Click()
    On Error Resume Next
    Inet1.Execute , "CLOSE"
    Call subDisConnected
End Sub
```

The **Close** command is, perhaps, the only one that operates instantaneously, so you don't need the **Do** loop here. The **subDisconnected** procedure enables and disables the appropriate Command buttons.

Reading a Text File

If you are "trolling" FTP sites instead of looking for specific files, look for files named **index.txt** and **readme.txt**. The readme file generally contains information about the site, including the site's rules, whereas the index file provides a list of directories and files on the site.

Clearly, you need a way to read the text files while you are online. The project needs one more form to display text files.

1. Add a new form to the project.

2. Add a Command button and a text box to the form.

3. Set the properties according to Table 18-30.

Table 18-30 Properties for **frmText**

Object	Property	Value
Form	Name	frmText
	Caption	"Text File"
	Height	4410
	Width	7110
	ControlBox	False
TextBox	Name	txtData
	Height	3735
	Left	120
	Locked	True
	MultiLine	True
	ScrollBars	'Both
	Top	120
	Width	6975

Object	Property	Value
CommandButton	Name	cmdDone
	Caption	"Done"
	Height	375
	Left	240
	Top	3960
	Width	975

The completed form is shown in Figure 18-20.
Open the Code window and add the code in Listing 18-24.

Listing 18-24 Code for frmText

```
Option Explicit

Private Sub cmdDone_Click()
Me.Hide
frmFTP.Show
End Sub

Private Sub Form_Load()
Form_Resize
End Sub

Private Sub Form_Resize()
txtData.Width = Me.ScaleWidth - 120
txtData.Height = cmdDone.Top - 240
End Sub
```

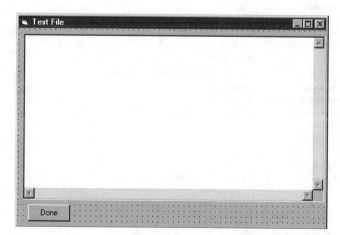

Figure 18-20
frmText at design
time

The only real work in this code is in the **Form_Resize** event, which sizes **txtData** to fill the form. Note, also, that the form is *hidden* by **cmdDone**, rather than unloaded. This is a supplementary form that is loaded and unloaded only by **frmFTP**.

You are finished with **frmText**.

1. Close the Object and Code windows of **frmText**.

2. Open the Code window of **frmFTP**.

3. Change the **Form_Load** procedure as shown below (changes are in bold).

```
Private Sub Form_Load()
Load frmText
lblWhat.Caption = "Enter Server Name"
End Sub
```

Add the code in Listing 18-25 to the **Click** event of **cmdReadText**.

Listing 18-25 Code for cmdReadText_Click

```
Private Sub cmdReadText_Click()
On Error GoTo Error_Handler
'    Read a text file -- display it on frmText
Dim sFileName As String
If lstDir.List(lstDir.ListIndex) = "" Then
    MsgBox "No file selected.", vbOKOnly, "Note:"
    Exit Sub
End If
If Right$(lstDir.List(lstDir.ListIndex), 3) <> "txt" Then
    MsgBox "File is not a text file!", vbOKOnly, "Note:"
    Exit Sub
End If
'    ok, got here so set up to read directory
'    Creat filename of directory
If txtDirectory = "/" Then    '    This is the root
    sFileName = txtServer & txtDirectory & lstDir.List(lstDir.ListIndex)
ElseIf Right$(txtDirectory, 1) = "/" Then    '    / is there
    sFileName = txtServer & "/" & _
        txtDirectory & lstDir.List(lstDir.ListIndex)
Else    '    slash is not there, add one
    sFileName = txtServer & "/" & _
        txtDirectory & "/" & lstDir.List(lstDir.ListIndex)
End If
iAction = intntGetText
'    Get file
'    Display activity
lblWhat = "Reading " & lstDir.List(lstDir.ListIndex)
DoEvents
sCommand = sFileName
'    Display command being sent
txtCommand = txtCommand & vbCrLf & sCommand
txtCommand.SelStart = Len(txtCommand.Text)
```

```
Call subBusy(True)
frmText.txtData.Text = Inet1.OpenURL(sCommand)
'   Wait until done before doing anything else
Do While Inet1.StillExecuting
    DoEvents
Loop
'   done reading, display the form
Call subBusy(False)
frmText.Show
lblWhat.Caption = ""
Exit_Normal:
    Exit Sub
Error_Handler:
    MsgBox Err & " " & Error, vbOKOnly, "Read Text"
    Select Case Err
        Case 35761: Inet1.Cancel      ' Timeout
        Case 35764: Inet1.Cancel      ' Still Executing
    End Select
    Resume Exit_Normal
End Sub
```

As always, the procedure starts by validating the request. It verifies that something is selected and that the selection is a really a text file. If the request passes the test, the procedure uses the **OpenURL** method to retrieve and display the text file. The **OpenURL** method copies the text file directly into the text box on **frmText**.

Downloading

Finally! The whole point of FTP is downloading files. Now that you can connect and read the supporting text files, it's time to download. Add the code in Listing 18-26 to **cmdDownlod_Click**.

Listing 18-26 Downloading files

```
Private Sub cmdDownLoad_Click()
'   Download the selected file
Dim sFileName As String, sTemp As String
Dim sDLName As String, iResponse As Integer
On Error GoTo Error_Handler
If lstDir.List(lstDir.ListIndex) = "" Then
    MsgBox "No file selected.", vbOKOnly, "Note:"
    Exit Sub
    '   No file selected, exit this procedure
End If
If Right$(lstDir.List(lstDir.ListIndex), 1) = "/" Then
    MsgBox "Directory selected.", vbOKOnly, "Note:"
    Exit Sub
    '   Not a file -- cannot download
End If
'   build the path and filename string
If txtDirectory = "/" Then
    '   Root directory
    sFileName = txtDirectory & lstDir.List(lstDir.ListIndex)
```

continued on next page

continued from previous page

```
ElseIf Right$(txtDirectory, 1) = "/" Then
    '    has slash. Build path/filename
    sFileName = txtDirectory & lstDir.List(lstDir.ListIndex)
Else
    '    no slash, add it to build path/filename
    sFileName = txtDirectory & "/" & lstDir.List(lstDir.ListIndex)
End If
sDLName = lstDir.List(lstDir.ListIndex)
If Len(Dir(DownLoadDir & sDLName)) Then
    '    File exists in download directory
    iResponse = MsgBox(sDLName & "already in " & DownLoadDir & _
        vbCrLf & "OverWrite?", vbOKCancel, "Warning!")
    ' No? Then exit sub
    If iResponse = vbCancel Then Exit Sub
    ' Yes, then delete old
    sTemp = DownLoadDir & sDLName
    Kill sTemp
End If
Call subBusy(True)
'    Start the download
With Inet1
    sCommand = "GET " & sFileName & " " & DownLoadDir & _
        sDLName
    '    Display command being sent
    txtCommand = txtCommand & vbCrLf & sCommand
    txtCommand.SelStart = Len(txtCommand.Text)
    .Execute , sCommand
    '    Wait until done before doing anything else
    Do While Inet1.StillExecuting
        lblWhat.Font.Bold = Not lblWhat.Font.Bold
        lblWhat.Caption = "Downloading " & lstDir.List(lstDir.ListIndex)
        DoEvents
    Loop
    lblWhat.Caption = "Done Downloading"
    Call subBusy(False)
    Beep
End With
Exit_Normal:
    Exit Sub
Error_Handler:
    MsgBox Err & " " & Error, vbOKOnly, "Download Error"
    Select Case Err
        Case 35761: Inet1.Cancel    ' Timeout
        Case 35764: Inet1.Cancel    ' Still Executing
    End Select
    Resume Exit_Normal
End Sub
```

Downloading is all but automatic. The code checks to be sure that something has been selected and that the selection is not a directory name. It also checks the download directory for a file of the same name. If it finds a match, it offers the option of overwriting the original or exiting from the download operation.

Finally, the code builds the **GET** command string, **sCommand**, and issues **.Execute** **sCommand** to the ITC. That done, all that remains is to wait in a **Do** loop until the download is complete. The loop alternates **lblWhat**'s **Font.Bold** property as an activity indicator.

Exiting

You can now log on to an FTP site, change directories, read text files, download files of any kind, and disconnect from the site. All that remains is a way to exit from the program itself, which is, of course, the reason for **cmdQuit**.

Add the following code to the **Click** event of **cmdQuit**:

```
Private Sub cmdQuit_Click()
'   Exit from the program
Unload Me
End
End Sub
```

Running the Program

Unlike the WebBrowser control, the Internet Transfer control does not start the logon process for you. Before you can connect to an FTP site with this program, you must connect to your Internet service provider (ISP).

Once that connection is made, enter **FTP.microsoft.com** into **txtServer** and press ⟨ENTER⟩ or click on Connect. Figure 18-21 shows the program connected to the Microsoft FTP site.

Note the response from the site in **txtCommand**.

Click on disclaimer.txt in the directory listing and then click on Read Text File. Figure 18-22 shows the program displaying the text file on **frmText**.

Now navigate through the directories. Double-click on DEVELOPR. When that directory is completely listed, click on BASIC and then click on Get Directory to switch to that directory. Finally, double-click on KB to change to the Visual Basic Knowledge Base directory.

Click on index.txt and then on Download File to download the Knowledge Base index to your computer. When the download is completed, explore the site to your heart's content.

Click on Close Connection, followed by Exit when you are finished.

Summary

The program in this lesson is a rudimentary FTP browser. Its main purpose is to demonstrate how to use the ITC to access FTP sites. If your project involves automatic download, many of the choices that this project leaves to the user—logging on, changing to the correct directory, and even downloading the file—can be done programmatically.

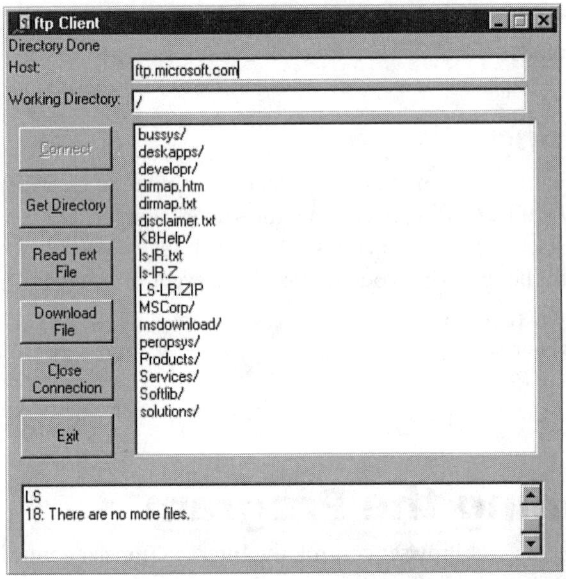

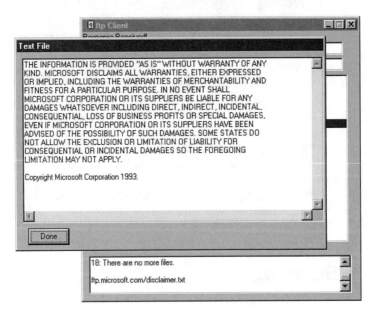

Figure 18-21
Connected!

Figure 18-22
Reading a text file

1. The term *FTP* stands for:
   a. Fine-tuned praxis
   b. File time priority
   c. File transfer protocol
   d. Files to practice

2. Sites that let anyone log on to download files are:
   a. Anonymous FTP sites
   b. Public FTP sites
   c. Free FTP sites
   d. Pirate FTP sites

3. The _____ method is used to start most FTP operations.
   a. `GoTo`
   b. `SendMessage`
   c. `GetChunk`
   d. `Execute`

4. Use the _____ method to read text files or directories.
   a. `GoTo`
   b. `SendMessage`
   c. `GetChunk`
   d. `Execute`

5. The Internet Transfer control responds to messages from the FTP site in the _____ event.
   a. `GotData`
   b. `StateChanged`
   c. `GotFocus`
   d. `State`

EXERCISE

Modify the FTP project from Lesson 5 to make it more useful as an FTP browser. At a minimum it should have

- A way to save and recall your favorite FTP sites

- A way to enter an original directory path

- A Cancel button

- A way to determine the size of a file before a download begins

GRAND FINALE

This is not really a lesson, but a message of congratulations. You have arrived at the end of the book, and you have done so in grand fashion!

If you have followed the lessons throughout this book and done all the exercises yourself, you have learned a great deal about Visual Basic 5. The objective throughout has been to show you the most-used features of the language and to build enough familiarity that you can approach almost any project with confidence.

Yes, there is more to learn—there is *always* more to learn. Computer programming is one of today's most challenging and most rewarding activities. Meet the challenges to reap the rewards!

APPENDIX A
QUIZ ANSWERS

CHAPTER 1 WHAT'S ALL THAT STUFF ON MY SCREEN?
Lesson 1 *Getting Started*
1. a
2. b
3. c
4. d
5. a

Lesson 2 *Customizing the Development Environment*
1. c
2. d
3. b
4. c
5. b

Lesson 3 *The Application Wizard*
1. d
2. b
3. b
4. d
5. c

Lesson 4 *Add-Ins*
1. d
2. c
3. c
4. d
5. a

Lesson 5 *Help!*
1. a
2. a
3. c
4. b
5. c

CHAPTER 2 OBJECT-ORIENTED PROGRAMMING
Lesson 1 *Objects*
1. d
2. b
3. d
4. a
5. b

Lesson 2 *Forms: Your First Program*
1. d
2. a
3. b
4. c
5. c

Lesson 3 *Getting Things Done*
1. d
2. a
3. b
4. d
5. c

Lesson 4 *The File Picker Gets Better*

1. c
2. d
3. c
4. a
5. d

Lesson 5 *The Development Environment*

1. a
2. c
3. d
4. a
5. a

Lesson 6 *Looking Closely at Forms*

1. b
2. c
3. a
4. d
5. b

Lesson 7 *The File Picker: Better Still*

1. d
2. d
3. a
4. d
5. b

Lesson 8 *It's a Wrap*

1. b
2. a
3. c
4. d
5. c

CHAPTER 3 VARIABLES, CONSTANTS, AND ASSOCIATED FUNCTIONS

Lesson 1 *Variables: Getting Started*

1. b
2. a
3. c

4. a
5. b

Lesson 2 *The Code Window Explored*

1. a
2. d
3. b
4. a
5. a

Lesson 3 If *and More Variable Types*

1. c
2. c
3. d
4. c
5. b

Lesson 4 *Introduction to Strings*

1. a
2. a
3. c
4. c
5. d

Lesson 5 *String Manipulation*

1. a
2. b
3. c
4. b
5. c

Lesson 6 *Times and Dates*

1. c
2. a
3. b
4. d
5. d

Lesson 7 *Other Date and Time Support Functions*

1. c
2. a

3. c
4. b
5. d

Lesson 8 *Variables Concluded*

1. b
2. b
3. d
4. b
5. a

CHAPTER 4 SUBROUTINES, FUNCTIONS, AND THE VISUAL BASIC 5 LANGUAGE
Lesson 1 *A Project Skeleton*

1. d
2. d
3. a
4. b
5. c

Lesson 2 For *Loops*

1. c
2. d
3. b
4. d
5. a

Lesson 3 *Other Loops*

1. b
2. d
3. a
4. c
5. a

Lesson 4 *Decision Statements*

1. d
2. b
3. c

4. d
5. a

Lesson 5 *Subroutines and Functions: Introduction*

1. a
2. c
3. c
4. c
5. d

Lesson 6 *Subroutines and Functions: The Sequel*

1. a
2. a
3. d
4. c
5. b

Lesson 7 *Argument Lists*

1. b
2. d
3. d
4. d
5. c

Lesson 8 *Arrays*

1. d
2. b
3. c
4. d
5. a

CHAPTER 5 CONTROLS
Lesson 1 *The TextBox Control*

1. d
2. b
3. d
4. a
5. b

Lesson 2 *Labels and the* `MsgBox` *Function*

1. b
2. c
3. d
4. c
5. a

Lesson 3 *Command Buttons and Check Boxes*

1. b
2. b
3. c
4. c
5. a

Lesson 4 *Option Buttons and Frames*

1. d
2. a
3. c
4. b
5. a

Lesson 5 *The ListBox Control*

1. a
2. c
3. c
4. d
5. a

Lesson 6 *Advanced ListBox Techniques and the ComboBox Control*

1. b
2. a
3. d
4. c
5. d

Lesson 7 *Control Arrays*

1. d
2. b

3. b
4. c
5. a

CHAPTER 6 FORMS, MENUS, AND MDI FORMS

Lesson 1 *Forms*

1. a
2. c
3. c
4. b
5. c

Lesson 2 *An MDI Application*

1. d
2. a
3. b
4. d
5. d

Lesson 3 *Creating Forms at Runtime*

1. c
2. a
3. b
4. a
5. c

Lesson 4 *Further Form Techniques*

1. d
2. d
3. d
4. a
5. b

Lesson 5 *Adding Menus to Your Project*

1. a
2. c
3. d
4. d
5. c

Lesson 6 *Filling In the Blanks: Programming the File Menus*

1. b
2. c
3. a
4. a
5. d

Lesson 7 *Filling In the Blanks: Programming the Edit Menus*

1. b
2. b
3. a
4. b
5. c

Lesson 8 *Filling In the Blanks: Finishing Up SuperPad*

1. a
2. c
3. d
4. b
5. b

CHAPTER 7 CLASSES
Lesson 1 *Classes and Objects*

1. d
2. b
3. c
4. d
5. d

Lesson 2 *The* Form *Class*

1. c
2. b
3. b
4. b
5. a

Lesson 3 *Control Classes*

1. d
2. c
3. d
4. b
5. b

Lesson 4 *Introducing User-Defined Classes*

1. b
2. d
3. b
4. c
5. c

Lesson 5 *A Class Act: Modifying SuperPad*

1. b
2. d
3. b
4. d
5. d

Lesson 6 *Collections*

1. d
2. a
3. c
4. d
5. b

Lesson 7 *User-Defined Properties*

1. b
2. c
3. a
4. c
5. d

Lesson 8 *Why Use Classes?*

1. a
2. d

3. b
4. c
5. d

CHAPTER 8 DISCOVERING THE COMMONDIALOG AND WINDOWS 95 CONTROLS
Lesson 1 *Introducing the CommonDialog Control*

1. b
2. b
3. c
4. a
5. d

Lesson 2 *The RichTextBox Control and the Font and Color Dialog Boxes*

1. d
2. a
3. b
4. c
5. a

Lesson 3 *The ToolBar and ImageList Controls*

1. d
2. c
3. b
4. c
5. a

Lesson 4 *The StatusBar Control*

1. c
2. d
3. a
4. c
5. a

Lesson 5 *The TabStrip Control*

1. b
2. a

Lesson 6 *The TreeView Control*

1. a
2. d
3. b
4. b
5. b

Lesson 7 *The ListView Control*

1. b
2. a
3. d
4. b
5. d

Lesson 8 *The ProgressBar and Slider Controls*

1. b
2. a
3. c
4. b
5. d

CHAPTER 9 PRINTING
Lesson 1 *Introducing Printing*

1. d
2. d
3. b
4. c
5. a

Lesson 2 *Using Fonts*

1. a
2. b
3. c
4. d
5. b

Lesson 3 *The Printer and the CommonDialog*

1. b
2. b
3. a
4. c
5. c

Lesson 4 *Printer Capabilities*

1. c
2. a
3. c
4. d
5. b

Lesson 5 *Combining Text and Graphics*

1. c
2. b
3. c
4. b
5. c

Lesson 6 *Printing Reports from Visual Basic*

1. b
2. d
3. d
4. a
5. c

Lesson 7 *Formatting Numeric Output*

1. d
2. d
3. c
4. a
5. b

Lesson 8 *Formatting Dates for Output*

1. a
2. a
3. b

4. b
5. b

CHAPTER 10 ERROR HANDLING AND DEBUGGING

Lesson 1 *Errors in Visual Basic 5 Programs*

1. a
2. c
3. c
4. c
5. a

Lesson 2 *Error Handlers*

1. a
2. d
3. a
4. a
5. a

Lesson 3 *Debugging: The Noble Art*

1. c
2. b
3. d
4. b
5. a

Lesson 4 *Debugger Bugs*

1. c
2. a
3. d
4. c
5. a

Lesson 5 *How to Write Code That Is Easy to Maintain*

1. a
2. a
3. d
4. c
5. a

Lesson 6 *Advanced Debugging Techniques*

1. a
2. c
3. b
4. d
5. a

CHAPTER 11 GRAPHICS
Lesson 1 *Understanding Coordinates*

1. d
2. a
3. c
4. a
5. b

Lesson 2 *Using Graphical Controls*

1. a
2. c
3. b
4. c
5. c

Lesson 3 *Using Graphical Methods*

1. b
2. b
3. a
4. c
5. a

Lesson 4 *Drawing Shapes*

1. c
2. b
3. a
4. d
5. d

Lesson 5 *Colors*

1. d
2. a

3. b
4. a
5. c

Lesson 6 *Picture Control Versus Image Control*

1. b
2. a
3. c
4. d
5. b

Lesson 7 *Simple Animation*

1. b
2. c
3. a
4. d
5. a

Lesson 8 *Miscellaneous Graphics Issues*

1. d
2. a
3. d
4. a
5. b

CHAPTER 12 FILES
Lesson 1 *Using the File System Controls*

1. d
2. b
3. b
4. b
5. a

Lesson 2 *Making the File System Controls Work Together*

1. c
2. c
3. b
4. d
5. d

Lesson 3 *Opening, Reading, and Closing a File*

1. c
2. b
3. b
4. c
5. a

Lesson 4 *Sequential and Random Access Files*

1. a
2. c
3. a
4. a
5. b

Lesson 5 *Binary File Access*

1. b
2. c
3. d
4. a
5. b

Lesson 6 *A Notepad Application*

1. d
2. a
3. c
4. b
5. b

Lesson 7 *Using Files in Development Time Versus Standalone Applications*

1. a
2. d
3. c
4. a
5. d

CHAPTER 13 DATA ACCESS

Lesson 1 *What Is a Database?*

1. a
2. c
3. d
4. b
5. b

Lesson 2 *Using the Data Control*

1. c
2. d
3. a
4. d
5. d

Lesson 3 *Accessing Data with Code*

1. c
2. a
3. a
4. d
5. b

Lesson 4 *Using the Bound Controls*

1. d
2. a
3. c
4. b
5. a

Lesson 5 *Managing Your Data with SQL*

1. d
2. c
3. b
4. b
5. c

Lesson 6 *Creating Reports*

1. d
2. b
3. a

4. d

5. b

Lesson 7 *Designing a Database*

1. c

2. a

3. b

4. d

5. b

Lesson 8 *Understanding ODBC*

1. c

2. a

3. d

4. a

5. b

CHAPTER 14 ADVANCED FEATURES
Lesson 1 *Using the Windows API*

1. b

2. c

3. d

4. b

5. a

Lesson 2 *Timer Control*

1. c

2. d

3. b

4. a

5. d

Lesson 3 *Understanding the Architecture*

1. d

2. a

3. b

4. c

5. a

Lesson 4 *Idle Time*

1. c

2. a

3. d

4. c

5. b

Lesson 5 *DDE*

1. d

2. b

3. a

4. c

5. c

Lesson 6 *Creating an Executable*

1. a

2. b

3. c

4. d

Lesson 7 *Using the Setup Wizard*

1. b

2. a

3. d

4. c

5. b

Lesson 8 *Application Optimization*

1. d

2. b

3. c

4. a

5. c

CHAPTER 15 INTERFACING WITH EXCEL AND OTHER PROGRAMS
Lesson 1 *What Is OLE?*

1. d

2. b

3. a

4. a

5. d

Lesson 2 *Using the OLE Container Control*

1. a

2. b

3. d

4. b

5. c

Lesson 3 *What Is OLE Automation?*

1. d

2. a

3. c

4. d

5. a

Lesson 4 *Object Hierarchy and the Object Browser*

1. d

2. c

3. a

4. a

5. b

Lesson 5 *Using OLE Automation with Microsoft Word and Microsoft Excel*

1. c

2. a

3. c

4. b

5. b

Lesson 6 *Exposing Your Own Classes: Creating OLE Servers*

1. d

2. d

3. a

4. c

5. a

Lesson 7 *Using Visual Basic Built-In Objects*

1. d

2. a

3. b

4. a

5. d

Lesson 8 *Thinking in Objects*

1. b

2. a

3. c

4. d

5. b

CHAPTER 16 ROLL YOUR OWN: CREATING YOUR OWN ACTIVEX CONTROLS

Lesson 1 *What Is ActiveX?*

1. c

2. c

3. a

4. d

5. c

Lesson 2 *Running the Control at Design Time*

1. d

2. b

3. c

4. d

5. b

Lesson 3 *The Key Events of a User Control Object*

1. a

2. b

3. c

4. d

5. d

Lesson 4 *Drawing the Control*

1. b
2. d
3. a
4. c
5. a

Lesson 5 *The Ins and Outs of Events*

1. c
2. b
3. c
4. c
5. d

Lesson 6 *Give Your Control a Property Page*

1. a
2. c
3. b
4. c
5. b

Lesson 7 *The Control Interface Wizard*

1. d
2. d
3. a
4. a
5. d

Lesson 8 *Compiling and Distributing Your Control*

1. a
2. b
3. c
4. d
5. b

CHAPTER 17 REGISTER YOUR PROGRAMS: USING THE WINDOWS REGISTRY

Lesson 1 *Using the Registry with Built-In VB Commands*

1. d
2. c
3. a
4. b
5. b

Lesson 2 *Using the Registry API*

1. d
2. a
3. c
4. d
5. b

Lesson 3 *Adding Values to Subkeys*

1. c
2. d
3. a
4. c
5. b

Lesson 4 *Reading Registry Values*

1. c
2. a
3. c
4. b
5. d

Lesson 5 *Deleting Values and Subkeys*

1. d
2. c
3. a
4. c
5. c

CHAPTER 18 VISUAL BASIC 5 COMMUNICATIONS
Lesson 1 *The MSComm Control*

1. b
2. d
3. a
4. d
5. a

Lesson 2 *More from the Modem*

1. c
2. a
3. d
4. d
5. a

Lesson 3 *Communications with MSComm*

1. d
2. a
3. b
4. b
5. c

Lesson 4 *Connect to the World Wide Web*

1. b
2. d
3. c
4. a
5. b

Lesson 5 *Files, Files, Files: Using FTP*

1. c
2. a
3. d
4. c
5. b

APPENDIX B

INTERNET EXPLORER 3.0: A FIELD GUIDE

A new day dawned. The sun reached its fingers over the digital outback. The mighty Navigators (*Netscapus navigatorus*)—a species that reproduced like rabbits and ran nearly as fast—covered the landscape. Yonder, on a cliff that seemed to be beyond the horizon, a trembling new creature looked out over the Internet jungle. This strange new creature, calling itself the Explorer (*Microsoftus interneticus explorus*), sniffed around, considering whether it should enter the fragile ecosystem. Netscape gators gnashed their teeth, but the Explorer was not daunted. Explorer was a formidable beast. It became a part of the jungle and thrived. And even though it began as a mere pup, it evolved, and it evolved and it evolved.

Now the jungle is rife with two intelligent species.

What follows is a guide to domesticating Internet Explorer. You will learn how to care for your Explorer and even how to teach it tricks. Before long, you shall find truth behind the old axiom that the Explorer is man's (and woman's) best friend.

INTRODUCING EXPLORER TO YOUR ECOSYSTEM

Whether you're running Windows NT or Windows 95, installing Explorer is easy. Explorer's own installation program makes setup a breeze, and you need only to select the appropriate file on the CD-ROM to launch this installer. Make sure the CD-ROM included with this book is in the CD-ROM drive; then, depending upon your system, follow the directions below for either Windows 95 or Windows NT.

Windows 95 Installation

1. Click the Start button in the lower left corner of your screen.

2. Click on the Run... option in the Start menu. A dialog box similar to the one shown in Figure B-1 appears.

3. Using the Run dialog box, type in a pathname and specify the location of the Explorer installation program. IE301M95.EXE is in the CD's \Explorer directory, so if your CD-ROM drive is designated as D:, you'd type

   ```
   d:\explorer\ie301m95.exe
   ```

   If your CD-ROM drive has a different designation letter, type in the appropriate drive designation letter in place of d:.

4. After typing the proper pathname, click the OK button to start the Explorer's installation program. Depending upon your system, it may take a moment to load.

5. Once the installation program loads, follow the on-screen prompts to set up Explorer on your computer.

Windows NT 4 Installation

1. Click the Start button in the lower left corner of your screen.

2. Click on the Run... option in the Start menu. A dialog box similar to the one shown in Figure B-2 appears.

Figure B-1
The Windows 95
Run dialog box

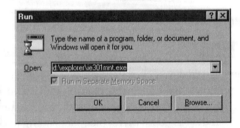

Figure B-2
The Windows NT
Run dialog box

3. Using the Run dialog box, type in a pathname and specify the location of the Explorer installation program. MSIE30M.EXE is in the CD's \Explorer directory, so if your CD-ROM drive is designated as D:, you'd type

```
d:\explorer\ie301mnt.exe
```

   If your CD-ROM drive has a different designation letter, type in the appropriate drive designation letter in place of d:.

4. After typing the proper pathname, click the OK button to start the Explorer's installation program. Depending upon your system, it may take a moment to load.

5. Once the installation program loads, follow the on-screen prompts to set up Explorer on your computer.

Once you've run the installation, you'll need to restart your system. You can then click on the Internet icon on your desktop. If you've already selected an Internet provider with Windows dial-up networking, you'll be connected. If not, you'll be walked through the dial-in process. You'll need to enter the phone number of your Internet provider, your modem type, and other related information. Ultimately, you'll be taken to Microsoft's home page, where you can register your Explorer and find out about its latest features.

 The Explorer is a constantly evolving animal. For the latest updates, plug-ins, and versions, be sure to regularly check out Microsoft's neck of the woods at http://www.microsoft.com/ie/.

Explorer Components

Explorer is more than a plain-Jane Web browser. As you work through the installation, you'll be able to choose a variety of components. You can select the following add-ons:

- *Internet Mail*—This is a comprehensive e-mail package. Using simple icons, you can write and read your mail off-line and then log on quickly to send and receive your latest batch of correspondence. See Figure B-3.

- *Internet News*—This is a window that lets you browse through thousands of newsgroups, read through the threads, and post your own messages. The News system is very easy to use. You can easily keep track of your favorite topics and automatically update with the latest news.

- *ActiveMovie*—This feature of Explorer lets you watch all sorts of video clips—MPEG, AVI, and QuickTime formats. It even supports a special streaming version of video that downloads movies as you watch them, letting you view video with little delay. The ActiveMovie system also lets you listen to all popular formats of audio files—AU, WAV, MIDI, MPEG, and AIFF. This makes it easy to add background sound to Web pages.

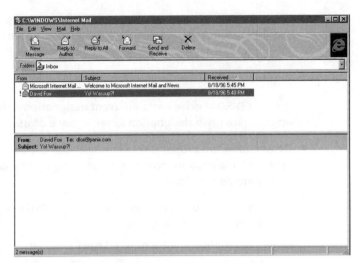

Figure B-3
The Internet Mail
main window

- *VRML Support*—This feature is a separate module that lets you download and coast through Virtual Reality Modeling Language worlds. This allows you to explore true 3D landscapes and objects.

- *NetMeeting*—This is a full-featured package that lets you hold entire meetings over the Internet. You can chat with one person or with dozens. If you have a microphone, you can use the Internet phone feature to hold voice conversations with other people. You can share applications. For example, you and a client can edit the same word processing document together. A whiteboard feature lets you draw on a "digital blackboard" that can be updated live across the Internet.

- *HTML Layout Control*—This tool lets Web page publishers create spiffy versions of HTML pages, the way professional designers would lay out a magazine page or a newspaper. Designers can choose exactly where to place elements within a Web page. You can make objects transparent and layer objects over each other, which helps make a Web page eye-catching yet uncluttered.

THE NATURE OF THE BEAST

Internet Explorer features very up-to-date HTML. It supports HTML 3.2, including the following:

- *Frames*—These break up the Web page window into several areas. For example, you can keep an unchanging row of navigation controls along the top of the page while constantly updating the bottom. You can use *borderless frames*, which split up the page without making it seem split.

A special type of frame known as the *floating frame* lets you view one Web page within another.

● *Cascading Style Sheets*—This allows all your Web sites to have the same general look and feel.

● *Tables*—You can create or view all sorts of fancy tables, with or without graphics, borders, and columns.

● *Embedded Objects*—Internet Explorer can handle Java applets, ActiveX controls, and even Netscape plug-ins. These objects are discussed later, in the Symbiotic Partners section of this appendix.

● *Fonts*—Explorer supports many fonts, allowing Web pages to have a variety of exciting designs.

From the get-go, Internet Explorer has included a few special bells and whistles. For example, it's easy to create and view marquees across Web pages. This lets you scroll a long, attention-drawing message, similar to a tickertape, that puts a great deal of information in a very small space.

TRAINING THE EXPLORER

By its very nature, the Explorer is a friendly beast. You can access the full range of the Explorer's talents by pushing its buttons. These buttons, which appear in the toolbar at the top of the screen as depicted in Figure B-4, are as follows:

● *Back*—Use this to return to the Web page you've just come from. This will help you retrace your steps as you take Explorer through the Internet maze.

● *Forward*—Use this after you've used the Back button, to jump forward again to the page from which you began.

● *Stop*—If a Web page is taking too long to load, press this button. Any text and graphics will immediately stop downloading.

● *Refresh*—If your Web page is missing some graphics, or if you've previously stopped its loading using the Stop button, you can reload it using Refresh.

● *Home*—This takes you to your pre-set home page. By default, this is Microsoft's main Web page, but you can set your home to any you'd like. See the Taming the Beast section.

● *Search*—This takes you to a special page that allows you to search for a Web page, using a number of cool search engines. See the Hunting Skills section.

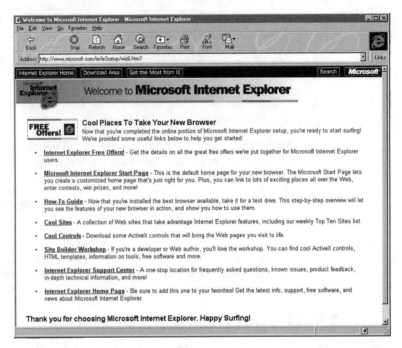

● *Favorites*—This button lets you access a list of your favorite Web sites. See the Favorite Haunts section.

● *Print*—This allows you to print out the current Web page, allowing you to keep a perfect hard copy of it.

● *Font*—Find yourself squinting at a Web page? Just click here to zoom in. The font size will grow several degrees. Too big now? Click a few more times and the size will shrink once again.

● *Mail*—This will launch the Internet Mail program, which allows you to send and receive e-mail and to access newsgroups.

PLAYING FETCH

Your Explorer is a devoted friend. It can scamper anywhere within the Internet, bringing back exactly what you desire.

If you know where you want to go, just type the URL into Explorer's Address box at the top of the screen. If you like, you can omit the `http://` prefix. The Web page will be loaded up. You can also search for a page or load up a previously saved page.

You can now click on any *hyperlink*—an underlined or colored word or picture—to zoom to that associated Web page or Internet resource. Some hyperlinked graphics may not be obvious. Explorer will tell you when you are positioned over a valid hyperlink, because the cursor will change into a pointing finger. Continue following these links as long as you like. It's not uncommon to start researching knitting needles and end up reading about porcupines.

Note

If you're an aspiring Web page writer, you might want to take a peek at the HTML source code to see how that page was created. Just select View|Source.

HUNTING SKILLS

If you want to find Web pages dealing with a specific category, the Explorer makes it easy to find them. Click the Search button. The Search screen will appear, as in Figure B-5. You can search for more than Web pages. With Explorer, it's easy to find

- Phone numbers, ZIP codes, and addresses
- Information on a number of topics—health, home, education, consumer affairs, finance, weather, sports, travel, and so on

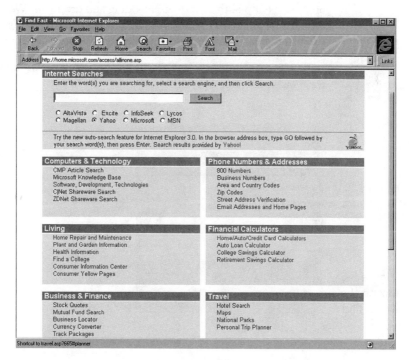

Figure B-5
The Search screen

- References—maps, a dictionary, a thesaurus, quotations, and an encyclopedia

- On-line books, newspapers, and magazines

You can also quickly hunt for any idea, word, or category. Simply type GO in the Address box at the top of the screen, followed by the word or phrase you want to search for.

FAVORITE HAUNTS

It's easy to keep track of the Web pages you visit most. When you want to save a page for future reference, simply click the Favorites button or choose the Favorites menu item. Select the Add To Favorites option. The current Web page will now be added to the list of favorites, which appears each time you click on the Favorites button or menu.

After a while, your list of favorites will get long and cluttered. It's simple to keep track of huge lists of favorites—just put them into separate folders. Organize your favorites, as shown in Figure B-6, by selecting Favorites|Organize Favorites.

To create a new folder, click on the New Folder icon (the folder with the little glint on it) at the top of the window. Now drag and drop your Web page bookmarks into the appropriate folders. You can also move, rename, or delete a folder by selecting it and using the corresponding buttons at the bottom of the screen.

You can even include or attach a favorite Web document within an e-mail message, the way you would attach any other file.

Figure B-6
Organizing the
Favorites list

On Windows systems, the Favorites list is actually a folder within your Windows directory. This reflects a Microsoft trend—treating the entire World Wide Web as just another folder to explore on your desktop. Eventually, you'll be able to drag and drop documents across the Internet as easily as you would within your own hard drive.

MEMORY

Internet Explorer keeps track of every Web page you visit. This is kept in a vast History list. You can view the entire History list, in chronological order, by clicking the View History button. Just click on any page you'd like to revisit.

The History list is cleared every 20 days—you can set this value within the Navigation properties sheets.

TAMING THE BEAST

Now that you and your Explorer are getting acquainted, why not tame it so that it acts and looks exactly like you want? Select View|Options and pick a tab at the top of the window to customize the following properties:

 General—The general properties sheet is illustrated in Figure B-7. Since multimedia content (such as sounds, movies, and graphics) takes longer to load in Web pages, you can choose not to load certain media types. You can also easily customize the color of the text and hyperlinks. Finally, you can decide how little or how much information appears in your toolbar.

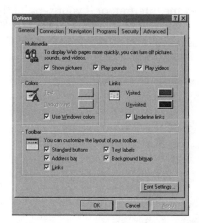

Figure B-7
The General
properties sheet

Note

You can change the size and position of your toolbar simply by clicking on its borders and dragging it to a desired location.

● *Connection*—You can adjust your connections settings, as shown in Figure B-8, by clicking on this tab. This lets you choose your Internet provider. If you're connecting to the Internet through a network firewall, you can also set your proxy server information here.

● *Navigation*—You can customize which page you'd like to use as your starting home page. Just enter its URL in the Address box here.

● *Programs*—This allows you to set which programs you'd like to use for e-mail and for Usenet news. By default, you can use Microsoft's Internet Mail and Internet News, which are included with Explorer. You can also tell Explorer how to handle various types of files by selecting the File Types button. It allows you to designate which program or plug-in should be launched whenever Explorer comes across various unfamiliar file formats.

● *Security*—You are able to customize how securely documents will be handled by Explorer. If you want to keep your computer extremely safe, you may tell Explorer not to download possible security risks such as ActiveX controls, Java applets, or other plug-ins. Another nice feature is a Content Advisor. Click on Settings; the Content Advisor window will appear as in Figure B-9. You may now decide which Web pages to skip based on Adult Language, Nudity, Sex, or Violence. Many questionable Web pages are written with certain tags so that the pages can be weeded out by people who don't want to see them. This is a great option to use if your kids surf the Internet, or if your sensibilities are offended. To turn ratings on, click on the Enable Ratings button. You can also lock this window with a password.

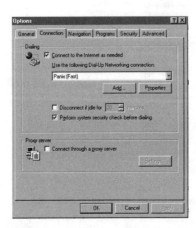

Figure B-8
The Connection
property sheet

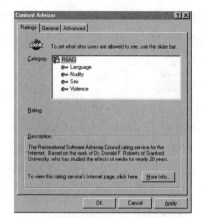

Figure B-9
The Content
Advisor window

● *Advanced*—This properties sheet lets you customize when Internet Explorer will issue warnings. This is useful if you deal with sensitive information and want to know which Web pages are secure and which are not. You can also set a number of other advanced Java and Security options here.

SYMBIOTIC PARTNERS

Explorer includes many of the latest Web technologies. These make your Web pages sing, dance, and even act as entire applications. The line between what a computer can do in general and what a computer can do over the Internet is thinning.

ACTIVEX

Microsoft's proprietary ActiveX technology lets you drop controls into your Web pages. Controls are software components such as specialized buttons, input forms, graphics viewers, sound players, and so forth.

When you load a page with an ActiveX control, Explorer will check if you already have that control on your system. If not, you'll be asked whether you'd like to download it. You'll be told whether the control has been authenticated by Microsoft. If the control is secure, it'll automatically be downloaded and installed for you. The resulting Web page may look more like a software program than a Web page. Don't be surprised to find all new types of buttons, such as the up and down arrow controls in Figure B-10.

SCRIPTS

Internet Explorer allows Web page writers to add different types of scripts right into the source code of the Web page itself. This means you can get instantaneous feedback and control of the Web browser, ActiveX controls, Java applets, and other plug-ins. This

Figure B-10
Loading a page
with an ActiveX
control

makes interactivity fast and easy. Internet Explorer supports Visual Basic, Scripting Edition and JavaScript languages.

JAVA

Finally, Explorer fully supports the popular Java language. Java is a programming language that lets you write full applications that run directly within your Web browser. Java is great for writing games, graphics demonstrations, databases, spreadsheets, and much more.

TOTAL MASTERY

Now that you are fully in control of Explorer, you can learn, work, and have fun using it with the greatest of ease. Wandering through the Internet faster than ever, you are ready to investigate new paths of adventure with your trusty, obedient Explorer guiding you every step of the way.

INDEX

Symbols

+ (addition) operator, 82

& (ampersand), adding accelerator keys to captions, 228-229

: (colon) separator, executing multiple statements, 176

, (commas), formatting print output, 458

/ (division) operator, 82

= (equality) operator, 93

= (equal sign), as assignment operator, 51

^ (exponentiation) operator, 82

> (greater than) operator, 93

>= (greater than or equal to) operator, 93

<< (inequality) operator, 93

\ (integer) operator, 82

< (less than) operator, 93

<= (less than or equal to) operator, 93

* (multiplication) operator, 82

- (negation) operator, 82

? (question mark), as notation for Print method, 169

; (semicolons), formatting print output, 458

A

About Box Application Wizard, 15

about boxes

    adding Image control, 323-325

    adding to projects, 321-323

About Microsoft Visual Basic option, 23

Abs function, 90

accelerator keys, *see* shortcut keys

Access databases, 663

accessing

    Color dialog box, 388, 390

    controls from outside forms, 68-69

    database data with code, 675-678

    default methods, 157

    files

        binary, 630-631

        random, 619-621

        sequential access, 619

    FTP sites, 973

    OLE objects, 790

    see also opening

Action property (Crystal Custom control), 721

Activate event, 313-314

ActiveForm property, 309

ActiveMovie, 1017

ActiveX, 788

    Component dialog box, 778

    Control Extension, *see* OCXs

    Control Interface Wizard, *see* Control Interface Wizard

    controls, 3, 837

        creating distribution copies, 882

        Design mode, 844-846

        disabling, 844

        distributing, 882

        Internet Explorer, 1025-1026

        licensing, 882-883

        shareware distribution, 883-884

        versioning issues, 884

        WebBrowser, see WebBrowser control (Microsoft)

        see also user controls

    defined, 20, 838

    Document Migration Wizard, 20

    documents, 3

Add button, creating recordsets, 679

Add Class Module dialog box, 345-346

Add Form command (Project menu), 55

Add method,

    adding objects to collections, 358

    TreeView Nodes collection, 424-425

AddNew method, 679

AddNew option, 671

Add Procedure , 853-856

Add Project command (File menu), 841

Add Property Page command (Project menu), 863

Add-ins, 3

    adding, 19

    APIViewer, 19

    Builder, 345-346

    Data Tools, 20

    defined, 18

    Manager, 676

    SQLDebugger, 20

    VBAdd-In toolbar, 20

    Visual Data Manager, 19

    see also wizards

AddForm function, 283-286
    calling, 285
    optimizing, 287
AddItem method, 252-253
Addition (+)operator, 82
Address Book project
    adding controls to, 116-117
    adding icons to, 104
    code, 106-112, 119-123
    properties, 104-105
    running, 113
Address picture boxes, properties, 964
Advanced properties sheet (Internet Explorer), 1025
Aggregate
    functions, 714
    queries, 713-714
algorithms, 34
Align property (Toolbar control), 396
Alignment property
    CheckBox control, 239-242
    Label control, 227
    status bar panels, 406
AlreadyAdded function, 189
American StandardCode for Information Interchange,
    see ASCII
Ampersand (&), adding accelerator keys to captions,
    228-229
And operator, 171-172
Animate project, 577-581
animation, 577-581
anonymous FTP sites, 977
ANSIBBS, connecting Chat to, 958
answers to quizzes, 1001-1013
APIs (Application Program Interfaces), 19
API Text Viewer, 745, 897-899
API Viewer add-in, 19
App object, 659, 829
Appearance property (TextBox control), 221
Application options (EXE Options dialog box), 772
Application program interfaces, see APIs
Application Wizard, 21
    creating database tables, 676-678
    screens, 13-16
    templates, 14
applications, see programs
Application Wizard, starting, 12
AppObject, 658
arguments
    defined, 86-87
    lists, 204-205
    optional, 206
    passing, 205, 215
arithmetic operators, 82

arrays, 209, 267-268
    control arrays, 266
        creating, 268
        Index property, 267
    declaring, 210
    dynamic sizing, 212-213
    Erase statement, 214
    For Each...Next loop, 213-214
    index numbering, 210-211
    LBound function, 214
    multiple dimensions, 211-212
    picture boxes, 414-415
    UBound function, 214
Asc function, 115, 122
ASCII (American Standard Code for Information
    Interchange), 118-119, 619
assigning variables, 148-150
Assignment operator (=), 51
assignments, 43, 51
Atn function, 90
attributes (Font property), 463
Authors project, 668
    adding text boxes to, 672
    properties, 669, 673-674
Auto Data Tips option, 503-504
Auto List Members option, 503
Auto Quick Info feature, 88, 503
Auto Syntax Check option, 502
AutoInc property (Graph control), 589
automatic persistence, 202
automatic syntax checking, 43
AutoRedraw property, 583-584
AutoSize property, 68, 406

B

Back button, 26, 1019
BackColor property, 565, 858-860
    adding to controls, 866-869
    Line control, 548
background processing (Timer control), 751-753
BackStyle property (Line control), 548
BBSs (Bulletin Board Services), connecting Chat to, 958
BeforeClick event (TabStrip control), 418
Bevel property, status bar panel, 406
binary files
    accessing, 630-631
    reading, 631
    writing, 631
Binary project
    adding data, 642-643
    CheckValidData function, 638
    code, 637-644

Binary project (*continued*)
  FillText procedure, 637
  Form_Activate procedure, 639-640
  Form_Load procedure, 638-639
  global declarations, 637
  Navigation buttons, 640-641
  properties, 631-632
    Command buttons, 635-636
    text boxes, 632-634
  running, 644
binding controls to database columns, 672-673
bitmaps, 573
bitwise operations, 173
BMP files, 573
BOF Action property (Data control), 671
Booleans, 96, 99
  logical operators, 171
  loops, 168-169
    break mode, 170-171
  variables, 97-98
BorderColor property (Line control), 548, 565
BorderStyle property
  adding about boxes to projects, 322
  Line control, 546, 548
BorderWidth property (Line control), 546, 548
boxes
  about boxes, *see* about boxes
  combo boxes, *see* combo boxes
  drawing, 557-559
branching statements, 92
Break button, 169, 512
Break mode
  Boolean expressions, 170-171
  entering, 169
  fixing code in, 532
breakpoints, 512, 525
Browse project, 598
  code, 606-607
  properties, 599, 603-605
browsers
  FTP (File Transfer Protocol), adding to programs,
    973-977
  Internet Explorer, *see* Internet Explorer 3.0
bugs
  debugging, 511-512
  see also errors
Bulletin Board Services, *see* BBSs
Button Group option, 398
buttons
  Add, creating recordsets, 679
  adding images, 399-400
  adding to toolbars, 396-398
  Back, 26
  Break, 169, 512
  Cancel, 69, 237-238

buttons (*continued*)
  Circle command, properties, 561-562
  Click event code, 653
  Delete, deleting recordsets, 680-681
  End (Debug toolbar), 512
  Exit, 129
  Find, 682-683
  Form templates (Application Wizard), 14
  frmBrowser, 963
  frmChat, 946
  Help topics, 26
  Internet Explorer toolbar, 1019-1020
  Navigation, Binary project, 640-641
  New, Click event code, 652
  OK, code, 234
  Open, Click event code, 652
  Options, 26
  radio, *see* OptionButton control
  Refresh, refreshing recordsets, 681
  RegClear, properties, 892-893
  Return, 257
  Save, 401, 653
  Snoop, 199
  Start (Debug toolbar), 511
  styles, 398
  TabStrip control, 413
  tooltips, 57
  Update, updating recordsets, 680
  View Mail Log, 196
ByRef method, passing arguments, 205
Byte variables, 96-97
ByVal keyword, 742
ByVal method, passing arguments, 205-206

C

cache, defined, 967
calculation functions, date/time, 140-143
Call Stack window (Debug Demo project), 521-522
calling
  Delete routine, 317
  DLLs (Dynamic Link Libraries), 740-744
  functions, 185, 188-189, 285
  routines, 189-190, 201
  SetupCSMenus, 307-308
  subroutines, 185, 187-188
Cancel button, 69, 236-238
Cancel property
  CommandButton control, 237-238
  ITCcontrol, 981
Caption property, 42
  Frame control, 246
  SButton control, 853
captions, 39
  adding to SButton control, 853-856
Carrier Detect (CD), 955

cascading style sheets, 1019
case-insensitivity, 43
case-sensitivity, 43-44
CD (Carrier Detect), 955
CDMaker, 76
    adding Label control to, 77, 84, 94
    adding picture box control to, 76
    computer calculations
        Computing average length and room left
            (listing 3.7), 86
        Forcing integer values (listing 3.8), 86
        Variables to hold computation results
            (listing 3.6), 84
    constants, 95-96
    declaring variables, 78-79
    initializing variables, 79-80
    manipulating variables, 80-82
    properties, 80
centering forms by writing subroutines, 334-335
Chalkboard project, 551-554
Change event
    form-level change flag, 303-305
    Slider control, 450
charts
    creating with Graph control, 588-590
    Excel
        embedding, property settings for OLE Container
            control, 796
        linking, 796
Chat, 938
    frmChat
        code, 950-954
        creating, 945-947
        OnComm event, 954-955
        properties, 939
        status bar, 949
        text boxes, 948
    frmSetup
        code, 943-944
        frames, 941-942
        option buttons, 941-942
        properties, 939-941
    project settings, 940
    running, 957-958
    unprintable characters, 956-957
Check Style option, 398
Checkbox control
    events, 26
    methods, 25
    properties, 25, 238-242
CheckValidData function (Binary project), 638
child nodes, 428-429
    finding parent, 435
ChkEcho, properties, 948-949

Chr function, 115, 123
Circle Command button, properties, 561-562
circles, drawing, 561-562
circuits, UART, 923
Class Builder utility, 21, 345-346
Class controls
    OCXs, *see* OCXs
    VBX, *see* VBX controls
Class modules
    components, 347
    creating, 345-346
    defined, 347
    properties, 349-350
Class property (OLE Container control), 365-366, 794
classes, 328
    Collection, 330
    control, *see* OCXs;VBX controls
    defineddesign, 328
    File, *646-649*
    Fomr1, creating Form1 objects, 332-333
    Font, 330
    Form, 331
    objects, 35-36, 329
    Picture, 330
    Printer, properties, 476
    single-instance, 329-330
    types, 329
    user-defined, 330, 343-344
clauses, 709-711
Clear method, 257
clearing breakpoints, 512
Click event, 43
    nodes, 434
    TabStrip control, 415-416
clients (OLE), 801
Clipboard object, 830
    copying text, 315-316
    deleting text, 316-317
    enabling/disabling Paste menu, 314-315
    pasting text, 319-320
Close command, 992
    confirming, 303-305
Close statement, 610
CloseFile method (File class), 646, 648
closing
    Control Design window, 849
    Design window, 844
    files, 610
    Project Explorer window, 7
    VBCalc, 826
    windows, 8
ClsDocument
    events, 353
    objects, adding to collections, 357-358
Cls method, 550

CmdClear, properties, 948-949
CmdSave_Click event, 107-112
code
    accessing database data, 675-678
    adding to Command_Click event, 910, 914-917
    adding to RegAPI.Bas, 910-911, 914-917
    adding to Resize event, 843-844
    Address Book, 107-113, 119-123
    Binary project, 637-644
    breakpoints, 512
    Browse project, 606-607
    case-sensitivity, 44
    components, 43
    Debug Demo project, 515-517
    dialer project, 935-936
    executing threads, 755
    fixing in Break mode, 532
    flxGrid project, 699-700
    flxMerge.pr, 702-703
    Font Demo project, 462, 465-467
    frmBrowser, 968-970
    frmChat, 660-664
    frmSetup, 943-944
    Good Code project, 530
    Goof project, 507-509
    Graph project, 591-595
    maximum number of lines in forms, 755
    MSComm project, 926-930
    native, 773, 755
    NotePad project, 652-654
    Ok button, 234
    optimizing, 291-292, 781-783
    P-code, 755
        compiling executable files, 773
    Picture Pusher project, 178-179
    PixLogo project, 586-587
    prjComm_2, 931-933
    procedures, 32
    property pages, 864-865
    Random project, 624-628
    referencing indexed controls, 270-271
    Registry API project, 899-902
        adding values to subkeys, 905-909
    remming, 875
    reusable, 370
    Sender project, 194-196
    SQL.vbp, 707-708
    spaghetti, 527-528
    StateChanged event, 982-983
    subroutines, 43
    TestCalc project, 823-825
    Timer event, 752-753
    Title project, 694-695
    writing, 526-529
    WWW.vbp project, 962

Code command (View menu), 55
Code window, 4, 42, 83, 192
    context-sensitive help, 88-89
collapsing nodes, 435
Collate check box, 473
collating printed copies, 473
collections, 355
    adding object references, 357-358
    classes, 330
    Count property, 363
    creating, 356-357
    destroying, 356-357
    Item method, 363
    removing objects from, 359
    searching with, 360-362
colon (:) separator, executing multiple statements, 176
Color dialog box, accessing, 388, 390
Color Selection dialog box, 868-869
colors, 564
    adding to forms, *565-567*
    controls, adding, 565-567
    functions, 565-569
    hexadecimal, 867-869
    restoring to original values, 858-860
    setting, 388, 390
Column Headers tab, 444-446
columns, 663
    binding controls to, 672-673
Columns property (ComboBox control), 259-260
combo boxes, 261
    drop-down, 263
    drop-down lists, 264
    promotions, 262
    simple, 264
ComboBox control, 259-263
    Data Bound, 686-688
ComEvCD event, 955
ComEvDSR event, 955
ComEvReceive event, 956
Command line, creating executable files, 773-774
CommandButton control, 236
    adding to TstShape project, 558-559
    Binary project, 635-636
    FTP project, 976-977
    properties, 236-238, 976-977
CommandDialog control, 376-379
commands
    assignments, 43
    Close, *303-305,* 992
    DoEvents, 419, *757-760*
    Edit menu, *246, 319-320,* 360
    Exit For, 162
    File menu
        Add Project, 841
        Load Text File, 897-899

commands (*continued*)
>> New Project, 12, 76
>> Print, 471
>> Save Project, 840
>> Save Project Group, 842
>> TestCalcEXE, 826
> FTP (File Transfer Protocol), 979-980
> GetObject, 810
> Insert menu, Module, 332
> Loadpicture, 574
> methods, *see* methods
> Print #, 626
> Project menu
>> Add Form, 55
>> Add Proeprty Page, 863
>> Properties, 58, 839-840
> Run to Cursor, 513
> Start menu, Run, 37
> Step commands, 513
> Tools menu
>> Add Procedure, 853
>> Custom Controls, 337-338
>> Menu Editor, 56
>> Options, 191
>> Spelling, 812
> View menu, Code, 55
Command_Click event, 910, 914-917
commas (,), formatting print output, 458
comments, writing code, 529
Common Dialog boxes, 377-380
> Color, 388
> File, 381-385
> Font, 388-390
> Open, 384-385
> Save As, 385
CommonDialog control
> adding to MDI forms, 379
> properties, 380-385
communications, 919
> Chat, 938
>> frmChat, 939, 945-954
>> frmSetup, 939-944
>> project settings, 940
>> running, 957-958
>> unprintable characters, 956-957
> interprocess, 762, 791-792
> modem
>> data transfers, 925
>> dialing out, 951
>> handshaking, 924-925
>> hanging up, 953
>> MSComm project code, 926-930
>> opening com ports, 952
>> phone dialer, 934-937

communications (*continued*)
>> setup properties, 923
>> waiting for calls, 951
> polled, 938
> serial, 920-924
comparing strings, 125-126
comparison operators, 93
compiling
> executable files, 773
> user controls, 879-881
Components dialog box, 837
compound documents, 788
computer screen
> points, 541
> Screen object, 539-540
concatenation, formatting print output, 458
conditional statements, 92
Confirm Dependencies dialog box, 778
Connect dialog box, 970
Connect property (Data control), 669
Connect Property Pages dialog box, 865-866
connecting
> property pages to controls, 865-866
> to Internet, 970
>> breaking connection, 991-992
Connection properties sheet (Internet Explorer), 1024
connectivity screen (Application Wizard), 13
constants, 95-96
> LineStyle property, 433
> Msg function, 232-233
> predefined, 231
> QBColor function, 567
> RGB function, 567
> StateChanged event, 981
> Style proeprty, 433
constituent controls, 852-853
context-sensitive menus, adding to projects
> Edit menus, 311-317, 319-321
> File Close menu, 309
> File New menu, 305
> forms collection, 306-308
> SuperPad, 301
control arrays, 266
> creating, 268
> defined, 267-268
> Index property, 267
Control classes, 336
> OCXs, *see* OCXs, 337
> VBXs, *see* VBX controls
Control data type, 340-341
Control design window, closing, 849
Control Interface Wizard
> Create Custom Interface Members dialog box, 871
> Finished! dialog box, 873-874
> modified declarations section, 874-878

Control Interface Wizard (*continued*)

   running, 870-871

   Set Attributes dialog box, 873

   Set Mapping dialog box, 872-873

controls, 4, 39, 219

   accessing from outside of forms, 68-69

   active, Design mode, 844-846

   ActiveX, *see* ActiveX, controls

   adding to

      Address Book, 116-117

      Font Demo project, 461-464

      forms, 40, 45-46

      frames, 246-249

      user controls, 852-853

   BackColor property, adding, 866-869

   binding to database columns, 672-673

   CheckBox, properties, 238-242

   class, *see* Class controls

   colors, adding, 565-567

   ComboBox, 259-263

      see also *combo boxes*

   CommandButton, 236-238

   CommandDialog, 376-379

   coordinates, setting multiple coordinates, 341-342

   CommonDialog

      adding to MDI forms, 379

      properties, 380-385

   constituent, 852-853

   copying, 268

   creating instances at runtime, 269-270

   Crystal Custom, 719-721

   Data, 667-668

      Data Bound controls passing values to, 688-689

      navigating recordsets, 671-672

      properties, 669-671

   Data Bound, 685

      ComboBox, 686-688

      Grid, 695-696

      ListBox, 686

      MSFlexGrid, 697-699, 704

      passing values to Data controls, 688-689

   Data Entry project, 222-224

   Debug Demo, 514-517

   DirListBox, 45-46, 600

      chaining DriveListBox control to, 602

      properties, 49

   disabling, 341

   DriveListBox, 45-46, 599-600

      chaining to DirListBox control, 602

      chaining to FileListBox control, 603

      properties, 49

   events, 26

      deleting to run Control Interface Wizard, 870-871

      see also *events*

controls (*continued*)

   File, 598, 600

      chaining, 602-603

      properties, 599, 601

   FileListBox, 45-46, 600

      chaining DriveListBox control to, 603

      Pattern property, 65-66

      properties, 49

      Text property, 66-67

   Form, properties for Animate project, 578

   Frame, 245

      properties, 246

      see also *frames*

   Graph, 588-590

   graphical, 544

      Line, 545-546

      Shape, 546-548

   groups, defining, 413

   HTML Layout, 1018

   Image, 572-573

      adding to About box, 323-325

      array properties for Animate project, 578-579

      compared to PictureBox control, 322-323, 575-576

      loading pictures, 574-575

   ImageList, 395

      adding images to toolbar buttons, 399-400

      disassociating image lists from controls, 441-442

      properties, 396-397

   intrinsic, 837

   ITC (Internet Transfer Control), 973

      methods, 978, 980-981, 983-985

      properties, 977

      StateChanged event, 981-983

   Label, 227

      adding to CDMaker, 77, 84, 94

      properties, 227-230

   lifetimes, 848-851

   ListBox

      adding items to list, 251-253

      multiselect list boxes, 255-256

      properties, 251

      removing items from, 256-257

      selecting items, 253-255

   ListView, 420-421, 437-438

      adding ListItems objects to, 439-446

      ColumnHeaders collection, 439-441

   mapping, 872-873

   maximum, 755

   methods, 25

   moving between

      changing tab order, 117-118

      tab order, 228

   MSComm, 920-921

      OnComm event, 938, 954-955

      properties, 921-926, 946

controls (*continued*)
    names, 268
    New, properties, 904-905
    Number Adder project, 154-155
    object variables, 338-339
    OCXs
        defined, 337-338
        referencing, 337-338
    OLE Container, 793
        adding sound effects to Number Adder project,
            156-157
        linking and embedding, 794-796
        properties, 794
    OptionButton, 243-245
    PictureBox, 67, 572-573
        adding to CDMaker, 76
        adding to frmOptions, 413-415
        compared to Image control, 322-323, 575-576
        loading pictures, 574-575
        see also *picture boxes*
    ProgressBar control, 448-449
    properties, *see* properties
    referencing, 270-271
    RichTextBox
        properties, 388-389
        replacing TextBox control with, 387-388
    SButton
        adding captions, 853-856
        color changes, 858-860
        events, 844, 849-850
        Line object properties, 845-846
        mapping properties, 873
        properties, 871
        raising events, 861-862
        testing, 881
    SButton User, 840
    sizing, 46
        shadow lines, 852-853
    Slide, properties for Animate project, 581
    Slider, 449-450
    StatusBar, 404-406
    TabIndex values, 229-230
    TabStrip, 410-413
        BeforeClick event, 418
        Click event, 415-416
        defining control groups, 413
        properties, 416
    TextBox, 65, 220
        binding to database columns, 673
        disabling, 341
        properties, 221-224
        replacing with RichTextBox control, 387-388
        SuperPad, 279
    Timer, 748
        background processing, 751-753

controls (*continued*)
        properties, 749
        properties for Animate project, 578
    Toolbar, 395-397
    TreeView, 420-421, 432
        adding to projects, 421-422
        displaying images, 425-427, 432-433
        Nodes collection, 424-425
    user
        adding property pages, 863-865
        adding standard property pages, 866-869
        compiling, 879-881
        connecting property pages to, 865-866
        creating with Control Interface Wizard, 870-878
        distributing, 880-881
        events, 848-850, 857-860
        raising events, 860-862
    VBX, 338-339
    WebBrowser, 960, 962-965
        frmBrowser code, 968-970
        methods, 965-967
    see also objects
conversions, data types, 743
cooperative multitasking vs. preemptive, 754
coordinate systems (print location), 479, 538
    controls, setting multiple, 341-342
    ScaleHeight values, 481-482
    ScaleMode values, 480, 542-543
    ScaleWidth property, 481-482
    Screen object, 539-541
    twips, 541
Copy menu, adding to projects, 315
copying
    controls, 268
    text to Clipboard, 315-316
CopiesToPrinter property (Crystal Custom control), 721
Cos function, 90
Count method, 307
Count property, collections, 363
Create a Setup Program option (Setup Wizard), 776
Create Custom Interface Members dialog box, 871-872
Create Internet Download Setup option
    (Setup Wizard), 776
CreateNewKey sub, 900-902
Create New Data Source dialog box, 733-735
Create New Report dialog box, 717-719
CreateObject command, 810
crippleware programs, 883
Crystal Custom control, 719-721
currency variables, 96, 100
Custom Controls
    command (Tools menu), 337-338
    dialog box, 337-338
Custom Properties dialog box, 399-400, 444-446
Customize window, 10

customizing
	development environment, 7-10
	Internet Explorer, 1024-1025
	toolbars, 9-10
Cut command (Edit menu), 246
Cut menu, adding to projects, 315-317

D

Data Bound controls, 685
	ComboBox, 686-688
	Grid, 695-696
	ListBox, 686
	MSFlexGrid, 697-699, 704
	passing values to Data controls, 688-689
Data control, 667-668
	Data Bound controls passing values to, 688-689
	navigating recordsets, 671-672
	properties, 669-671
Data Definition Language (DDE), 706
Data Entry project, 220-222
	controls, 222-224
	validating user input, 224-226
Data Form Wizard, 21
data hiding, 371
data management, SQL (Structured Query Language), 706
	Order By clause, 711
	Select statement, 709
	variables in statements, 711-712
	Where clause, 709-710
Data Manipulation Language (DML), 706
data segments, 756
Data source name, *see* DSN
data sources
	ODBC (Open Database Connectivity), 732
		adding, 733-735
data structures, fixed-length records, 619
	customer record (listing 12.12), 630
	fill characters, 620
	Random project code, 624-628
Data Tools add-in, 20
data transfers, modem communication, 925
data types
	Control, 340-341
	coversions, 743
	Date, 127-128
	delimiters, 710
	selecting, 618
data typesdata validation, Binary project, 638
data-centric programs
	MDI
		adding CommonDialog control to, 379
		SuperPad, see SuperPad
	SDI
		displaying within MDI form frames, 280
		vs. MDI, 274-275

data-centric programs (*continued*)
		Windows Notepad, 275-277
		WordPad, 275
DataAccess screen (Application wizard), 677-678
DatabaseName property (Data control), 670
databases, 662
	Access, 663
	accessing data with code, 675-678
	columns, binding controls to, 672-673
	design, 723-729
	foreign keys, 664, 666
	indexes, 664
	ODBC, 730-731
		data source, 732
		data source, adding, 733-735
		Jet Database engine, 735-736
	primary keys, 664, 666
	queries, 664
		duplicates, 713
		multiple tables, 713
	records, navigating, 671
	recordsets, 664, 670
		creating, 679
		deleting, 680-681
		finding, 682-683
		manipulating with code, 675-681
		navigating, 671-672
		refreshing, 681
		updating, 680
	relational, 663-665
	relationships, 665, 725, 727-728
	reports, *see* reports
	searches, 681-683
	SQL (Structured Query Language), 663
	tables, 663
Date
	data type, 127-128
	function, 132
	variables, 97
Date$ function, 750
DateAdd function, 140-141
DateDiff function, 142-143
dates
	formatting, 494-497
	functions, 131-143
	literals, 130-131
	manipulating, 131-140
DateSerial function, 137
DateValue function, 133
Day function, 134
DBGrid project, 695-696
DDE (Dynamic Data Exchange), 762
	compared to OLE, 791-792
	destinations, setup, 763-765
	links, establishing, 763-765
DDE (Data Definition Language), 706

Debug
    object, 830
    toolbar, 511-512, 518-522
    window, Resize event, 843
Debug Demo project, 514-517
    Call Stack window, 521-522
    Immediate window, 518-519
    Locals window, 521
    Quick Watch window, 520-521
    running, 517
    Watch window, 519-520
debugging, 511-512
    Debug Demo project, *see* Debug Demo project
    Debugger
        errors, 524-525
        testing procedures/functions, 533
Decimal variables, 96, 100-101
Declare statement, 741
declaring
    arrays, 210
    variables, 78-79
        Dim statement, 197-199
        explicit declarations, 144-145
        implicit declarations, 145
        Option Explicit statement, 147
        private declarations, 199-200
        public declarations, 199-200
        TypeName function, 145-146
decomposition, 32
DefaultExt property, 385
defaults
    CommandButton control, 236-237
    development environment, 4-6
    events, 43
    object methods, accessing, 157
    printer, 456-457
defining
    control groups, 413
    functions, 185-186
    subroutines, 185-186
Delete button, deleting recordsets, 680-681
Delete menu, 316-317, 681
Delete routine, calling, 317
DeleteSetting statement, 891
deleting
    events from controls to run Control Interface
        Wizard, 870-871
    nodes, 429
    recordsets, 680-681
    registry keys, 914-917
    text from Clipboard, 316-317
    see also removing
dependencies, 778
dependent objects, 805
Description property (err object), 505-506

delimiters, data types, 710
design
    classes, 328
    databases, 723-725, 727-728
        exercise, 726-729
        normalization, 725-726, 728-729
    object-oriented programming, 371-372
    OLE objects, 833-835
    software
        history, 32
        objects, 34
Design mode, ActiveX controls, 844-846
Design window, closing, 844
destination applications, 762, 764-765
Destination property (Crystal Custom control), 720
destroying
    collections, 356-357
    objects, 353-354
development environment
    accelerator keys, 228-230
    customizing, 7-10
    defaults, 4-6
    main screen, 54
    menu bar, 53
    toolbar, 57
    windows, *see* windows
development time, 658
Dialer project, 934
    code, 935-936
    running, 937
dialing out, modem communication, 951
DialNumber procedure, 951
dialog boxes, *see* individual names
Dim statement
    declaring arrays, 210
    declaring variables, 197-199
dimensioning arrays, 210-212
directories, changing FTP sites, 989-991
DirListBox control, 45-46, 600
    chaining DriveListBox control to, 602
    properties, 49
disabling
    ActiveX controls, 844
    menus, 301, 311-315
    Save button, 401
    TextBox controls, 341
disks
    directories, application distribution, 777
    opening files, 3
display speed, optimization, 783
displaying
    images in TreeView control, 425-427, 432-433
    SButton Designer window, 843
    tabs, 418-419

distributing
    ActiveX controls, 882-884
    applications, Setup Wizard, 775-780
    user controls, 880-881
Distribution Method dialog box, 777
Division (/) operator, 82
DLLs (Dynamic Link Libraries), 740
    calling, 740-741
        hDC property, 743
        hWnd property, 743
        SendMessage, 743-744
    data type conversions, 743
    files, 3
    ODBC (Open Database Connectivity), 731
    passing by reference, 741-742
    passing by value, 741-742
DML (Data Manipulation Language), 706
Document object, 344
    class modules, 347-350
    creating a class module, 345-346
Do loop, 165
Do Unitl loop, 166
Do Whatever project, 656-658
Do While loop, 166
Dockable
    property
        setting, 11
        viewing, 6
    windows, 6
Docking tab, 11
documentation, 883
documents
    ActiveX, 3
    defined, 274
    Word
        embedding, 798
        linking, 796, 798
        property settings for OLE Container control, 796
DoEvents command, 419
    creating idle loops, 757-760
double variables, 96, 100
DoVerb method, 157
downloading files, 995-996
drag and dropping, 10
drawing shapes, 556-557
    AutoRedraw property, 583-584
    boxes, 557-559
    circles, 561-562
    triangles, 560-561
DrawMode property (Line control), 548
DriveListBox control, 45-46, 599-600
    chaining to DirListBox control, 602
    chaining to FileListBox control, 603
    properties, 49

drivers, 920
drives, mapped, 657
dropdown combos, 263, 688
dropdown lists, 264, 688
DSN (Data Source Name), 732
duplicate queries, 713
Dynamic Data Exchange, see DDE
Dynamic Link Libraries, see DLLs
dynamic sizing, arrays, 212-213
Dynaset recordsets, 670

E
early-binding, 809-811
Edit menu, 298
    adding to projects, 311-317, 319-321
    adding to Setup routine, 311-312
    commands, 246, 319-320, 360
    NotePad, 277
editing
    text, nodes, 434
    text boxes, 288-292
    visual editing, 791
embedding (OLE), 789-791
    objects, internet Explorer, 1019
    OLE Container control, 794-796
    Word documents, 798
empty procedures (stubs), 416
empty values, variants, 148
Enabled property
    CheckBox control, 241
    Timer control, 749
    mapping, 873
enabling
    Enter key, 118
    menus, 311-315
encapsulation, 371
End button (Debug toolbar), 512
End statement, 43
EndDoc method, 456
Enter key, enabling, 118
EOF Action property (Data control), 671
EOF function, 611
Equal sign (=), as assignment operator, 51
Equality (=) operator, 93
Eqv (Equivalence) operator, 171-172
Erase statement, arrays, 214
Err object, 505-506, 830
Error function, 506
error handlers, 383, 505-506
    On Error statement, 506
    Resume statement, 506-508
error values, variants, 148
Error-Trapping method, File dialog boxes, 383-384

errors
  descriptions, 532
  error handlers, *see* error handlers
  in Debugger, 524-525
  logic, 501
  numbers, 532
  preventing
      Auto Data Tips, 503-504
      Auto List Members option, 503
      Auto Quick Info option, 503
      Auto Syntax Check option, 502
      Require Variable Declaration option, 502
  runtime, 500-501
  syntax, 499-500
  see also bugs
events, 42
  Activate, 313-314
  BeforeClick (TabStrip control), 418
  Change (Slider control), 450
  Click, 43
      nodes, 434
      TabStrip control, 415-416
  class modules, 347
  clsDocument, 353
  cmdSave_Click, 107-112
  ColorBack property, 859-860
  ComEvCD, 955
  ComEvDSR, 955
  ComEvReceive, 956
  Command_Click
      code (listing 17.7), 910
      code (listing 17.9), 914-917
  controls, 26, 850
  default, 43
  deleting from controls to run Control Interface Wizard,
      870-871
  idle time, 757-760
  Initialize (SButton control), 849
  KeyDown, 524
  KeyPress, 118-119, 223-224
  KeyUp, 313
  LinkClose, 765
  LinkError, 765
  LinkNotify, 765
  LinkOpen, 765
  Load, 60-61
  MouseDown, 524-525, 858-860
  MouseUp, 313
  objects, 35
  OnComm (MSComm control), 938, 954-955
  Property Get, 366-368
  Property Let, 366-368
  Property Set, 368
  Read Properties (SButton control), 849

events (*continued*)
  Resize
      adding code to, 843-844
      sizing text boxes, 289-290
  SButton control, 844, 849, 871
  Scroll (Slider control), 450
  SelChange, 407
  SendKey, 119
  SetFocus, 224-226
  StateChanged (ITC control), 981-983
  Terminate (SButton control), 850
  Unload, 304-305
  user controls, 848-850, 857-860
      raising, 860-862
  Validation, 671
Excel
  charts, property settings for OLE control in embedded
      charts, 796
  Macro Recorder, 816
  object hierarchy, 804-807
  OLE Automation, 813-815
  OLE project, 813-815
EXE files, 2-3
EXE Options dialog box, 772
executable files
  compiling, 773
  creating, 770-774
Execute method (ITC control), 978
executing
  code, threads, 755
  multiple statements with : (colon) separator, 176
Existing tab, 3
Exit button, 129, 653
Exit For command, 162
Exit routine, 78-79, 155
exiting
  FTP sites, 997
  programs, EndDoc method, 456
Exp function, 90
ExpandedImage property, 431-432
expanding
  nodes, 431-432, 435
  registry, 888
expiration, shareware distribution, 884
explicit declarations, variables, 144-145
Explorer (Internet) 3.0, *see* **Internet Explorer 3.0**
Exponentiation (^) operator, 82
exposed objects, 800, 805-807
extender events, user controls, 857-860
extensions (file)
  BMP, 573
  EXE, 2-3
  GIF, 573
  JPG, 573
  VBP, 53
  WMF, 573

F

False keyword, 87
Favorites button (Internet Explorer toolbar), 1020
Favorites list (Internet Explorer), 1022-1023
File class, 646-649
File Close routine, 309
File dialog boxes
    Error-Trapping method, 383-384
    Filter property, 381-382
    Flags property, 384-385
    Non-Error-Trapping method, 382
file extensions, *see* extensions (file)
File menu, 54, 298
    adding to projects, 305-309
    Notepad, 276
    commands
        Add Project, 841
        Load TextFile, 897-899
        Make TestCalcEXE, 826
        New Project, 12, 76
        Print, 471
        Save Group project, 842
        Save Project, 840
File New routine, 305
File Picker, 64
    objects, 48
    shutting down with Hide method, 67
File Summary dialog box, 779
File Transfer Protocol, *see* FTP
FileHandle property (File class), 646
FileListBox control, 45-46, 600
    chaining DriveListBox control to, 603
    Pattern property, 65-66
    properties, 49
    Text property, 66-67
FileMode parameter (Open statement), 620
FileName property (FileListBox control), 45
files
    access modes, 619-620
    accessing
        binary, 630-631
        random, 621
    Add-ins, *see* Add-Ins
    BMP, 573
    closing, 610
    controls, 598, 600
        chaining, 602-603
        properties, 599, 601
    data validation (Binary project), 638
    DLL, *see* DLLs (Dynamic Link Libraries)
    downloading, 995-996
    EXE, 2-3
    executable
        compiling, 773
        creating, 770-774

files (*continued*)
    File Picker, 64
        objects, 48
        shutting down with Hide method, 67
    GIF, 573
    hardcoding, 658
    help, *see* help
    JPG, 573
    metafiles, 573
    OCX, creating, 880-881
    opening, 609-610
        Binary project, 638
        from disk, 3
    picture, 573
    reading, 611-612
        binary, 631, 639-640
        random access, 621
        Seq project, 613-616
    readme, 992-994
    RTF (Rich Text Files), 391-393
    text, reading online, 992-994
    WMF, 573
    writing, 625
        binary, 631
        random files, 626
        sequential files, 626
fill characters, 620
FillColor property, 548, 565
FillDir procedure, 985
FillStyle property (Line control), 548
FillText procedure (Binary project), 637
Filter property (CommonDialog control), 381-382
Find button, 682-683
Find command (Edit menu), 360
FindFirst method, finding recordsets, 682
finding
    parent of child nodes, 435
    recordsets, 682-683
    see also searching
FindLast method, finding recordsets, 682
FindNext method, finding recordsets, 682
FindPrevious method, finding recordsets, 682
Find tab, 27-28
Finished! dialog box, 873
Finished! screen (Application Wizard), 16
Fix function, 90
fixed-length records, 619
    customer record (listing 12.12), 630
    fill characters, 620
    Random project code, 624-628
fixed-length strings, 106
flags
    defined, 966
    Font dialog box, 389-390
    Navigate method (WebBrowser control), 967
    Printer dialog, 470-471, 473

Flags property
    CommonDialog control, 381-382
    File dialog boxes, 384-385
floppy disks, application distribution, 777-780
FlxGrid project, 697-700
FlxMerge.prj project, 701-703
FMode property (File class), 646
focus, 62
Font button (Internet Explorer toolbar), 1020
Font classes, 330
Font Demo project, 461, 463-464
    code, 462, 465-467
    running, 463, 467
Font dialog box, 77, 379
    accessing, 388
    flags, 389-390
Font property
    attributes, 463
    Label control, 77
    Printer object, 462
fonts, 460-463
    Internet Explorer, 1019
    setting, 388-390
    TrueType, 460-463
footers, printing, 486-487
For Each...Next loop, arrays, 213-214
For...Next loop, 158-160
    Exit For command, 162
    nested loops, 162-163
    Step keyword, 161
ForeColor property, 565
foreign keys, 664, 666
Form Activate event routine, 314
Form class, 331
Form1 class, creating Form1 objects, 332-333
Form control, properties (Animate project), 578
Form Layout window, 5, 7-8
Form Templates button (Application Wizard), 14
Format function, 488
    date formats
        named, 494-495
        user-defined, 495-497
    formatting numbers, 489-493
formatting
    dates
        named formats, 495
        user-defined, 495-497
    numbers, 489
        named formats, 490-491
        user-defined formats, 491-493
    print output, 458-459
forms, 4, 38, 274
    Address Book, adding controls to, 116-117
    colors, adding, 565-567
    controls, *see* controls

forms (*continued*)
    creating at runtime, 283-287
    File Picker, *see* File Picker
    focus, 62
    Font Demo project, 461-464
    icons, 280-281
    instances, Me keyword, 290
    loading, Load event, 60-61
    maximum number of lines, 755
    MDI programs (multiple document interface), *see* MDI
        (Multiple Document Interface) programs
    modal, 63, 825
    modeless, 825
    object types, 334-335
    properties, *see* properties
    SDI programs, *see* SDI (Single Document Interface)
        programs
    Sender, 193-194
    startup, 39, 58
    text boxes, *see* text boxes
    variables, 285
    see also individual names
Forms collection, 307
Form_Activate procedure, Binary project, 639-640
Form_Load procedure, Binary project, 638-639
Forward button (Internet Explorer toolbar), 1019
frames
    adding controls to, 246-249
    Frame control, 245-246
    frmSetup, 941-942
    internet Explorer, 1018
frmBrowser (WWW.vbp project), 962, 965
    address picture box properties, 964
    code, 968-970
    toolbar buttons, 963
frmChat
    code
        dialing out, 951
        hanging up, 953-954
        opening Com port, 952
        startup, 950
        waiting for calls, 951
    creating, 945-947
    OnComm event, 954-955
    properties, 939
    status bar, 949
    text boxes, 948
FrmDocument, changes, 350-352
FrmFind, properties, 360-362
frmFTP, properties, 974-975
frmMain (WWW.vbp project)
    code, 962
    menus, 961
    properties, 961

frmOptions, 410
adding PictureBox controls to, 413-414
multiple picture boxes, 417-418
TabStrip control's Click event, 415-416
ZOrder, 415
FrmPublishers form, properties, 681
frmSetup
code, 943-944
frames, 941-942
option buttons, 941-942
properties, 939-941
frmText, properties, 992-994
frmVBCalc, properties, 820
FTP (File Transfer Protocol), 972
browser, adding to programs, 973-977
commands, 979-980
downloading files, 995-996
project, 973
CommandButton properties, 976-977
frmFTP properties, 974-975
ITC properties, 977
LstDir properties, 975
sites, 972
accessing, 973
anonymous, 977
changing directories, 989-991
exiting, 997
reading text files, 992-994
functions, 185, 191
Abs, 90
AddForm, 283-286
calling, 285
optimizing, 287
aggregate, 714
AlreadyAdded, 189
argument lists, 204-205
Asc, 115, 122
Atn, 90
calling, 185, 188-189, 285
CheckValidData (Binary project), 638
Chr, 115, 123
class modules, 347
colors, 565-567, 569
Cos, 90
Date, 132
Date$, 750
DateAdd, 140-141
DateDiff, 142-143
dates, 131-143
DateSerial, 137
DateValue, 133
Day, 134
defined, 86-87
defining, 185-186
EOF, 611
Error, 506

functions (*continued*)
Exp, 90
Fix, 90
Format, 488
date formats, 494-495
formatting numbers, 489-493
user-defined date formats, 495-497
GetAllSettings, 892
GetSetting, 890-891
GotFocus, 133
Hour, 135
Input, reading files, 611
InputBox, 252-253, 256-257
InStr, 106, 110-111
Int, 86-87, 90
IsDate, 133
LBound, arrays, 214
LCase, 115, 120
Left, 106, 112
Let, 106, 109
LoadPicture, 68
LOF, 611
Log, 90
LostFocus, 133
LSet, 116
LTrim, 115
math, 89-91
Mid, 112-113
Minute, 135
Month, 134
Msg, 231-233
Now, 132
ReadRegValue, 911-913
Right, 106, 112
Rnd, 90
RSet, 116
RTrim, 115
SafePath, 658-659
scope, 200
Second, 135
SendMessage, 743-744
Sgn, 91
Sin, 91
Space, 115, 123-124
Sqr, 91
Str, 150-151
StrComp, 116, 126
String, 116, 124
strings, 106-113, 115-116, 122-125
Sum, calling, 188-189
syntax, 200
Tan, 91
testing with debugger, 533
Time, 132
Time$, 750

functions (*continued*)
Timer, 139-140
times, 131-138
calculation, 140-143
TimeSerial, 137-138
TimeValue, 134
Trim, 115, 122
TypeName, 145-147, 341
UBound, arrays, 214
UCase, 115, 120
Val, 150
Weekday, 138-139
Windows API, 740-744
Year, 134
see also methods

G

General properties sheet (Internet Explorer), 1024-1025
General tab (Properties dialog box), 412
Generate Dependency File Only option
  (Setup Wizard), 776
generating executable files, 770
Get statement, 621
GetAllSettings function, 892
GetChunk method (ITC control), 980, 983-984
GetColor function, 569
GetDir procedure, 984-985
GetLineFromChar method, 407
GetObject command, 810
GetRecord procedure, 624
GetSetting function, 890-891
GIF files, 573
global declarations (Binary project), 637
Good Code project, 530
Goof project, 507-509
GotFocus function, 133
Graph control, 588-590
Graph project, 591-595
GraphData property (Graph control), 589
graphics, 537
adding to toolbar buttons, 399-400
controls, 544
Line, 545-546
Shape, 546-548
files, *see* picture files
methods, *549-551*
printing, 584
redrawing with AutoRedraw property, 583-584
see also images; pictures
graphs, creating with Graph control, 588-590
GraphType property (Graph control), 589
Greater than (>) operator, 93
Greater than or equal to (>=) operator, 93
Grid control (Data Bound), 695-696
groups, defining controls, 413

H

handshaking, 924-925
hardcoding, 658
HDC property, 743
headers, 966
printing, 486-487
Height property, 290-291
help, 22-23
About Microsoft Visual Basic option, 23
context-sensitive (Code window), 88-89
Microsoft on the Web option, 23
properties, 222
Search Master index, 23
Search Reference index, 23
tabs, 27-28
technical support, 23
tooltips, 57
topics, 23-26
Help menu, 298
NotePad, 277
Help Topics button, 26
hexadecimal colors, 867-869
Hidden properties, 371
Hide method, shutting down File Picker, 67
hiding data, 371
History list (Internet Explorer), 1023
Home button (Internet Explorer toolbar), 1019
Hour function, 135
HTML Layout control, 1018
HWnd property, 743

I

Icon property, 280-281
icons, 280-281
adding to Address Book, 104
idle loops, creating, 757-760
idle time, 757-760
Idleloop project, 758-760
If statement, 92-93, 176
Else, 177-179
ElseIf, 177-179
Image control, 572-573
adding to About box, 323-325
array properties (Animate project), 578-579
compared to PictureBox control, 322-323, 575-576
loading pictures, 574-575
ImageList control, 395
adding images to toolbar buttons, 399-400
disassociating image lists from controls, 441-442
properties, 396-397
images
displaying, 425-427, 432-433
see also graphics

Immediate window, 6, 8, 102
        Debug Demo project, 518-519
        printing, 103
Imp operator, 172
Implication operator, *see* Imp operator
implicit declarations, variables, 145
Index numbering, 210
        changing base index, 211
        specifying base with To keywrod, 211
Index property, control arrays, 267
Index tab, 27
indexes, 23, 664
Inequality (<<) operator, 93
Initialize event, 849-850
initializing variables, 79-80
InitProperties event, control lifetimes, 850
Inner Join query, 713
Input # statement, reading files, 612
Input function, reading files, 611
InputBox function, 252-253, 256-257
Insert Menu commans, Module, 332
Insert Object dialog box, 156, 795-796
Insert Procedure dialog box, 283-284
installing Internet Explorer, 1015
        Windows 95, 1016
        Windows NT 4, 1016-1017
instances, 36, 329
        controls, creating at runtime, 269-270
        forms, Me keyword, 290
        objects, 352-353
instantiating objects, 352-353
InStr function, 106, 110-111
Int function, 86-87, 90
Integer (\) operator, 82
Integers, 96
        variables, 99
Interface screen (Application Wizard), 13
Internet, 960
        connecting to, 970
        sites
                breaking connection, 991-992
                opening, 965
        World Wide Web, *see* WWW (World Wide Web)
Internet Explorer 3.0
        ActiveX controls, 1025-1026
        customizing properties, 1024-1025
        Favorites list, 1022-1023
        features, 1017-1019
        History list, 1023
        installing, 1015
                Windows 95, 1016
                Windows NT 4, 1016-1017
        Java, 1026
        ListView control, 421
        loading Web pages, 1020-1021
        scripts, 1025-1026

Internet Explorer 3.0 (*continued*)
        searching for information, 1021-1022
        toolbar buttons, 1019-1020
        TreeView control, 421
Internet Mail, 1017
Internet News, 1017
Internet Transfer Control, *see* ITC
interprocess communication, 762, 791-792
Interval property (Timer control), 749
intrinsic controls, 837
Is keyword (SelectCase statement), 181-182
IsDate function, 133
Is statement, referencing objects, 334
ISPs (Internet Service Providers), 997
IT control, StateChanged event, 981-983
ITC (Internet Transfer Control), 973
        connecting to FTP sites, 997
        methods, 978, 980-981, 983-985
        properties, 977
ItemData property, 260
Item method, collections, 363

J-K

Java, Internet Explorer, 1026
Jet Database engine, ODBC (Open Database Connectivity), 735-736
joining tables, 666
JPG files, 573

Key property, status bar panels, 406
KeyAscii, 118-119
KeyDown event, 524
KeyPress event, 118-119, 223-224
keys
        accelerator, 228-230
        adding objects to collections, 357-358
        Enter, enabling, 118
        foreign, 664, 666
        primary, 664, 666
        registry, 890
                adding values to, 904-909
                deleting, 914-917
KeyUp event, 313
keywords
        Auto Quick Info feature, 88
        ByVal, 742
        False, 87
        Is, Select Case statement, 181-182
        Let, 148-149
        Like, 683
        Me, 289-290 335
        MyVal, 742
        New, 285
        Nothing, removing objects from memory, 353-354
        ParamArray, 215
        Preserve, sizing one dimension of arrays, 213

keywords (*continued*)
>   Static, 203
>   Step, 161
>   To, specifying base index, 211
>   True, 87
>   TypeOf, 341
>   While, 166

L

Label control, 227
>   adding to CDMaker project, 77, 84, 94
>   properties, 77, 84, 227-230
LabelText property (Graph control), 590
Large Icon view, 437
LargeChange property (Slider control), 450
Late binding, 809-810
LBound function, arrays, 214
LCase function, 115, 120
Learnole project, 794-796
Left function, 106, 112
Left property, 290-291
Len function, 106, 109
Less than (<) operator, 93
Less than or equal to (<=) operator, 93
Let keyword, 148-149
licensing ActiveX controls, 882-883
life cycles, objects, 36
lifetimes, controls, 848-849
>   events, 850-851
Like keyword, 683
Line control, 545-546
Line Input # statement, reading files, 612
Line method, 482-484, 550-551
Line objects, properties, 845-846
LineStyle property
>   constants, 433
>   TreeView control, 432
LinkClose event, 765
LinkError event, 765
linking (OLE), 789-790
>   Excel charts, 796
>   OLE Container control, 794-796
>   Word documents, 796, 798
LinkItem property, 764
LinkMode property, 764
LinkNotify event, 765
LinkOpen event, 765
LinkPoke method, 765
LinkRequest method, 765
LinkSend method, 765
LinkTimeout property, 764
LinkTopic property, 764
list boxes
>   adding items to, 251-253
>   removing items from, 257
>   searching for items, 261

list boxes (*continued*)
>   selecting from, 253-256
>   sorting items in, 260-261
>   storing numbers in, 260
List property (ListBox control), 253-255
List view, 438, 444
ListBox control
>   adding items to list, 251-253
>   Data Bound, 686
>   multiselect list boxes, 255-256
>   properties, 251
>   removing items from list, 256-257
>   selecting items, 253-255
ListCount property (ListBox control), 253-255
ListIndex property (ListBox control), 253-255
listings
>   2.1 A change to the drive list box propagates a change to the directory box, 49-50
>   2.2 A change to the directory list box propagates a change to the file box, 50-51
>   2.3 Displaying the file picker form, 62
>   2.4 Code to end the program, 62
>   2.5 Showing the form in modal style, 63
>   2.6 Loading the picture, 69
>   2.7 The Cancel button, 69
>   3.1 The Exit routine, 78-79
>   3.2 Initializing values, 79-80
>   3.3 Variables to hold song lengths, 81
>   3.4 Giving the user more information, 81
>   3.5 Adding the lengths, 82
>   3.6 Variables to hold computation results, 84
>   3.7 Computing average length and room left, 86
>   3.8 Forcing integer values, 86-87
>   3.9 Making the controls visible, 87
>   3.10 Implementing a conditional statement, 94
>   3.11 Replacing numbers with meaningful constants helps readability, 97
>   3.12 Code fragment to assign a value to a Boolean, 98
>   3.13 Boolean flag example, 99
>   3.14 Testing the Immediate window, 103
>   3.15 The cmdSave_Click event, 107-112
>   3.16 The new code for Address Book, 121-122
>   3.17 The Exit button, 129
>   3.18 Assign the current date to the text box, 132
>   3.19 Give the user access to the system clock, 132
>   3.20 Validate the date the user entered, 133
>   3.21 Computing the time difference, 134
>   3.22 Displaying the date in the form caption, 134
>   3.23 Output the difference in a more readable format, 135
>   3.24 Viewing a date as a double, 138
>   3.25 The DateAdd function, 141
>   3.26 The TypeName function, 146-147
>   3.27 The Str function on a positive value, 150-151
>   3.28 The Str function on a negative value, 151
>   4.1 The familiar Exit routine, 155
>   4.2 Ta da!, 157

listings (*continued*)

4.3 Adding the numbers from 1 to 10, 159-160
4.4 Using the variable loop parameters, 160
4.5 Using a function's return value in a loop parameter, 160
4.6 The Exit For command, 162
4.7 Nested For loops, 162-163
4.8 The Do Until loop, 166
4.9 Checking Do Until exit condition, 166
4.10 Loop While, 167
4.11 Loop Until, 167-168
4.12 Combining Boolean expressions, 171
4.13 "Move" the pictures, 178
4.14 More readable routine with ElseIf, 179
4.15 Constants for Grocery program, 179
4.16 Expanded Grocery program, 180
4.17 Select Case with strings, 180
4.18 Case ranges, 180
4.19 Evaluating more than one condition, 181
4.20 Nested select Case statements, 181
4.21 Combining ranges, 182
4.22 The Output subroutine, 186-188
4.23 Calling the Output routine, 187-188
4.24 The Sum function, 188-189
4.25 The AlreadyAdded function, 189
4.26 Calling our routines, 189-190
4.27 The main form routine, 195
4.28 Sending text across forms, 195-196
4.29 Sender 1 form's first attempt at keeping a log, 196
4.30 Sender 1 form tries to read the log, 196
4.31 Private variables are separate, even if they have the same name, 197
4.32 Module scope, 198
4.33 Competing variables, 198-199
4.34 Sender 1 with module scope variables, 199
4.35 The Snoop button, 199
4.36 A public Sub in a standard module, 201
4.37 Calling a standard module routine, 201
4.38 Automatic persistence, 202
4.39 Static persistence, 202-203
4.40 Static in subroutine definition, 203
4.41 Passing parameters by value, 205-206
4.42 Optional arguments, 206
4.43 Array, 210
4.44 The Preserve keyword, 213
4.45 The ParamArray keyword, 215
5.1 Convert the key pressed to uppercase, 224
5.2 Validating user input, 225-226
5.3 The OK button, 234
5.4 The Cancel event routine, 238
5.5 Evaluate the check box value, 240-242
5.6 Enable a button if a value is checked, 242
5.7 Select Case is a natural way to access the Option button values, 244-245
5.8 Accessing the credit card info, 248-249
5.9 Adding a video title to the list box, 253

listings (*continued*)

5.10 Determining the selected item, 255
5.11 Finding selected items, 256
5.12 Removing selected items from a list, 257
5.13 The NewIndex property, 260-261
5.14 Filling the combo box, 263
5.15 Loading controls at runtime, 269-270
5.16 The controls so you can see them, 270
6.1 Add a new form at runtime, 284-286
6.2 The MDIForm_Load routine, 286
6.3 Optimized AddForm, 287
6.4 The Resize event routine, 289
6.5 Center SuperPad on any size screen, 292
6.6 Setting the form-level change flag, 303-304
6.7 The Unload event routine, 304-305
6.8 The File New routine, 305
6.9 Setting up context-sensitive menus, 306-307
6.10 Setting up the menus when a form is loaded, 307-308
6.11 Calling SetupCSMenus from Form_Unload, 308
6.12 The Closing variable, 308-309
6.13 The File Close routine, 309
6.14 Adding Edit menu to Setup routine, 311-312
6.15 Special cases for the Edit menu, 312-313
6.16 Calling Setup routine when user selects text, 313
6.17 The Form Activate event routine, 314
6.18 Copying text to the clipboard, 316
6.19 The Cut Menu item, 316
6.20 Calling the Delete routine, 317
6.21 The Paste command, 319-320
6.22 Select all the text, 320-321
6.23 Adding the date and time, 321
6.24 Dismissing the About box, 323
6.25 Calling the About box, 323
6.26 Code to rearrange the windows, 324-325
7.1 Loading a form via code, 332-333
7.2 Two variables reference the same form, 333-334
7.3 Passing a form as a procedure argument, 334-335
7.4 Centering any form on the screen, 335
7.5 Using a common routine for data checking, 339-340
7.6 Declaring the collection, 356
7.7 Destroying the collection, 356
7.8 frmMain's general declarations, 358
7.9 frmDocument's general declarations, 358
7.10 Assigning keys to collection members, 358
7.11 The Remove method, 359
7.12 mnuEditFind's Click event in frmMain, 361
7.13 Enable/disable the Find menu item in SetupCSMenus, 361
7.14 The Find form's Cancel button, 361
7.15 The Find routine, 362
7.16 The class module, 367-368
7.17 Updated Property Let and txtDocument_Change routines, 367-368
8.1 Bringing up the File Open dialog, 381-382

listings (*continued*)

8.2 Checking for Cancel without error handling, 383
8.3 Checking for Cancel with error handling, 383
8.4 FileSaveAs routine, 385
8.5 Letting the user change the font, 389
8.6 Activating the Color dialog, 390
8.7 Opening a rich text file, 391-392
8.8 The SaveAs routine, 392-393
8.9 The Save routine, 393
8.10 Making the toolbar context-sensitive, 401
8.11 Programming the toolbar, 401-402
8.12 Same routine, different variable name, 402
8.13 Routine to display a line number, 407
8.14 Calling DisplayLineNumber, 407
8.15 Calling DisplayLineNumber, 407
8.16 Update to the Unload event, 408
8.17 Bringing up the frmOptions dialog, 410-412
8.18 Unload the form, 411
8.19 Selecting the correct tab option, 416
8.20 Using the Move method to position the picture boxes, 418
8.21 Setting the Tab control's initial value, 419
8.22 Adding nodes to a tree, 423-425
8.23 Adding nodes with images, 426-427
8.24 Child nodes, 428-429
8.25 Sorting nodes, 430
8.26 The ExpandedImage property, 431-432
8.27 Testing the node's Click events, 434
8.28 Expanding nodes, 435
8.29 Expanding selected nodes, 435
8.30 The ListView demo, 440-441
8.31 Disassociating the shared ImageList, 442
8.32 Small icon view, 442-443
8.33 Report view demo, 445-446
8.34 Sorting the report, 446-447
8.35 ProgressBar demo, 449
8.36 Slider demo, 450
9.1 Viewing the Printers collection, 455
9.2 Uniquely identifying a printer, 455
9.3 The Print method and the Printer object, 457-458
9.4 Using Tab() and Spc(), 459
9.5 Code for cmdFixed and cmdProportional, 462
9.6 Completing the Font Demo program, 465-467
9.7 Displaying the Print Setup dialog box, 470
9.8 Bringing up the Print dialog box, 472-473
9.9 Checking supported paper sizes, 476-477
9.10 Using the ScaleMode property, 480
9.11 Improved code for drawing a line, 481-482
9.12 Using the Line method with the printer, 483-484
9.13 Routines to print headers and footers, 486-487
9.14 The named formats, 490-491
9.15 User-defined formats, 492-493
9.16 Named date format examples, 495
9.17 User-defined date format examples, 497
10.1 The code for Goofs.vbp, 507-508
10.2 An improved error handler, 509

listings (*continued*)

10.3 The Debug Demo project, 515-517
10.4 Spaghetti code, 528
10.5 The code for the Good Code project, 530
11.1 Draw Box Command button click event code, 559
11.2 Code to draw a triangle, 560-561
11.3 Adding a button to draw circles, 562
11.4 Loading possible QBColors into a combo box during form load, 568-569
11.5 GetColor function, 569
11.6 Circle Command button click event with color changing code, 570
11.7 Box Command button click event with color changing code, 570
11.8 Loading an icon at runtime, 575
11.9 Form load event initalization code, 580
11.10 The Timer controls timer event code to perform animation, 580-581
11.11 Code for PixLogo, 587
11.12 Code for the Graph project, 591-594
11.13 Adding a second data set, 594-595
12.1 Setting the directory list box drive, 603
12.2 Setting the file list box, 603
12.3 Setting search criteria, 606-607
12.4 Sequential I/O read code in Command button Click event, 614-616
12.5 Opening the file Random.dat in random access mode, 621
12.6 GetRecord procedure, 624
12.7 cmdNext Click event code, 624
12.8 cmdPrevious Click event code, 624-625
12.9 Form frmRandom Load event, 627-628
12.10 Creating and opening the file random.txt, 628
12.11 Writing random records to file random.txt, 628
12.12 Fixed-length customer record, 630
12.13 A Customer type for binary files, 630
12.14 Global declarations for Binary, 637
12.15 The FillText procedure, 637
12.16 The CheckValidData function, 638
12.17 The declarations and the Form_Load procedure, 638-639
12.18 Reading the file, 639-640
12.19 The Navigation Buttons, 640-641
12.20 Adding data and writing to the file, 642-643
12.21 The rest of the code, 644
12.22 Public property procedures for the property Mode, 647
12.23 OpenFile method, 647-648
12.24 CloseFile method, 648
12.25 ReadAll method, 648-649
12.26 WriteAll method, 649
12.27 Open button Clickevent code, 652
12.28 New button Click event code, 652-653
12.29 Save button Click event code, 653
12.30 Exit button Click event code, 653
12.31 Menu items Click event code, 654

listings (*continued*)

12.32 Using the Visual Basic App object, 659
13.1 New Form_Activate procedure, 679
13.2 Command button Find Click event code, 682-683

listings (*continued*)

13.3 Code for the Titles project
13.4 The code for the FlexGrid project, 699-700
13.5 Code for flxMerge
13.6 Code for the SQL demo project, 707-708
14.1 Code to fill ListBox in Form_Load event, 745
14.2 Calling APIfunction in Text_Change Event Command button, 746-747
14.3 Timer event code, 752-753
14.4 Start button Click event, 758-759
14.5 New start button Click event, 759-760
14.6 Command button cmdConversation Click event, 768
14.7 Command button cmdGetData Click event, 768
14.8 Textbox txtReceive LinkNotify event, 769
15.1 frmLearnOLE FormLoad event code, 797
15.2 cmbOLEComboBox Click event code, 797
15.3 mnuSpelling_Click event code, 811-812
15.4 Command button Click event code to control Excel via OLE, 814-815
15.5 Public property declarations for clsCalculator, 819
15.6 Methods for clsCalculator, 819
15.7 The ShowFormmethod for clcCalculator, 821
15.8 The code for TestCalc, 823-825
16.1 Code to observe the lifetime of a control, 848-849
16.2 Resizing the shadow lines, 852-853
16.3 Setting and getting the caption, 854
16.4 Saving and restoring the properties, 855-856
16.5 Color change on MouseDown and MouseUp, 859-860
16.6 Code for the Property page, 864-865
16.7 The BackColor property, 867
16.8 Adding the BackColor property, 867-869
16.9 The modified declarations section, 874-878
16.10 Some other changes from the Wizard, 874-875
16.11 Testing SButton, 881
17.1 The code for your first registry manipulation, 892-893
17.2 The code for the form, 899-900
17.3 The CreateNewKey sub, 900-902
17.4 The declaration of RegSetValueEx, 905
17.5 Additions to Command_Click, 905
17.6 The SetNewValueSub, 905-909
17.7 New code for the Command_Click event, 910
17.8 The ReadRegValue function, 911-913
17.9 The remaining code for Command_Click, 914-917
17.10 Declarations for RegDeleteValue and RegDeleteKey, 915
17.11 The code for DeleteRegValue, 915
17.12 The code for DeleteRegKey, 916-917
18.1 Making it work, 926-928
18.2 The ShowStatus procedure, 929
18.3 Changes to cmdStart_Click, 929-930

listings (*continued*)

18.4 Code for prjComm_2, 931-933
18.5 Code for frmSetup, 943-944
18.6 Code for ToolBar Private Sub DialNumber, 947
18.7 Startup code for frmChat, 950
18.8 Dialing out, 951-952
18.9 Waiting for a call, 951-952
18.10 Opening the Com port, 952
18.11 Hanging up, 953
18.12 Online and offline, 953-954
18.13 The OnCom event, 954-955
18.14 The ParseString procedure, 956-957
18.15 Code for frmMain, 962
18.16 Code for frmBrowser, 968-970
18.17 The StateChanged event, 982-983
18.18 The GetDir procedure, 984-985
18.19 The FillDir procedure, 985
18.20 Controlling the Command buttons, 986
18.21 Declarations and form events for frmFTP, 986-987
18.22 Code for txtServer and cmdConnect, 987-988
18.23 Code for cmdDirectory, 989-991
18.24 Code for frmText, 993-994
18.25 Code for cmdReadText_Click, 994-995
18.26 Downloading files, 995-996

ListItem objects, 437-438
    adding to ListView control, 439-446
ListView control, 420-421, 437-438
    adding ListItems objects to, 439-446
    ColumnHeaders collection, 439-441
literals, times, 130-131
Load event, 60-61
Load statement, creating instances of controls, 269-270
Load TextFile command (File menu), 897-899
LoadFile method, 392-393
loading
    forms, Load event, 60-61
    pictures, 574-575
    programs, optimization, 782-783
    RTF files, 391-393
LoadPicture function, 68
Locals window (Debug Demo project), 521
Log function, 90
logic errors, 501
logical database design, 723
    normalization, 725-726, 728-729
logical operators, 171-173
    Not, 133
Login Dialog screen (Application Wizard), 15
long variables, 96, 99
Lookup project, 686-688
Loop Until loop, 167-168
Loop While loop, 167
loops
    Boolean expressions, 168-169
    break mode, 170-171

loops (*continued*)

Do, 165
Do Until, 166
Do While, 166
For Each...Next, arrays, 213-214
For...Next, 158-160
Exit For command, 162
nested loops, 162-163
Step keyword, 161
idle, creating with DoEvents command, 757-760
Loop Until, 167-168
Loop While, 167
statements, 92
While Wend, 168
LostFocus function, 133
LSet function, 116
LSet statement, 125
LstDir properties, 975
LTrim function, 115

M

Macro Recorder (Microsoft), 816
Mail button (Internet Explorer toolbar), 1020
Make EXE dialog box, 772
Make Project dialog box, 771
Make TestCalcEXE command (File menu), 826
manipulating
dates, 131-140
strings, 115-116, 122-125
variables, 80-82
many-to-many relationships, 665
databases, 725, 727-728
mapped drives, 657
mapping, 872
Enabled property, 873
SButton control, 873
MaskColor property (Toolbar control), 396-397
Math functions, 89-91
maximizing windows, 7, 286
MDI (Multiple Document Interface) programs, 274
adding CommonDialog control to, 379
compared to SDI (Single Document Interface)
programs, 274-275
naming, 279
SuperPad, *see* SuperPad
MDIChild property, 280
Me keyword, 289-290, 335
memory
data segments, 756
leaks, 353-354
stack size, 755
memory MergeCells property, 703
Menu bar, 53
Menu Editor
adding menus to main screen, 56

Menu Editor (*continued*)
adding menus to projects
context-sensitive, 301, 306-308
Edit menus, 311-317, 319-321
File Close menu, 309
File New menu, 305
separator bars, 299-300
shortcut keys, 298-299
subordinate menu items, 296, 298
top-level menu items, 295
Word Wrap, 300-301
Menu Editor command (Tools menu), 56
menus
adding to main screen with Menu Editor, 56
adding to projects, *see* Menu Editor
Application Wizard, 13
Click event code, 654
defined, 294
disabling, 301, 311-314
Edit, 298, 311-312
enabling, 311-314
File, 54, 298
Help, 298
NotePad, 276-277
WWW.vbp project, 961
metafiles, 573
methods, 61
methods
Add
TreeView Nodes collection, 424-425
adding objects to collections, 358
AddItem, 252-253
AddNew, 679
ByRef, passing arguments, 205
ByVal, passing arguments, 205-206
Clear, 257
controls, 25
Count, 307
Delete, 681
DoVerb, 157
EndDoc, 456
err object, 505-506
error-trapping, 383-384
File class, 646-649
FindFirst, finding recordsets, 682
FindLast, finding recordsets, 682
FindNext, finding recordsets, 682
FindPrevious, finding recordsets, 682
GetLine, 407
graphical, 549-551
Hide, shutting down File Picker, 67
ITC, 978, 980-981, 983-985
Item, collections, 363
Line, 482-484
LinkPoke, 765
LinkRequest, 765

methods (*continued*)
    LinkSend, 765
    LoadFile, 392-393
    Move, 577-578
        optimizing code, 291-292
        positioning picture boxes, 418
    NewPage, 456
    Non-Error-Trapping, 382
    objects, 35, 157
    PaintPicture, 584-585
    Print, 103, 457-458
    Refresh, 681
    Remove
     deleting nodes, 429
    removing objects from collections, 359
    RemoveItem, 257
    SetText, 315-316
    Show, 62
    UpdateRecord, 680
    WebBrowser control, Navigate, 965-967
    see also functions
Microsoft Excel, *see* Excel
Microsoft on the Web option, 23
Microsoft Web site, 1017
Microsoft WebBrowser control, *see* WebBrowser control (Microsoft)
Mid function, 107, 112-113
Mid statement, 120
minimizing windows, 286
Minute function, 135
modal forms, 825
modal windows vs. modeless, 63
modeless windows vs. modal, 63
modems
    communications
        data transfers, 925
        handshaking, 924-925
        MSComm project, 926-930
        setup property parameters, 922
        setup string, 923
    dialing out, 951
    hanging up, 953
    opening Com ports, 952
    phone dialers, creating, 934-937
    waiting for calls, 951
Module command (Insert menu), 332
modules (class), 347
    components, 347
    creating, 345-346
    defined, 347
    maximum size, 755
    properties, 349-350
    scope, 198-199
    standard, adding to Sender project, 201
Modulo operator, 82
Month function, 134

mouse, drag and dropping, 10
MouseDown event, 524-525
    BackColor property, 858-860
MouseUp event, 313
    ColorBack property, 859-860
MoveLast otpion, 671
Move method, 577-578
    positioning picture boxes, 418
MSComm control, 920-921
    frmChat, 946
    OnComm event, 938, 954-955
    properties, 921-926
MSComm project, 920-921
    code, 926-930
    running, 928
MSFlexGrid control (Data Bound), 697-699, 704
MsgBox function, 231-233
MultiLine property (TextBox control), 222-223
Multiple Document Interface, *see* MDI (Multiple Document Interface) programs
Multiplication (*) operator, 82
Multiselect property (ListBox control), 255-256
multitasking, cooperative vs. preemptive, 754
multithreaded applications, 755
MyVal keyword, 742

N

nags, 883
Name property, 42, 349-350
names
    controls, 268
    MDI (Multiple Document Interface) applications, 279
    objects, 42
    variables, 76
    writing code, 529
native code, 755
    compiling executable files, 773
Navigate method (WebBrowser control), 965-967
navigating
    records, 671
    recordsets, 671-672
    Web pages, 967
Navigation buttons (Binary project), 640-641
Navigation properties sheet (Internet Explorer), 1024
Negation (-) operator, 82
nested loops, 162-163
Nested Select Case statements, 181
NetMeeting, 1018
New button (Click event code), 652
New Controls, properties, 904-905
New Form_Activate procedure, 679
New keyword, 285
New Project
    command (File menu), 12, 76
    dialog box, 838

New start button Click event, 759
New tab, 4
NewBtn project
    adding TestBtn project, 840-842
    creating, 838-840
    project properties pages, 839-840
NewBtn.vbp project, removing from project group, 880-881
NewBtnDemo project, running, 847
NewIndex property, 260-261
NewPage method, 456
newsgroups, 15
Node objects, 422
    adding to Nodes collection, 423-425
    collapsing nodes, 435
    deleting nodes, 429
    editing text in nodes, 434
    expanding nodes, 431-432, 435
    finding parent of child nodes, 435
    relationships, 427-429
    selecting nodes, 435
    sorting nodes, 430
    testing node's Click events, 434
Non-Error-Trapping method, 382
normalization, 725-726, 728-729
Not operator, 133, 172-173
Notepad (Windows), 275
    creating executable files, 770-773
    project, 645-646
        code, 652-654
        properties, 650-651
    user interface, 276-277
Nothing keyword, removing objects from memory, 353-354
Now function, 132
Null value, variants, 148
Number Adder project
    adding sound effects with OLE Container control, 156-157
    controls, 154-155
    Exit For command, 162
    nested loops, 162-163
    Step keyword, 161
numbers
    errors, 532
    formatting, 489-493
    storing in list boxes, 260

O

Object Browser, viewing exposed objects, 805-807
object hierarchy, 803
    dependent objects, 805
    Excel, 804-805
        viewing with Object Browser, 805-807
Object Linking and Embedding, see OLE
Object property (OLE Container control), 794

object-oriented programming, 21, 31
    design, 371-372
    objects, 34
objects, 32
    Address Book project, 104-105
    App, 658-659
    Authors project, 669, 673-674
    Binary project, 631-632
    CDMaker project, 76
    Chalkboard project, 552-554
    classes, 35-36
    Clipboard
        copying text, 315-316
        deleting text, 316-317
        enabling/disabling Paste menu, 314-315
        pasting text, 319-320
    clsDocument, adding to collections, 357-358
    collections, see collections
    CommandButton control, 236
    components, 800
    controls, see controls
    dependent, 805
    destroying with Nothing keyword, 353-354
    Document, 344
        class modules, 347
        creating a class module, 345-346
        see also class modules
    embedded, 1019
    err, 505-506
    events, see events
    exposed, 800, 805-807
    File Picker, 48
    flxGrid project, 698-699
    flxMerge.pr, 701-703
    focus, 62
    forms, see forms
    Frame control, 246
    Good Code project, 530
    idleloop project, 758-760
    instances, 329
    instantiating, 352-353
    Learnole project, 795-796
    life cycles, 36
    Line, properties, 845-846
    ListBox control, 251
    ListItem, 437-438
        adding to ListView control, 439-446
    methods, 35, 61, 157
    MSComm project, 920-921
    names, 42
    New controls, 904-905
    Node, see Node objects
    NotePad project, 650-651
    object-oriented programming, 34
    ODBC project, 736-737

objects (*continued*)

OLE, 788

accessing, 790

declaring variables for, 809-810

design, 833-835

OLE, *see* OLE, objects

OptionButton control, 244-245

Picture Pusher project, 177

PixLogo project, 585-586

Printer, *see* Printer object

private, 800

properties, *see* properties

public, 800

Random project, 622-623

references, 332

Is statement, 334

referencing multiple times, 333-334

removing from collections, 359

Republish project, 721Screen, 292, 539

Sender project, 193-194

Seq project, 613-614

single-instance, 330

Spagh project, 527-528

system, 828-831

TestCalc project, 822

test_DLL project, 744-746

Timesheet program, 128-129

Title project, 689-693

TstShape project, 556-557, 568

variables, 97, 332

controls, 338-339

referencing objects multiple times, 333-334

referencing with Is statement, 334

VBDest project, 766-768

VBSrc project, 766

see also controls

OCXs (ActiveX Control Extension), 337, 789

creating, 880-881

defined, 337-338

referencing, 337-338

ODBC (Open database Connectivity), 730-731

data source, 732-735

Jet Database engine, 735-736

project, 736-737

OK button, code, 234

OLE (Object Linking and Embedding), 762

clients, 801

compared to DDE (Dynamic Data Exchange), 791-792

defined, 788

embedding, 789

Word documents, 798

future considerations, 832

linking, 789

Excel charts, 796

Word documents, 796, 798

OLE (Object Linking and Embedding) (*continued*)

objects, 788

accessing, 790

adding sound efftcs to Number Adder project, 156

declaring variables for, 809-810

design, 833-835

servers, 802

creating, 817-819

out-of-process, 820-821

visual editing, 788, 791

OLE Automation, 789, 801-802, 809

defined, 800

Excel, 813-815

Word, 810-812

OLE Container control, 793

adding sound efects to Number Adder project, 156-157

linking and embedding, 794-796

properties, 794

OLE Custom Controls, *see* OCXs

OLEType property (OLE Container control), 794

OLETypeAllowed property (OLE Container control), 794

OnComm event (MSComm control), 938, 954-955

On Error statement, 506

one-to-many relationships, 665

databases, 725, 727-728

one-to-one relationships, databases, 725, 727-728

Open Database Connectivity, *see* ODBC

OOP (object-oriented programming), *see* object-oriented programming

Open button, Click event code, 652

Open dialog box, 384-385

Open statement, 609-610

FileMode parameter, 620

OpenCom procedure, 952-953

OpenFile method (File class), 646-648

opening

files, 609-610

Binary project, 638

from disk, 3

Internet sites, 965

windows, 8

see also accessing

OpenURL (ITC control), 980

operators

arithmetic, 82

bitwise, 173

comparison, 93

logical, 171-173

combining Boolean expressions, 171

Not, 133

optimizing

AddForm function, 287

code, Move method, 291-292

optimizing (*continued*)
　　programs, 781-783
　　　　display speed, 783
　　　　operating speed, 783-784
　　　　size, 784-785
Option Base statement, changing base index, 211
Option buttons (frmSetup), 941-942
Option Explicit statement, declaring variables, 147
optional arguments, 206
OptionButton control, 243
　　properties, 244-245
Options
　　button, 26
　　command (Tools menu), 191
　　dialog box, accessing, 410-412
Options Dialog for Custom Settings screen (Application
　　Wizard), 15
Order By clause, 711
Or operator, 172-173
out-of-process servers, 820-821
output, formatting print output, 458-459
Output subroutine
　　calling, 187-188
　　defining, 186
overriding, precedence, 82

P

P-code, 755
　　compiling executable files, 773
Page property (Printer object), 456
Pages option (Printing), 474
Paint event, control lifetimes, 850
PaintPicture method, 584-585
Panel Property dialog box, 405-406
panels
　　adding text to, 406-407
　　adding to status bar, 405-406
　　properties, 405-406
paper, size, 476-477
ParamArray keyword, 215
parameters
　　passing by reference, 741-742
　　passing by value, 741-742
　　see also arguments
ParseString procedure, 956-957
passing
　　control references to subroutines, 339-340
　　parameters, 205
　　　　by reference, 741-742
　　　　by value, 741-742
　　　　ParamArray, 215
Password property, 977
Paste command (Edit menu), 246, 319-320

Paste menu
　　adding to projects, 319
　　enabling/diabling, 314-315
pasting text from Clipboard, 319-320
paths, building with App object, 658-659
Pattern property (FileListBox control), 65-66
persistence
　　automatic, 202
　　static, 202-203
phone dialers, creating, 934-937
physical database design, 723
picture boxes
　　positioning, 418
　　see also PictureBox control
Picture classes, 330
picture files, 573
Picture property, 68
Picture Pusher project, 177
　　code, 178-179
PictureBox control, 67, 572-573
　　adding to CDMaker project, 76
　　adding to frmOptions, 413-414
　　　　multiple picture boxes, 417-418
　　　　TabStrip control's Click event, 415-416
　　　　ZOrder, 415
　　compared to Image control, 322-323, 575-576
　　loading pictures, 574-575
　　see also picture boxes
pictures
　　loading, 574-575
　　printing, 584
　　see also graphics;images
pixels, 539-541
PixLogo project, 585-586
　　code, 586-587
　　running, 587
Placeholder Style option, 398
points, 541
polled communications, 938
polymorphism, 370
Port property (Printer object), 455
ports, 920
positioning
　　picture boxes, 418
　　text to print, 459
PostData, 966
precedence
　　arithmetic operators, 82
　　overriding, 82
predefined constants, 231
preemptive multitasking vs. cooperative, 754
Preserve keyword, sizing one dimension of arays, 213
Primary keys, 664, 666
Print # command, 626

Print
button (Internet Explorer toolbar), 1020
command (File menu), 471
Print dialog box
displaying, 472-473
flags, 470-471, 473
print jobs, 455-456, 473
Print method, 103, 457-458
Print Setup dialog box, 378, 469
displaying, 470
Print to File option, 473
print zones, 458
Printer class, properties, 476
Printer object, 830
Font property, 462
attributes, 463
Page property, 456
Port property, 455
TrackDefault property, 456-457
printers, 454
capabilities, 475
changing, 457
collection, *454-455*
default, 456-457
paper size, 476-477
Printers window, 454
printing
collating copies, 473
coordinate system (print location), 479
ScaleHeight property, 481-482
ScaleMode property, 480
ScaleWidth property, 481-482
footers, 486-487
formatting output, 458-459
graphics, 584
headers, 486-487
Immediate window, 103
Pages option, 474
positioning text to print, 459
print jobs, 455-456, 473
Print method, 457-458
Print to File option, 473
print zones, 458
Selection option, 474
TrueType fonts, 460-463
virtual pages, 479
private declarations, declaring variables, 199-200
private objects, 800
private scope, 197
Private statement, declaring variables, 200
PrjComm_2
code, 931-933
running, 933-934
procedures, 32, 43
DialNumber, 951
empty (stubs), 416

procedures (*continued*)
FillDir, 985
FillText (Binary project), 637
Form_Activate (Binary project), 639-640
Form_Load (Binary project), 638-639
GetDir, 984-985
GetRecord, 624
New Form_Activate, 679
OpenCom, 952-953
ParseString, 956-957
scope, 200
ShowStatus, 929-930
WaitForRing, 951
product support, 883
program stubs, 416
programming
assignments, 51
languages, defined, 43
object-oriented, 21, 31, *371-372*
toolbars, 401-402
programs
break mode
Boolean expressions, 170-171
entering, 169
crippleware, 883
data segments, 756
data-centric, SDI, 274-277
development time, 658-659
distributing with Setup Wizard, 775-780
exiting (EndDoc method, 456
idle time, 757-760
loading (optimization, 782-783
multithreaded, 755
NotePad (creating executable files for, 770-773
optimizing, 781-783
display speed, 783
operating speed, 783-784
size, 784-785
running
instances, 329
Load event, 60
runtime errors, 500-501
toolbar reorganization, 403
scope, *see* scope
single-threaded, 755
stack size, 755
standalone, 658-659
stopping, Step commands, 513
see also projects
Programs properties sheet (Internet Explorer), 1024
ProgressBar control, 448-449
Project Explorer window, 5, 7
Project menu commands
Add Form, 55
Add Property Page, 863
properties, 58, 839-840

Project Options dialog box, 410-412, 771
Project window, 55
projects
    about boxes, adding, 321-323
    adding class modules to, 345-347
    Address Book, *see* Address Book project
    Animate, 577-581
    Authors, 668
        adding text boxes, 672
        properties, 669, 673-674
    Binary, *see* Binary project
    Browse, 598-599
        checkbox properties, 604-605
        code, 606-607
        frame properties, 604
        label properties, 603, 605
        text box properties, 605
    CDMaker, *see* CDMaker
    Chalkboard, 551-554
    controls, adding, 40
    creating, 76
    Data Entry, 220-222
        controls, 222-224
        validating user input, 224-226
    DBGrid, properties, 695-696
    Debug Demo, *see* Debug Demo project
    dialer, 934
        code, 935-936
        running, 937
    Do Whatever, 656-657
        development time, 658
    Excel OLE, 813-815
    flxGrid, 697-700
    flxMerge.prj, *701-703*
    Font Demo, 461, 463-464
        code, 462, 465-467
        running, 463, 467
    FTP, 973
        CommandButtonproperties, 976-977
        frmFTPproperties, 974-975
        ITCproperties, 977
        LstDirproperties, 975
    Good Code, 530
    Goof, *507-09*
    Graph, *591-595*
    idleloop, 758-760
    Learnole, 794-796
    Lookup, 686-688
    MDI forms, adding, 279
    menus
        adding, 294-296, 298
        context-sensitive, 301, 305-309, 311-317, 319-321
        defined, 294
        separator bars, 299-300
        shortcut keys, 298-299
        Word Wrap, 300-301

projects (continued)
    MSComm, 920-921
        code, 926-930
        running, 928
    NewBtn
        adding TestBtn, 840-842
        creating, 838-840
        project properties pages, 839-840
    NewBtn.vbp, removing from project group, 880-881
    NewBtnDemo, running, 847
    NotePad, 645-646
        code, 652-654
        properties, 650-651
    Number Adder
        controls, 154-155
        loops, 158-163
    ODBC, 736-737
    Picture Pusher, 177-179
    PixLogo, 585-586
        code, 586-587
        running, 587
    prjComm_2
        code, 931-933
        running, 933-934
    Random, 621
        code, 624-625, 627-628
        properties, 622-623
    Registry API
        adding values to subkeys, 904-909
        code, 899-902
        properties, 895-897
        running, 902
    Republish, 721
    reusable code, 370
    saving, 53
    SBtn.bmp, 879-881
    Sender, 193-194
        adding standard modules, 201
        code, 194-196
    Seq, 613-614
    SQL.vbp, 706-708Spagh, 527-528
    SpellPad, 811-812
    SuperPad, see SuperPad
    TestBtn, adding to NewBtn project, 840-842
    TestCalc, 821-825
    test_dd, 744-746timerapp, 749-751
    Timesheet, 128-129
    Titles
        code, 694-695
        properties, 689-693
    toolbars, adding, 395-397
    TstShape, 556-557
        color objects/properties, 568
        drawing boxes, 557-559
        drawing circles, 561-562
        drawing triangles, 560-561

projects (*continued*)

VBCalc, 818-819

closing, 826

VBDest, 766-768

VBSrc, 765-766

WWW.vbp, 960

frmBrowser, 962-965, 968-970

frmMain code, 962

frmMain menus, 961

frmMain properties, 961

running, 971

see also forms; programs

Promotions combo box, 262

properties, 5

ActiveForm, 309

Address Book project, 104-105

address picture boxes, 964

Align (Toolbar control), 396

Authors project, 669, 673-674

AutoRedraw, 583-584

AutoSize, 68

BackColor, 565, 858-860

adding to controls, 866-869

Binary project, 631-632

Commad buttons, 635-636

text boxes, 632-634

BorderColor, 565

BorderStyle, adding About boxes to projects, 322

Browse project

checkbox, 604-605

frame, 604

label, 603, 605

text box, 605

Caption, 42

SButton control, 853

CDMaker project, 76, 80

Chalkboard project, 552-554

CheckBox control, 238-242

chkEcho, 948-949

Circle Command button, 561-562

class modules, 347, 349-350

cmdClear, 948-949

ComboBox control, 259-260, 262-263

CommandButton control, 236, 558-559, 976-977

CommonDialog control, 380-385

Count, collections, 363

Crystal Custom control, 720-721

DBGrid project, 695-696

Debug Demo project, 514-517

DefaultExt, 385

dockable

setting, 11

viewing, 6

Enabled, mapping, 873

err object, 505-506

properties (*continued*)

ExcelOLE, 813-815

ExpandedImage, 431-432

File class, 646

File controls, 601

File Selection controls, 49

FileListBox control, 45

FillColor, 565

flxGrid project, 698-699

flxMerge.pr, 701-703

Font

Label control, 77

Printer object, 462-463

Font Demo project, 461-464

ForeColor, 565

Form control (Animate project), 578

Frame control, 246

frmChat, 939

frmFind, 360-362

frmFTP, 974-975

frmOptions, 410

FrmPublishers, 681

frmSetup, 939-941

frmText, 992-994

frmVBCalc, 820

Good Code project, 530

Graph control, 589-590

Height, 290-291

help, 222

hWnd, 743

Icon, 280-281

idleloop project, 758-760

Image control (Animate project), 578-579

ImageList control, 396-397

Index (control arrays), 267

Internet Explorer, customizing, 1024-1025

ITC, 977

ItemData, 260

Label control, 77, 84, 227-228

Learnole project, 795-796

Left, 290-291

Line control, 546

Line objects, 845-846

LineStyle

constants, 433

TreeView control, 432

LinkItem, 764

LinkMode, 764

LinkTimeout, 764

LinkTopic, 764

Listbox control, 251, 253-256

Lookup project, 687-688

LstDir, 975

MaskColor (ImageList control), 396-397

MergeCells, 703

properties (*continued*)

MSComm control, 921
>   *data transfer,* 925-926
>   *handshaking,* 924-925
>   *modem setup,* 922-924

Name, 42
New controls, 904-905
NewIndex, 260-261
NotePad project, 650-651
Number Adder form, 154-155
objects, 33-35, 290-291
>   *captions,* 39
>   *changing,* 291

ODBC project, 736-737
OLE Container control, 794
OptionButton control, 244-245
Page (Printer object), 456
Password, 977
Pattern (FileListBox control), 65-66
Picture, 68
Picture Pusher project, 177
PixLogo project, 585-586
Port (Printer object), 455
Printer class, 476
property pages, 864-865
Random project, 622-623
RegClear command button, 892-893
Registry API project, 895-897
Republish project, 721
RichTextBox control, 388-389
SButton control, 871
ScaleHeight, 481-482
ScaleMode, 480, 542-543
ScaleWidth, 481-482
SelLength, 312, 317
SelStart, 317
Sender project, 193-194
SQL.vbp, 706-707
Seq project, 613-614
setting for multiple controls, 84
Shape control, 547-548
Slide control (Animate project), 581
Slider control, 450
Spagh project, 527-528
status bar panels, 405-406
Style
>   *constants,* 433
>   *TreeView control,* 432

SuperPad program, 280
TabStrip control, 410-413, 416
TestCalc project, 822
test_DLL project, 744-746
Text (FileListBox control), 66-67
TextBox control, 65, 221-224
Timer control, 749
>   *Animate project,* 578

properties (*continued*)

timerapp project, 750-751
Timesheet program, 128-129
Title project, 689-693
Toolbar control, 396-397
Top, 290-291
TrackDefault (Printer object), 456-457
Triangle Command button, 560-561
TstShape project, 556-557
>   *colors,* 568

txtChat, 948-949
user-defined, 364-368
VBCalc project, 818
VBDest project, 766-768
VBSrc project, 766
Visible (Label control), 84
WebBrowser control, 965
Width, 290-291
WWW.vbp project, 961

Properties command (Project menu), 58, 839-840
Properties dialog box, 58
Properties Page dialog box, 396-400
Properties window, 8, 11, 39, 55
Property dialog box, 422
Property Get event, 366-368
Property Let event, 366-368
Property Set event, 368
Property Page Designer, 863-865
Property Page Wizard, 21
property pages

adding to user controls, 863-865
connecting to controls, 865-866
properties, 864-865

protocols, transfer, 938
Pset method, 550
Pseudo-code, *see* **P-code**
public declarations, declaring variables, 199-200
public objects, 800
Public statement, declaring variables, 200
Put statement, 626

Q-R

QBColor function, 566-567
queries, 664

aggregate, 713-714
duplicates, 713
filling Data Bound ComboBox control, 686-688
Inner Join, 713
multiple tables, 713

Question mark (?), as notation for Print method, 169
Quick Watch window (Debug Demo project), 520-521
quizzes, answers, 1001-1013

radio buttons, *see* **OptionButton control**
raising events, 860-862

Random access, 619-621
Random files, writing to, 626
Random project
    code, 624-625, 627-628
    properties, 622-623
Read Properties event (SButton control), 849
ReadAll method (File class), 646, 648-649
reading
    files, 611-612
        binary, 631
        Binary project, 639-640
        random access, 621
        Seq project, 613-616
    registry values, 910-913
Readme files, 992-994
ReadOnly property (Data control), 671
ReadProperties, control lifetimes, 850
ReadRegValue function, 911-913
Recent tab, 4
records, 619, 663
    customer record (listing 12.12), 630
    fill character, 620
    navigating, 671
    Random project code, 624-628
recordsets, 664, 670
    creating, 679
    deleting, 680-681
    finding, 682-683
    manipulating with code, 675-681
    navigating, 671-672
    refreshing, 681
    updating, 680
RecordSource property (Data control), 670
referencing
    indexed controls, 270-271
    objects
        Is statement, 334
        multiple times, 333-334
    OCXs, 337-338
References dialog box, 805-807
referential integrity, 663
Refresh button, 681, 1019
Refresh method, 681
refreshing recordsets, 681
RegAPI.Bas, adding code to, 910-911, 914-917
RegClear command button, properties, 892-893
registry
    DeleteSetting statement, 891
    entries, 892-893
    expanding, 888
    GetAllSettings function, 892
    GetSetting function, 890-891
    keys, 890
        adding values to, 904-909
        deleting, 914-917

registry (*continued*)
    reading values, 910-913
    roots, 889-890
    SaveSetting statement, 891
    viewing, 888
Registry API project
    adding values to subkeys, 904-909
    code, 899-902
    properties, 895-897
    running, 902
relationships, Node object, 427-429
relative nodes, 429
remming code, 875
removing
    list box items, 257
    nodes, 429
    objects from collections, 359
    see also deleting
RemoveItem method, 257
Replace dialog box, 351-352
Report Designer, creating reports, 716-719
ReportFileName property (Crystal Custom control), 720
reports, creating, 716-719
Report view, 438, 444-446
    sorting, 446-447
Republish project, 721
Require Variable Declaration option, 502
Resize event
    adding code to, 843-844
    control lifetimes, 850
    sizing text boxes, 289-290
resolution, screen, 292
resources, newsgroups, 15
Resources screen (Application Wizard), 13
Resume statement, 506-508
Return button, 257
reusable code, 370
RGB function, 566-567
Rich Text Format, *see* RTF
RichTextBox control
    properties, 388-389
    replacing TextBox control with, 387-388
Right function, 106, 112
Rnd function, 90
roots, registry, 889-890
routines
    calling, 189-190
        Delete, 317
        standard modules, 201
    Code window, 192
    defined, 185
    Delete, calling, 317
    Exit, 155
    File Close, 309
    File New, 305

routines (*continued*)
File SaveAs, 385
printing headers/footers, 486-487
Save, 393
SaveAs, 392-393
Setup, adding Edit menu, 311-312
RSet statement, 125
RTF (Rich Text Format), 387
loading files, 391-393
saving files, 391-393
RTrim function, 115
rows, 663
Run command (Start menu), 37
Run to Cursor command, 513
running
Binary project, 644
Chat, 957-958
Control Interface Wizard, 870-871
Debug Demo project, 517
dialer project, 937
Font Demo project, 463, 467
Goof project, 508
Graph project, 594
MSComm project, 928
NewBtnDemo project, 847
PixLogo project, 587
prjComm_2, 933-934
programs
instances, 329
Load event, 60
runtime errors, 500-501
toolbar reorganization, 403
Registry API project, 902
TestCalc project, 825
WWW.vbp project, 971
see also starting
runtime
creating forms, 283-287
creating instances of controls, 269-270
errors, 500-501
reorganizing toolbars, 403

S

SafePath function, 658-659
Save As dialog box, 385
Save button
Click event code, 653
disabling, 401
Save File As dialog box, 63
Save Group Project command (File menu), 842
Save Project command (File menu), 840
Save routine, 393
SaveAs routine, 392-393
Save Setting statement, 891

saving
projects, 53
RTF files, 391-393
SBtn.bmp project, 879-881
creating OCX file, 880-881
SButton control
adding captions, 853-856
color changes, 858-860
Designer window, 843
events, 844, 871
raising, 861-862
Initialize event, 849
Line object properties, 845-846
mapping properties, 873
properties, 871
Read Properties event, 849
Terminate event, 850
testing, 881
User control, 840
ScaleHeight property, 481-482
ScaleMode property, 480, 542-543
ScaleWidth property, 481-482
scope, 197
functions, 200
module, 198-199
private, 197
procedure, 200
subroutines, 200
Screen object, 292, 539, 830-831
screens
Application Wizard, 13-16
computer, Screen object, 539-540
resolution, 292
splash, optimization, 782-783
splitting, 85
scripts (Internet Explorer), 1025-1026
Scroll event (Slider control), 450
ScrollBars property (TextBox control), 223
SDI (Single Document Interface) programs, 274
compared to MDI (Multiple Document Interface)
programs, 274-275
displaying withing MDI form frames, 280
Windows Notepad, 275-277
WordPad, 275
Search button (Internet Explorer toolbar), 1019
Search Master index, 23
Search Reference index, 23
searching
list boxes, 261
with collections, 360-362
Second function, 135
Security properties sheet (Internet Explorer), 1024
See Also option (help topics), 24
SelChange event, 407
Select All menu, adding to projects, 320

Select Case statement, 179-180
  Is keyword, 181-182
  nested, 181
Select Interface Members dialog box, 870
Select statement, 709
Selected property (ListBox control), 256
SelectedItem property (TabStrip control), 416
selecting
  data types, 618
  nodes, 435
  text, 320-321
Selection option (printing), 474
SelLength property, 312, 317
SelStart property, 317
semicolons (:), formatting print output, 458
Sender project, 193-194
  adding standard modules, 201
  code, 194-196
SendKey event, 119
SendMessage function, 743-744
separator bars, adding to menus (SuperPad), 299-300
Separator option, 398
Seq project, 613-614
sequential access, 619
Sequential files, writing to, 626
serial communications, 920-921
  setup property parameters, 922-924
servers
  accessing OLE objects, 790
  OLE (Object Linking and Embedding), 802
    creating, 817-819
    out-of-process, 820-821
Set Attributes dialog box, 873
Set Mapping dialog box, 872-873
Set Next statement, 522
Set statement, 285
SetFocus event, 224-226
SetText method, 315-316
setting
  breakpoints, 512
  control properties, multiple controls, 84
  dockable property, 11
Setup routine, adding Edit menu, 311-312
Setup Wizard, 775-776
  creating distribution copies, 882
  distribution media, 777-780
Sgn function, 91
shadow lines, resizing controls, 852-853
Shape control, 546-548
shapes, drawing, 556-557
  AutoRedraw, 583-584
  boxes, 557-559
  circles, 561-562
  triangles, 560-561
sharing code, 370

shareware, distributing ActiveX controls, 883-884
shortcut keys, 228-229
  adding to menus, 298-299
  TabIndex values, 230
Show method, 62
simple combo boxes, 264
  Data Bound ComboBox control, 688
Sin function, 91
single directories, application distribution, 777
Single Document Interface, see SDI (Single Document
  Interface) programs
single-instance classes, 329-330
single variables, 96, 99-100
single-threaded applications, 755
sites, 972
  FTP (File Transfer Protocol), 972
    accessing, 973
    anonymous, 977
    changing directories, 989-991
    exiting, 997
    reading text files, 992-994
  Internet
    breaking connections, 991-992
    opening, 965
    Visual Basic
sizing
  arrays, dynamic sizing, 212-213
  controls, 46
    shadow lines, 852-853
  programs, optimizing, 784-785
  windows, 286
Slide control, properties (Animate project), 581
Slider control, 449-450
Small Icon view, 438, 442
SmallChange property (Slider control), 450
snapshot recordsets, 670
Snoop button, 199
software design
  history, 32
  objects, 34
sorting
  items in list boxes, 260-261
  nodes, 430
  Report view, 446-447
source applications, 762-765
Space function, 115, 123-124
Spagh project, 527-528
Spaghetti code, 527-528
Specifics option (help topics), 26
speed display, optimization, 783
Spelling command (Tools menu), 812
SpellPad project, 811-812
Splash screen
  Application Wizard, 15
  optimization, 782-783

splitting screens, 85
SQL (Structured Query Language), 663
     data management, 706
     Debugger, 20
     Order By clause, 711
     queries
         aggregate, 713-714
         duplicates, 713-714
         multiple tables, 713
     Select statement, 709
     statement variables, 711-712
     Where clause, 709-710
SQL.vbp project, 706
     code, 707-708
     properties, 707
stack size, 755
standalone progams, 658-659
Standard Forms
     dialog box, 14
     screen (Application Wizard), 14
standard modules, adding to Sender project, 201
Standard property pages, adding to controls, 866-869
Start button
     Click event, 758-759
     Debug toolbar, 511
Start menu commands, Run, 37
starting
     Application Wizard, 12
     Visual Basic 5, 2
     see also running
startup code, frmChat, 950
startup forms, 39 , 58
statements
     branching, 92
     Close, 610
     conditional, 92
     Declare, 741
     DeleteSetting, 891
     Dim
         declaring arrays, 210
         declaring variables, 197-199
     End, 43
     Erase, arrays, 214
     executing multiple statements with colon separator, 176
     Get, 621
     if, 92-93, 176
         Else, 177-179
         ElseIf, 177-179
     Input #, reading files, 612
     Is, referencing objects, 334
     Line Input #, reading files, 612
     Load, creating instances of controls at runtime, 269-270
     looping, 92
     LSet, 125
     Mid, 120
     On Error, 506

statements (*continued*)
     Open, 609-610
         FileMode parameter, 620
     Option Explicit, declaring variables, 147
     OptionBase, changing base index, 211
     Private, declaring variables, 200
     Public, declaring variables, 200
     Put, 626
     Resume, 506-508
     RSet, 125
     SaveSetting, 891
     Select, 709
     Select Case, 179-182
     Set, 285
     Set Next, 522
     variables, 711-712
     With, 341-342
static keyword, 203
static persistence, 202-203
status bar
     frmChat, 949
     panels, *405-407*
Status property (File class), 646
StatusBar control, 404-406
Step command, 513
Step Into command, 513
Step keyword, 161
Step Out command, 513
Step Over command, 513
Stop button (Internet Explorer toolbar), 1019
stopping programs, 513
storing numbers in list boxes, 260
Str function, 150-151
StrComp function, 116, 126
String function, 116, 124
strings, 67, 105-106
     comparing, 125-126
     defined, 102
     fixed-length, 106
     functions, 106-113, 115-116, 122-125
     manipulating, 115-116, 122-125
     modem communications, 923-924
     Select Case statement, 180
     TargetFrameName, 966
     variable-length, 106
Structured Query Language, *see* **SQLSqr function,** 91
stubs, 416
Style property
     ComboBox control, 263
     constants, 433
     status bar panel, 406
     TabStrip control, 413
     TreeView control, 432
styles, toolbar buttons, 398

subroutines, 43, 185, 191
argument lists, 204-205
calling, 185
syntax, 187-188
centering forms, 334-335
class modules, 347
defining, 185-186
output, *186-188*
passing control references to, 339-340
scope, 200
syntax, 200
see also routines
Sum function, calling, 188-189
Summary option (help topics), 26
SuperPad
frmDocument, changes, 350-352
frmFind, 360-362
centering on computer screens, 292
clsDocument, events, 353
context-sensitive menus, 301
Edit menus, 311-317, 319-321
File Close, 309
File New, 305
Forms collection, 306-308
Document object, *see* Document object
instances, 329
Print dialog box, 472
properties, 280
separator bars, 299-300
shortcut keys, 299
TextBox control, 279
user interface, creating, 278-279
Word Wrap, 300-301
support, 883
syntax errors, 499-500
System Info window, 17
system objects, 828-829
App, 829
Clipboard, 830
Debug, 830
Err, 830
Printer, 830
Screen, 830-831
System registry, *see* **registry**

T

Tab order, 228
changing, 117-118
Tab tab (Properties dialog box), 412
TabIndex property (Label control), 228
TabIndex values, 229
accelerator keys, 230

tables, 663, 1019
Column Headers, 444-446
displaying, 418-419
Docking, 11
Existing, 3
Find, 27-28
General (Properties dialog box), 412
help, 27-28
index, 27
joining, 666
multiple queries, 713
New, 4
Recent, 4
recordsets, 670
Tabs (Properties dialog box), 412
TabStrip control, 413
TabStop property (Label control), 230
TabStrip control, 410-413
BeforeClick event, 418
Click event, 415-416
defining control groups, 413
properties, 416
tagging documents, 353
Tan function, 91
TargetFrameName string, 966
technical support, 23
telephone dialers, creating, 934-937
templates (Application Wizard), 14
Terminate event, 850-851
TestBtn project, adding to NewBtn project, 840-842
TestCalc project, 821-822
code, 823-825
running, 825
testing
code with debugger, 533
SButton control, 881
Test_dll project, 744-746
text
adding to status bar panels, 406-407
copying to Clipboard, 315-316
deleting from Clipboard, 316-317
nodes, editing, 434
pasting from Clipboard, 319-320
positioning to print, 459, 482-484
selecting, 320-321
TextBox control
binding to database columns, 673
disabling, 341
text boxes
adding to Authors project, 672
Binary project, 632-634
editing, 288-290
properties, 291-292
frmChat, 948
properties, 290-291

text files, reading online, 992-994
Text property
    FileListBox control, 66-67
    ListBox control, 253-255
    TextBox control, 222
TextBox control, 65, 220
    properties, 221-224
    replacing with RichTextBox control, 387-388
    SuperPad program, 279
ThisPoint property (Graph control), 589
threads, 755
Time function, 132
Time/Date menu, adding to projects, 320-321
Timer control, 748-749
    background processing, 751-753
Timer
    event, code, 752-753
    function, 139-140
Timerapp project, 749-751
times
    functions, 131-*143*
    literals, 130-131
TimeSerial function, 137-138
Timesheet program, 128-129
TimeValue function, 134
title bars
    NotePad, 276
    SuperPad, 279-280
Titles project
    code, 694-695
    properties, 689-693
To keyword, specifying base index, 211
Toolbar control, 395
    properties, 396-397
toolbars, 5, 8, 57
    adding buttons, 396
    adding to projects, 395-397
    buttons
        adding, 397-398
        adding images, 399-400
        disabling Save button, 401
        frmBrowser, 963
        frmChat, 946
        styles, 398
    customizing, 9-10
    Debug, 511-512, *518-522*
    programming, 401-402
    reorganizing at runtime, 403
    tooltips, 402
    VBAdd-In, 20
Toolbox, 8, 377
Tools menu commands, 337-338
    Add Procedure, 853
    Menu Editor, 56
    Options, 191
    Spelling, 812

Tooltips, 40, 57, 402
Top property, 290-291
TrackDefault property (Printer object), 456-457
transfer protocols, 938
TreeView control, 420-421, 432
    adding to projects, 421-422
    displaying images, 425-427, 432-433
    Nodes collection, 424-425
Triangle Command button, properties, 560-561
triangles, drawing, 560-561
Trim function, 115, 122
True keyword, 87
TrueType fonts, 460-463
TstShape project, 556-557
    color objects/properties, 568
    drawing boxes, 557-559
    drawing circles, 561-562
    drawing triangles, 560-561
twips, 480, 541
TxtChat, properties, 948-949
type declaration characters, assigning variables, 149-150
typefaces, 460-463
TypeName function, 145-147, 341
TypeOf keyword, 341

U

UARTcircuits, 923
UBound function, arrays, 214
UCase function, 115, 120
Unload event, 304-305
unprintable characters, Chat, 956-957
Update button, updating recordsets, 680
UpdateRecord method, 680
updating recordsets, 680-681
URLs (Uniform Resource Locators), defined, 966
UseMnemonic property (Label control), 229
user controls
    adding controls to, 852-853
    adding property pages, 863-*869*
    compiling, 879-881
    connecting property pages to, 865-866
    creating with Control Interface Wizard, 870-878
    distributing, 880-881
    events, 848-850, 857-*862*
    mapping, 872-873
    see also ActiveX, controls
user-defined classes, 330, 343-344
user-defined properties, 364-366
    Class, 365-366
    Property Get event, 366-367
    Property Let event, 366-367
    Property Set event, 368
user input, validating (DataEntry project), 224-226

user interfaces
creating for Superpad, 278-279
Windows NotePad, 276-277
user-defined formats, 491-493

V

Val function, 150
Validation event, 671
validating
data, Binary project, 638
user input, Data Entry project, 224-226
Value property (CheckBox control), 240-242
variable-length strings, 106
variables, 96
arrays, *see* arrays
assigning, 148-150
Boolean, 96-99
Byte, 96-97
Currency, 96, 100
Date, 97
Decimal, 96, 100-101
declaring, 78-79
Dim statement, 197-199
explicit declarations, 144-145
implicit declarations, 145
Option Explicit statement, 147
private declarations, 199-200
public declarations, 199-200
TypeName function, 145-146
double, 96, 100
form, 285
initializing, 79-80
Integer, 96, 99
long, 96, 99
manipulating, 80-82
names, 76
objects, 332
controls, 338-339
referencing multiple times, 333-334
referencing with Is statement, 334
persistence, *202-203*
scope, *197-200*
Select Case statement, 180
single, 96, 99-100
in SQL statements, 711-712
variants, 97, 148
variants, 97, 148
VB Add-In toolbar, 20
VBApplication Wizard, 3
VBCalc project, 818-819, 826
VBDest project, properties, 766-768
VBP file extension, 53

VBSrc project, 765-766
VBX controls, 338-339
Version information options (EXE Options dialog box), 772
Version Number options (EXE Options dialog box), 772
versioning issues, developing ActiveX controls, 884
View Mail Log button, 196
View menu commands, Code, 55
viewing
dockable property, 6
exposed objects with Object Browser, 805-807
Printers collection, 455
registry, 888
views
Large Icon, 437
List, 438, 444
Report, 438, 444-447
Small Icon, 438, 442
virtual pages, 479
Visible property (Label control), 84
Visual Basic 5
resources, 15
starting, 2
Web site, 15
Visual Data Manager add-in, 19
visual editing, 788, 791
VRML Support feature (Internet Explorer), 1018

W-Z

WaitForRing procedure, 951
Watch window (Debug Demo project), 519-520
Wdith property, 290-291
Web browsers, Internet Explorer, *see* Internet Explorer 3.0
Web pages, navigating, 967
Web sites
Microsoft, 1017
Visual Basic, 15
WebBrowser control (Microsoft), 960, 962-964
frmBrowser code, 968-970
methods, Navigate, 965-967
properties, 965
Weekday function, 138-139
Where clause, 709-710
While keyword, 166
While...Wend loop, 168
With statement, 341-342
Window list menu, adding to projects, 324-325
windows, 4
Call Stack (Debug Demo project), 521-522
closing, 8
Code, 4, 42, 83
context-sensitive, 88-89
routines, 192

windows (*continued*)
  Control Design, closing, 849
  Customize, 10
  Debug, Resize event, 843
  Design, closing, 844
  dockable, 6
  Form Layout, 5-8
  Immediate, 6, 8, 102
    Debug Demo project, 518-519
    printing, 103
  Locals (Debug Demo project), 521
  maximizing, 7, 286
  minimizing, 286
  modal vs. modeless, 63
  opening, 8
  Printers, 454
  Project Explorer, 5
    closing, 7
  Properties, 8, 11, 39, 55
  Quick Watch (Debug Demo project), 520-521
  SButton Designer, 843
  System Info, 17
  Watch (Debug Demo project), 519-520
Windows 95, installing Internet Explorer, 1016
Windows API
  functions
    calling in DLLs, 740-741
    hDC property, 743
    hWnd property, 743
    SendMessage, 743-744
  registry settings, 895-897
  Text Viewer, 745
Windows API Text Viewer, 897-899
Windows Notepad, *see* **Notepad (Windows)**
Windows NT, installing Internet Explorer, 1016-1017
Wizard Manager, 21
wizards
  ActiveX Document Migration, 20
  Application, 21
    creating database tables, 676-678
    screens, 13-16
    templates, 14
  Control Interface, 20
    Create Custom Interface Members dialog box, 871
    Finished! dialog box, 873-874
    modified declarations section, 874-878
    running, 870-871
    Set Attributes dialog box, 873
    Set Mapping dialog box, 872-873
  Data Form, 21

wizards (*continued*)
  Property Page, 21
  Setup, 775-776
    distribution media, 777-780
  VBApplication, 3
  Wizard Manager, 21
  see also add-ins
WMF files, 573
Word
  documents
    embedding, 798
    property settings for OLE control in embedded
      charts, 796
  Macro Recorder, 816
  OLE Automation, 810-812
Word Wrap
  adding to menus (SuperPad), 300-301
  adding to projects, 321
WordPad, 275
World Wide Web, *see* **WWW**
WriteAll method (File class), 646, 649
WriteProperties event, control lifetimes, 851
writing
  code, 526-528
    guidelines, 529
  files, 625
    binary, 631
    random files, 626
    sequential files, 626
WWW (World Wide Web), 15, 960
  navigating, 967
  sites, *see* Web sites
WWW.vbp project, 960
  frmBrowser, 962, 965
    address picture box properties, 964
    code, 968-970
    toolbar buttons, 963
  frmMain code, 962
  frmMain menus, 961
  frmMain properties, 961
  running, 971

X properties (Line control), 546
Xor operator, 172-173

Y properties (Line control), 546
Year function, 134

ZOrder, adding PictureBox controls to frmOptions, 362, 415
  Click event, 415-416
  multiple picture boxes, 417-418

Books have a substantial influence on the destruction of the forests of the Earth. For example, it takes 17 trees to produce one ton of paper. A first printing of 30,000 copies of a typical 480-page book consumes 108,000 pounds of paper, which will require 918 trees!

Waite Group Press™ is against the clear-cutting of forests and supports refor-estation of the Pacific Northwest of the United States and Canada, where most of this paper comes from. As a publisher with several hundred thousand books sold each year, we feel an obligation to give back to the planet. We will therefore support organi-zations that seek to preserve the forests of planet Earth.

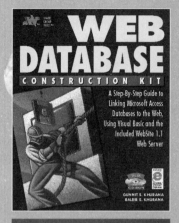
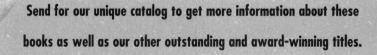

Message from the
Publisher

WELCOME TO OUR NERVOUS SYSTEM

Some people say that the World Wide Web is a graphical extension of the information superhighway, just a network of humans and machines sending each other long lists of the equivalent of digital junk mail.

I think it is much more than that. To me, the Web is nothing less than the nervous system of the entire planet—not just a collection of computer brains connected together, but more like a billion silicon neurons entangled and recirculating electro-chemical signals of information and data, each contributing to the birth of another CPU and another Web site.

Think of each person's hard disk connected at once to every other hard disk on earth, driven by human navigators searching like Columbus for the New World. Seen this way the Web is more of a super entity, a growing, living thing, controlled by the universal human will to expand, to be more. Yet, unlike a purposeful business plan with rigid rules, the Web expands in a nonlinear, unpredictable, creative way that echoes natural evolution.

We created our Web site not just to extend the reach of our computer book products but to be part of this synaptic neural network, to experience, like a nerve in the body, the flow of ideas and then to pass those ideas up the food chain of the mind. Your mind. Even more, we wanted to pump some of our own creative juices into this rich wine of technology.

TASTE OUR DIGITAL WINE

And so we ask you to taste our wine by visiting the body of our business. Begin by understanding the metaphor we have created for our Web site—a universal learning center, situated in outer space in the form of a space station. A place where you can journey to study any topic from the convenience of your own screen. Right now we are focusing on computer topics, but the stars are the limit on the Web.

If you are interested in discussing this Web site or finding out more about the Waite Group, please send me e-mail with your comments, and I will be happy to respond. Being a programmer myself, I love to talk about technology and find out what our readers are looking for.

Sincerely,

Mitchell Waite

Mitchell Waite, C.E.O. and Publisher

200 Tamal Plaza
Corte Madera, CA 94925
415-924-2575
415-924-2576 fax

Website:
http://www.waite.com/waite

CREATING THE HIGHEST QUALITY COMPUTER BOOKS IN THE INDUSTRY

Waite Group Press

Come Visit
WAITE.COM
Waite Group Press
World Wide Web Site

Now find all the latest information on Waite Group books at our new Web site, **http://www.waite.com/waite**. You'll find an online catalog where you can examine and order any title, review upcoming books, and send e-mail to our authors and editors. Our FTP site has all you need to update your book: the latest program listings, errata sheets, most recent versions of Fractint, POV Ray, Polyray, DMorph, and all the programs featured in our books. So download, talk to us, ask questions, on **http://www.waite.com/waite**.

The New Arrivals Room has all our new books listed by month. Just click for a description, Index, Table of Contents, and links to authors.

The Backlist Room has all our books listed alphabetically.

The People Room is where you'll interact with Waite Group employees.

Links to Cyberspace gets you in touch with other computer book publishers and other interesting Web sites.

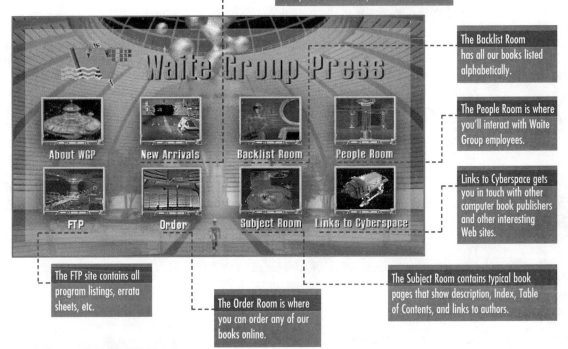

The FTP site contains all program listings, errata sheets, etc.

The Order Room is where you can order any of our books online.

The Subject Room contains typical book pages that show description, Index, Table of Contents, and links to authors.

World Wide Web:

COME SURF OUR TURF—THE WAITE GROUP WEB

http://www.waite.com/waite
Gopher: gopher.waite.com
FTP: ftp.waite.com

This is a legal agreement between you, the end user and purchaser, and The Waite Group®, Inc., and the authors of the programs contained in the disk. By opening the sealed disk package, you are agreeing to be bound by the terms of this Agreement. If you do not agree with the terms of this Agreement, promptly return the unopened disk package and the accompanying items (including the related book and other written material) to the place you obtained them for a refund.

SOFTWARE LICENSE

1. The Waite Group, Inc. grants you the right to use one copy of the enclosed software programs (the programs) on a single computer system (whether a single CPU, part of a licensed network, or a terminal connected to a single CPU). Each concurrent user of the program must have exclusive use of the related Waite Group, Inc. written materials.

2. The program, including the copyrights in each program, is owned by the respective author and the copyright in the entire work is owned by The Waite Group, Inc. and they are therefore protected under the copyright laws of the United States and other nations, under international treaties. You may make only one copy of the disk containing the programs exclusively for backup or archival purposes, or you may transfer the programs to one hard disk drive, using the original for backup or archival purposes. You may make no other copies of the programs, and you may make no copies of all or any part of the related Waite Group, Inc. written materials.

3. You may not rent or lease the programs, but you may transfer ownership of the programs and related written materials (including any and all updates and earlier versions) if you keep no copies of either, and if you make sure the transferee agrees to the terms of this license.

4. You may not decompile, reverse engineer, disassemble, copy, create a derivative work, or otherwise use the programs except as stated in this Agreement.

GOVERNING LAW

This Agreement is governed by the laws of the State of California.

LIMITED WARRANTY

The following warranties shall be effective for 90 days from the date of purchase: (i) The Waite Group, Inc. warrants the enclosed disk to be free of defects in materials and workmanship under normal use; and (ii) The Waite Group, Inc. warrants that the programs, unless modified by the purchaser, will substantially perform the functions described in the documentation provided by The Waite Group, Inc. when operated on the designated hardware and operating system. The Waite Group, Inc. does not warrant that the programs will meet purchaser's requirements or that operation of a program will be uninterrupted or error-free. The program warranty does not cover any program that has been altered or changed in any way by anyone other than The Waite Group, Inc. The Waite Group, Inc. is not responsible for problems caused by changes in the operating characteristics of computer hardware or computer operating systems that are made after the release of the programs, nor for problems in the interaction of the programs with each other or other software.

THESE WARRANTIES ARE EXCLUSIVE AND IN LIEU OF ALL OTHER WARRANTIES OF MERCHANTABILITY OR FITNESS FOR A PARTICULAR PURPOSE OR OF ANY OTHER WARRANTY, WHETHER EXPRESS OR IMPLIED.

EXCLUSIVE REMEDY

The Waite Group, Inc. will replace any defective disk without charge if the defective disk is returned to The Waite Group, Inc. within 90 days from date of purchase.

This is Purchaser's sole and exclusive remedy for any breach of warranty or claim for contract, tort, or damages.

LIMITATION OF LIABILITY

THE WAITE GROUP, INC. AND THE AUTHORS OF THE PROGRAMS SHALL NOT IN ANY CASE BE LIABLE FOR SPECIAL, INCIDENTAL, CONSEQUENTIAL, INDIRECT, OR OTHER SIMILAR DAMAGES ARISING FROM ANY BREACH OF THESE WARRANTIES EVEN IF THE WAITE GROUP, INC. OR ITS AGENT HAS BEEN ADVISED OF THE POSSIBILITY OF SUCH DAMAGES.

THE LIABILITY FOR DAMAGES OF THE WAITE GROUP, INC. AND THE AUTHORS OF THE PROGRAMS UNDER THIS AGREEMENT SHALL IN NO EVENT EXCEED THE PURCHASE PRICE PAID.

COMPLETE AGREEMENT

This Agreement constitutes the complete agreement between The Waite Group, Inc. and the authors of the programs, and you, the purchaser.

Some states do not allow the exclusion or limitation of implied warranties or liability for incidental or consequential damages, so the above exclusions or limitations may not apply to you. This limited warranty gives you specific legal rights; you may have others, which vary from state to state.

MACMILLAN COMPUTER PUBLISHING USA

A VIACOM COMPANY

Technical ---┐
        └--- **Support:**

If you need assistance with the information in this book or with a CD/Disk
accompanying the book, please access the Knowledge Base on our Web
site at **http://www.superlibrary.com/general/support**. Our most
Frequently Asked Questions are answered there. If you do not find the
answer to your questions on our Web site, you may contact Macmillan
Technical Support **(317) 581-3833** or e-mail us at **support@mcp.com**.